CONTENTS

ACKNOWLEDGMENTS

It would have been impossible to complete such an enormous project without the help of many people. And so we would like to express our appreciation to the following: Mrs. Willard D. White and Miss Bonnie L. Wirts for their hours of extra service; Miss Mary Campfield, Mrs. Clarence J. Fields, Mrs. Lewis C. Hash, Mrs. Walter Kahler, and Mrs. Frank G. Peck, all of the Essex Community College Library; Mr. George T. Bachmann, Miss Judith Cobb, Mrs. Thos. W. Farndon, Miss Ellen B. Fletcher, Miss Sharon Moylan, Mrs. Marjorie E. Plitt, and Mrs. William J. Ritter of the Catonsville Community College Library; Mrs. James C. Brownlow of the Baltimore County Library, Essex branch and Mrs. James E. Grumbach of the North Point branch; Dr. Royce Hanson, Director of the Washington Center for Metropolitan Studies; Mr. Donald A. Hobbs, Associate Professor, Sociology, Catonsville Community College; Dr. David T. Lewis, Chairman, Division of Social Sciences, University of Maryland; Mr. Stanley Z. Mazer, Associate Professor and Chairman of the Department of Urban Affairs, Community College of Baltimore; Mr. Jerome Garitee, Associate Professor, History, Essex Community College; Mrs. Robert Smelkinson, Maryland Center for Public Broadcasting; and Mrs. James Kopelke, Coordinator of Early Childhood Curriculums, Maryland Department of Education; and Miss Priscilla A. Haines, Instructor, Essex Community College.

We also wish to thank Mr. Alan B. Lesure of Prentice-Hall for his confidence and persistence; Mrs. Barbara Christenberry for her editorial assistance; Mr. Richard Reiner for the idea; Mrs. Paul Naden who helped us through the long galleys; and the staff of Senator Edmund Muskie and Congressman Jonathan Bingham for their invaluable aid.

And a special thanks to Eleni and Jackie who saw the project through with patience and encouragement far beyond the call of feminine duty.

The book's deficiencies are clearly the fault of the authors who can only hope that they have made a reasonable contribution to the understanding of contemporary urban life.

FOREWORD

TOWARDS A NEW URBAN ERA

THE FRAGILE BALANCE OF URBAN LIFE

In recent times, magazines, newspapers, television, and radio have been full of news about "ecology." We can all remember the old textbook pictures the word "ecology" conjures up: a leafy environment . . . trees . . . ferns . . . moss . . . animals crawling around. But modern man knows—or soon must learn—that ecology is not just a pastoral word. Our mountains and our forests do not stand alone in needing the conservationists' touch.

As this provocative anthology shows, the nature of contemporary events has made it quite clear that urban life too is dangerously vulnerable to the distortions of man's ingenuity. As a focal point for man's happenings, the urban scene is often subjected to the brunt of man's mistakes and the horrors of his shortsightedness. The "ecology" that governs the city, therefore, is as frail as that of nature itself; and at times, it is more mysterious.

A VIEW FROM THE SENATE

In the past the nation has failed to cope with the problems of the cities because people—legislators included—have had a tendency to take a narrow and unrelated view of the urban environment. Because of the pressure of events, it is not unusual for a Senator's concept of the city to be conditioned by his chosen field of expertise or committee assignment.

For example, as a member of the Senate's Public Works Committee, the city, to me and to many of my colleagues, was mainly a conglomeration of poor housing, growing unemployment, congested traffic, inferior architecture, wretched planning, and bad land usage.

As chairman of the Subcommittee on Air and Water Pollution, I viewed the city as a center of smog and pollution. It was an environmental disaster that needed more stringent enforcement of water and air pollution regulations.

My work on the Banking and Currency Committee took me into the jungle of urban economics, a field that to this day remains one of the land's richest mysteries. In those committee sessions, the city meant vast urban renewal and public housing projects.

And I am chairman of the Senate Government Operation's Subcommittee on Intergovernmental Relations, a body devoted to the prospect of making sense out of governments regardless of size, shape, or level. There I have viewed the urban environment as the chief victim of an almost unfathomable game of duplication, bureaucracy, and what can only be described as medieval sorcery. Competition between the hundreds of little sovereignties which have developed in our major cities is often incredible. Housing officials will not talk with road builders; road builders will not sit with planners; planners will not meet with architects; and on and on.

In an interesting sidelight, in our subcommittee hearings, we have also discovered that the suburbs are not immune from the difficulties facing the cities. In some areas, notably in the south and west, the traditional disparity between city and suburb is completely reversed. The suburbs often reflect a higher level of poverty than the city. A 1966 report of the Advisory Commission on Intergovernmental Relations also indicated that "cities and suburbs showed little difference in the proportion of their adult populations with less than 4 years of high school . . . or in their high school drop out rates. Under-education of young and adults," it went on, "is an equally serious problem in both urban and suburban segments of most metropolitan areas."

A VIEW FROM THE HUSTINGS

Even with these viewpoints—public works, pollution control, banking and intergovernmental relations, it was not until I campaigned for the Vice Presidency that the harsh reality of the urban condition really crashed down on me. My home state has its cities but they tend to be in the 25,000 and 50,000 size. And although the problems that exist in Portland and Bangor are at times difficult and complex, at least to me they always seem comprehensible. Campaigning across this great and vast nation exposed me to some other patterns.

We traveled across the country to urban communities as large as New York and as small as Hot Springs. We walked through black ghettos and Polish wards; we caravaned down main streets and central avenues in scores of municipalities. We spoke with and listened to urban residents, rested in their homes and hotels, ate in their restaurants, toured their day care centers, their mental institutions, their factories and businesses. We hopped from college to college, speaking with the young and with their instructors. We met with police chiefs and patrolmen, and with black militants and bankers. We talked with union chiefs and rank and filers. Every day, for weeks, the urban scene flashed before us—with all its tensions, its charms, its aspirations. We discovered the hard way that if you've seen one city—you obviously have *not* seen them all.

I had a view of the cities from the bottom up—a view that made me realize all the more those ingredients that tie urban life together rather than separate it. My lasting impression was that the American urban environment is a remarkable way of life that is neither threatening nor harmful. And it possesses enormous potential.

THE FEDERAL GOVERNMENT AND THE URBAN ENVIRONMENT

Improving urban life is not an unreasonable task. Cities are not evil; cities are not unmanageable; cities will not respond glowingly to violence or to ineptitude.

They will react, however, to rational and forceful direction, to creative design, to sensitive and practical planning, to humane and relevant programs. Spasmodic responses to immediate crises provide none of these. Therefore, the first and most urgent requirement to improve urban life is a total and unrelenting national pledge to do just that. The "new national commitment" to the city must be a profound, radical, and penetrating effort to marshal the country's ingenuity and resources against urban decay.

Despite all the volumes of literature and the barrels of Rhetoric, the nation to this day has not established a comprehensive urban policy outlining what we want our cities to be. It has not assumed a national commitment to make American cities the best in the world. A nation that has landed on the dark side of the moon seems incapable of coping with garbage collection in the dark side of a ghetto alley.

Up Against The Urban Wall shows clearly and forcefully that until the nation is willing to make this vital commitment to its cities, they can have no real future. Making the commitment will be difficult; fulfilling it may be even more so. It will require daring experimentation, hard-headed realism and exceptional national political leadership. That leadership must choose its priorities wisely and its alternatives prudently.

At the very minimum, it must:

1. *Establish a "tax sharing" program that gives urban areas a definite priority in the distribution of shared revenues.* As economist Walter Heller pointed out: "Economic growth creates a glaring fiscal gap; it bestows its revenue bounties on the federal government, whose progressive income tax is particularly responsive to growth, and imposes the major part of its burdens on state and local governments." A national program that will distribute monies

back to the states and urban communities through formula that offers fairness and incentive will permit a more flexible and more effective use of tax dollars to cope with urban problems.

2. *Reform the national welfare program to provide a guaranteed minimum income for all citizens,* eliminating the stigma and paternalism so degradingly associated with the current system. It is difficult to comprehend how the nation has remained so attached to a welfare system that is detested both by those who rely on it for sustenance and by those who foot the bill. The most sensible alternative deals with establishng a minimum income for all citizens. That income should permit a family head to seek meaningful employment without fear of losing payments he can receive by mere idleness—perhaps the most sinful fault of the present system.

3. *Undertake a massive employment program for the inner city area.* Along with housing and education, employment is probably the single most critical issue facing the ghettos. Unemployment in the ghettos ranges seven and eight times higher than in the nation as a whole. Unskilled black workers are the last to be hired; the first to be dismissed; the lowest on the apprenticeship list; and the most difficult to train. But a man without a job is a driftless soul who can demand no respect from his family and maintain no confidence in himself. The nation must find jobs for the ghetto residents.

The most immediate way is to initiate a vast urban physical renewal program geared to hiring local ghetto residents to work on projects designed to provide the ghetto with needed facilities. These include medical clinics, community day care centers and neighborhood recreational facilities. In order to coordinate the employment program with improving education standards, schools would work intimately with the workers offering courses in the various trades and arranging for incentives to be based on school promotion.

Under such a plan employment would be meaningful and effective. It would not provide an isolated individual with an isolated job that may or may not exist tomorrow. It would offer a full range of employment opportunities, highly visible to local residents, on projects that would improve local conditions. It would have academic incentives to encourage drop outs to stay in school.

4. *Undertake a vast inner city low and middle income housing program to make some headway in the estimated 600,000 new dwelling units the country needs every year.* This project will require creative and efficient prefabricated housing techniques already used to great advantage in a number of European countries. America can and must do the same.

5. *Vigorously enforce open housing regulations and school desegregation guidelines that have stifled balanced urban expansion beyond arbitrary geographical city lines.*

6. *Encourage the development of "new towns", which can be an important ingredient in alleviating the pressures of increased population and mobility.* By offering appropriate features of a progressive urban environment,

"new towns" promise cities that will remain new and dynamic for succeeding generations. Many of our contemporary urban ills can be laid directly to the period of heavy industrialization and urban migration that caught the city flat-footed. Today these conditions have caught up with us.

New town planners, blessed with insight on what makes a city decay and what makes a city thrive, can eliminate many of those factors that distort urban life. To do this they will require government help to assemble land and secure the tremendous financing required for such undertakings. Building "new towns," however, cannot be confined to rural or suburban areas. The same imagination and creativity must be applied to building "new neighborhoods" within existing urban settings.

7. *Improve the educational opportunities of slum children by undertaking an "impacted aid" program for ghetto schools similar to the impacted aid programs for Federal installations.* We must also expand the opportunity for community colleges and other local institutions of higher learning to identify with and focus on neighborhood needs.

8. *Demand a more enlightened view by industrial leaders of the environment in general and the urban environment specifically.* A major industry located in a suburban community has a great deal of leverage in improving the attitude of that community toward open housing and toward an inner city resident who must find a reasonable relationship between his employment and his home. "Manufacturers," said Jeanne Lowe, Urban Affairs Consultant for the *Saturday Review,* "are uniquely capable of . . . severing the suburban 'White Noose' around our core cities, making the metropolitan housing-real estate market work the same for the Negro as for the White, and forcing exclusionist suburbs, exurbs, and smaller cities to accept nonwhites and lower-income families in significant volume and in a harmonious manner."

9. *Increase the level of cooperation between local, State and Federal Agencies, between suburban and urban officials, between private and public citizens.* This cooperation involves concepts such as metropolitan councils of government, special authorities, and local control of special community functions including education, welfare, and housing.

10. *Seek new government units that are more visible, more responsive and more alert to the intimacies of local conditions and community patterns.*

11. *Secure surplus food programs to feed the hungry, medical aid to comfort the impoverished, day care centers to aid working mothers, and community health centers to care for ghetto as well as suburban neighborhoods.* When it comes to health, there is no doubt that ghetto Americans are victims of national indifference. The Urban Coalition's Task Force on health revealed the startling facts that the poor have four to eight times the incidence of such chronic conditions as heart disease, arthritis, hypertension and visual impairment as the nonpoor. It also showed that the ratio of doctors in the ghettos is from one-fifth to one-half that of the city as a whole.

12. *Improve the sophistication of contemporary urban police forces, vastly overhaul and streamline local judicial systems to provide speedy and equitable justice.*

13. *Provide for a more orderly migration of work forces from one community to another through aggressive planning relating to growth and demands.* "Most of the present urban crisis," The Violence Commission reported, "derives from the almost total absence of positive policies to cope with the large scale migration of Southern Negroes into northern and western cities over the past century, when the number of Negroes living in cities rose from 2.7 to 14.8 million.

14. *Overhaul archaic zoning laws, building codes, and urban land use policies. Presently these are based on principles that are at best outmoded and at worse discriminatory.*

15. *Improve the quantity and quality of research into urban oriented problems such as the effectiveness of contemporary educational programs and the realities of drug use and abuse.*

16. *Provide for a national urban growth report to summarize annually for the Congress and the public the basic trends of urbanization, an evaluation of these trends, and an assessment of the public and private progress in meeting these trends.*

17. *Demand that the federal government reform its own practices so that it no longer is guilty of illicit behavior we condemn in others—including mediocre architectural design; environmental pollution; insensitive planning; favoritism and corruption in the distribution of funds; and shortsightedness and hardheadedness concerning legitimate citizen views and complaints.*

18. *Initiate a more healthy and positive dialogue between inner city blacks and suburban whites.* We need this dialogue to lessen antagonism, to prove that continued hostility is disastrous and to show that the good American is ultimately neither silent nor militant but one who cherishes his neighbor whatever his color or ethnic background.

Let's be frank. A large part of the urban issue today is race. Blacks and whites stare at each other from across irrational geographic lines and irrational personal barriers. Blacks resent white institutions reflecting white attitudes and promoting white culture. Whites resent black militancy advocating black power and reflecting a new sense of black identity. The nation must reconcile these differences, must create institutions that are free of racism, and must find ways of sharing the abundance of our society.

A NEW NATIONAL URBAN COMMITMENT

Once the nation has committed itself to undertaking a healthy and invigorating national program to transform contemporary American cities, then it must face the second and equally essential part of the task.

A commitment to improve urban life is useless if that commitment is made in a vacuum. The city cannot be considered in isolation. It is a vital part of an overall environment that will rise or fall according to remote, often obscure, forces. The American city can prosper only if American society is prospering. And, conversely, society can advance only if the city is advancing.

Again, it is a matter of "ecology." The city cannot improve if suburban attitudes remain rigid, inflexible, and hostile. Inner city citizens cannot increase their opportunities if white Americans move their plants and their homes beyond the temporary friction. Nor can the city hope to prosper if it continues to be the dumping ground for rural poor, who seek a refuge from the destitution of the countryside and merely add their grief to the city's existing woes. This inbound migration aggravates the urban crisis, further stimulates the outbound migration of whites, which in turn stimulates the urban crises. It is a vicious "ecological" circle that escalates the crisis as each separate element seeks its own separate salvation.

In December 1969, on behalf of the Advisory Commission on Intergovernmental Relations, I introduced in the Senate the balanced urbanization policy and planning act. The bill authorizes a full analysis of urban and rural growth for the development of a national urban policy. It provides additional assistance to State and local governments for developing comprehensive program planning and coordination. And by placing the power to coordinate urban affairs directly within the executive office of the President the bill would initiate a process at the national level of government to hammer out a balanced urban policy that could ultimately resolve the nightmarish spread of rural decay, central city deterioration, suburban sprawl, and metropolitan fragmentation.

There is room in this nation for central cities and for suburbs—compact or sprawling; and for rural areas—remote and insulated, but not if each views its condition as separate and isolated from its neighbor. There is but one America and that America is a complex interaction of forces and people.

This leads directly to the next phase of that "national commitment" we have been discussing. The nation must be equally prepared to invest in its future by investing in the improvement of its total environment. It will mean cleaning rivers and eliminating smog; it will mean resurrecting rural areas and improving rural education; it will mean balanced economic growth and altered social attitudes.

It will mean an excruciating reappraisal of national policies that have encouraged violence, militancy, crime, confrontation, and alienation. It will mean creative, at times radical, institutional adjustments to meet these issues.

This will require not only great moral leadership but also a great amount of money, probably it may take billions of dollars. That money must come from local and state governments, but especially from the federal government which has wider and fairer sources of revenue.

It must come from a nation that has reassessed its priorities, diminished its military investments and increased its social obligations.

It must also come from citizens and institutions in the private sphere. One of the greatest needs in this nation today is to direct the latent talents of American industrial and business ingenuity toward social problems. Mr. David Rockefeller, of Chase Manhattan, addressing a Senate Committee, suggested that businessmen often feel that "government officials tend to look upon them as rivals in competition rather than as partners in progress." This impression must be wiped away and a new spirit of unity between the private and public sector must emerge.

THE CHALLENGE FOR THE YOUNG

I would like to direct a special word to the students who are reading this important book and who will be wrestling with the urban problems of the future. You did not make the city what it is, nor are you directly responsible for the conditions of society in general. But you will share the responsibility for saving it.

The society of the future will be even more urban than the society of the past. The streets of the next decade will be more crowded than the streets of today. More schools and more medical facilities will be necessary. Citizens will be crying for better homes and additional recreational space. The gap between the poor and the affluent may be even more severe and, what is worse, it may be more visually apparent.

That's why your generation will have no alternative but to fathom the mysteries of the urban environment, plunge willingly into the morass of relationships that direct and govern its growth and commit yourself to reshaping and redirecting those forces. If the rift between black and white continues . . . if urban education is no more meaningful and urban housing conditions no more tolerable . . . if the suburbs do not open more windows . . . if business does not show more courage and government more flexibility . . . if hunger and poverty are not eradicated in urban slums as well as rural shacks . . . then the next generation of Americans will suffer the horrible consequences of an urban society that could not sustain an important and decent way of life.

You have challenged your elders to seek a new and better way of life; you have demanded reason and tolerance; you have picketed for new priorities and marched to stop hunger and erase poverty and prejudice; you have clamored for commitment and involvement.

The cities will not survive without any of these ingredients. And so we ask whether you will be able to do for us what we could not do for you. Balance the nation's power with the nation's conscience so that the urban citizen is the benefactor, not the victim, of man's victory over nature.

I think you can.

Senator Edmund S. Muskie

THE SOULLESS CITY

Daniel P. Moynihan

There is to be encountered in one of the Disraeli novels a gentleman described as a person "distinguished for ignorance" as he had but one idea and that was wrong. It is by now clear that future generations will perforce reach something of the same judgment about contemporary Americans in relation to their cities, for what we do and what we say reflect such opposite poles of judgment that we shall inevitably be seen to have misjudged most extraordinarily either in what we are saying about cities or in what we are doing about them. We are, of course, doing very little, or rather, doing just about what we have been doing for the past half century or so, which can reflect a very great deal of activity but no very considerable change. Simultaneously, and far more conspicuously, we are talking of crisis. The word is everywhere: on every tongue; in every pronouncement. The President has now taken to sending an annual message to Congress on urban subjects. In 1968 it was bluntly titled *The Crisis of the Cities.* And indeed, not many weeks later, on Friday, April 5, to be exact, he was issuing a confirming proclamation of sorts:

> *Whereas I have been informed that conditions of domestic violence and disorder exist in the District of Columbia and threaten the Washington metropolitan area, endangering life and property and obstructing execution of the laws, and the local police forces are unable to bring about the prompt cessation . . . of violence and restoration of law and order. . . .*

The excitement is nothing if not infectious. In a recent joint publication, *Crisis: The Condition of the American City,* Urban America, Inc. and the League of Women Voters noted that during 1967 even the Secretary of Agriculture devoted most of his speeches to urban problems. At mid-1968, the president of the University of California issued a major statement entitled, "What We Must Do: The University and the Urban Crisis." The bishops of the United States Catholic Conference came forth with their own program, entitled "The Church's Response to the Urban Crisis." At its 1968 convention the Republican party, not heretofore known for an obsession with the subject, adopted a platform plank entitled "Crisis of the Cities," while in an issue featuring a stunning black coed on the cover, *Glamour* magazine, ever alert to changing fashion, asked in appropriate form the question many have posed themselves in private—"The Urban Crisis: What Can One Girl Do? "

Daniel P. Moynihan, "The Soulless City," **AMERICAN HERITAGE,** *April, 1969.*
Reprinted by permission of the publisher, American Heritage Publishing Co., Inc.

Academics who have been involved with this subject might be expected to take some satisfaction that the alarums and jeremiads of the past decades seem at last to have been heard by the populace, and yet even those of us most seized with what Norman Mailer has termed the "middle-class lust for apocalypse" are likely to have some reservations about the current enthusiasm for the subject of urban ills. It is not just a matter of the continued disparity between what we say and what we do: it is also, I suspect, a matter of *what* we are saying, and the manner of our saying it. A certain bathos comes through. One thinks of Sean O'Casey's Captain Boyle and Joxer in that far-off Dublin tenement: no doubt the whole world was even then in a "state of chassis" but precious little those two could or would do about it, save use it as an excuse to sustain their own weakness, incompetence, and submission to the death wishes of the society about them. One wonders if something not dissimilar is going on in this nation, at this time. Having persistently failed to do what it was necessary and possible to do for urban life on grounds that conditions surely were not so bad as to warrant such exertion, the nation seems suddenly to have lurched to the opposite position of declaring that things are indeed so very bad that probably nothing will work anyway. The result either way is paralysis and failure. It is time for a measure of perspective.

I take it Lewis Mumford intended to convey something of this message in his most recent book, *The Urban Prospect,* which he begins with a short preface cataloguing the ills of the modern city with a vigor and specificity that command instant assent from the reader. Exactly! one responds. That is precisely the way things are! Mumford is really "telling it like it is." (A measure of *négritude* has of late become the mark of an authentic urban-crisis watcher.) One reads on with increasing recognition, mounting umbrage, only to find at the end that this foreword was in fact written for the May, 1925, edition of *Survey Graphic.* Things have changed, but not that much, and in directions that were, in a sense, fully visible to the sensitive eye nearly a half century ago. To be sure, at a certain point a matter of imbalance becomes one of pathology, a tendency becomes a condition, and for societies as for individuals there comes a point when mistakes are no longer to be undone, transgressions no longer to be forgiven. But it is nowhere clear that we have reached such a point in our cities.

Continuity and change. These are the themes of all life, and not less that of cities. However, as in so many aspects of our national experience, Americans seem more aware of, more sensitive to modes of change than to those of continuity. This is surely a survival from the frontier experience. There has not, I believe, ever been anything to match the rapidity, nay, fury with which Americans set about founding cities in the course of the seventeenth, eighteenth, and nineteenth centuries. Only just now is the historical profession beginning to catch up with that breathless undertaking. Before long we are likely to have a much clearer idea than we do now as to how it all began. But it is still possible at this early state, as it were, to identify a half dozen or so persistent themes in the American urban experience which seem to evolve from earlier to later stages in a process that some would call growth, and others decay, but in a manner that nonetheless constitutes change.

The first theme is that of violence. Through history—the history, that is, of Europe and Asia and that great bridge area in between—cities have been, nominally at least, places of refuge, while the countryside has been the scene of insecurity and exposure to misfortune and wrongdoing. Obviously the facts permit of no generalization, but there is at least a conceptual validity, a persistence over time, of the association of the city with security. In the classical and feudal world, to be without the gates was to be in trouble. Writing of the destruction of Hiroshima and Nagasaki, the critic George Steiner evokes the ancient certainty on this point, and suggests the ways in which it lives on.

In these two cities, the consequences have been more drastic and more specialized. Therein lies the singularity of the two Japanese communities, but also their symbolic link with a number of other cities in history and with the role such cities have played in man's consciousness of his own vulnerable condition—with Sodom and Gomorrah, visited by such fiery ruin that their very location is in doubt; with Nineveh, raked from the earth; with Rotterdam and Coventry; with Dresden, where in 1944, air raids deliberately kindled the largest, hottest pyre known to man. Already, in the "Iliad," the destruction of a city was felt to be an act of peculiar finality, a misfortune that threatens the roots of man. His city smashed, man reverts to the unhoused, wandering circumstance of the beast from which he so uncertainly emerged. Hence the necessary presence of the gods when a city is built, the mysterious music and ceremony that often attend the elevation of its walls. When Jerusalem was laid waste, says the Haggada, God Himself wept with her.

Little of this dread is to be encountered in the United States, a society marked by the near absence of internal warfare once the major Indian conflicts were over. Warfare, that is to say, between armies. We have, on the other hand, been replete with conflict between different groups within the population, classified in terms of race, class, ethnicity, or whatever, and this conflict has occurred in our cities, which in consequence have been violent places.

An account of the draft riots in New York City in 1863 strikes a surpassingly contemporary note.

Nothing that we could say, could add to the impressiveness of the lesson furnished by the events of the past year, as to the needs and the dangerous condition of the neglected classes in our city. Those terrible days in July—the sudden appearance, as if from the bosom of the earth, of a most infuriated and degraded mob; the helplessness of property-holders and the better classes; the boom of cannon and rattle of musketry in our streets; the skies lurid with conflagrations; the inconceivable barbarity and ferocity of the crowd toward an unfortunate and helpless race; the immense destruction of property—were the first dreadful revelations to many of our people of the existence among us of a great, ignorant, irresponsible class, who were growing up here without any permanent interest in the welfare of the community or the success of the Government—the proletaires of the European capitals. Of the gradual formation of this class, and the dangers to be feared from it, the agents of this Society have incessantly warned the public for the past eleven years.

*—Eleventh Annual Report
Children's Aid Society, New York*

In some degree this violence—or the perception of it—seems to have diminished in the course of the 1930's and 1940's. James Q. Wilson, a professor of government at Harvard, has noted the stages by which, for example, the treatment of violence as an element in American politics steadily decreased in successive editions of V. O. Key's textbook on American politics that appeared during the latter part of this period. It may be that depression at home and then war abroad combined to restrict opportunity or impulse. In any event, there was a lull, and in consequence all the more alarm when violence reappeared in the mid-1960's. But it was only that: a reappearance, not a beginning.

Yet with all this it is necessary to acknowledge a transformation howsoever subtle and tentative. The tempo of violence seems to have speeded up, the result, more or less direct, of change in the technology of communications, which now communicate not simply the fact but also the spirit of violent events, and do so instantaneously. More ominously, there appears to have been a legitimation of violence, and a spread of its ethos to levels of society that have traditionally seen themselves, and have been, the repositories of stability and respect for, insistence upon, due process. It is one thing to loot clothing stores— Brooks Brothers was hit in 1863—to fight with the police, to seize sections of the city and hold out against them. It is another thing to seize university libraries, and that is very much part of the violence of our time, a violence that arises not only among the poor and disinherited, but also among the well-to-do and privileged, with the special fact that those elements in society as a whole have been peculiarly unwilling, even unable, to protest the massive disorders of recent times.

A second theme is migration. The American urban experience has been singular in the degree to which our cities, especially those of the North and East, have been inundated by successive waves of what might be called rural proletarians, a dispossessed peasantry moving—driven from—other people's land in the country to other people's tenements in the city. American cities have ever been filled with unfamiliar people, acting in unfamiliar ways, at once terrified and threatening. The great waves of Catholic Irish of the early nineteenth century began the modern phase of this process, and it has never entirely stopped, not so much culminating as manifesting itself at this time in the immense folk migration of the landless southern Negro to the northern slum. In small doses such migrations would probably have been easily enough absorbed, but the sheer mass of the successive migrations has been such as to dominate the life of the cities in their immediate aftermath. The most dramatic consequence was that popular government became immigrant government: in the course of the nineteenth century, great cities in America came to be ruled by men of the people, an event essentially without precedent in world history—and one typically deplored by those displaced from power in the course of the transformation. Let me cite to you, for example, a schoolboy exercise written in 1925 by a young Brahmin, the bearer of one of Boston's great names, on the theme "That there is no more sordid profession in the world than *Politics.* "

> The United States is one of the sad examples of the present form of government called democracy. We must first remember that America is made up of ignorant, uninterested, masses, of foreign people who follow the saying, "that the sheep are many but the shepards are few." And the shepards of our government are wolves in sheeps clothing. From Lincoln's Gettysburg address let me quote the familiar lines "a government of the people, for the people, and by the people." In the following lines I shall try and show you how much this is carried out in modern times.
>
> Let us take for example the position of our mayors. They are elected by majority vote from the population in which they live. Let us take for a case Mayor Curley of Boston. He tells the Irish who make up the people of Boston that he will lower their taxes, he will make Boston the greatest city in America. He is elected by the Irish mainly because he is an Irishman. He is a remarkable politician: he sur-

rounds himself by Irishmen, he bribes the Chief Justice of the court, and although we know that the taxes that we pay all find a way into his own pocket we cannot prove by justice that he is not a just and good maayor.

But such distaste was not wholly groundless. The migrant peasants did and do misbehave: as much by the standards of the countryside they leave behind, as of the urban world to which they come. The process of adapting to the city has involved great dislocations in personality and manners as well as in abode. From the first, the process we call urbanization, with no greater specificity than the ancient medical diagnosis of "bellyache" or "back pain," has involved a fairly high order of personal and social disorganization, almost always manifesting itself most visibly in a breakdown of social controls, beginning with the most fundamental of controls, those of family life. The Children's Aid Society of New York was founded in response to the appearance of this phenomenon among the immigrant Irish. Let me quote from their first annual report:

> *It should be remembered, that there are no dangers to the value of property or to the permanency of our institutions, so great as those from the existence of such a class of vagabond, ignorant, ungoverned children. This "dangerous class" has not begun to show itself, as it will in eight or ten years, when these boys and girls are matured. Those who were too negligent or too selfish to notice them as children, will be fully aware of them as men. They will vote. They will have the same rights as we ourselves, though they have grown up ignorant of moral principle, as any savage or Indian. They will poison society. They will perhaps be embittered at the wealth, and the luxuries, they never share. Then let society beware when the outcast, vicious, reckless multitude of New York boys, swarming now in every foul alley and low street, come to know their power and use it!*

Mumford in his new book speaks of precisely the same phenomenon:

> *One of the most sinister features of the recent urban riots has been the presence of roaming bands of children, armed with bottles and stones, taunting and defying the police, smashing windows and looting stores. But this was only an intensification of the window-breakings, knifings, and murders that have for the past twenty years characterized "the spirit of youth in the city streets."*

And note the continuity of his last phrase, which alludes, of course, to Jane Addams' book *The Spirit of Youth and the City Streets*, in which she describes just those conditions at the turn of the century in terms that William James declared "immortal" and which, we must allow, were hardly ephemeral.

Yet here, too, technology seems to have been playing us tricks, accentuating and exacerbating our recent experience. The newest migrants come upon an urban world that seems somehow to need them less, to find them even more disturbing and threatening, and to provide them even less secure a place in the scheme of things than was ever quite the case with those who preceded them. I take this to be almost wholly a function of changing employment patterns consequent upon changing technology. But this very technology has also provided an abundance of material resources—and a measure of social conscience—so that people who are not especially needed are nonetheless provided for: by 1968, after seven years of unbroken economic expansion, there were 800,000 persons living on welfare in New York City, with the number expected to reach 1,000,000 in 1969. In part this is a phenomenon of birth rates. One person in ten, but one baby in six today is Negro. The poor continue to get children, but those children no longer succumb to cholera, influenza, and tuberculosis. Thus progress more and more forces us to live with the consequences of social injustice. In a more brutal age the evidence soon disappeared!

A third theme of the American urban experience has been the great wealth of our cities. Those who have moved to them have almost invariably improved their standard of life in the not-very-long run. Nor has this been wholly a matter of the consumption of goods and services. "City air makes men free," goes the medieval saying, and this has not been less true for industrial America. The matter was settled, really, in an exchange between Hennessey and Dooley at the turn of the century. The country, said that faithful if not always perceptive patron, is where the good things in life come from. To which the master responded, "Yes, but it is the city that they go to." Technology is at the base of this process. The standard of life in American cities rises steadily, and there are few persons who do not somehow benefit. And yet this same technology—wealth—takes its toll. More and more we are conscious of the price paid for affluence in the form of manmade disease, uglification, and the second- and third-order effects of innovations which seem to cancel out the initial benefits.

Nathan Keyfitz, a sociologist at the University of Chicago, has nicely evoked the paradox implicit in many of the benefits of technology. Plenty encourages freedom. It also encourages density. Density can be managed only by regulation. Regulation discourages freedom. The experienced, conditioned city dweller learns, of course, to live with density by maintaining, as Keyfitz puts it, "those standards of reserve, discretion, and respect for the rights of others" that keep the nervous system from exhausting itself from the overstimulus available on any city street. The traditional assertion of Manhattan apartment dwellers that they have never met their neighbors across the hall is not a sign of social pathology: to the contrary, it is the exercise of exemplary habits of social hygiene. Borrowing the meter from George Canning's account of the failings of the Dutch, the rule for the modern cliff dweller might be put as follows:

> In the matter of neighbors,
> The sound thing to do,
> Is nodding to many
> But speaking to few.

It may be speculated, for example, that a clue to the transformation of the roistering, brawling, Merrie England of tradition into that somber land where strangers dare not speak to one another in trains lies *in the fact of the trains.* Technology—in this case the steam engine that created the vast nineteenth-century complexes of London and Manchester—brought about urban desities which required new forms of behavior for those who wished to take advantage of technology's advances and yet retain a measure of internal balance. The British, having been first to create the densities, were first to exhibit the telltale *sang-froid* of the modern urban dweller.

It may also be speculated that the "disorganized" life of the rural immigrants of today arises in some measure at least from an inability to control the level of stimulus: to turn down the radio, turn off the television, come in off the streets, stay out of the saloons, worry less about changing styles of clothes, music, dance, whatever. Lee Rainwater, a professor of sociology at the University of Washington, has provided us with painful accounts of the feeling of helplessness of the mothers of poor urban families in the face of the incursions from the streets: the feeling, literally, that one cannot simply close one's door in the housing project and refuse to allow family, friends, neighbors, and God knows who else to come and go at will. This makes for lively neighborhoods, which from a distance seem almost enviable. But also for very disturbed people.

When such groups became large enough, when densities become ominous, government regulation becomes necessary, or at least all but invariably makes its appearance, so that even for the disciplined urbanite, technology at some point begins to diminish freedom. Keyfitz writes:

> George Orwell's 1984 is inconceivable without high population density, supplemented by closed circuit television and other devices to eliminate privacy. It exhibits in extreme form an historical process by which the State has been extending its power at the expense of the Church, the Family, and the Local Community, a process extending over 150 years.

There are few bargains in life, especially in city life.

A fourth theme of the American urban experience is mobility. Cities are not only places where the standards of life improve, but also very much—and as much now as ever—they are places where men rise in social standing. Otis Dudley Duncan and Peter M. Blau in their powerful study. The American Occupational Structure have made this abundantly clear. American cities are places where men improve their position, as well as their condition. Or at least have every expectation that their sons will do so. The rigidities of caste and class dissolve, and opportunity opens. Yet this has never been quite so universally agreeable an experience as one could be led to suppose from the accounts of those for whom it has worked. In the city men first, perhaps, come to know success. There also men, especially those from the most caste-ridden rural societies, first come to know failure. It seems to me that this is a neglected aspect of the urban experience. I would argue that the rural peasant life of, let us say, the Irish, the Poles, the Slavs, the Italians, the Negro Americans who have migrated over the past century and a half was characterized by a near total absence of opportunity to improve one's position in the social strata, but also it was characterized by the near impossibility of observing others improve theirs. Rarely, in either absolute or relative terms, did individuals or families of the lowest peasant classes experience decline and failure: that in a sense is the law of a non-contingent society. Only with arrival in the city does that happen, and I would argue that for those who lose out in that competition, the experience can be far more embittering than that brought on by the drab constancy of country life.

Again technology—again television, for that matter—plays its part. Stephan Thernstrom in Poverty and Progress has noted that the immigrant workers of nineteenth-century New England, earning $1.50 a day when they had work, nonetheless managed in surprising numbers to put aside some money and to buy a piece of property and respectability before their lives were out, despite the fact that their incomes rarely permitted them to maintain what the social workers of the time calculated to be the minimum standard of living. The difference, Thern-

strom notes, was that for the migrants a minimum standard of living was potatoes. Period. So long as they did not share the expectations of those about
them—even the small expectations of social workers—they were not deprived.
But advertising and television, and a dozen similar phenomena, have long since
broken down that isolation, and the poor and newly arrived of the American
city today appear to be caught up in a near frenzy of consumer emotions:
untouched by the disenchantment with consumption of those very well off, and
unrestrained by the discipline of household budgets imposed on those in between. The result, as best such matters can be measured, is a mounting level of
discontent, which seems to slide over from the area of consumption as such to
discontent with levels of social status that do not provide for maximum levels of
consumption. Thus, even those who seem to be succeeding in the new urban
world feel they are not succeeding enough, while others are suffused with a sense
of failure.

*A fifth theme of the American urban experience relates not to the experi-
ence of the poor and the newly arrived so much as to that of the well-to-do and
the comparatively well settled: the persistent, one almost says primal, distaste
for the city of educated Americans.* In *The Intellectual Versus the City,* Morton
and Lucia White point out that "enthusiasm for the American city has not been
typical or predominant in our intellectual history. Fear has been the more common reaction." Fear, distaste, animosity, ambivalence. "In the beginning was the
farm," or so the Jeffersonian creed asserts. And the great symbol—or perhaps
consummation would be the better term—of this belief was the agreement
whereby in return for the Jeffersonian willingness to have the federal government accept the debts acquired by states during the Revolutionary War, the
capital of the new nation would be transferred from the city of New York to a
swamp on the banks of the Potomac. Do not suppose that that agreement has
not affected American history. New York remains the capital of the nation, as
that term is usually understood, in the sense of the first city of the land. It is the
capital of finance, art, theatre, publishing, fashion, intellect, industry . . . name
any serious human endeavor other than politics, and its center in the United
States will be found in New York City. In years of hard-fought presidential
primaries, it is even for many purposes the political capital of the nation. But the
seat of government is in Washington, which is only just beginning to respond to
the fact that for half a century now ours has been a predominantly urban
society.

Once again technology seems to be interacting with a pre-existing tendency. As the American city came more and more to be the abode of the
machine, the alarm of American intellectuals, if anything, was intensified. And
to a very considerable degree legitimated, for surely machines have given a
measure of reality to alarums that were previously more fantasy than otherwise.
To this has been added an ever more persistent concern for social justice, so that
American intellectuals of the present time now conclude their expanding cata-
logues of the horrors of urban life with ringing assertions that the cities must be
saved. But it is to be noted that this comes almost as an afterthought: the
conviction that in the cities will be found the paramount threat to the life of the
Republic has changed hardly at all. But at long last what they have been saying
may be beginning to be true.

A sixth theme of the American urban experience, and the last with which I shall deal, has been and continues to be the singular ugliness of the average American city. That there are great and stunning exceptions is as much a matter of accident as anything. The essential fact is that for all the efforts to sustain and assert a measure of elite concern for urban aesthetics—of the kind one associates with historical preservation societies—and for all the occasional bursts of energy within the urban planning profession, the American city remains an ugly place to live, pretty much because we like it that way. A measure, no doubt, of this persisting condition can be attributed to the business and propertied interests of the nation that have resisted municipal expenditure, notably when it passed through the hands of egalitarian city halls. But it is more than that. Somehow, somewhere, in the course of the development of democratic, or demagogic, tradition in this nation the idea arose that concern for the physical beauty of the public buildings and spaces of the city was the mark of—what? — crypto-deviationist antipeople monumentalism—and in any event an augury of defeat at the polls. The result has been a steady deterioration in the quality of public buildings and spaces, and with it a decline in the symbols of public unity and common purpose with which the citizen can identify, of which he can be proud, and by which he can know what he shares with his fellow citizens. For the past seven years, as an example, I have been involved with efforts to reconstruct the center of the city of Washington, an attempt that begins with the assertion of the validity and viability of L'Enfant's plan of the late eighteenth century. In this effort we have had the tolerant to grudging co-operation of a fairly wide range of public and private persons, but let me say that we have had at no time the enthusiasm of any. And now I fear we may have even less, since of late there has arisen the further belief that to expend resources on public amenities is in effect to divert them from needed areas of public welfare. The very persons who will be the first to demand increased expenditures for one or another form of social welfare will be the last to concede that the common good requires an uncommon standard of taste and expenditure for the physical appointments of government and the public places of the city.

This attitude was perhaps unintentionally evoked by the respected Episcopal bishop of New York who in 1967 announced that in view of the circumstances of the poor of the city he would not proceed with the completion of the Cathedral of St. John the Divine, the largest such building ever begun, situated on a magnificent site overlooking the flat expanse of Harlem. Why? Meaning no disrespect, is it the plan of the church to liquidate its assets and turn them over to the poor? How much would that come to per head? But even so, would not the completed cathedral be an asset? If men need work, could they not be given jobs in its construction? The French— *toujours gai,* as mehitable would have it—built Sacre Coeur as an act of penance for the excesses of the Commune. Could not the Episcopalians build St. John the Divine—a perfect symbol of rebirth—as a gesture of penance for all that Brahmin disdain which, in one form or another, to use Max Ways's phrase, taught us to despise our cities until they became despicable? If the phenomenon of ugliness, the last of my urban themes, can be thought to have arisen from more or less abstract qualities of American society in the present and foreseeable future its principal cause is visible, concrete, and ubiquitous, which is to say it is the automobile. More than any other single factor it is the automobile that has wrecked the twentieth-century American city, dissipating its strength, destroying its form, fragmenting its life. So pervasive is the influence of the automobile that it is possible almost not to notice it at all. Indeed, it is almost out of fashion to do so: the men who first sought to warn us have almost ceased trying, while those who might have followed have sought instead formulations of their own, and in that manner diverted attention from the essential fact that in the age of the automobile, cities, which had been places for coming together, have increasingly become machines for moving apart, devices whereby men are increasingly insulated and isolated one from the other.

A coda of sorts that has persisted through the elaboration of the themes of this paper has been the recent role of technology in accentuating and in a sense exacerbating long-established tendencies. The impact of technology on human society—on all forms of life—is the pre-eminent experience of the modern age, and obviously of the city as well. But only of late, one feels, has any very considerable appreciation developed that a change in quantity becomes after a point a change in quality, so that a society that begins by using technology can end by being used by it, and in the process, somehow, lose such control of its destiny as past human societies can be said to have had. Technology being so outwardly rational, it has been assumed by many that those who have been concerned about its directions have not really understood it. People easily come to fear what they do not understand, and it has been suspected, not always without foundation, that a certain amount of criticism of technology has been a latter-day form of rick burning.

One begins to think that this may not be so. Take the family automobile: a simple, easily enough comprehended (or seemingly so), unthreatening, and convenient product of folk technology rather than of modern science. Who would imagine any great harm coming from the automobile? Yet consider a moment. With its advent, everyday citizens, for the first time in human history, came into possession of unexampled physical energy: the powers of the gods themselves became commonplace. And from the very outset, violence ensued. It is said, for example, that when there were only four gasoline-powered vehicles in Missouri, two of them were in St. Louis and managed to collide with such impact as to injure both drivers, one seriously. Thus was introduced a form of pathology that was to grow steadily from that year to this. Today, something between one quarter and two thirds of the automobiles manufactured in the United States end up with blood on them. Indeed so commonplace and predictable have collisions become that the U.S. Court of Appeals for the Eighth Circuit recently ruled that a crash must be considered among the "intended uses" of a motor vehicle, and the manufacturers accordingly responsible to provide for such contingency in their design.

It becomes increasingly clear that the major environment, or, if you will, vehicle, in which incidents of uncontrolled episodic violence occur within the population is that of the automobile. Whether access and exposure to this environment have increased the incidence of such episodes, or whether the urban environment now largely created and shaped by the automobile has generally increased the violence level is uncertain at best (there has, of course, been a great decline in violence directed toward animals), but with the number of deaths and injuries at the present ongoing rates, and the number of vehicles in use approaching the one-hundred-million mark, it is a matter worth pondering.

Crashes are but one form of pathology. Each year in the United States automobiles pour eighty-six million tons of carbon monoxide, oxides of nitrogen and sulfur, hydrocarbons, lead compounds and particulates into the air we breathe. Recently my younger son came home with a button that announced, "Clean air smells funny." Dr. Clare C. Patterson of the California Institute of Technology put it another way in testimony before a congressional committee: "The average resident of the United States is being subject to severe chronic lead insult," originating in lead tetraethyl. Such poisoning can lead to severe intellectual disability in children: so much that Patterson feels it is dangerous for youth to live long periods of time near freeways.

ecology

But that is only the beginning, hardly the end of the impact of this particular form of technology on the society at this time. In consequence of the management of the automobile traffic system by means of traditional rules of the road, the incidence of armed arrest of American citizens is the highest of any civilization in recorded history. In 1965, for example, the California highway patrol alone made one million arrests. Indeed so commonplace has the experience become that a misdemeanor or felony committed in a motor vehicle is no longer considered a transgression of any particular consequence, and to be arrested by an armed police officer is regarded as a commonplace. That is precisely what Orwell told us would happen, is it not?

There are some 13,600,000 accidents a year, with some thirty million citations for violations issued each twelve months. And at this point, ineluctably, technology begins to have an effect on the most fundamental of civil institutions, the legal system itself. Largely in consequence of the impact of traffic-crash litigation, it now takes an average of 32.4 months to obtain a civil jury trial for a personal injury case in the metropolitan areas of the nation. In Suffolk County, New York, it is 50 months. In the Circuit Court of Cook County, serving Chicago, it is 64 months. This past winter in Bronx County, New York, the presiding judge of the appellate division announced he was suspending civil trials altogether while he tried to catch up with criminal cases. The courts are inundated; the bar is caught up, implicated and confused; the public knows simply that somehow justice is delayed and delayed. All of which is a consequence of this simplest form of technology, working its way on the institutions of an essentially pretechnological society.

It sometimes happens that a work of art appearing at a particular moment in time somehow simultaneously epitomizes and reveals the essential truths of the time. In a most astonishing and compelling way this has happened for the American city, and it has done so, most appropriately, on Forty-second Street in Manhattan, in the persona of the Ford Foundation headquarters, designed by Kevin Roche, John Dinkeloo & Associates—a great firm, successor to Eero Saarinen & Associates whose first large commission was, of course, the General Motors Technical Center outside Detroit. Saarinen, and now Roche, have gathered a group of artist/technicians whose work, from the Dulles Airport at Chantilly, Virginia, to the Trans World Airlines Terminal at Kennedy Airport and the Columbia Broadcasting headquarters in New York City, has evoked the power and purpose of the age of technology as perhaps no other organization has.

Here in the Ford Foundation headquarters is expressed the very highest purposes of modern technological power: compassionate and potent concern for the betterment of man's lot. The building is everything a building could be: a splendid work place, a gift to the city in the form of a public park, a gift to the world simply as a work of imagination and daring. If it is a reproach of sorts to the public and private builders of the nation who by and large show little of either, it is a gentle reproach, more show than tell. In that favored form of foundation giving, it is a kind of demonstration project: an example of what can, and what therefore in an age of technology must, be done.

The exterior of the building is quiet and unassertive: it is not *that* big a building, and it seeks rather to understate both its size and importance. No-nonsense shafts of Cor-ten steel rise from the ground, here and there sheathed with a blue-brown granite and interspersed with large rectangular glass panels. Rather in the mode of a cathedral, the portals do not so much impart as suggest the experience to come. It is only on entering—Chartres, say, or Vézelay—and encountering the incomparable space, shaped and reserved for a single purpose only, that one leaves off observing the building and begins to be shaped by it: the eye rises, the mind turns to last things. So with the Ford Foundation headquarters. One passes through revolving doors to enter a garden. Truly a garden, a small park, like nothing anywhere else to be encountered, a third of an acre, lush and generous, climbing a small hill that follows the terrain of Manhattan at this point, illuminated by the now vast windows that climb nine stories toward heaven itself, and there only to be met by a glass roof. Water moves slightly in a pool—a font? Attendants move quietly, and are helpful. One notices that vegetation sprouts from beams and ledges on the third and fourth and even the fifth floors. One is awestruck by the wealth and power of the foundation, and the sheer authority of its intent to do good. Only the gray-white light is not quite what it should be: as in those French and German cathedrals whose stained glass was lost to war or revolution or Protestantism.

But this is only the entering light. As in any such edifice, there is a light within. In this case a very monstrancelike golden-brown glow that shines forth from the offices of the foundation executives, who from the floor of the park are to be seen at their work behind glass panels formed and reticulated by the same rusted beams that frame the colorless glass of two sides of the building. (Cor-ten steel seals itself by rusting and need not be painted.) At this point one perceives readily enough that the building has been built as a factory. Not precisely as a factory—any more than the Gothic Revival built office buildings precisely as medieval monasteries—but rather to evoke the style and somehow the spirit of a great plant. The huge, heavy lateral beams, from which elsewhere would be suspended the giant hoists that roam back and forth amidst the clatter and roar; the sawtooth roof; the plant managers' eyrie hung from the ceiling, keeping an eye on everything; the perfectly standardized, interchangeable fixtures in each office; the seriousness and competence of it all, even the blue-black, somehow oily granite of the cheerless rest rooms (No Loitering in the Can— magically, stunningly, trimphantly, evoke the style and spirit of the primeval capitalist factory. Cor-ten. Red. Rouge. River Rouge. Of course! And why not, for $16,000,000 of Henry Ford's money? He was that kind of man. Knew how to make automobiles and obviously liked to. Else he could hardly have done it so well. All black, just as the Ford Foundation headquarters is all brown. Same principle. So also the panopticon effect of the exposed offices wherein the presumptively interchangeable officers at their perfectly inter-changeable desks labor at their good works in full view of management and public alike. (The public serving, perhaps, as the visitors to Jeremy Bentham's prospective model prison: a "promiscuous assemblage of unknown and therefore unpaid, ungarbled and incorruptible inspectors"?) Critics, at least in the first reviews, seem to have missed most of this, but no matter: the architecture needs no guidebook; the intellectual and aesthetic effect is not to be avoided, even when the intent is least perceived. All in all it is just as McGeorge Bundy proclaimed it in the 1968 annual report of the foundation: "Kevin Roche's triumph."

But it is more than that. Or rather, there is more than is to be perceived at one time. A great work of art has levels of meaning at once various and varying. Standing in the park, gazing upward, following the factory motif, the mind is of a sudden troubled. Something is missing. Noise. Factories are places of noise. Of life. Clatter. Roar. There is no noise here. Only quiet. The quiet of the . . .? The mind oscillates. It is a factory, all right. But a *ruined* factory! The holocaust has come and gone: hence the silence. The windows have blown out, and only the gray light of the burned out world enters. The weather has got in, and with it nature now reclaiming the ravaged union of fire and earth. The factory floor has already begun to turn to forest. Vegetation has made its way to ledges halfway up the interior. The machine tools are gone. Reparations? Vandalism? Who knows. But the big machines will no longer be making little machines. Gone too is the rational, reforming, not altogether disinterested purpose of the pan-opticon. One is alone in the ominous gloom of a Piranesi prison, noting the small bushes taking hold in the crevices of the vast ruined arches.

Is it the past or the future that has taken hold of the mind? Certainly the ruined steel frame is a good enough symbol of the twentieth century so far. (Where had one last seen that color? Of course. Pingree Street in Detroit after the riot. A year later there it was again, on Fourteenth Street in Washington: the fiery orange-red of the twisted steel shopping centers' framing after the looting and arson has passed.) Or is it the future? There is a *sur real* quality that comes of standing in the ruined half of the building, watching the life going on behind the glass walls of the intact half, seemingly oblivious to the devastation without. Can ruin advance slowly like rot? No. Yes. Did the automobile start all this? No. Surely it is all this that started automobiles. One quarter to two thirds of which end up with blood on them. Blood. Red. Rouge. River Rouge.

Enough.

But then why has the American architect Joseph Stein built the Ford Foundation headquarters in New Delhi immediately adjacent the Lodi Tombs, symbols of death sensual to the point of necrophilia? Did not Bentham remark that he could legislate wisely for all India from the recesses of his study? There's a panopticon in your future.

No. Enough.

And yet it comes together in a way. *"Le Siècle de la machine,"* Le Corbusier wrote in 1924, *"a réveillé l'architecte."* Not least because the machine destroys so much of that experience of community that the architect seeks to create. A biographer describes Eero Saarinen's purpose thus: "What . . . [he] wished to renew, maintain, and improve was the organic expression of the *civitas* which he found weakened or destroyed virtually everywhere in modern civilization, with one significant exception—the university campus." And so Roche built a ruined machine-for-making-machines as the headquarters of a great philantropic foundation whose principal concerns have been to support the universities of the nation, and to seek to strengthen the community life of its cities.

The research of James Q. Wilson and Edward C. Banfield at Harvard University is now beginning to produce results surprisingly similar to the visions of the architect/artist. As Wilson puts it, "After a decade or more of being told by various leaders that what's wrong with our large cities is inadequate transportation, or declining retail sales, or poor housing, the resident of the big city is beginning to assert his own definition of that problem—and this definition has very little to do with the conventional wisdom on the urban crisis." Wilson and his colleague asked one thousand Boston homeowners what *they* thought to be the biggest urban problem of this time.

> The *"conventional"* urban problems—housing, transportation, pollution, urban renewal, and the like—were a major concern of only 18 per cent of those questioned, and these were expressed disproportionally by the wealthier, better-educated respondents. Only 9 per cent mentioned jobs and employment, even though many of those interviewed had incomes at or even below what is often regarded as the poverty level. The issue which concerned more respondents than any other was variously stated—crime, violence, rebellious youth, racial tension, public immorality, delinquency. However stated, the common theme seemed to be a concern for improper behavior in public places.
>
> What these concerns have in common, and thus what constitutes the *"urban"* problem for a large percentage (perhaps a majority) of urban citizens, is a sense of the failure of community.

And yet cities, by definition, destroy community. Or is it only when they are too big, too unsettled, that they do this? Is it only when social conditions are allowed to arise which lead inevitably to assaults on the private communities that experienced city dwellers create for themselves which in turn lead to more collective regulation and, in consequence, less of the self-imposed decision to behave properly and as expected, which is the essence of community?

We do not know. "Them what gets the apple gets the worm," goes an old folk saying. Is that what the Ford Foundation building represents: a shining exterior, rotting from within? A civilization whose cancerous growth has already devoured half its offspring, and is moving toward the unthinking, untroubled other half? We shall see. Hopefully, in the meantime we shall also think about it a bit. Mumford, unfailingly, has sorted out the levels of immediacy and difficulty of the current crisis.

> To go deeper into this immediate situation we must, I suggest, distinguish between three aspects, only one of which is open to immediate rectification. We must first separate out the problems that are soluble with the means we have at hand: this includes such immediate measures as vermin control, improved garbage collection,

cheap public transportation, new schools and hospitals and health clinics. Second, those that require a new approach, new agencies, new methods, whose assemblage will require time, even though the earliest possible action is urgent. And finally there are those that require a reorientation in the purposes and ultimate ideals of our whole civilization—solutions that hinge on a change of mind, as far-reaching as that which characterized the change from the medieval religious mind to the modern scientific mind. Ultimately, the success of the first two changes will hinge upon this larger— and, necessarily, later—transformation. So, far from looking to a scientifically oriented technology to solve our problems, we must realize that this highly sophisticated dehumanized technology itself now produces some of our most vexatious problems, including the unemployment of the unskilled.

But something more than thinking will be required. A certain giving of ourselves with no certainty of what will come of it. It is the only known way, and imperfectly known at that.

Attend to Mrs. Boyle at the end of *Juno and the Paycock*, pleading for the return of a simpler life, a life before all things had become political, before all men were committed, before all cities somehow seemed in flames:

Sacred Heart o' Jesus, take away our hearts o' stone, and give us hearts o' flesh! Take away this murdherin' hate, an' give us Thine own eternal love!

THE URBAN UNEASE: COMMUNITY VS. CITY

James Q. Wilson

One of the benefits (if that is the word) of the mounting concern over "the urban crisis" has been the emergence, for perhaps the first time since the subject became popular, of a conception of what this crisis really means, from the point of view of the urban citizen. After a decade or more of being told by various leaders that what's wrong with our large cities is inadequate transportation, or declining retail sales, or poor housing, the resident of the big city, black and white alike, is beginning to assert his own definition of that problem—and this definition has very little relationship to the conventional wisdom on the urban crisis.

This common man's view of "the urban problem," as opposed to the elite view, has several interesting properties. Whereas scholars are interested in poverty, this is a national rather than a specifically urban problem; the common man's concern is with what is unique to cities and especially to large cities. Racial discrimination deeply concerns blacks, but only peripherally concerns whites; the problem that is the subject of this article concerns blacks and whites alike, and intensely so. And unlike tax inequities or air pollution, for which

James Q. Wilson, "The Urban Unease: Community vs. City," **THE PUBLIC INTEREST**, *Summer 1968. Copyright 1968 by National Affairs, Inc., and reprinted by permission of the author and publisher.*

government solutions are in principle available, it is far from clear just what, if anything, government can do about the problem that actually concerns the ordinary citizen.

This concern has been indicated in a number of public opinion surveys, but, thus far at least, the larger implications of the findings have been ignored. In a poll of over one thousand Boston home owners, that I recently conducted in conjunction with a colleague, we asked what the respondent thought was the biggest problem facing the city. The "conventional" urban problems—housing, transportation, pollution, urban renewal, and the like—were a major concern of only 18 per cent of those questioned, and these were expressed disproportionately by the wealthier, better-educated respondents. Only 9 per cent mentioned jobs and employment, even though many of those interviewed had incomes at or even below what is often regarded as the poverty level. *The issue which concerned more respondents than any other was variously stated—crime, violence, rebellious youth, racial tension, public immorality, delinquency. However stated, the common theme seemed to be a concern for improper behavior in public places.*

For some white respondents this was no doubt a covert way of indicating anti-Negro feelings. But it was not primarily that, for these same forms of impropriety were mentioned more often than other problems by Negro respondents as well. And among the whites, those who indicated, in answer to another question, that they felt the government ought to do *more* to help Negroes were just as likely to mention impropriety as those who felt the government had already done too much.

Nor is this pattern peculiar to Boston. A survey done for *Fortune* magazine in which over three hundred Negro males were questioned in thirteen major cities showed similar results. In this study, people were not asked what was the biggest problem of their city, but rather what was the biggest problem they faced as individuals. When stated this generally, it was not surprising that the jobs and education were given the highest priority. What is striking is that close behind came the same "urban" problems found in Boston—a concern for crime, violence, the need for more police protection, and the like. Indeed, these issues ranked *ahead* of the expressed desire for a higher income. Surveys reported by the President's Commission on Law Enforcement and Administration of Justice showed crime and violence ranking high as major problems among both Negro and white respondents.

THE FAILURE OF COMMUNITY

In reading the responses to the Boston survey, I was struck by how various and general were the ways of expressing public concern in this area. "Crime in the streets" was *not* the stock answer, though that came up often enough. Indeed, many of the forms of impropriety mentioned involved little that was criminal in any serious sense—rowdy teenagers, for example, or various indecencies (lurid advertisements in front of neighborhood movies and racy paperbacks in the local drugstore).

What these concerns have in common, and thus what constitutes the "urban problem" for a large percent (perhaps a majority) of urban citizens, is *a sense of the failure of community.* By "community" I do not mean, as some do, a metaphysical entity or abstract collectivity with which people "need" to affiliate. There may be an "instinct" for "togetherness" arising out of ancient or tribal longings for identification, but different people gratify it in different ways, and for most the gratification has little to do with neighborhood or urban conditions. When I speak of the concern for "community," I refer to a desire for the observance of standards of right and seemly conduct in the public places in which one lives and moves, those standards to be consistent with—and supportive of—the values and life styles of the particular individual. Around one's home, the places where one shops, and the corridors through which one walks there is for each of us a public space wherein our sense of security, self-esteem, and propriety is either reassured or jeopardized by the people and events we encounter. Viewed this way, the concern for community is less the "need" for "belonging" (or in equally vague language, the "need" to overcome feelings of "alienation" or "anomie") than the concerns of any rationally self-interested person with a normal but not compulsive interest in the environment of himself and his family.

A rationally self-interested person would, I argue, take seriously those things which affect him most directly and importantly and over which he feels he can exercise the greatest influence. Next to one's immediate and particular needs for shelter, income, education, and the like, one's social and physical surroundings have perhaps the greatest consequence for oneself and one's family. Furthermore, unlike those city-wide or national forces which influence a person, what happens to him at the neighborhood level is most easily affected by his own actions. The way he behaves will, ideally, alter the behavior of others; the remarks he makes, and the way he presents himself and his home will shape, at least marginally, the common expectations by which the appropriate standards of public conduct in that area are determined. How he dresses, how loudly or politely he speaks, how well he trims his lawn or paints his house, the liberties he permits his children to enjoy—all these not only express what the individual thinks is appropriate conduct, but in some degree influence what his neighbors take to be appropriate conduct.

These relationships at the neighborhood level are to be contrasted with other ways in which a person might perform the duties of an urban citizen. Voting, as a Harvard University colleague delights in pointing out, is strictly speaking an irrational act for anyone who does not derive any personal benefit from it. Lacking any inducement of money or esteem, and ignoring for a moment the sense of duty, there is for most voters no rational reason for casting a ballot. The only way such an act would be reasonable to such a voter is if he can affect (or has a good chance to affect) the outcome of the election—that is, to make or break a tie. Such a possibility is so remote as to be almost nonexistent. Of course, most of us do vote, but primarily out of a sense of duty, or because it is fun or makes us feel good. As a way of influencing those forces which in turn influence us, however, voting is of practically no value.

Similarly with the membership one might have in a civic or voluntary association; unless one happens to command important resources of wealth, power, or status, joining such an organization (provided it is reasonably large) is not likely to affect the ability of that organization to achieve its objective.. And if the organization *does* achieve its objectives (if, for example, it succeeds in getting taxes lowered or an open occupancy law passed or a nuisance abated), nonmembers will benefit equally with members. This problem has been carefully analyzed by Mancur Olson in *The Logic of Collective Actions*[1] in a way that calls into serious question the ability of any organization to enlist a mass following when it acts for the common good and gives to its members no individual rewards. Some people will join, but because they will get some personal benefit (the status of influence that goes with being an officer, for example), or out of a sense of duty or, again, because it is "fun." As a way of shaping the urban citizen's environment, however, joining a large civic association is not much more rational than voting.

CONTROLLING THE IMMEDIATE ENVIRONMENT

It is primarily at the neighborhood level that meaningful (i.e., potentially rewarding) opportunities for the exercise of urban citizenship exist. And it is the breakdown of neighborhood controls (neighborhood self-government, if you will) that accounts for the principal concerns of urban citizens. When they can neither take for granted nor influence by their actions and those of their neighbors the standards of conduct within their own neighborhood community, they experience what to them are "urban problems"—problems that arise directly out of the unmanageable consequences of living in close proximity.

I suspect that it is this concern for the maintenance of the neighborhood community that explains in part the overwhelming preference Americans have for small cities and towns. According to a Gallup Poll taken in 1963, only 22 per cent of those interviewed wanted to live in cities, 49 per cent preferred small towns, and 28 per cent preferred suburbs. (Only among Negroes, interestingly enough, did a majority prefer large cities—perhaps because the costs of rural or small town life, in terms of poverty and discrimination, are greater for the Negro than the costs, in terms of disorder and insecurity, of big-city life.) Small towns and suburbs, because they are socially more homogeneous than large cities and because local self-government can be used to reinforce informal neighborhood sanctions, apparently make the creation and maintenance of a proper sense of community easier. At any rate, Americans are acting on this preference for small places, whatever its basis. As Daniel Elazar has pointed out, the smaller cities are those which are claiming a growing share of the population; the largest cities are not increasing in size at all and some, indeed, are getting smaller.

A rational concern for community implies a tendency to behave in certain ways which some popular writers have mistakenly thought to be the result of conformity, prejudice, or an excessive concern for appearances. No doubt all of these factors play some role in the behavior of many people and a dominant role in the behavior of a few, but one need not make any such assumptions to

[1] Cambridge: Harvard University Press, 1965.

explain the nature of most neighborhood conduct. In dealing with one's immediate environment under circumstances that make individual actions efficacious in constraining the actions of others, one will develop a range of sanctions to employ against others and one will, in turn, respond to the sanctions that others use. Such sanctions are typically informal, even casual, and may consist of little more than a gesture, word, or expression. Occasionally direct action is taken—a complaint, or even making a scene, but resort to these measures is rare because they invite counterattacks ("If that's the way he feels about it, I'll just show him! ") and because if used frequently they lose their effectiveness. The purpose of the sanctions is to regulate the external consequences of private behavior—to handle, in the language of economists, "third-party effects," "externalities," and "the production of collective goods." I may wish to let my lawn go to pot, but one ugly lawn affects the appearance of the whole neighborhood, just as one sooty incinerator smudges clothes that others have hung out to dry. Rowdy children raise the noise level and tramp down the flowers for everyone, not just for their parents.

Because the sanctions employed are subtle, informal, and delicate, not everyone is equally vulnerable to everyone else's discipline. Furthermore, if there is not a generally shared agreement as to appropriate standards of conduct, these sanctions will be inadequate to correct such deviations as occur. A slight departure from a norm is set right by a casual remark; a commitment to a different norm is very hard to alter, unless of course the deviant party is "eager to fit in," in which case he is not committed to the different norm at all but simply looking for signs as to what the preferred norms may be. Because of these considerations, the members of a community have a general preference for social homogeneity and a suspicion of heterogeneity—a person different in one respect (e.g., income, or race, or speech) may be different in other respects as well (e.g., how much noise or trash he is likely to produce).

PREJUDICE AND DIVERSITY

This reasoning sometimes leads to error—people observed to be outwardly different may not in fact behave differently, or such differences in behavior as exist may be irrelevant to the interests of the community. Viewed one way, these errors are exceptions to rule-of-thumb guides or empirical generalizations; viewed another way, they are manifestations of prejudice. And in fact one of the unhappiest complexities of the logic of neighborhood is that it can so often lead one wrongly to impute to another person some behavioral problem on the basis of the latter's membership in a racial or economic group. Even worse, under cover of acting in the interests of the neighborhood, some people may give vent to the most unjustified and neurotic prejudices.

However much we may regret such expressions of prejudice, it does little good to imagine that the occasion for their expression can be wished away. We may even pass laws (as I think we should) making it illegal to use certain outward characteristics (like race) as grounds for excluding people from a neighborhood. But the core problem will remain—owing to the importance of community to most people, and given the process whereby new arrivals are inducted into and constrained by the sanctions of the neighborhood, the suspicion of heterogeneity will remain and will only be overcome when a person proves by his actions that his distinctive characteristic is not a sign of any disposition to violate the community's norms.

Such a view seems to be at odds with the notion that the big city is the center of cosmopolitanism—by which is meant, among other things, diversity. And so it is. A small fraction of the population (in my judgment, a *very* small fraction) may want diversity so much that it will seek out the most cosmopolitan sections of the cities as places to live. Some of these people are intellectuals, others are young, unmarried persons with a taste for excitement before assuming the responsibilities of a family, and still others are "misfits" who have dropped out of society for a variety of reasons. Since one element of this group—the intellectuals—writes the books which define the "urban problem," we are likely to be confused by their preferences and assume that the problem is in part to maintain the heterogeneity and cosmopolitanism of the central city—to attract and hold a neat balance among middle-class families, young culture-lovers, lower-income Negroes, "colorful" Italians, and big businessmen. *To assume this is to mistake the preferences of the few for the needs of the many.* And even the few probably exaggerate just how much diversity they wish. Manhattan intellectuals are often as worried about crime in the streets as their cousins in Queens. The desired diversity is "safe" diversity—a harmless variety of specialty stores, esoteric bookshops, "ethnic" restaurants, and highbrow cultural enterprises.

ON "MIDDLE-CLASS VALUES"

At this point I had better take up explicitly the dark thoughts forming in the minds of some readers that this analysis is little more than an elaborate justification for prejudice, philistinism, conformity, and (worst of all) "middle-class values." The number of satirical books on suburbs seem to suggest that the creation of a sense of community is at best little more than enforcing the lowest common denominator of social behavior by means of *kaffee klatsches* and the exchange of garden tools; at worst, it is the end of privacy and individuality and the beginning of discrimination in its uglier forms.

I have tried to deal with the prejudice argument above, though no doubt inadequately. Prejudice exists; so does the desire for community; both often overlap. There is no "solution" to the problem, though stigmatizing certain kinds of prejudgments (such as those based on race) is helpful. Since (in my opinion) social class is the primary basis (with age and religion not far behind) on which community-maintaining judgments are made, and since social class (again, in my opinion) is a much better predictor of behavior than race, I foresee the time when racial distinctions will be much less salient (though never absent) in handling community problems. Indeed, much of what passes for "race prejudice" today may be little more than class prejudice with race used as a rough indicator of approximate social class.

With respect to the charge of defending "middle-class values," let me stress that the analysis of "neighborhood" offered here makes no assumptions about the substantive values enforced by the communal process. On the contrary, the emphasis is on the process itself; in principle, it could be used to enforce any set of values. To be sure, we most often observe it enforcing the injunctions against noisy children and lawns infested with crabgrass, but I suppose it could also be used to enforce injunctions against turning children into "sissies" and being enslaved by lawn-maintenance chores. In fact, if we turn our attention to the city and end our pre-occupation with suburbia, we will find many kinds of neighborhoods with a great variety of substantive values being enforced. Jane Jacobs described how and to what ends informal community controls operate in working-class Italian sections of New York and elsewhere. Middle-class Negro neighborhoods tend also to develop a distinctive code. And Bohemian or "hip-pie" sections (despite their loud disclaimers of any interest in either restraint or constraint) establish and sustain a characteristic ethos.

PEOPLE WITHOUT COMMUNITIES

Viewed historically, the process whereby neighborhoods, in the sense intended in this article, have been formed in the large cities might be thought of as one in which order arose out of chaos to return in time to a new form of disorder.

Immigrants, thrust together in squalid central-city ghettos, gradually worked their way out to establish, first with the aid of streetcar lines and then with the aid of automobiles, more or less homogeneous and ethnically distinct neighborhoods of single-family and two-family houses. In the Boston survey, the *average* respondent had lived in his present neighborhood for *about twenty years.* When asked what his neighborhood had been like when he was growing up, the vast majority of those questioned said that it was "composed of people pretty much like myself"—similar, that is, in income, ethnicity, religion, and so forth. In time, of course, families—especially those of childrearing age—began spilling out over the city limits into the suburbs, and were replaced in the central city by persons lower in income than themselves.

Increasingly, the central city is coming to be made up of persons who face special disabilities in creating and maintaining a sense of community. There are several such groups, each with a particular problem and each with varying degrees of ability to cope with that problem. One is composed of affluent whites without children (young couples, single persons, elderly couples whose children have left home) who either (as with the "young swingers") lack an interest in community or (as with the elderly couples) lack the ability to participate meaningfully in the maintenance of community. But for such persons, there are alternatives to community—principally, the occupancy of a special physical environment that in effect insulates the occupant from such threats as it is the function of community to control. They move into high-rise buildings in which their apartment is connected by an elevator to either a basement garage (where they can step directly into their car) or to a lobby guarded by a doorman and perhaps even a private police force. Thick walls and high fences protect such open spaces as exist from the instrusion of outsiders. The apartments may even be air conditioned, so that the windows need never be opened to admit street noises. Interestingly, a common complaint of such apartment-dwellers is that, in the newer buildings at least, the walls are too thin to ensure privacy—in short, the one failure of the physical substitute for community occasions the major community-oriented complaint.

A second group of noncommunal city residents are the poor whites, often elderly, who financially or for other reasons are unable to leave the old central-city neighborhood when it changes character. For many, that change is the result of the entry of Negroes or Puerto Ricans into the block, and this gives rise to the number of anti-Negro or anti-Puerto Rican remarks which an interviewer encounters. But sometimes the neighborhood is taken over by young college students, or by artists, or by derelicts; then the remarks are anti-youth, anti-student, anti-artist, or anti-drunk. The fact that the change has instituted a new (and to the older resident) less seemly standard of conduct is more important than the attributes of the persons responsible for the change. Elderly persons, because they lack physical vigor and the access to neighbors which having children facilitates, are especially vulnerable to neighborhood changes and find it especially difficult to develop substitutes for community—except, of course, to withdraw behind locked doors and drawn curtains. They cannot afford the high-rise buildings and private security guards that for the wealthier city-dweller are the functional equivalent of communal sanctions.

In the Boston survey, the fear of impropriety and violence was highest for those respondents who were the oldest and the poorest. Preoccupation with such issues as the major urban problem was greater among women than among men, among those over sixty-five years of age than among those under, among Catholics more than among Jews and among those earning less than $5,000 a year more than among those earning higher incomes. (Incidentally, these were *not* the same persons most explicitly concerned about and hostile to Negroes—anti-Negro sentiment was more common among middle-aged married couples who had children and modestly good incomes.)

The third group of persons afflicted by the perceived breakdown of community are the Negroes. For them, residential segregation as well as other factors have led to a condition in which there is relatively little spatial differentiation among Negroes of various class levels. Lower-class, working-class, and middle-class Negroes are squeezed into close proximity, one on top of the other, in such a way as to inhibit or prevent the territorial separation necessary for the creation and maintenance of different communal life styles. Segregation in the housing market may be (I suspect it is) much more intense with respect to lower-cost housing than with middle-cost housing, suggesting that middle-class Negroes may find it easier to move into previously all-white neighborhoods. But the constricted supply of low-cost housing means that a successful invasion of a new area by middle-class Negroes often leads to that break being followed rather quickly by working- and lower-class Negroes. As a result, unless middle-class Negroes can leapfrog out to distant white (or new) communities, they will find themselves struggling to assert hegemony over a territory threatened on several sides by Negroes with quite different life styles.

This weakness of community in black areas may be the most serious price we will pay for residential segregation. It is often said that the greatest price is the perpetuation of a divided society, one black and the other white. While there is some merit in this view, it overlooks the fact that most ethnic groups, when reasonably free to choose a place to live, have chosen to live among people similar to themselves. (I am thinking especially of the predominantly Jewish suburbs.) *The real price of segregation, in my opinion, is not that it forces blacks and whites apart but that it forces blacks of different class positions together.*

WHAT CITY GOVERNMENT CANNOT DO

Communal social controls tend to break down either when persons with an interest in, and the competence for, maintaining a community no longer live in the area or when they remain but their neighborhood is not sufficiently distinct, territorially, from areas with different or threatening life styles. In the latter case especially, the collapse of informal social controls leads to demands for the imposition of formal or institutional controls—demands for "more police protection," for more or better public services, and the like. The difficulty, however, is that there is relatively little government can do directly to maintain a neighborhood community. It can, of course, assign more police officers to it, but there are real limits to the value of this response. For one thing, a city only has so many officers and those assigned to one neighborhood must often be taken away from another. And perhaps more important, the police can rarely manage all relevant aspects of conduct in public places whatever may be their success·in handling serious crime (such as muggings or the like). Juvenile rowdiness, quarrels among neighbors, landlord-tenant disputes, the unpleasant side effects of a well-patronized tavern—all these are matters which may be annoying enough to warrant police intervention but not to warrant arrests. Managing these kinds of public disorder is a common task for the police, but one that they can rarely manage to everyone's satisfaction—precisely because the disorder arises out of a dispute among residents over what *ought* be the standard of proper conduct.

In any case, city governments have, over the last few decades, become increasingly remote from neighborhood concerns. Partly this has been the consequence of the growing centralization of local government—mayors are getting stronger at the expense of city councils, city-wide organizations (such as newspapers and civic associations) are getting stronger at the expense of neighborhood-based political parties, and new "superagencies" are being created in city hall to handle such matters as urban renewal, public welfare, and anti-poverty programs. Mayors and citizens alike in many cities have begun to react against this trend and to search for ways of reinvolving government in neighborhood concerns: mayors are setting up "little city halls," going on walking tours of their cities, and meeting with neighborhood and block clubs. But there is a limit to how effective such responses can be, because whatever the institutional structure, the issues that most concern a neighborhood are typically those about which politicians can do relatively little.

For one thing, the issues involve disputes among the residents of a neighborhood, or between the residents of two adjoining neighborhoods, and the mayor takes sides in these matters only at his peril. For another, many of the issues involve no tangible stake—they concern more the *quality* of life and competing standards of propriety and less the dollars-and-cents value of particular services or programs. Officials with experience in organizing little city halls or police-community relations programs often report that a substantial portion (perhaps a majority) of the complaints they receive concern people who "don't keep up their houses," or who "let their children run wild," or who "have noisy parties." Sometimes the city can do something (by, for example, sending around the building inspectors to look over a house that appears to be a firetrap or by having the health department require someone to clean up a lot he has littered), but just as often the city can do little except offer its sympathy.

POVERTY AND COMMUNITY

Indirectly, and especially over the long run, government can do much more. First and foremost, it can help persons enter into those social classes wherein the creation and maintenance of community is easiest. Lower-class persons are (by definition, I would argue) those who attach little importance to the opinions of others, are preoccupied with the daily struggle for survival and the immediate gratifications that may be attendant on survival, and inclined to uninhibited, expressive conduct. (A lower-*income* person, of course, is not necessarily lower *class;* the former condition reflects how much money he has, while the latter indicates the attitudes he possesses.) Programs designed to increase prosperity and end poverty (defined as having too little money) will enable lower-income persons who do care about the opinions of others to leave areas populated by lower-income persons who don't care (that is, areas populated by lower-class persons).

Whether efforts to eliminate poverty by raising incomes will substantially reduce the size of the lower class is a difficult question. The progress we make will be much slower than is implied by those who are currently demanding an "immediate" and "massive" "commitment" to "end poverty." I favor many of these programs, but I am skeptical that we really know as much about how to end our social problems as those persons who blame our failure simply on a lack of "will" seem to think. I suspect that know-how is in as short supply as will power. But what is clear to me is that *programs that seek to eliminate poverty in the cities will surely fail,* for every improvement in the income and employment situation in the large cities will induce an increased migration of more poor people from rural and small-town areas to those cities. The gains are likely to be wiped out as fast as they are registered. To end urban poverty it is necessary to end rural poverty; thus, programs aimed specifically at the big cities will not succeed, while programs aimed at the nation as a whole may.

The need to consider poverty as a national rather than an urban problem, which has been stated most persuasively by John Kain and others, is directly relevant to the problem of community. *Programs that try to end poverty in the cities, to the extent they succeed, will probably worsen, in the short run, the problems of maintaining a sense of community in those cities—and these communal problems are, for most persons, the fundamental urban problems.* People migrate to the cities now because cities are, on the whole, more prosperous than other places. Increasing the advantage the city now enjoys, without simultaneously improving matters elsewhere, will increase the magnitude of that advantage, increase the flow of poor migrants, and thus make more difficult the creation and maintenance of communal order, especially in those working-class areas most vulnerable to an influx of lower-income newcomers. This will be true whether the migrants are white or black, though it will be especially serious for blacks because of the compression effects of segregation in the housing market.

THE DIFFERENCES AMONG PEOPLE

It is, of course, rather misleading to speak in global terms of "classes" as if all middle-class (or all working-class) persons were alike. Nothing could be further from the truth; indeed, the failure to recognize intraclass differences in life style has been a major defect of those social commentaries on "middle-class values" and "conformity." The book by Herbert J. Gans on Levittown is a refreshing exception to this pattern, in that it calls attention to fundamental cleavages in life style in what to the outside observer appears to be an entirely homogeneous, "middle-class" suburb. Partly the confusion arises out of mistaking economic position with life style—some persons may be economically working-class but expressively middle-class, or vice versa.

To what extent can persons with low incomes display and act upon middle-class values? To what extent is there a substitute for affluence as a resource permitting the creation and maintenance of a strong neighborhood community? Apparently some Italian neighborhoods with relatively low incomes nonetheless develop strong communal controls. The North End of Boston comes to mind. Though economically disadvantaged, and though the conventional signs of "middle-class values" (neat lawns, quiet streets, single-family homes) are almost wholly absent, the regulation of conduct in public places is nonetheless quite strong. The incidence of street crime is low, "outsiders" are carefully watched, and an agreed-on standard of conduct seems to prevail.

Perhaps a strong and stable family structure (as among Italians) permits even persons of limited incomes to maintain a sense of community. If so, taking seriously the reported weakness in the Negro family structure becomes important, not simply because of its connection with employment and other individual problems, but because of its implications for communal order. Indeed, substantial gains in income in areas with weak family and communal systems may produce little or no comparable gain in public order (and I mean here order as judged by the residents of the affected area, not order as judged by some outside observer). What most individuals may want in their public places they may not be able to obtain owing to an inability to take collective action or to make effective their informal sanctions.

"BLACK POWER" AND COMMUNITY

It is possible that "Black Power" will contribute to the ability of some neighborhoods to achieve communal order. I say "possible"—it is far from certain, because I am far from certain as to what Black Power implies or as to how dominant an ethos it will become. As I understand it, Black Power is not a set of substantive objectives, much less a clearly worked-out ideology, but rather an attitude, a posture, a communal code that attaches high value to pride, self-respect, and the desire for autonomy. Though it has programmatic implications ("neighborhood self-control," "elect black mayors," and so forth), the attitude is (to me) more significant than the program. Or stated another way, the cultural implications of Black Power may in the long run prove to be more important than its political implications.

In the short run, of course, Black Power—like any movement among persons who are becoming politically self-conscious, whether here or in "developing" nations—will produce its full measure of confusion, disorder, and demagoguery. Indeed, it sometimes appears to be little more than a license to shout slogans, insult "whitey," and make ever more extravagant bids for power and leadership in black organizations. But these may be only the short-term consequences, and I for one am inclined to discount them somewhat. The long-term implications seem to be a growing pride in self and in the community, and these are prerequisites for the creation and maintenance of communal order.

Historians may some day conclude that while Negroes were given emancipation in the nineteenth century, they had to win it in the twentieth. The most important legacy of slavery and segregation was less, perhaps, the inferior economic position that Negroes enjoyed than the inferior cultural position that was inflicted on them. To the extent it is possible for a group to assert communal values even though economically disadvantaged, Negroes were denied that opportunity because the prerequisite of self-improvement—self-respect—was not generally available to them. The present assertion of self-respect is an event of the greatest significance and, in my view, contributes more to explaining the civil disorders and riots of our larger cities than all the theories of "relative deprivation," "economic disadvantages," and the like. The riots, from this perspective are expressive acts of self-assertion, not instrumental acts designed to achieve particular objectives. And programs of economic improvement and laws to guarantee civil rights, while desirable in themselves, are not likely to end the disorder.

The fact that these forms of self-expression cause such damage to the black areas of a city may in itself contribute to the development of communal order; the people who are paying the price are the Negroes themselves. The destruction they have suffered may lead to an increased sense of stake in the community and a more intense concern about the maintenance of community self-control. Of course, no amount of either self-respect or commitment to community can overcome a serious lack of resources—money, jobs, and business establishments.

NO INSIDE WITHOUT AN OUTSIDE

Because the disorders are partly the result of growing pride and assertiveness does not mean, as some have suggested, that we "let them riot" because it is "therapeutic." For one thing, whites who control the police and military forces have no right to ignore the interests of the nonrioting black majority in favor of the instincts of the rioting black minority. Most Negroes want *more* protection and security, not less, regardless of what certain white radicals might say. Furthermore, the cultural value of Black Power or race pride *depends in part on its being resisted by whites.* The existence of a "white enemy" may be as necessary for the growth of Negro self-respect as the presumed existence of the "capitalist encirclement" was for the growth of socialism in the Soviet Union. As James Stephens once said, there cannot be an inside without an outside.

Nor does Black Power require that control over all political and economic institutions be turned over forthwith to any black organization that happens to demand it. Neighborhoods, black or white, should have control over some functions and not over others, the decision in each case requiring a rather careful analysis of the likely outcomes of alternative distributions of authority. Cultures may be invigorated and even changed by slogans and expressive acts, but constitutions ought to be the result of deliberation and careful choices. The reassertion of neighborhood values, by blacks and whites alike, strikes me as a wholly desirable reaction against the drift to overly bureaucraticized central city governments, but there are no simple formulas or rhetorical "principles" on the basis of which some general and all-embracing reallocation of power can take place. Those who find this reservation too timid should bear in mind that functions given black neighborhoods will also have to be given to white neighborhoods—it is not politically feasible (or perhaps even legally possible) to decentralize power over black communities but centralize it over white ones. Are those radicals eager to have Negro neighborhoods control their own police force equally eager to have adjoining working-class Polish or Italian neighborhoods control theirs?

In any case, no one should be optimistic that progress in creating meaningful communities within central cities will be rapid or easy. The fundamental urban problems, though partly economic and political, are at root questions of values, and these change or assert themselves only slowly, if at all. And whatever gains might accrue from the social functions of Black Power might easily be outweighed by a strong white reaction against it and thus against blacks. The competing demands for territory within our cities is intense and not easily managed, and for some time to come the situation will remain desperately precarious. [Summer 1968]

OUR CITIES, THE UPTIGHT LIFE

Ira Mothner

We are all afraid now. Panic can make an edgy white man read vengeance in every black face; and black men see the terror, and it burns them, because it adds another affront to the day.

We clash eyes with the man beside us when a seat opens on the bus, stare each other down for a taxi or a table. We're vulnerable to an elbow in the belly or a crack at our pride. "What vital service will blow next?" we ask. "What union will strike?" We hate the grit and sooty air, the din and the feeling that there's nothing we can do about any of it; no one we can blame or curse or ask to make it right.

Cities were never made for the meek. They are rude, abrasive places, and they forge sharp types who take turmoil with the street wisdom no city kid ever forgets. Art, commerce and ideas thrive in these messy surroundings. They always have. The ambiance, cheap lodgings and artists drew talented youngsters from the sticks long before there were museums and schools. Culture in a "center" is already stuffed and mounted; back street, offbeat failures make it grow, feed it new forms and new blood. What lights up the city is the urban flux, the jarring contact of different styles and different peoples; for cities are the vital center of the metropolitan sprawl where two-thirds of the nation live.

Most Americans stick to the soft outer edges. Suburbs clicked off gains of better than 11 million people between 1960 and 1966. The cities picked up about one-and-a-half million by 1963, then stopped cold.

The nation never cherished its cities. Jefferson chose to stick the capital in a swamp rather than New York, and thought yellow fever wasn't too terrible if it discouraged "the growth of great cities." Our legendary heroes are woodsmen and cowboys, not artists or inventors. We rejected cities first because they weren't woodsy enough, then turned on them because they weren't quite civilized. They were filled with noisy, smelly immigrants sweating their hopes out over machines that made America rich.

Now, the cities are feared for their problems. Well, who dumped them here? What happens to the drifters and the drunks when they get run out of small towns and suburbs? Where do your local homosexuals go, your runaways? Can a junkie make a connection in Moose Lake? When you move

Ira Mothner, "Our Cities, The Uptight Life," **LOOK MAGAZINE,** *June 11, 1968.* Copyright 1968 by Cowles Communications, Inc. Reprinted by permission of the editors.

monster machines onto the land and have to pay minimum wages to farm workers, where do they go after you fire them?

The city imports failure—ignorance, addiction, poverty and perversion—and keeps it. The talent and energy that come in, it exports as success. That hustling young graduate starts career-making in Big Town. But where does he go when he begins his family? The odds are he doesn't fight for a decent-sized apartment and worry about city schools. He takes off greenward, and his money goes with him. (During the five years after 1960, American families had a median-income jump of $900. Suburban homes did $150 better, while city families got $150 less.)

Suburbs defy their metropolitan nature. They're not little cities, but anti-cities. Against the urban disarray, the clash of class and the more touchy confrontation of race, they set up ordered streets and rows of similarity. His family tucked behind the hedge stockade, safe from rude encounters, crime and miseducation, Daddy braves the urban wilds to bring back the sirloin.

Who comes to town and stays? Mostly, those who can't get out—usually Negroes. More than a million black people moved into central cities between 1960 and 1966, while better than four times as many whites left. (The Negro population of our 25 largest cities doubled between 1950 and 1966.)

Negroes are not only pushed off the farm toward town, they've quit the South for the North and West. They come for jobs, but without skills or the kind of education it takes to get work. And they come with black faces that make the difference.

The city can't help most of them over the big hump into middle-class America. Black unemployment in big cities is now four times greater than white and the cities are strapped to meet Negro needs. Just about all local costs doubled between 1955 and 1966, education went up one-and-a-half times. (New York's welfare bills have jumped from $900 million to $1.4 billion in the past two years alone.) The cities are almost bankrupt, yet they haven't even started on the job that has got to be done.

"The Negro *is* the city problem" is too easy an answer. He's the latest, the most urgent, but he sits under the whole pile of urban inadequacies. The urban crisis is continual, but it doesn't stop the music, the excitement, the opportunity that pull the eager young to big towns each year. Most leave in time, but there will always be those who, knowing the problems, choose to remain.

CITIES: IT'S WHERE THEY HAVE TO LIVE

John and David, Harlem

They don't riot, bust into stores, use drugs or go to school. They're both 16 and smart. Only, "too much was happening on the street" for them to stick in junior high. David didn't get a diploma ("He was the brightest kid who ever came into my class," says his English teacher). Nor did John. Passed on to high school, they stayed three weeks.

John might still be there if he'd found a part-time job, "so I could buy clothes. Even teachers pay more attention to kids with the bucks to dress." Now, the pair lug groceries or shove a hand truck around the garment district. "Some guys do that for a living," says David. But these two have ambitions. Big, stolid John wants to be an engineer; David, a doctor. And they can tell you why it'll never happen. "I'm restless, impatient," insists the thin, keyed-up David. "You need a foreign language for college," says John.

David's mother is a hotel maid; his father, a custodian. (John's father is a crippled widower.) "See the kind of work we had to do," the parents argue. But the street argues louder: "Hustlers never went to school, have big cars, pretty women and smack you in the face with a wad of money." They pay fast cash for pushing drugs in schools, but John and David pass it up.

Both boys live way up Park Avenue, where commuter trains clank by and junkies hang out. They wouldn't leave: "There's always something happening in Harlem." While John allows, "I got no great love for the white man, but he's no devil," he's down on "the junkies, Uncle Toms, store owners." What burns the boys is, "When a guy gets an education, he's gone, and the hustlers are still there."

Each day, they weigh going back to school; they still figure to catch up. "One more day won't hurt," David says. "I'll start back Monday." But he knows, "Monday, it'll be something different." And if he never gets back, he blankly admits, "I'll be a failure."

Anthony Polcari, Boston

"He was the best pocketmaker in Boston," says his son, but Anthony sank his savings in a coffee roaster (a friend showed him how to work it) and went into business. That was 35 years ago, when more than 40,000 people lived in the North End, and almost every one of them was Italian. "Then they throw all the houses down," the old man complains, to build highways that sliced off edges of the district. (Population now: 12,098, and only 67.5 percent Italian.) Students are moving in for cheap housing. "Beatniks dirtied up the neighborhood," a customer tells. "They had to leave." Few Negroes try it. "We simply will not allow a colored person to live down here," says another shopper.

"It's the best place," Anthony swears, near downtown, close-knit by church and clubs, with a tradition of order. ("The element" shot people, but women were safe, and the North End was clean—no drugs.) His daughter and bachelor son Ralph (he runs the store now) still climb to the old man's flat and eat the tripe, *linguine vongole,* all the old-country dishes he loves to cook. Could he ever leave the North End? "Never. Where I going to go to make friends? I'm 70 years."

CITIES: THEY COME TO DO THEIR THING OR MAKE A BUCK

The key dealers, San Francisco

A key is a kilogram, 2.2 pounds of marijuana. The dealer here and his hippie household move 500 kilos a month in Haight-Ashbury. They get $75 or

$85 a brick and make a five-buck profit. (Cut into one-ounce "lids," the brick is worth $200 to $300.) "We believe the key dealers are saints," say the householders, three young men and their girls. ("She's my pupil. I'm her guru," one explains.) They preach a gospel of "grass": "It's a holy thing." There's a warm, puppy-litter feel to their half-a-house. "When we make a whole lot of bread, we go to the park, hand out food and grass." Police don't bother them: "The San Francisco cops are groovy. The only way you can get into trouble is to do something stupid." But thieves do: 23 bricks were stolen; five more went in a holdup.

They talk about buying a country house or an island. Cut off from parents, they put down that generation: "They're going to die pretty soon. Then, we'll be running the country." One girl went back to her family, returned, and says with sad certainty, "This is the only home I've ever had."

Joanne Hedge, Washington

"If I'd stayed in Grosse Pointe Shores, I'd be married by now," But suburbs bored her. New York scared her; so she went to Washington, worked around and settled at antipoverty headquarters. "This town is tailored for young people," but not for a girl "dying to meet a fellow." It's the randomness she goes for: "You happen on to things. You can't bring that great Greek pastry lady to the suburbs." She hates concrete—"They should have grassy paths"—and has learned caution: "In suburbs you can afford to be naive." But the city costs femininity, and "If I'm going to work all day with the boys, damn if I don't want to be treated like a downright woman at night."

Mike Curb, Los Angeles

He's 23. He makes music—and music has made him a very rich boy. In turtleneck and blazer, he leads the producers, musicians and business-side types of Sidewalk Productions, his wholly owned, three-year-old company. (It grossed a million last year.) Off and composing at 18, Mike now produces movie scores and records, runs two publishing companies, three recording studios and a teen-fan newspaper.

Mike works. He rarely dates (and the girl is likely to end up auditioning singers), doesn't think about politics and urban problems except smog. "I like L.A.," he says. "Record companies are here, hippies, teen clubs. We're getting a lot out of the city." His sister adds, "L.A.'s the only place you can make a million dollars overnight."

Paul Shapiro, Boston

"You can do your own thing in the city, without being bothered." Paul's is painting—mostly on canvas. "Painting a model is an experiment, and it's fun," but it's nothing like the careful mandalas he usually creates—symbolic paintings that supposedly aid meditation.

Teaching part-time at a small art school, whanging guitar with a rock group and painting, he chews his day into very small pieces. His wife and two young children "will get their time when we get out of town and have a peaceful life," he says. Like most of us, Paul is ambivalent about urban life: "Boston is good for the artist." The city gives "good vibrations." Then again, he insists, "The city has ripped down all the studios and lofts." (Paul rents space in a vast old piano factory.) Cops have it in for "people like me," and he seethes about rats and rubbish in his alley. "Exhaust pipes blast in your kids' faces," his wife complains. "Parks are for perverts," he says, and believes, "Public schools would destroy my children." Still, for here and now, "The city is the easiest place to operate."

James Cleveland, Cleveland

"A guy can make a buck now," and Jim does. An ex-Army sergeant, he couldn't get a break in Warren, Ohio, and moved on. In Cleveland, he pumped gas, tried and failed to start a service station with his brother and was making $7,000 a year ("That was good money for me") when Shell asked him to try again. Jim only rents his station near the surly Hough ghetto, but clears $15,000 to $16,000.

He lives on the far side of the city line—in Shaker Heights. "Schools were the only reason we moved out," he says, but segregation played a part: "Why should I buy in an area that's going to become a slum? " If riots come, he won't protect his station: "Let it burn." He works with Hough kids in his church group: "These kids have a need—they'll just kill you."

James Morris, Detroit

He'd make out better on welfare, but he's honest, religious, hardworking—and desperate. A brake assembler, earning $107.02 a week, he takes home $84 after taxes, dues and debt. Welfare pays about $120 a week to a family with ten children.

He tried welfare when he was laid off (15 weeks last year). "Why does your wife have babies so often? " the lady asked. He explained about their Pentecostal faith. "You're killing your wife. I'm not going to give you nothing."

He doesn't rage, his church forbids it: "If it weren't for that, I'd have robbed somebody back when everyone was pressing me for bills and the gas was shut off." "I'm scarce of beds," his wife explains, so all the children double up. "We just manage to buy food." It's the cheapest kind of food, often greens and a pot of beans. Yet, when he remembers the riots last summer, he just shakes his head: "I don't know why all this happened."

CITIES: LIVE ROCKY-HARD OR SILK-LINED SMOOTH

Lester Rogers, New York

He's worked logging camps in Washington, harvest crews in Montana; poured steel, washed dishes and ended up "on a Broadway traffic island, sitting on a bench and shaking. I'd been drinking, didn't have a damn thing."

Lester is 64 and an alcoholic, lives in an SRO (single-room occupancy) building, an old apartment house chopped into singles. New York's SRO owners get $15 to $18 a week from their 30,000 tenants (mostly alcoholics and addicts, the aged and mentally ill) for drab rooms without baths. On one block of West 85th Street, there are 700 SRO dwellers (those on welfare cost half a million dollars a year). Lester's building is no worse than others: "They broke into my room twice, got my shoes and brand-new coat. . . . There are some bad boys in the building. Guys get slugged in the elevators." He shuns other drinkers and junkies, scorns "guys who mix it, get high on wine and goofballs."

On welfare and off the bottle, he hangs out at a friendship center for alcoholics, trying to stay dry. He hasn't made it all the way yet.

A small, feisty old man with nearly bare gums ("What do I want with teeth? I live on stew"), he has a touching love for the city: "You go down to Riverside Park when you're hot and can't sleep, lie on the grass and watch the boats go upriver, the lights, the foghorns. It gets to you. I've been all over the States, and I like it here, the upper West Side. Thank God," he says, "I never had to live on the Bowery."

Burt Sugarman, Los Angeles

That's almost $20,000 worth of car and a lot of girl. Burt's 29, single and a swinger-businessman. Starting in college, at 17, with 20 used cars, he now cuts a sugary slice of L.A. action: six used car lots, a finance company, real estate, stocks and a Ghia-Maserati-Excalibur agency. Work and play merge, for "this is the nation's fun business center," he says.

He keeps horses, skis at Aspen, water-skis at Acapulco, golfs at Palm Springs. Ducking the discotheques, his idea of a great night is "going down to Malibu to play volleyball." He owns a beach house there, a house in town and bought a third for its tennis court. He drives the rare red Maserati Ghibli, plus a Rolls, Bentley, Excalibur and a Pontiac station wagon. "Pay $400,000 or $600,000 for a house, and who can see the extra $200,000; but buy a $15,000 car, and people really look—quicker than they look at a girl."

No urbanite ("Paris is just a town, London has only night life"), he talks up L.A.'s restaurants (never eats at home), its art museum (he went two years ago) and its cultural center (he saw Nureyev and Fonteyn). He catches Southern Cal's home games, the Rams, the Dodgers and the city's new hockey team. Casual, he owns two suits, "wear them to court and funerals."

He dismisses crime as a problem, "in our part of town," and keeps an attack-trained German shepherd, a gun by his bed and a burglar alarm.

CITIES: THEY WANT OUT, THEY COME BACK

Minnie Parker, Birmingham

Back in rural New Castle, she'd been doing all right. When her husband walked out, she worked in a motel until she got sick. On welfare, she fleshed out the family diet with homegrown chickens, pigs, corn, peas and collards.

But her father wanted her back in Birmingham ("I was Daddy's child").

Then Daddy died, and her soldier son went AWOL to attend the funeral. He was court-martialed, and his allotment stopped. Now, there was just $118 a month from welfare.

Minnie couldn't pay rent in October and was evicted. They moved everything out, and her gas stove was stolen. She cooks on a coal heater in her new place, a three-room half-house with no hot water, stopped-up plumbing and a broken window. Rent is $35 a month, and rats skitter through the rubbish outside. One rat made it into bed with the child next door.

Angel, 15, was sleeping in class and had to give up his job washing dishes. He'd been working eight hours a night for four dollars. The kids haven't seen a movie since he quit. They eat lots of rice, and Minnie buys big packs of bacon ends and pigs' tails, sometimes a precious pound of chopped meat. She wishes, "the girls had clothes to go to church and could get things to join the Girl Scouts."

Sorry she ever left New Castle, Minnie hopes for a place in the projects, for "they say these houses will be torn down." She couldn't go North and leave her mother: "It's too far. It takes money to take all these children. I really don't care what happens," she says with weary patience. But she does care, and she's grown afraid: "I'm not going to give up my children."

Richard Watson, Philadelphia

"Little League and that sort of thing is not our bag." When the Watsons' home in outer-city Chestnut Hill got too small, they first rented a farmhouse further out. "It was straight out of John O'Hara," says Dick. "These people were worried about Italians moving in." Looking in Philadelphia's Society Hill redevelopment area, a short walk from downtown, they found a burned-out shell for $5,000. It took another $20,000 to make it livable.

The youngsters go to an integrated public school, but the number of black students is falling as more white families move in. Dick, an urbanologist, is delighted that six-year-old Brendan is becoming "a real tough urban kid." For the girls, "The city is Valhalla." Eden, nine, pops off to the movies alone, goes skating, sees plays and ballets. "All these people lugging their kids to children's plays. We give them a buck and send them around the corner."

For Dick and Joan, the joy is deciding to see a play, hear a concert, go out to dinner or a hockey game—and then just go. "If you plan carefully, you *can* live out of the city and still do all this. But the fact is that you *don't*."

Parking is a problem. Joan quit as PTA president "because all we were supposed to do was sell cookies." The house next door has been robbed. And there's the dirt. "Occasionally," Dick admits, "I'd say the hell with it if I could find someplace where the streets are clean." His wife hates July, when the children come home "filthy, sweaty." But they get away for August and can always get out for good. "We're here because we want to be here. People with less money feel trapped, and that makes them afraid."

CITIES: AND THEY HARDLY EVER TOUCH EACH OTHER

Richard Freeman, New Orleans

He has power ("Leadership tends to live in the city to have a voice in city affairs"), and he carries a load of civic and charitable offices. Chairman of Delta

Air Lines' finance committee, he owns four Coca-Cola plants and hunts investments to "fill a void" in the city.

He preaches better planning and a rapid-transit system for New Orleans, doesn't worry about crime and believes the schools are "in good shape."

In the comfortable district where the Freemans live, homes go for better than $100,000. He hunts duck, quail and dove, keeps a 52-foot powerboat on Lake Pontchartrain and a summer place on the Mississippi shore.

Middle-class whites are slipping out of town, while Negroes remain; and the city should soon have a black majority. Freeman is surprised there are no black members on the city council.

"We've pretty well identified the hard-core unemployed," he says, "but haven't met the problem with any success." He finds unskilled jobs hardest to fill: "Somehow, this group has been told they're not to do menial work."

He looks to Washington for money, not for leadership: "Federal programs kill people's desire to help the less fortunate." The voluntary way, he maintains, "gives greater benefits with less cost and more kindness."

Andrew Laskowitz, St. Louis

"We've talked about moving out since the day we moved in. But all our friends with bigger homes have two jobs or else the wife works." Their son goes to parochial school; Andy coaches a kids baseball team. They keep making improvements that won't raise the price of their little house. Young home hunters want newer, suburb-built models.

The neighborhood will be integrated when they go. There's no panic selling, "only whites aren't looking here any more." Andy doesn't balk at Negro neighbors, "not working people raising children. I wouldn't want *anybody* who'd throw trash in our yard."

Mark Carpenter, Chicago

The machine is an image plane digitizer. It feeds facts to a computer from movies of electrons passing through a bubble chamber. The student is more complicated. From Miles City, Montana, Mark picked the University of Chicago for its redhot physics department. He wasn't prepared for nearby black Woodlawn, the muggings, the rapes—and the fear.

Mark hits the art museum, the symphony—but not too hard. Now a junior, he plans to work in astrophysics. He"ll live in the suburbs, away from racial tension," and not raise his children in town: "It seems an unwholesome atmosphere to grow up in."

Gloria Raines, Newark

"We get programmed and studied, inspected, injected, dissected," because "people on welfare aren't considered people." An angry lady, Gloria heads the welfare rights group in Newark's Central Ward and has a chestful of griefs: "If they pay us more money than Mississippi, are we supposed to clap hands and say goody, goody? To get enough food, you can't buy clothes. Caseworkers don't tell you what you can get, just what to do. They want to find men's clothes. If they do, they keep your check." She keeps hammering, "We don't *want* to raise our children on welfare," and charges, "They aim to keep us like this."

Gloria has been on and off welfare since 1959. She had her son Kevin bused to another district, and he was told, "This isn't your school, you're just borrowing it." Cut cold at a PTA meeting, Gloria walked outside, where neighborhood kids threw rocks at her. She fights the filth at home: "The landlord doesn't care, not if he let me move in with five kids.

"I don't want to throw stones and yell, 'We hate Whitey.' I just want us to have what you've got. This is a slum, but it doesn't have to look so slummy." She points to the huge trees no one has tended since the whites moved out. Most of them are dead.

Abe Ptachik, New York

"The Hudson is still there, more beautiful than any river in Europe," but everything else is changing. "This used to be one of the finest neighborhoods in the city," and Abe lived here for 30 years, since he was married and moved into the residence hotel across the street. Now, "The area [the upper West Side] has been invaded," he says. "You can't go out at night," claims his wife. "They knock you down when you get out the door." So, the Ptachiks shouldn't mind leaving—and they must. The hotel is evicting them, "Throwing us out on the sidewalk," because the owners plan to turn the building into a nursing home. "It's not the money, it's being dislocated. You get accustomed to things. We have lots of friends here."

Across town, the area around Abe's Army-Navy store has flipped the other way, and rents are escalating. He doubts he'll renew his lease next time. Then, that will be it for the business his father started 50 years ago.

While they've talked of retiring and moving away, they hesitate. But New York is no longer the city they knew. He remembers walking home with his mother, crossing the Park at night with no fear: "There were block parties then, times when you got to know your neighbors. But not today. Now, you're afraid to be neighborly."

Our cities just don't work very well—for anybody. But they give the worst deal to the people who need the most help. If you've got money, you've got choice. If you haven't, you take whatever the system dishes out. People like Richard Watson can say, "Who needs this?" and get out. With homes selling at a median $23,600 (up $1,200 this past year), it's not a cheap alternative. Nor is it open to everyone. Only one percent of VA and FHA mortgages are written for Negroes.

Still, Jim Cleveland made it across the city line. He moved for better schools; most parents do. There's no argument that suburban schools are a couple of cuts above city ones. It's a simple equation: more middle-class kids equal better schools, no matter what color the kids, no matter where the schools. That's why middle-class city parents have swamped private schools. But money can't always swing this deal either. It takes social skills (connections or prestige) to land a place today. Parochial schools are also overcrowded, and many must raise or start charging tuition, dumping more poor children onto the public system. Poor children are likely to be black children. Between 1960 and 1966, city public school enrollment of Negro youngsters bounced up 30 percent, while white enrollment dropped one percent. Black students sit behind one out of three big-city public school desks—and most of their desks are packed into black schools.

Danger, too, sends families scurrying out of town: the crime rate in our largest cities jumped 23 percent last year. But with enough money, you can hire private patrolmen to watch over your neighborhood, the way Richard Freeman and his friends do. You can keep attack-trained dogs and guns or install a burglar alarm like Burt Sugarman.

What's bad in the city is worse in the ghetto—schools, crime and housing. In New York, almost 35 percent of all Negro housing is "deteriorated or dilapidated." In Pittsburgh, the figure is closer to 50 percent. The simple solution is to knock down all this wretched real estate, and that's what urban renewal was supposed to be all about. But urban renewal demolished twice as many houses and apartments as it replaced during its first 15 years. Poor people's homes came down; all sorts of other things (including high-rent apartments) went up.

Concert halls, museums, parks, libraries, public malls and city centers delight city planners and most solid citizens. They make poor people rage, for the builders must first smash their steel balls into what little low-cost housing remains. Can't public housing take up the slack? Not with fewer than 700,000 "dwelling units" built since New Deal days.

Nor has public housing been such a happy solution. The huge projects are bleak, depressing compounds. ("We don't have trees; muggers could hide behind them.") Critics call them "vertical slums," and tenants often live up to the description with filth and vandalism. ("Why is public housing so lousy? " asked a New York block worker. "Graft," one tenant told him. "Then who," pressed the worker, "pays the guy for pissing in the elevator? ")

While there are now more pleasant ways to provide public housing, even the early eyesores are filled, and waiting lists are years long. Families like Minnie Parker's can do no better; for outside the projects, the true slums begin.

On a block of East 117th Street, not far from where John and David live, one building is now abandoned. There was a fire there last December. "Suspicious origins," said the firemen; "Junkies," said the neighbors; "Hazardous stairwell," said the Department of Buildings, and ordered everyone out. Within two weeks, everything salvageable had been stripped by addicts. The owner had been losing money, so he gave up on the building, didn't even bother to board it up. Now, junkies camp in the doorway, children scramble through treacherous hallways, and neighbors fear this will happen to their home next.

It's a little late to crack down on the slumlords. The slum kings got away, sold out a long time back. Deteriorated buildings were taken over by smaller operators; profits shrank while upkeep kept growing. Most ghetto landlords now are small investors who made a big mistake. Strict code enforcement only forces them to abandon more buildings.

The East Harlem Tenants Council knows this, but keeps after the owners. "These tenants can't pay their way as people do in middle-class neighborhoods," they argue. "The price of profits here is exploitation." If enough buildings are abandoned, they figure the city will have to do something.

The notion of straining the system until it breaks is a familiar strategy these days. The welfare-rights movement, which Gloria Raines pushes in Newark, was first designed to short-circuit the whole welfare system. By welfare standards, the poor are due twice the money that's now passed out. If they organized, got every possible client (like James Morris) to apply for every last nickel, then the whole rattletrap apparatus might finally collapse.

Only, who would pick up the pieces? The cities can barely totter along as they are. "No one has any operating money," says New York's John Lindsay. They can borrow capital money to get things built, but they have a rough time covering regular expenses. New York is in a particular bind. "The whole state is in trouble," the Mayor explains. "We underestimated the care of the poor." Maybe the short-circuit strategy is working.

Meanwhile, the poor must do with what they get. Both Gloria Raines and Minnie Parker depend on public medical care. When Gloria's baby had pneumonia, "He was sent home from the hospital with a collapsed lung," she says. "He was sent home to die." But he didn't. Minnie's son Angel should have his arm broken and reset, only the clinic charges 50 cents a visit, and Minnie owes them. "The woman at the desk, she's a real devil. If you don't have the fifty cents, she won't take you."

Packs of antipoverty money have gone to shore up weak services to the poor. Still, lots of goodhearted people agree with Richard Freeman and believe the job should be left to charity. More enlightened types want to help Negroes fight for things like welfare rights. A crew of white suburban ladies works with the welfare mothers in Newark. But the time has passed for even this kind of action. "There's no room for Whitey in the ghetto," the people there say. "If things are going to change, black people will have to go it alone."

The city is just not coming across for them (or for the Puerto Ricans and Mexican-Americans) the way it did for their predecessors in the slums. There's not much call for brute labor, and Negroes have long since pulled their share of that without getting much to show for it.

Since the last of the old immigrant groups made it up and out, the cities have been professionalized and reformed. We threw monkey wrenches into the machines, drove out the bosses and created a system that is less corrupt and probably more efficient—but indifferent. The ward-heeled organization had a heart and ears, and it ran the city. There was a pipeline to downtown from the neighborhood clubhouse, and a citizen had a chance to get his beefs squared. Now, civil service regulations protect the great bureaucratic baronies that dispense city services with even-handed disregard for customers. They can ignore the people. They can ignore City Hall. "The Mayor is interfering with the police department," New Yorkers were told, as though Lindsay had insulted a foreign power. Reluctant to change, the engineers and educators shrug off most suggestions with the explanation, "You're not professionals."

Rebuffed by bureaucratic resistance, Negroes want to straighten out the ghetto themselves, run the schools, maybe the police, take over the businesses and build a community. They'll need outside help, and they figure it's owed them.

But not everyone believes black people are due any kind of a break. Who objects? "The guy with blinders on," says Lindsay of the man with a narrow class and ethnic point of view. "He corrupts the whole system by demanding everything stand still. He has the most to lose. Yet he's the kind we want in the city because he's got a stake here too."

He drives a cab, walks a beat, works in a union Negroes can't crack. He remembers a generation back and will tell you, "My father was proud to sweep the streets of Boston . . . Baltimore . . . New York . . . Chicago . . . Philadelphia. He never asked for special favors."

Suburban liberals and the city's upper middle class aren't the ones who'll have to move over much. Let them cluck their tongues about "racism"; they aren't threatened. What's brewing in the cities now is an old-style, impolite, political brawl between Negroes and people just a step or two up the ladder. This is what Black Power means to most black people, a chance to confront someone who won't agree with them and won't say, "Isn't it a shame."

CITIES: WHO CAN SAVE THEM?*

As in most self-diagnosis, we tend to interpret the sharp pain our cities are giving us as a sign of deadly cancer or pass it off as the hot dog we ate at lunch. I traveled 10,000 miles around the country to learn from our best city thinkers that things are neither that bad nor that simple.

We must stop kidding ourselves about our cities. This was brought home to me when I talked to insurance vice president Bruce Hayden. He had just visited Soviet Russia with an Urban Land Institute group. "I tried to see things as though I were the head of a newly emerging Asian or African nation who had been exposed to Moscow and Leningrad after visiting New York and Chicago. Judging America and Russia by what he would see, I think it is pretty likely he would draw the wrong conclusion.

"Eight-hundred-year-old Moscow is today a better planned, more livable city than New York by a fairly substantial margin. I found it a thoroughly modern city of six-and-one-half-million people, providing, in a planned fashion, boulevards, parks, skyscrapers, perhaps the world's best mass-transportation system, and satisfactory, if relatively stereotyped, new housing at a very rapid rate. Our visiting head of state perhaps wouldn't notice a lot of other things, like a much lower standard of living than the average American's, because his own nation's standard of living is so far below even the Russian level."

The blunt fact is that the U.S. is far behind many modern nations in city building. One of the best indications that things may improve is the Urban Coalition. John Gardner, recently Secretary of Health, Education and Welfare and now behind the executive desk in the Coalition's Washington headquarters, explains, "We have an ample supply of handwringers. We have an ample supply of critics. We are in very short supply of people willing to lend a hand, to take an honest look at their community and do something about it. The purpose of the Urban Coalition is to make that kind of action possible. It brings the mayors, business leaders, labor leaders, minority-group leaders, religious leaders, etc., together. You cannot solve the problems of our cities without some kind of an alliance of the key figures who affect the life of the city. They do not have to have a perfect understanding. There can be plenty of arguments. But they must agree that it is their city and that they must share in the solution of its problems.

*This section was written by **LOOK** Editor John Peter.

"The business world," says Gardner, "is more concerned than ever with what it ought to do. This awareness has gone through a number of stages, and it's on a new level now. It is not just a feeling that the image of business has to be improved. It is not just a matter of conscience that requires commitment. Many corporation leaders now recognize that it is a question of whether this complex society *can be made to work*— whether we can gain command of the problems that threaten to overwhelm us. Business has a tremendous stake, as all of us do, in whether that question is answered in the affirmative."

Not all would agree with Gunnar Myrdal, the Swedish economist and sociologist, who told me: "The American citizen is generally a much more broad-minded individual, prepared to act more in line with American ideals, when he acts at the national level." But there is widespread agreement among city thinkers on the importance of the Federal Government, especially when it comes to money. Cities, which used to collect more than 70 percent of all taxes, today collect only about 15 percent. Meanwhile, our cities have responsibilities multiplying and needs unattended. Four times, in Woodrow Wilson's Administration, FDR's, Truman's, and now LBJ's, war has diverted money from urban tasks.

John Kenneth Galbraith, author and economic adviser to Presidents, sprawled on a comfortable Eames chair in his office at Harvard's School of Political Science as he talked: "In the 1930's, the years of the great farm crisis, we federalized rural problems. Now, in the years of the great urban crisis, we should federalize the problems of the big cities. We should take over the No. 1 city problem by federalizing the relief program. The strategy of this is important, for the welfare load is the heaviest in the big cities. You give the greatest amount of relief to the area with the greatest need. If you do this in the nature of a guaranteed income, you also slow down the urbanization process. People move into Harlem not because it's good but because it's better than where they have been."

The success of Operation Bootstrap in raising the level of living in Puerto Rico, for example, has achieved something like that. It has now balanced the inflow and outflow of islanders over the "air bridge" to New York City. This kind of interrelationship between rural, suburban, city and central city has forced many thinkers to look for national rather than local solutions. It is even forcing the various departments of the Federal Government that are involved in cities to begin to plan together.

The beginnings of interrelationships between the U.S. departments of Housing and Urban Development, Transportation, Interior, Commerce and Agriculture and their move toward comprehensive thinking led me to a new group of thinkers who may well prove to be one of the best things that ever happened to our cities.

For quite a while, many people have wondered if the same systems-engineering techniques developed for national defense and space programs might not be applied to more down-to-earth problems in our cities. This hope made sense, for the systems approach, as it has evolved, is not just a way of producing expensive hardware but fundamentally a method of tackling complex problems and organizing their solutions. It views problems not in isolation but as part of a system. Like any other disciplinary pursuit, it follows an established procedure through a series of given steps. In the systems approach, you start with a study or exploratory phase, defining the boundaries of the system. Next, you gather and analyze all relevant data for possible solutions. Then, you take the most promising possibilities and move into the "action" phase, in which these solutions become projects or prototypes for testing and evaluation. Finally, you take the best answer and go ahead with it. All this sounds sufficiently logical, but a private language littered with phrases like simulation modeling, input-output techniques, cost-effective formulas, linear and nonlinear programming, feedback theory, queuing theory and other esoteric physical scientisms has created a throbbing aura of mystery around the whole procedure.

In a sunlit Santa Monica building that looks like a cross between a factory and a university, Henry Rowen, president of the RAND Corporation, the most celebrated think tank in the land, said, "The systems approach is not a gadget, not a panacea, not a mystique possessed by a small group of priests. It is simply a matter of putting together people who are disciplined and organized with relevant skills and keeping them together, working in a serious way on the problem. All of which is very commonsensical, very unfancy and very rarely done."

Rowen is convinced that the systems approach can help with the problems of the city and has signed a history-making study contract with New York City to prove it. "What is needed," Rowen argues, "is to overcome the relative lack in our key institutions of a way to really attack the problem more comprehensively. We have to look at city problems more comprehensively and *keep at it.* In the defense business, where some of this work has been done, one important characteristic is that people do not presume that problems get solved in the way that the group can disband and go to work on something else. The problems get transformed, new ones crop up, but you *keep at them.*"

From the systems men like Rowen, we have to learn that the good old Gung-Ho-American-Way of solving the problem won't work any better with the cities than it does in other areas like defense. We have got to get over what people in our national capital call the Jimmy Stewart syndrome: Mr. Smith goes to Washington and solves *the* problem. The problems at home, like those of what to do about Russia, China and the bomb, are not going to be solved by any one idea. The afflictions of our cities are ones we are going to have to work at all our lives and for generations beyond. They are what engineers call ongoing, or open-ended, problems. This may not make us any happier about them, but it should make us more mature.

Not one of the systems men I talked with thought the problems of the city were going to be solved by any invention, but they felt that one—the computer —could help. In a quiet conference room near the center of the security-tight Lockheed Missiles and Space complex in Palo Alto, Calif., Kenneth Larkin outlined the contribution the information sciences might make toward solving urban ills: "The problem of health care, for instance, is not one of medical research. It has prospered and made great progress. Yet large sections of our population get zero health care. When you come right down to it, the problem lies in the health-care delivery system—not in knowing what to do but how to get it done. We have put together a working association with parts of the medical profession and the Mayo Clinic. We began with over 100,000 work-sample measurements in one hospital alone, to find out qualitatively where the moneys go, the limitation of personnel, why the long waiting lines, etc. We postulated a system, a nationwide series of computer centers, to serve urban areas. We are in the process of installing the first part of that system. It will take on the not-so-modest task of putting in computer format the entire body of medical knowledge, and *we are going to get that done.* It holds the promise that any physician anywhere in the U.S., no matter how or where he was trained, will have the information to practice at the highest level of the art. We can begin to see a great many other ways to even more considerably increase the productivity of our health system."

Systems men contradict the tradition of the "specialist" engineer. They look for the broad problems and often prefer to attack them from imaginative, unorthodox angles. For example, Thomas Paine, general manager at GE's TEMPO, in the quiet Southern California mission town of Santa Barbara, questions whether we *should* be attempting to attract industry into the slums. "This is a movement to gild the ghetto. We should make reasonable efforts to improve things there, but fundamentally, we are dealing with an obsolete urban area, the streets, sewers, transportation, etc. To bring a modern factory into that and expect it to compete with a factory out on the crossroads of a couple of superhighways is pretty unrealistic. The alternative would be to move the people out to the suburban part of the city, where there are some clean houses near some factories that offer job opportunities after we give them some training. There may be people in the city who might not like to move—and I realize a lot of lily-white communities don't want them to—but I would like to give these people some real options.

"I don't expect this to happen overnight, but it *is* happening. It *is* going to happen, and in our long-range planning, it seems to me that speeding it up is the sound direction to go. Let's make exits bigger and the aisle wider. We should look at the city and state as a geographic social system which will encourage people to do what they want to do.

"There are institutions that have become," Paine insists, "and institutions that are becoming. Cities are inherently the second. They never should be finished. Americans are criticized by Europeans as being in a throwaway society. We should be criticized; but only because we built too permanently. We should make things with fairly short useful lives so we can rearrange our structures to meet the need of living people. Harlem is just a plain horse-and-buggy place for a large number of sweatshop people who once worked in the downtown lofts. The things that made it are gone, but the structures are left.

"Our big office buildings are an artifact of the paper-and-typewriter society, and already, we see the handwriting on the wall in the magnetic blips of microwave communication that will obsolete it. Lincoln Center is more the wave of the future than the Pan Am Building. The city is going to be the place for leisure-time activities, for government and the industry that runs industry, the command and control center, the knowledge and the communication and decision-making center."

The systems approach is not a quick "technological fix" for our uptight cities. It is a new, virtually unused planning tool in the hands of society. Every systems man like Paine, who has been appointed deputy administrator of NASA, emphasized that our cities represent a problem of a completely different order of magnitude from a moon shot. Bewilderingly complicated though it is, putting a man on the moon is simply a matter of time and money. We can pace a rocket along a critical development path, even if we have to invent new technology as we go, but when dealing with urban people, with their customs and traditions, no one can control the time scale. One systems specialists describes their difficulty in relation to the cities this way: "We don't even know where the moon is yet."

In the temporarily housed Housing and Urban Development agency on K Street in northwest Washington, D.C., undersecretary and ex-MIT Professor Robert Wood voiced the question this way: "What kind of communities do we want to build for those hundred million new Americans who are going to arrive in this country in the next twenty years?"

The men who would save the cities believe that we have been too inclined to look at them as a study in fatal illness. Our cities are not going to die. We have the resources, if we have the will, to make them *the* place to live.

THE FUTURE OF THE CITIES

NATIONAL ADVISORY COMMISSION

INTRODUCTION

We believe action of this kind outlined [in this report] can contribute substantially to control of disorders in the near future. But there should be no mistake about the long run. The underlying forces continue to gain momentum.

The most basic of these is the accelerating segregation of low-income, disadvantaged Negroes within the ghettos of the largest American cities.

By 1985, the 12.1 million Negroes segregated within central cities today will have grown to approximately 20.8 million—an increase of 72 percent.[1]

Prospects for domestic peace and for the quality of American life are linked directly to the future of these cities.

Two critical questions must be confronted: Where do present trends now lead? What choices are open to us?

---

[1] Notes [on population growth] appear at end of [article].

REPORT OF THE NATIONAL ADVISORY COMMISSION ON CIVIL DISORDERS, *"The Future of the Cities" (Washington, D.C.: U.S. Government Printing Office, 1968), Chap. 16.*

I. THE KEY TRENDS

Negro Population Growth[2]

The size of the Negro population in central cities is closely related to total national Negro population growth. In the past 16 years, about 98 percent of this growth has occurred within metropolitan areas, and 86 percent in the central cities of those areas.

A conservative projection of national Negro population growth indicates continued rapid increases. For the period 1966 to 1985, it will rise to a total of 30.7 million, gaining an average of 484,000 a year, or 7.6 percent more than the increase in each year from 1960 to 1966.

CENTRAL CITIES

Further Negro population growth in central cities depends upon two key factors: in-migration from outside metropolitan areas, and patterns of Negro settlement within metropolitan areas.

From 1960 to 1966, the Negro population of all central cities rose 2.4 million, 88.9 percent of total national Negro population growth. We estimate that natural growth accounted for 1.4 million, or 58 percent of this increase, and in-migration accounted for 1 million, or 42 percent.

As of 1966, the Negro population in all central cities totaled 12.1 million. By 1985, we have estimated that it will rise 72 percent to 20.8 million. We believe that natural growth will account for 6 million of this increase and in-migration for 2.7 million.

Without significant Negro out-migration, then, the combined Negro populations of central cities will continue to grow by an average of 316,000 a year through 1985.

This growth would increase the proportion of Negroes to whites in central cities by 1985 from the present 20.6 percent to between an estimated 31 and 35.6 percent.

LARGEST CENTRAL CITIES

These, however, are national figures. Much faster increases will occur in the largest central cities where Negro growth has been concentrated in the past two decades. Washington, D.C., and Newark are already over half Negro. A continuation of recent trends would cause the following 11 major cities to become over 50 percent Negro by the indicated dates:

New Orleans	1971	St. Louis	1978
Richmond	1971	Detroit	1979
Baltimore	1972	Philadelphia	1981
Jacksonville	1972	Oakland	1983
Gary	1973	Chicago	1984
Cleveland	1975		

[2] Tables and explanations of the projections on which they are based appear at the end of the [article].

These cities, plus Washington, D.C. (now over 66 percent Negro), and Newark, contained 12.6 million people in 1960, or 22 percent of the total population of all 224 American central cities. All 13 cities undoubtedly will have Negro majorities by 1985, and the suburbs ringing them will remain largely all white, unless there are major changes in Negro fertility rates,[3] in-migration, settlement patterns or public policy.

Experience indicates that Negro school enrollment in these and other cities will exceed 50 percent long before the total population reaches the mark. In fact, Negro students already comprise more than a majority in the public elementary schools of 12 of the 13 cities mentioned above. This occurs because the Negro population in central cities is much younger and because a much higher proportion of white children attend private schools. For example, St. Louis' population was about 36 percent Negro in 1965; its public elementary school enrollment was 63 percent Negro. If present trends continue, many cities in addition to those listed above will have Negro school majorities by 1985, probably including:

Dallas	Louisville
Pittsburgh	Indianapolis
Buffalo	Kansas City, Mo.
Cincinnati	Hartford
Harrisburg	New Haven
Atlanta	

Thus, continued concentration of future Negro population growth in large central cities will produce significant changes in those cities over the next 20 years. Unless there are sharp changes in the factors influencing Negro settlement patterns within metropolitan areas, there is little doubt that the trend toward Negro majorities will continue. Even a complete cessation of net Negro in-migration to central cities would merely postpone this result for a few years.

Growth of the Young Negro Population

We estimate that the nation's white population will grow 16.6 million, or 9.5 percent, from 1966 to 1975, and the Negro population 3.8 million, or 17.7 percent, in the same period. The Negro age group from 15 to 24 years of age, however, will grow much faster than either the Negro population as a whole, or the white population in the same age group.

From 1966 to 1975, the number of Negroes in this age group will rise 1.6 million, or 40.1 percent. The white population aged 15 to 24 will rise 6.6 million, or 23.5 percent.

This rapid increase in the young Negro population has important implications for the country. This group has the highest unemployment rate in the nation, commits a relatively high proportion of all crimes, and plays the most significant role in civil disorders. By the same token, it is a great reservoir of underused human resources which are vital to the nation.

[3] The fertility rate is the number of live births each year per 1,000 women aged 15 to 44. [Population projections at end of article].

The Location of New Jobs

Most new employment opportunities do not occur in central cities, near all-Negro neighborhoods. They are being created in suburbs and outlying areas—and this trend is likely to continue indefinitely. New office buildings have risen in the downtowns of large cities, often near all-Negro areas. But the out-flow of manufacturing and retailing facilities normally offsets this addition significantly —and in many cases has caused a net loss of jobs in central cities.

Providing employment for the swelling Negro ghetto population will require society to link these potential workers more closely with job locations. This can be done in three ways: by developing incentives to industry to create new employment centers near Negro residential areas; by opening suburban residential areas to Negroes and encouraging them to move closer to industrial centers; or by creating better transportation between ghetto neighborhoods and new job locations.

All three involve large public outlays.

The first method—creating new industries in or near the ghetto—is not likely to occur without government subsidies on a scale which convinces private firms that it will pay them to face the problems involved.

The second method—opening up suburban areas to Negro occupancy—obviously requires effective fair housing laws. It will also require an extensive program of federally-aided, low-cost housing in many suburban areas.

The third approach—improved transportation linking ghettos and suburbs —has received little attention from city planners and municipal officials. A few demonstration projects show promise, but carrying them out on a large scale will be very costly.

Although a high proportion of new jobs will be located in suburbs, there are still millions of jobs in central cities. Turnover in those jobs alone can open up a great many potential positions for Negro central city residents—if employers cease racial discrimination in their hiring and promotion practices.

Nevertheless, as the total number of Negro central city job-seekers continues to rise, the need to link them with emerging new employment in the suburbs will become increasingly urgent.

The Increasing Cost of Municipal Services

Local governments have had to bear a particularly heavy financial burden in the two decades since the end of World War II. All United States cities are highly dependent upon property taxes that are relatively unresponsive to changes in income. Consequently, growing municipalities have been hard-pressed for adequate revenues to meet rising demands for services generated by population increase. On the other hand, stable or declining cities have not only been faced with steady cost increases but also with a slow-growing, or even declining, tax base.

As a result of the population shifts of the post-war period, concentrating the more affluent parts of the urban population in residential suburbs while leaving the less affluent in the central cities, the increasing burden of municipal taxes frequently falls upon that part of the urban population least able to pay them.

Increasing concentrations of urban growth have called forth greater expenditures for every kind of public service: education, health, police protection, fire protection, parks, sewage disposal, sanitation, water supply, etc. These expenditures have strikingly outpaced tax revenues.

The story is summed up below:

LOCAL GOVERNMENT REVENUES, EXPENDITURES AND DEBT

(Billions of dollars)

	1950	*1966*	*Increase*
Revenues	11.7	41.5	+29.8
Expenditures	17.0	60.7	+43.7
Debt outstanding	18.8	77.5	+58.7

The fact that the problems of the cities are a national problem is seen in the growth of federal assistance to urban areas under various grant-in-aid programs, which reached the level of $10 billion in the current fiscal year.

Nevertheless, the fiscal plight of many cities is likely to grow even more serious in the future. Local expenditures inevitably will continue to rise steeply as a result of several factors, including the difficulty of increasing productivity in the predominantly service activities of local governments, and the rapid technologically-induced increases in productivity in other economic sectors.

Traditionally, individual productivity has risen faster in the manufacturing, mining, construction, and agricultural sectors than in those involving personal services.

However, all sectors compete with each other for talent and personnel. Wages and salaries in the service-dominated sectors generally must keep up, therefore, with those in the capital-dominated sectors. Since productivity in manufacturing has risen about 2.5 percent per year compounded over many decades and even faster in agriculture, the basis for setting costs in the service-dominated sectors has gone up, too.

In the postwar period, costs of the same units of output have increased very rapidly in certain key activities of local government. For example, education is the single biggest form of expenditure by local governments (including school districts), accounting for about 40 percent of their outlays. From 1947 to 1967, costs per pupil-day in United States public schools rose at a rate of 6.7 percent per year compounded—only slightly less than doubling every ten years.[4] This major cost item is likely to keep on rising rapidly in the future, along with other government services like police, fire, and welfare activities.

---

[4] It is true that the average pupil-teacher ratio declined from 28 to about 25, and other improvements in teaching quality may have occurred. But they cannot account for anything approaching this rapid increase in costs. [See notes, end of article.]

Some increases in productivity may occur in these fields, and some economies may be achieved through use of semi-skilled assistants such as police and teachers' aides. Nevertheless, with the need to keep pace with private sector wage scales, local government costs will keep on rising sharply.

This and other future cost increases are important to future relations between central cities and suburbs. Rising costs will inevitably force central cities to demand more and more assistance from the federal government. But the federal government can obtain such funds through the income tax only from other parts of the economy. Suburban governments are, meanwhile, experiencing the same cost increases along with the rising resentment of their constituents.

II. CHOICES FOR THE FUTURE

The complexity of American society offers many choices for the future of relations between central cities and suburbs and patterns of white and Negro settlement in metropolitan areas. For practical purposes, however, we see two fundamental questions:

Should future Negro population growth be concentrated in central cities, as in the past 20 years, and should Negro and white populations become even more residentially segregated?

Should society provide greatly increased special assistance to Negroes and other relatively disadvantaged population grouups?

For purposes of analysis, the Commission has defined three basic choices for the future embodying specific answers to these questions:

The Present Policies Choice

Under this course, the nation would maintain approximately the share of resources now being allocated to programs of assistance for the poor, unemployed and disadvantaged. These programs are likely to grow, given continuing economic growth and rising federal revenues, but they will not grow fast enough to stop, let alone reverse, the already deteriorating quality of life in central-city ghettos.

This choice carries the highest ultimate price, as we will point out.

The Enrichment Choice

Under this course, the nation would seek to offset the effects of continued Negro segregation and deprivation in large city ghettos. The Enrichment Choice would aim at creating dramatic improvements in the quality of life in disadvantaged central-city neighborhoods—both white and Negro. It would require marked increases in federal spending for education, housing, employment, job training, and social services.

The Enrichment Choice would seek to lift poor Negroes and whites above poverty status and thereby give them the capacity to enter the mainstream of American life. But it would not, at least for many years, appreciably affect either the increasing concentration of Negroes in the ghetto or racial segregation in residential areas outside the ghetto.

The Integration Choice

This choice would be aimed at reversing the movement of the country toward two societies, separate and unequal.

The Integration Choice—like the Enrichment Choice— would call for large-scale improvement in the quality of ghetto life. But it would also involve both creating strong incentives for Negro movement out of central-city ghettos and enlarging freedom of choice concerning housing, employment, and schools.

The result would fall considerably short of full integration. The experience of other ethnic groups indicates that some Negro households would be scattered in largely white residential areas. Others—probably a larger number—would voluntarily cluster together in largely Negro neighborhoods. The Integration Choice would thus produce both integration and segregation. But the segregation would be voluntary.

Articulating these three choices plainly oversimplifies the possibilities open to the country. We believe, however, that they encompass the basic issues—issues which the American public must face if it is serious in its concern not only about civil disorder, but the future of our democratic society.

III. THE PRESENT POLICIES CHOICE

Powerful forces of social and political inertia are moving the country steadily along the course of existing policies toward a divided country.

This course may well involve changes in many social and economic programs—but not enough to produce fundamental alterations in the key factors of Negro concentration, racial segregation, and the lack of sufficient enrichment to arrest the decay of deprived neighborhoods.

Some movement towards enrichment can be found in efforts to encourage industries to locate plants in central cities, in increased federal expenditures for education, in the important concepts embodied in the "War on Poverty," and in the Model Cities Program. But so far congressional appropriations for even present federal programs have been so small that they fall short of effective enrichment.

As for challenging concentration and segregation, a national commitment to this purpose has yet to develop. This is seen in the history of national open housing legislation, pending in Congress, which the President has again urged the Congress to enact.

Of the three future courses we have defined, the Present Policies Choice— the choice we are now making—is the course with the most ominous consequences for our society.

The Probability of Future Civil Disorders

Under the Present Policies Choice, society would do little more than it is now doing against racial segregation, fundamental poverty, and deprivation. What effect would this have on the potential for major civil disorders?

We believe for two reasons that this choice would lead to a larger number of violent incidents of the kind that have stimulated recent major disorders.

First, the Present Policies Choice does nothing to raise the hopes, absorb the energies, or constructively challenge the talents of the rapidly-growing number of young Negro men in central cities. Therefore, the proportion of unemployed or underemployed among them will remain very high. These young men have contributed disproportionately to crime and violence in cities in the past, and there is danger, obviously, that they will continue to do so.

Second, under these conditions, a rising proportion of Negroes in disadvantaged city areas might come to look upon the deprivation and segregation they suffer as proper justification for violent protest or for extending support to now isolated extremists who advocate civil disruption by guerrilla tactics.

More incidents, however, would not necessarily mean more or worse riots. For the near future, there is substantial likelihood that even an increased number of incidents could be controlled before becoming major disorders. Such control should be possible if society undertakes to improve police and National Guard forces so that they can respond to potential disorders with more prompt and disciplined use of force.

In fact, the likelihood of incidents mushrooming into major disorders would be only slightly higher in the near future under the Present Policies Choice than under the other two possible choices. For no new policies or programs could possibly alter basic ghetto conditions immediately. And the announcement of new programs under the other choices would immediately generate new expectations. Expectations inevitably increase faster than performance: in the short run, they might even increase the level of frustration.

In the long run, however, the Present Policies Choice risks a seriously greater probability of major disorders, worse, possibly, than those already experienced.

If the Negro population as a whole developed even stronger feelings of being wrongly "penned in" and discriminated against, many of its members might come to support not only riots, but the rebellion now being preached by only a handful.

If large-scale violence resulted, white retaliation would follow. This spiral could quite conceivably lead to a kind of urban *apartheid* with semi-martial law in many major cities, enforced residence of Negroes in segregated areas, and a drastic reduction in personal freedom for all Americans, particularly Negroes.

The same distinction is applicable to the cost of the Present Policies Choice. In the short run, its costs—at least its direct cash outlays—would be far less than for the other choices.

Any social and economic programs likely to have significant lasting effect would require very substantial annual appropriations for many years. Their cost would well exceed the direct losses sustained in recent civil disorders. Property damage in all the disorders we investigated, including Detroit and Newark, totalled less than $100 million. The casualty toll was far smaller than that for automobile accidents on an average weekend.

But it would be a tragic mistake to view the Present Policies Choice as cheap. Damage figures measure only a small part of the costs of civil disorder. They cannot measure the costs in terms of the lives lost, injuries suffered, minds and attitudes closed and frozen in prejudice, or the hidden costs of the profound disruption of entire cities.

Ultimately, moreover, the economic and social costs of the Present Policies Choice will far surpass the cost of the alternatives. The rising concentration of improverished Negroes and other minorities within the urban ghettos will constantly expand public expenditures for welfare, law enforcement, unemployment and other existing programs without reversing the tendency of older city neighborhoods toward decay and the breeding of frustration and discontent. But the most significant item on the balance of accounts will remain largely invisible and incalculable—the toll in human values taken by continued poverty, segregation and inequality of opportunity.

Polarization

Another and equally serious consequence is the fact that this course would lead to the permanent establishment of two societies: one predominantly white and located in the suburbs, in smaller cities, and in outlying areas, and one largely Negro located in central cities.

We are well on the way to just such a divided nation.

This division is veiled by the fact that Negroes do not now dominate many central cities. But they soon will, as we have shown, and the new Negro mayors will be facing even more difficult conditions than now exist.

As Negroes succeed whites in our largest cities, the proportion of low-income residents in those cities will probably increase. This is likely even if both white and Negro incomes continue to rise at recent rates, since Negroes have much lower incomes than whites. Moreover, many of the ills of large central cities spring from their age, their location, and their physical structures. The deterioration and economic decay stemming from these factors have been proceeding for decades and will continue to plague older cities regardless of who resides in them.

These facts underlie the fourfold dilemma of the American city:

Fewer tax dollars come in, as large numbers of middle-income taxpayers move out of central cities and property values and business decline;

More tax dollars are required, to provide essential public services and facilities, and to meet the needs of expanding lower-income groups;

Each tax dollar buys less, because of increasing costs;

Citizen dissatisfaction with municipal services grows as needs, expectations and standards of living increase throughout the community.

These trends already grip many major cities, and their grip is becoming tighter daily.

These are the conditions that would greet the Negro-dominated municipal governments that will gradually come to power in many of our major cities. The Negro electorates in those cities probably would demand basic changes in present policies. Like the present white electorates there, they would have to look for assistance to two basic cources: the private sector and the federal government.

With respect to the private sector, major private capital investment in those cities might have ceased almost altogether if white-dominated firms and industries decided the risks and costs were too great. The withdrawal of private capital is already far advanced in most all-Negro areas of our large cities.

Even if private investment continued, it alone would not suffice. Big cities containing high proportions of low-income Negroes and block after block of deteriorating older property need very substantial assistance from the federal government to meet the demands of their electorates for improved services and living conditions. In fact, all large cities will need such assistance.

By that time, however, it is probable that Congress will be more heavily influenced by representatives of the suburban and outlying city electorate. These areas will comprise 41 percent of our total population by 1985, compared with 33 percent in 1960. Central cities will decline from 31 percent to 27 percent.[5] Without decisive action toward integration, this influential suburban electorate would be over 95 percent white and much more affluent than the central city population.

Yet even the suburbs will be feeling the squeeze of higher local government costs. Hence, Congress might resist providing the extensive assistance which central cities will desperately need. Many big-city mayors are already beseeching the federal government for massive aid.

Thus the Present Policies Choice, if pursued for any length of time, might force simultaneous political and economic polarization in many of our largest metropolitan areas. Such polarization would involve large central cities—mainly Negro, with many poor, and nearly bankrupt—on the one hand, and most suburbs—mainly white, generally affluent, but heavily taxed—on the other hand.

Some areas might avoid political confrontation by shifting to some form of metropolitan government designed to offer regional solutions for pressing urban problems such as property taxation, air and water pollution and refuse disposal, and commuter transport. Yet this would hardly eliminate the basic segregation and relative poverty of the urban Negro population. It might even increase the Negro's sense of frustration and alienation if it operated to prevent Negro political control of central cities.

The acquisition of power by Negro-dominated governments in central cities is surely a legitimate and desirable exercise of political power by a minority group. It is in an American political tradition exemplified by the achievements of the Irish in New York and Boston.

But such Negro political development would also involve virtually complete racial segregation and virtually complete spatial separation. By 1985, the separate Negro society in our central cities would contain almost 21 million citizens. That is about 72 percent larger than the present Negro population of

[5] Based on Census Bureau Series D projections.

central cities. It is also larger than the current population of every Negro nation in Africa except Nigeria and Ethiopia.

If developing a racially integrated society is extraordinarily difficult today when 12.5 million Negroes live in ghettos, then it is quite clearly going to be virtually impossible in 1985 when almost 21 million Negroes—still much poorer and less educated than most whites—will be living there.

Can Present Policies Avert Extreme Polarization?

There are at least two possible developments under the Present Policies Choice which might avert such polarization. The first is a faster increase of incomes among Negroes than has occurred in the recent past. This might prevent central cities from becoming even deeper "poverty traps" than they now are. It suggests the importance of effective job programs and higher levels of welfare payments for dependent families.

The second possible development is migration of a growing Negro middle class out of the central city. This would not prevent competition for federal funds between central cities and outlying areas, but it might diminish the racial undertones of that competition.

There is, however, no evidence that a continuation of present policies would be accompanied by any such movement. There is already a significant Negro middle class. It grew rapidly from 1960 to 1966. Yet in these years, 88.9 percent of the total national growth of Negro population was concentrated in central cities—the highest in history. Indeed, from 1960 to 1966, there was actually a net total in-migration of Negroes from the urban fringes of metropolitan areas into central cities. The Commission believes it unlikely that this trend will suddenly reverse itself without significant changes in private attitudes and public policies.

IV. THE ENRICHMENT CHOICE

The Present Policies Choice plainly would involve continuation of efforts like Model Cities, manpower programs, and the War on Poverty. These are in fact enrichment programs, designed to improve the quality of life in the ghetto.

Because of their limited scope and funds, however, they constitute only very modest steps toward enrichment—and would continue to do so even if these programs were somewhat enlarged or supplemented.

The premise of the Enrichment Choice is performance. To adopt this choice would require a substantially greater share of national resources—sufficient to make a dramatic, visible impact on life in the urban Negro ghetto.

The Effect of Enrichment on Civil Disorders

Effective enrichment policies probably would have three immediate effects on civil disorders.

First, announcement of specific large-scale programs and the demonstration of a strong intent to carry them out might persuade ghetto residents that genuine remedies for their problems were forthcoming, thereby allaying tensions.

Second, such announcements would strongly stimulate the aspirations and hopes of members of these communities—possibly well beyond the capabilities of society to deliver and to do so promptly. This might increase frustration and discontent, to some extent cancelling the first effect.

Third, if there could be immediate action on meaningful job training and the creation of productive jobs for large numbers of unemployed young people, they would become much less likely to engage in civil disorders.

Such action is difficult now, when there are about 583,000 young Negro men aged 16 to 24 in central cities—of whom 131,000, or 22.5 percent, are unemployed and probably two or three times as many are underemployed. It will not become easier in the future. By 1975, this age group will have grown to nearly 700,000.

Given the size of the present problem, plus the large growth of this age group, creation of sufficient meaningful jobs will require extensive programs, begun rapidly. Even if the nation is willing to embark on such programs, there is no certainty that they can be made effective soon enough.

Consequently, there is no certainty that the Enrichment Choice would do much more in the near future to diminish violent incidents to central cities than would the Present Policies Choice. However, if enrichment programs can succeed in meeting the needs of residents of disadvantaged areas for jobs, education, housing and city services, then over the years this choice is almost certain to reduce both the level and frequency of urban disorder.

The Negro Middle Class

One objective of the Enrichment Choice would be to help as many disadvantaged Americans as possible—of all races—to enter the mainstream of American prosperity, to progress toward what is often called middle-class status. If the Enrichment Choice were adopted, it could certainly attain this objective to a far greater degree than would the Present Policies Choice. This could significantly change the quality of life in many central city areas.

It can be argued that a rapidly enlarging Negro middle class would promote Negro out-migration, and thus the Enrichment Choice would open up an escape hatch from the ghetto. This argument, however, has two weaknesses.

The first is experience. Central cities already have sizable and growing numbers of middle-class Negro families. Yet, as noted earlier, only a few have migrated from the central city.

The past pattern of white ethnic groups gradually moving out of central-city areas to middle-class suburbs has not applied to Negroes. Effective open-housing laws will help make this possible. It is probable, however, that other more extensive changes in policies and attitudes will be required—and these would extend beyond the Enrichment Choice.

The second weakness in the argument is time. Even if enlargement of the

Negro middle class succeeded in encouraging movement out of the central city, could it do so fast enough to offset the rapid growth of the ghetto? To offset even *half* the growth estimated for the ghetto by 1975 would call for the out-migration from central cities of 217,000 persons a year. This is eight times the annual increase in suburban Negro population—including natural increase—which occurred from 1960 to 1966. Even the most effective enrichment program is not likely to accomplish this.

A corollary problem derives from the continuing migration of poor Negroes from the South to Northern and Western cities.

Adoption of the Enrichment Choice would require large-scale efforts to improve conditions in the South sufficiently to remove the pressure to migrate. It should, however, be recognized that less than a third of the estimated increase in Negro central-city population by 1985 will result from in-migration—2.7 million out of total increase of 8.7 million.

Negro Self-Development

The Enrichment Choice is in line with some of the currents of Negro protest thought that fall under the label of "Black Power." We do not refer to versions of Black Power ideology which promote violence, generate racial hatred, or advocate total separation of the races. Rather, we mean the view which asserts that the American Negro population can assume its proper role in society and overcome its feelings of powerlessness and lack of self-respect only by exerting power over decisions which directly affect its own members. A fully integrated society is not thought possible until the Negro minority within the ghetto has developed political strength—a strong bargaining position in dealing with the rest of society.

In short, this argument would regard predominatly Negro central cities and predominatly white outlying areas not as harmful, but as an advantageous future.

Proponents of these views also focus on the need for the Negro to organize economically and politically, thus tapping new energies for self-development. One of the hardest tasks in improving disadvantaged areas is to discover how deeply deprived residents can develop their own capabilities by participating more fully in decisions and activities which affect them. Such learning-by-doing efforts are a vital part of the process of bringing deprived people into the social mainstream.

Separate But Equal Societies?

The Enrichment Choice by no means seeks to perpetuate racial segregation. In the end, however, its premise is that disadvantaged Negroes can achieve equality of opportunity with whites while continuing in conditions of nearly complete separation.

This premise has been vigorously advocated by Black Power proponents. While most Negroes originally desired racial integration, many are losing hope of ever achieving it because of seemingly implacable white resistance. Yet they cannot bring themselves to accept the conclusion that most of the millions of Negroes who are forced to live racially segregated lives must therefore be condemned to inferior lives—to inferior educations, or inferior housing, or inferior status.

Rather, they reason, there must be some way to make the quality of life in the ghetto areas just as good. And if equality cannot be achieved through integration then it is not surprising that some Black Power advocates are denouncing integration and claiming that, given the hyprocrisy and racism that pervade white society, life in a black society is, in fact, morally superior. This argument is understandable, but there is a great deal of evidence that it is false.

The economy of the United States and particularly the sources of employment are preponderantly white. In this circumstance, a policy of separate but equal employment could only relegate Negroes permanently to inferior incomes and economic status.

The best evidence regarding education is contained in recent reports of the Office of Education and Civil Rights Commission which suggest that both racial and economic integration are essential to educational equality for Negroes. Yet critics point out that, certainly until integration is achieved, various types of enrichment programs must be tested, and that dramatically different results may be possible from intensive educational enrichment—such as far smaller classes, or greatly expanded pre-school programs, or changes in the home environment of Negro children resulting from steady jobs for fathers.

Still others advocate shifting control over ghetto schools from professional administrators to local residents. This, they say, would improve curricula, give students a greater sense of their own value, and thus raise their morale and educational achievement. These approaches have not yet been tested sufficiently. One conclusion, however, does seem reasonable: any real improvement in the quality of education in low-income, all-Negro areas will cost a great deal more money than is now being spent there—and perhaps more than is being spent per pupil anywhere. Racial and social class integration of schools may produce equal improvement in achievement at less total cost.

Whether or not enrichment in ghetto areas will really work is not yet known, but the Enrichment Choice is based on the yet-unproved premise that it will. Certainly, enrichment programs could significantly improve existing ghetto schools if they impelled major innovations. But "separate but equal" ghetto education cannot meet the long-run fundamental educational needs of the central-city Negro population.

The three basic educational choices are: providing Negro children with quality education in integrated schools; providing them with quality education by enriching ghetto schools; or continuing to provide many Negro children with inferior education in racially segregated school systems, severely limiting their life-time opportunities.

Consciously or not, it is the third choice that the nation is now making, and this choice the Commission rejects totally.

In the field of housing, it is obvious that "separate but equal" does not mean really equal. The Enrichment Choice could greatly improve the quantity, variety, and environment of decent housing available to the ghetto population. It could not provide Negroes with the same freedom and range of choice as whites with equal incomes. Smaller cities and suburban areas together with the central city provide a far greater variety of housing and environmental settings than the central city alone. Programs to provide housing outside central cities, however, extend beyond the bounds of the Enrichment Choice.

In the end, whatever its benefits, the Enrichment Choice might well invite a prospect similar to that of the Present Policies Choice: separate white and black societies.

If enrichment programs were effective, they could greatly narrow the gap in income, education, housing, jobs, and other qualities of life between the ghetto and the mainstream. Hence the chances of harsh polarization—or of disorder—in the next 20 years would be greatly reduced.

Whether they would be reduced far enough depends on the scope of the programs. Even if the gap were narrowed from the present, it still could remain as a strong source of tension. History teaches that men are not necessarily placated even by great absolute progress. The controlling factor is relative progress—whether they still perceive a significant gap between themselves and others whom they regard as no more deserving. Widespread perception of such a gap— and consequent resentment—might well be precisely the situation 20 years from now under the Enrichment Choice, for it is essentially another way of choosing a permanently divided country.

V. THE INTEGRATION CHOICE

The third and last course open to the nation combines enrichment with programs designed to encourage integration of substantial numbers of Negroes into the society outside the ghetto.

Enrichment must be an important adjunct to any integration course. No matter how ambitious or energetic such a program may be, few Negroes now living in central-city ghettos would be quickly integrated. In the meantime, significant improvement in their present environment is essential.

The enrichment aspect of this third choice should, however, be recognized as interim action, during which time expanded and new programs can work to improve education and earning power. The length of the interim period surely would vary. For some it may be long. But in any event, what should be clearly recognized is that enrichment is only a means toward the goal; it is not the goal.

The goal must be achieving freedom for every citizen to live and work according to his capacities and desires, not his color.

We believe there are four important reasons why American society must give this course the most serious consideration. First, future jobs are being created primarily in the suburbs, but the chronically unemployed population is increasingly concentrated in the ghetto. This separation will make it more and more difficult for Negroes to achieve anything like full employment in decent jobs. But if, over time, these residents began to find housing outside central cities, they would be exposed to more knowledge of job opportunities. They would have to make much shorter trips to reach jobs. They would have a far better chance of securing employment on a self-sustaining basis.

Second, in the judgment of this Commission, racial and social-class integration is the most effective way of improving the education of ghetto children.

Third, developing an adequate housing supply for low-income and middle-income families and true freedom of choice in housing for Negroes of all income levels will require substantial out-movement. We do not believe that such an out-movement will occur spontaneously merely as a result of increasing prosperity among Negroes in central cities. A national fair housing law is essential to begin such movement. In many suburban areas, a program combining positive incentives with the building of new housing will be necessary to carry it out.

Fourth, and by far the most important, integration is the only course which explicitly seeks to achieve a single nation rather than accepting the present movement toward a dual society. This choice would enable us at least to begin reversing the profoundly divisive trend already so evident in our metropolitan areas—before it becomes irreversible.

VI. CONCLUSIONS

The future of our cities is neither something which will just happen nor something which will be imposed upon us by an inevitable destiny. That future will be shaped to an important degree by choices we make now.

We have attempted to set forth the major choices because we believe it is vital for Americans to understand the consequences of our present failure to choose—and then to have to choose wisely.

Three critical conclusions emerge from this analysis:

1. The nation is rapidly moving toward two increasingly separate Americas.

Within two decades, this division could be so deep that it would be almost impossible to unite:

> a white society principally located in suburbs, in smaller central cities, and in the peripheral parts of large central cities; and
> a Negro society largely concentrated within large central cities.

The Negro society will be permanently relegated to its current status, possibly even if we extend great amounts of money and effort in trying to "gild" the ghetto.

2. In the long run, continuation and expansion of such a permanent division threatens us with two perils.

The first is the danger of sustained violence in our cities. The timing, scale, nature, and repercussions of such violence cannot be foreseen. But if it occurred, it would further destroy our ability to achieve the basic American promises of liberty, justice, and equality.

The second is the danger of a conclusive repudiation of the traditional American ideals of individual dignity, freedom, and equality of opportunity. We will not be able to espouse these ideals meaningfully to the rest of the world, to ourselves, to our children. They may still recite the Pledge of Allegiance and say "one nation . . . indivisible." But they will be learning cynicism, not patriotism.

3. We cannot escape responsibility for choosing the future of our metropolitan areas and the human relations which develop within them. It is a responsibility so critical that even an unconscious choice to continue present policies has the gravest implications.

That we have delayed in choosing or, by delaying, may be making the wrong choice, does not sentence us either to separatism or despair. But we must choose. We will choose. Indeed, we are now choosing.

ON POPULATION GROWTH

[1] The Census Bureau publishes four projections of future population growth based upon differing assumptions about future fertility rates (the fertility rate is the annual number of live births per 1,000 women aged 15 to 44). Series A assumes fertility rates similar to those prevalent from 1962 to 1966; Series B through D assume lower rates. Assuming that Negro fertility rates will continue to decline, we have used the average of Series C and D—which make the *lowest* assumptions about such rates. We have also converted the Census Bureaus non-white population projections into Negro projections by assuming Negroes will continue to comprise about 92 percent of all nonwhites. If, however, fertility rates remain at their present levels, then the total Negro population in 1985 would be 35.8 million rather than 30.7 million. The average annual rate of increase from 1966 to 1985 would be 753,000, rather than 484,000—55 percent higher. The projection is as follows:

			Increase from the Previous Date Shown		
	Total U.S. Negro Population (in millions)	*Negroes As % of Total U.S. Population*	*Total Increase*		
Date			*Number (in millions)*	*Percent*	*Annual Average*
1960	18.8 (actual)	10.4 %	—	—	—
1966	21.5 (actual)	10.9	2.7	14.4	450,000
1970	23.2	11.3	1.7	7.9	425,000
1975	25.3	11.6	2.1	9.1	420,000
1980	28.1	12.1	2.8	11.1	560,000
1985	30.7	12.4	2.6	10.9	520,000

[2] The general concept of a metropolitan area is of an integrated, economic and social unit with a recognized large population nucleus. Statistically, it is called a Standard Metropolitan Statistical Area—one which contains at least one central city of at least 50,000 inhabitants. It covers the county of the central city and adjacent counties found to be economically and socially integrated with that county.

A Central City is the largest city of an SMSA and that which gives the SMSA its name.

"Core city" or "inner city" is a popular expression sometimes meaning central city and sometimes meaning the central business district and densely populated downtown neighborhoods of generally poorer residents.

The array of statistical materials for metropolitan areas by "central city" and "outside central city" categories carries with it some dangers which can trap the unwary. The general proposition made in such displays is that the Negro population is concentrated in the central city and is kept out of the suburbs. Certainly this is true.

The danger arises from the inference which the reader may make about the character of "outside central city" and "suburb." "Outside central city" means the whole metropolitan area outside the city or cities whose names are given to the Standard Metropolitan Statistical Area. This is not a homogeneous, affluent, white-only collection of bedroom communities or housing developments. It is a wide-ranging assortment of these and more. Some are attractive communities with trees, grass and fresh air. Others are grimy, industrial towns with all the problems commonly associated with the central city. There are in fact 246 cities of over 25,000 "hidden" in the concept "outside central city." Seventy-seven of these had over 50,000 population in 1960. Many are white only or close to it. Many are not. Some even have higher proportions of Negroes to total population than the central cities of the metropolitan areas of which they are a part. Some of these cities are new. Some are old and have to fight the same battles against urban blight as the central cities of many metropolitan areas.

[3] We have considered two projections of this population. The first projection assumes no further in-migration or out-migration of Negroes to be from central cities. This assumption is unrealistic, but it provides a measure of how much the central-city Negro population is likely to expand through natural increase alone. The second projection assumes that central cities will continue to contain 88.9 percent of all Negro population growth, as they did from 1960 to 1966.

Total U.S. Central-City Negro Population (in millions)

Date	Based on Natural Increase from the Existing Base Only	Based on 88.9% of All Future Negro Growth In Central Cities
1966 (actual)	12.1	12.1
1970	13.8	14.5
1975	14.9	16.0
1980	16.3	18.5
1985	18.1	20.8

Thus, even assuming *no* Negro migration into central cities, the total Negro population would increase six million, 49.6 percent, by 1985. Under the more realistic assumption of both continued in-migration (at present rates) and natural growth, total Negro population of central cities would increase by 8.7 million Negroes, 72 percent.

[4] We have arrived at these estimates by making three different assumptions about future white central city population shifts: (a) that it will remain constant at its 1966 level of 46.4 million; (b) that it will decline, as it did from 1960 to 1966, by an amount equal to half the increase in central-city Negro population. In all three cases, we assume that Negro central city population will continue to account for 88.9 percent of all Negro population growth. These projections embrace both estimates that are probably unrealistically high *and* low. The full projections are as follows:

PROPORTION OF TOTAL CENTRAL CITY POPULATION NEGRO IF:

Date	White Population Remains Constant at 1966 Level	White Population Declines at an Absolute Annual Rate Equal to: One-Half Negro Population Gains	Total Negro Population Gains
1966 (actual)	20.6%	20.6%	20.6%
1975	25.6	26.4	27.3
1985	31.0	33.1	35.6

The first assumption requires a rise in total central-city population from 58.5 million in 1966 to 67.2 million in 1985. Since many of the largest central cities are already almost fully developed, so large an increase is probably unrealistic. On the other hand, the third assumption involves no change in the 1966 central city population figure of 58.5 million. This may be unrealistically low. But in any event, it seems likely that continued concentration will cause the total proportion of Negroes in central cities to reach at least 25 percent by 1975 and 31 percent by 1985.

CITIES FOR 3,000 MILLION PEOPLE

Barbara Ward

The modern city is grounded in paradox. Nothing seems more solid than the towering buildings, the deep underground apparatus of supply and movement and disposal, the square miles of concrete and bricks. Yet much of this urban setting is no more stable than a sandcastle. A speeded-up picture of an urban settlement taken from outer space would show a hard, rugose membrane of construction spreading over the land, its levels rising and falling with the obsolescence and replacement of buildings, its surface criss-crossed with reversible flows of flood-like traffic, every cranny alive with swarming activity; and this picture would present a truer picture of the modern city than any image of a congealed and settled urban landscape.

Change, mobility, expansion are the medium of modern urban life, whether it is the physical mobility of the day's journeys or the social mobility of a would-be equal society or the psychological mobility of educated, increasingly affluent citizens who ask questions, look for new goods and forget old pieties. In fact, one can best analyse the needs, the hopes and failures of the modern city in terms of these inter-related factors of growth, choice and mobility, for they have made the urban pattern what it is, their pressures are inexorably increasing and, unchanged and undirected, they could by the end of the century produce widespread urban breakdown—a fundamental risk when one remembers that by the year 2000 at least 50 percent of a humanity which will have doubled in size will live in cities of more than 100,000 inhabitants.

In developed countries, the proportion will be closer to 90 per cent and the planners must allow not only for people but for cars as well. The two-car family may by then be the norm in America, the one car family elsewhere. Thus the urban order must accommodate not only the new millions of men and women but the ton weight of moving metal which they take with them on at least half their external errands. In concrete terms this means that between now and the year 2000, 150 million more Americans and their cars will have to be given a manageable urban environment. Britain—where over 90 per cent of the people are city dwellers now—must find room for nearly 20 million more. Gen-

Barbara Ward, "Cities for 3,000 Million People," **THE ECONOMIST,** *July 8, 1967. Reprinted by permission of the publisher.*

eral de Gaulle aims at a 50 million increase, the majority, inexorably, in the cities. And these additions are only trickles compared with the flood that could bring a Calcutta or a Bombay to 30 million in thirty years.

Upwards of three billion people will have to be accommodated to a mainly urban way of life in not much more than three decades—more than all the people drawn into cities from the dawn of history to the present day. This is the growth that has to be jammed in and around existing urban areas which all too often seem already congested to the point of suffocation. For it is not simply a question of absorbing the new multitudes. The present container does not properly serve its present purposes. Urban settlements have to grow but they must also be transformed at the same relentless speed. This is the scale of the urban revolution. It is like trying to rebuild and raise a dam when the lake is already full—and to do so largely without agreed specifications.

The Way They Burst

Change, choice and mobility created the modern metropolis. Once industry brought production out of the fields into city barracks and lofts and split up manufacturing into thousands of different specialisations, the great city began to grow since workers had to live near their work and managers needed quick access to each other's concerns. Economy and convenience dictated the early centralisation. They underlie much of it to this day. But of course "nearness" and "access" have wholly different meanings in the age of the train, the automobile and the teleprinter. The peak of urban density in many western cities was passed as early as 1860. Thereafter, the train and then the car brought with them increased mobility and hence greater choice and set in motion a new cycle of change. People with better incomes began their escape from the dirty, workworn, overcrowded yet expensive city centre to the ever widening suburban ring, and then came the following outward wave of shops following the shoppers, of industry needing more space and offices now able to keep in touch by telephone. Both these movements, of residence and of work, have created the metropolitan area—sometimes called the "spread city"—with its dense urban core, its satellite dormitories, its scattered shops and services, its lifelines of road and rail and its often vestigial open spaces, parks and playing fields all covering a hundred and more square miles of built-up territory.

Today, in many regions, "conurbations" are starting to overlap: for instance, along the Great Lakes or America's Atlantic seaboard. A continuous built-up belt from London to Manchester is not inconceivable; Belgium from Antwerp to Ghent is the very pattern of urban "fall out." So are the shores of Tokyo Bay. Not all town dwellers live in a metropolis; yet such areas are the world's dominant urban form in that they are growing a hundred per cent faster than medium-size cities. They appear to be what successful cities will become.

Yet the word "successful" has a certain irony. Choice and mobility may have shaped the modern metropolis. But in many ways the pattern that has emerged frustrates them both now, and threatens worse restrictions for tomorrow. Of course, one should not exaggerate. Most modern city-dwellers are better off than their Victorian forebears. People in London died of cholera as late as the 1850s. No longer do vagrants with the blue faces of gin addicts stumble through peasoup fogs. Children who may be delinquents today had in those days been bundled off to blacking factories before they were ten. Even so, Fagin and Bill Sykes hardly suggest a tranquil, law-abiding, urban order. It can be argued that modern evils have much less brutish effects. But evils and gross inconveniences are a fact and all of them turn precisely on the frustration of that mobility and choice which modern man demands as a first priority of his city and his way of life.

The two are interdependent. Obviously, the city offers richness of choice and variety only if citizens have access to them. There is no need to underline how the present structure of cities with their congested working centres and ever-spreading dormitories frustrates the ideal of easy access. Peak densitits morning and evening on the journey to and from work exhaust the users of both public and private transport. At the weekends, escape from a uniform and boring built-up landscape involves almost comparable densities on the roads to and from the hills or the sea.

Cars and Claustrophobia

The motor car contributes a further edge of irony to these frustrations. In theory, it confers on the family extraordinary powers of free decision over personal mobility. Its appeal has proved irresistible even to the puritan and collective Russians. In practice, packed in increasing numbers into cities framed in the pre-automobile age, it has become one of the chief architects of immobility as it jams the main routes at peak hours, infiltrates the by-streets with heavy traffic, fills up the quiet squares and leaves pile after pile of metal at every curb. New Yorkers may be used to the halt called to midtown traffic at the end of the Manhattan working day when 4 million commuters are on the move. But Mr. Henry Barnes, their Commissioner of Traffic, calls this positive mobility compared with Oxford Street at 4:30 on a weekday afternoon.

And all this is occurring before the next wave of new citizens hits the cities, before the two-car family becomes the norm. Professor Buchanan's report on "Traffic in Towns" has set out a number of suggested changes to combine populations and car ownership both rising on the expected scale by 1980 with the present shape of "spread cities." But estimates based on his proposals indicate that the capital sums needed for an acceptable transport network in a city the size of Leeds would amount to as much as £200 million—a sum not far short of Britain's total present budget for roads.

These obstacles to physical mobility imposed by the structure of the modern city affect all its citizens. But the structure imposes other deeper and more damaging immobilities on smaller groups. Wherever the old working areas of main-streets and old houses are left—in the centre-city, in the inner ring of suburbs—it is here that the poor remain or arrive when the better-off have moved on. If racial differences are added to poverty—Negroes in America, Jamaicans in London, Algerians in the *bidonvilles*—they are often literally trapped since housing is segregated in newer districts while service jobs, which can absorb the semi-skilled, follow the incomes out to the better suburbs and deprive the ghettoes of accessible work. A poverty from which there is no escape creates the preconditions of continuing poverty, lack of knowledge, lack of skill, lack of hope for the children. That violence erupts from such despairs to ignite the riots of Watts or Rochester is a surprise only to those—all too many—for whom a slum is a flash of buildings seen from the passing car. Yet the American metropolitan trend, unchecked, is towards black, rundown centre-cities surrounded by rings of white affluent suburbia. It is the very recipe for civic violence and breakdown. Like imperial Rome, the modern urban order could begin to rot from the core.

These are the extreme evils of social immobility, the social starvation induced by almost total deprivation. But men and women can be wretchedly undernourished, far short of famine, if their diets have inadequate protein. Many of the suburbs have this quality of depletion. One-class, one-income, one-age-group, during weekdays almost one-sex, they belie the urban promise of variety and choice. They breed the fears fed on ignorance and exclusion which allow America's contemporary Nazis to incite white youths in the Cicero suburb of Chicago to stone Negroes and spit at nuns. And perhaps they also breed the aimless violence of Mods and Rockers or the zany anarchism of Amsterdam's provos. With the tensions of scarce housing added, they may in part explain the drunken hooliganism of Russian youths which in the past year has demanded a whole new ministry to correct it. Some observers even detect similar pressures in China's Red Guards.

Prisons of Resentment

Cities built only to work and sleep in—drab, uniform, continuous, without parks and swimming pools—become prisons of resentment to adolescents, some without work, others with more in their pay packets than in their minds or dreams. And if the oncoming millions of new citizens are simply to be crammed into the traditional mould, the risks are of a further decline in urban quality— more sprawl at the edges, more violence and decay at the core, more frustration along the roadways, less access to the non-urban world, further megalopolitan overlap—London spreading to cover southeast England, Washington meeting Boston, Holland becoming the first "spread-nation" and everywhere choice and mobility distorted and lessened by the pressures of unco-ordinated growth.

Is there much hope of reversing the trend? Perhaps the most promising fact about city planning today is that ideas derived from mobility and growth tend now to replace earlier, more static ideas of the city. This advance to realism could open the way to much more workable and successful planning.

A COPERNICAN REVOLUTION

For most of the first half of this century, when reformers thought about improving cities, they aimed at a better version of the same thing. Towns were seen as static entities with defined limits and a traditional inner structure—an important business and cultural centre, more or less segregated manufacturing sectors and separate residential neighbourhoods, all linked by a traffic network converging on the city core. To prevent the concentric rings of urban growth from producing too many commuters for the centre to carry, the device of green belts was evolved. Beyond them, population would be drawn into new settlements built on the traditional town model. Urban obsolescence—slum clearance —would be dealt with by rehousing people largely in the same area with the same roads and services. Old patterns improved, not a rethinking of the urban order, dominated the planners' ideas.

But the pattern was breaking down even while they worked on it. The pressures of growth in the big cities led would-be commuters to leap-frog the green belts and turn new communities into old domitories. Green belts, falling between urban and rural life, all too often carried the neglect of both in half-hearted poultry farms, abandoned shacks and all the debris of a purposeless landscape. At the same time rural land beyond the new settlements suffered indiscriminate, bungaloid invasions. In any case, the green belt concept tends to be officially whittled away as more and more people look for houses with reasonable access to the centre-city where the bulk of the work and almost all the better entertainment are still to be found. Far from ending the sprawl, the policy confirms it as new towns like Crawley or Stevenage follow Hemel Hempstead and Welwyn into the vast metropolitan conurbation.

The pull of the centre-city is not lessened by the new satellite towns. For this reason, it may well be that projects such as the Greater Stockholm or Washington's Year 2000 plans, which link a starlike pattern of satellite communities by rapid transit to the parent city, may be defeated by the pressure of more millions still pressing into the centre. It is perhaps ominous that Swedish planners first designed Vällingby, 30 minutes away from Stockholm by train, as a self-contained community employing at least half its own inhabitants. Today, the great majority still commute.

The most dramatic illustration of the virtual impossibility of fixing ideal limits to city growth comes not from the open societies of the West but from Soviet Russia where, in the past, government cannot be said to have been impeded by consumer pressue or the lobbying of private developers or the cupidities of a free market in land. As early as 1931, the Russian planners concluded that Moscow and Leningrad had reached the limit of desirable growth. The decision was taken to ban all new enterprises in both cities. They then contained between two and three million inhabitants. In 1962, both had over six million. A similar decision was taken in 1939 for such cities as Rostov, Gorky, and Sverdlovsk. Since then, Rostov has grown by 30 per cent, Gorky by 59 per cent, Sverdlovsk has doubled.

In other cities—Tashkent, Novosibirsk, Minsk—population in 1962 had already surpassed the figure proposed for 1975. Such unexpected urban migrations have introduced considerable incoherence into the Soviet Union's theoretical ability—through total control of land use and resources—to evolve an urban policy. New cities, planned with services and industries for one level of population, have to be transformed in mid-construction to take four and five times as many. It is not surprising that in the early 1960s about half of Russia's 80 designated "planning regions" had no plans, and that in city after city planning has become something of a rolling readjustment—a tendency which must be enormously reinforced by the decision to add the private car to road systems originally planned without it.

Breaking the Straitjacket

The concept of the city as a fixed hierarchical structure rising to a central area and surrounded by subordinate districts even survives in one of the most notable attempts made to concentrate public attention on the problem of movement. The Buchanan Report represented in Britain an absolutely indispensable exercise in foresight and warning. It has been the starting point of a whole new ferment of study and experiment. Yet its critics are right in pointing out that its main recommendations still assume a virtually unchanged pattern of urban life and try, at vast cost, to accommodate to it the movements, public or private, which people must or want to make.

At its core lies the unresolved problem of the avalanche-like journey of workers to and from the centre. Give consumer choice free rein, bring in more people by car, then tremendous expense in tunnelling, parking and split-level roadbuilding must be incurred to give people at the centre some chance of safe and reasonable daylight activity. Increase the load on public transport, deny the motorist unlimited access to the centre—and the authorities must run counter to some of the strongest preferences of a consumer democracy, while still incurring heavy expense in up-grading and probably also subsidising public movement. In either case, after investment in building and compensation of astronomical size, the network must operate in the most wasteful fashion, alternating between over-capacity at peak hours and under-use at all others.

This is not to say that the effort to accommodate the car to traditional urban structures has been wasted. On the contrary, the design of such actual or potential new British towns as Runcorn and Hook shows a far greater ability to combine an increased use of the car with central areas than do the first generation of postwar plans—for Harlow or Crawley or Luton. Moreover, the exercise of projecting future traffic flows and trying to work out their implications for the centre-city has laid bare the sheer physical limits set to any reliance on cars alone. In the New York metropolitan region it is estimated that if every bridge, tunnel and freeway were doubled in capacity and the centre of the city given over to as much road and parking space as central Los Angeles—where it has reached 70 per cent—only 22 per cent of all the commuters could come and go by private car. In short, whether one looks at cost or convenience or practicality or even the minimum likelihood that plans, once made, can be realised, the coming pressures of men and machines confront the world's evolving urban order with a series of impasses. Within the present structures of cities, it looks as though the fundamental desire of modern man for widening choice and opportunity cannot be fully satisfied.

This, undoubtedly, is one central reason why planners today are trying to think about cities in new terms—of growth rather than size, of mobility rather than settlement, of alternatives and choices rather than of a rooted environment. This new thinking begins from the supposition that change, not fixity, is the medium of modern living. In spite of all their apparent monumentality, their vast investment, their cloud-capped towers and gorgeous palaces, the cities should in fact be seen as part of a system in flux. The starting points of a creative urban order must be choice—the mobility of man's desires—and move-

Boochin

ment—the mobility of man in pursuit of them. It is perhaps a Copernician revolution in urban thought. And it is not yet ten years old.

HOW DETROIT IS FACING UP TO IT

The new principles can best be studied in three major studies all published in 1966 and all to a certain degree an expression of the new order of thinking. Two are British—the preliminary report on urban development in the Swindon region prepared for the Ministry of Housing and Local Government by Llewellyn Davis and Associates[1] and the proposals for a new urban region in South Hampshire, also prepared for the ministry, by Colin Buchanan and Partners.[2] The third comes from America and is not yet complete—a study of the Detroit metropolitan region planned jointly by one of America's largest power companies, Edison, by Wayne State University and the town-planning consultants, Doxiadis Associates.

In all three projects it is possible to distinguish a new approach—a new stress on openness and mobility, a new effort to incorporate choice and change even into something as apparently fixed, substantial and unyielding as the form of an urban settlement, a readiness to make movement itself a servant of neighbourhood. One sees these concepts operating at three levels—in the whole metropolitan region, in the particular urban or city area and then in the localities. The Detroit plan, being still at a high level of generalisation, does not yet offer specifics at the local level. These are to be worked out over the next two years.

All three studies accept the fact that no effective town-planning is possible now unless it embraces the whole metropolitan or regional context. Cities are part of a growing, changing field of force; action on the fringes can directly effect changes at the core and vice versa. The truth about south-east England, into which three and a half million more people and their cars have to be fitted by 1980, is that without some form of positive planning, they will drift into London's magnetic field and there complete the combination of overload on the centre and "conurbation" on the fringes that already seriously stultify human choice and movement. The sucking pull of London, as the Swindon plan's careful mapping of movements and concentrations of population makes plain, already reaches beyond Reading. Build a new centre even as far out as Didcot and it will still go the way of Harlow or Crawley, turning towards London and contributing to overloads of traffic, longer commuting and wider sprawl. The planners' advocacy of Swindon as a city to grow to half a million rests on their belief that its position allows it to exercise an effective counterpull and to divert future population from Greater London.

The same purpose suggests the choice of an urban region to lie along the Hampshire coast, from Southampton to Portsmouth. It is already an area where people want to come. It has excellent opportunities for industrial and commer-

[1] Ministry of Housing and Local Government: *A New City—a study of urban development in an area including Newbury, Swindon and Didcot;* London HMSO 1966.
[2] South Hampshire Study: Colin Buchanan and Partners in association with Economic Consultants Ltd. HMSO 1966.

cial growth, whether or not the decision is taken to make Southampton a port for freight as well as passengers. Between downs and sea and straddling three river valleys, it can, properly designed, offer really imaginative openings for recreation. And it lies beyond the present pull of London. Indeed, when one compares the range of services and opportunities likely to be available in South Hampshire with those of an even much expanded Swindon, it is probable that the Hampshire metropolis will be a more effective counterpoise to London growth. Only cities of a certain size can counterbalance the megalopolises. Otherwise, more varied work, wider chances of education, more frequent first nights still pull the commuters in to the great wen.

The most systematic attempt yet made to plot a metropolitan region as an interdependent area of pressure and counterforce appears in the plan for metropolitan Detroit. Detroit lies at about the geographical heart of one of the great conurbations of the future—the Great Lakes Megalopolis which will spread from Milwaukee to Buffalo. But the role it will play in this new "field of force" is not clear. Today it cannot be called a very distinguished place. The heart of the city on the Detroit river has been razed and partly rebuilt, admitting new throughways with conference halls and hotels beside and above them. But wholesale demolition has, as usual, pushed urban blight a dozen blocks further back and the city planners have published a rueful map which proves that by the time the present core of blight will have been eliminated, deterioration looks like being larger than it was when the present project of renewal began. Detroit is thus faced with a large opportunity—of becoming the vital centre of one of America's most dynamic urban concentrations—and with an equal risk—of slipping into greater obsolescense.

This is the background of the plan for greater Detroit. It began a couple of years ago with a complete inventory of trends in the region—growth, movement and density of population, sales of agricultural land, implications of lines and modes of traffic, length of commuting journeys, concentrations of industry extrapolated to the year 2000 and it became apparent at once that unless some fresh and dramatic initiatives were made either Detroit would be crushed by the new pressure of traffic and business—thus expanding the existing blight in the inner city—or it would try to accommodate the pressure as Los Angeles has done and turn its centre into an uncentre of traffic lanes and parking lots. Either way, it would lose its place as a vital capital of the greater megalopolis.

The next stage of the plan was therefore to examine alternatives covering Detroit's whole regional "field of force" and its place in the wider patterns of movement which criss-cross the region, linking it northwards to Canada and in every direction to other dynamic areas of growth and change in the United States. Four or five major criteria were chosen—the siting of urban centres, major concentrations of industry, harbours, airports, the larger educational and research centres—and then tested against such alternatives as density of population, networks of traffic, speed of movement, maximum travelling time. Even so, with only a few essential presuppositions, possible solutions, when run through the computers, still reached tens of millions. However, the number of routes that major lines of communication can in fact take across the region is limited. Large concentrations of activity must cluster round their intersections. These considerations reduce the number of possible locations to a more manageable number and this is further reduced by testing their efficiency as centres against differing densities of population, speeds and ease of movement and commuting time. The most workable solutions at this level of complexity have been chosen and used as the framework for a new set of comparisons.

At this stage, the enquiry increases in detail. The region is divided into smaller areas—in the Detroit plan they are six miles by six miles—and the impact of various alternatives on vital physical resources—water, land, topography, beauty—as well as on human movement and convenience are studied. A new set of optimum possibilities emerges. They in turn are related to even more specific areas—downtown Detroit, existing shopping centres, university campuses—and to detailed budgets covering the cost and time of alternative programmes. This process—of progressively eliminating alternatives and increasing the detail of application—finally converges on one solution which, in terms of cost, practicability, amenity and convenience, gives the best answer to the region's future.

The method itself clearly has revolutionary possibilities for the effective study of dynamic regions where growth and movement are as much a part of the landscape as hills and streams. But in the Detroit plan, the conclusion itself has considerable significance for all planners struggling to find solutions within the gravitational field of megalopolis. The conclusion in the Detroit region is that the city itself can prosper and play its role in the region only if present uncoordinated pressures of growth are relieved.

Fifteen million more people—and their cars and artefacts—will drive central Detroit either to final obsolescence or to a concrete-asphalt takeover by traffic. The best alternative is to construct, at another node or intersection of movement, a completely new twin-city, Port Huron, which will permit both cities to flourish and does not exclude the expansion of Toledo as a third major centre in the 21st century. This pattern keeps movement and density manageable, spares the areas of beauty and good farming, permits wide experiments in new technologies—of construction, of transport networks—in the new city and gives the old city time to breathe and reorganise creatively for the pressures to come.

ENGLAND TAKES TO THE GRID

The two more detailed studies—of South Hampshire and Swindon—now take us from the metropolitan and regional level to the working of the system in the cities themselves. In both these plans we see applied at the local level the same attempt—as in the whole Detroit region—to get away from a single overloaded centre-city and to restore a greater range of unimpeded movement. In the words of the Swindon plan.

> *The urban form proposed . . . is derived from consideration of the relationship of the new development to the existing town of Swindon. As the first phase of the development involves bringing in a new population equal to that of present-day Swindon and the ultimate development will lead to a population four times that of Swindon, it is clear that a simple concentric development working outwards from the present town . . . would not be a satisfactory solution. A concentric urban form would mean that the new developments would all depend on the existing town centre of Swindon for*

central functions. The scale of development is such that the present central area of Swindon could not meet the demands of such a massive new population. To rebuild it so that it could handle four times the present demand on its services would involve wholesale destruction of much comparatively modern building and impossibly expensive roadway developments, with major new roads cutting through the existing fabric of Swindon. But on the other hand it would be wrong to develop any single major new centre with the idea that this would eventually take over all central functions for the expanded city, thus depriving the present flourishing centre of Swindon of its role.

In the case of the South Hampshire study, the proposed urban region already has two concentrated city centres in Southampton and Portsmouth. A simple concentric pile-up of people round each centre, particularly round the awkward restricted island site of Portsmouth, would simply lead to unworkable pressures of traffic and movement on already inadequate facilities. The plan therefore proposes that both centres be incorporated in a much wider urban network which allows for a third centre at Southwick and consciously aims at equalising the flow and pressure of traffic over the whole area.

These interesting and new thoughts together suggest that the concept of a multiplicity of centres within a wider urban field has taken firm hold on British town planning. The impression is strengthened by its reappearance in the proposals for the new town of Washington in the north of England; and the Minister of Housing and Local Government made his own attitude plain in his comments on the proposed new city for 250,000 people in Buckinghamshire, the plan for Milton Keynes. Urban centres already to be found within the proposed city area—Bletchley, Wolverton, Stony Stratford—are to be preserved as "nodes of high density" in the wider urban field of force.

This brings us to the next principle—that the lines of movement and hence of force in the urban region should follow the pattern not of concentric rings but of a grid. The word easily conjures up horrific pictures of hundreds of American cities, all divided into regular and indistinguishable square blocks, all streets marching onwards in faceless uniformity, all recognising their fundamental inadequacy by calling themselves by numbers, not names. But this is not what a grid means. Street systems can twist and turn, they can skirt hills and preserve valley bottoms, they can equally serve large universities and small stores without losing the character of a grid. The grid simply means that communication is kept open in all directions and that lines of movement and growth are not turned back upon themselves. Applied to all the means of movement within an urban region, it can give the citizen the largest opportunities of unimpeded mobility and if it is imaginatively combined with the siting of facilities—for work, for learning, for play—it can also give him the widest selection of unimpeded choice.

The suggested new pattern for Swindon is based upon the grid since it proposes a number of urban communities, some of about the same size as the existing city, some smaller, each with a number of facilities—shops, offices, health centres, schools—but none all-inclusive and all depending in some measure on neighbouring communities for a full range of activity and linked to them by the open communications of the grid. The wife whose children are in the neighbourhood schools has the chance of employment, full or part-time, nearby but she travels north for university courses and joins her husband south for an evening concert. The de-concentration of activity prevents lemminglike surges of traffic and this in itself helps to conserve speedy movement and keeps the urban community as a whole in touch and in some measure a neighbourhood.

Perhaps the clearest way of studying the new approach is to examine the idea for South Hampshire. The scheme set out in the plan is misleading. It suggests a rigid grid whereas actual streets and centres would follow the contours and exhibit every kind of difference in style and elevation of building. But the points it underlines are openness of movement, dispersion of centres, variety of choices and a sorting out of different kinds of traffic—all the way from small low-velocity roadways and pedestrian paths in residential areas to the big six-lane highways and railways which link the total urban organism to the wider arterial system of the whole south-east.

Incidentally, by getting away from the concentric pattern and combining different types and speeds of traffic with the open grid, the South Hampshire plan makes more possible the vision of *Traffic in Towns*—that of unimpeded movements through connecting corridors devoted to different purposes and constructed for different speeds. It also preserves, within the city, open spaces which run on and out to join the sea and the great beauties of downland to the north. Thus the urban areas do not close themselves off behind barbaric barricades of concrete. The non-urban world reaches in and out, providing variety and access to another range of choice.

Balanced Traffic

The third principle is already implicit in what has been said. If uncluttered movement is taken to be one of urban man's chief but most frustrated goals, the relationships between the networks of movement and the uses to which they may be put move to the centre of urban planning. It is not simply a question of avoiding the more lunatic schizophrenias such as building a 90-story Pan-Am Building in the heart of Manhattan without a single widening of the approach routes—unless one counts a small, noisy and selective helicopter service from the roof. It is the whole matter of trying to see facilities—factories, hospitals, schools, shopping centres—as the generators of traffic and trying to disperse them so that more balanced movement is possible all over the city.

This does not mean an even all-over dispersion of a depressing and monotonous kind. The areas of activity can be intensified in nodes or centres of a higher order. Hierarchies of activity can be introduced from primary communities such as the grouping of the neighbourhood store, the residential neighbourhood and the primary school all the way to the city administrative block with art gallery, concert hall and repertory theatre alongside. But there must be a variety of such hierarchies and they must be linked not up single ladders leading hierarchically from small to large communities, but laterally and diagonally through a traffic system designed to carry the flows simultaneously in all directions and to cope with the dispersed demand which dispersed activities make possible. The South Hampshire plan shows this dispersion. Swindon aims at it. Both represent the arrival of mobility at the core of the planners' thought.

JUST MORE LIKE LOS ANGELES

But is it a real breakthrough? A number of major criticisms tend to be made of the suggestion that some new principles have genuinely emerged. One is that they simply sanctify failure. What you describe, the critics say, is Los Angeles lightly covered with a fig leaf of theory. More dispersed, interconnected "nodes of higher density," all linked in a mesh of traffic, make up precisely the pattern which has turned Los Angeles into an "un-community," into "twenty suburbs in search of a city," into the archetypal "slurb." This development may be inevitable in the wake of affluence and the automobile, but do not dignify it in the name of principle and planning.

But, in fact, it is not the same. On the contrary, Los Angeles is a warning of what happens when the city's obsolescence takes the form not of overloading but of doing away with the centre and indeed with most coherent sub-centres as well. Los Angeles is not a grid of interconnected and coherent communities. It tends much more towards the pattern of a large, shapeless, sprawl of semi-urban "happenings," very unevenly linked by haphazard connections which, for all their apparent look of high power and capacity, do not distinguish between different purposes and needs. Through traffic, industrial traffic, commuting traffic jam the same lanes on the big freeways; yet a community like Watts is condemned to unemployment because it has not access it can afford to the city's places of employment. Lack of jobs quite as much as racial resentment started up the rest in 1965.

Public transport is vestigial. The almost total substitution of the private car has hastened the disappearance of coherent centres of heightened activity under a rising tide of parking places. At the same time, the dispersal of people spins the city out so that it fills the coastal plain almost to San Diego to the south and reaches up towards Santa Barbara. The ocean and the mountains do, it is true, set limits and give the millions escape from the city. But this is good geography, not good planning; and meanwhile the real estate operators are felling and gouging all the hills they can reach. In short, the pattern is not one of unimpeded movement between a variety of reasonable choices but rather one of immobility for the poor, escape for the rich and a mixture of commuting and marooning for the people in the middle. The lack of contact and community produced by this pattern may well be one factor in Los Angeles's peculiar and disturbing addiction to the politics of the radical right.

Another related criticism alleges that by accepting the concept of the grid, and raising mobility and easy access to the dignity of first principles, this type of planning undermines man's fundamental need for a neighbourhood, for having roots in a particular locality and making contact face-to-face with fellow citizens. Impersonality, the critics say, is at the root of adolescent alienation.

But again, this misinterprets the approach. It does not in any way exclude the small neighbourhoods with primary schools reachable on foot over paths or streets where a six-year-old can maneuver himself without danger. Nor does it abolish local shopping centres and small-scale services. These will grow up naturally at intersections of the grid, small ones between minor roads, larger ones where, say, local roads meet cross-city highways or stations for rapid transit. All the planners say is that in modern life a citizen does not find all his friends and all his activities in the locality. They argue that it is not alienation but sheer boredom that encourages much of the delinquency in neighbourhoods without variety or stimulus.

Today, more and more citizens have connections all over the city—of professional life, of municipal responsibility, of artistic interest. Indeed, they probably have further connections all over the world and one of the preconditions of "neighbourhood" may be a quick access to the airport, which is becoming a growing centre for meeting, conferring and entertaining. A city which permits its inhabitants to move about easily is, in a true sense, more neighbourly than one which provides them with supposedly self-sufficient communities and then tends to shut them off. In any case, it cannot be done. Britain's new towns were no substitutes for London. People simply went on moving in and out.

But, say the critics, why suppose that the new concepts of open access and easy mobility will serve London or other large cities any better? What has the new pattern to offer old entrenched cities? They cannot make themselves over—except at a cost which, on the analogy of *Traffic in Towns*, is far more than the community can afford to pay. Meanwhile, are they simply to carry on, balancing between obsolescence or disintegration?

The short answer is, of course, that the current plans, like the satellite towns of Stockholm or Paris or Washington, are designed not to recreate the big cities' inner structure but to prevent further massive overloading of what exists now. But there are other advantages, even if they are less direct. For instance, provided the expansion of the new centres is also designed to take some overspill and is carried out speedily, the new plans can reduce existing urban pressures by increasing the number of middle-income and low-income houses on the market. This need is especially urgent in America, where racial segregation further distorts a public housing programme which, incredibly, is not providing many more houses than in the 1920s. The planners can also argue that if they produce in South Hampshire or Port Huron new cities designed to maximise choices and open up the flows of traffic, a general pattern of renewal will have been set, on which more piecemeal changes in existing cities can be modelled. After all, a new attention to overall planning will not end smaller schemes of urban renewal. Some can perhaps be combined. If a metropolis like New York takes advantage of the federal money which may become available for "demonstration cities," it might well attempt to graft the new principles even on to old surroundings. It could distinguish types of traffic—pedestrian pathways leading to malls and parks and carrying threads of green all through the city, limited access roads to schools and shopping centres, connections, possibly underground, to the roads and subways linking the locality with the rest of the city and the surrounding land—and attempt to secure easy access and maximum communication by distributing its houses, shops, schools, factories and recreation centres round the whole sector according to the flow of traffic each facility tends to promote.

Success would, of course, remain limited by the tendency of traffic networks outside the new sector to remain in their present over-loaded and incoherent state. But once again, in America, there is new interest in the possibilities of building comfortable, rapid mass-transit systems; renewed city sectors may be able, like small electrical systems, to wire themselves into better and more reliable grids of movement. It is significant that political leaders as alert to trends as Senator Robert Kennedy and Charles Percy are proposing new forms of public-private co-operation of the "Comsat" type to undertake Government-renewal low-cost housing.

Last of all, there are the critics of scale. They argue that to plan with the scope implied in Detroit or South Hampshire defeats itself in part because the variables are too great, in part because the sums involved are too large. But the first criticism disregards the revolutions in planning made possible by the computer, the second ignores the fact that the expenditure will in fact be made because the people will, irretrievably and irreversibly, be there. They cannot simply be dumped, homeless, all over the landscape. Twenty million more British people must be housed somewhere. Whether American plans are better or worse, 150 million more Americans in the next three decades will entail over $100 million of expenditure a year in homes and services. The only choice is between doing it well and doing it badly.

There are new insights into urban planning. There are new technologies available to give the plans a solid base in fact and extrapolation. There are myriad inventions—in power, in traffic control, in automation—waiting to be applied to urban problems. And there are the resources which will in any case be spent. What is lacking so far is the unifying vision of the whole urban order as a proper field of co-ordinated inquiry and action. Until it is achieved, men may well remain more visionary about their outer space than their inner space and give themselves a rougher landing in the city than on the moon.

tion against intruders. In some urban neighborhoods, nearly on
residents wish to move because of high rates of crime, and very
have moved for that reason. In fear of crime, bus drivers in many cities
carry change, cab drivers in some areas are in scarce supply, and some merchants
are closing their business. Vigilante-like groups have sprung up in some areas.

Fear of crime is destroying some of the basic human freedoms which any
society is supposed to safeguard—freedom of movement, freedom from harm,
freedom from fear itself. Is there a basis for this fear? Is there an unprecedented
increase in violent crime in this country? Who and where are most of the violent
criminals and what makes them violent? What can we do to eliminate the causes
of that violence?

I. PROFILE OF A VIOLENT CRIME

Between 1960 and 1968, the national rate of criminal homicide per
100,000 population increased 36 percent, the rate of forcible rape 65 percent, of
aggravated assault 67 percent, and of robbery 119 percent. These figures are
from the *Uniform Crime Reports* published by the Federal Bureau of Investigation. These Reports are the only national indicators we have of Crime in America. But, as the FBI recognizes, they must be used with caution.

There is a large gap between the reported rates and the true rates. In 1967
the President's Commission on Law Enforcement and Administration of Justice
stated that the true rate of total major violent crime was roughly twice as high as
the reported rate.[2] This ratio has probably been a changing one. Decreasing
public tolerance of crime is seemingly causing more crimes to be reported.
Changes in police practices, such as better recording procedures and more intensive patrolling, are causing police statistics to dip deeper into the large well of
unreported crime. Hence, some part of the increase in reported rates of violent
crime is no doubt due to a fuller disclosure of the violent crimes actually
committed.

Moreover, while current rates compare unfavorably, even alarmingly, with
those of the 1950's, fragmentary information available indicates that at the
beginning of this century there was an upsurge in violent crime which probably
equaled today's levels. In 1916, the city of Memphis reported a homicide rate
more than seven times its present rate. Studies in Boston, Chicago and New York
during the years of the First World War and the 1920's showed violent crime
rates considerably higher than those evident in the first published national crime
statistics in 1933.

> *Despite all these factors, it is still clear that* significant and disturbing increases in
> the true rates of homicide and, especially, of assault and robbery have occurred over
> the last decade.

While the reported incidence of forcible rape has also increased, reporting diffi-

---

[2] Reasons for the gap include failure of citizens to report crimes because they believe
police cannot be effective in solving them; others do not want to take the time to
report, some do not know how to report, and others fear reprisals.

culties associated with this crime are too great to permit any firm conclusion on the true rate of increase.

Violent crimes are not evenly distributed throughout the nation. Using new data from a Victim-Offender Survey conducted by our staff Task Force on Individual Acts of Violence, standard data from the FBI, and facts from other recent studies, we can sketch a more accurate profile of violent crime in the United States than has hitherto been possible. We note, however, that our information about crime is still unsatisfactory and that many critical details in the profile of violent crime remain obscure. Moreover, we strongly urge all who study this profile to keep two facts constantly in mind. First, violent crime is to be found in all regions of the country, and among all groups of the population— not just in the areas and groups of greatest concentration to which we draw attention. Second, despite heavy concentrations of crime in certain groups, the overwhelming majority of individuals in these groups are law-abiding citizens.

(1) *Violent crime in the United States is primarily a phenomenon of large cities. This is a fact of central importance.*

The 26 cities with 500,000 or more residents and containing about 17 percent of our total population contribute about 45 percent of the total reported major violent crimes. Six cities with one million or more residents and having ten percent of our total population contribute 30 percent of the total reported major violent crimes.

Large cities uniformly have the highest reported violent crime levels per unit of population. Smaller cities, suburbs and rural areas have lower levels. The average rate of major violent offenses in cities of over 250,000 inhabitants is eleven times greater than in rural areas, eight times greater than in suburban areas, and five and one-half times greater than in cities with 50,000 to 100,000 inhabitants.[3]

For cities of all sizes, as well as for suburbs and rural areas, there has been a recent upward trend in violent crime; the increase in the city rate has been much more dramatic than that for the other areas and subdivisions.

The result in our larger cities is a growing risk of victimization: in Baltimore, the nation's leader in violent crime, the risk of being the victim of a reported violent crime is one in 49 per year. Thus, in the context of major crimes, the popular phrase "urban crisis" is pregnant with meaning.

(2) *Violent crime in the city is overwhelmingly committed by males.*

Judgments about overall trends and levels of violent crime, and about variations in violent crime according to city size, can be based upon reported offense data. But conclusions about the sex, age, race and socioeconomic status

[3] The direct correlation between city size and violent crime rates may not be as uniform in the south as in other regions. Available data indicate higher suburban violent crime rates relative to center city rates in the south, suggesting the possibility that smaller city rates may also be higher relative to larger city rates in the south (although direct evidence on this point is not presently available).

Also, it should be kept in mind that the relationships noted in the text are for cities within certain population ranges (*e.g.*, more than 250,000, 100,000—250,000, etc.), not for individual cities. Thus the five cities with the highest metropolitan violent crime rates in 1968—Baltimore, Newark, Washington, San Francisco and Detroit—had

of violent offenders can be based only on *arrest* data. Besides the gap previously mentioned between true offense rates and reported offense rates, we must now deal also with the even larger gap between *offenses reported* and *arrests made.* Accordingly, conclusions in these areas must be drawn with extreme care, especially since arrests, as distinguished from convictions, are made by policemen whose decisions in apprehending suspects thus determine the nature of arrest statistics.[4]

In spite of the possibly wide margins of error, however, one fact is clearly indisputable: violent crimes in urban areas are disproportionately caused by male offenders. To the extent that females are involved, they are more likely to commit the more "intimate" violent crimes like homicide than the "street crimes" like robbery. Thus, the 1968 reported male homicide rate was five times higher than the female rate; the robbery rate twenty times higher.

(3) *Violent crime in the city is concentrated especially among youths between the ages of fifteen and twenty-four.*

Urban arrest rates for homicide are much higher among the 18-24 age group than among any other; for rape, robbery and aggravated assault, arrests in the 15-24 age group far outstrip those of any other group. Moreover, it is in these age groups that the greatest increases in all arrest rates have occurred. Surprisingly, however, there have also been dramatic and disturbing increases in arrest rates of the 10-14 age group for two categories—a 300 percent increase in assault between 1958 and 1967, and 200 percent in robbery in the same period.

(4) *Violent crime in the city is committed primarily by individuals at the lower end of the occupational scale.*

Although there are no regularly collected national data on the socioeconomic status of violent offenders, local studies indicate that poor and uneducated individuals with few employment skills are much more likely to commit serious violence than persons higher on the socioeconomic ladder. A forthcoming University of Pennsylvania study of youthful male offenders in Philadelphia, for example, will show that boys from lower income areas in the city have delinquency rates for assaultive crimes nearly five times the rates of boys from higher income areas; delinquency rates for robbery are six times higher.[5] Other

---

smaller populations than some very large cities with somewhat lower rates of violent crime.

[4] According to the FBI Uniform Crime Reports, about half of all arrests for serious crimes result in pleas of guilty or convictions: in only 88 percent of all arrests does the prosecutor decide he has sufficient evidence to try the case, and of these cases that are prosecuted, only 62 percent result in a plea of guilty or a conviction, often for a lesser offense than the one originally charged. A wide margin of error thus exists between the making of an arrest and proof that the person arrested has committed an offense.

[5] This is a study of 9945 males born in 1945 and who lived in Philadelphia at least from age 10 to 18. Of this group, 3475, or 35 percent, were taken into custody by the police for delinquent offenses other than traffic violations. Race, socio-economic status and many other variables are analyzed in this study, supported by NIMH, to be published shortly by Thorsten Sellin and Marvin E. Wolgang under the title, *Delinquence in a Birth Cohort.*

studies have found higher involvement in violence by persons at the lower end of the occupational scale. A succession of studies at the University of Pennsylvania, using Philadelphia police data, show that persons ranging from skilled laborers to the unemployed constitute about 90-95 percent of the criminal homicide offenders, 90 percent of the rape offenders and 92-97 percent of the robbery offenders. A St. Louis study of aggravated assault found that blue collar workers predominate as offenders. The District of Columbia Crime Commission found more than 40 percent of the major violent crime offenders to be unemployed.

(5) *Violent crime in the cities stems disproportionately from the ghetto slum where most Negroes live.*

Reported national urban arrest rates are much higher for Negroes than for whites in all four major violent crime categories, ranging from ten or eleven times higher for assault and rape to sixteen or seventeen times higher for robbery and homicide.[6] As we shall show, these differences in urban violent crime rates are not, in fact, racial; they are primarily a result of conditions of life in the ghetto slum. The gap between Negro and white crime rates can be expected to close as the opportunity gap between Negro and white also closes—a development which has not yet occurred.

The large national urban arrest differentials between Negroes and whites are also found in the more intensive Philadelphia study previously cited. Of 10,000 boys born in 1945, some 50 percent of the three thousand non-whites had had at least one police contact by age 18, compared with 20 percent of the seven thousand whites. (A police contact means that the subject was taken into custody for an offense other than a traffic violation and a report recording his alleged offense was prepared and retained in police files.) The differences were most pronounced for the major violent offenses: of fourteen juveniles who had police contacts for homicide, all were non-whites; of 44 who had police contacts for rape, 86 percent were non-whites and fourteen percent whites; of 193 who had police contacts for robbery, 90 percent were non-whites and ten percent whites; and of 220 who had police contacts for aggravated assault, 82 percent were non-whites and eighteen percent whites. When the three sets of figures for rape, robbery and assault are related to the number of non-whites and whites, respectively, in the total group studied (3,000 vs. 7,000), the differences between the resulting ratios closely reflect the differentials in the national urban arrest rates of non-whites and whites in the 10-17 age group.

(6) *The victims of assaultive violence in the cities generally have the same characteristics as the offenders: victimization rates are generally highest for males, youths, poor persons, and blacks. Robbery victims, however, are very often older whites.*

There is a widespread public misconception that most violent crime is

[6] Because some police commonly associate violence with Negroes more than with whites, Negroes may be disproportionately arrested on suspicion, thus producing a higher report Negro involvement in crime than is the true situation.

committed by black offenders against white victims. This is not true. Our Task Force Victim-Offender Survey covering seventeen cities has confirmed other evidence that serious assaultive violence in the city—homicide, aggravated assault and rape—is predominantly between white offenders and white victims and black offenders and black victims. The majority of these crimes involves blacks attacking blacks, while most of the remainder involve whites victimizing whites. Indeed, our Survey found that 90 percent of urban homicide, aggravated assaults and rapes involve victims and offenders of the same race.

In two-thirds of homicides and aggravated assaults in the city, and in three-fifths of the rapes, the victim is a Negro. Rape victims tend strongly to be younger women; the victims of homicide and aggravated assault are usually young males but include a higher proportion of older persons. Nearly four-fifths of homicide victims and two-thirds of the assault victims are male. Generalizing from these data, we may say that the typical victim of a violent assaultive crime is a young Negro male, or in the case of rape, a young Negro woman.

Robbery, on the other hand, is the one major violent crime in the city with a high inter-racial component: although about 38 percent of robberies in the Survey involve Negro offenders and victims, 45 percent involve Negroes robbing whites—very often young black males robbing somewhat older white males. In three-fifths of all robberies the victim is white and nearly two-thirds of the time he or she is age 26 or over. Four-fifths of the time the victim is a man.

Data collected by the Crime Commission indicate that victimization rates for violent crimes are much higher in the lower-income groups. This is clearly true for robbery and rape, where persons with incomes under $6,000 were found to be victimized three to five times more often than persons with incomes over $6,000. The same relation held, but less strongly, for aggravated assault, while homicide victimization rates by income could not be computed under the investigative techniques used.

(7) *Unlike robbery, the other violent crimes of homicide, assault and rape tend to be acts of passion among intimates and acquaintances.*

The Victim-Offender Survey shows that homicide and assault usually occur between relatives, friends or acquaintances (about two-thirds to three-fourths of the cases in which the relationship is known). They occur in the home or other indoor locations about 50-60 percent of the time. Rape is more likely to be perpetrated by a stranger (slightly over half of the cases), usually in the home or other indoor location (about two-thirds of the time). By contrast, robbery is usually committed outside (two-thirds of the cases) by a stranger (more than 80 percent of the cases).

The victim, the offender, or both are likely to have been drinking prior to homicide, assault, and rape, and the victim often provokes or otherwise helps precipitate the crime. The ostensible motives in homicide and assault are often relatively trivial, usually involving spontaneous altercations, family quarrels, jealous rages, and the like. The two crimes are similar; there is often no reason to believe that the person guilty of homicide sets out with any more intention to harm than the one who commits an aggravated assault. Except for the seriousness of the final outcomes, the major distinction is that homicides most often involve handguns while knives are most common in assault.[7]

(8) By far the greatest proportion of all serious violence is committed by repeaters.

While the number of hard-core repeaters is small compared to the number of one-time offenders, the former group has a much higher rate of violence and inflicts considerably more serious injury. In the Philadelphia study, 627 of the 10,000 boys were chronic offenders, having five or more police contacts. Though they represented only six percent of the boys in the study, they accounted for 53 percent of the police contacts for personal attacks—homicide, rape and assault—and 71 percent of the contacts for robberies.

Offenders arrested for major criminal violence generally have long criminal histories, but these careers are mainly filled with offenses other than the final serious acts. Generally, though there are many exceptions, the more serious the crime committed, the less chance it will be repeated.

(9) Americans generally are no strangers to violent crime.

Although it is impossible to determine accurately how many Americans commit violent crimes each year, the data that are available suggest that the number is substantial, ranging from perhaps 600,000 to 1,200,000—or somewhere between one in every 300 and one in every 150 persons.[8] Undoubtedly, a far greater number commit a serious violent crime at some time in their lives. The Philadelphia study found that of about 10,000 boys 35 percent (3475) were taken into police custody for delinquency, and of the delinquents ten percent (363) were apprehended once or more for a major crime of violence before age eighteen.

A comparison of reported violent crime rates in this country with those in other modern, stable nations shows the United States to be the clear leader. Our homicide rate is more than twice that of our closest competitor, Finland, and from four to twelve times higher than the rates in a dozen other advanced

[7] In another report, this Commission has indicated that gun attacks are fatal in one out of five cases, on the average; knife attacks are fatal in one out of twenty.

[8] The FBI has reported that in 1968, 588,000 violent crimes occurred. This is about 300 crimes of major violence per each 100,000 Americans. It is generally estimated that only about half of all violent crimes are reported; if this is true, the total number of violent crimes per year is in the range of 1,200,000 or 600 per 100,000 people. These are *offenses,* not *offenders.* Since violent crimes often involve several offenders committing a single crime—particularly among the large number of juvenile offenders —a fair guess might be that twice as many offenders (2,400,000) were involved. But some offenders account for more than one crime per year. If we assume the commission of two crimes per year per offender, the total number of offenders drops back to 1,200,000; if we assume the commission of four crimes per year per offender, the total number of offenders is 600,000. Thus the number of Americans who commit violent crimes each year appears to be somewhere between these figures—between one in every 150 and one in every 300 Americans. Since children under twelve and adults over 45 commit relatively few crimes, the rate for persons between 12 and 45 is even higher.

countries including Japan, Canada, England and Norway. Similar patterns are found in the rates of other violent crimes: averages computed for the years 1963-1967 show the United States rape rate to be twelve times that of England and Wales and three times that of Canada; our robbery rate is nine times that of England and Wales and double that of Canada; our aggravated assault rate is double that of England and Wales and eighteen times that of Canada.

II. CAUSES OF VIOLENT CRIME

Violent crime occurs in many places and among all races but we have just shown that it is heavily concentrated in large cities and especially among poor black young men in the ghettoes. We must, therefore, focus on the conditions of life for the youth of the inner-city to find the root causes of a high percentage of violent crime.

Much has been written about inner-city slums where crime and delinquency are bred. Social scientists have analyzed slum conditions and their causal link to crime and violence, writers and artists have dramatized the sordidness and the frustrations of life in the inner-cities, and a number of Commissions prior to this one have produced comprehensive reports on this subject.[9] In its 1967 Report the Crime Commission described the linkage between violent crime and slum conditions in large cities as "one of the most fully documented facts about crime." Referring to numerous studies conducted over a period of years, the Commission found that violent crime, its offenders and its victims are found most often in urban areas characterized by:

low income
physical deterioration
dependency
racial and ethnic concentrations
broken homes
working mothers
low levels of education and vocational skills
high unemployment
high proportions of single males
overcrowded and substandard housing
high rates of tuberculosis and infant mortality
low rates of home ownership or single family dwellings
mixed land use
high population density.[10]

A series of studies by Clifford Shaw and Henry McKay remains the classic investigation of these ecological patterns.[11] Extensive data on the distribution

[9] President's Commission on Law Enforcement and Administration of Justice, *The Challenge of Crime in a Free Society* (Washington, D.C.: Government Printing Office, 1967); *Report of the National Advisory Commission on Civil Disorders* (Washington, D.C.: Government Printing Office, 1968); National Commission on Urban Problems, *Building the American City* (Washington, D.C.: Government Printing Office, 1968).

[10] *The Challenge of Crime in a Free Society,* op. cit., p. 35.
[11] Shaw & McKay, *Juvenile Delinquency and Urban Areas,* Chicago, 1969.

of delinquency among neighborhoods were collected in a number of large American cities, and the results for Chicago have recently been updated to cover the period from 1900 through 1965. Finding uniformly high correlations between delinquency and areas having the characteristics listed above, Shaw and McKay focused on the process of change in the communities studied.

Neighborhoods disrupted by population movements and social change contained high proportions of delinquents. Although the same central core areas tended to experience social change and high delinquent rates over time, high or low delinquent rates were not permanently associated with any particular ethnic or racial group. The newest immigrant or migrant groups tended to settle initially in the core areas and be responsible for the highest delinquency rates in each city; yet the rates for these groups went down as the groups either moved outward to better areas or achieved a more stable community structure. In Chicago, first the Germans and Irish, then the Poles and Italians, and finally Southern Negroes and Spanish-speaking peoples replaced one another as the newest groups settling in the inner-city and producing the highest delinquency rates. Consistent with these findings has been a regular decline in delinquency rates from the innermost to the outermost areas around the centers of each city examined.[12] Crime and delinquency are thus seen as associated with the disorganization and deprivation experienced by new immigrant or migrant groups as they strive to gain a foothold in the economic and social life of the city.

Negroes, however, have not been able, even when they have improved their economic condition, to move freely from the central cities. Therefore, movement of Negroes with higher income has tended merely to extend the ghetto periphery. The Southern Negro migrants who have now been concentrated in the cities for two generations—as well as Negroes who have been living under conditions of urban segregation even longer—have experienced the same disorganizing forces as the earlier European settlers, but there are a number of reasons why the impact of these forces has been more destructive in the case of the Negro. Discrimination by race in housing, employment and education has been harder to overcome than discrimination based on language or ethnic background. With changes in the economy, there has been less demand for the Negro's unskilled labor than for that of the earlier immigrants. The urban political machines which furthered the political and economic interests of earlier immigrants had declined in power by the time the Negroes arrived in large numbers. The cultural experience which Negroes brought with them from the segregation and discrimination of the rural South was of less utility in the process of adaptation to urban life than was the cultural experience of many of the European immigrants. The net effect of these differences is that urban slums have tended to become *ghetto* slums from which escape has been increasingly difficult.

The National Commission on Urban Problems observed in its Report last year that "one has to see and touch and smell a slum before one appreciates the real urgency of the problem." Some of the urgency comes through, however, even in a simple verbal description of the facts and figures of slum life. Before

[12]One expert testifying before this Commission reported his finding in Chicago: a person living in the inner-city faced a risk each year of 1 in 77 of being assaulted; a risk of only 1 in 2,000 in the better areas of the city, and 1 in 10,000 in the rich suburbs.

presenting this description (much of which is drawn from the Reports of the Crime Commission and the Kerner Commission), we emphasize again that many slum residents manage to live peaceful and decent lives despite the conditions that surround them, and that the characterizations which follow are typical only of the ghetto core and those who fall into delinquency. They do not describe all neighborhoods or all residents of the inner city.

The Home. If the slums in the United States were defined strictly on the basis of dilapidated housing, inadequate sanitary facilities, and overcrowding, more than five million families, or one-sixth of the urban population, could be classified as slum inhabitants. To the inner-city child, home is often characterized by a set of rooms shared by a shifting group of relatives and acquaintances, furniture shabby and sparse, many children in one bed, plumbing in disrepair, plaster falling, roaches and sometimes rats, hallways dark or dimly lighted, stairways littered, air dank and foul.

In such circumstances, home has little holding power for a child, adolescent or young adult. Physically unpleasant and unattractive, it is not a place to bring friends; it is not even very much the reassuring gathering place of one's own family. Indeed, the absence of parental supervision early in the slum child's life is not unusual, a fact partly due to the condition of the home.

The Family. Inner-city families are often large. Many are fatherless, permanently or intermittently; others involve a conflict-ridden marital relationship; in either instance the parents may communicate to their offspring little sense of permanence and few precepts essential to an orderly, peaceful life.

Loosely organized, often with a female focus, many inner-city families bestow upon their children what has been termed "premature autonomy." Their children do not experience adults as being genuinely interested or caring persons. These children may, rather, experience adults as more interested in their own satisfactions than those of their children. Consequent resentment of authority figures, such as policemen and teachers, is not surprising. With a lack of consistent, genuine concern for children who are a burden to them, the parents may vacillate from being unduly permissive to being overly stern. Child rearing problems are exacerbated where the father is sometimes or frequently absent, intoxicated, or replaced by another man; where coping with everyday life with too little money for the size of the family leaves little time or energy for discipline; or where children have arrived so early and unbidden that parents are too immature to put their child's needs above their personal pleasure.

The seeds of delinquency in young boys are shown, studies suggest,[13] in families where there is an absence of consistent affection from both parents, and where there is lacking consistent parental direction. Identification of the boy with a stable positive male image is difficult when the father is frequently absent, erratic in his behavior, often unemployed, unfair in his discipline, or treated without respect by others. Conversely, studies indicate that a stable

[13]See studies cited in "The Family and Violence," Chapter 9 of *Law and Order Reconsidered,* the Report of this Commission's staff Task Force on Law and Law Enforcement (Washington, D.C.: Government Printing Office, 1969) and in "Juvenile Delinquency and the Family," Appendix L of the Crime Commission's *Task Force Report on Juvenile Delinquency* (Washington, D.C.: Government Printing Office, 1967).

integrated family life can do much to counteract powerful external influences that pull young men toward delinquency.[14] If the inner-city family, particularly the ghetto black family, were stronger and more secure, with good family relationships, more of its offspring could avoid criminal behavior. However, even where there is a stable family which wishes to avoid the problems of slum-ghetto life, continuing racial discrimination makes it difficult for them to remove themselves and their children from the pernicious influences of the slums.

The Neighborhood. In many center city alleys are broken bottles and snoring "winos"—homeless, broken men, drunk constantly on cheap wine. Yards, if any, are littered and dirty. Fighting and drunkenness are everyday occurrences. Drug addiction and prostitution are rampant. Living is crowded, often anonymous. Predominantly white store ownership and white police patrols in predominantly black neighborhoods are frequently resented, reviled, and attacked, verbally and physically. Municipal services such as garbage collection, street repairs and utilities maintenance and the like are inadequate and, at times, all but non-existent.

Many ghetto slum children spend much of their time—when they are not watching television—on the streets of this violent, poverty-stricken world. Frequently, their image of success is not the solid citizen, the responsible, hardworking husband and father. Rather, the "successful" man is the cynical hustler who promotes his own interests by exploiting others—through dope selling, numbers, robbery and other crimes. Exploitation and hustling become a way of life.

The School. The low-income ghetto child lives in a home in which books and other artifacts of intellectual interest are rare. His parents usually are themselves too poorly schooled to give him the help and encouragement he needs. They have not had the time—even had they the knowledge—to teach him basic skills that are routinely acquired by most middle-class youngsters: telling time, counting, learning the alphabet and colors, using crayons and paper and paint. He is unaccustomed to verbalizing concepts or ideas. Written communication is probably rare in his experience.

The educational system in the slums is generally poorly equipped. Most schools in the slums have outdated and dilapidated buildings, few text and library books, the least qualified teachers and substitute teachers, the most overcrowded classrooms, and the least developed counseling and guidance services. These deficiencies are so acute that the school cannot hold the slum child's interests. To him it is boring, dull, and apparently useless, to be endured for awhile and then abandoned.

The school experience often represents the last opportunity to counteract the forces in a child's life that are influencing him toward crime and violence. The public school program has always been viewed as a major force for the transmission of legitimate values and goals, and some studies have identified a good school experience as a key factor in the development of "good boys out of bad environments." The link between school failure and delinquency is not completely known, but there is evidence that youth who fail in school con-

---

[14]*E.g.,* U.S. Dept. of Labor, Office of Policy Planning and Research, *The Negro Family: The Case for National Action* (Washington, D.C.: Government Printing Office, 1965), pp. 38-40.

tribute disproportionately to delinquency. One estimate is that the incidence of delinquency among drop-outs is ten times higher than among youths who stay in school.[15]

The Job. Getting a good job is harder than it used to be for those without preparation, for an increasing proportion of all positions require an even higher level of education and training. To be a Negro, an 18-year-old, a school dropout, a resident of the slums of a large city, is to have many times more chances of being unemployed than a white 18-year-old high school graduate living a few blocks away. Seventy-one percent of all Negro workers are concentrated in the lowest paying and lowest skilled occupations. They are the last to be hired. Union practices, particularly in the building trades, have always been unduly restrictive toward new apprentices (except those related to union members), and this exclusionary policy has a major impact on young blacks. The unemployment rate, generally down in the last few years, remains twice as high for non-whites as for whites; and for black teenagers in central cities in 1968 the unemployment rate was 30 percent, up a third over 1960.

Success in job hunting is dependent on information about available positions. Family and friends in middle-class communities are good sources for obtaining information about employment. In the ghetto, however, information about job openings is limited by restricted contact with the job market. The slum resident is largely confined to his own neighborhood, where there are few new plants and business offices, and unfortunately State Employment Services have been generally ineffective even when used.

Most undereducated youngsters do not choose a job. Rather, they drift into one. Since such jobs rarely meet applicants' aspirations, frustration typically results. Some find their way back to school or into a job training program. Some drift fortuitously among low paying jobs. Others try crime and, if successful, make it their regular livelihood; others lack aptitude and become failures in the illegal as well as the legal world—habitues of our jails and prisons. And there are those who give up, retreat from conventional society, and search for a better world in the private fantasies induced by drink and drugs.

The realities of the employment problem faced by ghetto Negroes are reflected in the data on family income. Negro family income in the cities is only sixty-eight percent of the median white family income. One-third of Negro families in cities live on $4,000 a year or less, while only sixteen percent of the whites do so.

When poverty, dilapidated housing, high unemployment, poor education, over-population, and broken homes are combined, an inter-related complex of powerful criminogenic forces is produced by the ghetto environment. These social forces for crime are intensified by the inferiority-inducing attitudes of the larger American society—attitudes that today view ghetto blacks as being suspended between slavery and the full rights and dignity of free men.

The competitive road to success is accorded great emphasis in American life. Achievement often tends to be measured largely in material terms. Our

[15] See "Violence and Youth," Chapter 14 of the Report of our staff Task Force on Individual Acts of Violence. Thirty-nine percent of Negroes and 23 percent of whites in cities fail to complete four years of high school.

consumer-oriented culture pressures us to desire goods and services and to feel successful if one obtains them, unsuccessful if one does not. The network of mass communications spreads a culture of consumer desires over a vast audience. Happiness, we are endlessly reminded, is obtaining and having things. Most Americans operate on the premise that in the race to material success all men have an equal chance at the starting line, and that anyone who falls behind has only himself to blame. Yet not all can be at the front of the pack, especially not those who started far behind in the first place. And the race has different rules for different participants.

There are many ways of coping with the frustration of failure. Some take solace in the fact that others are even further behind. Some withdraw entirely from the race; alcohol, drugs, mental illness and even suicide are avenues of escape. Others, especially college youth whose parents have succeeded in the race, experiment with "alternative life-styles" such as those associated with the hippie phenomenon. In the inner-city, where the chances of success are less, many adopt illegal means in the effort to achieve their goals of securing more money and higher status among their peers.

To be a young, poor male; to be undereducated and without means of escape from an oppressive urban environment; to want what the society claims is available (but mostly to others); to see around oneself illegitimate and often violent methods being used to achieve material success; and to observe others using these means with impunity—all this is to be burdened with an enormous set of influences that pull many toward crime and delinquency. To be also a Negro, Mexican or Puerto Rican American and subject to discrimination and segregation adds considerably to the pull of these other criminogenic forces.

Believing they have no stake in the system, the ghetto young men see little to gain by playing according to society's rules and little to lose by not. They believe the odds against their success by legitimate means are greater than the odds against success by crime. The step to violence is not great, for in an effort to obtain material goods and services beyond those available by legitimate means, lower-class persons without work skills and education resort to crimes for which force or threat of force has a functional utility, especially robbery, the principal street crime.

But the slum ghetto does more than generate frustration that expresses itself in violent acquisitive crime. It also produces a "subculture" within the dominant American middle-class culture in which aggressive violence tends to be accepted as normal in everyday life, not necessarily illicit. In the contemporary American city we find the necessary conditions not only for the birth but also for the accelerated development of violent subcultures, and it is in these settings that most violent aggressive crimes in fact occur.[16]

From the perspective of dominant middle-class standards, the motives in most criminal homicides and other assaults—altercations, family quarrels, jeal-

---

[16] The subculture of violence is not the product of our cities alone: the Thugs of India, the *vedetta barbaricina* in Sardinia, the *mafioso* in Sicily and the Ku Klux Klan, for example, have existed for many years. Nor is violence absent from the established middle-class culture of the majority in our society. It is simply the greater frequency and approval of illegitimate violence that distinguishes the subculture of violence from the dominant cultural pattern.

ousy—are cheap issues for which people give their lives or suffer serious injury. Similarly, the transient gratifications to be obtained from the rape or the robbery do not seem to warrant the risk of punishment or the burden of guilt that is presumably involved. Yet these events are much more reasonable to those in the ghetto slum subculture of violence, where a wide range of situations is perceived as justifying violent responses.[17] An altercation with overtones threatening a young man's masculinity, a misunderstanding between husband and wife, competition for a sexual partner, the need to get hold of a few dollars—these "trivial" events can readily elicit a violent response in an environment that accepts violence as a norm, allows easy access to weapons, is physically and culturally isolated from the rest of the wider American community, and has limited social controls—including inadequate law enforcement.

Violence is actually often used to enable a young man to become a successful member of ghetto society. In the subculture of violence, proving masculinity may require frequent rehearsal of the toughness, the exploitation of women, and the quick aggressive responses that are characteristic of the lower-class adult male. Those who engage in subcultural violence are often not burdened by conscious guilt, because their victims are likely to belong to the same subculture or to a group they believe has exploited them. Thus, when victims see their assaulters as agents of the same kind of aggression they themselves represent, violent retaliation is readily legitimized.

Moreover, if the poor, young, black male is conditioned in the ways of violence by his immediate subculture, he is also under the influence of many forces from the general, dominant culture. As we have said in another statement, violence is a pervasive theme in the mass media. The frequency of violent themes in myriad forms in the media tends to foster permissive attitudes toward violence. Much the same can be said about guns in American society. The highest gun-to-population ratio in the world, the glorification of guns in our culture, and the television and movie displays of guns by heroes surely contribute to the scope and extent of urban violence.

Taking all the foregoing facts and circumstances into account, perhaps we should marvel that there is not more violent crime in the cities of our nation.

III. THE RISE IN VIOLENT CRIME

If, as we believe, the conditions of life for inner-city populations are responsible for the sharp difference in violent crime rates between these populations and other groups in our society, there remains a puzzling paradox to be considered: Why, we must ask, have urban violent crime rates increased substantially during the past decade when the conditions that are supposed to cause violent crime have not worsened—have, indeed, generally improved?

The Bureau of the Census, in its latest report on trends in social and economic conditions in metropolitan areas, states that most "indicators of well-

[17]We are here drawing upon Marvin E. Wolfgang and Franco Ferracuti, *The Subculture of Violence,* London: Tavistock Publications; New York: Barnes and Noble, 1967.

being point toward progress in the cities since 1960."[18] Thus, for example, the proportion of blacks in cities who completed high school rose from 43 percent in 1960 to 61 percent in 1968; unemployment rates dropped significantly between 1960 and 1968; the median income of families living in cities rose by 16 percent between 1959 and 1967 (from $6,720 to $7,813), and the median family income of blacks in cities increased from 61 percent to 68 percent of the median white family income during the same period. Also during the same period the number of persons living below the legally-defined poverty level in cities declined from 11.3 million to 8.3 million.

There are some important counter-trends. The unemployment rate for blacks, though lower, continued to be about twice that for whites; and, as previously noted, unemployment among black teenagers in cities increased by a third between 1960 and 1968 (to 30 percent, two and one-half times the urban white teenager rate). Moreover, figures indicating a closing of the family income gap between blacks and whites in the 1960's do not reflect a number of critical details, such as the fact that in cities black men who worked the year round in 1967 earned about seven-tenths as much as white workers and that this fraction was unchanged since 1959, or the fact that the "dependency ratio"—the number of children per thousand adult males—for blacks is nearly twice that for whites, and the gap widened sharply in the 1960's.[19] The degree of poverty among the Negro poor in metropolitan areas remained severe, half the families reporting incomes $1,000 or more below the Social Security Administration's poverty budget of $3,335 for a family of four. We also find a significant increase in the number of children growing up in broken homes, especially among Negroes and lower income families in the cities. Among Negroes in the cities in 1968 with incomes below $4,000, only one-fourth of all children were living with both parents, as compared to one-half for white families of the same income level. Significantly, for families with incomes of $10,000 per year, this difference between white and black families disappears.

Whatever may be the correct over-all judgment on the change in inner-city living conditions over the past ten years, it is clear, however, that the change has been less dramatic than the change in violent crime rates during this period. How is this discrepancy to be explained?

In seeking an acceptable answer, we must keep in mind two qualifications which to a degree mitigate the seriousness of the discrepancy: First, while, as we have said, serious increases have occurred in major crimes involving violence, these increases are not so dramatic as FBI data suggest. Undoubtedly our crime reporting system is gradually dipping deeper into the well of previously unreported crime. Second, substantial portions of such increases as have occurred are to some extent attributable to demographic shifts in the population, particularly

[18]U. S. Bureau of the Census, *Current Population Reports,* Series P-23, Special Studies (formerly Technical Studies), No. 27, "Trends in Social and Economic Conditions in Metropolitan Areas," U. S. Government Printing Office, Washington, D. C., 1969.

[19]Also, such closing of the family income gap as has occurred all took place after 1965; for the previous 15 years there was no change. See *Law and Order Reconsidered, op. cit.,* at 103.

increases in the young population and increasing urbanization of the population.[20]

Even with these two factors taken into account, however, an important
part of the original question remains. Why, if a high percentage of the crime in
our cities is caused by factors such as poverty and racial discrimination, has it
increased in a period of unprecedented prosperity for most Americans and in a
time of painfully slow and uneven but genuine progress toward racial equality?
These questions are not susceptible to precise scientific answers, but it is possible
to offer informed judgments about them. In our considered opinion, the following factors have been significantly operative in the increasing levels of violent
crime in the inner cities:

(1) The United States has been changing with bewildering rapidity—
scientifically, technologically, socially, and politically. Americans literally are
changing how we work, how we live, how we think, how we manage our vast
enterprise. Other rapidly changing nations—Israel, Japan, Western European
countries—also have experienced rapid rises in crime rates, though at a much
lower level than ours. Sociologists and anthropologists have long observed that
rapid social change leads to a breakdown of traditional social roles and institutional controls over the behavior of young and old alike—but particularly the
young, who, because of the social change, are less likely to be socialized into
traditional ways of doing things (and not doing them) and, hence, ineffectively
constrained by these traditional ways. This process includes the breakdown in
traditional notions of civility, respect for elders and the institutions and patterns
of conduct they represent, property rights, ways of settling disputes, relations
between the sexes and many other matters.

With economic and technical progress in the United States has come increased affluence for most—but not all—of the members of our society. This
combination of rapid social change and unevenly distributed affluence is
devastating. At a time when established ways of doing things, traditions of
morality, and attitudes about personal and property rights are changing, rising
levels of affluence, interacting with public promises of a better life and television
displays of still more affluence, have created expectations that have outstripped
reality, particularly among the poor and especially the poor black. Rising income
statistics look reassuring until one focuses on the continuing gap between black
and white incomes.

We have in this country what has been referred to as a "revolution of rising
expectations" born of unprecedented prosperity, changes in the law, wars on
poverty, space spectaculars, and a host of other features of contemporary life.
But, as one of the research contributions in this Commission's Task Force on
Historical and Comparative Perspectives points out,[21] a rapid increase in human

[20] Computations set forth in the Report of our staff Task Force on Individual Acts of
Violence suggest that 18% of the increase in the volume of violent crime between
1950 and 1965 is attributable solely to urbanization, and 12% to age redistribution
alone.

[21] See Davies, "The J—Curve of Rising and Declining Satisfactions as a Cause of Some
Great Revolutions and a Contained Rebellion," in *Violence in America,* the Report
of our staff Task Force on Historical and Comparative Perspectives (Washington, D.C.:
Government Printing Office, 1969).

expectations followed by obvious failure to meet those expectations has been and continues to be a prescription for violence. Disappointment has manifested itself not only in riots and violent demonstrations—but may also be reflected in the increasing levels of violent crime.

As we analyze in other parts of our reports, we are allowing law enforcement to falter, the handgun census to approach 25 million, and an increasing number of crimes to go unpunished. Every successful crime is an inducement to further crime: it advertises society's inability to enforce generally accepted rules of conduct. Weaknesses of our criminal justice system have had a multiplier effect upon the rise of violent crime.

(3) Public order in a free society does not and cannot rest solely on applications or threats of force by the authorities. It must also rest on the people's acceptance of the legitimacy of the rule-making institutions of the political and social order and of the rules these institutions make. Persons obey the rules of society when the groups with which they identify approve those who abide by the rules and disapprove those who violate them. Such expressions of approval and disapproval are forthcoming only if the group believes that the rule-making institutions are in fact entitled to rule—that is, are "legitimate." What weakens the legitimacy of social and political institutions contributes to law-breaking, including violent crime.

In recent years a number of forces have converged to weaken the legitimacy of our institutions. We repeat what we have said elsewhere: the spectacle of governors defying court orders, police unlawfully beating demonstrators, looters and rioters going unapprehended and unpunished, and college youth attacking society's rules and values, makes it easier, even more "logical," for disadvantaged young people, whose attachment to law-abiding behavior already is tenuous, to slip into law-breaking behavior when the opportunity presents itself. Too, the pervasive suspicion that personal greed and corruption are prevalent among even the highest public officials has fed the idea among the poor that nearly everyone is "on the take," and that the real crime is in getting caught.

The beliefs that some claim to be widely held among poor young ghetto males—that the "system" in the United States is collectively guilty of "white racism" and of prosecuting an "immoral" war in Vietnam—have also tended to impair the moral impact upon them of our nation's institutions and laws and weakened the sense of guilt that otherwise would have restrained the commission of violent crimes against society.

These three factors—disappointments of minorities in the revolution of rising expectations, the weakening of law enforcement, and the loss of institutional legitimacy in the view of many—have had their effects on crime rates throughout our society. It is not surprising, however, that their greatest impact has been in the inner-cities, among the young, the poor, the male, the black. It is there that reality most frustrates expectations, that law enforcement provides the least protection, and that the social and political institutions of society serve the needs of the individual least effectively. It is in the inner-city that a subculture of violence, already flourishing, is further strengthened by the blockage of aspirations whose fulfillment would lead out of the subculture, by the failure of a criminal justice system that would deter adherence to undesirable subcultural values, and by the weakness of institutions which would inculcate a competing set of values and attitudes.

LIKE IT IS IN THE ALLEY

Robert Coles

"In the alley it's mostly dark, even if the sun is out. But if you look around, you can find things. I know how to get into every building, except that it's like night once you're inside them, because they don't have lights. So, I stay here. You're better off. It's no good on the street. You can get hurt all the time, one way or the other. And in buildings, like I told you, it's bad in them, too. But here it's o.k. You can find your own corner, and if someone tries to move in, you fight him off. We meet here all the time, and figure out what we'll do next. It might be a game, or over for some pool, or a coke or something. You need to have a place to start out from, and that's like it is in the alley; you can always know your buddy will be there, provided it's the right time. So you go there, and you're on your way, man."

Like all children of nine, Peter is always on his way—to a person, a place, a "thing" he wants to do. *"There's this here thing we thought we'd try tomorrow,"* he'll say; and eventually I'll find out that he means there's to be a race. He and his friends will compete with another gang to see who can wash a car faster and better. The cars belong to four youths who make their money taking bets, and selling liquor that I don't believe was ever purchased, and pushing a few of those pills that *"go classy with beer."* I am not completely sure, but I think they also have something to do with other drugs; and again, I can't quite be sure what their connection is with a "residence" I've seen not too far from the alley Peter describes so possessively. The women come and go—from that residence and along the street Peter's alley leaves.

Peter lives in the heart of what we in contemporary America have chosen (ironically, so far as history goes) to call an "urban ghetto." The area was a slum before it became a ghetto, and there still are some very poor white people on its edges and increasing numbers of Puerto Ricans in several of its blocks. Peter was not born in the ghetto, nor was his family told to go there. They are Americans and have been here *"since way back before anyone can remember."* That is the way Peter's mother talks about Alabama, about the length of time she and her ancestors have lived there. She and Peter's father came north *"for freedom."* They did not seek out a ghetto, an old quarter of Boston where they were expected to live and where they would be confined, yet at least some of the time solidly at rest, with kin, and reasonably safe.

No, they sought freedom. Americans, they moved on when the going got *"real bad,"* and Americans, they expected something better someplace, some

Robert Coles, "Like It Is In The Alley," **DAEDALUS,** Fall, 1968. Reprinted by permission from **DAEDALUS,** Journal of the American Academy of Arts and Sciences, Boston, Massachusetts, Volume 97, Number 4.

other place. They left Alabama on impulse. They found Peter's alley by accident. And they do not fear pogroms. They are Americans, and in Peter's words:
*"There's likely to be another riot here soon. That's what I heard today. You
hear it a lot, but one day you know it'll happen."*

Peter's mother fears riots too—among other things. The Jews of Eastern
Europe huddled together in their ghettos, afraid of the barbarians, afraid of the
Goyim, but always sure of one thing, their God-given destiny. Peter's mother has
no such faith. She believes that *"something will work out one of these days."*
She believes that *"you have to keep on going, and things can get better, but
don't ask me how."* She believes that *"God wants us to have a bad spell here,
and so maybe it'll get better the next time—you know in Heaven, and I hope
that's where we'll be going."* Peter's mother, in other words, is a pragmatist, an
optimist, and a Christian. Above all she is American: *"Yes, I hear them talk
about Africa, but it don't mean anything to us. All I know is Alabama and now
it's in Massachusetts that we are. It was a long trip coming up here, and sometimes I wish we were back there, and sometimes I'd just as soon be here, for all
that's no good about it. But I'm not going to take any more trips, no sir. And
like Peter said, this is the only country we've got. If you come from a country,
you come from it, and we're from it, I'd say, and there isn't much we can do but
try to live as best we can. I mean, live here."*

What is "life" like for her over there, where she lives, in the neighborhood
she refers to as "here"? A question like that cannot be answered by the likes of
me, and even her answer provides only the beginning of a reply: *"Well, we does
o.k., I guess. Peter here, he has it better than I did, or his daddy. I can say that. I
tell myself that a lot. He can turn on the faucet over there, and a lot of the time,
he just gets the water, right away. And when I tell him what it was like for us, to
go fetch that water—we'd walk three miles, yes sir, and we'd be lucky it wasn't
ten—well, Peter, it doesn't register on him. He thinks I'm trying to fool him, and
the more serious I get, the more he laughs, so I've stopped.*

*"Of course, it's not all so good, I have to admit. We're still where we were,
so far as knowing where your next meal is coming from. When I go to bed at
night I tell myself I've done good, to stay alive and keep the kids alive, and if
they'll just wake up in the morning, and me too, well then, we can worry about
that, all the rest, come tomorrow. So there you go. We do our best, and that's all
you can do."*

She may sound fatalistic, but she appears to be a nervous, hard-working,
even hard-driven woman—thin, short, constantly on the move. I may not know
what she "really" thinks and believes, because like the rest of us she has her
contradictions and her mixed feelings. I think it is fair to say that there are some
things that she can't say to me—or to herself. She is a Negro, and I am white. She
is poor, and I am fairly well off. She is very near to illiterate, and I put in a lot of
time worrying about how to say things. But she and I are both human beings,
and we both have trouble—to use that word—"communicating," not only with
each other, but with ourselves. Sometimes she doesn't tell me something she
really wants me to know. She has forgotten, pure and simple. More is on her
mind than information I might want. And sometimes I forget too: *"Remember
you asked the other day about Peter, if he was ever real sick. And I told you he
was a weak child, and I feared for his life, and I've lost five children, three that*

was born and two that wasn't. Well, I forgot to tell you that he got real sick up here, just after we came. He was three, and I didn't know what to do. You see, I didn't have my mother to help out. She always knew what to do. She could hold a child and get him to stop crying, no matter how sick he was, and no matter how much he wanted food, and we didn't have it. But she was gone—and that's when we left to come up here, and I never would have left her, not for anything in the world. But suddenly she took a seizure of something and went in a half hour, I'd say. And Peter, he was so hot and sick, I thought he had the same thing his grandmother did and he was going to die. I thought maybe she's calling him. She always liked Peter. She helped him be born, she and my cousin, they did."

Actually, Peter's mother remembers quite a lot of things. She remembers the "old days" back South, sometimes with a shudder, but sometimes with the same nostalgia that the region is famous for generating in its white exiles. She also notices a lot of things. She notices, and from time to time will remark upon, the various changes in her life. She has moved from the country to the city. Her father was a sharecropper and her son wants to be a pilot (sometimes), a policeman (sometimes), a racing-car driver (sometimes), and a baseball player (most of the time). Her husband is not alive. He died one year after they all came to Boston. He woke up vomiting in the middle of the night—vomiting blood. He bled and bled and vomited and vomited and then he died. The doctor does not have to press very hard for "the facts." Whatever is known gets spoken vividly and (still) emotionally: *"I didn't know what to do. I was beside myself. I prayed, and in between I held his head and wiped his forehead. It was the middle of the night. I woke up my oldest girl and I told her to go knocking on the doors. But no one would answer. They must have been scared or have suspected something bad. I thought if only he'd be able to last into the morning, then we could get some help. I was caught between things. I couldn't leave him to go get a policeman. And my girl, she was afraid to go out. And besides, there was no one outside, and I thought we'd just stay at his side, and somehow he'd be o.k. because he was a strong man, you know. His muscles, they were big all his life. Even with the blood coming up, he looked too big and strong to die, I thought. But I knew he was sick. He was real bad sick. There wasn't anything else, no sir, to do. We didn't have no phone and even if there was a car, I never could have used it. Nor my daughter. And then he took a big breath and that was his last one."*

When I first met Peter and his mother, I wanted to know how they lived, what they did with their time, what they liked to do or disliked doing, what they believed. In the back of my mind were large subjects like "the connection between a person's moods and the environment in which he lives." Once I was told I was studying "the psychology of the ghetto," and another time the subject of "urban poverty and mental health." It is hoped that at some point large issues like those submit themselves to lives; and when that is done, when particular but not unrepresentative or unusual human beings are called in witness, their concrete medical history becomes extremely revealing. I cannot think of a better way to begin knowing what life is like for Peter and his mother than to hear the following and hear it again and think about its implications: *"No sir, Peter has never been to a doctor, not unless you count the one at school, and she's a nurse I believe. He was his sickest back home before we came here, and* you know there was no doctor for us in the country. In Alabama you have to pay a white doctor first, before he'll go near you. And we don't have but a few colored ones. (I've never seen a one.) There was this woman we'd go to, and she had gotten some nursing education in Mobile. (No, I don't know if she was a nurse or not, or a helper to the nurses, maybe.) Well, she would come to help us. With the convulsions, she'd show you how to hold the child, and make sure he doesn't hurt himself. They can bite their tongues real, real bad.

"Here, I don't know what to do. There's the city hospital, but it's no good for us. I went there with my husband, no sooner than a month or so after we came up here. We waited and waited, and finally the day was almost over. We left the kids with a neighbor, and we barely knew her. I said it would take the morning, but I never thought we'd get home near suppertime. And they wanted us to come back and come back, because it was something they couldn't do all at once—though for most of the time we just sat there and did nothing. And my husband, he said his stomach was the worse for going there, and he'd take care of himself from now on, rather than go there.

"Maybe they could have saved him. But they're far away, and I didn't have money to get a cab, even if there was one around here, and I thought to myself it'll make him worse, to take him there.

"My kids, they get sick. The welfare worker, she sends a nurse here, and she tells me we should be on vitamins and the kids need all kinds of check-ups. Once she took my daughter and told her she had to have her teeth looked at, and the same with Peter. So, I went with my daughter, and they didn't see me that day, but said they could in a couple of weeks. And I had to pay the woman next door to mind the little ones, and there was the carfare, and we sat and sat, like before. So, I figured, it would take more than we've got to see that dentist. And when the nurse told us we'd have to come back a few times—that's how many, a few—I thought that no one ever looked at my teeth, and they're not good, I'll admit, but you can't have everything, that's what I say, and that's what my kids have to know, I guess."

What *does* she have? And what belongs to Peter? For one thing, there is the apartment, three rooms for six people, a mother and five children. Peter is a middle child with two older girls on one side and a younger sister and still younger brother on the other side. The smallest child was born in Boston: "*It's the only time I ever spent time in a hospital. He's the only one to be born there. My neighbor got the police. I was in the hall, crying I guess. We almost didn't make it. They told me I had bad blood pressure, and I should have been on pills, and I should come back, but I didn't. It was the worst time I've ever had, because I was alone. My husband had to stay with the kids, and no one was there to visit me.*"

Peter sleeps with his brother in one bedroom. The three girls sleep in the living room, which is a bedroom. And, of course, there is a small kitchen. There is not very much furniture about. The kitchen has a table with four chairs, only two of which are sturdy. The girls sleep in one big bed. Peter shares his bed with his brother. The mother sleeps on a couch. There is one more chair and a table in the living room. Jesus looks down from the living room wall, and an undertaker's calendar hangs on the kitchen wall. The apartment has no books, no records. There is a television set in the living room, and I have never seen it off.

Peter in many respects is his father's successor. His mother talks things over with him. She even defers to him at times. She will say something; he will disagree; she will nod and let him have the last word. He knows the city. She still feels a stranger to the city. *"If you want to know about anything around here, just ask Peter,"* she once said to me. That was three years ago, when Peter was six. Peter continues to do very poorly at school, but I find him a very good teacher. He notices a lot, makes a lot of sense when he talks, and has a shrewd eye for the ironic detail. He is very intelligent, for all the trouble he gives his teachers. He recently summed up a lot of American history for me: *"I wasn't made for that school, and that school wasn't made for me."* It is an old school, filled with memories. The name of the school evokes Boston's Puritan past. Pictures and statues adorn the corridors—reminders of the soldiers and statesmen and writers who made New England so influential in the nineteenth century. And naturally one finds slogans on the walls, about freedom and democracy and the rights of the people. Peter can be surly and cynical when he points all that out to the visitor. If he is asked what kind of school he would *like*, he laughs incredulously. *"Are you kidding? No school would be my first choice. They should leave us alone, and let us help out at home, and maybe let some of our own people teach us. The other day the teacher admitted she was no good. She said maybe a Negro should come in and give us the discipline, because she was scared. She said all she wanted from us was that we keep quiet and stop wearing her nerves down, and she'd be grateful, because she would retire soon. She said we were becoming too much for her, and she didn't understand why. But when one kid wanted to say something, tell her why, she told us to keep still, and write something. You know what? She whipped out a book and told us to copy a whole page from it, so we'd learn it. A stupid waste of time. I didn't even try; and she didn't care. She just wanted an excuse not to talk with us. They're all alike.*

Actually, they're *not* all alike, and Peter knows it. He has met up with two fine teachers, and in mellow moments he can say so: *"They're trying hard, but me and my friends, I don't think we're cut out for school. To tell the truth, that's what I think. My mother says we should try, anyway, but it doesn't seem to help, trying. The teacher can't understand a lot of us, but he does all these new things, and you can see he's excited. Some kids are really with him, and I am, too. But I can't take all his stuff very serious. He's a nice man, and he says he wants to come and visit every one of our homes; but my mother says no, she wouldn't know what to do with him, when he came here. We'd just stand and have nothing to talk about. So she said tell him not to come; and I don't think he will, anyway. I think he's getting to know."*

What is that teacher getting to know? What *is* there to know about Peter and all the others like him in our American cities? Of course, Peter and his friends who play in the alley need better schools, schools they can feel to be theirs, like the ones they *have* in fact met on occasion. But I do not feel that a reasonably good teacher in the finest school building in America would reach and affect Peter in quite the way, I suppose, people like me would expect and desire. At nine Peter is both young and quite old. At nine he is much wiser about many things than my sons will be at nine, and maybe nineteen. Peter has in fact taught me a lot about his neighborhood, about life on the streets, about survival: *"I get up when I get up, no special time. My mother has Alabama in her. She gets up with the sun, and she wants to go to bed when it gets dark. I try to tell her that up here things just get started in the night. But she gets mad. She wakes me up. If it weren't for her shaking me, I might sleep until noon. Sometimes we have a good breakfast, when the check comes. Later on, though, before it comes, it might just be some coffee and a slice of bread. She worries about food. She says we should eat what she gives us, but sometimes I'd rather go hungry. I was sick a long time ago, my stomach or something— maybe like my father, she says. So I don't like all the potatoes she pushes on us and cereal, all the time cereal. We're supposed to be lucky, because we get some food every day. Down South they can't be sure. That's what she says, and I guess she's right.*

"Then I go to school. I eat what I can, and leave. I have two changes of clothes, one for everyday and one for Sunday. I wait on my friend Billy, and we're off by 8:15. He's from around here, and he's a year older. He knows everything. He can tell you if a woman is high on some stuff, or if she's been drinking, or she's off her mind about something. He knows. His brother has a convertible, a Buick. He pays off the police, but Billy won't say no more than that.

"In school we waste time until it's over. I do what I have to. I don't like the place. I feel like falling off all day, just putting my head down and saying good-bye to everyone until three. We're out then, and we sure wake up. I don't have to stop home first, not now. I go with Billy. We'll be in the alley, or we'll go to see them play pool. Then you know when it's time to go home. You hear someone say six o'clock, and you go in. I eat and I watch television. It must be around ten or eleven I'm in bed."

Peter sees rats all the time. He has been bitten by them. He has a big stick by his bed to use against them. They also claim the alley, even in the daytime. They are not large enough to be compared with cats, as some observers have insisted; they are simply large, confident, well-fed, unafraid rats. The garbage is theirs; the land is theirs; the tenement is theirs; human flesh is theirs. When I first started visiting Peter's family, I wondered why they didn't do something to rid themselves of those rats, and the cockroaches, and the mosquitoes, and the flies, and the maggots, and the ants, and especially the garbage in the alley which attracts so much of all that "lower life." Eventually I began to see some of the reasons why. A large apartment building with many families has exactly two barrels in its basement. The halls of the building go unlighted. Many windows have no screens, and some windows are broken and boarded up. The stairs are dangerous; some of them have missing timber. (*"We just jump over them,"* says Peter cheerfully.) And the landowner is no one in particular. Rent is collected by an agent, in the name of a "realty trust." Somewhere in City Hall there is a bureaucrat who unquestionably might be persuaded to prod someone in the "trust"; and one day I went with three of the tenants, including Peter's mother, to try that "approach." We waited and waited at City Hall. (I drove us there, clear across town, naturally.) Finally we met up with a man, a not very encouraging or inspiring or generous or friendly man. He told us we would have to try yet another department and swear out a complaint; and that the "case" would have to be "studied," and that we would then be "notified of a decision."

We went to the department down the hall, and waited some more, another hour and ten minutes. By then it was three o'clock, and the mothers wanted to go home. They weren't thinking of rats anymore, or poorly heated apartments, or garbage that had nowhere to go and often went uncollected for two weeks, not one. They were thinking of their children, who would be home from school and, in the case of two women, their husbands who would also soon be home. *"Maybe we should come back some other day,"* Peter's mother said. I noted she didn't say *tomorrow*, and I realize that I had read someplace that people like her aren't precisely "future-oriented."

Actually, both Peter and his mother have a very clear idea of what is ahead. For the mother it is *"more of the same."* One evening she was tired but unusually talkative, perhaps because a daughter of hers was sick: *"I'm glad to be speaking about all these things tonight. My little girl has a bad fever. I've been trying to cool her off all day. Maybe if there was a place near here, that we could go to, maybe I would have gone. But like it is, I have to do the best I can and pray she'll be o.k."*

I asked whether she thought her children would find things different, and that's when she said it would be *"more of the same"* for them. Then she added a long afterthought: *"Maybe it'll be a little better for them. A mother has to have hope for her children, I guess. But I'm not too sure, I'll admit. Up here you know there's a lot more jobs around than in Alabama. We don't get them, but you know they're someplace near, and they tell you that if you go train for them, then you'll be eligible. So maybe Peter might someday have some real good steady work, and that would be something, yes sir it would. I keep telling him he should pay more attention to school, and put more of himself into the lessons they give there. But he says no, it's no good; it's a waste of time; they don't care what happens there, only if the kids don't keep quiet and mind themselves. Well, Peter has got to learn to mind himself, and not be fresh. He speaks back to me, these days. There'll be a time he won't even speak to me at all, I suppose. I used to blame it all on the city up here, city living. Back home we were always together, and there wasn't no place you could go, unless to Birmingham, and you couldn't do much for yourself there, we all knew. Of course, my momma, she knew how to make us behave. But I was thinking the other night, it wasn't so good back there either. Colored people, they'd beat on one another, and we had lot of people that liquor was eating away at them; they'd use wine by the gallon. All they'd do was work on the land, and then go back and kill themselves with wine. All then there'd be the next day—until they'd one evening go to sleep and never wake up. And we'd get the Bossman and he'd see to it they got buried.*

"Up here I think it's better, but don't ask me to tell you why. There's the welfare, that's for sure. And we get our water and if there isn't good heat, at least there's some. Yes, it's cold up here but we had cold down there, too, only then we didn't have any heat, and we'd just die, some of us would, every winter with one of those freezing spells.

"And I do believe things are changing. On the television they talk to you, the colored man and all the others who aren't doing so good. My boy Peter, he says they're putting you on. That's all he sees, people 'putting on' other people. But I think they all mean it, the white people. I never see them, except on

television, when they say the white man wants good for the colored people. I think Peter could go and do better for himself later on, when he gets older, except for the fact that he just doesn't believe. He don't believe what they say, the teacher, or the man who says it's getting better for us—on television. I guess it's my fault. I never taught my children, any of them, to believe that kind of thing; because I never thought we'd ever have it any different, not in this life. So maybe I've failed Peter. I told him the other day, he should work hard, because of all the 'opportunity' they say is coming for us, and he said I was talking good, but where was my proof. So I went next door with him, to my neighbor's, and we asked her husband, and you know he sided with Peter. He said they were taking in a few here and a few there, and putting them in the front windows of all the big companies, but that all you have to do is look around at our block and you'd see all the young men, and they just haven't got a thing to do. Nothing. "

Her son also looks to the future. Sometimes he talks—in his own words— "big," He'll one day be a bombardier or *"something like that."* At other times he is less sure of things: *"I don't know what I'll be. Maybe nothing. I see the men sitting around, hiding from the welfare lady. They fool her. Maybe I'll fool her, too. I don't know what you can do. The teacher the other day said that if just one of us turned out o.k. she'd congratulate herself and call herself lucky."*

A while back a riot excited Peter and his mother, excited them and frightened them. The spectacle of the police being fought, of white-owned property being assaulted, stirred the boy a great deal: *"I figured the whole world might get changed around. I figured people would treat us better from now on. Only I don't think they will."* As for his mother, she was less hopeful, but even more apocalyptic: *"I told Peter we were going to pay for this good. I told him they wouldn't let us get away with it, not later on."* And in the midst of the trouble she was frightened as she had never before been: *"I saw them running around on the streets, the men and women, and they were talking about burning things down, and how there'd be nothing left when they got through. I sat there with my children and I thought we might die the way things are going, die right here. I didn't know what to do: if I should leave, in case they burn down the building, or if I should stay, so that the police don't arrest us, or we get mixed up with the crowd of people. I've never seen so many people, going in so many different directions. They were running and shouting and they didn't know what to do. They were so excited. My neighbor, she said they'd burn us all up, and then the white man would have himself one less of a headache. The colored man is a worse enemy to himself than the white. I mean, it's hard to know which is the worst."*

I find it as hard as she does to sort things out. When I think of her and the mothers like her I have worked with for years, when I think of Peter and his friends, I find myself caught between the contradictory observations I have made. Peter already seems a grim and unhappy child. He trusts no one white, not his white teacher, not the white policeman he sees, not the white welfare worker, not the white storekeeper, and not, I might add, me. There we are, the five of us from the 180,000,000 Americans who surround him and, of course, 20,000,000 others. Yet, Peter doesn't really trust his friends and neighbors, either. At nine he has learned to be careful, wary, guarded, doubtful, and calculating. His teacher may not know it, but Peter is a good sociologist, and a good political scientist, a good student of urban affairs. With devastating accuracy he can reveal how much of the "score" he knows; yes, and how fearful and sad and angry he is: *"This here city isn't for us. It's for the people downtown. We're here because, like my mother said, we had to come. If they could lock us up or sweep us away, they would. That's why I figure the only way you can stay ahead is get some kind of deal for yourself. If I had a choice I'd live someplace else, but I don't know where. It would be a place where they treated you right, and they didn't think you were some nuisance. But the only thing you can do is be careful of yourself; if not, you'll get killed somehow, like it happened to my father."*

His father died prematurely, and most probably, unnecessarily. Among the poor of our cities the grim medical statistics we all know about become terrible daily experiences. Among the black and white families I work with—in nearby but separate slums—disease and the pain that goes with it are taken for granted. When my children complain of an earache or demonstrate a skin rash I rush them to the doctor. When I have a headache, I take an aspirin; and if the headache is persistent, I can always get a medical check-up. Not so with Peter's mother and Peter; they have learned to live with sores and infections and poorly mended fractures and bad teeth and eyes that need but don't have the help of glasses. Yes, they can go to a city hospital and get free care; but again and again they don't. They come to the city without any previous experience as patients. They have never had the money to purchase a doctor's time. They have never had free medical care available. (I am speaking now of Appalachian whites as well as Southern blacks.) It may comfort me to know that every American city provides some free medical services for its "indigent," but Peter's mother and thousands like her have quite a different view of things: *"I said to you the other time, I've tried there. It's like at City Hall, you wait, and they pushes you and shove you and call your name, only to tell you to wait some more, and if you tell them you can't stay there all day, they'll say 'lady, go home, then.' You get sick just trying to get there. You have to give your children over to people or take them all with you; and the carfare is expensive. Why if we had a doctor around here, I could almost pay him with the carfare it takes to get there and back for all of us. And you know, they keep on having you come back and back, and they don't know what each other says. Each time they starts from scratch."*

It so happens that recently I took Peter to a children's hospital and arranged for a series of evaluations which led to the following: a pair of glasses; a prolonged bout of dental work; antibiotic treatment for skin lesions; a thorough cardiac work-up, with the subsequent diagnosis of rheumatic heart disease; a conference between Peter's mother and a nutritionist, because the boy has been on a high-starch, low-protein, and low-vitamin diet all his life. He suffers from one attack of sinus trouble after another, from a succession of sore throats and earaches, from cold upon cold, even in the summer. A running nose is unsurprising to him—and so is chest pain and shortness of breath, due to a heart ailment, we now know.

At the same time Peter is tough. I have to emphasize again *how* tough and, yes, how "politic, cautious and meticulous," not in Prufrock's way, but in another way and for other reasons. Peter has learned to be wary as well as angry; tentative as well as extravagant; at times controlled and only under certain circumstances defiant: *"Most of the time, I think you have to watch your step. That's what I think. That's the difference between up here and down in the South. That's what my mother says, and she's right. I don't remember it down there, but I know she must be right. Here, you measure the next guy first and then make your move when you think it's a good time to.*

He was talking about *"how you get along"* when you leave school and go *"mix with the guys"* and start *"getting your deal."* He was telling me what an outrageous and unsafe world he has inherited and how very carefully he has made his appraisal of the future. Were I afflicted with some of his physical complaints, I would be fretful, annoyed, petulant, angry—and moved to do something, see someone, get a remedy, a pill, a promise of help. He has made his "adjustment" to the body's pain, and he has also learned to contend with the alley and the neighborhood and *us,* the world beyond: *"The cops come by here all the time. They drive up and down the street. They want to make sure everything is o.k. to look at. They don't bother you, so long as you don't get in their way."*

So, it is live and let live—except that families like Peter's have a tough time living, and of late have been troubling those cops, among others. Our cities have become not only battlegrounds, but places where all sorts of American problems and historical ironies have converged. Ailing, poorly fed, and proud Appalachian families have reluctantly left the hollows of eastern Kentucky and West Virginia for Chicago and Dayton and Cincinnati and Cleveland and Detroit, and even, I have found, Boston. They stick close together in all-white neighborhoods—or enclaves or sections or slums or ghettos or whatever. They wish to go home but can't, unless they are willing to be idle and hungry all the time. They confuse social workers and public officials of all kinds because they both want and reject the city. Black families also have sought out cities and learned to feel frightened and disappointed.

I am a physician, and over the past ten years I have been asking myself how people like Peter and his mother survive in mind and body and spirit. And I have wanted to know what a twentieth-century American city "means" to them or "does" to them. People cannot be handed questionnaires and asked to answer such questions. They cannot be "interviewed" a few times and told to come across with a statement, a reply. But inside Peter and his brother and his sisters and his mother, and inside a number of Appalachian mothers and fathers and children I know, are feelings and thoughts and ideas—which, in my experience, come out casually or suddenly, by accident almost. After a year or two of talking, after experiences such as I have briefly described in a city hall, in a children's hospital, a lifetime of pent-up tensions and observation comes to blunt expression: *"Down in Alabama we had to be careful about ourselves with the white man, but we had plenty of things we could do by ourselves. There was our side of town, and you could walk and run all over, and we had a garden you know. Up here they have you in a cage. There's no place to go, and all I do is stay in the building all day long and the night, too. I don't use my legs no more, hardly at all. I never see those trees, and my oldest girl, she misses planting time. It was bad down there. We had to leave. But it's no good here, too, I'll tell you. Once I woke up and I thought all the buildings on the block were falling down on me. And I was trying to climb out, but I couldn't. And then the next thing I knew, we were all back South, and I was standing near some sunflowers—you know, the tall ones that can shade you if you sit down.*

"No, I don't dream much. I fall into a heavy sleep as soon as I touch the bed. The next thing I know I'm stirring myself to start in all over in the morning. It used to be the sun would wake me up, but now it's up in my head, I guess. I know I've got to get the house going and off to school."

Her wistful, conscientious, law-abiding, devoutly Christian spirit hasn't completely escaped the notice of Peter, for all his hardheaded, cynical protestations: *"If I had a chance, I'd like to get enough money to bring us all back to Alabama for a visit. Then I could prove it that it may be good down there, a little bit, even if it's no good, either. Like she says, we had to get out of there or we'd be dead by now. I hear say we all may get killed soon, it's so bad here; but I think we did right to get up here, and if we make them listen to us, the white man, maybe he will."*

To which Peter's mother adds: *"We've carried a lot of trouble in us, from way back in the beginning. I have these pains, and so does everyone around here. But you can't just die until you're ready to. And I do believe something is happening. I do believe I see that."*

To which Peter adds: *"Maybe it won't be that we'll win, but if we get killed, everyone will hear about it. Like the minister said, before we used to die real quiet, and no one stopped to pay notice."*

Two years before Peter spoke those words he drew a picture for me, one of many he has done. When he was younger, and when I didn't know him so well as I think I do now, it was easier for us to have something tangible to do and then talk about. I used to visit the alley with him, as I still do, and one day I asked him to draw the alley. That was a good idea, he thought. (Not all of my suggestions were, however.) He started in, then stopped, and finally worked rather longer and harder than usual at the job. I busied myself with my own sketches, which from the start he insisted I do. Suddenly from across the table I heard him say he was through. Ordinarily he would slowly turn the drawing around for me to see; and I would get up and walk over to his side of the table, to see even better. But he didn't move his paper, and I didn't move myself. I saw what he had drawn, and he saw me looking. I was surprised and a bit stunned and more than a bit upset, and surely he saw my face and heard my utter silence. Often I would break the awkward moments when neither of us seemed to have anything to say, but this time it was his turn to do so: *"You know what it is?"* He knew that I liked us to talk about our work. I said no, I didn't—though in fact the vivid power of his black crayon had come right across to me. *"It's that hole we dug in the alley. I made it bigger here. If you fall into it, you can't get out. You die."*

He had drawn circles within circles, all of them black, and then a center, also black. He had imposed an X on the center. Nearby, strewn across the circles, were fragments of the human body—two faces, an arm, five legs. And after I had taken the scene in, I could only think to myself that I had been shown *"like it is in the alley"*—by an intelligent boy who knew what he saw around him, could give it expression, and, I am convinced, would respond to a different city, a city that is alive and breathing, one that is not for many of its citizens a virtual morgue.

OVERCROWDING AND HUMAN AGGRESSION

George M. Carstairs

When statisticians warn us about the inevitable consequences if recent population trends are allowed to continue unchecked during the next few generations, our first concern has naturally been over the basic question of survival: Will the world's resources suffice to feed all those extra billions? No sooner have we heard the arguments on this than we find ourselves facing the next question: What will be the quality of the life led by the inhabitants of an overcrowded planet? In particular, what will be the effects of overcrowding on the manifestations of aggression within and between societies?

In former centuries, disease and early death exercised so effective a form of population control that the vast majority of mankind could not indulge in the luxury of aspiring to a high standard of living. Simply to survive into late adulthood, at the same level of subsistence as one's forefathers, was good fortune enough. From the time of the earliest prehistoric civilizations to the present day, in almost every human society, only the privileged elite were in a position to cultivate their sensibilities and to expand the boundaries of human experience and understanding. In London, as recently as the beginning of the present century, the very chances of survival through early infancy were more than twice as high for the children of the rich as for the children of the poor. Throughout the contemporary world, survival has become generally attainable, for rich and poor alike; and now, for the first time in the history of mankind, education, self-awareness, and the aspiration for a meaningful and satisfying life experience are being shared by a majority of people.

Inevitably, once the killing diseases and the threat of starvation have been averted, people become increasingly aware of, and discontented with, minor forms of discomfort or unhappiness. One of the striking changes in morbidity in both highly developed and in developing countries during recent decades has been the apparent increase in neurosis and psychosomatic disorders. These functional illnesses—which some people would prefer to regard as manifestations of "problems of living" rather than of disease—have long been recognized among the privileged classes. Already in 1689, Thomas Sydenham declared that half of his non-fertile patients, that is, one-sixth of his total practice, were hysterical; and in 1733, George Cheyne (in his book entitled *The English Disease*) stated that a third of his patients were neurotic.

Both Sydenham and Cheyne were fashionable physicians, most of whose

George M. Carstairs, "Overcrowding and Human Aggression," **THE HISTORY OF VIOLENCE IN AMERICA** *(New York: Bantam Books, Inc., 1969), Chap. 21.*

clientele was drawn from the wealthy minority of the English society of their day. Sydenham himself observed that hysteria was commoner among women of the leisured classes than among those who had to toil. It is only in the present day that the working classes have been in a position to enjoy the luxury of being neurotic; but recent surveys, both in Asia[1] and in Manhattan,[2] have shown that the rates for almost every form of mental illness are highest among the socio-economically underprivileged sections of contemporary societies.

It must be emphasized that the very marked increase in the "visibility" of mental disorders in most countries of the world is partly due to the better control of infections and other serious physical illnesses. Neurosis is a by-product of a raised level of expectation of the quality of life experience when these higher expectations are denied fulfillment. It can, at times, be manifested as what Charles Kingsley called "divine discontent," a spur toward the further enhancement of the standard of living—provided, of course, that steps can be taken to remedy the adverse environmental factors to which the symptoms have drawn our attention.

There are, however, many situations in which individuals feel themselves powerless to better their state: conspicuous instances can be found in the socially disorganized slum areas of great cities, especially in periods of very rapid growth such as that experienced by Chicago and Detroit in the early decades of this century, and by such cities as Tokyo, Calcutta, Rio de Janeiro, and other conurbations after the Second World War. Here we are confronted by this vital question: What will be the consequences, for mental health, of a continuing massive increase in human populations?

As yet, the science of human behavior is not sufficiently developed to be able to answer this question with precision, or even with confidence. Nevertheless it is possible to learn from studies of animals, both in their natural environment and under experimental conditions, and to note certain regularly occurring consequences of severe overcrowding: with due caution, one can infer some similar repercussions of overcrowding in man. There are also a number of direct observations, in human populations, on the interrelationships between overcrowding and certain indices of mental health, from which we can predict with greater confidence the likely consequences of overcrowding on a still larger scale.

STUDIES OF ANIMAL BEHAVIOR

At first sight, it might seem that much could be learned from observations on species such as lemmings or voles, which are subject to periodic fluctuations of population size. There is still a good deal of controversy among naturalists as to whether these fluctuations are esssentially determined by rather gross environmental factors of food supply or infection or whether social interactions also play an important role. Films of lemmings taken during one of their mass migra-

---

[1] T. Y. Lin, "A Study of the Incidence of Mental Disorder in Chinese and Other Cultures," *Psychiatry*, vol. XVI (1953), pp. 313 ff.
[2] L. Srole, T. S. Langer, S. T. Michael, M. K. Opler, and T. A. C. Rennie, *Mental Health in the Metropolis* (New York: McGraw-Hill, 1962).

tions have shown that although scarcity of food may be one factor, the movement of the whole population takes on a cumulative momentum as the result of repeated, frenetic interactions, which have been described as showing a hysterical quality.

In recent years the work of ethologists has taught us a great deal about the interaction of innate, biological propensities and learning experiences in many animal species. At a relatively crude level, this can be demonstrated by a modification of the animal's adrenal size and activity. The adrenals play an essential role in an animal's response to stress, whether by fighting or by taking flight. There is a conspicuous difference between the size of the adrenals in wild rats and in rats which have been bred for generations in captivity, the latter having much smaller adrenal glands. When wild rats are caged, and allowed to breed, a diminution in adrenal size becomes apparent in a few generations. In colonies in which there is a great deal of fighting, the mean size of the rats' adrenals increases by up to 30 percent—and this is true both of the aggressors and the victims. Observations in nature have shown marked diminution in adrenal size when rat populations are depleted. For example, the rat population in the sewers of Hamburg at one time became alarmingly large. A vigorous campaign of extermination succeeded literally in decimating their numbers. It was found that the size of the adrenals (in relation to total body size) significantly diminished after the reduction in the rat population. Similar findings were observed when numbers were reduced in an overcrowded herd of deer.

Adrenal activity is stimulated by social interaction, especially by the challenge of attack and the need for counterattack in self-defense. One interesting finding is that the quality of the stress response takes on a different character for the animal that is victorious in the contest. Such an animal can go from strength to strength, able to fight one battle after another; in the intervals of fighting, its sexual potency is also at a high level. In contrast, an animal which undergoes a series of defeats becomes debilitated, even although suffering no obvious physical injury, and is sexually less active. A biologist, Anthony Barnett, has shown that prolonged exposure to even moderate hostility can lead to weakness and death. He has epitomized this reaction as follows: "evidently the bodily response to humiliation resembles, in some ways, that to danger to life or limb."[3] Usually the loser in such contests is able to survive by escaping from the scene of battle and thereafter refraining from challenging its victor; but there are situations, both in the wild and in the captive state, where animals are unable to escape, and are repeatedly confronted by the threat of a contest in which they are doomed to defeat. There are well-authenticated observations, in rats, of the weaker animal's sudden death under such circumstances, and even careful postmortem examination has failed to show any organic trauma sufficient to account for these deaths.[4]

Another instance of the interaction of biological and social factors in the response to stress can be found in observation on the toxicity of amphetamine drugs, whose action is similar to that of adrenalin, the secretion of the medulla of the adrenal gland. A relatively small dose of amphetamine will prove fatal to a

---

[3] S. A. Barnett, "The Biology of Aggression," *Lancet* (1964), p. 803.
[4] *Ibid.*

rat that is confined in a cage with many other rats, whereas a rat that is kept in isolation can survive doses of amphetamine up to four times greater. It is presumed that the effect of the drug is greatly enhanced, in the former situation, by the numerous stressful interactions, with the other rats, each of which stimulates the output of more adrenalin until complete exhaustion supervenes.

These, of course, represent extremes of overstimulation. Many species of animals and birds have evolved self-protective behavior patterns to insure that such extremes will not occur. Typical of these behavior patterns is the "peck orders" or status hierarchy, by virtue of which a group of animals whose members meet each other regularly first fight each other, and then mutually agree to a rank order of ascendancy, after which the animal of inferior status invariably concedes in the face of a challenge from those above him in rank. More detailed studies have shown that status hierarchies can be either *absolute*, whereby every member of a group of animals invariably remains in the same position in relation to each of his fellows, or *relative* in which under different circumstances of time or place, the individual's respective degrees of ascendancy over another may change.[5] Absolute status hierarchies are most likely to be found where all the animals in a group share the same living space; they become most clearly defined when that space is a restricted one. Under such circumstances, Barnett has shown that adrenal size becomes inversely correlated with height in the social hierarchy.

Relative dominance is seen most clearly in animals that have individual territories. When on their home ground, they are often able to vanquish an intruder and compel him to retreat, whereas if they are challenged by the same individual on his home territory, they in turn will admit defeat. Many species of birds, and most mammals (including man), exhibits this kind of territorial behavior. Not only football teams, but all of us, tend to perform best on our home ground—mental as well as physical—and to resist anyone who ventures to challenge us there. Naturalists have recognized in territorial behavior, and in the varying degrees of dominance associated with the center and the periphery of the territory, a self-regulating mechanism that insures an optimal degree of dispersion of the species.[6]

When animals such as domestic cats, which customarily enjoy quite a wide range of movement, are crowded together in a limited space, there tends to emerge one particularly tyrannical "despot" who holds all the others in fear and also one or more whom Leyhausen terms "pariahs," at the bottom of the status hierarchy.[7] These unfortunate creatures, he observes, are "driven to frenzy and all kinds of neurotic behavior by continuous and pitiless attack by all the others." Although these "pariahs" bear the severest brunt, the whole community of cats held in such close confinement is seen to sufferer. These cats "seldom relax,

[5] P. Leyhausen, "The Communal Organization of Solitary Mammals," *Symposium of the Zoological Society (London),* vol. XIV (1965), pp. 249 ff., and V. C. Wynne-Edwards, *Animal Dispersion in Relation to Social Behavior* (Edinburgh and London: Oliver & Boyd, 1962).

[6] See Konrad Lorenz, *On Aggression* (New York: Harcourt, Brace & World, 1966), and Robert Ardrey, *The Territorial Imperative* (New York: Atheneum, 1961).

[7] P. Leyhausen, "The Sane Community—a Density Problem? *Discovery,* vol. XXVI (Sept. 1965), pp. 27 ff.

they never look at ease, and there is continuous hissing, growling and even fighting. Play stops altogether, and locomotion and exercise are reduced to a minimum."[8]

This clearly represents a pathological social situation, in which overcrowding and confinement conspire to accentuate disturbing confrontations between individuals. Another observer, studying the behavior of colonies of rats under different degrees of over-population, observed similar changes in their customary interrelationships. Where overcrowding was most marked, the enforced social interactions were seen to interfere with the satisfaction of quite basic biological needs such as feeding, nest building, and the care of their young. Normally mother rats whose nest is disturbed will carry their young, one by one, to a place of safety, but in overcrowded pens this behavior pattern was lost, and the rats' general maternal care became so faulty that in one experiment 80 percent and in another 96 percent of all the young died before reaching maturity. Among the males, some became ascendant over their fellows but others showed a number of disturbances of behavior, of which two patterns were particularly striking: some males appeared to opt out of sexual and social interaction altogether, sulking alone on the periphery of the group, while others became morbidly pensexual, mounting female rats, whether receptive or not, whenever they could do so without being attacked by one of the ascendant males. These hyperactive rats contravened many of the norms of behavior of their group, even becoming cannibal toward the young of their own kind.[9]

It has been maintained by some writers that the human species is unique in its tendency to destroy its own kind; but this is not quite true. Colonies of rats will frequently attack, and even exterminate, single newcomers or groups of "alien" rats that are introduced into their midst. On the other hand, if several rats, previously reared in separate cages, are simultaneously introduced into a strange pen, they will spend several hours exploring the confines of the pen, and each other, without showing aggression; but after a relatively short interval any additional stranger introduced into this newly formed group will be liable to be attacked and killed.

It is, of course, a far cry from the behavior of rats and cats to that of humans; but observations on the behavior of higher primates have a more immediate relevance. Recent studies of apes and monkeys in their natural habitat have greatly modified earlier preconceptions about the frequency of both fighting and sexual behavior. These beliefs were much influenced by observations made by Zuckerman upon apes in zoos, which displayed almost incessant fighting and sexual competitition;[10] but this has proved to be only a travesty of their conduct in their natural surroundings. Instead, it is the product of their being confined in over-crowded conditions without the possibility of escape. In the wild state, protective mechanisms operate to control the frequency of both the above types of behavior; but when groups of primates outgrow their territory, the frequency of quarreling and fighting increases.[11]

[8] *Ibid.*

[9] J.B. Calhoun, "Population Density and Social Pathology," in L. J. Duhl, ed., *The Urban Condition* (New York: Basic Books, 1963), p. 33.

[10] S. G. Zuckerman, *The Social Life of Monkeys and Apes* (London: Kegan Paul, 1932).

[11] I. DeVore, *Primate Behaviour* (New York: Treubner King, 1965).

OBSERVATIONS ON HUMANS

It is perhaps significant that Leyhausen and Lorenz, the two naturalists who have devoted more attention than almost any others to the disruptive effects of overcrowding, themselves both underwent the painful experience of being closely confined in prisoner-of-war camps for several years. Their personal observations, which have been corroborated by other medical and psychiatric witnesses (e.g., Bettelheim, Cochrane, Gibbens),[12] were that when a group of men was penned up together in close quarters for many months on end, its members tended to become hyper-irritable, and to find each other's small mannerisms positively intolerable.

These, too, like the observations on caged cats and rats, were instances of extreme conditions; and yet one must realize that there are many impoverished groups in the world whose conditions of life today are scarcely better. In theory, of course, they can escape from their surroundings; but in practice the "culture of poverty" can induce a sense of despair of ever being able to escape.[13] One is tempted to draw an analogy between the rat that is subjected to a series of physical defeats, or the "pariahs" in an overcrowded colony of cats, and the members of problem families in our city slums who display a seeming inability to make a successful social adaptation. It appears that social institutions and transmitted value systems can create a sense of confinement no less demoralizing than the bars of a cage.

Many years ago, Farris and Dunham[14] drew attention to the ecological concentration of certain forms of mental illness in those parts of a large city where both overcrowding and social disorganization—or *anomie* as Durkheim[15] had earlier described it—were most marked. Subsequent research has challenged Dunham's specific contention that schizophrenia is generated by the conditions of life in a socially disorganized community; but many other studies have confirmed his finding that alcoholism, illegitimacy, divorce, delinquency, and numerous other forms of social pathology are most prevalent in such areas.

There remains, however, an interesting contrast in the social correlates of two particular manifestations of social pathology, namely, suicide and attempted suicide—at least, as they are observed in cities of the Western World. Suicide rates are highest in areas where many people live in a state of social isolation, bereft of the support of family, or of any other primary group. On the other hand, studies of attempted suicide have shown that the most important social correlate is overcrowding. Typically, the person who makes a nonfatal suicidal gesture has been harassed beyond endurance by recurrent friction within the

[12] Bruno Bettlelheim, "Individual and Mass Behavior in Extreme Situations," *Journal of Abnormal and Social Psychology,* vol. XXXVIII (1943), pp. 417 ff.; A. L. Cochrane, "Notes on the Psychology of Prisoners of War," *British Medical Journal,* vol. I (1946), pp. 282 ff.; and T. C. N. Gibbens, *The Psychology and Psychopathology of Prisoners of War,* M. D. thesis, University of London, 1947.

[13] Oscar Lewis, *Five Families: Mexican Case Studies in the Culture of Poverty* (New York: Basic Books, 1959).

[14] R. E. L. Farris and H. W. Dunham, *Mental Disorders in Urban Areas* (Chicago: University of Chicago Press, 1939).

[15] Emile Durkheim, *Le Suicide* (Paris: Ancienne Libraire Germer Bailliere, 1897).

domestic group, in cramped and overcrowded premises. Here, too, as in the instance of rats' dose resistance to amphetamine, one can see the mutual reinforcement of multiple factors. A majority of those who attempt suicide are relatively young men and women, who often have had a bad start in life with unstable or absent parent figures. These patients tend to experience great difficulty, in their turn, in forming stable interpersonal relationships: they are often at the same time demanding and inconsiderate toward others, and yet are themselves emotionally immature and dependent. Their deficiencies prompt them to seek out partners from whom they hope to derive support, but all too often the partner whom they select is handicapped in much the same way; so far from meeting each other's dependency needs, these unfortunates only succeed in making each other's state even worse than before. Often, too, they turn to drink or drugs to allay their need for dependence, and this in turn further impoverishes their ability to form rewarding personal relationships.[16]

During recent years many countries have been obliged to take stock of increasing rates of alcoholism, crimes of violence, and attempted suicide. Sociological and social-psychiatric research has shown that there are clusters of disturbances that are found most commonly in overpopulated, underprivileged sectors of large cities; but several interacting factors, in addition to that of overcrowding, are believed to contribute to their appearance. In recent years mass outbreaks of violence have quickened attention to these phenomena. It is disquieting to be reminded that even in countries that have experienced an overall improvement in their standard of living during the last quarter century, an increasing number of people feel alienated from the goals, and the rewards, to which their fellow citizens aspire—and alienated so profoundly that they despair of ever being able to get back into the mainstream of humanity.

Alienation and despair are the product of extreme situations—such as, for example, were realized in the grotesque, doomed societies of the Nazi concentration camps. Many, if not most, of the inmates of such camps found themselves surrendering their customary standards of behavior and their values, becoming completely disoriented by the inhuman conditions under which they were forced to live.[17]

There have been crises in the course of human history when quite large sectors of mankind experienced this sense of alienation from participation in the life of their fellow countrymen. Sometimes after prolonged deprivation their discontents have exploded in outbreaks of revolution, as a result of which a new social order has been created; but at other times leaderless masses of the dispossessed have shown themselves only too ready to become the dupes of mentally unstable yet charismatic demagogues, who promised them a magical deliverance from their miseries. The historian Norman Cohn has shown how often in European history periods of social and economic disruption have resulted in the demoralization of large populations. Cohn has identified a number of social circumstances in which this is liable to occur. Conspicuous among these have

[16]W. I. N. and J. W. McCulloch, "Repeated Acts of Self-Poisoning and Self-Injury," *Proceedings of the Royal Society of Medicine,* vol. LIX (1966), pp. 89 ff.
[17]L. Eitinger, *Concentration Camp Survivors in Norway and Israel* (London: Allen & Unwin, 1961).

been occasions in which long-settled means of production and traditional occupations have been rapidly superseded by new techniques, throwing many individuals out of work; circumstances in which different sectors of a population experience widely contrasting standards of living; and situations where traditional values are weakened, and customary authorities cease to fulfill their protective function. Common to all these circumstances is an all-pervading sense of uncertainty about the future.[18]

George Kennan has epitomized the consequences of such periods of uncertainty with his customary eloquence:

> *Whenever the authority of the past is too suddenly and too drastically undermined—whenever the past ceases to be the great and reliable reference book of human problems—whenever, above all; the experience of the father becomes irrelevant to the trials and searchings of the son—there the foundations of man's inner health and stability begin to crumble, insecurity and panic begin to take over, conduct becomes erratic and aggressive.*[19]

Just how erratic and aggressive conduct can become in such situations is amply illustrated in Cohn's monograph. He shows that the rootless, uncertain populations who are the victims of too rapid social change tend to regress emotionally, and to clutch at magical solutions for their plight. Nor have leaders been lacking to offer them just such magical solutions, promising a millennium of effortless bliss just around the corner.

A characteristic of these millennial movements has been their tendency to begin on a note of generosity, brotherliness, and willingness to let all share equally in the plenty which is soon to be available. This was the case with the followers of Tanchelm, who inspired a vast following among the poor in Flanders in the early 12th century, and with those of Eudes de l'Etoile, who preached a millennium of universal riches to hordes of peasants in Brittany rendered landless by successive years of famine. Both of these leaders were worshiped as divine during their short hey-days.

Two hundred years later, the English "Peasants' Revolt"—fundamentally a rebellion against the feudal relic of villeinage, which restricted laborers' freedom to avail themselves of new forms of employment in trades and manufacturing— found a more down-to-earth leader in John Ball, who contrasted the "natural state of man," born equal and entitled to his fair share of the world's goods, with existing social inequalities. The peroration of one of his addresses went: "Good folk, things cannot go well in England nor ever shall until all things are in common and there is neither villein nor noble, but all of us are of one condition."

The most remarkable of all the European millennial movements was the 2-year reign (1534-36) of the Anabaptist sect in the German town of Münster. Members of this sect proclaimed a universal brotherhood, and held all their possessions in common; but like all their predecessors, they met with vigorous opposition from the established authorities, and this opposition, in every case,

---

[18] Norman R. C. Cohn, *The Pursuit of the Millennium* (London: Secker & Warburg, 1957).
[19] George Kennan, *Realities of American Foreign Policy* (Princeton: Princeton University Press, 1954).

provoked counter aggression that was all the more extreme because it was fired with righteous indignation. The benign, ascetic Tanchelm surrounded himself with a ferocious bodyguard; Eudes was executed, threatening to return "on the third day" and wreak vengeance on the oppressors; John Ball soon began to advocate the extermination of all great lords, justices, and priests as a necessary prelude to the Kingdom of the Saints; and the Anabaptists of Münster found themselves tyrannized by a fanatical leader who personally and publicly executed anyone who questioned his "divine" authority.

In parentheses, it is interesting to observe a somewhat similar sequence of events during the past 5 years of student protest. In almost every case, these protests have occurred in vast, rapidly expanded campuses (Berkeley, Columbia, Paris, Rome, Tokyo, etc.) where students felt themselves alienated both personally from their teachers and ideologically from the aims of the university courses. Typically student protest movements have started with generous, not to say utopian ideals and have taken an ugly turn only when they were confronted with measures of control that were not merely firm, but openly violent. When this happens, the naive slogans of "Flower Power" are soon replaced by cries of "Kill the Pig."

One of Cohn's purposes, in reviewing earlier millennial cults, was to show the similarity between their origins, their magical expectations, and their decline into orgies of "highprincipled" killings and the corresponding sequence of events in Hitler's "thousand-year Reich." Similar outbreaks of unreason have occurred in recent times in less developed societies, typically in one of two social situations. The first occurs when a technologically undeveloped community is suddenly confronted with the material products of the industrialized West. This happened during both World Wars, and led to the outbreak of a series of Cargo Cults that bore a striking resemblance to the earlier European millennial movements, and that like them, began optimistically with promises of magical abundance, encountered the inevitable frustration of the hopes so aroused, and then frequently ended in bitterness and bloodshed.[20] The second situation, familiar to many of the newly liberated colonial countries, is that in which large numbers of the community have developed aspirations for a standard of living long before the economic and political institutions of their country have advanced to the point where these expectations could be fulfilled.

The common theme in all of these examples of the abrogation of commonsense, of contact with reality, and, in the face of frustrations, of the unleashing of extremes of violent and destructive behavior, has been the simultaneous arousal of extravagant aspirations together with the shock of realizing that these aspirations are not going to be. The mere juxtaposition of wealth and poverty is not sufficient by itself to excite a spirit of revolt. The stimulus to develop impossible expectations seems to come from a sense of inner insecurity and hopelessness, a total loss of confidence in one's own future. During the postwar era, this has been nowhere more apparent than in the ghettos of the great cities, both in the relatively rich, highly developed societies and in the hungry half of the world. The situation is aggravated when, as a result of uncontrolled population increase, standards of living actually begin to decline at the very time when,

---

[20] Peter Worsley, *The Trumpet Shall Sound* (London: MacGibbon & Kee, 1957).

by marginal, vicarious participation in a "consumer culture," a people's material aspirations have been raised to new levels.

Today's underprivileged differ from those of previous generations in two respects: their actual poverty is much less severe, and their level of information about their better-off fellows is much greater, thanks to the mass media. As Dr. Sukarno put it, in a much-quoted speech:

> The motion picture industry has provided a window on the world, and the colonized nations have looked through that window and have seen the things of which they have been deprived. It is perhaps not generally realized that a refrigerator can be a revolutionary symbol—to a people who have no refrigerators. A motor car owned by a worker in one country can be a symbol of revolt to a people deprived of the necessities of life.

What he says of undeveloped societies applies with equal force to the impact of movies and television on the aspirations of the less privileged citizens of the technologically advanced countries.

In summary, it seems that overpopulation only aggravates the widespread threat to social stability presented by masses of our population who are basically unsure of their personal future, who have lost confidence in their chance of ever attaining a secure place in their community. It is imperative that we recognize the gravity of this threat because mankind today commands such destructive powers that we cannot afford to risk outbreaks of mass violence; and yet the lesson of history points to the threat of just such disasters. Unless the masses of our city poor can be persuaded that there is a future for them too in the Great Society, their morale is likely to crumble until vast human communities degenerate into the semblance of concentration camp inmates, if not even to that of Zuckerman's pathologically belligerent apes.

2. A DECLINING ECONOMY

THE WHITE EXODUS TO SUBURBIA STEPS UP

Herbert J. Gans

In this unpredictable world, nothing can be predicted quite so easily as the continued proliferation of suburbia. Not only have American cities stopped growing for more than a generation, while the metropolitan areas of which they are a part were continuing to expand lustily, but there is incontrovertible evi-

Herbert J. Gans, "The White Exodus to Suburbia Steps Up," THE NEW YORK TIMES MAGAZINE, *January 7, 1968.* ©*1968 by The New York Times Company. Reprinted by permission of the author and publisher.*

dence that another huge wave of suburban home building can be expected in the coming decade.

Between 1947 and about 1960, the country experienced the greatest baby boom ever, ending the slowdown in marriages and childbirths created first by the Depression and then by World War II. Today, the earliest arrivals of that baby boom are themselves old enough to marry, and many are now setting up house-keeping in urban or suburban apartments. In a few years, however, when their first child is 2 to 3 years old, and the second is about to appear, many young parents will decide to buy suburban homes. Only simple addition is necessary to see that by the mid-seventies, they will be fashioning another massive suburban building boom, provided, of course, that the country is affluent and not engaged in World War III.

The new suburbia may not look much different from the old; there will, however, be an increase in the class and racial polarization that has been develop-ing between the suburbs and the cities for several generations now. The suburbs will be home for an ever larger proportion of working-class, middle-class and upper-class whites; the cities, for an ever larger proportion of poor and non-white people. The continuation of this trend means that, by the nineteen-seventies, a greater number of cities will be 40 to 50 per cent non-white in population, with more and larger ghettos and greater municipal poverty on the one hand, and stronger suburban opposition to open housing and related policies to solve the city's problems on the other hand. The urban crisis will worsen, and although there is no shortage of rational solutions, nothing much will be done about the crisis unless white America permits a radical change of public policy and undergoes a miraculous change of attitude toward its cities and their popula-tions.

Another wave of suburban building would develop even if there had been no post-World War II baby boom, for American cities have always grown at the edges, like trees, adding new rings of residential development every generation as the beneficiaries of affluence and young families sought more modern housing and "better" neighborhoods. At first, the new rings were added inside the city limits, but ever since the last half of the 19th century, they have more often sprung up in the suburbs.

Although these trends may not be so apparent to New Yorkers, who live in a world capital rather than in a typical American city, both urban and suburban growth have almost always taken the form of single family houses, first on large lots and later, as less affluent city dwellers could afford to move out, on smaller lots. Even inside most American cities—again, other than New York and a few others—the majority of people live in single family homes.

Moreover, studies of housing preferences indicate that the majority of Americans, including those now living in the city, want a suburban, single family house once they have children, and want to remain in that house when their children have grown up. This urge for suburban life is not limited to the middle class or just to America; the poor would leave the city as well if they could afford to go, and so would many Europeans.

The only people who clearly do not want to live in the suburbs are the single and some of the childless couples, and that handful of urban middle-class professionals and intellectuals living in New York and a few other cosmopolitan cities. For everyone else, suburbia means more housing space at less cost, a backyard and an up-to-date community—all of which make raising children significantly easier for the mother, more compatible neighbors, cleaner air, a chance to leave the dirt and congestion behind and, in recent years, a chance also to escape the expansion of Negro and poor neighborhoods. Even some of the dedicated urbanites move to the suburbs when their children are young, although they—but only they—miss the cultural facilities of the big city and are often unhappy in suburbia.

Obviously, the popular antisuburban literature, which falsely accuses the suburbs of causing conformity, matriarchy, adultery, divorce, alcoholism and other standard American pathologies, has not kept anyone from moving to the suburbs, and even the current predictions of land shortages, longer commuting and urban congestion in the suburbs will not discourage the next generation of home buyers. Most, if not all, metropolitan areas still have plenty of rural land available for suburban housing. Moreover, with industry and offices now moving to the suburbs, new areas previously outside commuting range become ripe for residential development to house their employees. Thus, for several years now, more than half the suburbanites of Nassau County have been commuting to jobs inside Nassau County; in the next decade, they will probably be joined by new commuters living in Suffolk County. Of course, all this leads to increasing suburban congestion, but most suburbanites do not mind it. They do not leave the city for a rural existence, as the folklore has it; they want a half acre or more of land and all their favorite urban facilities within a short driving distance from the house.

In some metropolitan areas, or in parts of them, land may indeed be too scarce and thus too expensive to permit another round of old-style suburbanization. There, people will move into "townhouses" and semidetached houses, which have less privacy than single family houses, but still provide private yards and a feeling of separateness from the next-door neighbors. The recent failure of Reston, Va., the much praised new town near Washigton, D. C., suggests, however, that the exquisitely designed communal recreational areas cannot substitute for private space. Most home buyers do not seem to want that much togetherness, and Reston's townhouses, which lacked front or backyards, sold too slowly.

It goes without saying that almost all the new suburbanities—and the developments built for them—will be white and middle-income, for, barring miracles in the housing industry and in Federal subsidies, the subdivisions of the seventies will be too expensive for any family earning less than about $7,500 (in 1967 dollars). Thus, even if suburbia were to be racially integrated, cost alone would exclude most nonwhites. Today, less than 5 per cent of New York State's suburban inhabitants are nonwhite, and many of them live in ghettos and slums in the small towns around which suburbia has developed.

Nevertheless, the minuscule proportion of nonwhite suburbanites will increase somewhat in the future, for, if the current affluence continues, it will benefit a small percentage of Negroes and Puerto Ricans. Some of them will be able to move into integrated suburban communities, but the majority will probably wind up in existing and new middle-class ghettos.

If urban employment is available, or if the ongoing industralization of the South pushes more people off the land, poverty-stricken Negroes will continue to come to the cities, overcrowding and eventually enlarging the inner-city ghettos. Some of the better-off residents of these areas will move to "outer-city" ghettos, which can now be found in most American cities; for example, in Queens. And older suburbs like Yonkers and Mount Vernon will continue to lose some of the present residents and attract less affluent newcomers, as their housing, schools and other facilities age. As a result of this process, which affects suburbs as inevitably as city neighborhoods, some of their new inhabitants may be almost as poor as inner-city ghetto residents, so that more and more of the older suburbs will face problems of poverty and social pathology now thought to be distinctive to the city.

That further suburban growth is practically inevitable does not mean it is necessarily desirable, however. Many objections have been raised, some to suburbia itself, others to its consequences for the city. For example, ever since the rise of the postwar suburbs, critics have charged that suburban life is culturally and psychologically harmful for its residents, although many sociological studies, including my own, have shown that most suburbanites are happier and emotionally healthier than when they lived in the city. In addition, the critics have charged that suburbia desecrates valuable farm and recreation land, and that it results in "suburban" sprawl.

Suburbia undoubtedly reduces the supply of farm acreage, but America has long suffered from an oversupply of farmland, and I have never understood why allowing people to raise children where other people once raised potatoes or tomatoes desecrates the land. Usually, the criticism is directed to "ugly, mass-produced, look-alike little boxes," adding a class bias to the changes, as if people who can only afford mass-produced housing are not entitled to live where they please, or should stay in the city.

Suburban developments sometimes also rise on recreational land, although state and Federal funds are now available to save such land for public leisure-time use. Even so, I find it difficult to believe that child raising and the at-home recreation that goes on in a suburban house is a less worthy use of land than parks, which people only visit during part of the year. Furthermore, there is no reason why we cannot have both suburbia and parks, the latter built farther out, with high-speed expressways and mass transit to bring them closer to visitors.

Suburban sprawl scatters residential developments over large areas because single-family houses take up so much more acreage than multiple dwellings. As a result, highways, transit systems, utility lines and sewers must be longer and, therefore, more expensive. These added costs are not a steep price for affluent suburbanites; they want low-density housing more than economy, and they do not care that sprawl looks ugly to the trained eye of the architect. There may even be somewhat less sprawl in the future, partly because of townhouse developments, partly because high land costs at the far edges of the suburbs may induce builders to fill up vacant land left in the existing suburban rings during earlier periods of residential construction. Moreover, the next wave of suburbia may finally generate sufficient political support for the building of high-speed mass transit systems, now languishing on the planners' drawing boards, to connect the parts of the sprawling area.

The harmful effects of suburbia on the city are a more important criticism. One charge, made ever since the beginning of suburbanization in the 19th century, is that the suburbs rob the city of its tax paying, civic-minded and culture-loving middle class. Actually, however, middle-class families are often a tax liability for the city; they demand and receive more services, particularly more schools, than their taxes pay for. Nor is there any evidence that they are more civic-minded than their non-middle-class neighbors; they may be more enthusiastic joiners of civic organizations, but these tend to defend middle-class interests and not necessarily the public interest. Moreover, many people who live in the suburbs still exert considerable political influence in the city because of their work or their property holdings and see to it that urban power structures still put middle-class interests first, as slum organizations, whose demands for more antipoverty funds or public housing are regularly turned down by city hall, can testify.

The alleged effect of the suburbs on urban culture is belied by the vast cultural revival in the city which occurred at the same time the suburban exodus was in full swing. Actually, most suburbanites rarely used the city's cultural facilities even when they lived in the city, and the minority which did, continues to do so, commuting in without difficulty. Indeed, I suspect that over half the ticket buyers for plays, art movies, concerts and museums, particularly outside New York, are—and have long been—suburbanites. Besides, there is no reason why cultural institutions cannot, like banks, build branches in the suburbs, as they are beginning to do now. Culture is no less culture by being outside the city.

A much more valid criticism of suburbanization is its effect on class and racial segregation for the fact that the suburbs have effectively zoned out the poor and the nonwhites is resulting in an ever-increasing class and racial polarization of city and suburb. In one sense, however, the familiar data about the increasing polarization are slightly misleading. In years past, when urban census statistics showed Negroes and whites living side by side, they were actually quite polarized socially. On New York's Upper West Side, for example, the big apartment buildings are *de facto* segregated for whites, while the rotting brownstones between them are inhabited by Negroes and Puerto Ricans. These blocks are integrated statistically or geographically, but not socially, particularly if white parents send their children to private schools.

Nor is suburbanization the sole cause of class and racial polarization; it is itself an effect of trends that have gone on inside the city as well, and not only in America. When people become more affluent and can choose where they want to live, they choose to live with people like themselves. What has happened in the last generation or two is that the opportunity of home buyers to live among compatible neighbors, an opportunity previously available only to people in the middle- and lower-middle-income brackets. This fact does not justify either class or racial segregation, but it does suggest that the polarization resulting from affluence would have occurred even without suburbanization.

Class and racial polarization are harmful because they restrict freedom of housing choice to many people, but also because of the financial consequences for the city. For one thing, affluent suburbia exploits the financial bankrupt city; even when payroll taxes are levied, suburbanites do not pay their fair share of the city's cost in providing them with places of work, shopping areas and cultural facilities and with streets and utilities, maintenance, garbage removal and police protection for these facilities.

More important, suburbanites live in vest-pocket principalities where they can, in effect, vote to keep out the poor and the nonwhites and even the not very affluent whites.

As a result, the cities are in a traumatic financial squeeze. Their ever more numerous low-income residents pay fewer taxes but need costly municipal services, yet cities are taking in less in property taxes all the time, particularly as the firms that employ suburbanites and the shops that cater to them also move to the suburbs. Consequently, city costs rise at the same time as city income declines. To compound the injustice, state and Federal politicians from suburban areas often vote against antipoverty efforts and other Federal funding activities that would relieve the city's financial troubles, and they also vote to prevent residential integration.

These trends are not likely to change in the years to come. In fact, if the present white affluence continues, the economic gap between the urban have-nots and the suburban haves will only increase, resulting on the one hand in greater suburban opposition to integration and to solving the city's problems, and on the other hand to greater discontent and more ghetto rebellions in the city. This in turn could result in a new white exodus from the city, which, unlike the earlier exodus, will be based almost entirely on racial fear, making suburbanites out of the middle-aged and older middle-class families who are normally reluctant to change communities at this age and working-class whites who cannot really afford a suburban house. Many of them will, however, stay put and oppose all efforts toward desegregation, as indicated even now by their violent reaction to integration marches in Milwaukee and Chicago, and to scattered-site public housing schemes which would locate projects in middle-income areas in New York and elsewhere.

Ultimately, these trends could create a vicious spiral, with more ghetto protest leading to more white demands, urban and suburban, for repression, resulting in yet more intense ghetto protests, and culminating eventually in a massive exodus of urban whites. If this spiral were allowed to escalate, it might well hasten the coming of the predominantly Negro city.

Today, the predominantly Negro city is still far off in the future, and the all-Negro city is unlikely. Although Washington, D.C.'s population is already about 60 per cent Negro, and several other cities, including Newark, Gary and Richmond, hover around the 50 percent mark, recent estimates by the Center for Research in Marketing suggest that only five of the country's 25 largest cities and 10 of the 130 cities with over 100,000 population will be 40 per cent or more Negro by 1970. (New York's Negro population was estimated at 18 per cent in 1964, although in Manhattan, the proportion of Negroes was 27 per cent and of Negroes and Puerto Ricans, 39 per cent.)

Moreover, these statistics only count the nighttime residential population, but who lives in the city is, economically and politically, a less relevant statistic than who works there, and the daytime working population of most cities is today, and will long remain, heavily and even predominantly white.

Still, to a suburbanite who may someday have to work in a downtown surrounded by a black city, the future may seem threatening. A century ago, native-born WASPs must have felt similarly, when a majority of the urban population consisted of foreign-born Catholics and Jews, to whom they attributed the same pejorative racial characteristics now attributed to Negroes. The city and the WASPs survived, of course, as the immigrants were incorporated into the American economy, and suburban whites would also survive.

Today's nonwhite poor play a more marginal role in the urban economy, however, raising the possibility that if the city became predominantly Negro, many private firms and institutions, which hire relatively few Negroes, would leave to build a new downtown elsewhere, a phenomenon already developing on a small scale in Arlington Va., just outside Washington, D.C., and in Clayton, Mo., just outside St. Louis. If this trend became widespread, someday in the distant future only public agencies and low-wage industries, which boast integrated work forces, would remain in the present downtown area.

Many white suburbanites might welcome this development, for it would cut their remaining ties to the city altogether. Some Negroes might also prefer a predominantly black city, partly because they would be able to move into the good housing left by whites, and partly because they would take over political control of the city, thus promising the rank-and-file ghetto resident more sympathetic, if not necessarily better, treatment than he now gets from the white incumbents of city hall.

Nevertheless, the predominantly black city is undesirable, not only because it would create apartheid on a metropolitan scale, but because it would be a yet poorer city, less able to provide the needed public services to its low-income population and less likely to get the funds it would need from a predominantly white Federal Government.

Unfortunately, present governmental policies, local, state and Federal, are doing little to reverse the mounting class and racial polarization of city and suburb. Admittedly, the strong economic and cultural forces that send the middle classes into the suburbs and bring poor nonwhite people from the rural areas into the city in ever larger numbers are difficult to reverse even by the wisest government action.

Still, governmental policies have not been especially wise. The major efforts to slow down class and racial polarization have been these: legislation to achieve racial integration; programs to woo the white middle class back to the city; plans to establish unified metropolitan governments, encompassing both urban and suburban governmental units. All three have failed. None of the open housing and other integration laws now on the books have been enforced sufficiently to permit more than a handful of Negroes to live in the suburbs, and the more recent attempt to prevent the coming of the predominantly black city by enticing the white middle class back has not worked either.

The main technique used for this last purpose has been urban renewal, but there is no evidence—and, in fact, there have been no studies—to show that it has brought back a significant number of middle-class people. Most likely, it has only helped confirmed urbanites find better housing in the city. The attractions of suburbia are simply too persuasive for urban renewal or any other governmental program to succeed in bringing the middle class back to the city.

Even most older couples, whose children have left the suburban house empty, will not return; they have just paid off the mortgage and are not likely to give up a cheap and familiar house for an expensive city apartment, not to mention their gardens, or the friends they have made in the suburbs. At best, some may move to suburban apartments, but most American cities other than

New York have too few downtown attractions to lure a sizable number of people back to the center.

Metropolitan government is, in theory, a good solution, for it would require the suburbs to contribute to solving the city's problems, but it has long been opposed by the suburbs for just this reason. They have felt that the improvements and economies in public services that could be obtained by organizing them on a metropolitan basis would be offset by what suburbanites saw as major disadvantages, principally the reduction of political autonomy and the loss of power to keep out the poor and the nonwhites.

The cities, which have in the past advocated metropolitan government, may become less enthusiastic as Negroes obtain greater political power. Since the metropolitan area is so predominantly white, urban Negroes would be outvoted every time in any kind of metropolitan government. Some metropolitanization may nevertheless be brought about by Federal planning requirements, for as Frances Piven and Richard Cloward point out in a recent New Republic article, several Federal grant programs, particularly for housing and community facilities, now require a metropolitan plan as a prerequisite for funding. Piven and Cloward suggest that these requirements could disfranchise the urban Negro, and it is, of course, always possible that a white urban-suburban coalition in favor of metropolitan government could be put together deliberately for precisely this purpose. Under such conditions, however, metropolitan government would only increase racial conflict and polarization.

What, then, can be done to eliminate this polarization? One partial solution is to reduce the dependence of both urban and suburban governments on the property tax, which reduces city income as the population becomes poorer, and forces suburbs to exclude low-income residents because their housing does not bring in enough tax money. If urban and suburban governments could obtain more funds from other sources, including perhaps the Federal income tax, parts of the proceeds of which would be returned to them by Washington, urban property owners would bear a smaller burden in supporting the city and might be less opposed to higher spending. Surburbanites would also worry less about their tax rate, and might not feel so impelled to bar less affluent newcomers, or to object to paying their share of the cost of using city services.

Class polarization can be reduced by rent- or price-supplement programs which would enable less affluent urbanites to pay the price of suburban living and would reduce the building and financing costs of housing. But such measures would not persuade the suburbs to let in Negroes; ultimately, the only solution is still across-the-board residential integration.

The outlook for early and enforceable legislation toward this end, however, is dim. Although election results have shown time and again that Northern white majorities will not vote for segregation, they will not vote for integration either. I cannot imagine many political bodies, Federal or otherwise, passing or enforcing laws that would result in significant amounts of suburban integration; they would be punished summarily at the next election.

For example, proposals have often been made that state and Federal governments should withdraw all subsidies to suburban communities and builders practicing *de facto* segregation, thus depriving the former of at least half their school operating funds, and the latter of Federal Housing Authority (F.H.A.)

insurance on which their building plans depend. However desirable such legislation is, the chance that it would be passed is almost nil. One can also argue that Washington should offer grants-in-aid to suburban governments which admit low-income residents, but these grants would often be turned down. Many suburban municipalities would rather starve their public services instead, and the voters would support them all the way.

The best hope now is for judicial action. The New Jersey Supreme Court ruled some years back that builders relying on F.H.A. insurance had to sell to Negroes, and many suburban subdivisions in that state now have some Negro residents. The United States Supreme Court has just decided that it will rule on whether racial discrimination by large suburban developers is unconstitutional. If the answer turns out to be yes, the long, slow process of implementing the Court's decisions can at least begin.

In the meantime, solutions that need not be tested at the ballot box must be advanced. One possibility is new towns, built for integrated populations with Federal support, or even by the Federal Government alone, on land now vacant. Although hope springs eternal in American society that the problems of old towns can be avoided by starting from scratch, these problems seep easily across the borders of the new community. Even if rural governments can be persuaded to accept new towns in their bailiwicks and white residents could be attracted, such towns would be viable only if Federal grants and powers were used to obtain industries—and of a kind that would hire and train poorly skilled workers.

Greater emphasis should be placed on eliminating job discrimination in suburban work places, particularly in industries which are crying for workers, so that unions are less impelled to keep out non-white applicants. Mass transit systems should be built to enable city dwellers, black and white, to obtain suburban jobs without necessarily living in the suburbs.

Another and equally important solution is more school integration—for example, through urban-suburban educational parks that will build up integrated student enrollment by providing high-quality schooling to attract suburban whites, and through expansion of the busing programs that send ghetto children into suburban schools. Although white suburban parents have strenuously opposed bussing their children into the city, several suburban communities have accepted Negro students who are bussed in from the ghetto; for example, in the Boston area and in Westchester County.

And while the Supreme Court is deliberating, it would be worthwhile to persuade frightened suburbanites that, as all the studies so far have indicated, open housing would not mean a massive invasion of slum dwellers, but only the gradual arrival of a relatively small number of Negroes, most of them as middle-class as the whitest suburbanite. A massive suburban invasion by slum dwellers of any color is sheer fantasy. Economic studies have shown the sad fact that only a tiny proportion of ghetto residents can even afford to live in the suburbs. Moreover, as long as Negro workers lack substantial job security, they need to live near the center of the urban transportation system so that they can travel to jobs all over the city.

In addition, there are probably many ghetto residents who do not even want suburban integration now; they want the same freedom of housing choice as whites, but they do not want to be "dispersed" to the suburbs involuntarily.

Unfortunately, no reliable studies exist to tell us where ghetto residents do want to live, but should they have freedom of choice, I suspect many would leave the slums for better housing and better neighborhoods outside the present ghetto. Not many would now choose predominantly white areas, however, at least not until living among whites is psychologically and socially less taxing, and until integration means more than just assimilation to white middle-class ways.

Because of the meager success of past integration efforts, many civil-rights leaders have given up on integration and are now demanding the rebuilding of the ghetto. They argue persuasively that residential integration has so far and will in the future benefit only a small number of affluent Negroes, and that if the poverty-stricken ghetto residents are to be helped soon, that help must be located in the ghetto. The advocates of integration are strongly opposed. They demand that all future housing must be built outside the ghetto, for anything else would just perpetuate segregation. In recent months, the debate between the two positions has become bitter, each side claiming only its solution has merit.

Actually there is partial truth on both sides. The integrationists are correct about the long-term dangers of rebuilding the ghetto; the ghetto rebuilders (or separatists) are correct about the short-term failure of integration. But if there is little likelihood that the integrationists' demands will be carried out soon, their high idealism in effect sentences ghetto residents to remaining in slum poverty.

Moreover, there is no need to choose between integration and rebuilding, for both policies can be carried out simultaneously. The struggle for integration must continue, but if the immediate prospects for success on a large scale are dim, the ghetto must be rebuilt in the meantime.

The primary aim of rebuilding, however, should not be to rehabilitate houses or clear slums, but to raise the standard of living of ghetto residents. The highest priority must be a massive antipoverty program which will, through the creation of jobs, more effective job-training schemes, the negative income tax, children's allowances and other measures, raise ghetto families to the middle-income level, using outside resources from government and private enterprise and inside participation in the planning and decision-making. Also needed are a concerted effort at quality compensatory education for children who cannot attend integrated schools; federally funded efforts to improve the quality of ghetto housing, as well as public services; some municipal decentralization to give ghetto residents the ability to plan their own communities and their own lives, and political power so that the ghetto can exert more influence in behalf of its demands.

If such programs could extend the middle-income standard of living to the ghetto in the years to come, residential integration might well be achieved in subsequent generations. Much of the white opposition to integration is based on stereotypes of Negro behavior—some true, some false—that stem from poverty rather than from color, and many of the fears about Negro neighbors reflect the traditional American belief that poor people will not live up to middle-class standards. Moreover, even lack of enthusiasm for integration among ghetto residents is a result of poverty; they feel, rightly or not, that they must solve their economic problems before then can even think about integration.

If ghetto poverty were eliminated, the white fears—and the Negro ones— would begin to disappear, as did the pejorative stereotypes which earlier Ameri-

cans held about the "inferior races"—a favorite 19th-century term for the European immigrants—until they achieved affluence. Because attitudes based on color
differences are harder to overcome than those based on cultural differences, the
disappearance of anti-Negro stereotypes will be slower than that of anti-
immigrant stereotypes. Still, once color is no longer an index of poverty and
lower-class status, it will cease to arouse white fears, so that open-housing laws
can be enforced more easily and eventually may even be unnecessary. White
suburbanites will not exclude Negroes to protect their status or their property
values, and many, although not necessarily all, Negroes will choose to leave the
ghetto.

Morally speaking, any solution that does not promise immediate integration is repugnant, but moral dicta will neither persuade suburbanites to admit
low-income Negroes into their communities, nor entice urbane suburbanites to
live near low-income Negroes in the city. Instead of seeking to increase their
middle-income population by importing suburban whites, cities must instead
make their poor residents middle-income. The practical solution, then, is to
continue to press for residential integration, but also to eliminate ghetto poverty
immediately, in order to achieve integration in the future, substituting government antipoverty programs for the private economy which once created the jobs
and incomes that helped poorer groups escape the slums in past generations.
Such a policy will not only reduce many of the problems of the city, which are
ultimately caused by the poverty of its inhabitants, but it will assure the ultimate dissappearance of the class and racial polarization of cities and suburbs.

There is only one hitch: This policy is not likely to be adopted. Although
white voters and their elected officials are probably more favorable to ghetto
rebuilding than to integration, they are, at the moment, not inclined or impelled
to support even the former. They lack inclination to rebuild the ghetto because
they do not want to pay the taxes that would raise ghetto incomes; they are not
so impelled because neither the problems of the ghetto nor even its rebellions
touch their lives directly and intimately. So far, most of them still experience
the ghetto only on television. Until many white Americans are directly affected
by what goes on in the ghetto, they will probably support nothing more than a
minuscule antipoverty program and a token effort toward racial integration.

THE SAGGING FINANCES OF STATES AND CITIES—
HOW WASHINGTON CAN HELP

Murray L. Weidenbaum

Guns or butter is still pretty much the rule—despite the protests of the administration to the contrary. And in recent years it's been guns. Yet it is not too early to begin speculating about possible changes in government spending after the Vietnam war—particularly in view of the fact that those budgeting innovations made necessary by the war may have an important and salutary effect on the civilian, domestic services (butter, if you will) we can have after the expenditure for guns goes down.

One place where change is needed is in the fiscal relations between the federal government and state and local governments. It is there that some interesting problems have arisen. I take my text from John Kenneth Galbraith (from whom I usually take only exception):

> *"The great economic anachronism of our time is that economic growth gives the federal government the revenues while, along with the population increase, it gives the states and especially the cities the problems. The one unit of government gets the money, the other gets the work."*

Although Galbraith has somewhat overstated his case, he is essentially correct. The fact is that state and local tax structures are, in the main, "regressive." They depend on property taxes and sales taxes, and—as the general income rises—the percentage that goes for state and local taxes declines. The federal tax structure is, on balance, "progressive." Washington gets most of its revenue from individual and corporate income taxes, which take a larger and larger percentage as a taxpayer's income rises. The federal revenues are thus automatically responsive to economic growth; state and local governments, however, must raise assessments and tax rates to keep up with economic expansion.

When we turn to what these governments do with the money they take in, we again find quite a different picture. With the exception of periods of hot war, such as we are experiencing now, total federal spending for existing programs tends to rise more *slowly* than the overall level of economic activity. Despite the variety and importance of federal domestic programs, they simply do not require—or at least do not call forth—the massive expenditures of a shooting war. In the cold-war years of 1955 through 1964, federal spending rose less rapidly

*Murray L. Weidenbaum, "The Sagging Finances of States and Cities—How Washington Can Help," **TRANS-action**, July/August, 1968. Copyright© 1968 by **TRANS-action** **MAGAZINE**, New Brunswick, New Jersey. Reprinted by permission of the publisher.*

than the gross national product or federal revenues; defense spending tended to be fairly stable, or to rise slowly.

The financial requirements of existing state and local government programs, on the other hand, rise far more *rapidly* than the economy as a whole. This is especially true of educational requirements, which now account for nearly half of local-government spending.

More is being spent for education because more children are in school. The U.S. Office of Education, using cautious—or even pessimistic—assumptions, has estimated that in the next decade spending for public education will rise by 50 percent. Among the agency's assumptions was that during that time there would be *no improvement in educational quality.*

Another reason why local spending will rise rapidly is the increasing suburbanization of the United States. By 1975, three out of four Americans will live in urban or suburban areas. This continued growth and movement will put greater demands upon local governments and economies to provide public services, utilities, and transportation.

Where does all this leave us? With no change in either tax rates or sources of income, and even with no new programs, local and state governments will face a large excess of demands over available revenues. At the same time, Washington is likely to have more revenue than it needs for current programs.

Of course, neither the federal nor the local governments will be standing still. Since World War II, state and local governments have broadened their revenue sources—not only by raising assessments and taxes on property, but through new taxes, federal grants-in-aid, and additional debt financing, and by canceling, postponing, or stretching out many programs. While these revenue sources will continue to be used, some may be used with more and more reluctance. Over the past 15 years, the national debt rose 21 percent, while local-government debt rose 236 percent. Legal limits on debts and on tax rates, as well as similar restrictions, are beginning to curtail the local government's reliance on existing revenue sources. Even without legal limits, state and local taxpayers are voting against new bond issues and higher taxes.

The people's resistance to higher taxes is certainly one problem faced by elected leaders who want to be re-elected. But the leaders are also fearful that higher taxes will drive out old industry and discourage new industry. No one can escape federal taxes, but state taxes are something else. The existence of state, county, and city borders—and the mobility of people, trade, and industry—are facts of life that keep state and local taxes far under the federal level.

On the other hand, federal aid to states and cities, in the form of specific grants, will continue to expand after the war is over—as indicated by the trends in the anti-poverty program and the general program of aid to education. It is unlikely, however, that federal grants-in-aid will grow enough to bridge the gap between a local government's revenues from existing local taxes and the rising costs of already established local programs.

The solution to this problem—more money at the federal level, and less money and more to do with it on the state and local level—is fairly obvious. Let the federal government, in some fashion, give money to the smaller governmental units. This idea has had considerable application in American history.

Thomas Jefferson, in his second inaugural address in 1805, suggested that the excess revenues from import duties—then the major source of federal funds —"may, by a just repartition among the states . . . be applied, in time of peace, to rivers, canals, roads, arts, manufactures, education, and other great objects within each State." A bill that would have distributed among the states the dividends from the federal subscription to the second national bank was vetoed by James Madison, on constitutional grounds. But in 1837 Congress did vote on a distribution of $37 million in surplus funds, which was more than twice the annual federal budget of those days. This $37 million was a result of an unbroken string of surpluses from 1825 to 1836, the longest in our history, during which time the national debt was virtually eliminated.

The variety of uses to which the states devoted this windfall is interesting. Some used the money to capitalize state banks. Others used it to pay off state debts or to build public works. Most of the interest and some of the principal was applied to education. The state of Maine, after spending some of its $900,000 on education, simply divided up the rest per capita, "a trifling sum to each," as a contemporary observer remarked. The Georgia legislature stated that the share was being accepted only to prevent it from being divided among the other states. Georgia then invested some of the money in a railroad line which terminated in a collection of cabins that grew to be the city of Atlanta (the state still owns the rail line). The rest of Georgia's money seems to have been frittered away.

Another distribution of surplus federal funds was proposed in the 1880s, but in spite of great public interest no Congressional action was taken. More recently, the Eisenhower administration offered to shift some federal revenue sources to the states, along with some spending obligations, but though new revenue was greater than new obligations, the states ignored the bait.

Today, economists and federal and local executives have been discussing six proposals for redistributing the governmental wealth to the states and cities. These are direct federal expenditures; conditional ("tied") grants-in-aid; unconditional ("block") grants; tax sharing; tax credits; and federal tax reductions.

None of these proposals is likely to satisfy everybody, so I will examine them from a number of viewpoints. The five criteria I have used are:
—tendency to expand, or reduce, the role of the federal government in the national economy generally;
—tendency to increase, or decrease, federal influence on the states;
—effect on the progressiveness, or regressiveness, of the total governmental tax structure;
—impact on the power of the tax structure to stabilize the economy;
—tendency to strengthen, or weaken, the role of the cities in relation to the states. (While the states and the federal government share sovereignty under the U.S. Constitution, the cities are creations of the state under state constitutions.)

I shall take up six proposals one by one. Table I contains a summary.

Most of the proposed programs, clearly, would not change the present situation. The federal role in the economy is strengthened in only one case; likewise, federal influence on the states is strengthened in only one case. Tax progressivity and built-in stabilization are reduced in three programs. And in two programs the role of the cities would be reduced. Now let me discuss the six proposals one by one.

DIRECT FEDERAL EXPENDITURES

Increases in federal revenues above the needs of existing programs could be devoted to new programs. For example, the government could begin new programs of an interstate character, such as facilities to control air and water pollution. This approach, however, leaves no room for state or local participation—one common explanation is that there is little administrative talent at the lower levels. And it would mean a greater federal role in the economy, and greater federal intervention in the states.

TIED GRANTS

Grants to states and cities for specific uses would avoid direct federal intervention. But they would make the federal government an even more important influence on state and local operations. Since such grants often call for matching funds, they would also influence state and local budgeting. As many local politicians say, "We can't afford to lose the federal money."

BLOCK GRANTS

Much attention has been paid to the Heller Plan—unconditional federal grants to local governments. One such arrangement would set up a permanent trust fund to distribute to the states 2 percent of the federal income-tax base. This would reduce the role of the federal government in the national economy, and maintain the independence of state fiscal affairs. The cities, however, would probably have to fight for a "fair" share of the funds in the legislature. (A suggested modification would be to require states to transfer a share of the money to local governments.)

TAX SHARING

Under this plan, federal revenues would be parceled out according to the source of the revenues—so that high-income states would receive the larger shares. Again, the federal role in the economy and the states would be reduced; again, the cities would face a fight in the state houses. And, of course, the wealthy states would get a little wealthier.

TAX CREDITS

The state and local income taxes paid by an individual or corporation would be deducted from federal tax bills. This would help both state and local governments soften popular resistance to increased state and local taxes. Again, the wealthier states would tend to benefit the most.

FEDERAL TAX REDUCTION

This would be an *indirect* assist to state and local government. It would permit local units to increase taxes—without increasing the total tax bills of the average citizen. Unlike the tax-credits plan, though, there would be no necessary connection in the citizen's mind between the federal and state actions, except his noticing that federal taxes were dropping while state taxes were rising. Again, the federal role in state government and the private sector would be reduced; and again, state and regional economic rivalries would be a question.

TABLE 1   COMPARING PROPOSALS TO REDISTRIBUTE FEDERAL INCOME

	Federal Role in Economy	Federal Influence on States	Tax Progressivity	Built-in Stabilizers	Role of Cities
Direct federal programs	+	0	0	0	0
Tied grants	0	+	0	0	0
Block grants	0	0	0	0	—
Tax credits	0	0	—	—	0
Tax sharing	0	0	—	—	—
Federal tax reduction	0	0	—	—	0

+ = Increase   0 = No change   — = Decrease

Now, the main purpose of these summaries has been to show that a choice among the six proposals will not be easy. Our society has plural objectives; no single federal policy would satisfy more than a few of them. As we have seen, direct federal spending may expand worthy programs, but bypass state and local governments. A tax reduction meets state and local needs only indirectly, if at all. Tax sharing and block grants leave the spending up to the states, which are presumably familiar with the needs and desires of their residents, but make little or no provision for the growing financial needs of smaller units—counties, school districts, cities, and towns.

The greatest danger, however, is that we will not agree upon *any* of these approaches. Instead, we might use up increases in national revenues for low-priority federal programs. Meanwhile, state and local programs of much greater worth would either languish, or depend upon local tax increases—which adversely affect the nation's economic ability, or which weigh most heavily on the poor.

What we need is some technique that will help us decide how to allocate public resources in a better way. It is here that the ill wind of Vietnam has blown some good. What I have in mind is the planning-programming-budgeting system (P.P.B.S.), which is being established in the major departments of the federal government. P.P.B.S. is a tool of modern business management, and since 1961 government agencies have been using it—with varying success. It was Robert McNamara's extensive use of P.P.B.S. in the Defense Department that gave it prominence, and that prompted President Johnson's directive of August 25, 1965, ordering the application of P.P.B.S. to all large federal agencies.

What P.P.B.S. does is shift the emphasis in budgeting from agencies and inputs to the major purposes to be accomplished by the government as a whole. P.P.B.S. throws down a fundamental challenge: Can we accomplish the basic purposes of government in a more effective and economical way? It provides a format for presenting the data, and a method for analyzing the data, what will enable us to meet this challenge with greater ease. Although the system is now organized within agencies, if it proves successful, it can be applied to the entire federal budget.

P.P.B.S. is clearly no panacea for all financial problems, and its implementation to date indicates numerous shortcomings (some of the initial enthusiastic claims of its influencing policy were, for instance, certainly premature). Nevertheless, the basic idea of consciously allocating government resources to those areas that promise the greatest among of benefit to the nation is inherently desirable.

P.P.B.S. works through four major steps. The first is to identify the special goals that are deemed appropriate for the government. This is no simple matter, as we shall see.

Second, the broad goals must be related to specific programs, and a selection must be made of those programs with the most promise of achieving these goals efficiently. This, too, is difficult. In practice, the typical government agency may have clear and precise Congressional directives on how much money may be spent in what fashion on what programs. Or Congressional guidance may be so vague and conflicting as to imply no goal at all. The trick needed here is to infer the goals from the programs authorized by Congress, and then to conjure up new or improved programs to achieve these goals.

Third, the costs of alternative programs must be estimated in order to determine which is the most efficient approach to the goal. A glance at benefit/cost studies of water-resources projects, or cost/effectiveness analysis of weapons systems, will show that this third step is not easily reached.

Finally, the manpower, facilities, and other needs of the program have to be translated into budget dollars. And then management decisions can be made.

This orientation toward a goal is in sharp contrast with the usual practice in government. For many years, the government has been oriented to organizational units and to inputs—such as office equipment, travel costs, and so forth.

Federal agencies are also being urged to consider comparable programs elsewhere, even though this might mean the loss of a program to another bureau. The result may be greater competition in government operations, and thus greater effectiveness from the limited resources available for a given program.

Over time, the decision-making process in Washington will probably undergo substantial change as executives become accustomed to using such sophisticated managerial tools as benefit/cost, cost/effectiveness, and systems analysis. There will probably be less tendency for executives to make decisions on individual programs in isolation, using subjective, intuitive judgments. Computers and systems analysis will not replace managers in making decisions, nor will staff analysts supplant line management, nor will economic analysis—even economic analysis accounting for all sorts of nonfiscal costs—fill the role of political decision-making. But, if P.P.B.S. works, it helps the decision-makers by giving them better tools of management.

The use of P.P.B.S. may indicate some new directions for the government. Preliminary work indicates that such tools as benefit/cost analysis will show that people-oriented expenditures—investments in education, training, and health—yield a greater "profit," or excess of benefits over costs, than the more traditional physical-capital investments and public-works programs. This tendency is already being felt by state and local officials through sharply accelerated grants-in-aid for a wide variety of anti-poverty efforts. A better understanding of the way the federal government allocates funds is bound to be of some help to the hard-pressed men in state and local government. They will find themselves dealing with increasingly sophisticated government managers, who will expect to have proposals and requests for grants in a form they can use for the federal P.P.B.S. analysis. And, of course, understanding P.P.B.S. will enable local officials to make better use of the money they have on hand, of which federal grants are as yet only a small part.

To some degree, at least eight states and many major counties and cities (including New York) are using P.P.B.S. techniques. The Ford Foundation has joined with five states in studying P.P.B.S. applications—Wisconsin, California, Michigan, Vermont, and New York; with five counties—Los Angeles County, Wayne County (Detroit), Dade County (Miami), Davidson County (Nashville, Tenn.), and Nassau County (N.Y.); and with five cities—San Diego, Denver, Dayton, New Haven, and Detroit.

Such studies are bound to become more important. In opening this discussion, I focused on the rigid constraints on local-government finance. The cities in particular are doubly restrained—by their dependence on property taxes, and by their dependence on state legislatures to give them rein to take action. I assumed in this discussion that there would be no changes in tax sources or programs. But even with no changes, the position of the cities was difficult. Yet there are changes—some for the better and some for the worse—that make rational allocation all the more necessary to the continued operation of city governments.

The range of functions performed and services rendered by city governments is increasing. In 1902, local governments spent 27.1 percent of their budgets on schools and 19.5 percent on highways; 6.3 percent on health, hospitals, and welfare and 23.6 percent on police, fire, and other control activities. By 1963, local governments spent 45.0 percent on schools and only 8.8 percent on highways; 12.1 percent on welfare, health, and hospitals and 11.4 percent on control. Education costs and percentages will continue to rise as the quality of schooling improves.

The tax structure of local government is being broadened. The property tax is still king, but in 1940 it provided 90 percent of general revenue in the nation's cities, while in 1963 it provided only 78 percent. Various forms of sales taxes and income taxes have been the major new sources of revenue.

The state and federal role in providing revenues to local governments is being expanded. Such outside financing has risen from 8 percent in the 1920s to 13 percent in the 1930s and to 27 percent in the 1960s. Most of this aid has come from the states, and reapportionment may lend further impetus to this trend.

Following peace in Vietnam, we will probably see a major expansion of federal aid, possibly involving a basic change in kind. I have in mind some switch to local control, such as the Heller block-grant plan. Since P.P.B.S. analysis seems to indicate that people-oriented services yield greater economic returns, and since the cities are concentrating more on people-oriented services, the uses of such grants may also be different.

An important new planning and budgeting concept will be available to local governments. If P.P.B.S. continues to influence federal budgeting, local officials will be learning more and more about it—in order to talk to federal officials. And as they learn more about it, they are beginning to apply it to their own governmental operations. A likely result is an increase in the efficiency and rationality of local government.

In sum, even though government budgeting and financing problems will probably not be solved easily in coming years, we have traveled a considerable distance. After all, at one time a chart with the title "The Tools of Budgeting" hung in the office of the Budget Bureau Director. The chart showed only three tools—a crystal ball, two dice, and a pair of scissors.

Further Reading Suggested by The Author

New Dimensions of Political Economy by Walter W. Heller (New York: W. W. Norton, paperback, 1967). This is the authoritative statement by the recent chairman of the President's Council of Economic Advisers on the role of the new economics in Washington and on the nature of the Heller Plan for federal aid to states.

Intergovernmental Fiscal Relations in the United States by Fremont J. Lyden and Ernest G. Miller, Editors, *Planning-Programming-Budgeting: A Systems Approach to Management* (Chicago: Markham Publishing Company, 1967).

Planning for a Nation of Cities edited by Samuel B. Warner (Cambridge: MIT Press, 1966). This volume contains a variety of political, economic, and sociological analyses of the various problems faced by the modern city.

WHITE GANGS

Walter B. Miller

If one thinks about street corner gangs at all these days, it is probably in the roseate glow of *West Side Story,* itself the last flowering of a literary and journalistic concern that goes back at least to the late 40's. Those were the days when it seemed that the streets of every city in the country had become dark battlefields where small armies of young men engaged their honor in terrible trials of combat, clashing fiercely and suddenly, then retiring to the warm succor of their girl cohorts. The foreword to a 1958 collection of short stories, *The Young Punks,* captures a bit of the flavor:

> These are the stories behind today's terrifying headlines—about a strange new frighten-ing cult that has grown up in our midst. Every writer whose work is included in this book tells the truth. These kids are tough. Here are knife-carrying killers, and thirteen-year-old street walkers who could give the most hardened callgirl lessons. These kids pride themselves on their "ethics": never go chicken, even if it means knifing your own friend in the back. Never rat on a guy who wears your gang colors, unless he rats on you first. Old men on crutches are fair game. If a chick plays you for a sucker, blacken her eyes and walk away fast.

Today the one-time devotee of this sort of stuff might be excused for wondering where they went, the Amboy Dukes and all those other adolescent warriors and lovers who so excited his fancy a decade ago. The answer, as we shall see, is quite simple—nowhere. The street gangs are still there, out on the corner where they always were.

The fact is that the urban adolescent street gang is as old as the American city. Henry Adams, in his *Education,* describes in vivid detail the gang fights between the Northsiders and Southsiders on Boston Common in the 1840's. An observer in 1856 Brooklyn writes: ". . . at any and all hours there are multitudes of boys . . . congregated on the corners of the streets, idle in their habits, dissolute in their conduct, profane and obscene in their conversation, gross and vulgar in their manners. If a female passes one of the groups she is shocked by what she sees and hears. . . ." The Red Raiders of Boston have hung out on the same corner at least since the 1930's; similarly, gang fighting between the Tops and Bottoms in West Philadelphia, which started in the 30's, is still continuing in 1969.

Walter B. Miller, "White Gangs," TRANS-action, *September, 1969. Copyright©1969 by* TRANS-action MAGAZINE, *New Brunswick, New Jersey. Reprinted by permis-sion of the publisher.*

Despite this historical continuity, each new generation tends to perceive the street gang as a new phenomenon generated by particular contemporary conditions and destined to vanish as these conditions vanish. Gangs in the 1910's and 20's were attributed to the cultural dislocations and community disorganization accompanying the mass immigration of foreigners; in the 30's to the enforced idleness and economic pressures produced by the Great Depression; in the 50's to the emotional disturbance of parents and children caused by the increased stresses and tensions of modern life. At present, the existence of gangs is widely attributed to a range of social injustices; racial discrimination, unequal educational and work opportunities, resentment over inequalities in the distribution of wealth and privilege in an affluent society, and the ineffective or oppressive policies of service agencies such as the police and the schools.

There is also a fairly substantial school of thought that holds that the street gangs are disappearing or have already disappeared. In New York City, the stage of so many real and fictional gang dramas of the 50's and early 60's, *The Times* sounded their death-knell as long ago as 1966. Very often, the passing of the gang is explained by the notion that young people in the slums have converted their gang-forming propensities into various substitute activities. They have been knocked out by narcotics, or they have been "politicized" in ways that consume their energies in radical or reform movements, or their members have become involved in "constructive" commercial activities, or enrolled in publicly financed education and/or work-training programs.

As has often been the case, these explanations are usually based on very shaky factual grounds and derived from rather parochial, not to say self-serving, perspectives. For street gangs are not only still widespread in United States cities, but some of them appear to have again taken up "gang warfare" on a scale that is equal to or greater than the phenomenon that received so much attention from the media in the 1950's.

In Chicago, street gangs operating in the classic formations of that city—War Lords, High Supremes, Cobra Stones—accounted for 33 killings and 252 injuries during the first six months of 1969. Philadelphia has experienced a wave of gang violence that has probably resulted in more murders in a shorter period of time than during any equivalent phase of the "fighting gang" era in New York. Police estimate that about 80 gangs comprising about 5,000 members are "active" in the city, and that about 20 are engaged in combat. Social agencies put the total estimated number of gangs at 200, with about 80 in the "most hostile" category. Between October 1962 and December 1968, gang members were reportedly involved in 257 shootings, 250 stabbings and 205 "rumbles." in the period between January 1968 and June 1969, 54 homicides and over 520 injuries were attributed to armed battles between gangs. Of the murder victims, all but eight were known to be affiliated with street gangs. The assailants ranged in age from 13 to 20, with 70 percent of them between 16 and 18 years old. Most of these gangs are designated by the name of the major corner where they hang out, the 12th and Poplar Streeters, or the 21 W's (for 21st and Westmoreland). Others bear traditional names such as the Centaurs, Morroccos and Pagans.

Gangs also continue to be active in Boston. In a single 90-minute period on May 10, 1969, one of the two channels of the Boston Police radio reported 38 incidents involving gangs, or one every 2 1/2 minutes. This included two gang fights. Simultaneous field observation in several white lower-class neighborhoods turned up evidence that gangs were congregating at numerous street corners throughout the area.

Although most of these gangs are similar to the classic types to be described in what follows, as of this summer the national press had virtually ignored the revival of gang violence. *Time* magazine did include a brief mention of "casual mayhem" in its June 27 issue, but none of the 38 incidents in Boston on May 10 was reported even in the local papers. It seems most likely, however, that if all this had been going on in New York City, where most of the media have their headquarters, a spate of newspaper features, magazine articles and television "specials" would have created the impression that the country was being engulfed by a "new" wave of gang warfare. Instead, most people seem to persist in the belief that the gangs have disappeared or that they have been radically transformed.

This anomalous situation is partly a consequence of the problem of defining what a gang is (and we will offer a definition at the end of our discussion of two specific gangs), but it is also testimony to the fact that this enduring aspect of the lives of urban slum youth remains complex and poorly understood. It is hoped that the following examination of the Bandits and the Outlaws—both of Midcity—will clarify at least some of the many open questions about street corner gangs in American cities.

Midcity, which was the location of our 10-year gang study project (1954-64), is not really a city at all, but a portion of a large one, here called Port City. Midcity is a predominantly lower-class community with a relatively high rate of crime, in which both criminal behavior and a characteristic set of conditions—low-skill occupations, little education, low-rent dwellings, and many others—appeared as relatively stable and persisting features of a developed way of life. How did street gangs fit into this picture?

In common with most major cities during this period, there were many gangs in Midcity, but they varied widely in size, sex composition, stability and range of activities. There were about 50 Midcity street corners that served as hangouts for local adolescents. Fifteen of these were "major" corners, in that they were rallying points for the full range of a gang's membership, while the remaining 35 were "minor," meaning that in general fewer groups of smaller size habitually hung out there.

In all, for Midcity in this period, 3,650 out of 5,740, or 64 percent, of Midcity boys habitually hung out at a particular corner and could, therefore, be considered members of a particular gang. For girls, the figure is 1,125 out of 6,250, or 18 percent. These estimates also suggest that something like 35 percent of Midcity's boys, and 80 percent of its girls, did *not* hang out. What can be said about them? What made them different from the approximately 65 percent of the boys and 20 percent of the girls who did hang out?

Indirect evidence appears to show that the practice of hanging out with a gang was more prevalent among lower-status adolescents, and that many of those who were not known to hang out lived in middle-class or lower-class I (the higher range of the lower-class) areas. At the same time, however, it is evident that a fair proportion of higher-status youngsters also hung out. The question of status, and its relation to gang membership and gang behavior is very complex, but it should be borne in mind as we now take a closer look at the gangs we studied.

THE BANDIT NEIGHBORHOOD

Between the Civil War and World War II, the Bandit neighborhood was well-known throughout the city as a colorful and close-knit community of Irish laborers. Moving to a flat in one of its ubiquitous three-decker frame tenements represented an important step up for the impoverished potato-famine immigrants who had initially settled in the crowded slums of central Port City. By the 1810's the second generation of Irish settlers had produced a spirited and energetic group of athletes and politicos, some of whom achieved national prominence.

Those residents of the Bandit neighborhood who shared in some degree the drive, vitality and capability of these famous men assumed steady and fairly remunerative positions in the political, legal, and civil service world of Port City, and left the neighborhood for residential areas whose green lawns and single houses represented for them what Midcity had represented for their fathers and grandfathers. Those who lacked these qualities remained in the Bandit neighborhood, and at the outset of World War II made up a stable and relatively homogeneous community of low-skilled Irish laborers.

The Bandit neighborhood was directly adjacent to Midcity's major shopping district, and was spotted with bars, poolrooms and dance halls that served as meeting places for an active neighborhood social life. Within two blocks of the Bandits' hanging-out corner were the Old Erin and New Hibernia dance halls, and numerous drinking establishments bearing names such as the Shamrock, Murphy and Donoghue's, and the Emerald Bar and Grill.

A number of developments following World War II disrupted the physical and social shape of the Bandit community. A mammoth federally-financed housing project sliced through and blocked off the existing network of streets and razed the regular rows of wooden tenements. The neighborhood's small manufacturing plants were progressively diminished by the growth of a few large establishments, and by the 1950's the physical face of the neighborhood was dominated by three large and growing plants. As these plants expanded they bought off many of the properties which had not been taken by the housing project, demolished buildings and converted them into acres of black-topped parking lots for their employees.

During this period, the parents of the Bandit corner gang members stubbornly held on to the decreasing number of low-rent, deteriorating, private dwelling units. Although the Bandits' major hanging corner was almost surrounded by the housing project, virtually none of the gang members lived there. For these families, residence in the housing project would have entailed a degree of financial stability and restrained behavior that they were unable or unwilling to assume, for the corner gang members of the Bandit neighborhood were the scions of men and women who occupied the lowest social level in Midcity. For them low rent was a passion, freedom to drink and to behave drunkenly a sacred privilege, sporadic employment a fact of life, and the social welfare and law-enforcement agencies of the state, partners of one's existence.

The Bandit Corner was subject to field observation for about three years—from June 1954 to May 1957. Hanging out on the corner during this period were six distinct but related gang subdivisions. There were four male groups: The Brigands, aged approximately 18 to 21 at the start of the study period; the Senior Bandits, aged 16 to 18; the Junior Bandits, 14 to 16, and the Midget Bandits, 12 to 14. There were also two distinct female subdivisions: The Bandettes, 14 to 16, and the Little Bandettes, 12 to 14.

The physical and psychic center of the Bandit corner was Sam's Variety Store, the owner and sole employee of which was not Sam but Ben, his son. Ben's father had founded the store in the 1920's, the heyday of the Irish laboring class in the Bandit neighborhood. When his father died, Ben took over the store, but did not change its name. Ben was a stocky, round-faced Jew in his middle 50's, who looked upon the whole of the Bandit neighborhood as his personal fief and bounden responsibility—a sacred legacy from his father. He knew everybody and was concerned with everybody; through his store passed a constant stream of customers and noncustomers of all ages and both sexes. In a space not much larger than that of a fair-sized bedroom, Ben managed to crowd a phone booth, a juke box, a pinball machine, a space heater, counters, shelves and stock, and an assorted variety of patrons. During one 15-minute period on an average day Ben would supply $1.37 worth of groceries to 11-year-old Carol Donovan and enter the sum on her mother's page in the "tab" book, agree to extend Mrs. Thebodeau's already extended credit until her A.D.C. check arrived, bandage and solace the three-year-old Negro girl who came crying to him with a cut forefinger, and shoo into the street a covey of Junior Bandits whose altercation over a pinball score was impeding customer traffic and augmenting an already substantial level of din.

Ben was a bachelor, and while he had adopted the whole of the Bandit neighborhood as his entended family, he had taken on the 200 adolescents who hung out on the Bandit corner as his most immediate sons and daughters. Ben knew the background and present circumstances of every Bandit, and followed their lives with intense interest and concern. Ben's corner-gang progeny were a fast-moving and mercurial lot, and he watched over their adventures and misadventures with a curious mixture of indignation, solicitude, disgust, and sympathy. Ben's outlook on the affairs of the world was never bland; he held and freely voiced strong opinions on a wide variety of issues, prominent among which was the behavior and misbehavior of the younger generation.

This particular concern was given ample scope for attention by the young Bandits who congregated in and around his store. Of all the gangs studied, the Bandits were the most consistently and determinedly criminal, and central to Ben's concerns was how each one stood with regard to "trouble." In this respect, developments were seldom meager. By the time they reached the age of 18, every one of the 32 active members of the Senior Bandits had appeared in court at least once, and some many times; 28 of the 32 boys had been committed to a correctional institution and 16 had spent at least one term in confinement.

Ben's stout arm swept the expanse of pavement which fronted his store. "I'll tell ya, I give up on these kids. In all the years I been here, I never seen a worse bunch. You know what they should do? They should put up a big platform with one of them stocks right out there, and as soon as a kid gets in trouble, into the stocks with 'im. Then they straighten out. The way it is now, the kid tells a sob story to some soft-hearted cop or social worker, and pretty soon he's back at the same old thing. See that guy just comin' over here? That's what I mean. He's hopeless. Mark my word, he's gonna end up in the electric chair."

The Senior Bandit who entered the store came directly to Ben. "Hey, Ben, I just quit my job at the shoe factory. They don't pay ya nothin,' and they got some wise guy nephew of the owner who thinks he can kick everyone around. I just got fed up. I ain't gonna tell Ma for awhile, she'll be mad." Ben's concern was evident. "Digger, ya just gotta learn you can't keep actin' smart to every boss ya have. And $1.30 an hour ain't bad pay at all for a 17-year-old boy. Look, I'll lend ya 10 bucks so ya can give 5 to ya Ma, and she won't know."

In their dealings with Ben, the Bandits, for their part, were in turn hostile and affectionate, cordial and sullen, open and reserved. They clearly regarded Ben's as "their" store. This meant, among other things, exclusive possession of the right to make trouble within its confines. At least three times during the observation period, corner boys from outside neighborhoods entered the store, obviously bent on stealing or creating a disturbance. On each occasion these outsiders were efficiently and forcefully removed by nearby Bandits, who then waxed indignant at the temerity of "outside" kids daring to consider Ben's as a target of illegal activity. One consequence, then, of Ben's seigneurial relationship to the Bandits was that his store was unusually well protected against theft, armed and otherwise, which presented a constant hazard to the small-store owner in Midcity.

On the other hand, the Bandits guarded jealously their own right to raise hell in Ben's. On one occasion, several Senior Bandits came into the store with a cache of pistol bullets and proceeded to empty the powder from one of the bullets onto the pinball machine and to ignite the powder. When Ben ordered them out they continued operations on the front sidewalk by wrapping gunpowder in newspaper and igniting it. Finally they set fire to a wad of paper containing two live bullets which exploded and narrowly missed local residents sitting on nearby doorsteps.

Such behavior, while calculated to bedevil Ben and perhaps to retaliate for a recent scolding or ejection, posed no real threat to him or his store; the same boys during this period were actively engaged in serious thefts from similar stores in other neighborhoods. For the most part, the behavior of the Bandits in and around the store involved the characteristic activities of hanging out. In warm weather the Bandits sat outside the store on the sidewalk or doorstoops playing cards, gambling, drinking, talking to one another and to the Bandettes. In cooler weather they moved into the store as the hour and space permitted, and there played the pinball machine for such cash payoffs as Ben saw fit to render, danced with the Bandettes to juke box records, and engaged in general horseplay.

While Ben's was the Bandits' favorite hangout, they did frequent other hanging locales, mostly within a few blocks of the corner. Among these was a park directly adjacent to the housing project where the boys played football and baseball in season. At night the park provided a favored locale for activities such as beer drinking and lovemaking, neither of which particularly endeared them to the adult residents of the project, who not infrequently summoned the police to clear the park of late-night revellers. Other areas of congregation in the local neighborhood were a nearby delicatessen ("the Delly"), a pool hall, and the apartments of those Bandettes whose parents happened to be away. The Bandits also ran their own dances at the Old Erin and New Hibernia, but they had to conceal their identity as Bandits when renting these dance halls, since the proprietors had learned that the rental fees were scarcely sufficient to compensate for the chaos inevitably attending the conduct of a Bandit dance.

The Bandits were able to find other sources of entertainment in the central business district of Port City. While most of the Bandits and Bandettes were too young to gain admission to the numerous downtown cafes with their rock 'n' roll bands, they were able to find amusement in going to the movies (sneaking in whenever possible), playing the coin machines in the penny arcades and shoplifting from the downtown department stores. Sometimes, as a kind of diversion, small groups of Bandits spent the day in town job-hunting, with little serious intention of finding work.

One especially favored form of downtown entertainment was the court trial. Members of the Junior and Senior Bandits performed as on-stage participants in some 250 court trials during a four-year period. Most trials involving juveniles were conducted in nearby Midcity Court as private proceedings, but the older Bandits had adopted as routine procedure the practice of appealing their local court sentences to the Superior Court located in downtown Port City. When the appeal was successful, it was the occasion for as large a turnout of gang members as could be mustered, and the Bandits were a rapt and vitally interested audience. Afterwards, the gang held long and animated discussions about the severity or leniency of the sentence and other, finer points of legal procedure. The hearings provided not only an absorbing form of free entertainment, but also invaluable knowledge about court functioning, appropriate defendant behavior, and the predilections of particular judges—knowledge that would serve the spectators well when their own turn to star inevitably arrived.

THE SENIOR BANDITS

The Senior Bandits, the second oldest of the four male gang subdivisions hanging out on the Bandit corner, were under intensive observation for a period of 20 months. At the start of this period the boys ranged in age from 15 to 17 (average age 16.3) and at the end, 17 to 19 (average age 18.1). The core group of the Senior Bandits numbered 32 boys.

Most of the gang members were Catholic, the majority of Irish background; several were Italian or French Canadian, and a few were English or Scotch Protestants. The gang contained two sets of brothers and several cousins, and about one third of the boys had relatives in other subdivisions. These included a brother in the Midgets, six brothers in the juniors, and three in the Marauders.

The educational and occupational circumstances of the Senior Bandits were remarkably like those of their parents. Some seven years after the end of the intensive study period, when the average age of the Bandits was 25, 23 out of the 27 gang members whose occupations were known held jobs ordinarily classified in the bottom two occupational categories of the United States census. Twenty-one were classified as "laborer," holding jobs such as roofer, stock boy, and trucker's helper. Of 24 fathers whose occupations were known, 18, or 83 percent, held jobs in the same bottom two occupational categories as their sons; 17 were described as "laborer," holding jobs such as furniture mover and roofer. Fathers even held jobs of similar kinds and in similar proportions to those of their sons, e.g., construction laborers: sons 30 percent, fathers 25 percent; factory laborers: sons 15 percent, fathers 21 percent. Clearly the Senior Bandits were not rising above their fathers' status. In fact, there were indications of a slight decline, even taking account of the younger age of the sons. Two of the boys' fathers held jobs in "public safety" services—one policeman and one fireman; another had worked for a time in the "white collar" position of a salesclerk at Sears; a fourth had risen to the rank of Chief Petty Officer in the Merchant Marine. Four of the fathers, in other words, had attained relatively elevated positions, while the sons produced only one policeman.

The education of the Senior Bandits was consistent with their occupational status. Of 29 boys whose educational experience was known, 27 dropped out of school in the eighth, ninth, or tenth grades, having reached the age of 16. Two did complete high school, and one of these was reputed to have taken some post-high-school training in a local technical school. None entered college. It should be remarked that this record occurred not in a backward rural community of the 1800's, nor in a black community, but in the 1950's in a predominantly white neighborhood of a metropolis that took pride in being one of the major educational centers of the world.

Since only two of the Senior Bandits were still in school during the study, almost all of the boys held full-time jobs at some time during the contact period. But despite financial needs, pressure from parents and parole officers and other incentives to get work, the Senior Bandits found jobs slowly, accepted them reluctantly, and quit them with little provocation.

The Senior Bandits were clearly the most criminal of the seven gangs we studied most closely. For example, by the time he had reached the age of 18 the average Senior Bandit had been charged with offenses in court an average of 7.6 times; this compared with an average rate of 2.7 for all five male gangs, and added up to a total of almost 250 separate charges for the gang as a whole. A year after our intensive contact with the group, 100 percent of the Senior Bandits had been arrested at least once, compared with an average arrest figure of 45 percent for all groups. During the 20-month contact period, just about half of the Senior Bandits were on probation or parole for some period of time.

LAW VIOLATION, CLIQUES AND LEADERSHIP

To a greater degree than in any of the other gangs we studied, crime as an occupation and preoccupation played a central role in the lives of the Senior Bandits. Prominent among recurrent topics of discussion were thefts successfully executed, fights recently engaged in, and the current status of gang members who were in the process of passing through the successive states of arrest, appearing in court, being sentenced, appealing, re-appealing and so on. Although none of the crimes of the Senior Bandits merited front-page headlines when we were close to them, a number of their more colorful exploits did receive newspaper attention, and the stories were carefully clipped and left in Ben's store for circulation among the gang members. Newspaper citations functioned for the Senior Bandits somewhat as do press notices for actors; gang members who made the papers were elated and granted prestige; those who did not were often disappointed; participants and non-participants who failed to see the stories felt cheated.

The majority of their crimes were thefts. The Senior Bandits were thieves *par excellence,* and their thievery was imaginative, colorful, and varied. Most thefts were from stores. Included among these was a department store theft of watches, jewelry and clothing for use as family Christmas presents; a daylight raid on a supermarket for food and refreshments needed for a beach outing; a daytime burglary of an antique store, in which eight gang members, in the presence of the owner, stole a Samurai sword and French duelling pistols. The gang also engaged in car theft. One summer several Bandits stole a car to visit girl friends who were working at a summer resort. Sixty miles north of Port City, hailed by police for exceeding speed limits, they raced away at speeds of up to 100 miles an hour, overturned the car, and were hospitalized for injuries. In another instance, Bandits stole a car in an effort to return a drunken companion to his home and avoid the police; when this car stalled they stole a second one parked in front of its owner's house; the owner ran out and fired several shots at the thieves, which, however, failed to forestall the theft.

The frequency of Senior Bandit crimes, along with the relative seriousness of their offenses, resulted in a high rate of arrest and confinement. During the contact period somewhat over 40 percent of the gang members were confined in correctional institutions, with terms averaging 11 months per boy. The average Senior Bandit spent approximately one month out of four in a correctional facility. This circumstance prompted one of the Bandettes to remark, "Ya know, them guys got a new place to hang—the reformatory. That bunch is never together—one halfa them don't even know the other half. . . ."

This appraisal, while based on fact, failed to recognize an important feature of gang relationships. With institutional confinement a frequent and predictable event, the Senior Bandits employed a set of devices to maintain a high degree of group solidarity. Lines of communication between corner and institution were kept open by frequent visits by those on the outside, during which inmates were brought food, money and cigarettes as well as news of the neighborhood and other correctional facilities. One Midcity social worker claimed that the institutionalized boys knew what was going on in the neighborhood before most neighborhood residents. The Bandits also developed well-established methods for arranging and carrying out institutional escape by those gang members who were so inclined. Details of escapes were arranged in the course of visits and inter-inmate contacts; escapees were provided by fellow gang members with equipment such as ropes to scale prison walls and getaway cars. The homes of one's gang fellows were also made available as hideouts. Given this set of arrangements, the Bandits carried out several highly successful escapes, and one succeeded in executing the first escape in the history of a maximum security installation.

This means by which the Senior Bandits achieved group cohesion in spite of recurrent incarcerations of key members merit further consideration— both because they are of interest in their own right, and because they throw light on important relationships between leadership, group structure, and the motivation of criminal behavior. Despite the assertion that "one halfa them guys don't know the other half," the Senior Bandits were a solidaristic associational unit, with clear group boundaries and definite criteria for differentiating those who were "one of us" from those who were not. It was still said of an accepted group member that "he hangs with us"—even when the boy had been away from the corner in an institution for a year or more. Incarcerated leaders, in particular, were referred to frequently and in terms of admiration and respect.

The system used by the Senior Bandits to maintain solidarity and reliable leadership arrangements incorporated three major devices: the diffusion of authority, anticipation of contingencies, and interchangeability of roles. The recurring absence from the corner of varying numbers of gang members inhibited the formation of a set of relatively stable cliques of the kind found in the other gangs we studied intensively. What was fairly stable, instead, was a set of "classes" of members, each of which could include different individuals at different times. The relative size of these classes was fairly constant, and a member of one class could move to another to take the place of a member who had been removed by institutionalization.

The four major classes of gang members could be called key leaders, standby leaders, primary followers, and secondary followers. During the intensive contact period the gang contained five key leaders—boys whose accomplishments had earned them the right to command; six standby leaders—boys prepared to step into leadership positions when key leaders were institutionalized; eight primary followers—boys who hung out regularly and who were the most dependable followers of current leaders; and 13 secondary followers—boys who hung out less regularly and who tended to adapt their allegiances to particular leadership situations.

Predictably, given the dominant role of criminal activity among the Senior Bandits, leadership and followership were significantly related to criminal involvement. Each of the five key leaders had demonstrated unusual ability in criminal activity; in this respect the Senior Bandits differed from the other gangs, each of which included at least one leader whose position was based in whole or in part on a commitment to a law-abiding course of action. One of the Senior Bandits' key leaders was especially respected for his daring and adeptness in theft; another, who stole infrequently relative to other leaders, for his courage, stamina and resourcefulness as a fighter. The other three leaders had proven themselves in both theft and fighting, with theft the more important basis of eminence.

Confinement statistics show that gang members who were closest to leadership positions were also the most active in crime. They also suggest, however, that maintaining a system of leadership on this basis poses special problems. The more criminally active a gang member, the greater the likelihood that he would be apprehended and removed from the neighborhood, thus substantially diminishing his opportunities to convert earned prestige into operative leadership. How was it possible, then, for the Senior Bandits to maintain effective leadership arrangements? They utilized a remarkably efficient system whose several features were ingenious and deftly contrived.

First, the recognition by the Bandits of five key leaders—a relatively large number for a gang of 32 members—served as a form of insurance against being left without leadership. It was most unlikely that all five would be incarcerated at the same time, particularly since collective crimes were generally executed by one or possibly two leaders along with several of their followers. During one relatively brief part of the contact period, four of the key leaders were confined simultaneously, but over the full period the average number confined at any one time was two. One Bandit key leader expressed his conviction that exclusive reliance on a single leader was unwise: ". . . since we been hangin' out [at Ben's corner] we ain't had no leader. Other kids got a leader of the gang. Like up in Cornerville, they always got one kid who's the big boss . . . so far we ain't did that, and I don't think we ever will. We talk about 'Smiley and his boys,' or 'Digger and his clique,' and like that. . . ."

It is clear that for this Bandit the term "leader" carried the connotation of a single and all-powerful gang lord, which was not applicable to the diffuse and decentralized leadership arrangements of the Bandits. It is also significant that the gangs of Cornerville which he used as an example were Italian gangs whose rate of criminal involvement was relatively low. The "one big boss" type of leadership found in these gangs derives from the "Caesar" or "Il Duce" pattern so well established in Italian culture, and it was workable for Cornerville gangs because the gangs and their leaders were sufficiently law-abiding and/or sufficiently capable of evading arrest as to make the removal of the leader an improbable event.

A second feature of Bandit leadership, the use of "standby" leaders, made possible a relatively stable balance among the several cliques. When the key leader of his clique was present in the area, the standby leader assumed a subordinate role and did not initiate action; if and when the key leader was committed to an institution, the standby was ready to assume leadership. He knew, however, that he was expected to relinquish this position on the return of the key leader. By this device each of the five major cliques was assured some form of leadership even when key leaders were absent, and could maintain its form, identity and influence vis-à-vis other cliques.

A third device that enabled the gang to maintain a relatively stable leadership and clique structure involved the phenomenon of "optimal" criminal involvement. Since excellence in crime was the major basis of gang leadership, it might be expected that some of those who aspired to leadership would assume that there was a simple and direct relationship between crime and leadership: the more crime, the more prestige; the more prestige, the stronger the basis of authority. The flaw in this simple formula was in fact recognized by the actual key leaders: in striving for maximal criminal involvement, one also incurred the maximum risk of incarceration. But leadership involved more than gaining prestige through crime; one had to be personally involved with other gang members for sufficiently extended periods to exploit won prestige through wooing followers, initiating noncriminal as well as criminal activities, and effecting working relationships with other leaders. Newly-returned key leaders as well as the less criminally-active class of standby leaders tended to step up their involvement in criminal activity on assuming or reassuming leadership positions in order to solidify their positions, but they also tended to diminish such involvement once this was achieved.

One fairly evident weakness in so flexible and fluid a system of cliques and leadership was the danger that violent and possibly disruptive internal conflict might erupt among key leaders who were competing for followers, or standby leaders who were reluctant to relinquish their positions. There was, in fact, surprisingly little overt conflict of any kind among Bandit leaders. On their release from confinement, leaders were welcomed with enthusiasm and appropriate observances both by their followers and by other leaders. They took the center of the stage as they recounted to rapt listeners their institutional experiences, the circumstances of those still confined, and new developments in policies, personnel and politics at the correctional school.

When they were together Bandit leaders dealt with one another gingerly, warily and with evident respect. On one occasion a standby leader, who was less criminally active than the returning key leader, offered little resistance to being displaced, but did serve his replacement with the warning that a resumption of his former high rate of crime would soon result in commitment both of himself and his clique. On another occasion one of the toughest of the Senior Bandits (later sentenced to an extended term in an adult institution for ringleading a major prison riot) returned to the corner to find that another leader had taken over not only some of his key followers but his steady girl friend as well. Instead of taking on his rival in an angry and perhaps violent confrontation, he reacted quite mildly, venting his hostility in the form of sarcastic teasing, calculated to needle but not to incite. In the place of a direct challenge, the newly returned key leader set about to regain his followers and his girl by actively throwing himself back into criminal activity. This course of action—competing for followers by successful performance in prestigious activities rather than by brute-force confrontation—was standard practice among the Senior Bandits.

THE JUNIOR BANDITS

The leadership system of the Junior Bandits was, if anything, even farther removed from the "one big boss" pattern than was the "multi-leader power-balance" system of the Seniors. An intricate arrangement of cliques and leadership enabled this subdivision of the gang to contain within it a variety of individuals and cliques with different and often conflicting orientations.

Leadership for particular activities was provided as the occasion arose by boys whose competence in that activity had been established. Leadership was thus flexible, shifting, and adaptable to changing group circumstances. Insofar as there was a measure of relatively concentrated authority, it was invested in a collectivity rather than an individual. The several "situational" leaders of the dominant clique constituted what was in effect a kind of ruling council, which arrived at its decisions through a process of extended collective discussion generally involving all concerned. Those who were to execute a plan of action thereby took part in the process by which it was developed.

A final feature of this system concerns the boy who was recognized as "the leader" of the Junior Bandits. When the gang formed a club to expedite involvement in athletic activities, he was chosen its president. Although he was an accepted member of the dominant clique, he did not, on the surface, seem to possess any particular qualifications for this position. He was mild-mannered, unassertive, and consistently refused to take a definite stand on outstanding issues, let alone taking the initiative in implementing policy. He appeared to follow rather than to lead. One night when the leaders of the two subordinate factions became infuriated with one another in the course of a dispute, he trailed both boys around for several hours, begging them to calm down and reconcile their differences. On another occasion the gang was on the verge of splitting into irreconcilable factions over a financial issue. One group accused another of stealing club funds; the accusation was hotly denied; angry recriminations arose that swept in a variety of dissatisfactions with the club and its conduct. In the course of this melee, the leader of one faction, the "bad boys," complained bitterly about the refusal of the president to take sides or assume any initiative in resolving the dispute, and called for a new election. This was agreed to and the election was held—with the result that the "weak" president was re-elected by a decisive majority, and was reinstated in office amidst emotional outbursts of acclaim and reaffirmation of the unity of the gang.

It was thus evident that the majority of gang members, despite temporary periods of anger over particular issues, recognized on some level the true function performed by a "weak" leader. Given the fact that the gang included a set of cliques with differing orientations and conflicting notions, and a set of leaders whose authority was limited to specific areas, the maintenance of gang cohesion required some special mechanisms. One was the device of the "weak" leader. It is most unlikely that a forceful or dominant person could have controlled the sanctions that would enable him to coerce the strong-willed factions into compliance. The very fact that the "weak" leader refused to take sides and was noncommittal on key issues made him acceptable to the conflicting interests represented in the gang. Further, along with the boy's nonassertive demeanor went a real talent for mediation.

THE OUTLAW NEIGHBORHOOD

The Outlaw street corner was less than a mile from that of the Bandits, and like the Bandits, the Outlaws were white, Catholic, and predominantly Irish, with a few Italians and Irish-Italians. But their social status, in the middle range of the lower class, was sufficiently higher than that of the Bandits to be reflected in significant differences in both their gang and family life. The neighborhood environment also was quite different.

Still, the Outlaws hung out on a classic corner—complete with drugstore, variety store, a neighborhood bar (Callahan's Bar and Grill), a pool hall, and several other small businesses such as a laundromat. The corner was within one block of a large park, a convenient locale for card games, lovemaking, and athletic practice. Most residents of the Outlaw neighborhood were oblivious to the deafening roar of the elevated train that periodically rattled the houses and stores of Midcity Avenue, which formed one street of the Outlaw corner. There was no housing project in the Outlaw neighborhood, and none of the Outlaws were project residents. Most of their families rented one level of one of the three-decker wooden tenements which were common in the area; a few owned their own homes. In the mid-1950's, however, the Outlaw neighborhood underwent significant changes as Negroes began moving in. Most of the white residents, gradually and with reluctance, left their homes and moved out to the first fringe of Port City's residential suburbs, abandoning the area to the Negroes.

Prior to this time the Outlaw corner had been a hanging locale for many years. The Outlaw name and corner dated from at least the late 1920's, and perhaps earlier. One local boy who was not an Outlaw observed disgruntledly that anyone who started a fight with an Outlaw would end up fighting son, father, and grandfather, since all were or had been members of the gang. A somewhat drunken and sentimental Outlaw, speaking at a farewell banquet for their field worker, declared impassionedly that any infant born into an Outlaw family was destined from birth to wear the Outlaw jacket.

One consequence of the fact that Outlaws had hung out on the same corner for many years was that the group that congregated there during the 30-month observation period included a full complement of age-graded subdivisions. Another consequence was that the subdivisions were closely connected by kinship. There were six clearly differentiated subdivisions on the corner: the Marauders, boys in their late teens and early twenties; the Senior Outlaws, boys between 16 and 18; the Junior Outlaws, 14 to 16; and the Midget Outlaws, 11 to 13. There were also two girls groups, the Outlawettes and the Little Outlawettes. The number of Outlaws in all subdivisions totalled slightly over 200 persons, ranging in age, approximately, from 10 to 25 years.

The cohesiveness of the Outlaws, during the 1950's, was enhanced in no small measure by an adult who, like Ben for the Bandits, played a central role in the Outlaws' lives. This was Rosa—the owner of the variety store which was their principal hangout—a stout, unmarried woman of about 40 who was, in effect, the street-corner mother of all 200 Outlaws.

THE JUNIOR OUTLAWS

The Junior Outlaws, numbering 24 active members, were the third oldest of the four male subdivisions on the Outlaw Corner, ranging in age from 14 to 16. Consistent with their middle-range lower-class status, the boys' fathers were employed in such jobs as bricklayer, mechanic, chauffeur, milk deliveryman; but a small minority of these men had attained somewhat higher positions, one being the owner of a small electroplating shop and the other rising to the position of plant superintendent. The educational status of the Junior Outlaws was higher than that of the Bandit gangs, but lower than that of their older brother gang, the Senior Ourlaws.

With regard to law violations, the Junior Outlaws, as one might expect from their status and age, were considerably less criminal than the lower-status Bandits, but considerably more so than the Senior Outlaws. They ranked third among the five male gangs in illegal involvement during the observation period (25 involvements per 10 boys per 10 months), which was well below the second-ranking Senior Bandits (54.2) and well above the fourth-ranking Negro Kings (13.9). Nevertheless, the two-and-a-half-year period during which we observed the Juniors was for them, as for other boys of their status and age group, a time of substantial increase in the frequency and seriousness of illegal behavior. An account of the events of this time provides some insight into the process by which age-related influences engender criminality. It also provides another variation on the issue, already discussed in the case of the Bandits, of the relation of leadership to criminality.

It is clear from the case of the Bandits that gang affairs were ordered not by autocratic ganglords, but rather through a subtle and intricate interplay between leadership and a set of elements such as personal competency, intra-gang divisions and law violation. The case of the Junior Outlaws is particularly dramatic in this regard, since the observation period found them at the critical age when boys of this social-status level are faced with a serious decision—the amount of weight to be granted to law-violating behavior as a basis of prestige. Because there were in the Junior Outlaws two cliques, each of which was committed quite clearly to opposing alternatives, the interplay of the various elements over time emerges with some vividness, and echoes the classic morality play wherein forces of good and evil are locked in mortal combat over the souls of the uncommitted.

At the start of the observation period, the Juniors, 13-, 14- and 15-year-olds, looked and acted for the most part like "nice young kids." By the end of the period both their voices and general demeanor had undergone a striking change. Their appearance, as they hung out in front of Rosa's store, was that of rough corner boys, and the series of thefts, fights, and drinking bouts which had occurred during the intervening two-and-one-half years was the substance behind that appearance. When we first contacted them, the Juniors comprised three main cliques; seven boys associated primarily with a "good boy" who was quite explicitly oriented to law-abiding behavior; a second clique of seven boys associated with a "bad boy" who was just starting to pursue prestige through drinking and auto theft; and a third, less-frequently congregating group, who took a relatively neutral position with respect to the issue of violative behavior.

The leader of the "good boy" clique played an active part in the law-abiding activities of the gang, and was elected president of the formal club organized by the Juniors. This club at first included members of all three cliques; however, one of the first acts of the club members, dominated by the "good boy" leader and his supporters, was to vote out of membership the leader of the "bad boy" clique. Nevertheless, the "bad boy" leader and his followers continued to hang out on the corner with the other Juniors, and from this vantage point attempted to gain influence over the uncommitted boys as well as members of the "good boy" clique. His efforts proved unsuccessful, however, since during this period athletic prowess served for the majority of the Juniors as a basis of greater prestige than criminal behavior. Disgruntled by this failure, the "bad boy" leader took his followers and moved to a new hanging corner, about two blocks away from the traditional one.

From there, a tangible symbol of the ideological split within the Juniors, the "bad boy" leader continued his campaign to wean away the followers of the "good boy" leader, trying to persuade them to leave the old corner for the new. At the same time, behavior at the "bad boy" corner became increasingly delinquent, with, among other things, much noisy drinking and thefts of nearby cars. These incidents produced complaints by local residents that resulted in several police raids on the corner, and served to increase the antagonism between what now had become hostile factions. Determined to assert their separateness, the "bad boy" faction began to drink and create disturbances in Rosa's store, became hostile to her when she censured them, and finally stayed away from the store altogether.

The antagonism between the two factions finally became sufficiently intense to bring about a most unusual circumstance—plans for an actual gang fight, a "jam" of the type characteristic of rival gangs. The time and place for the battle were agreed on. But no one from either side showed up. A second battle site was selected. Again the combatants failed to appear. From the point of view of intragang relations, both the plan for the gang fight and its failure to materialize were significant. The fact that a physical fight between members of the same subdivision was actually projected showed that factional hostility over the issue of law violation had reached an unusual degree of bitterness; the fact that the planned encounters did not in fact occur indicated a realization that actual physical combat might well lead to an irreversible split.

A reunification of the hostile factions did not take place for almost a year, however. During this time changes occurred in both factions which had the net effect of blunting the sharpness of the ideological issue dividing them. Discouraged by his failure to win over the majority of the Outlaws to the cause of law-violation as a major badge of prestige, the leader of the "bad boy" clique began to hang out less frequently. At the same time, the eight "uncommitted" members of the Junior Outlaws, now moving toward their middle teens, began to gravitate toward the "bad boy" corner—attracted by the excitement and risk of its activities. More of the Juniors than ever before became involved in illegal drinking and petty theft. This trend became sufficiently pronounced to draw in members of the "good boy" clique, and the influence of the "good boy" leader diminished to the point where he could count on the loyalty only of his own brother and two other boys. In desperation, sensing the all-but-irresistible appeal of illegality for his erstwhile followers, he increased the tempo of his own delinquent behavior in a last-ditch effort to win them back. All in vain. Even his own brother deserted the regular Outlaw corner, although he did not go so far as to join the "bad boys" on theirs.

Disillusioned, the "good boy" leader took a night job that sharply curtailed the time he was able to devote to gang activities. Members of the "bad boy" clique now began a series of maneuvers aimed at gaining control of the formal club. Finally, about two months before the close of the 30-month contact period, a core member of the "bad boy" clique was elected to the club presidency. In effect, the proponents of illegality as a major basis of prestige had won the long struggle for dominance of the Junior Outlaws. But this achievement, while on the surface a clear victory for the "bad boy" faction, was in fact a far more subtle process of mutual accommodation.

The actions of each of the opposing sides accorded quite directly with their expressed convictions; each member of the "bad boy" faction averaged about 17 known illegal acts during the observation period, compared to a figure of about two per boy for the "good boy" faction. However, in the face of these sharp differences in both actions and sentiments respecting illegality, the two factions shared important common orientations. Most importantly, they shared the conviction that the issue of violative behavior as a basis of prestige was a paramount one, and one that required a choice. Moreover, both sides remained uncertain as to whether the choice they made was the correct one.

The behavior of both factions provides evidence of a fundamental ambivalence with respect to the "demanded" nature of delinquent behavior. The gradual withdrawal of support by followers of the "good boy" leader and the movement toward violative behavior of the previously "neutral" clique attest to a compelling conviction that prestige gained through law-abiding endeavor alone could not, at this age, suffice. Even more significant was the criminal experience of the "good boy" leader. As the prime exponent of law-abiding behavior, he might have been expected to serve as an exemplar in this respect. In fact, the opposite was true; his rate of illegal involvement was the highest of all the boys in his clique, and had been so even before his abortive attempt to regain his followers by a final burst of delinquency. This circumstance probably derived from his realization that a leader acceptable to both factions (which he wanted to be) would have to show proficiency in activities recognized by both as conferring prestige.

TO BE A MAN

It is equally clear, by the same token, that members of the "bad boy" faction were less than serenely confident in their commitment to law-violation as an ideal. Once they had won power in the club they did not keep as their leader the boy who had been the dominant figure on the "bad boy" corner, and who was without question the most criminally active of the Junior Outlaws, but instead elected as president another boy who was also criminally active, but considerably less so. Moreover, in the presence of older gang members, Seniors and Marauders, the "bad boy" clique was far more subdued, less obstreperous, and far less ardent in their advocacy of crime as an ideal. There was little question that they were sensitive to and responsive to negative reactions by others to their behavior.

It is noteworthy that members of both factions adhered more firmly to the "law-violation" and "law-abiding" positions on the level of abstract ideology than on the level of actual practice. This would suggest that the existence of the ideologies and their corresponding factions served important functions both for individual gang members and for the group as a whole. Being in the same orbit as the "bad boys" made it possible for the "good boys" to reap some of the rewards of violative behavior without undergoing its risks; the presence of the "good boys" imposed restraints on the "bad" that they themselves desired, and helped protect them from dangerous excesses. The behavior and ideals of the "good boys" satisfied for both factions that component of their basic orientation that said "violation of the law is wrong and should be punished"; the behavior and ideals of the "bad boys" that component that said "one cannot earn manhood without some involvement in criminal activity."

It is instructive to compare the stress and turmoil attending the struggle for dominance of the Junior Outlaws with the leadership circumstances of the Senior Bandits. In this gang, older and of lower social status (lower-class III), competition for leadership had little to do with a choice between law-abiding and law-violating philosophies, but rather with the issue of which a number of competing leaders was *best* able to demonstrate prowess in illegal activity. This virtual absence of effective pressures against delinquency contrasts sharply with the situation of the Junior Outlaws. During the year-long struggle between its "good" and "bad" factions, the Juniors were exposed to constant pressures, both internal and external to the gang, to refrain from illegality. External sources included Rosa, whom the boys loved and respected; a local youth worker whom they held in high esteem; their older brother gangs, whose frequent admonitions to the "little kids" to "straighten out" and "keep clean" were attended with utmost seriousness. Within the gang itself the "good boy" leader served as a consistent and persuasive advocate of a law-abiding course of action. In addition, most of the boys' parents deplored their misbehavior and urged them to keep out of trouble.

In the face of all these pressures from persons of no small importance in the lives of the Juniors, the final triumph of the proponents of illegality, however tempered, assumes added significance. What was it that impelled the "bad boy" faction? There was a quality of defiance about much of their delinquency, as if they were saying—"We know perfectly well that what we are doing is regarded as wrong, legally and morally; we also know that it violates the wishes and standards of many whose good opinion we value; yet, if we are to sustain our self-respect and our honor as males we *must*, at this stage of our lives, engage in criminal behavior." In light of the experience of the Junior Outlaws, one can scarcely argue that their delinquency sprang from any inability to distinguish right from wrong, or out of any simple conformity to a set of parochial standards that just happened to differ from those of the legal code or the adult middle class. Their delinquent behavior was engendered by a highly complex interplay of forces, including, among other elements, the fact that they were males, were in the middle range of the lower class and of critical importance in the present instance, were moving through the age period when the attainment of manhood was of the utmost concern.

In the younger gang just discussed, the Junior Outlaws, leadership and clique structure reflected an intense struggle between advocates and opponents of law-violation as a prime basis of prestige.

THE SENIOR OUTLAWS

Leadership in the older Senior Outlaws reflected a resolution of the law-conformity versus law-violation conflict, but with different results. Although the gang was not under direct observation during their earlier adolescence, what we know of the Juniors, along with evidence that the Senior Outlaws themselves had been more criminal when younger, would suggest that the gang had in fact undergone a similar struggle, and that the proponents of conformity to the law had won.

In any case, the events of the observation period made it clear that the Senior Outlaws sought "rep" as a gang primarily through effective execution of legitimate enterprises such as athletics, dances, and other non-violative activities. In line with this objective, they maintained a consistent concern with the "good name" of the gang and with "keeping out of trouble" in the face of constant and ubiquitous temptations. For example, they attempted (without much success) to establish friendly relations with the senior priest of their parish—in contrast with the Junior Outlaws, who were on very bad terms with the local church. At one point during the contact period when belligerent Bandits, claiming that the Outlaws had attacked one of the Midget Bandits, vowed to "wipe out every Outlaw jacket in Midcity," the Senior Outlaws were concerned not only with the threat of attack but also with the threat to their reputation. "That does it," said one boy, "I knew we'd get into something. There goes the good name of the Outlaws."

Leadership and clique arrangements in the Senior Outlaws reflected three conditions, each related in some way to the relatively low stress on criminal activity: the stability of gang membership (members were rarely removed from the area by institutional confinement), the absence of significant conflict over the prestige and criminality issue, and the importance placed on legitimate collective activities. The Senior Bandits were the most unified of the gangs we observed directly; there were no important cleavages or factions; even the distinction between more-active and less-active members was less pronounced than in the other gangs.

But as in the other gangs, leadership among the Senior Outlaws was collective and situational. There were four key leaders, each of whom assumed authority in his own sphere of competence. As in the case of the Bandit gangs there was little overt competition among leaders; when differences arose between the leadership and the rank and file, the several leaders tended to support one another. In one significant respect, however, Outlaw leadership differed from that of the other gangs; authority was exercised more firmly and accepted more readily. Those in charge of collective enterprises generally issued commands after the manner of a tough army sergeant or work-gang boss. Although obedience to such commands was frequently less than flawless, the leadership style of Outlaw leaders approximated the "snap-to-it" approach of organizations that control firmer sanctions than do most corner gangs. Compared to the near-chaotic behavior of their younger brother gang, the organizational practices of the Senior appeared as a model of efficiency. The "authoritarian" mode of leadership was particularly characteristic of one boy, whose prerogatives were somewhat more generalized than those of the other leaders. While he was far from an undisputed "boss," holding instead a kind of *primus inter pares* position, he was as close to a "boss" as anything found among the direct-observation gangs.

His special position derived from the fact that he showed superior capability in an unusually wide range of activities, and this permitted him wider authority than the other leaders. One might have expected, in a gang oriented predominantly to law-abiding activity, that this leader would serve as an exemplar of legitimacy and rank among the most law-abiding. This was not the case. He was, in fact, one of the most criminal of the Senior Outlaws, being among the relatively few who had "done time." He was a hard drinker, an able street-fighter a skilled football strategist and team leader, an accomplished dancer and smooth ladies' man. His leadership position was based not on his capacity to best exemplify the law-abiding orientation of the gang, but on his capabilities in a variety of activities, violative and non-violative. Thus, even in the gang most concerned with "keeping clean," excellence in crime still constituted one important basis of prestige. Competence as such rather than the legitimacy of one's activities provided the major basis of authority.

We still have to ask, however, why leadership among the Senior Outlaws was more forceful than in the other gangs. One reason emerges by comparison with the "weak leader" situation of the Junior Bandits. Younger and of lower social status, their factional conflict over the law-violation-and-prestige issue was sufficiently intense so that only a leader without an explicit commitment to either side could be acceptable to both. The Seniors, older and of higher status, had developed a good degree of intragang consensus on this issue, and showed little factionalism. They could thus accept a relatively strong leader without jeopardizing gang unity.

A second reason also involves differences in age and social status, but as these relate to the world of work. In contrast to the younger gangs, whose perspectives more directly revolved around the subculture of adolescence and its specific concerns, the Senior Outlaws at age 19 were on the threshold of adult work, and some, in fact, were actively engaged in it. In contrast to the lower-status gangs whose orientation to gainful employment was not and never would be as "responsible" as that of the Outlaws, the activities of the Seniors as gang members more directly reflected and anticipated the requirements and conditions of the adult occupational roles they would soon assume.

Of considerable importance in the prospective occupational world of the Outlaws was, and is, the capacity to give and take orders in the execution of collective enterprises. Unlike the Bandits, few of whom would ever occupy other than subordinate positions, the Outlaws belonged to that sector of society which provides the men who exercise direct authority over groups of laborers or blue collar workers. The self-executed collective activities of the gang—organized athletics, recreational projects, fund-raising activities—provided a training ground for the practice of organizational skills—planning organized enterprises, working together in their conduct, executing the directives of legitimate superiors. It also provided a training ground wherein those boys with the requisite talents could learn and practice the difficult art of exercising authority effectively over lower-class men. By the time they had reached the age of 20, the leaders of the Outlaws had experienced in the gang many of the problems and responsibilities confronting the army sergeant, the police lieutenant and the factory foreman.

The nature and techniques of leadership in the Senior Outlaws had relevance not only to their own gang but to the Junior Outlaws as well. Relations between the Junior and Senior Outlaws were the closest of all the intensive-contact gang subdivisions. The Seniors kept a close watch on their younger fellows, and served them in a variety of ways, as athletic coaches, advisers, mediators and arbiters. The older gang followed the factional conflicts of the Juniors with close attention, and were not above intervening when conflict reached sufficient intensity or threatened their own interests. The dominant leader of the Seniors was particularly concerned with the behavior of the Juniors; at one point, lecturing them about their disorderly conduct in Rosa's store, he remarked, "I don't hang with you guys, but I know what you do. . . ." The Seniors did not, however, succeed in either preventing the near-break-up of the Junior Outlaws or slowing their move toward law-breaking activities.

THE PREVALENCE OF GANGS

The subtle and intricately contrived relations among cliques, leadership and crime in the four subdivisions of the Bandits and Outlaws reveal the gang as an ordered and adaptive form of association, and its members as able and rational human beings. The fascinating pattern of intergang variation within a basic framework illustrates vividly the compelling influences of differences in age and social status on crime, leadership and other forms of behavior—even when these differences are suprisingly small. The experiences of Midcity gang members show that the gang serves the lower-class adolescent as a flexible and adaptable training instrument for imparting vital knowledge concerning the value of individual competence, the appropriate limits of law-violating behavior, the uses and abuses of authority, and the skills of interpersonal relations. From this perspective, the street gang appears not as a casual or transient manifestation that emerges intermittently in response to unique and passing social conditions, but rather as a stable associational form, coordinate with and complementary to the family, and as an intrinsic part of the way of life of the urban low-status community.

How then can one account for the widespread conception of gangs as somehow popping up and then disappearing again? One critical reason concerns the way one defines what a gang is. Many observers, both scholars and non-scholars, often use a *sine qua non* to sort out "real" gangs from near-gangs, pseudo-gangs, and non-gangs. Among the more common of these single criteria are: autocratic one-man leadership, some "absolute" degree of solidarity or stable membership, a predominant involvement in violent conflict with other gangs, claim to a rigidly defined turf, or participation in activities thought to pose a threat to other sectors of the community. Reaction to groups lacking the *sine qua non* is often expressed with a dismissive "Oh, them. That's not a *gang*. That's just a bunch of kids out on the corner."

ON THE CORNER AGAIN

For many people there are no gangs if there is no gang warfare. It's that simple. For them, as for all those who concentrate on the "threatening" nature of the gang, the phenomenon is defined in terms of the degree of "problem" it poses: A group whose "problematic" behavior is hard to ignore is a gang; one less problematic is not. But what some people see as a problem may not appear so to others. In Philadelphia, for example, the police reckoned there were 80 gangs, of which 20 were at war; while social workers estimated there were 200 gangs, of which 80 were "most hostile." Obviously, the social workers' 80 "most hostile" gangs were the same as the 80 "gangs" of the police. The additional 120 groups defined as gangs by the social workers were seen as such because they were thought to be appropriate objects of social work; but to the police they were not sufficiently

In view of this sort of confusion, let me state our definition of what a gang is. A gang is a group of urban adolescents who congregate recurrently at one or more nonresidential locales, with continued affiliation based on self-defined criteria of inclusion and exclusion. Recruitment, customary places of assembly and ranging areas are based in a specific territory, over some portion of which limited use and occupancy rights are claimed. Membership both in the gang as a whole and in its subgroups is determined on the basis of age. The group maintains a versatile repertoire of activities, with hanging out, mating, recreational and illegal activity being of central importance; and it is internally differentiated on the basis of authority, prestige, personality and clique-formation.

The main reason that people have consistently mistaken the prevalence of gangs is the widespread tendency to define them as gangs on the basis of the presence or absence of one or two characteristics that are thought to be essential to the "true" gang. Changes in the forms of frequencies or particular characteristics, such as leadership, involvement in fighting, or modes of organization, are seen not as normal variations over time and space, but rather as signs of the emergence or disappearance of the gangs themselves. Our work does not support this view; instead, our evidence indicates that the core characteristics of the gang vary continuously from place to place and from time to time without negating the existence of the gang. Gangs may be larger or smaller, named or nameless, modestly or extensively differentiated, more or less active in gang fighting, stronger or weaker in leadership, black, white, yellow or brown, without affecting their identity as gangs. So long as groups of adolescents gather periodically outside the home, frequent a particular territory, restrict membership by age and other criteria, pursue a variety of activities, and maintain differences in authority and prestige—so long will the gang continue to exist as a basic associational form.

Further Reading Suggested by the Author

The Gang: A Study of 1313 Gangs in Chicago by Frederic M. Thrasher (Chicago: University of Chicago Press, 1927) is the classic work on American youth gangs. Although published in the 1920's, it remains the most detailed and comprehensive treatise on gangs and gang life ever written.

Delinquent Boys: The Culture of the Gang by Albert K. Cohen (Glencoe, Ill.: Free Press, 1955) is the first major attempt to explain the behavior of gang members using modern sociological theory.

Delinquency and Opportunity: A Theory of Delinquent Gangs by Richard A. Cloward and Lloyd E. Ohlin (Glencoe, Ill.: Free Press, 1960) explains the existence, both of gangs, and major types of gangs. It has had a profound impact on American domestic policy.

Group Process and Gang Delinquency by James F. Short Jr. and Fred L. Strodtbeck (Chicago: University of Chicago Press, 1965). An empirical "test" of divergent theories of gangs and delinquency, it includes the first extensive application of statistical techniques and the first systematic application of the social-psychological conceptual framework to the study of gangs.

WATCH OUT, WHITEY: NEGRO YOUTH GANGS AND VIOLENCE

Lewis Yablonsky

Displaying a twisted smile of defiance, the Negro gang youth who had "done the thing" during the Watts riots, told me: "Our 'weekend activity' [Negro gang fighting] has stopped for a while. I don't know whether we'll ever fight each other again. We're all tight [close together] now. Most of us now know that Whitey is our only real enemy." This may be a unique comment by one gang boy, or it may be a prophecy of a new style of gang behavior. Negro gangs that fought each other on weekends may train their sights—if not a few rifles—on the "real enemy."

The phrase "burn-baby-burn," a chant expressed by a Negro Los Angeles disc jockey was considered, before the riot, simply a "hip" comment. The rioters picked it up as a slogan and acted it out. The first night of the riot, gang members in Watts, like other Negroes, met casually in their hangouts to observe the scene. When the imminent holocaust began to clarify itself, the outside enemy becoming apparent, a destructive camaraderie developed; gang youths banded together; many former gang enemies became partners in the looting.

Some intricacies of the Negro gang were revealed to me by 10 Negro youths who participated in the riot. Here are some of the things I learned:

> Gangs were not tight cohesive entities, but an impending battle could produce several hundred members from their own territory.
> Gang leaders were "big men" in the neighborhood and well-known.
> Although these boys were not book readers, one of James Baldwin's comments seemed to fit their emotional condition: "To be a Negro in this country and to be relatively conscious is to be in a rage almost all the time."

They deeply hated *all* white men. I asked them, "How can you hate me when you don't even know me?" Two told me my white face was all they needed.

"Social workers don't know what the hell they are doing and cause more trouble than help." There was a uniform attitude that people trying to do social work in the neighborhood who lived outside were "fools," to be exploited as much as possible. (Several weeks after the riot a white social-welfare worker was shot twice by a 19-year-old Negro gang youth.)

There is a greater solidarity in the Negro youth community today than in the past.

There may be another riot soon. A next move is being discussed. It appears that these youth will not be able to go back to the old, false and pre-riot rational of self-hatred. The tie is blood, the foe now is Whitey—"the man who put us in this rotten prison."

In the modern disorganized slum, the gang has been for many Negro youths their only source of identity, status and emotional satisfaction. Ill-trained to participate with any degree of success in the dominant middle-class world of rigid ideas, community centers and adult demands, they construct their own community. They set goals that are achievable; they build an empire, partly real and partly fantasy, that helps them live through the confusion of adolescence.

The gang member is not, from his point of view, attacking anyone when he fights with a gang. He is defending himself or getting even with the "white devil." A young Negro mixed up in a brutal gang killing describes his uncontrollable need to go along this way: "I started thinking about it inside; then I have my mind made up I'm not going to be in no gang. Then I go on inside. Something comes up, then here comes all my friends coming to me. Like I said before, I'm intelligent and so forth. They be coming to me—then they talk to me about what they gonna do. Like, 'Man we'll go out here and kill this guy.' I say, 'Yeah.' They kept on talking and talking. I said, 'Man, I just gotta go with you.' Myself, I don't want to go, but when they start talking about what they gonna do, I say, 'So, he isn't gonna take over my rep. I ain't gonna let him be known more than me.' And I go ahead just for selfishness."

No one is going to take away his hard-won status in the only situation in which he feels capable of success. He will kill if need be to maintain his position of self-styled integrity in the gang.

For the Negro youngster growing up in places like Watts or Harlem, the schools, community centers, even the modern Job Corps are foreign lands with values and expectations beyond him. He doesn't understand their demands (scheduled activities, forms, dues) or have the skills to join in their activities. The demands for performance and responsibility in the violent gang, however, are readily adapted to his personal needs. Usually, the criteria for membership are vague. In many gangs, a youth can say he belongs one day and quit the next without necessarily telling any other gang member. Some boys say that the gang is organized for protection and that one role of a gang member is to fight. How, when, with whom and for what reason he is to fight have in the past been unclear. However, the civil rights fight has given clear focus to the Negro gang boys' feelings. The gang provides a vehicle for consolidating hurt feelings. Among the "sanctioned" opportunities the gang provides a youth in his confused search for "success" are robbing and assault. Other ways to Nirvana include alcohol, drug addiction and thrill-seeking kicks based on assault and violence. If only in caricature, he can become a "success" and at the same time strike back at society.

"Kicks" have a very special meaning here. In extreme, the main purpose of life for the "cat" is to experience the "kick." A "kick" seems to be any act tabooed by "squares" that exaggerates and intensifies the present moment of experience. "Kicks" provide a temporary relief from boredom. Senseless violence or drugs can produce this change of feeling. As one gang boy expressed it: "If I didn't get my 'kicks' I'd just as soon be dead."

In the violent gang, he can become a gang president, or war lord, control vast domains and generally act out a powerful even though fantasized success image. The boys can mutually expand the degree of their shared and highly valued success by reinforcing each other's fantasies of power.

The unwritten contractual agreement is, "Don't call my bluff and I won't call yours"; "I'll support your big man gang image if you'll support mine." This lends prestige to all involved in the "charade." Aside from real addiction common among Negro youths, the violent gang can serve as a social narcotic. No special ability is required to commit violence—not even a plan—and the guilt connected with it is minimized by the gang code of approval—especially if the violence fulfills the gang's idealized standards of a swift, sudden and senseless outbreak. ("A knife or a gun makes you 10 feet high.")

But a homicide or assault in the gang picture frame with a "I got Whitey" thrown in is much more valid than the outburst of a psychotic mind. It provides a cloak of self-immunity. And although these emotionally disturbed youths may only be a handful in a rioting mob that has other motives, they are both sparks and generators.

Some Negro youths who committed a brutal gang homicide several years ago expressed themselves in the following words:

"I didn't want to be like . . . you know, different from the other guys. Like they hit him, I hit him. In other words, I didn't want to show myself as a punk."

"It makes you feel like a big shot. You know, some guys think they're big shots and all that. They think, you know, they got the power to do everything they feel like doing. They say, like 'I wanna stab a guy.' And then the other guy says, 'Oh, I wouldn't dare do that.' You know, he thinks I'm acting like a big shot. That's the way he feels. He probably thinks in his mind, 'Oh, he probably won't do that.' Then, when we go to a fight, you know, he finds out what I do."

"I didn't have a knife, if I would of get a knife, I would have stabbed him. That would have gave me more of a buildup. People would have respected me for what I've done and things like that. They would say, 'There goes a cold killer.'"

THE ONES YOU'RE AGAINST

Although there is some evidence that the violent gang pattern is disapproved on the surface by the members' parents, it may be encouraged by them on a covert level. There are many cases of minority group parents, and this was seen in the Watts riots, consciously and unconsciously provoking their children to "get the bastards."

Racial prejudice, however, is not always clear-cut in the gang world. This is partially shown by a white gang boy who came to see me when I was working with gangs in New York City back in 1955. He entered my office very excited and told me how on the previous evening a very dark-complexioned ("He was Negro") man in his twenties had approached him and tried to draft him into a gang. The Negro attempting to draft the white youth said (in a Spanish accent): "We want everyone around here to join our gang so we can burn [kill] all the niggers."

The complexity of discrimination in the gang is evidenced here. The drafter, who was both Negro and Puerto Rican (depending on his self—or other definition), was trying to disassociate himself from any Negro background by becoming a Puerto Rican who hated Negroes. Gang activity was his special escape from the discriminatory "box" in which society had placed him.

In another case it was not a matter of skin color, but retaliation against the unfair majority group. As told by Professor James Coleman in his book on *Contemporary Social Problems:* "A young mathematician from England was recently at the University of Chicago for a short period. When he was walking across the Midway, he was accosted by several Negro boys who demanded his wallet. He objected, one of them produced a knife, and they led him over toward bushes beside the walk. The ensuing conversation went something like this, according to his later account: One boy said, 'Come on, now, give us your wallet, or we'll have to get tough with you,' He replied, 'Look here, I don't want to give up my wallet to you. Besides, I've just arrived here from England, and I don't think this is the way to treat someone who's a visitor here.' The boys looked at one another, and then one said, 'Oh. We thought you were one of those white guys,' and they quickly went away.

"To these Negro boys, 'white guys' had nothing to do with skin color per se, for the English mathematician was white. 'White guys' were their fellow community members, the whites from whom they felt alienated because there had been no processes to create common identity between them, only those creating hostility. The Englishman was not a 'white guy' against whom a reserve force of hostility had been built up."

Recognized Negro leaders have had little meaningful communication with or control over the violent minority. An exhaustive FBI report on the summer riots of 1964 in nine cities concluded that: "In most of the communities, respected Negro and other civic leaders, clergymen and public officials made every effort to halt the riots. Many of them went to the scene of the riot at considerable personal risk, others made strong statements which were published in the press or went on television and radio, urging the restoration of order without apparent effect.

"In almost all cases only massive and vigorous police action or the arrival of state police or the national guard finally brought about a termination of the riots and the restoration of law and order."

The Watts experience revealed something quite special: "Whitey's cops" were vulnerable. They had to call out the Army, in direct contradiction to Los Angeles Police Chief Parker's incendiary comment: "We're on top and they're on bottom." The Negro gang youths I interviewed feel very much on top of the lawman.

And what has the official power structure of Los Angeles learned from the holocaust? There are pious pronouncements about the need for more jobs, welfare funds and rebuilding the community. All true. But have any of these programs ever come close to the hard-core gang youth who need attention? And even if they could, once the immediate guilt for the riot no longer grips the conscience of the White establishment, its leaders drift back to the same political battlegrounds and bureaucratic mazes that tie up both money and people who might be of help. The police look straight into the TV camera and ask. "Where are the complaints of police brutality?" They do this knowing full well that most victims of police indignities either feel they deserve to be insulted, are afraid to complain or don't really know how to get through the paperwork. The sheer physical structure of a police station or city hall represents an ominous threat to most Negroes.

THE IRRELEVANT COMMISSION

Another inept response is the "commission" investigation. There are about four such groups currently operating in Los Angeles. Most commission members are political appointees who have a limited comprehension of the deeply buried and complex social-psychological forces that produce riots. Not one of the four commissions has on it a sociologist or a psychologist. None of these "blue-ribbon" commissions has one member (even the usual token Negro appointee) who knows the neighborhood scene or has *the ability to communicate directly* with the core rioter—the gang youth turned into a defender and hero of the race struggle by his violence.

What is needed is honest, open and direct communication with the people who help to incite and may perpetuate the riot condition: Some kind of forum where the young gang man strangling on his status-violence-whitey-hatred-syndrome can tell the well-insulated investigators the truth. In reverse the politicians (and from the gang youth's view, the "poverty cats") have to come to terms directly with people they mistakenly categorize and treat as subservient clients.

Phony "window dressing" commissions and temporary political gestures that have appeared in the wake of the Watts riots keep misunderstanding on the boil. The Negro community clearly sees these sideshows in their true light and becomes more outraged. The main answer seems to lie in some greater knowledge and understanding of the Negro gang youth, and the foot-on-his-neck problem that he encounters. If these forces of knowledge and action are not put in motion soon, we will be hit by conflagrations that won't be acted out simply in the Negro community.

CHALLENGING OUR YOUTH

*The National Commission on The Causes
and Prevention of Violence*

One key to much of the violence in our society lies with the young. Our youth account for an ever-increasing percentage of crime—greater than their increasing percentage of population. Arrest rates for violent urban crime are two to three times higher among youth aged 15 to 24 than among older groups in the urban population. The cutting edge of protest, and the violence which has sometimes accompanied it, has been honed largely by the young in the streets and on the campuses. In cities experiencing ghetto riots more than half of the persons arrested were teenagers and young adults. Most of the people involved in the violence during the Chicago Convention demonstrations in August of 1968 were under 25 years of age.

Violence by the young, as by persons of all ages, has multiple causes, involving many elements of personality and social environment. Some young people, even those raised in affluence, may rob for the thrill involved, others for what they hope will be material gain. A few maladjusted individuals may engage in wholesale killing; others may commit murder in a particular moment of rage or calculated coolness. Some may engage in violent forms of protest as a deliberate tactic; others may do so out of excitement and response to mob psychology.

Many of the young people in the nation today, however, are highly motivated by the ideals of justice, equality, candor, peace—fundamental values which their intellectual and spiritual heritage has taught them to honor. The youth of today have not been called on by their elders to defend these values by service in causes which young and old alike believe to be urgent and important, such as the war against the Axis powers or the struggle to end the depression of the thirties. Instead, they face the prospect of having to fight in a war most of them believe is unjustified, or futile, or both.

Moreover, they speak eloquently and passionately of the gap between the ideals we preach and the many social injustices remaining to be corrected. They see a nation which has the capacity to provide food, shelter, and education for all, but has not devised the procedures, opportunities, or social institutions that bring about this result. They see a society built on the principle of human equality that has not assured equal opportunity in life. With the fresh energy and

The National Commission on The Causes and Prevention of Violence, **COMMISSION STATEMENT ON CHALLENGING OUR YOUTH** *(Washington, D.C.: U.S. Government Printing Office, November 26, 1969).*

idealism of the young, they are impatient with the progress that has been made and are eager to attack these and other key problems. A combination of high ideals, tremendous energy, impatience at the rate of progress, and lack of constructive means for effecting change has led some of today's youth into disruptive and at times violent tactics for translating ideals into reality.

At the same time, our urban slums abound with youths who have few opportunities to perform constructive roles of any kind. They often receive little help from social institutions, or from their equally disadvantaged parents. Too often, in fact, they have no father in the home to provide a male model for acceptable conduct. They are the last to be employed, and the first to suffer social injustices. Recognizing no stake in the values of an orderly society, they often turn to crime, either individually or in gangs. The highest crime rate in the nation is among these young people.

The nation cannot afford to ignore lawlessness, or fail to enforce the law swiftly and surely for the protection of the many against the depredations of the few. We cannot accept violent attacks upon some of our most valuable institutions, or upon the lives of our citizens, simply because some among the attackers may be either idealistically motivated or greatly disadvantaged.

It is no less permissible for our nation to ignore the legitimate needs and desires of the young. Law enforcement must go hand in hand with timely and constructive remedial action. In a position paper issued earlier this year, this Commission stated its view that students should be given a useful role in shaping the future of the university, as well as responsibility of working directly with faculty members and administrators to develop standards for acceptable student conduct and responses of the institution in the face of deviations from these standards. Whether in the inner city, in a suburb or on a college campus, today's youth must be given a greater role in determining their own destiny and in shaping the future course of the society in which they live.

I.

Despite their increasing share of the highly educated population—indeed 18-year-olds are now better educated than were 21-year-olds when our nation was born—today's youth remain almost entirely disenfranchised. In 1950, two and a quarter million young men and women were attending college, as compared to the more than seven million today. In the same time span we have seen a decline in farmers and agricultural workers from eight million to less than four million. Yet, the latter exercise considerable political influence, while the growing college population remains excluded from participation in the electoral process. Political realities have changed while our laws and institutions lag behind.

Today only two of our states (Georgia and Kentucky) permit eighteen-year-olds to vote, and two others permit voting before the age of 21. Yet, in virtually every other respect, we expect that eighteen-year-olds behave and assume responsibility as adults. At that age, some are in college, and many are married with families and, along with others, are working taxpayers. In most states, eighteen-year-olds are treated as adults by the criminal law. We demand the ultimate service, the highest sacrifice, when we require them to perform military service. Many young men have become battle-tried veterans and some have died on the battlefield before they could vote. Their way of life—and, for some, even the duration of life itself—is dictated by laws made and enforced by men they do not elect. This is fundamentally unjust. Accordingly—

We recommend that the Constitution of the United States be amended to lower the voting age for all state and federal elections to eighteen.

Presidents Eisenhower, Kennedy, Johnson and Nixon and many elected representatives of both parties have expressed support for such an amendment. In the first session of the 91st Congress, 48 joint resolutions calling for the eighteen-year-old vote were introduced. And over the years, a number of states have raised the issue in popular referenda, but the results have been disappointing.[1]

Today's youth are capable of exercising the right to vote. Statistically they constitute the most highly educated group in our society. More finish high school than ever before and more of them go on to higher education. The mass media—television, news and interpretative magazines, and an unprecedented number of books on national and world affairs—have given today's youth knowledge and perspective and made them sensitive to political issues. We have seen the dedication and conviction they brought to the civil rights movement, and the skill and enthusiasm they have infused into the political process, even though they lack the vote.

The anachronistic voting age-limitation tends to alienate them from systematic political processes and to drive them into a search for alternative, sometimes violent, means to express their frustrations over the gap between the nation's ideals and actions. Lowering the voting age will not eliminate protest by the young. But it will provide them with a direct, constructive, and democratic channel for making their views felt and for giving them a responsible stake in the future of the nation.

A significant focal point of dissent by the young has been the issue of draft reform. To many, the draft symbolizes the inflexibility of our institutions and all that is wrong with the government's treatment of the young. Further, the inequities of the system have been set in sharp relief by the reality of the on-going war that many youth believe to be immoral and futile. The "oldest-first" order of draft calls produces a period of prolonged uncertainty for young men that profoundly affects their education, career and marriage decisions—a condition which is made more unacceptable by the lack of uniform deferment and exemption standards and by the wide variation in the exercise of discretion by local boards. Draft reform will not take the sting out of student anti-war protest or other manifestations of student discontent, but it could go far to reduce the tensions and frustrations that now lead some young men to seek

---

[1] In referenda on November 4, 1969, voters in Ohio and New Jersey defeated amendments lowering the voting age to nineteen and eighteen, respectively. The unofficial Ohio vote was close: 51 percent against and 49 percent for. In New Jersey, unofficial results show the amendment defeated by a 3 to 2 margin.

Voting participation by 21 to 24-year-olds generally falls below the national average. Of the total population eligible to vote, 67.8 percent did so in the 1968 national elections, as compared to only 51.2 percent of 21 to 24 year-olds.

refuge abroad and others to destroy Selective Service records, burn draft cards, or disrupt induction centers.

A random lottery system which would subject all to equal treatment at age nineteen, would take the youngest rather than the oldest first, and would reduce the period of prime draft vulnerability from the present seven years to one year, appears to be the fairest and most promising alternative to the existing draft system. Undergraduate deferments would be continued, but with the understanding that the year of maximum vulnerability would come whenever the deferment expired. It would be far less disruptive in the lives of young men while fully consistent with national security needs. The President has recommended such a proposal to the Congress. We are pleased to note that the Congress has approved the random lottery feature.

We also strongly endorse the balance of President Nixon's proposal for reform of the draft system, which are similar to that recommended in 1967 by the Marshall Commission and the Clark Panel.[2] To the extent these proposals require further legislation, we urge the Congress to enact it.

Assuming the enactment of random selection system, however, the area of discretion for local draft boards is enormous and is likely to remain so.

We, therefore, urge that renewed attention be given to the recommendations of the Marshall Commission for building a greater measure of due process into the exercise of draft board discretion.

Youth should also be given a role on local draft boards.

We, therefore, recommend that in exercising his power to appoint the members of local draft boards, the President name at least one person under 30 years of age to each local board.[3]

II.

At present, the Selective Service System calls only about a third of the eligible young men for the draft each year. Reform of the system will not alter this, but by taking the youngest first and by reducing the period of uncertainty from seven years to one, it will free many young men to make firm decisions about their futures. The federal government should do much more to provide these young men, as well as other young men and women in all walks of life, with the opportunities for service to their communities and the nation. As the Peace Corps and VISTA experiences bear out, many young people are eager to

[2] *In Pursuit of Equity: Who Serves When Not all Serve?* Report of the National Advisory Commission on Selective Service (Washington, D.C.: Government Printing Office, 1967); U.S., Congress, Senate, *Report of the Civilian Advisory Panel on Military Manpower Procurement,* H. Doc. 374, 90th Cong., 2d Sess., 1968. Our recommendations, of course, refer only to the present draft system and are intended to apply only so long as it continues. The question of whether the draft should be replaced for the long term by a form of volunteer service in the armed forces is not under consideration by another Presidential commission.

[3] As suggested by Joseph A. Califano, Jr., in his book *The Student Revolution,* W. W. Norton & Co., Inc., New York, 1970. The Marshall Commission found that the average aged local board members was 58. One fifth of all the nearly 17,000 board members were over 70. While twelve were over 90, only one was under 30.

assist the less fortunate to achieve social justice and willing to devote a part of their lives to tasks for which the major reward is the satisfaction of helping others.

We do not suggest that voluntary service of this kind should be an alternative to military service. Rather, we suggest that public service opportunities be made available, regardless of military service, to young men and young women, high school and college graduates, inner city, suburban, and rural youth—as justified by the nation's needs.

We are convinced that youth will grasp meaningful opportunities for attacking constructively the problems and injustices that, too often, now drive them to attacks aimed at the destruction of useful institutions, rather than at their reform. But we recognize their skepticism of government-sponsored programs and their increasing unwillingness to become involved in social action programs in which they have no voice. Consequently, we believe that a new and flexible approach to youth service opportunities is required, one that is tailored to individual talents and desires.

We urge the President to seek legislation to expand the opportunities for youth to engage in both full-time and part-time public service, by providing federal financial support to young people who wish to engage in voluntary, non-military service to their communities and to the nation.

We do not suggest the creation of another federally-administered program, or set of programs, comparable to the Peace Corps or VISTA. Instead we suggest that a large number of full- and part-time public service options be opened to youth—opportunities which the youths themselves can be expected to seek out and to improve upon, and which can be filled and administered at the local level if federal financial support is made available. We have in mind such possibilities as teaching and reading assistants, tutors and counselors in the elementary and secondary schools; hospital orderlies and nurses' aides; personnel for neighborhood service and recreation centers; auxiliary aides to local law enforcement and social service agencies; and many others.

The service opportunities would be approved by a central federal agency. The authorizing statute should set general standards of agency approval, eligibility, and levels of compensation. The choice of the particular public service opportunity from the large approved list of public and private institutions and groups should be left to the volunteers, and the initiative, direction and control of the activities would remain entirely with the approved local entity.[4]

The program might be launched to recruit 100,000 young people each year for four or five years, as experience was accumulated. The eventual goal might be as high as 1,000,000 active youth volunteers in service at any given

[4] One considerable virtue of the approach to youth service suggested here is that it involves a "market strategy" rather than a "monopoly service" strategy: the multitude of public and private agencies would have to compete for the services of the federally-supported youth workers by offering them meaningful, satisfying opportunities for achievement of desired goals; less successful, unrewarding programs would fail to attract volunteers and hence would not waste the public funds being committed to youth service. Cf. the discussion of the importance of market-type incentives for success in public programs in Moynihan, "Toward a National Urban Policy," The Public Interest (No. 17, fall 1969).

time, depending upon experience and developing national needs. As is now true for Peace Corps and similar existing programs, the compensation to be paid should be set at a student subsistence level and should not be financially competitive with other employment opportunities. As a special inducement, however, we recommend that completion of two years of full-time public service entitle the participant to educational assistance comparable to that available to veterans under the GI Bill of Rights, with lesser amounts of assistance for service periods between six months and two years.[5]

Voluntary public service could contribute to reduction of the large backlog of unmet social needs, and thus could be an important step toward a more human reordering of national priorities. And youth service could signify to the young that our nation is committed to the achievement of social justice, as well as to military security.

III.

Young people in the inner city slums often grow up in a stultifying physical environment and in unstable or broken families. They face poverty and racial discrimination. They are trained in overcrowded and inadequate schools, and the failure of the educational process, added to residual racial prejudice, results in thwarted job opportunity. Forced by lack of money and racial exclusion to remain in the most deteriorated part of the city, the slum ghetto youth's sense of alienation and powerlessness is confirmed and reinforced by the lack of recreational, medical and social services in the community.

Even should his parents wish to leave the slum ghetto, non-ghetto neighborhoods that they can afford to move into are those that tend to be most resistant to them. The Fair Housing Act and the Supreme Court's 1968 decision in *Jones* v. *Alfred H. Mayer Co.* make it illegal to discriminate in housing sales or rentals, but community resistance and the slow process of case-by-case enforcement combine to retard the elimination of housing discrimination in fact. Thus, many black parents who try to inculcate values supporting lawful behavior must stay in communities where their children are subjected to the destructive influences of slum life.

Only by a massive effort to improve life in our inner cities and to eliminate private barriers to the dispersal of racial groups beyond the inner city can we begin to root out the basic causes of crime and violence in these concentrated areas. As part of this large effort, we urgently need programs that can effectively intervene at the critical juncture in a slum ghetto youth's life when he is torn between the forces that may lead him into crime and those which may lead him into socially constructive pursuits.[6]

Reaching the alienated slum youth is not easy. To expect youth programs to succeed where parents and schools already have failed is to hope for a great deal. Yet recent experience gives reason for optimisim.

---

[5] Depending on the availability of funds, educational assistance could be limited on the basis of demonstrated need.

[6] Despite these criminogenic forces, studies show that a large number of ghetto youth never have a police arrest and only a small percentage become repeated offenders.

Several recently organized youth programs have reached directly into the street and gang culture to draw upon indigenous talent and leadership. In the past, many youth programs, devised and imposed by adults, were alien to the life-styles and problems of the youths they were designed to help. They failed. Youth involvement in the planning and operation of programs characterized several new approaches that commanded the allegiance of the young. These innovative and strikingly successful youth programs may show the way to wider effort.

In Philadelphia, what began in 1966 as a film-making project for the Twelfth and Oxford Street gang—with youths writing, acting, and filming a story depicting the life and death of a gang leader—has bloomed into a full-fledged corporation which is now involved in a wide range of community-oriented projects. Youths who were formerly "warlords," "ministers of defense," and "guardians of weapons" are now the directors of a successful non-profit corporation. Initial financial successes in film-making attracted further assistance from private and governmental sources. Today the Twelfth and Oxford Street Film Corporation owns three properties in the neighborhood (one of which has been renovated for rental to five low-income families in the community), several of its members are receiving training in housing rehabilitation from the Philadelphia Housing Corporation and in marketing and survey from Temple University's School of Business, and plans are now being developed for opening the Twelfth and Oxford Restaurant and a Teen Age Record Company, both of which will provide additional opportunities for on-the-job training and utilization of youth's talents and skills.

Throughout the program's three-year development, motivation has remained high, and delinquency rates among the Twelfth and Oxford group have declined. Due to the skill of adult leadership, youths are given genuine responsibility and a sense of fulfillment. Its success, thus far, is a striking demonstration that the negative influences of the ghetto can be broken; that when urban youths are given a fair opportunity to run their own affairs, to develop their potentials in meaningful pursuits, they can become important agents of community change.

The same ingredients of success are evident in another youth program, this one in Washington D.C., Pride, Inc., which originally began as a modest summer work program for 1,000 inner city youth to clean up cluttered streets and exterminate rats, has now become a year-round operation with economic and manpower development as its central theme. Pride directors initially hired 21 street-corner leaders as recruiters. Within three days every job was filled and, since then, the organization has reached some of the city's most deprived and alienated youth. It operates a landscaping and gardening division which employs 30 young men and a gasoline station at which 15 youths are being trained, as well as a program for some 700 participants who work in cooperation with the D.C. Health and Sanitation Departments. Responsibility for supervision and administration of the clean-up programs in various parts of the city is delegated according to ability, and beginners work with the encouragement of knowing that there are possibilities for promotion.

Because Pride, Inc. is recruiting the most difficult of the hard-core unemployed, the organization has had to develop the capacity to deal with young men who are living in a state of crisis and to offer rudimentary supportive services in continuing education, orientation, recreation, health and legal services. On the whole, the results of Pride's efforts to date are good. Evaluations conducted on behalf of the Department of Labor, a major financial supporter of the program, showed that while 67 percent of Pride members had been arrested in the six months prior to joining the program only 24 percent were arrested during a like period after joining.

Pride, Inc. and the Twelfth and Oxford Street program.are by no means unique. Across the country are other youth programs suited to the life-styles of those involved. Program ingredients vary; the key elements to success are the broadened perspective and increased confidence that come with the feeling of responsible participation by the young people.

A number of programs are carried on by residential centers for rehabilitation and treatment of wayward and delinquent youth. One long-established and remarkably successful program of youth rehabilitation, involving young men of high school age, is Boys Republic in Southern California. Many teenage boys, usually from broken families and in difficulty with the law, are offered by the courts the option of attending Boys Republic voluntarily (there are no guards) or being assigned to one of the State's youth rehabilitation institutions. Boys Republic receives ten times as many court-controlled applications for admission as it can accept, for its facilities and funds are limited. The youths who are accepted are intimately involved in all aspects of the operational program, including making of decisions affecting their lives, work and education. A substantial portion of the funds needed to maintain the institution is earned by the boys themselves who operate a large farm and manufacture and sell the famous "Della Robbia" Christmas wreaths. The amazing long-time record of this effort in rehabilitation is that ninety percent of the young men who attend the institution and voluntarily remain until they complete the rehabilitation program never again have trouble with the police.

Examples of some comparable non-governmental residential centers for youth rehabilitation are the Berkshire Farm for Boys, Children's Village, and Lincoln Hall in New York State. Of the many state-administered institutions, the Kansas Boys' Industrial School is exemplary.

Junior Achievement, 4-H Clubs, Future Farmers of America, the Boy Scouts, Girl Scouts, YMCA and YWCA, the Catholic Youth Organization, Boys Club, Police Athletic League, Chicago Area Project, and many other youth programs, some church-sponsored, are so well known as to require no comment by this Commission, save perhaps the reminder that all of these stress maximum responsibility by the young people themselves in deciding what is to be done, what policy will govern their actions, how the projects are to be conducted, what will be done with earned funds, if any, and all related questions and policies. Even so, existing programs reach only a fraction of our youth, ghetto youth least of all. This fact emphasizes the importance of the new Philadelphia and Washington, D. C. experimental projects which we have briefly described.

Experience has shown that as youths become involved in meaningful activities such as film-making, housing rehabilitation, landscaping, running a gas station, operating a farm, or making Christmas wreaths, their needs for further education and business skills become apparent to them. All the aspects of running a business or community project—accounting, advertising, financing, marketing, manufacturing, selling, law—can stimulate youths to seek training and advice. This is a solid foundation upon which to develop relevant education or job-training programs, to persuade drop-outs to complete high school, and even to guide the ablest and most highly motivated on to college.

Because some youth programs deal with the most deprived and alienated, special supportive services in drug rehabilitation, legal aid, and health care are sometimes essential. Although youth programs can go far to counteract the negative influences of the street culture, drug abuse, delinquency, and illness remain ever-present possibilities. To some extent existing community services can be reoriented to meet the special needs of youth. But it may prove necessary to establish supportive services linked directly to the overall program effort. With respect to health care, group health insurance might be made part of any youth program once underway.

We urge the President, the Congress, and the Federal agencies that normally provide funding for youth programs—notably the Office of Economic Opportunity, the Department of Labor, and the Department of Health, Education, and Welfare—to take the risks involved in support of additional innovative programs of opportunity for innercity youth.

Imagination and flexibility are essential qualities which may be enhanced by greater involvement of young people in the operations of the granting agency.

IV.

Our main concern in this statement is to stress the importance of challenging the young people of the nation to become full partners in the enterprise of building a better society. But we must also add a word on one increasingly acute aspect of the present "generation gap"—the problem of drugs, particularly marijuana.

The development of drug subcultures among many of today's youth is particularly troubling to those who are older. Increased education about the physical and psychological hazards of the use of addictive drugs, LSD, the amphetamines and other dangerous substances is essential if the health of young people and their children is to be properly safeguarded. In addition, the older generation must answer, in good faith and on the basis of better knowledge, the question raised by many young people as to whether present proscriptions on marijuana use go too far.

The startling recent increase in marijuana use by many young people has intensified the conflict between generations and posed enormous problems in the enforcement of drug laws. Possession and/or use of marijuana is treated severely by the law. In most states such possession or use is a felony, whereas the use or possession of the more dangerous LSD is only a misdemeanor.[7] This lack

[7] A felony is a serious crime usually punishable by imprisonment for an extended period (under federal law for a year or more); a misdemeanor is a lesser offense punishable by a fine or imprisonment of less than a year. In many states, a felony conviction results in a loss of voting rights, jury service, and the right to enter various professional occupations; a misdemeanor conviction does not.

of elementary logic and justice has become a principal source of frustration and alienation contributing markedly to youth's often bitter dissatisfaction with today's society. We believe that action must be taken to put the whole situation into rational perspective.

Scientific knowledge about marijuana remains sparse, but some of its pharmacological properties have been established: marijuana is not a narcotic or an opiate and is not addicting.[8] There is as yet no evidence as to the relationship it bears to the use of harder drugs.[9]

We recommend that the National Institutes of Health, working with selected universities, greatly expand research on the physical and psychological effects of marijuana use.[10]

The Congress should enact laws and appropriate adequate funds for this purpose. Much remains to be learned about the drug's psychological effects, particularly with respect to the expectation and personality types of users and the total emotional mood of the environment and the persons in it. Many experienced users have had at least one "bad trip" and some cases have been reported of extremely traumatic reactions to marijuana. It may be that marijuana use can be damaging to individuals with a history of mental instability or other personality disorders. Similarly, little is known about its possible psychological effects, including psychological dependency, on adolescents who are in the process of learning to cope with the demands of adult life. And we most assuredly need to know if marijuana users have a predisposition to use harder drugs.

Despite all existing evidence to the contrary, state and federal laws alike treat marijuana as a narcotic, and penalties for its sale and use in some states are extreme. In one state, the penalty is two years to life imprisonment for a first offense of possession. In at least two others, the penalty for an adult convicted of selling marijuana to a minor is death. According to the latest available Justice Department figures, the average length of sentence imposed for violation of state laws was 47.7 months. In 1967 the federal government made 706 arrests for marijuana offenses, as compared to the State of California alone which made 37,513 arrests, 10,907 of them juveniles under eighteen.

Erroneously classifying marijuana as a narcotic, this patchwork of federal and state laws, inconsistent with each other and often unenforceable on their merits, has led to an essentially irrational situation. Respect for the law can hardly be inculcated under these circumstances. Since many of our youths believe marijuana to be relatively harmless and, yet, are faced with legal sanctions, they are led into a practice of law evasion which contributes to general disrespect for the law. Furthermore, enforcement of laws generally deemed harsh and unjust seem nonetheless to encourage police practices—*e.g.*, raids without prob-

---

[8] Addiction is a physiological and psychological dependence on a drug, with definite symptoms occurring when the drug is withdrawn.

[9] In Testimony on October 14, 1969 before the House of Representatives Select Committee on Crime, Dr. Robert O. Egeberg, Assistant Secretary of Health, Education and Welfare for Health and Scientific Affairs, stated that "there is no scientific evidence to demonstrate that the use of marijuana *in itself* predisposes an individual to progress to 'hard' drugs."

[10] A similar provision is contained in H.R. 10019 by Rep. Edward Koch, N.Y.

able cause, entrapment—which infringe on personal liberties and safeguards. The situation is reminiscent of the problems encountered in enforcement of Prohibition during the 1920's. The present harsh penalties for possession and use of marijuana are a classic example of what legal scholars call "overcriminalization"—treating as a serious crime private personal conduct that a substantial segment of the community does not regard as a major offense; prosecutors, judges and juries tend to moderate the severity of the statutory sanctions, and the resulting hypocrisy of all concerned diminishes respect for the law.

In view of the urgency of the marijuana problem, we believe that legislative reform of the existing marijuana penalty structure should not wait several years until further research is completed.

We recommend that federal and state laws make use and incidental possession of marijuana no more than a misdemeanor until more definitive information about marijuana is at hand and the Congress and State Legislatures have had an opportunity to revise the permanent laws in light of this information. (Pending further study, we do not recommend a similar reduction in the penalty for those who traffic in marijuana for profit.)

Instead of the existing inequitable criminal penalties (including imprisonment) for mere possession and use of the drug, interim legislation might well provide only for civil penalties such as the confiscation of the drug and fines. If the interim legislation does provide for prison sentences, it should at least grant wide discretion to the trial judge to suspend sentence or release on probation.

We were heartened by the recommendation recently submitted to the Congress by several leading officials of the Executive Branch of the government—recommendations which seek immediate change in the provisions of federal law affecting drug use. Among other things, these officials indicated that use and incidental possession of marijuana should be declared to be no more than a misdemeanor.

The above recommendations should not, of course, be taken as suggesting either that we approve the use of marijuana, or that we favor any relaxation of society's efforts to discourage the use of the clearly dangerous drugs.

Expert testimony offered to this Commission indicates that the so-called hard drugs, such as heroin, do not in themselves make users prone to commit other crimes, but that the daily use of such drugs involves exorbitant costs; hence users often undertake lives of burglary and armed robbery in order to obtain funds for the continued purchase of drugs. Further, drug importation and distribution, like certain forms of gambling, constitute part of the life-blood of organized crime—an empire of its own, ruthless, rich, pervasive, corrupting, and skillful at avoiding the reaches of the law.

We cannot usefully add to all that has been written by other Commissions, the Department of Justice, and many State authorities about the need for stopping the importation of the hard drugs, and for vigorously prosecuting the traffickers in those drugs. Nor can we add to the urgent recommendations that have been made by others to eliminate from our society the empires of organized crime.

But we do most emphatically declare that classifying marijuana users with the users of the hard drugs is scientifically wrong, a wrong recognized by the young, a wrong that makes them contemptuous of the drug laws and to some extent of all law. They wonder why the federal and State Governments do not insist upon more widespread research to establish facts and to change laws in harmony with the facts as developed.

V.

In this statement we have stressed the importance of genuinely involving young people in the political process as well as in planning and carrying on useful social projects. In our view, the lack of such alternatives has contributed to the spread of young lifestyles which depend on drugs or which stress hustling, vandalism, robbery, and even murder.

In stressing such remedies, we do not mean to suggest that until they are provided, violent behavior by young people should be tolerated or excused. Violent and unlawful conduct must be controlled by vigorous law enforcement at the same time that measures to eliminate the basic causes of violence are vigorously pursued.

We add a final statement on the apparently growing antagonism between young and old.[11]

In a sense, our immortality is our children. Youth represent the next step for our society, since they are the population which will join us in determining our directions and implementing our hopes. Yet we are aware that our youth are at times unstable, unpredictable and engaged in a major struggle to find their place in the world as they assert their adult capacities, physically and emotionally, politically and socially.

The older generation is faced with the challenge of making available to young people adequate opportunities to participate meaningfully in coping with society's problems, and thus facilitating individual emotional growth and maturity. All too often, the society—parents, school and university administrators, law enforcement personnel, community leaders—become identified in the eyes of youth with obstruction and repression, inflexibly protecting the status quo against the "onslaught" of youth.

There are many things each citizen can do to help resolve these problems. The challenge will not be met by new laws alone, or new programs directed to work with problem youth. Each citizen has a responsibility to participate— indeed, only as there is an increasing commitment on the part of all citizens toward understanding the problems of one another can we expect violence to diminish.

Understanding might more readily be achieved by observing the following guidelines:

It is important to acknowledge openly the existence of problems between the generations when they occur. Too often, people are so threatened by conflict in opinions that they refuse to acknowledge a contrary view, and suppress that challenging view.

It is imperative for all parties to listen carefully and respectfully to one

---

[11] This statement is largely the work of W. Walter Menninger, M.D.

another, with sincere consideration for differing opinions or ideas. Listening is not an easily practiced art.

Stated issues are often a red herring. At times, the conflicts cannot be resolved until underlying causal issues are identified and dealt with.

The resolution of any conflict will be profoundly affected by the expectations of the adversaries. If leaders are perceived by youth as unreasonable and are approached with that expectation, the leaders are themselves provoked into being unreasonable, and vice versa.

All must acknowledge the inevitability of change. The older generation can wear itself out trying to fight the tide or it can turn the energy of youth to advantage for the benefit of all.

Resolution of conflict depends on finding areas of agreement. Instead of emphasis on differences, which promotes polarization, it is necessary to identify points in common, such as the fact that people seek a voice in determining their destiny and dignity as human beings.

As a society founded on the principle that every individual has certain inalienable rights and privileges, it is important to keep the value of the individual high, in spite of the population explosion and the complications of modern society. Youth are entitled to full respect as persons. Youth in turn must accord respect to persons they identify as the "older generation."

The older generation has difficulty in dealing with problems of young people because of its awareness that it has not yet created the perfect world. We don't like to be challenged, especially by our juniors. If we are to cope effectively with youth, we must courageously acknowledge our mistakes and recognize that our offspring may surpass us. Indeed, if we have been successful in our child-rearing, they certainly should surpass us. We must take extra effort to understand their criticism of our ways, and be pleased that these suggestions are coming from our most important products, our youth who will prove our ultimate worth.

The younger generation has the difficulties of its impatience and its assumption that all people of a certain age are the same. With all its defects—and today's youth are not the first to criticize those defects—constitutional representative government is still the best form that man has devised. Youth should acknowledge that there are still opportunities for individuals to leave their mark and to prompt change in an orderly manner within our system. At the same time, young people must be aware of the psychological fact that their inner pressures may prompt them to refight childhood battles, artificially appointing well meaning people to play the same adversary role in which a child's parents are cast.

The first step for all of us is to look at ourselves, and to deal understandingly with the problems and conflicts we have with others. It is easier to blame others, and to see violence as being caused by others. But we must look inward as well as outward to the causes and prevention of violence.

3

THE BRUTALITY
OF URBAN POLITICS

As a science, urban politics is both imposing and messy. Elected mayors or appointed managers discover inevitably that running a city, a town, or a sprawling suburb is a hazardous enterprise, frequently requiring wisdom and foresight beyond the reach of ordinary men.

To begin with, the mechanical structure of urban government is burdensome, at times ruinous. Mayors and county executives do not share the impressive tradition reserved for presidents and governors. States are sanctified by the federalism of American constitutional government. Cities, counties and other minor jurisdictions owe their legal existence to state constitutions or statutes. The mayor of Philadelphia may be capable of performing certain tasks but only because the state has granted his city home rule. Even in New York, perhaps the world's most fascinating city, the mayor must operate within state requirements that frequently handicap or limit his ability to act.

Beyond legal restrictions, urban executives face an excess of jurisdictional problems. Assuming that a mayor or county executive can successfully control and direct the scores of agencies under his supervision, and assuming that he can secure the reasonable cooperation of other elected officials, his career can nevertheless be ruined by a recalcitrant metropolitan authority or an obstinate neighboring official over whom he has no real power. With a metropolitan authority, his power is invariably shared; with a neighboring official, it stems solely from gentle persuasion or hard bargaining where one item is sacrificed to secure assistance on another. A mayor, for example, who must negotiate with surrounding officials on water rights or garbage disposal facilities, may be reluctant to press publicly his efforts to persuade those officials to provide low income housing to alleviate the city's distressing housing shortage. A mayor who needs help from suburban delegates to secure additional state aid may squelch his desires for a commuter's tax on suburban residents, for fear of losing that support. Add to this the incredible array of program specialists spawned by federal programs who, with the lure of "matching grants," can quite frequently bypass or discomfort the mayor.

Unquestionably, the chief executives of urban communities are at the cutting edge of the democratic process. They are on the critical level of the traditional "local-state-federal" layers of governmental authority. They are at the spear's point of contemporary demands of community involvement and community control. Local governments wrestle daily with demands of local poverty boards or pleas of elected model cities representatives. Local governments must survive the social trauma frequently caused by obstinate citizens who dominate these groups, and must escape the political embarrassment stirred by a new breed of citizen who is determined to cut through bureaucracy and make city hall take notice. Local governments must bear the belligerent pressure of hyperactive legions of local vigilantes who demand more police and less sex education, who resist integration and think that "bussing" is a communist plot.

Urban governments have also become the centers of burgeoning metropolitan and regional bodies designed to coordinate overlapping activities of neighboring communities. Vast bodies have emerged to deal with rivers and parks, snow removal and police protection, toll facilities and jet ports, long range planning and short range zoning, building codes and garbage disposal, mass transit systems and water resources. These commissions, an increasing part of the urban scene, have the advantage of sharing leadership and coordinating joint enterprises. They have the disadvantage of diffusing power, confusing authority, creating additional levels of bureaucracy that further remove local government from citizens who want more, and more direct, communication with the public officials who shape their environment.

Mastering the structure of urban government is a difficult task to which is added the burden of complicated substantive issues. Few if any urban issues are clear cut. Securing additional tax revenues for needed services is far from simple. The ramifications of increasing property taxes versus creating new tax sources or banking on additional state or federal revenues are varied and frequently beyond the understanding of most citizens. The issues between races and within social classes are complex and bitter. One has only to listen to the rhetoric of local elections to be aware of the antagonisms that split factions. The location of a new school, standards to diminish air pollution, enforcement of water pollution regulations or housing codes lead to the development of pressure groups and power alignments difficult for public officials to withstand.

In New York, prominent authors and celebrities have frequently organized to fight destructive highways or mediocre renewal. In Washington, D.C. students have stood in the path of bulldozers to stall off the construction of another bridge across the Potomac. In Florida, massive public pressure prevented a jet port in the Everglades. Californians are constantly fighting to preserve remnants of their environment. It is not easy to determine who is right and who is wrong on these issues. But since the public seldom has the staying power of the constituted agencies, the burden of proof must be on the authorities, not the citizens.

And finally, as if the structure and the substance of urban government were not sufficiently complicated to make one marvel at the survival of local political institutions, there comes the raucous political process itself. The process frequently forces individuals to perform degrading, if not supercilious acts. An American election is a rather gruesome and reckless affair that seldom brings out the best in men or groups. The air is filled with charges and allegations; rational debate, heady dialogue, and reasoned solutions to complex issues are casualties of energies determined to create images and illusions. The process is always enervating, and at times humiliating. And although there is evidence that some men learn and mature from the experience, there is considerable proof that many are corrupted and others simply drained by it.

Obviously urban politics has undergone changes. For one thing, the old era of political bosses telling people what to do and handing them a few dollars to be sure that they did it—except for a few notably large-sized hamlets—has ended. In many places the bureaucrats have taken over. Successive civil service laws, increased status, and the advent of government employee unions have made the removal of inept or insensitive bureaucrats an impossibility. Urban communities have also experienced the arrival and the passing of reformers who inevitably discover that it is easier to talk than to act. Institutions have a way of warding off assault. The constant clamor from blacks and youth to bring down institutions is not an unreasonable clamor when one analyzes the implacable nature of institutions toward change. As a matter of fact, at least for those who have come up against the problem, it is often easier to simply abandon, let's say, an effective welfare bureau, than to improve it.

Recently some Mayors have even abandoned their jobs. These were bright and articulate men who suddenly found the burdens of governance intolerable. Rather than continue to face frustrations and confrontations, they bowed out gracefully. As Fred Powledge pointed out in an article entitled "The Flight From City Hall," these were frequently men who entered government with hopes and dreams; they were part of the 'new frontier,' with a determination to do something about urban life. Now the sixties have ended; politics and passions have taken their toll; these men are leaving the scene, and some of the bitterness is felt in the sting of their comments. Asked why he chose not to run again, for example, Detroit's Jerome Cavenaugh replied, "after a while you get punchy on a job like this. It's almost like a fighter who answers the bell. In the first few rounds you're coming out, right off that stool, and then by the tenth or twelfth round you're just dragging off that stool wishing the bell wouldn't ring."[1]

Both cities and suburbs are going through other transitions. Cities have had their bosses and their reformers. Now they will have blacks. Already Cleveland, Ohio and Gary, Indiana have elected black mayors. Already Newark and Washington, D. C. have black majorities. By 1985, it is estimated that the proportion of blacks to whites will rise from the present 21% to 35%. In key cities, the rise

---

[1] Fred Powledge, "The Flight From City Hall," *Harper's Magazine,* November, 1969.

will occur at a much faster rate. By 1975, New Orleans, Richmond, Baltimore, Jacksonville, Gary, and Cleveland will have black populations over 50%. By 1985 St. Louis, Detroit, Philadelphia, Oakland, and Chicago will join that list. The political ramifications are, of course, dramatic. Black power—probably in a more modest tone—will be more than a cry; in the city it will reflect the reality of the majority. How much change will occur with the passing of city power from whites to blacks is hard to predict. Cleveland, Gary, and Washington, D. C. have all experienced black leadership; but they are still burdened with critical needs and ineffective devices to meet those needs. Urban issues transcend the ability of men to resolve them because they happen to be one color or another, as in the past they transcended a man's particular ethnic status. In each cycle of history, however, the rise to power of individuals identified with the hopes and aspirations of the immediately dispossessed has kept a lid on revolution—not on violence or antagonism—but at least on revolution. Finding a home within the power structure for those who have felt left out is an acceptable way of trimming resentment and redirecting passions. That in itself may be the most important result of the increase of black participants in the urban decision-making process.

The suburbs which have had courthouse cronies and reformers will continue to have arch-conservatives, products of the backlash to black success in the city. This is inevitable—just as cities will develop larger black majorities, suburbs will develop larger and more conservative white majorities. In the past, suburban militancy has been expressed negatively in opposition to open housing, metropolitan agencies, urban renewal, zoning reform, school bussing, and other "race" related issues. Whether future white conservatism will drive suburban politicians to a more aggressive posture remains to be seen.

The fact is that the suburbs need to be "turned on" rather than "turned off." And the task of "radicalizing" suburbia or at least developing ways that bring the cities and the suburbs together could be one of the nation's most fascinating and absorbing activities. "I've come to see very clearly," Saul Alinsky said recently, "that this country is predominatingly middle-class economically. Almost four-fifths of our people are in that bracket, so that's where the power is. Hell, we would have to be blind not to see that this is where organization has to go."[2]

The brutality of urban politics has stimulated efforts to de-emphasize politics and allow urban officials to escape the pressures of public exposure. But the evidence is still inconclusive as to whether an urban environment can best be run by appointed experts with little link to the electorate or by elected officials with total obeisance to the electorate. Even those places that have attempted to combine the two—a county manager selected by an elected county council, for example—eventually change to something else. Cities still prefer partisan mayors. Although many have turned to nonpartisan elections, the process is basically the

[2] Saul Alinsky, "The Professional Radical, 1970," *Harper's Magazine,* January, 1970.

same, only political labels are diminished. For suburban counties the swing is toward elected county executives with authority and prestige similar to mayors. The commission form of government continues to be the favorite of less urbanized counties but even here, local municipalities usually elect mayors and councilmen.

Some contemporary urbanologists feel that running a city is beyond the capacity of any single man and are advocating that urban areas—particularly large cities—establish boards of directors. New York University Professor Leo J. Margolin, for example, asking if "one mayor is enough" suggested a "team" of mayors chosen by competitive civil service examinations each of whom would preside over a series of super agencies dealing with fourteen basic urban areas: administration, finance, personnel relations, community relations, air and water pollution and garbage disposal, education, intergovernmental relations, housing and rents, welfare, industry relations, nongovernmental labor relations, public safety, health and, finally, ceremonials, charm, fun and games (a job the professor estimates in New York City alone could keep a man going to 300 affairs a day). The chief executive officer would be selected by the fourteen board members from outside their own group. Not to insulate the process entirely from public opinion, Dr. Margolin suggested that the chairman of the board of mayors maintain some responsibility to the elected city council.[3]

How Americans, in an age of involvement, would accept such a proposal is difficult to imagine. One suspects that, as pendulums swing, reformers of the future will demand that board members "run" for their positions in order to establish closer public ties.

The fact is that issues change; public needs alter. Institutions that were once adequate must be reformed if only for the exercise. Today bosses are mute; bureaucrats are ensconced. Now the cry is to throw out the bureaucrats. That cry is heard through the increasing pressures for decentralization and community control, through the active involvement of local citizens and the intensive organizing of civic groups and neighborhood associations, through the readiness of people to take to the picket line in support of a public issue whether that issue is to provide kindergartens or to remove school boards. Local control is a plea to make government less remote and bureaucracy less insensitive. Whether those who carry the pickets realize it or not, total citizen involvement is a radical venture designed to shake up institutions and, if necessary, topple them. Although many consider the process skeptically and challenge its legitimacy, it is a vital part of the purging of passions important to the survival of any democracy that values human needs. After all, when things go wrong you simply can't fire all the bureaucrats in town—some are competent and others are relatives; so it becomes necessary to take away some of their autonomy and tear down some of their insulation.

[3] Leo J. Margolin, "Is One Mayor Enough Anymore," Christian Science Monitor, May 24, 1969.

This chapter of the anthology deals with the complicated issues of urban politics and power. Since much of the contemporary political fuss deals with what is happening in the city, the first portion of the chapter considers city hall—its grandeur and its weaknesses. Gus Tyler, the former labor leader, opens with a very fundamental question: "Can Anyone Run A City?" The reason most men can't, Tyler offers, is "density." "Where cities foresaw density and planned accordingly, the situation is bad but tolerable. Where exploding populations hit unready urban areas, they are in disaster. Where ethnic and political conflict add further disorder, the disease appears terminal."

The second article is by journalist and novelist, Norman Mailer, who examined the disease affecting New York and convinced Jimmy Breslin that the two of them should do something about it. "Sweet Sunday" was their plea; "Vote the Rascals In," they teased. They were trounced. What the electorate did to two great writers is a sin, perhaps unpardonable. But the experience was worth it and what Mailer says in this article, written before the campaign had ended, when in all campaigns there is that feeling of pride and euphoria, when victory is only weeks away, is worth attention. And what would they have done if they had won? ". . . never," Mailer says, ". . . never have a good time again. . . ."

But not so with America's super Mayor, Richard Daley of Chicago. One is convinced from what David Halberstam says in his article that, no matter what, Mayor Daley enjoys being mayor. He rules with toughness and with skill. He brooks no nonsense with rebels or reformers—ignoring them if the occasion warrants, making them full members of his entourage if it is called for. Mayor Daley, as Mr. Halberstam shows, believes deeply in the system. This is a vexing account of how that system has worked for one man and one city.

In the final article of the section, John Lindsay describes, from his own experience, the pain, the frustration, and the challenge, as mayor of one of the world's largest cities.

The second section of the chapter deals with a broader concept of the urban political scene—the concept of power. In any diverse state power is not entirely political. Charles Hamilton discusses the concept of "Black Power," its objectives and aims, offering a reasonable frame of reference for those citizens who hear it only as the anguish of angry militants. No doubt black power means to do some institution toppling; but Hamilton believes its force can be positive, constructive and progressive. "Black power," he says "is concerned with organizing the rage of black people and with putting new, hard questions and demands to white America." The responses white America makes to those questions will determine the ultimate path of black power.

Then there is the power of the community: the power of local citizens to determine their own future and govern their own events. Nathan Glazer's article deals with the complicated question of local control and decentralization, two concepts of power that have become essential ingredients of the urban process. Community control means local citizens controlling local affairs; decentralization means outside officials controlling local affairs, but doing it locally. "You can have decentralization," Glazer says, "without community control. You cannot have community control without some substantial measure of decentralization." In an era where programs have failed in their expectations because of inadequate forethought and insensitive administration, the plea for local power is important to understand.

There is a frequent tendency to dismiss black power moves, particularly the more militant ones, as unnecessary. Immigrants, the argument goes, faced similar conditions and were able ultimately to secure power through legitimate means. The Irish took over the precincts of Boston and elected mayors and governors. Italians did the same in Baltimore, the Poles in Chicago, and Jews in New York. All that may be true—the powerless can secure power through legitimate channels—at least if they are white. The black experience has been different, and power has not come readily or without brutality. The Kerner Commission Report, taken in large part from work done by Professor Herbert J. Gans, shows unmistakably that the immigrant and Negro experiences are difficult to compare, and that power comes less easily to some than to others.

Edward Banfield's article casts some light on the competing urban power structures that hinder and motivate government action. In a rather pessimistic thrust Banfield suggests that urban problems are beyond solution because their solution would be totally incompatible with contemporary political attitudes and institutional behavior. "However attractive they may otherwise be, all 'solutions' that are incompatible with the basic principles of our political system must be considered unavailable—that is, beyond the bounds of possibility." After listing a series of programs that should be considered if urban life is to progress in a fruitful way, Banfield remarks: "Perhaps the most palpable reason for the political infeasibility of most of the items on the list is that they would be instantly squashed by some interest group (or groups) if they were ever put forward."

1. THE RISE AND FALL OF CITY HALL

CAN ANYONE RUN A CITY?

Gus Tyler

Can anyone run a city? For scores of candidates who have run for municipal office across the nation this week, the reply obviously is a rhetorical yes. But if we are to judge by the experiences of many mayors whose terms have brought nothing but failure and despair, the answer must be no. "Our association has had a tremendous casualty list in the past year," noted Terry D. Schrunk, mayor of Portland, Oregon, and president of the U.S. Conference of Mayors. "When we went home from Chicago in 1968, we had designated thirty-nine mayors to sit in places of leadership. . . . Today, nearly half of them are either out of office or going out . . . most of them by their own decision not to run again." Since that statement, two of the best mayors in the country—Jerome P. Cavanagh of Detroit and Richard C. Lee of New Haven—have chosen not to run again.

Why do mayors want out? Because, says Mayor Joseph M. Barr of Pittsburgh, "the problems are almost insurmountable. Any mayor who's not frustrated is not thinking." Thomas G. Currigan, former mayor of Denver, having chucked it all in mid-term, says he hopes "to heaven the cities are not ungovernable, [but] there are some frightening aspects that would lead one to at least think along these lines." The scholarly Mayor Arthur Naftalin of Minneapolis adds his testimony: "Increasingly, the central city is unable to meet its problems. The fragmentation of authority is such that there isn't much a city can decide anymore: it can't deal effectively with education or housing."

Above all, the city cannot handle race. Cavanagh, Naftalin, and Lee—dedicated liberal doers all—were riot victims. Mayor A. W. Sorensen of Omaha had to confess that after he'd "gone through three-and-a-half years in this racial business," he'd had it.

Although frictions over race relations often ignite urban explosives, the cities of America—and the world—are proving ungovernable even where they are ethnically homogeneous. Tokyo is in hara-kiri, though racially pure. U Thant, in a statement of the U.N.'s Economic and Social Council, presented the urban problem as world-wide: "In many countries the housing situation . . . verges on disaster. . . . Throughout the developing world, the city is failing badly."

What is the universal malady of cities? The disease is density. Where cities foresaw density and planned accordingly, the situation is bad but tolerable. Where exploding populations hit unready urban areas, they are in disaster. Where ethnic and political conflict add further disorder, the disease appears terminal.

Some naturalists, in the age of urban crisis, have begun to study density as a disease. Crowded rats grow bigger adrenals, pouring out their juices in fear and fury. Crammed cats go through a "Fascist" transformation, with a "despot" at the top, "pariahs" at the bottom, and a general malaise in the community, where the cats, according to P. Leyhausen, "seldom relax, they never look at ease, and there is continuous hissing, growling, and even fighting."

How dense are the cities? The seven out of every ten Americans who live in cities occupy only 1 per cent of the total land area of the country. In the central city the situation is tighter, and in the inner core it is tightest. If we all lived as crushed as the blacks in Harlem, the total population of America could be squeezed into three of the five boroughs of New York City.

This density is, in part, a product of total population explosion. At some point the whole Earth will be as crowded as Harlem—or worse—unless we control births. But, right now, our deformity is due less to overall population than to the lopsided way in which we grow. In the 1950s, half of all the counties in the U.S. actually lost population; in the 1960s, four states lost population. Where did these people go? Into cities and metropolitan states. By the year 2000, we will have an additional 100 million Americans, almost all of whom will end up in the metropolitan areas.

The flow of the population from soil to city has been underway for more than a century, turning what was once a rural nation into an urban one by the early 1900s. Likewise, the flow from city to suburb has been underway for almost half a century. "We shall solve the city problem by leaving the city," advised Henry Ford in a high-minded blurb for his flivver. But, in the past decade, the flow has become a flood, modern know-how dispossessed millions of farmers, setting in motion a mass migration of ten million Americans from rural, often backward, heavily black and Southern counties to the cities. They carried with them all the upset of the uprooted, with its inherent ethnic and economic conflict. American cities, like Roman civilization, were hit by tidal waves of modern vandals. Under the impact of this new rural-push/urban-pull, distressed city dwellers started to move—then to run—out. Hence, the newest demographic dynamic: urban-push and suburban-pull. In the 1940s, half the metropolitan increase was in the suburbs; in the 1950s, it was two-thirds; in the 1960s, the central cities stopped growing while the suburbs boomed.

Not only people left the central city; but jobs, too, thereby creating a whole new set of economic and logistic problems. Industrial plants (the traditional economic ladder for new ethnic populations) began to flee the city in search of space for factories with modern horizontal layouts. Between 1945 and 1965, 63 per cent of all new industrial building took place outside the core. At present, 75 to 80 per cent of new jobs in trade and industry are situated on the metropolitan fringe. In the New York metropolitan area from 1951 to 1965, 127,753 new jobs were located in the city while more than three times that number (387,873) were located in the suburbs. In the Philadelphia metropolis, the city *lost* 49,461 jobs, while the suburbs gained 215,296. For the blue-collar worker who could afford to move to the suburbs or who could commute (usually by car) there were jobs. For those who were stuck in the city, the alternatives were work in small competitive plants hungry for cheap labor and no work at all.

Ironically, the worthwhile jobs that did locate in the cities were precisely those most unsuited for people of the inner core, namely, white-collar clerical, administrative, and executive positions. These jobs locate in high-rise office buildings with their vertical complexes of cubicles, drawing to them the more affluent employees who live in the outskirts and suburbs.

This disallocation of employment, calling for daily commuter migrations, has helped turn the automobile from a solution into a problem, as central cities have become stricken with auto-immobility; in midtown New York, the vehicular pace has been reduced from 11.5 mph in 1907 to 6 mph in 1963. To break the traffic jam, cities have built highways, garages, and parking lots that eat up valuable (once taxable) space in their busy downtowns: 55 per cent of the land in central Los Angeles, 50 per cent in Atlanta, 40 per cent in Boston, 30 per cent in Denver. All these "improvements," however, encourage more cars to come and go, leaving the central city poorer, not better.

Autos produce auto-intoxication: poisoning of the air. While the car is not the only offender (industry causes about 18 per cent of pollution; electric generators, 12 per cent; space heaters, 6 per cent; refuse disposal, 2.5 per cent), it is the main menace spewing forth 60 per cent of all the atmospheric filth. In 1966, a temperature inversion in New York City—fatefully coinciding with a national conference on air pollution—brought on eighty deaths. In 1952, in London, 4,000 people died during a similar atmospheric phenomenon.

The auto also helped to kill mass transit, the rational solution to the commuter problem. The auto drained railroads of passengers; to make up the loss, the railroad boosted fares; as fares went up, more passengers turned to autos; faced with bankruptcy, lines fell behind in upkeep, driving passengers to anger and more autos. Between 1950 and 1963, a dozen lines quit the passenger business; of the 500 intercity trains still in operation, fifty have applied to the ICC for discontinuance. Meanwhile, many treat their passengers as if they were freight.

Regional planners saw this coming two generations ago and proposed networks of mass transportation. But the auto put together its own lobby to decide otherwise: auto manufacturers, oil companies, road builders, and politicians who depend heavily on the construction industry for campaign contributions.

The auto is even failing in its traditional weekend role as the means to get away. On a hot August weekend this year, Jones Beach had to close down for a full hour, because 60,000 cars tried to get into parking lots with a capacity of 24,000. The cars moved on to the Robert Moses State Park and so jammed the 6,000-car lot there as to force a two-hour shutdown.

Overcrowding of the recreation spots is due not only to more people with more cars but to the pollution of waters by the dumping of garbage—another by-product of metropolitan density.

Viewed in the overall, our larger metropolises with their urban and suburban areas are repeating the gloomy evolution of our larger cities. When Greater New York was composed of Manhattan (then New York) and the four surround-

ing boroughs, the idea was to establish a balanced city: a crowded center surrounded by villages and farms. In the end, all New York became citified.
Likewise, the entire metropolitan area is becoming urbanized with the suburbanite increasingly caught up in the city tangle.

The flow from city to suburb does not, surprisingly, relieve crowding
within the central city, even in those cases where the city population is no longer
growing. The same number of people—especially in the poor areas—have fewer
places to live. In recent years, some 12,000 buildings that once housed about
60,000 families in New York City have been abandoned, with tenants being
dispossessed by derelicts and rats; 3,000 more buildings are expected to be
abandoned this year. The story of these buildings, in a city such as New York,
reads like a Kafkaesque comedy. For the city to tear down even one of these
menaces involves two to four years of red tape; to get possession of the land
takes another two to four years. Meanwhile, the wrecks are inhabited by human
wrecks preparing their meals over Sterno cans that regularly set fire to the
buildings. By law, the fire department is then charged with the responsibility of
risking men's lives to put out the fire, which they usually can do. However, when
the flames get out of hand, other worthy buildings are gutted, leaving whole
blocks of charred skeletons—victims of the quiet riot.

Other dwellings are being torn down by private builders to make way for
high-rise luxury apartments and commercial structures. *Public* action has destroyed more housing than has been built in all federally aided programs. As a
result, the crowded are more crowded than ever. Rehabilitation instead of renewal doesn't work. New York City tried it only to discover that rehabilitation
costs $38 a square foot— a little *more* than new luxury housing.

The result of all this housing decay and destruction (plus FHA money to
encourage more affluent whites to move to the suburbs) has been, says the
National Commission on Urban Problems, "to intensify racial and economic
stratification of America's urban areas."

While ghetto cores turn into ghost towns, the ghetto fringes flare out. The
crime that oozes through the sores of the diseased slum chases away old neighbors, a few of whom can make it to the suburbs; the rest seek refuge in the
"urban villages" of the low-income whites. Cities become denser and tenser than
they were. In the process, these populous centers of civilization become—like
Europe during the Dark Ages—the bloody soil on which armed towns wage their
inevitable wars over a street, a building, a hole in the wall. Amid this troubled
terrain, the free-lance criminal adds to the anarchy.

All these problems (plus welfare, schooling, and militant unions of municipal employees) hit the mayors at a time when, according to the National Commission on Urban Problems, "there is a crisis of urban government finance . . .
rooted in conditions that will not disappear but threaten to grow and spread
rapidly." The "roots" of the "crisis"? The mayor starts with a historic heavy
debt burden. His power to tax and borrow is often tethered by a rural-minded
state legislature. He has lost many of the city's wealthy payers to the suburbs.
His levies on property (small homes) and sales are prodding Mr. Middle to a tax
revolt. The bigger (richer) the city is the worse off it is. As population increases,
per capita cost of running a city goes up—not down: density makes for frictions
that demand expensive social lubricants. Municipalities of 100,000 to 299,000

spend $14.60 per person on police; those of 300,000 to 490,000 spend $18.33; and those of 500,000 to one million spend $21.88. New York City spends $39.83. On hospitalization, the first two categories spend $5 to $8 per person; those over 500,000 spend $12.54; New York spends $55.19.

Expanding the economy of a city does not solve the problem; it makes it worse. Several scholarly studies have come up with this piece of empiric pessimism: if the gross income of a city goes up 100 per cent, revenue rises only 90 per cent, and expenditures rise 110 per cent. Consequently, when a city's economy grows, the city's budget is in a worse fix than before. This diseconomy of bigness and richness applies even when cities merely limit themselves to prior levels of services. But cities, unable to cling to this inadequate past, have had to step up services to meet the rising expectations of city dwellers.

The easy out for a mayor is to demand that the federal coffers take over cost or hand over money. But is that the real answer? The federal income tax as presently levied falls most heavily on an already embittered middle class—our alienated majority. Unable to push this group any harder and unwilling to "soak the rich," an administration, such as President Nixon's, comes up with revenue-sharing toothpicks with which to shore up mountains. Nixon has proposed half a billion for next year and $5-billion by 1975, while urban experts see a need for $20- to $50-billion each year for the next decade. A Senate committee headed by Senator Abe Ribicoff calls for a cool trillion.

But even if a trillion were forthcoming, it might be unable to do the job. To build, a city must rebuild: bulldoze buildings, redirect highways, clear for mass transportation, remake streets—a tough task. But even tougher, a city must bulldoze people who are rigidified in resistant economic and political enclaves. The total undertaking could be more difficult than resurrecting a Phoenix that was already nothing but a heap of ashes.

What powers does a mayor bring to these complex problems? Very few. Many cities have a weak mayor setup, making him little more than a figurehead. If he has power, he lacks money. If he has power and money, he must find real—not symbolic—solutions to problems in the context of a density that turns "successes" into failures. If a mayor can, miraculously, come up with comprehensive plans, they will have to include a region far greater than the central city where he reigns.

A mayor must try to do all this in an era of political retribalism, when communities are demanding more, not less, say over the governance of their little neighborhoods. In this hour, when regional government is needed to cope with the many problems of the metropolitan area as a unity, the popular mood is to break up and return power to those warring factions—racial, economic, religious, geographic—that have in numerous cases turned a city into a no man's land.

Is there then no hope? There is—if we putter less within present cities and start planning a national push-pull to decongest urban America. Our answer is not in new mayors but in new cities; not in urban renewal but in urban "newal," to use planner Charles Abrams's felicitous word.

We cannot juggle the 70 per cent of the American people around on 1 per cent of the land area to solve the urban mess. We are compelled to think in terms of new towns and new cities planned for placement and structure by public action with public funds. "All of the urbanologists agree," reported *Time* amidst the 1967 riot months, "that one of the most important ways of saving cities is simply to have more cities." The National Committee on Urban Growth Policy proposed this summer that the federal government embark on a program to create 110 new cities (100 having a population of 100,000, and ten even larger) over the next three decades. At an earlier time, the Advisory Commission on Intergovernmental Relations proposed a national policy on urban growth, to use our vast untouched stock of land to "increase, rather than diminish, Americans' choices of places and environments," to counteract our present "diseconomics of scale involved in continuing urban concentration, the locational mismatch of jobs and people, the connection between urban and rural poverty problems, and urban sprawl."

New towns would set up a new dynamic. In the central cities, decongestion could lead to real urban renewal, starting with the clearing of the ghost blocks where nobody lives and ending with open spaces or even some of those dreamy "cities within a city." The new settlements could be proving grounds for all those exciting ideas of city planners whose proposals have been frustrated by present structures—physical and political. "Obsolete practices such as standard zoning, parking on the street, school bussing, on-street loading, and highway clutter could all be planned out of a new city," notes William E. Finley in the Urban Growth report. These new towns (cities) could bring jobs, medicine, education, and culture to the ghost towns in rural America, located in the counties that have lost population—and income—in the past decades. Finally, a half-century project for new urban areas would pick up the slack in employment when America, hopefully, runs out of wars to fight.

The cost would be great, but no greater than haphazard private developments that will pop up Topsy-like to accommodate the added 100 million people who will crowd America by the year 2000. Right now we grow expensively by horizontal or vertical accretion. We sprawl onto costly ground bought up by speculators and builders looking for a fast buck. Under a national plan, the federal government could buy up a store of ground in removed places at low cost or use present government lands. Where private developers reach out for vertical space, they erect towers whose building costs go up geometrically with every additional story. On the other hand, as city planners have been pointing out for a couple of decades, "it has been proved over and over again by such builders as Levitt, Burns, and Bohannon" that efficient mass production of low-risers "can and do produce better and cheaper houses." Cliff dwellings cost more than split-levels.

The idea of new towns is not untested. "There is little precedent in this country, but ample precedent abroad," notes the Committee on Urban Growth. "Great Britain, France, the Netherlands, the Scandinavian countries—all have taken a direct hand in land and population development in the face of urbanization, and all can point to examples of orderly growth that contrast sharply with the American metropolitan ooze." To the extent that the U.S. has created new communities it has done so as by-products: Norris, Tennessee, was built for TVA to house men working on a dam; Los Alamos, Oak Ridge, and Hanford were built for the Atomic Energy Commission "to isolate its highly secret operations."

What then is the obstacle to this new-cities idea? It runs contrary to the traditional wisdom that a) where cities are located, they should be located, and b) that the future ought to be left to private enterprise. Both thoughts are a hangover from a hang-up with laissez faire, a Panglossian notion that what is, is best.

The fact is, however, that past reasons for locating cities no longer hold—at least, not to the same extent. Once cities grew up at rural crossroads; later at the meeting of waters; still later at railroad junctions; then near sources of raw material. But today, as city planner Edgardo Contini testified before a Congressional committee, these reasons are obsolete. "Recent technological and transportation trends—synthesis rather than extraction of materials, atomic rather than hydroelectric or thermoelectric power, air rather than rail transportation— all tend to expand the opportunities for location of urban settlements." Despite this, the old cities, by sheer weight of existence, become a magnetic force drawing deadly densities.

Furthermore, concluded Mr. Contini and a host of others, "the scale of the new cities program is too overwhelming for private initiative alone to sustain, and its purposes and implications are too relevant to the country's future to be relinquished to the profit motive alone." The report of the Urban Growth Committee stresses the limited impact of new towns put up by private developers such as Columbia, Maryland and Reston, Virginia. "They are and will be in the first place, few in number, serving only a tiny fraction of total population growth. A new town is a 'patient' investment, requiring large outlays long before returns begin; it is thus a non-competitive investment in a tight money market. Land in town-size amounts is hard to find and assemble without public powers of eminent domain. Privately developed new towns, moreover, by definition must serve the market, which tends to fill them with housing for middle- to upper-income families rather than the poor."

The choice before America is really not between new cities and old. Population pressure will force outward expansion. But by present drift, this will be unplanned accretion—plotted for quick profit rather than public need. What is needed is national concern for the commonweal in the location and design of new cities: a kind of inner space program.

WHY ARE WE IN NEW YORK?

Norman Mailer

How is one to speak of the illness of a city? A clear day can come, a morning in early May like the pride of June. The streets are cool, the buildings have come out of shadow, and silences are broken by the voices of children. It is as if the neighborhood has slept in the winding sheet of the past. Forty years go by—one can recollect the milkman and the clop of a horse. It is a great day. Everyone speaks of the delight of the day on the way to work. It is hard on such mornings to believe that New York is the victim "etherized on a table."

Yet by afternoon the city is incarcerated once more. Haze covers the sky, a grim, formless glare blazes back from the horizon. The city has become unbalanced again. By the time work is done, New Yorkers push through the acrid lung-rotting air and work their way home, avoiding each other's eyes in the subway. Later, near midnight, thinking of a walk to buy The Times, they hesitate—in the darkness a familiar sense of dread returns, the streets are not quite safe, the sense of waiting for some apocalyptic fire, some night of long knives hangs over the city. We recognize one more time that the city is ill, that our own New York, the Empire City, is not too far from death.

Recollect: When we were children, we were told air was invisible, and it was. Now we see it shift and thicken, move in gray depression over a stricken sky. Now we grow used to living with colds all year, and viruses suggestive of plague. Tempers shorten in our hideous air. The sick get sicker, the violent more violent. The frayed tissue of New York manners seems ready to splatter on every city street. It is the first problem of the city, our atrocious air. People do not die dramatically like the one-day victims of Donora, rather they dwindle imperceptibly, die five years before their time, 10 years before, cough or sneeze helplessly into the middle of someone else's good mood, stroll about with the hot iron of future asthma manacled to their lungs. The air pollution in New York is so bad, and gives so much promise of getting worse, that there is no solution to any other problem until the air is relieved of its poisonous ingestions. New York has conceivably the worst air of any city in the universe today—certainly it is the worst air in the most technologically developed nation in the world, which is to say it is the air of the future if the future is not shifted from its program. Once Los Angeles was famous for the liver-yellow of its smog; we have surpassed her.

That is our pervasive ill. It is fed by a host of tributary ills which flow into the air, fed first by our traffic, renowned through the world for its incapacity to move. Midtown Manhattan is next to impenetrable by vehicle from midday to evening—the average rate of advance is, in fact, 6 miles an hour, about the speed of a horse at a walk. Once free of the center, there is the threat of hourlong tie-ups at every bridge, tunnel and expressway if even a single car breaks down in a lane. In the course of a year, people lose weeks of working time through the sum of minutes and quarter-hours of waiting to crawl forward in traffic. Tempers blow with lost schedules, work suffers everywhere. All the while stalled cars gun their motors while waiting in place, pumping carbon monoxide into air already laden with caustic sulphuroxide from fuel oil we burn to make electricity.

Given this daily burden, this air pollution, noise pollution, stagnant transport, all-but-crippled subways, routes of new transportation 20 years unbuilt— every New Yorker sallies forth into an environment which strips him before noon of his good cheer, his charity, his calm nerve, and his ability to discipline his anger.

Yet, beneath that mood of pestilential clangor, something worse is ticking away—our deeper sense of a concealed and continuing human horror. If there are eight million people in New York, one million live on welfare, no, the figure is higher now, it will be one million two hundred thousand by the end of the year. Not a tenth of these welfare cases will ever be available for work; they are women and children first, then too old, too sick, too addicted, too illiterate, too unskilled, too ignorant of English. Fatherless families and motherless families live at the end of an umbilical financial cord which perpetuates them in an embryonic economic state. Welfare is the single largest item in the city budget— two years ago it surpassed the figure we reserve for education, yet it comes down to payments of no more than $3,800 a year for a family of four. Each member of that family is able to spend a dollar a day for food, at most $1.25 a day.

Still, it is worse than that. If one of eight people in New York is on welfare, half as many again might just as well be on welfare because their minimum wage brings in no more than such a check. So the natural incentive is to cease working. Close to $1.5-billion is spent on welfare now. The figure will go up. Manpower Training, in contrast, spends about a twenty-fifth as much. Looking to skill the poor for work, it will train as many as 4,000 men a year, and place perhaps 10,000 men out of 100,000 applicants in bad jobs without foreseeable future, the only jobs indeed available for the untrained. Sometimes in the Job Corps it cost $13,000 to train a man for a job where he might be able to make $6,000 a year if he could find a job, but the skills he had learned were not related to the jobs he might return to at home. Poverty lies upon the city like a layer of smog.

Our housing offers its unhappy figures. If we have calculated that it is necessary to build 7,500 new low-income apartments a year, merely to keep on the same terms with the problem, we end in fact with 4,000 units constructed. Never mind how most of it looks—those grim, high-rise, new-slum prisons on every city horizon. Face rather the fact that we lose near to the same number of units a year as old buildings which could have been saved run down into a state requiring condemnation. Of the $100,000,000 the city spends each budget year for new housing, $20,000,000 goes into demolition. If four times as much were spent by present methods on low- and middle-income housing, 36,000 new and rehabilitated units could be provided a year, but housing needs would still be huge and unmet—the average family could wait 25 years to benefit from the program.

Our finances are intolerable. If New York State delivers $17-billion in income tax and $5-billion in corporate taxes to the Federal Government, it is conservative to assume that $14-billion of the total of $22-billion has come from the people of New York City. But our city budget is about $7.5-billion: of that sum only $3-billion derives from the State and from Washington. New York must find another $4.5-billion in real estate and other local taxes. Consider then: We pay $14-billion in income tax to the Federal Government and to Albany: back comes $3-billion. We put out 5 dollars for every dollar which returns. So we live in vistas of ironbound civic poverty. Four of those lost 5 dollars are going to places like Vietnam and Malmstrom in North Dakota where the ABM will find a site, or dollars are going to Interstate highways which pass through regions we probably will never visit. In relation to the Federal Government, the city is like a sharecropper who lives forever in debt at the company store.

Yes, everything is wrong. The vocations of the past disintegrate. Jewish teachers who went into the education system 20 years ago to have security for themselves and to disseminate enlightenment among the children of the poor, now feel no security in their work, and are rejected in their liberal sociological style of teaching. The collective ego of their life style is shattered. They are forced to comprehend that there are black people who would rather be taught by other black people than by experts. The need for authenticity has become the real desire in education. "Who am I? What is the meaning of my skin, my passion, my dread, my fury, my dream of glories undreamed, my very need for bread?"—these questions are now become so powerful they bring the pumps of blood up to pressure and leave murder in the heart. What can education be in the womb of a dying city but a fury to discover for oneself whether one is victim or potential hero, stupid or too bright for old pedagogical ways? Rage at the frustration of the effort to find a style became the rage at the root of the uproar in the schools last year, and the rage will be there until the schools are free to discover a new way to learn. Let us not be arrogant toward the ignorant—their sensitivity is often too deep to dare the knowledge of numbers or the curlicue within a letter. Picasso, age of 11, could still not do arithmetic because the figure 7 looked like a nose upside down to him.

Among the poor, genius may stay buried behind the mask of the most implacable stupidity, for if genius can have no issue in a man's life, he must conceal it, and protect it, reserve it for his seed, or his blessing, or, all else gone, for his curse. No wonder we live with dread in our heart, and the nicest of the middle class still padlock their doors against the curse. We are like a Biblical city which has fallen from grace. Our parks deteriorate, and after duty our police go home to suburbs beyond the city—they come back to govern us from without. And municpal employes drift in the endless administrative bogs of Wagnerian systems of apathy and attrition. Work gets done at the rate of work accomplished by a draft army in peacetime at a sullen out-of-the-way post. The Poverty Program staggers from the brilliance of its embezzlements. But, of course, if you were a bright young black man, might you not want to steal a million from the Feds?

Here, let us take ourselves to the problem. It goes beyond the Durham gang. Our first problem is that no one alive in New York can answer with honesty the question: Can New York be saved? None of us can know. It is possible people will emigrate from New York in greater and greater numbers, and administration will collapse under insufferable weights, order will be restored from without. Then, everyone who can afford it will redouble his efforts to go, and New York will end as the first asylum of the megacity of the technological future. We who leave will carry with us the infection of the cowardice and apathy, the sense of defeat of the terminal years. We will move into other cities similarly affected or into a countryside wary of us, for we are then packers and peddlers from an expiring social world. So our first problem is to find whether we can find a way to rally our morale.

Part of the tragedy, part of the unbelievable oncoming demise of New York is that none of us can simply believe it. We were always the best and the strongest of cities, and our people were vital to the teeth. Knock them down eight times and they would get up with that look in the eye which suggests the fight has barely begun. We were the city of optimists. It is probably why we settled so deep into our mistakes. We simply couldn't believe that we weren't inexhaustible as a race—an unspoken race of New Yorkers.

Now all our problems have the magnitude of junkie problems—they are so coexistent with our life that New Yorkers do not try to solve them but escape them. Our fix is to put the blame on the blacks and Puerto Ricans. But everybody knows that nobody can really know where the blame resides. Nobody but a candidate for Mayor. It is the only way he can have the optimism to run. So the prospective candidate writing these words has the heart to consider entering the Democratic primary on June 17 because he thinks he sees a way out of the swamp: better, he believes he glimpses a royal road.

The face of the solution may reside in the notion that the Left has been absolutely right on some critical problems of our time, and the Conservatives have been altogether correct about one enormous matter—which is that the Federal Government has no business whatever in local affairs. The style of New York life has shifted since the Second World War (along with the rest of the American cities) from a scene of local neighborhoods and personalities to a large dull impersonal style of life which deadens us with its architecture, its highways, its abstract welfare, and its bureaucratic reflex to look for government solutions which come into the city from without (and do not work). So the old confidence that the problems of our life were roughly equal to our abilities has been lost. Our authority has been handed over to the Federal power. We expect our economic solutions, our habitats, yes, even our entertainments, to derive from that remote abstract power, remote as the other end of a television tube. We are like wards in an orphan asylum. The shaping of the style of our lives is removed from us—we pay for huge military adventures and social experiments so separated from our direct control that we do not even know where to begin to look to criticize the lack of our power to criticize. We cannot—the words are now a cliché, the life has gone out of them—we cannot forge our destiny. So our condition is spiritless. We wait for abstract impersonal powers to save us, we despise the abstractness of those powers, we loathe ourselves for our own apathy. Orphans.

Who is to say that the religious heart is not right to think the need of every man and woman alive may be to die in a state of grace, a grace which for atheists and agnostics may reside in the basic act of having done one's best, of having found some part of a destiny to approach, and having worked for the view of it? New York will not begin to be saved until its men and women begin to believe that it must become the greatest city in the world, the most magnificent, most creative, most extraordinary, most just, dazzling, bewildering and balanced of cities. The demand upon us has come down to nothing less than that.

How can we begin? By the most brutal view, New York City is today a legislative pail of dismembered organs strewn from Washington to Albany. We are without a comprehensive function or a skin. We cannot begin until we find a function which will become our skin. It is simple: Our city must become a state. We must look to become a state of the United States separate from New York State: the Fifty-First, in fact, of the United States. New York City State, or The State of New York City. It is strange on the tongue, but not so strange.

Think on the problem of this separation. People across the state are oriented toward Buffalo or Albany or Rochester or Montreal or Toronto or Boston or Cleveland. They do not think in great numbers of coming to New York City to make their life. In fact the good farmers and small-town workers of New York State rather detest us. They hear of the evils of our city with quiet thin-lipped glee; in the State Legislature they rush to compound those evils. Everytime the city needs a program which the state must approve, the city returns with a part of its package—the rest has been lost in deals, compromises and imposts. The connection of New York City to New York State is a marriage of misery, incompatibility and abominable old quarrels.

While the separation could hardly be as advantageous to New York State as it would be for the city, it might nonetheless begin the development of what has been hitherto a culturally undernourished hinterland, a typically colorless national tract.

But we will not weep for New York State—look, rather, to the direct advantages to ourselves. We have, for example, received no money so far for improving our city transit lines, yet the highway program for America in 1968 was $5-billion. Of this, New York State received at least $350,000,000 for its roads. New York City received not a dollar from Washington or Albany for reconstruction of its 6,000 miles of streets and avenues.

As a city-state we could speak to the Federal Government in the unmistakable tones of a state. If so many hundreds of millions go to Pennsylvania and Oklahoma and Colorado and Maine for their highway programs, then we could claim that a comparable amount is required for our transportation problems which can better be solved by the construction of new rapid transit. Add the monies attainable by an increased ability as the Fifty-First State to press for more equitable return on our taxes. Repeat: we give to Washington and Albany almost 5 tax dollars for every dollar which returns; Mississippi, while declaiming the virtues and inviolability of states' rights, still gets four Federal dollars for every income-tax dollar she pays up.

As the center of the financial and communications industries, as the first victim of a nuclear war, the new State of the City of New York would not have the influence of one state in fifty-one, but rather would exist as one of the two or three states whose force and influence could be felt upon every change in the country's policy. With the power implicit in this grip, it may not be excessive to assume that divorce from Albany would produce an extra billion in real savings and natural efficiency, and still another billion (not to mention massive allocations for transit problems) could derive from our direct relation with the Federal Government: The first shift in our ability to solve our problems might have begun.

It would not, however, be nearly enough. The ills of New York cannot be solved by money. New York will be ill until it is magnificent. For New York must be ready to show the way to the rest of Western civilization. Until it does, it will be no more than the first victim of the technological revolution no matter how much money it receives in its budget. Money bears the same relation to social solutions that water does to blood.

Yet the beginning of a city-state and the tonic of a potential budget of $8- or $9- or $10-billion would offer a base on which to build. Where then could we take it? How would we build?

We could direct our effort first against the present thickets of the City Charter. The Charter is a formidable document. There are some who would say it is a hideous document. Taken in combination with the laws of New York State, it is a legal mat guaranteed to deaden the nerve of every living inquiry. The Charter in combination with the institutional and municipal baggage surrounding it is guaranteed to inhibit any honest man from erecting a building, beginning an enterprise, organizing a new union, searching for a sensible variety of living zone, or speaking up for local control in education. It would strangle any honest Mayor who approached the suffocations of air pollution or traffic, tried to build workable on-the-job training, faced the most immediate problems of law and order, attacked our shortage of housing or in general even tried to conceive of a new breath of civic effort. There is no way at present to circumvent the thicket without looking to power-brokers in the trade unions, the Mafia and real estate.

Only if the people of New York City were to deliver an overwhelming mandate for a city-state could anything be done about the thicket. Then the legal charter of the new state could rewrite the means by which men and women could work to make changes in the intimate details of their neighborhoods and their lives.

Such a new document would most happily be built upon one concept so fundamental that all others would depend upon it. This concept might state that power would return to the neighborhoods.

Power to the neighborhoods! In the new city-state, every opportunity would be offered to neighborhoods to vote to become townships, villages, hamlets, sub-boroughs, tracts or small cities, at which legal point they would be funded directly by the fifty-first state. Many of these neighborhoods would manage their own municipal services, their police, sanitation, fire protection, education, parks, or, like very small towns, they could, if they wished, combine services with other neighborhoods. Each neighborhood would thus begin to outline the style of its local government by the choice of its services.

It may be recognized that we are at this point not yet vastly different from a patch of suburbs and townships in Westchester or Jersey. The real significance of power to the neighborhoods is that people could come together and constitute themselves upon any principle. Neighborhoods which once existed as separate towns or districts, like Jamaica or New Utrecht or Gravesend, might wish to become towns again upon just such a historic base. Other neighborhoods with a sense of unity provided by their geography like Bay Ridge, Park Slope, Washington Heights, Yorkville, Fordham Road, Riverdale, Jackson Heights, Canarsie or Corona might be able without undue discussion to draw their natural lines.

Poorer neighborhoods would obviously look to establish themselves upon their immediate problems, rather than upon historical or geographical tradition. So Harlem, Bedford-Stuyvesant and the Barrio in East Harlem might be the first to vote for power to their own neighborhoods so that they might be in position to administer their own poverty program, own welfare, their own education systems, and their own—if they so voted—police and sanitation and fire protection for which they would proceed to pay out of their funds. They would then be able to hire their own people for their own neighborhood jobs and services. Their own teachers and communities would, if they desired, control their own schools. Their own union could rebuild their own slums. Black Power would be a political reality for Harlem and Bedford-Stuyvesant. Black people and, to the extent they desired, Puerto Rican people, could make separate but thoroughgoing attacks upon their economic problems, since direct neighborhood funding would be available to begin every variety of economic enterprise. Black militants interested in such communal forms of economic activity as running their own factories could begin to build economies, new unions and new trades in their neighborhoods.

Power to the neighborhoods would mean that any neighborhood could constitute itself on any principle, whether spirtual, emotional, economical, ideological or idealistic. Even prejudicial principles could serve as the base—if one were willing to pay. It could, for example, be established in the charter of the city-state that no principle of exclusion by race or religion would be tolerated in the neighborhoods unless each such neighborhood was willing to offer a stiff and proper premium for this desire in their taxes.

In reaction to this, each and every liberal, Negro and white, who would detest the relinquishment of the principle that no prejudice was allowed by law, might also consider the loss of the dream of integration as the greatest loss in the work of their lives. They would now be free to create neighborhoods which would incorporate on the very base of integration itself—Integration City might be the name of the first neighborhood to stand on the recapture of the old dream. Perhaps it might even exist where now is Stuyvesant Town.

On the other hand, people who wished anonymity or isolation from their neighbors could always choose large anonymous areas, neighborhoods only in name, or indeed could live in those undifferentiated parts of the city which chose no neighborhood for themselves at all. The critical point to conceive is that no neighborhood would come into existence because the mayoralty so dictated. To the extent that they had been conditioned for years by the notion that the government was the only agency large enough and therefore effective

enough to solve their problems, so to that extent would many people be reluctant to move to solutions which came from themselves.

To the degree, however, that we have lost faith in the power of the
government to conduct our lives, so would the principle of power to the neighborhoods begin to thrive, so too would the first spiritual problem of the 20th
century—alienation from the self—be given a tool by which to rediscover oneself.

In New York, which is to say, in the 20th century, one can never know
whether the world is vastly more or less violent than it seems. Nor can we
discover which actions in our lives are authentic or which belong to the art of
the put-on. Conceive that society has come to the point where tolerance of
others' ideas has no meaning unless there is benumbed acceptance of the fact
that we must accept their lives. If there are young people who believe that
human liberty is blockaded until they have the right to take off their clothes in
the street—and more! and more!—make love on the hood of an automobile—
there are others who think it is a sin against the eyes of the Lord to even
contemplate the act in one's mind. Both could now begin to build communities
on their separate faith—a spectrum which might run from Compulsory Free Love
to Mandatory Attendance in Church on Sunday! Grant us to recognize that
wherever there is a common desire among people vital enough to keep a
community alive, then there must be also the presence of a clue that some kind
of real life resides in the desire. Others may eventually discern how.

Contained beneath the surface of the notion is a recognition that the 20th
century has lost its way—the religious do not know if they believe in God, or even
if God is not dead; the materialist works through the gloomy evidence of socialism and bureaucracy; the traditionalist is hardly aware any longer of a battlefield
where the past may be defended; the technician—if sensitive—must wonder if the
world he fashions is evil, insane, or rational; the student rebellion stares into the
philosophical gulf of such questions as the nature of culture and the students'
responsibility to it; the blacks cannot be certain if they are fundamentally deprived, or a people of genius, or both. The answers are unknown because the
questions all collide in the vast empty arena of the mass media where no price
has ever to be paid for your opinion. So nobody can be certain of his value—one
cannot even explore the validity of one's smallest belief. To wake up in New
York with a new idea is to be plunged into impotence by noon, plunged into
that baleful sense of boredom which hints of dread and future violence.

So the cry of Power to the Neighborhoods may yet be heard. For even as
marriage reveals the balance between one's dream of pleasure and one's small
real purchase upon it, even as marriage is the mirror of one's habits, and the
immersion of the ego into the acid of the critic, so life in the kind of neighborhood which contains one's belief of a possible society is a form of marriage
between one's social philosophy and one's private contract with the world. The
need is deeper than we could expect, for we are modern, which is to say we can
never locate our roots without a voyage of discovery.

Perhaps then it can be recognized that power to the neighborhoods is a
most peculiar relocation of the old political directions. It speaks from the left
across the divide to conservatism. Speaking from the left, it says that a city
cannot survive unless the poor are recognized, until their problems are under-
lined as not directly of their own making; so their recovery must be based upon

more than their own private efforts, must be based in fact upon their being capitalized by the city-state in order that the initial construction of their community economics, whether socialist or capitalist or both, can begin.

Yet with power in the neighborhoods, so also could there be on-the-job training in carpentry, stone-masonry, plumbing, plastering, electrical work and painting. With a pool of such newly skilled workers, paid by the neighborhood, the possibility is present to rebuild a slum area *room by room.*

Better! The occupant of an apartment who desires better housing could go to work himself on his own apartment, using neighborhood labor and funds, patching, plastering, painting, installing new wiring and plumbing—as the tenant made progress he could be given funds to continue, could own the pride of having improved his housing in part through his own efforts.

So power to these poor neighborhoods still speaks to conservative principles, for it recognizes that a man must have the opportunity to work out his own destiny, or he will never know the dimensions of himself, he will be alienated from any sense of whether he is acting for good or evil. It goes further. Power to all neighborhoods recognizes that we cannot work at our destiny without a context—that most specific neighborhood which welcomes or rejects our effort, and so gives a mirror to the value of our striving, and the distortion of our prejudice. Perhaps it even recognizes the deepest of conservative principles—that a man has a right to live his life in such a way that he may know if he is dying in a state of grace. Our lives, directed by abstract outside forces, have lost that possibility most of all. It is a notion on which to hit the campaign trail.

Which is where we go now—into the campaign: to talk in the days ahead of what power to the neighborhoods will mean. We will go down the steps of the position papers and talk of jobs and housing and welfare, of education, municipal unions and law and order, finance, the names of laws, the statistics of the budget, the problems of traffic and transportation. There will be a paucity of metaphor and a taste of stale saliva to the debates, for voters are hard-working people who trust the plain more than the poetic. How then can Mailer and Breslin, two writers with reputations notorious enough for four, ever hope to convince the voting hand of the electorate? What would they do if, miracle of political explosions, they were to win?

Well, they might cry like Mario Procaccino, for they would never have a good time again; but they would serve, they would learn on the job, they would conduct their education in public. They would be obliged to. And indeed the supposition could remain that they might even do well, better than the men before them. How else could they have the confidence to run? They might either have supposed that the Lord was not dead but behind them or they must have felt such guilt about the years of their lives that only the long running duties of office could satisfy the list of their dues.

As for the fact that they were literary men—that might be the first asset of all. They would know how to talk to the people—they would be forced to govern by the fine art of the voice. Exposed by their own confession as amateurs they might even attract the skill of the city to their service, for the community would be forced to swim in full recognition of the depth of the soup. And best of all, what a tentative confidence would reign in the eye of New York that her literary men, used to dealing with the proportions of worlds hitherto created only in the mind, might now have a sensitive nose for the balances and the battles, the tugs, the pushing, the heaves of that city whose declaration of new birth was implicit in the extraordinary fact that *him,* Mailer! and *him,* Breslin! had been voted in. . . .

DALEY OF CHICAGO

David Halberstam

In the political year 1968, Richard J. Daley surveyed the city of Chicago and was master of it. He exercised power as probably no man outside of Washington exercised it, and he was by most norms of the American ethic, particularly his own, a towering success. The poor of his city were afraid of him and the powerful of the nation deferred to him.

It was his city to an extraordinary degree, and now his party was coming to his city to choose a President. The more contested the nomination would be, the more the poor blacks and the long-haired white kids worked in the primaries to offset the Democratic party establishment, why, yes, the more powerful Richard J. Daley would be in August; and he was aware of this, aware that in his own way he could dominate the convention, and though there might be other men more popular, more handsome, more beloved, the final decisions would be made by Mayor Daley. (Early in the year, when Robert Kennedy made his entrance into the race and a reporter asked a Daley man which hotel in Chicago Kennedy would be taking over, the Daley man answered, with the sense of certainty that only the very powerful have, "Bobby Kennedy isn't taking over anything in *this* city.") He would walk into the convention erect and powerful (particularly if his city were not in flames), and his words would be sought by the nation's foremost reporters, though surely they would be platitudinous, for he specialized in platitudes. He had learned long ago that if possible you spoke platitudes or you spoke not at all.

Everywhere there would be reminders to the guests that they were in Dick Daley's Chicago. In a profession where municipal officials keeled over like flies after one or two terms, especially if they were effective, thrown out by angry undertaxed constituents who felt themselves overtaxed, who hated the parking and the air and their neighbors, Richard J. Daley reigned supreme, King Richard as he was called in Chicago.

Four times he was elected, the fourth by his largest majority, 74 per cent. His years of success had virtually left Chicago without an electoral process, *that* was his achievement; in a city where few new buildings had been started before him, the sky was pierced again and again by new skyscrapers, each bigger and more gleaming than the last, and ever-grateful rich and aristocratic businessmen taught from the cradle to shun the Democratic party—that party of the machine and the Irish—competed to enlist in Republicans for Daley, vowed to give bigger contributions, while the most famous political scientists of Chicago, hawks and doves, liberals and conservatives, joined Professors for Daley. Municipal experts, technocrats with their measuring sticks, were in general agreement that Daley was the most successful Mayor in America—good cost accounting, good police department, good fire department, good social-economic programs. He was a politician with a smooth-functioning political machine in an age when machines were not supposed to function. (When one reporter for a local paper saw him at a meeting, a man who knew a machine when he saw one, Daley would say simply, "Organization, not machine. Get that. Organization, not machine.")

His city vibrated with those traditional American ingredients, vitality, energy, ambition, business drive, and racial failure, and it was because of these that Daley's role in history seemed curiously in doubt, for all his great achievements. In America now, when everything else failed, when the family failed and the churches failed and the system failed, the good Mayor would get the blame, not the Mayors of Natchez, Mississippi, or Clarksdale, Mississippi, or of thousands of other towns which had exported so many illiterate young Negroes North in the last fifteen years: the blame would be on the Mayor of the city which received them and which, as they had been failed once before, failed them again.

For Richard Daley presided over a city which had burned once and had a special tinderbox quality. It contained angry backlashing whites, some of the greatest backlashers in America who had finally managed to buy little homes in Chicago and paid their taxes there; and angry, frustrated, forelashing blacks. It was a city which contained one great Negro ghetto and another area which was not even a ghetto; it was a jungle, the kids alley-tough, totally outside the system, larger kids shaking down the smaller ones, youth gangs with organizational charts like the Army. Other cities were this bad, and some were worse, and in many of the older ways Richard J. Daley had done more for the Negro, to use that term, than many other Mayors. But there was also a suspicion that part of the problem was Daley, that his machine had been too smart for itself, and that finally Daley was perhaps not equipped to understand the complexity and the intense pressures of new times. Even his image seemed wrong, a point about which his staff was particularly sensitive. One of Daley's press people could point to a photograph of John Lindsay on the cover of *Life* and gloat over the headline, "Small acts and big plans," saying, "We could kill Lindsay with that. We could run against him and destroy him. Lindsay? What's he ever done? What programs has he got? Lindsay's people come out here for lessons in government."

It was not just Daley, it was America, with all the chickens, one hundred years or more in flight, coming home to roost. "Daley may well personify the Achilles' heel of America," one Negro critic said. "He's taken many positions not because he's outside the mainstream of America, but precisely because he's in it, which doesn't say a hell of a lot for either Daley or America."

For in a sense Chicago seemed to be the real capital of America, a strong, tough, vital city where the American business ethic worked, a city largely without reform influence ("We think of reform as being an effete Easterner idea," said one transplanted New Yorker). Nelson Algren, Chicago's uncrowned poet laureate, could write in his "Ode to Lower Finksville":

> *City of the big gray-flanneled shoulders*
> *Fierce as a dog with tongue lapping for action*
> *How come you spend all that great ferocity*
> *On the windpipes of The Down, The Out and The Defenseless*
> *And keep all that great lapping for overfed real-estate hogs?*

So Daley and Chicago seemed to symbolize America; he was ours, for better and for worse, in sickness and in health.

OTHER CHOICES, OTHER TIMES

Richard J. Daley is the product of the politics of another time. "I think one of the real problems he has with Negroes is understanding that the Irish are no longer the out-ethnic group," one Negro says. He would be doomed in the cosmetology of today's politics: those jowls, that heavy-set look. He doesn't look like a modern municipal leader, a cost-accounting specialist; he looks, yes, exactly like a big city boss, right out of the smoke-filled room. "Daley will never really get a fair judging on his abilities as a mayor because of the way he looks," an admiring Chicago political scientist says. "He's much better than people think."

When he was first elected he spoke badly—"dese" and "dems"—but he has worked hard and now has very considerable control over most of his political appearances; there has also been a sharp decline in his malapropisms, though some Chicago reporters still collect them. Two of the best are *we will reach greater and greater platitudes of achievement,* and *they have vilified me, they have crucified me, yes they have even criticized me.* He is not good on the tube, but it is a mistake to underestimate his power and charm in person. "He exudes" one fellow Irishman says, "the confidence and power of a man who has achieved everything he set out to do and then a little more, but he also has the black moods of an Irishman and if you catch him in one of those it can be pretty frightening."

He dominates Chicago and he knows it, and this adds to his confidence. "People are always coming to me and telling me that they're going down to see the Mayor and tell him off," one Negro remarks, "and off they go, and of course he charms them completely and they come back and I ask, 'Well, brother, how did it go?' and they tell me, 'Why the Mayor's a fine man and we *know*'—get that, we know—'he's going to do the right thing.' " But clever, resounding speech is not his forte, and he has learned that the less you say now, the less you have to regret later, and indeed the problem may go away by then. He has made a political virtue out of being inarticulate. He has been satisfied with being Mayor, has consolidated his base there, has never let his ambition run away with him; this is part of the explanation for his power. He has sat there with a power base, slowly adding to it, incorporating new men as they rose, always looking for winners. Above all else Richard Daley loves power and winners. An aide of John

Kennedy's remembers arriving in Chicago in 1960 for the first television debate, and Kennedy asking again and again, "Where's Daley, where's Daley," with no Daley to be found. "But after the debate," the aide recalls, "the first person to break through into the studio, with his flunkies around him like a flying wedge, was Daley. He knew he had a winner."

He was a poor Irish boy, born in a time when the Irish felt themselves despised in Protestant America. One reason, according to friends, that he was so close to Joseph Kennedy was that they both shared the same boyhood scars. Daley's father was a sheet-metal worker and an early union activist, blacklisted at several plants. There were few avenues open to an ambitious young Irish boy in those days and one of them was politics; though he is widely admired by all of Chicago's business giants today for his financial acumen, it is a fact of life, of which both are sharply aware, that he could not have made it in their world at that time.

More than most great men of power in America he is what he was. He lives in the same neighborhood where he was born, in the same house in which he has lived all his married life. He attends early Mass every day and observes the same basic tenets of the Catholic faith that he has based his life upon. His friends are the same small cluster of men, very much like himself, whom he has always known. His success has thrown him into the orbit of newer and more important men, but he has never crossed the line between association and friendship. His personal views remain rigid and he expects others to have the same; one reporter remembers a Daley son coming back from college recently with an unduly long haircut; Daley simply nodded at Matt Danaher, one of his deputies, and the boy was taken out for a trimming.

He is now the acknowledged master of the Democratic party machinery which gave him his start. The machine ethic was based upon hard work and loyalty; you worked your way up level by level. But loyalty rather than brilliance or social conscience or originality was the determining characteristic. It was and is a profession which abounded in limited men and hacks, of small men trying to throw around the power of bigger men, which often they only sniff at. Daley, apprenticing in a world of hacks, was and is no hack. He is an intelligent, strong-willed man, enormously hard-working. He set out within the party organization and mastered it, working his way up from precinct captain to committeeman to state legislator, a good one, easily distinguished from most of the men in Springfield, in his room every night studying the legislation. He was a young man who played by the rules of the game. He never frightened anyone, never looked too ambitious, accumulating political due bills all the time. He also mastered the art of finance as few active politicians in America have, eventually becoming director of revenue for Governor Adlai Stevenson.

In the view of several professional politicians, Daley helped protect Stevenson from less scrupulous politicians. He after all knew how and where the crooks might steal; it was the beginning of a relationship which would prove mutually beneficial to both until 1960 when Daley, given Stevenson's silence and Joe Kennedy's pressure, went for John Kennedy. As part of his loyalty ethic, however, Daley aided Stevenson's son, Adlai III, now Illinois State Treasurer, in his start in politics, trying to give him good advice, suggesting that he play down his criticism of Vietnam. The other regular pols were bitterly opposed to young

Stevenson. They considered him arrogant, uppity, and a man who had not done his apprenticeship. They were prepared to let him go on the slate this year for U. S. Senator, thus getting him out of Illinois; the machine has always preferred sending its reformers to Washington rather than Springfield. Stevenson, an attractive and intelligent politician and a somewhat rumpled version of his father, instead went before the slate-makers and told everyone in a rather long speech—normally, one goes in, hat in hand for thirty seconds—that he was the best and strongest candidate for Governor. The regulars were appalled and threw him out.

Daley told him that he could still get on the slate for the Senate if he would plead loyalty on Vietnam. Back in he went, up came the question of Vietnam, out came Stevenson's doubts and his talk about conscience, and off the ticket he came. "Jesus, that guy is even worse than his father," one professional pol said. The result is that the Democrats are fielding a very weak ticket this year, with neither Stevenson nor Sargent Shriver on it. It was a case of divided loyalty for Daley, but apparently it would have required more of a fight than he was prepared to make. Not getting into futile fights may explain how he manages to conserve power.

CHICAGO'S BRAND OF TOUGHNESS

Chicago is rougher than other cities. Even today its more sophisticated citizens take a quiet pleasure in talking about not only its past sins but its present vices and the current power of the crime Syndicate. The city's rough edge is often a little hard for Easterners to understand. A few years ago a Negro alderman named Ben Lewis was shot down in cold blood. A correspondent for an Eastern magazine was immediately cabled by his New York office for a piece which would include, among other things, the outraged reaction of the good people of Chicago. There was no outrage at all, he cabled back. "The feeling is that if he's an alderman, he's a crook, and if he's a crook then that's their business."

The kind of money which focuses on reform politics in New York simply does not exist in Chicago and the machine has traditionally understood the reformers better than the reformers have understood the machine. Reformers have one district locally from which their candidates harass the machine (this year one of the ablest reformers, Abner Mikva, is running for Congress with the support of the machine, a truce not uncommon in Chicago politics), and indeed are occasionally placed on the ticket statewide to broaden its base and serve as a safety valve to keep reformers from going after the machine, though, as far as the machine is concerned, a U. S. Senate seat, and the Governorship are minor offices. The races for state's attorney and state assessor (who can investigate and harass the machine) are much more important.

Thus in 1948, the year that Stevenson was running for Governor and Paul Douglas for the Senate, a golden year, a liberal happened to run into Colonel Jacob Arvey, then boss of the machine. "How's the election going?" the reformer asked. "Fine fine, couldn't be better," Arvey answered. "The polls show Boyle [state's attorney] way way ahead."

The Chicago machine had prospered under the New Deal, prospered to the point of venality, until it made Chicago probably the most corrupt city in the country. Everything could be bought or sold. The police force was largely concerned with street-corner traffic courts and the downtown center of the city was dying fast. So a reform movement was started behind Martin Kennelly, a clean and handsome businessman. He ran in 1951 as a reform candidate and won. The reformers were delighted; so were the Syndicate and the machine. It became easier to steal than before; underneath the surface honesty almost everything went wrong. Kennelly was totally naïve about a very tough city. To this day, a lot of Daley critics, knowing his faults and failings, think of John Lindsay and see Martin Kennelly.

The local Chicago establishment was so disturbed about the Kennelly years that an informal meeting was held to decide what to do about the Mayor. The first thing, they decided, was to destroy the myth that they themselves had created of the Good Reform Mayor. So they decided to approach a nationally known magazine writer and have him come in to expose Kennelly. Tom Stokes was selected and a leading lawyer was duly sent to visit him. Stokes proceeded to give him a lecture on why a nice businessman with high morals and fine ideals could never govern a city as tough as Chicago; he could never understand the balance between what the city required and what the politicians and crooks would permit. Chicago needed, Stokes said, a tough professional politician who understood the underside of Chicago life and how to control it.

HIS SECRET CLOUT

Enter Richard J. Daley. When he decided to run for Mayor he already wore an important political hat, clerk of Cook County, which was like being Secretary of State for the machine; it allowed him to dispense much of the machine's patronage. Before making the race he reportedly promised Colonel Arvey that he would give up the organizational job (which he didn't and it became the secret of his success). The primary was particularly bitter and it was repeatedly charged that electing Daley would be like throwing the rascals back in.

"I would not unleash the forces of evil," he countered. "It's a lie. I will follow the training my good Irish mother gave me—and Dad. If I am elected, I will embrace mercy, love, charity, and walk humbly with my God."

The machine was split (in the same ward one precinct went for Kennelly 485 to 7, while another precinct went for Daley 400 to 10). A number of reformers such as Stevenson came out for Daley, and with the help of Bill Dawson, Lord of the Negro wards, Daley won. In the general election he was opposed by Robert Merriam, an attractive Republican candidate who gave him a hard race. It was a hard fought campaign, the question being, who's going to control Chicago, State Street or the Neighborhoods (the rich or the poor)? Daley won again, decided to be both Mayor and organization chairman, thus to a degree breaking with Arvey. Most of his success has stemmed from that decision; it is an extraordinary achievement to hold both jobs with so little opposition for so long. (He was aided in the beginning by other polls, who underestimated him and felt he would be relatively easy to control.)

Daley's municipal ambition is backed up, to use the Chicago expression, with political clout. When he wants something done, it gets done. He knows every minuscule aspect of the city, both municipally and politically, knows the balance and has the political power to handle the people who don't measure up. As one Daley aide says, "I don't know how many times the Mayor told Bob Wagner there in New York to do the same thing, to go one way or another, either to be a reformer or to be like him, but to make a choice. But your city is different in New York—you people all have more illusions about yourselves."

From the time he took over almost thirteen years ago, Daley has steadily increased his power; where new power outside his sphere has risen up he has moved quickly and ably to incorporate it, to make it his. Where problems have arisen he has quickly appointed committees, often filled with former business foes, and then subtly moved the committees over to his own position. When there has been opposition, he has moved to embrace it (carrying always the threat of his real power if it didn't come along), to make it part of his consensus. Typically, several years ago the Republicans were prepared to run an excellent group of lawyers as judges. Daley went to them and said that if they ran as Republicans he would move Heaven and earth to beat them; if they ran as Democrats he would guarantee there would be no opposition. Most ran as Democrats.

As his power increased, so did his ability to accommodate people, and his ability to tell them to get on the team or be frozen out. Though Daley was strongly opposed by State Street in his first race, he has since practically destroyed the Republican party as a force within the city. He has given the business leaders what they want, a new downtown area, an expressway, a decent police force, confidence in the city's economic future (and if the school system is deteriorating, their children can always go to private or suburban schools). In return he has had his projects carried out with their support, and has gotten their political backing and campaign funds. The result of this is that it has been very difficult for a serious Republican candidate to make a challenge. It takes an estimated $1.5 million to run for Mayor of Chicago and any candidate would have a hard time raising $200,000 to run against Daley.

The Democratic primary is the decisive election within the city, much more so than in New York, and within the primary, all other things being equal, the machine is the dominant force. For it still functions well. Each ward committeeman has about 500 jobs (the eleventh ward, Daley's own in the Bridgeport neighborhood, has at least twice as many), and that means that each committeeman has a base in his own area of 500 families or more from which to operate. In general, the apparatus controls about 35,000 jobs and is considered to be worth about 100,000 votes in an election. Daley is very good about seeing that every committeeman gets his fair share of patronage, but it all comes down from the Mayor; he watches the organization to see who can still cut it and who can't. Through this system there is intense local control; if one block doesn't come through, everyone from top to bottom will know whose fault it is. The people just below Daley, the key committeemen, make their money selling insurance and real estate in their fiefs. But Daley has never been touched by scandal and probably never will be. The idea that he might be interested in money instead of sheer power would shock most Chicagoans. "It is Daley's greatest success that he has managed to convince the public that he is totally honest while at the same time conveying to the pols that he will permit clean graft so long as it is not abused and does not embarrass him," one newspaperman says. But even when there are abuses, he tries to take care of the offender; it is part of the ethic of loyalty. When he was first elected Daley had to clean out the Loop, which had become the center of crime. He carefully took all the hoods and semi-hoods who made their living there and put them in the Sanitation Department. About six years later the Sanitation Department began to go rotten and they had to be transferred again.

He has managed to keep the machine viable, to bring cost accounting to the city government, to keep up with many reforms in the New Deal tradition, and in the words of one political scientist, "to make the machine a limited instrument for social progress." He has bound together this unnatural consensus at a particularly difficult time, and part of the reason comes from the consensus itself; each member of it is aware of the others and of the counterpressure on the Mayor. This acts as a restraint; they will not push too far for fear of rocking the boat. Part of the reason, too, is that Daley simply works harder than his opponents. He is at early Mass when his enemies are still sleeping, and he is still working on city problems at night when they've all gone to bed or are out drinking. He pays enormous attention to detail; he goes over every job application, to a ridiculously low level. Finally he knows more about the petty details of Chicago than almost any of his critics. They, as Dr. Martin Luther King did, criticize the broad outlines of life in Chicago; he comes in armed with details of its daily life, what he is doing and what he would like to do but can't. "The Mayor could go on television tomorrow night and wave a wand to end discrimination but the next day life would be the same," says an aide.

He tries to control dissent in Chicago as much as he can, and outspoken critics from some papers and radio stations have occasionally left Chicago allegedly because of City Hall pressure; even in City Hall, when meetings are about to be called, there is what is known as the Ruly Crowd, made up of faithful followers ready to sit in at any meeting to keep out a potential Unruly Crowd. He avoids the press except on his own terms; reporters are avoided, though publishers are not; by Daley's maxim publishers have power and reporters do not. Besieged by magazine writers in the spring of this year he consented to see most of them. He was very gracious to me, sounding a little like Martin Luther King talking about race; yet I had the sense of being a mosquito bite, which once scratched would never itch again.

There was a sense that Daley was an American genius of sorts, a pragmatic man with a sense of man's corruptibility. He was successful where social reformers might have failed. He embodied many of the qualities which distinguish Chicago; he was as tough, as shrewd, ambitious, and sentimental as that city. When the Negroes, in their anger, burned Chicago, his city, his sentimental love for the place was almost childlike. He despaired; how could they do that to his city, how could they do that to him after all he had done for them? Why didn't the Negroes come forth now and show to the world how much they loved Chicago?

But Richard Daley knew more than most men where power existed, and it did not exist among the black citizens of the city. Part of this was his fault, but it was very late in the game. Now sixty-six, in what is almost surely his last term as Mayor, concerned more than anything else with his place in history, he presided over a city seething with racial problems, of steadily intensifying polarization, of a school system which was often useless; and many of the black people of the city saw him more than anyone else in the city, or the country, as the symbol of what was wrong with America. (A young Negro playwright named Ronald Fair could write a bitter play, *The Emperor's Parade,* about an Irish mayor who brings over an imported Irish leprechaun for his greatest day, the St. Patrick's Day parade, and goes berserk when it is ruined by black civil-rights marchers.) It was one of the ironies of Daley's rule of Chicago that because he had succeeded so much in other areas his failures on race relations seemed so marked. Unlike other mayors, one sensed that he had the power to do something.

BLACK POWER, LIMITED

For Chicago, despite all Daley's successes, is like other American cities: a place which is rotting. The pattern is not unusual—whites leaving the inner city as soon as they can afford to, jobs leaving the city too; Negroes taking over more of their old areas, Negroes bitter about their lack of jobs, their lack of power, their shabby schools, becoming more violent, their violence driving out more and more whites. The Poles and the other ethnic groups are angry and tense about the blacks *because they get all the attention,* because the country *is being run for them, all the politicians have sold out to them.* The ethnic groups hold onto their houses, bought after long and hard saving, by sheer dint of organized neighborhood feeling against the Negroes. White Congressmen from Polish neighborhoods, old-style New Deal liberals, are backtracking fast on civil rights, attacking school bussing, telling their friends, *What can I do, I try and explain, but they won't listen, they just won't listen.* The liberals are worried about the city but are moving to the suburbs faster and faster, while the traditionally liberal University of Chicago district becomes blacker and blacker. ("By the time the city is liberal enough to have a Jewish Mayor, it will have a black Mayor," one Jew says.) Those in our cities who are left to integrate with the blacks are those least prepared to understand and accept the problems of the blacks.

Perhaps 30 per cent of Chicago is black. Yet the black ghettos of Chicago are curiously powerless: they have little political bargaining power, and they have fewer jobs. A recent Urban League study on black power in Chicago showed that though Negroes composed 30 per cent of the population, they had only 2.6 per cent of policy-making positions in government and finance, and even that figure was probably optimistic.

Negro political leaders in Chicago have traditionally opted to play the machine's game, so that blacks in general have repeatedly been sold out by their own people; their representatives are ward politicians first, and Negroes second. "They can say no to us without checking higher up," one Negro said, "but they can never say yes without checking higher up." "I sometimes wonder," one white official remarked, "why so many of the Negroes on the City Council are so docile in this day and age, and then I realize that if they weren't docile they wouldn't be there."

The black community is thus divided against itself; its representatives are largely machine politicians interested in the traditional patronage and financial benefits, sensitive about intruding or being pushy in a white man's world, downplaying civil rights—just some of the boys mimicking the style of their white colleagues. "They're not even Toms," one Negro said. "There's no pretense at all to them. They play the game. That's what it's all about."

When on occasion a new Negro leader rises up and reflects power, Daley will try to accommodate and offer new and special privileges, with the alternative being a freeze-out. "So you have a tradition of people selling out, getting eroded. It's all too much for them," one white liberal who formerly served in the legislature said. "I know that white liberals will sit next to Negroes in the House and then the Negroes will occasionally encourage them on some liberal legislation. But when the vote comes the Negroes aren't there. So you ask them what the hell's going on, and they say, 'Look man, it's all right for you, you've got your own base, and you have something to fall back on. But this is all I've got, and if I don't do what they want, then I'm out of here.'"

All of this has probably tended to lull Daley's own view of reality. As one politician said, "The thing about him is that his machine is too successful for his own good. He allows these people so many jobs and so many positions and he thinks that he has real Negroes there and that the black community is satisfied. He doesn't realize that the community thinks that these people work for him, not for them. Then he sees the votes for him in the black wards and they're terrific votes because by the time the electoral process gets around, there's not much opposition and a lot of those people are scared to death anyway. So he decides that all this talk by civil-rights people is just talk, talk."

This, of course, is true only of the South Side, which is Chicago's older, more traditional ghetto. The South Side has some organizational form, some black representation. The West Side, in contrast, is a jungle. It is the port of entry for all the young illiterate blacks coming up from the South, and it is a wild, disorganized, and pitiful section. Those Negroes who make it go on to the South Side. Those who can't remain on the West Side, hopeless, without jobs, changing homes several times a year; the business establishments on the West Side are mostly all owned by whites who live elsewhere, the landlords are largely white and absentee, even the political machinery is controlled by whites, largely by Jews who once lived there and moved away, but have kept the political control. Inside it the kids are alienated and angry, totally outside the system.

After the murder of Dr. King the West Side burned. "Now," says A. A. Rayner, an independent alderman from the South Side, "they're building it back up just the way it was before, no decisions on the part of the people who live there, just the same people from the outside making all the decisions. If they put it up the same way, then it'll surely come down the same way again."

THE OUTLOOK FROM BRIDGEPORT

Daley would deal with these people if they had power, but they are so hopeless they are disinterested in the electoral process, their needs too great for the ballot. For twelve years they have gotten crumbs and the Mayor has manipulated them, confident that Chicago's Negroes have nowhere else to go in a showdown. If it is a choice between siding with them and with the white ethnic neighborhoods, which would have somewhere else to go (and with whom he has a basic sympathy and identity), he will edge more toward the whites. Thus black power in Chicago has stayed so small that finally in their anger and bitterness the blacks have a power, but it is a negative one, a power to destroy.

It is really a clash of two different cultures and ethics. Daley is from and of Bridgeport, a small Irish-American community which holds steadfastly to what it was. Going through it, the small bungalows, incredibly well kept up, sparkling with paint, the Blue Star flags in the windows, one has a sense of another time and place in America. Daley has lived in the same house for more than thirty years; he goes home for lunch every day. It is a neighborhood which has produced the last three Mayors of Chicago, and it has an unusually high percentage of people with city jobs. "Just about every house on the street has someone with political connections," one critic says. It is suspicious of outsiders and new ideas; Negroes do not walk its streets at night. Nor do they buy its property.

By dint of much effort, church centered, the property is kept up and the neighborhood is maintained. Negroes are not permitted to buy. A few years ago an unduly liberal resident sold to a Negro and riots resulted, windows were smashed, and the Negro's belongings were bodily moved out and the local Democratic organization moved two whites into the house.

Daley, of course, is better than Bridgeport, but he is still a part of it, and it influences the way he looks at social problems. He is deeply religious, but his religion is pre-Ecumenical, pre-John XXIII, where there is individual sin, but little social sin. He can tolerate small and petty graft, excuse an occasional roaring drunk, a failing of business virtue, but he cannot excuse adultery, and cannot understand or tolerate a man who fathers a family and then deserts it. He seems unable to understand the forces which create these failings.

He is a product of a time when the American ethic was to succeed, and those who didn't succeed at least respected those who did. He does not like poverty programs, in part because they represent a threat to his power—federal money going directly to black neighborhoods, without his control, diluting his base and creating a new base for an organization outside his machine, *financing his opposition.* Moreover, he doesn't think these people, what one lawyer calls "the underclass," are capable of leading and governing. "In his heart of hearts," one longtime associate says, "I think he would like to grab those people by their lapels, shake them and say *Get to work."* Two years ago a nun who was a militant civil-rights activist on the West Side went to see Daley and pleaded with him to come out there, to see the conditions, to look at the schools, to see the children.

"Look, Sister," the Mayor answered, "you and I come from the same background. We know how tough it was. But we picked ourselves up by our bootstraps."

WHEN KING CAME TO TOWN

The great challenge to Richard Daley's control of Chicago came in 1966 when Martin Luther King came to town. This became an almost classic conflict of two great forces: Daley with a tightly organized American political base—layer supporting layer of organizational structure, votes tangible, deliverable—pitted against a man whose power base was vague by traditional American terms, and was more moral than practical. In the immediate sense Daley certainly won, though the King people have a strong sense of social insight; it may be that years from now people will trace subsequent black victories and black awakenings to forces loosed by King's visit.

There is now some doubt among Chicagoans that Daley's victory was so wise. Some people feel that it was classic shortsightedness, that this time Daley really mixed the two jobs of politician and Mayor and viewed the challenge only as a politician, that King may have represented a chance to help save the city in spite of itself, that he might have helped give the kind of order to the black wards of Chicago that no white man can now do. "I'm not sure if Daley had to do it over again he wouldn't think twice," one reporter said, and then corrected himself. "No, that's me thinking. He'd do the same thing again."

King was unprepared for the immensity and complexity of Chicago. He and his people had never been noted for their organizational skill, but in the past they had operated in middle-sized Southern cities where they had a certain routine—find out who the best local people are, organize through them, pick out your targets, create your enemy, dramatize your fight against him, force them to make the mistakes.

In Chicago it was far more complicated. King just didn't have enough people. The city had different layers and different islands of Negro communities, and most of the existing black establishment saw King as a threat. ("Listen, don't tell us how well King's doing," a City Hall man told a reporter at the beginning of King's drive. "He had only forty people at his meeting last night and twenty of them were ours.")

As for Daley, he would be no Bull Connor; he would not be anyone's easy villain. Where King pushed, he would give away. Above all he would try and protect King and his people. Finally, King and his staff had no precise organizational plan of their own; it was their first venture into the North and they were deliberately biting off more than they could chew. If they could break Chicago, they could make it anywhere.

NO PROGRAM BUT A VISION

Early in their drive they invited Leon Despres, a white alderman who is Daley's foremost adversary in Chicago and a man who understands the Daley operation at least as well as the Mayor, to meet with them. Despres went before a large meeting and gave a precise description of how the machine worked—precinct by precinct, ward by ward, where it was vulnerable and what it would require in the way of hard work to beat it for aldermanic and legislative races. When he finished the crowd was enthusiastic. Then the Reverend James Bevel, a King deputy who was in charge of the Chicago program, a brilliant man but something of a mystic, said, "I believe in politics too. But if we do what this man wants then we're descending to the level of the opposition. We can't do that, we can't win and then end up like they are. That's not what we want."

Since Bevel was in charge of the program, the movement became largely speeches and street demonstrations; these demonstrations had their effect, and indeed terrified the white community by unleashing so much hatred. But if King had gone deeper, trying to match the organizational root in 1966, anti-Daley black politicians would probably be having an easier time in 1968.

Daley studied King, watched him move, sensed that he would not respond in a traditionally political way. ("Daley was always a little relieved and grateful that King had not come up here to become Mayor of Chicago," one lawyer said.) Finally, after feeling King out, Daley had a meeting with him. The meeting surprised Daley. He expected King to arrive with a long list of specific proposals (after all, Daley always went places with specific proposals). Daley's own staff was carefully rehearsed, and each member recited just exactly what his department was doing, where each swimming pool was being built.

None of these statistics and briefings had very much effect on King, who was concerned with the broad social ills of Chicago, who felt that Daley treated symptoms rather than causes, and who suspected that Daley was more interested in his machine than his people. The meeting broke up with Daley sure he could take King. "That King," one of Daley's press people said, "he didn't have any program. We had all these programs and we said, 'Why don't you help us? Why don't you do something for your people? Why don't you support Mayor Daley's programs? If you went on television and endorsed them do you realize how much good it would do? But, oh no, not him. And then that King left, and held a press conference and criticized the Mayor."

Even so, even without political power, King nearly brought Chicago to its knees. His street demonstrations touched off something very ugly in America. White racism exploded in the various ethnic neighborhoods. Day after day the scene repeated itself, the Negroes marching, the whites reacting with rocks and bricks, the replays on television, Daley's police forced again and again to arrest whites. Each day the establishment was more and more worried about the growing white racism.

Finally, King and Daley conferred again; it was the eve of King's proposed march into the tough Cicero neighborhood. As one white liberal described it, "The establishment would have given King almost anything not to make that march—it was worried sick what was going to happen. But King was too Christian, you know, and he was worried in his own mind about the Cicero march and what would happen to his own people and his responsibility for their lives—that's one difference between King and these younger people coming along now, they aren't going to worry very much about it—so he went into that room and the first thing he did was he gave away that Cicero march. They would have given him almost anything not to make it, and he gave it away at the beginning of the meeting." The result was a mild compromise of sorts—one of the usual citizens committees which sparkle throughout Chicago and America.

In the end, King's presence stirred many things in Chicago, including Operation Breadbasket (in which Negroes demanded jobs in proportion to their purchasing power, a very effective economic pressure). But though they encouraged others to challenge the system, and created forces which might someday help destroy the machine, it was a fact that King and his people had not developed a broad base in the poor black areas. In 1968 after King was slain, when the riots ensued and Richard Daley gave his shoot-to-kill order, the bulk of Daley's power was based upon the votes of poor blacks.

THE MAN WHO SWINGS COOK COUNTY

William L. Dawson made Dick Daley Mayor. And probably Harry Truman and John Kennedy President. And endless other smaller officeholders. For generations Bill Dawson has controlled and brokered the black vote in Chicago's South Side, a vote which could swing Cook County, Illinois, and ultimately the nation. Congressman Dawson is a Negro politician of the old school. ("He thinks like a machine man, not like a black man," one critic says.) His part of the machine in the poor black wards of the South Side is particularly well run; machines run better among the poor than among the rich. It is tightly organized. It runs on the basic patronage and the tiny—infinitesimal to white America—economic favors, gifts which went out as a political force in white America some sixteen years ago.

His is an almost classic political story. He is a Georgia Negro gone North; he served in World War I, and was wounded there. (One of his few memorable speeches in recent years came during the Korean war when there was an amendment before the House which would allow reservists to pick their units by race. Dawson delivered an eloquent speech describing his own service, his own wounds and bad medical service, and asked America how long it would inflict second class status on those who were dying for it.) Back to Chicago to work as a tailor, he made a hesitant entry into Republican politics, for the Republicans in those days were the party of the Negroes. He became the most successful precinct captain the Republicans had, and soon an alderman. With the coming of the New Deal and Franklin Roosevelt, he switched to the Democratic party, like many other Negro politicians of that era. He became a part of the Kelly-Nash machine, and hence more and more of a professional politician. ("The Kelly-Nash machine, you know they got their money's worth out of people, you never dealt with them for free," says Sammy Rayner, Dawson's opponent. "They said to him come along, we'll take care of you, and they did and he has never wanted since.")

He soon dominated the entire South Side, and in his time he was considered a great spellbinding speaker. Yet though he has always been for civil rights in his career, he has been under increasing attack from other blacks in the past decade; they feel he has been silent on too many things, and too much of an organization man.

"He's from a different generation," one of his critics says. "He does some good things, but he does them under cover—it's as if he feels there's something to be ashamed about, a black man demanding things. He believes if you make speeches, you make enemies." His opponents feel mainly that his organization has helped neutralize any new forces in the black community. Even his seniority in Congress—twenty-five years and chairman of the important Government Operations Committee—has done the Negro little good, they believe. A recent Urban League report cited Dawson, though not by name, as symbolic of the frustration of black people in Chicago: ". . . theoretically he is in a more strategic position to influence government operations than any other Chicago Congressman. Yet only 2 per cent of the top federal jobs located in Chicago were held by Negroes in 1965. Such limits on the ability of an individual to act for major race ends is grounded in his dependency on the institution either to maintain his post or to gain minor racial concessions. . . ."

In recent years Dawson's power has been limited even within the machine. At one time he was a broker for all the Negro aldermen, but several years ago Daley, not wanting any sub-brokers in Chicago, made alliances with other Negroes which broke part of Dawson's power. In addition there has been some criticism of Dawson by nonreform blacks who feel he has permitted Italians to take over the rackets in the South Side and hence sold out his own people.[1]

Dawson is old now; his age is listed at eighty-two, and some people believe he may even be ninety. He suffered a stroke several years ago and he does not see the public very often now. His office is often closed, he has little contact with civil-rights leaders. When a group of Chicago businessmen visited him in late May, they were stunned to hear him talk about Martin Luther King as if King were still alive. "That King is stealing money from these people and sending it to a bank in Geneva," he told them.

Thus by any normal standards, given the rising feeling in the ghettos, defeating Dawson in the primary should be relatively easy. It isn't. Though he does not campaign at all in the traditional sense, the machine virtually runs itself; there are some strong deputies to Dawson who find the present situation very profitable and are not about to see it disappear.

There are some chinks—the changing temper of Negroes, the increasing number of the Negro middle class, with the middle class votes strongly anti-Dawson (the District is gerrymandered to keep whites out). But much of the District is still poor. The Negroes live on welfare and in public housing ("high-rise vertical dungeons," one young Negro calls them) and they are frightened. They have been told over and over again they will lose their welfare and their housing by representatives of the organization, who also happen to sell them their insurance, visiting them monthly since Negro insurance is not sold long-term.

Thus the pols keep a close and friendly touch on the poor; they know every name and make sure every name votes. "Man, you whites think that King and those other preachers know these people," one black organization worker told a reporter recently. "They don't know these people. These people here, they don't want no talk. They can't eat that. You think any of these new preachers ever visited these people? They're too busy talking to white people like you. We talk to these people and we know them. We the ones get it done.

---

[1] The Urban League report adds: "Exclusion of Negroes is not limited to legal and legitimate spheres of activity. Thirty years ago gambling was one of the few areas in which Negroes held tangible power. Although the Syndicate with its billion dollar a year Chicago operation was not included in this formal survey, it is worthwhile noting recent data on the structure of this organization which wields power and political influence. No Negroes held positions among the alleged thirteen leaders in the crime Syndicate. There are five Negroes in the Chicago Crime Commission's 1967 list of 216 major Syndicate members; only one of these is reputed to have even minor authority. . . ."

Remember that. We the ones get it done." These poor housing developments turn out votes of twenty to one for the machine.

DISSENTER MAKES NEWS

The signs of Alabama A. A. (Sammy) Rayner say very simply: "If not Sammy . . . Who? If not now . . . When?" Rayner is something unique in Chicago, white or black. He is an open and strong-willed opponent of the machine, working in a rough alliance with another Negro, Bill Cousins, and Despres as the Opposition. Rayner, fifty, does not need to be a politician. He is an undertaker and with his father owns four funeral homes. He entered the race, he says, because there was no one else to do it. Four years ago he ran against Dawson and made a surprisingly good race: Dawson received 46,000 and Rayner, one of four others running, got 24,000. ("Sammy's a bit of a nut, you know," one white politician says. "If I had run that well against Dawson I'd have called it victory and made the machine deal with me, but no, Sammy Rayner got up there and told us he'd been defeated.")

Since then he has been elected to the City Council, knocking off one of Dawson's people. In the Council he fights Daley regularly, despite the frequent opportunity to play ball with the machine. One benefit of his opposition is that he, Despres, and Cousins get very good television coverage. Since most of the Council goes along with everything Daley does (one member simply attends and at every meeting keeps saying, "Thank God for Mayor Daley, Thank God for Mayor Daley! ") the dissenters make the news.

He has other things going for him. In an area where there is a tradition of dissenting politicians soon selling out, Rayner had stayed clean. In addition, though he is successful and has the backing of the middle class, he is a free-spirited and joyous man. (When I arrived the first thing he did was show me a postcard showing some African Watusi on the cover, and saying, "Dear Alderman. This is your brother. He needs your ability to build slums because you are the best at it.") He talks easily with all blacks. "Sammy," one young man with a natural haircut said, "talks good soul."

Yet he has enormous problems, based on the traditional divisions within the black community. When he first announced for the race, the young Black Nationalists told him not to run against another black man, that he was playing into the white man's hands. (Part of the reason was that some of the Nationalists were more loyal to Gus Savage, a black man making a highly possible race against a white incumbent in another district. It was a decision among some people in the black community to make the Savage race the priority campaign.)

Now in the last week in May, with the election scheduled for June 11, some of the Nationalists and younger kids were beginning to come around for Rayner ("Well, can you imagine them with their natural-style hairdos walking into the machine offices and working there? " Rayner laughed.) On occasions in his uphill fight Rayner was a little optimistic, but few of his white friends were. "Sammy doesn't even have voter lists," one said. "You know, lists of every voter in every building. That's what makes it go round in this city."

(To a degree this formula was right; when the primary vote finally came in,

Dawson ran strongly enough in the housing developments to win, 28,038 to 18,573; it was the closest anyone had come since the insurgents started going after Dawson in 1962, and Dawson's own vote was down about 15,000 votes from the total he received in the 1966 primary. But the machine marched on.)

It is a difficult campaign run at many levels. It is not well financed. Rayner, a peace candidate, thought he was going to get money from white people opposed to the war, but when President Johnson pulled out the money dried up. One night in late May, with four stops at middle-class houses where receptions were being organized over a current school fight, was typical. The meetings were quite proper, and Rayner was trying to get people to work and vote for him: "You know, I was with Charles Evers in Mississippi and down there black people weren't allowed to vote, and Charles can't understand us, no he can't understand it at all, what we do up here where we can vote, and we don't do anything." There is a murmur of assent from the people in the room. One of the women scribbles down the name of a Dawson precinct captain who wants to come over. "I've had a lot of them lately, these old boys. They lost a lot of jobs in the county, because the Republicans have county offices and when jobs go, why it's Negro jobs which go first," he says. Another woman, worried because in her polling place the Dawson people always hand out fried chicken and canned peas, asked one final question. What should she do? "Eat the chicken and vote for me," Rayner says.

"YOU FRIGHTENED?"

On to the next meeting. This one also middle-class. Most of the people here have made a nominal success in America; with husband and wife working, the incomes are probably over $12,000 a year, and yet they still live in ghettos with terrible schools and problems of crime. When the Jews and Irish made it, they were able to move to better neighborhoods; when the Negroes make it, they are still boxed in. There is particular anger at this meeting because the high school, less than ten years old, is now at 200 per cent of capacity and the floors are all condemned.

Rayner talks to them about this, about the need to have their own representatives, and he jokes with them about the difference between being black and Negro: "The other day Bill Cousins [Harvard-educated] was talking before the City Council and he started saying, 'The Negroes of Chicago feel—I beg your pardon—the blacks of Chicago . . .'" Another young Negro, running for the state legislature, is there and he talks against the new black mood for separatism. His remarks seem to go over reasonably well at the meeting. But later Rayner says the young man will have to learn to cool the integration thing, it isn't the time and place for it; they want to hear separatism now—"Maybe the other will come back some day."

Late at night the last stop is at a Nationalist meeting, which also seems to be a discotheque. Everyone is in Mod-Afro dress with natural hair styles. It is dark (fortunately for me) and the air is filled with bitter anti-white rhetoric. Rayner is welcomed with real enthusiasm. "Now there are these politicians, and they are *Negro* politicians, and we know what *Negro* means," one young man is saying. "It means they work for the white man instead of the black man. Means they work in the white man's kitchens. We have here a man who's black. A black politician. At least he's pretty black. Sammy Rayner. Sammy does some of the things that all politicians have to do, but he has to. But he's blacker than most. So our black friend, our soul brother, Sammy Rayner."

Rayner is a little annoyed by the introduction, but he smiles and acknowledges it nevertheless. He does not speak. Then on with black rhetoric. It is very ugly, and I am a little frightened, not so much for myself as for what is happening in this country. Rayner pushes me over to a dim corner and tells me to sit down. He stands in front of me so that the speakers will not see me and use me as a foil. The words spew out: "Kill the honkies. They like to kill niggers, we'll kill the honkies . . . We got soul, we got beauty, black people come to soul like flies come to sugar. . . . And so the honkies are like snakes and maybe they don't think they're snakes, but if its grandmother was a snake, and its mother was a snake, maybe it's a snake too, and so if they're going to get me, why on the way I'm goin' to kill me some snakes."

There is more rhetoric, all of it curiously disjointed, and the moment it stops we slip away. Rayner looks at me. "You frightened?" he asks. "Yes," I answered, for it reminds me of being in Bessemer, Alabama, at Klan meetings. "All they do is talk," he says, "just talk. probably anything happened they'd all disappear. Probably none of them is registered to vote."

Three days later I had lunch with a Negro youth leader from the same area. The leader is a well-known militant. He is angry about black powerlessness. At the end I asked him about how good Sammy Rayner's chances were. "Not too good," he said. "When is that election? November?"

A DAY IN THE LIFE

John V. Lindsay

The Mayor of New York presides over a city of 8 million people. During the working hours that population swells by several million people and tens of thousands of cars as the suburbanites flock to the core of Manhattan to work, shop and play. He presides over a city budget of $6.6 billion—greater than the budget of any single state. His city builds almost $2 billion a year in facilities. It employs 350,000 people. It teaches a million elementary and secondary school pupils every day. It puts 32,000 policemen on its streets each day to help protect safety. It tows away 100,000 illegally parked cars a year from midtown

John V. Lindsay, **THE CITY,** *Chapter 3. New York: W. W. Norton & Co., copyright ©
1969, 1970. Reprinted by permission of the publisher.*

Manhattan alone, and hauls away 60,000 more cars that have simply been abandoned by their owners. It runs a court system that rivals that of any state.

The numbers are staggering. Each of them, in one way or another, touches my life every day. Each of them defines a small part of the job that a Mayor of New York has; each of them poses new demands on an overtaxed, undernourished city treasury; each of them demands more productivity from a governmental structure that can barely keep pace with outmoded definitions of its job.

For beyond these numbers are the cold, hard facts of city life. With such an enormous number of people, with such a disparate collection of facilities, a statistically small fraction can mean tremendous burdens. Of 8 million people, a certain percentage get sick every day, and some of them cannot afford their own medical care. That means a system of twenty municipal hospitals employing thousands of doctors and nurses who must care for numbers far greater than the system's capacity for proper treatment because it lacks funds.

A small portion of a $2 billion capital construction budget is inevitably going to be delayed. What that means is that in some neighborhoods important facilities are behind schedule, and a community is up in arms because something it needs is not ready.

On any given day some of the thousands of miles of road will be in disrepair—but in a city as densely populated and traffic-choked as New York the closing of a single lane of traffic on a single midtown street can snarl traffic for hours and send new waves of frustration coursing through the veins of the city.

In New York, in other words, every problem—even those that are statistically small—are large. And in cases where the problems are relatively large—such as in the achievement levels of city schoolchildren or the number of people on welfare—you have a crisis of major proportions on your hands.

Then, too, you begin to recognize what may be the prime fact of municipal life—the essential interdependency of problems and solutions.

Take air pollution. That seems like a simple, single problem: pass stiff legislation to put polluters out of business. Force them to improve their machinery or shut down. But it isn't that simple.

Every time you shut down an incinerator, you increase the amount of garbage on the city streets. Every time you do that, you either have to put more street-cleaning forces out or face the fact that you are going to have a dirtier city. If incinerators can't burn garbage, it's going to be out on the street to be collected—or not collected. And that means that we are going to have to find the money to collect that garbage and to dispose of it rapidly, assuming we can find a place to bury it, before it builds up to the point where it engulfs us completely. So you cannot solve the pollution problem without solving the sanitation problem, and you can't solve either problem without money.

Or take traffic congestion. For years, people have been urging New York City to shut midtown Manhattan to private automobiles, which clog the streets and make midtown passage a challenge for Ulysses. But you cannot shut Manhattan to cars unless you are sure you are providing alternative transportation. That means mass transit—even more than we are now planning and engineering—from outlying areas into Manhattan, the core business and shopping district of the city.

Further, before you ban cars from midtown, you must listen to the arguments of the handicapped, United Nations diplomats and foreign consuls, garage operators, commuting businessmen, department store owners, merchants of every variety, the Automobile Association of America, and other powerful interests. And if you are not positive that you have designed an alternative to autos that works, you have lost not only an argument but also some of your credibility, without which any further attempt at city planning becomes virtually a lost cause. Thus the act of banning autos from midtown Manhattan is far from a unitary act of planning. It raises a wide range of other political, economic, and planning questions that are difficult to answer.

These are the kinds of question the Mayor is asked regularly. Because of the sheer size of the city and its government, almost every day brings with it basic planning decisions—decisions that will set the course of the city for years to come. If you approve a transit route, the location of a new industrial park, or a major housing project, you are committing great sums of money and great amounts of time on a single project that in turn will affect the entire life style of the surrounding area. And the city is so big that these decisions, which the Mayor of an average city may have to make once or twice in his term, are made by the Mayor of New York daily. Projects that would completely dominate the attention of most other towns are all but lost in the sheer enormousness of New York.

The only effective way I know to meet this problem is to get as much information as possible—information, and more information—and getting it determines much of my life. A typical day usually begins well before 8:00 A.M. on the telephone, an instrument that is a critical part of my life. Until well past midnight I am asking questions and answering them, listening to people and talking to them, on the phone or face to face, in an effort to know as much as possible about the consequences of each decision I must make.

Twice a week I meet with the principal policy makers of the city, the commissioners and administrators of the city departments and agencies. It is their prime responsibility to keep the basic city machinery running well and to design machinery to help it run better.

The City Planning Commission, for example, should know what the Economic Development Administration thinks about a proposed new city park site. Might it affect a decision of a major business firm to locate here? If so, are there alternative sites for a park? What is the increased cost of that alternative, and does the Budget Bureau think the greater costs are merited? Or would we risk losing a business that may move to the city because of the social benefit of that park at that time?

What is happening with the Regional Manpower Centers, designed to train and equip people with job skills? Are the centers behind schedule? If so, why? Are we lagging on capital-construction projects in this field, and if so is there anything we can do about it? Is the relevant agency hiring teachers and renting classroom space? If not, is it a lack of money? Is the Budget Bureau slowing down the program? If so, why?

By the time such a meeting is over the backlog of calls has already mounted. A call to Washington to an official in the Health, Education, and Welfare Department. For the fourth time, I argue for a total scrapping of the welfare system and a wholesale replacement by a federally funded program emphasizing job placement and advancement. A check with our Washington office to see whether or not the national administration has changed its mind on the proposal, and a reminder to find out when the funds that we were promised under the Housing Act will actually be reserved for us so we can start in with construction of low-income housing. A call from the leader of a public employees' union to tell me that a new vacation policy of a city department is in violation of a collective-bargaining provision and may trigger a strike. A call from a high school principal advising us of disorder in his school, coupled with a request for more police protection. A call from our Albany office to warn me that a bill is pending that will "mandate" certain unwanted costs on the city and its already bursting budget.

While all this is going on a community group may be waiting in another room in City Hall for a long-promised meeting. As I have already mentioned, almost every group in the city at one point or another wants to meet with the Mayor, because he is the highest elected official of the most immediate form of government. The problem is that the answers I give to their legitimate questions cannot, by definition, be satisfactory, unless the demand is for a specific, relatively low-cost request like a traffic light outside a school or the acceleration of an already-approved project.

Usually, however, the complaints are about more basic problems in the city. We don't have enough police. The garbage isn't picked up frequently enough. The subway system is a disgrace (in fact, the city does not even have authority over the subway system—it's the province of a state agency, the Metropolitan Transit Authority).

I listen to their inquiries and answer them the best way I can. But it won't do to say that every neighborhood wants more police—the questioner doesn't live in "every neighborhood," he lives in *this* neighborhood, and he does not want danger on *his* streets.

In late morning I may be meeting with any one of my assistants who are responsible for specific areas of city government—poverty, housing, environmental protection, sanitation. Such meetings are necessary to bring me up to date on developments within that agency: on programs that are or are not working well, on conflicts between the agency and other forces, either inside or outside of city government. If a crisis is serious enough, it may mean forty-five minutes of hastily called meetings or phone calls, throwing me further behind schedule.

Meanwhile, the calls keep coming. The director of our Washington office calls about the status of a program and wants me to call a Cabinet officer or a member of the Congress. A state senator or city councilman asks about a specific problem in his district. The Press Secretary has an inquiry from a newspaper that requires a fast answer about a politically sensitive subject. Someone from Albany says that the state legislature wants to know more about a tax-reform bill before taking action.

Or, if there is a scheduled press conference—generally, I have two a week—Tom Morgan, my Press Secretary, will meet with me and a small staff for the briefing. Here we'll try to plan our message and map out in advance a strategy for avoiding political traps that an innocent-looking press conference can produce. Finally, you must rely on your wits, and those of a good press secretary, to protect yourself from the dangers of a press conference: making policy through carelessly thought-out answers, giving off-the-cuff responses to unanticipated questions. So the press briefing may last a full hour to cover in advance as many questions as possible, straight or curved.

On any given day chances are I will give a talk somewhere at lunchtime (dinnertime as well). It may be the Queens-Brooklyn Rotary club, which wants specific problems about their region solved (What about the master plan for economic development of Jamaica? What is your proposal to reduce the welfare burden on New York?). It may be a conference on an issue directly affecting New York, such as pollution control or addiction. Speeches like these give me a chance to measure some of our progress. Four years ago I was talking about problems—today I am talking more about solutions.

After lunch, which is often a sandwich at my desk or in the car, I may go up to Gracie Mansion and spend the rest of the day working there. City Hall has been correctly labeled a gold-fish bowl, and there is no such thing as a private meeting. Any visitor is duly noticed by the press and accosted for comment on the way in or out. Gracie Mansion offers a far greater degree of privacy. It's also a less prepossessing, more comfortable place than City Hall, and meetings tend to be more congenial, as a general rule.

If it's time to plan the city's budget, I will be spending several days with officials from the budget Bureau and city agencies going over our budget requests for each department. Budget time is probably the roughest time of all for me. I spend much of my day during this period in the office of the Budget Director, Fred Hayes, where budget teams are available and where there is less pressure from the phone. Coffee is consumed by the gallon. No other process demonstrates more graphically what is meant by the city's chronic shortage of money. To someone looking at a city budget, a $6.6 billion municipal budget seems insanely high. How could any budget request not be met? In a city of 8 million people the answer to that question is all too simple: our expenses keep going up far faster than our revenues, because the sources from which we get our money are basically stagnant. They do not grow with a growing economy.

At budget-setting time we receive and review agency requests. How much is this new program going to cost? What specifically will the social costs be if we do not adopt this program? If this program of medical services is not adopted, where is the impact likely to be felt? Increased hospital costs for certain communities? If it's an addiction center that can't be funded, what does it tell us about the potential crime rate, and doesn't that justify the cost? How many housing units must be scrapped? How many summer jobs for high school students will we have to cut back on? These are the kinds of questions no Mayor wants to answer, for the choices are always impossible. But that is what it means to be Mayor at its most frustrating moments, for you choose not between two grandiose programs but between two essential services, attempting to figure out how best to distribute the thin resources that are available. Moreover, you do it knowing with dead certainty that next year at this same time you will be going through the same process—except worse—again, unless the Congress and state governments begin to recognize the full dimensions of city needs that have gone unmet.

After the budget retreat (or rout, as it sometimes has been), other specific problems may arise—frequently only in passing, since there is never enough time for commissioners, administrators, staff assistants, and others to schedule formal meetings. It may be that a conflict of judgment between two forces has arisen that I must resolve. It may be that an outside source is willing to underwrite the cost of a private program of help to the city, if we can convince that source of its importance. At any event, it means more time on the telephone.

By late afternoon the tempo has reached its peak (particularly if some important decision has made news, which is often). It reflects the simple fact that each decision the city makes sets in motion a series of other decisions—and for each of these there must be consultations with different city agencies, discussions with city groups that may be affected and an attempt to find out whether that decision has proved to be the right one.

For example, we were battling last year for the passage of a bill in the state legislature to enable us to put another platoon of policemen on the city streets. As part of the state's domination of city government, the state had enacted a law telling the city when and how to deploy its own police forces, which are funded by the city and its taxpayers. Several times before the vote I had been on the telephone and held meetings concerning this issue with editorialists on New York newspapers and with key state legislators who were helping to push the bill through. Finally the fight was won, but then it was vital to put the change through with a minimum of dispute. This meant a series of talks with the Police Commissioner to discuss his plans for implementing the fourth platoon and our efforts to deal with the lawsuit the Patrolmen's Benevolent Association was instituting to invalidate the new law.

It meant talks between the Corporation Counsel and the Commissioner to buttress the legal case against the suit. It meant a short call to the president of the PBA to tell him that if we won the fight we would work with him and the Association to minimize any hardships that might arise from the new law. And it meant initial planning to decide when the fourth platoon would begin, and where—and what kind of criteria we would use to judge the effectiveness of putting a substantially greater number of men on the streets at night.

Then, before the afternoon ends, there may be a meeting of the Executive Committee of the Urban Coalition, or possibly a meeting with the U.S. Ambassador to the United Nations and our new UN Advisory Committee, designed to make New York a better host city to the hundreds of UN families in our midst.

It's a constant battle to try to hold dinnertime for my wife and children, and I'm successful only about once or twice a week, usually on the weekend. Given the realities of public life in New York, I am out almost every night making speaking engagements or attending meetings to drum up support for such major programs as summer youth recreational and employment programs, which depend on the willingness of those in the private sector to shoulder their burden. But at the infrequent family dinner I try to spend the time on strictly family matters. It usually doesn't work out that way. At some point during the meal a phone call will require an instant decision: delegating authority to make an on-the-spot decision on a specific city project, getting information about a suddenly erupting crisis, or just catching up on the phone calls that did not get completed during the day. More often, I work straight through until 10 or 11 and then have dinner on a tray near the phone in the library of Gracie Mansion. My wife had a warmer installed in the kitchen of the Mansion that works remarkably well, and can keep a cooked dinner fresh all night (it's too bad they can't do the same for a Mayor). Often Mary will join me while I eat, working on her own mountain of mail.

On the rare occasions that I am home with Mary and the children for dinner, I'm usually off afterward to whatever meeting has been arranged by me and my staff for that evening. As often as not, the schedule during the day has become so tight that I'm forced to hold some appointments in the car while traveling from Gracie Mansion to a speaking engagement and back. It's not a satisfactory way of doing business, particularly if five people are wedged into the back seats, but it is frequently the only alternative to putting off appointments indefinitely—and where a decision is required, there is no real choice. The city moves too fast to stop.

There is, you may have noticed, only one flaw in this tightly packed schedule. It leaves me almost no room for thinking. There are those, I know, who don't believe it is part of an executive's job to think: he is just supposed to decide by listening to all the options and checking one of three boxes. I can't work that way. Possibly because of a law-school background, I try to read the documents involved with a basic policy decision. And that means that I'm usually up until 1:00 A.M. and beyond.

There is, further, one part of a Mayor's job that cannot be scheduled. And that is the possibility of a crisis—a sudden interruption of normality by an unpredictable event. During the teachers' strike in New York City the desperate search for a solution brought my involvement in most other phases of city government virtually to a standstill. During threats of disorder over the first three summers of my administration there were long, unscheduled hours devoted to personal walks on the city streets and constant efforts to follow up on promises to open up communications between tense communities and the city.

But somehow, even when the crises come, the city still keeps running. It makes you wonder sometimes about all the effort you put in during the normal days, even with full knowledge that "normal" is far from good enough.

This, at any event, is a general picture of the way I spend my time. But the more important question is the goal of this effort. What is it we are trying to do in New York City?

I can briefly answer that question. We're trying to hold this city together against the forces that are steadily eating away at it. We're trying to keep it together and at the same time we're hoping to change it in fundamental ways. To better understand this job, it's probably necessary to examine the state of New York City as it had become before I took office, and to recognize why we felt the new administration would face an enormous burden.

2. THE NOT SO GENTLE GAME OF "URBAN POWER"

AN ADVOCATE OF BLACK POWER
DEFINES IT

Charles V. Hamilton

Black Power has many definitions and connotations in the rhetoric of race relations today. To some people, it is synonymous with premeditated acts of violence to destroy the political and economic institutions of this country. Others equate Black Power with plans to rid the civil-rights movement of whites who have been in it for years. The concept is understood by many to mean hatred of and separation from whites; it is associated with calling whites "honkies" and with shouts of "Burn, baby, burn! " Some understand it to be the use of pressure-group tactics in the accepted tradition of the American political process. And still others say that Black Power must be seen first of all as an attempt to instill a sense of identity and pride in black people.

Ultimately, I suspect, we have to accept the fact that, in this highly charged atmosphere, it is virtually impossible to come up with a single definition satisfactory to all.

Even as some of us try to articulate our idea of Black Power and the way we relate to it and advocate it, we are categorized as "moderate" or "militant" or "reasonable" or "extremist." "I can accept your definition of Black Power," a listener will say to me. "But how does your position compare with what Stokely Carmichael said in Cuba or with what H. Rap Brown said in Cambridge, Md.? " Or, just as frequently, some young white New Left advocate will come up to me and proudly announce: "You're not radical enough. Watts, Newark, Detroit—that's what's happening, man! You're nothing but a reformist. We've got to blow up this society. Read Che or Debray or Mao." All I can do is shrug and conclude that some people believe that making a revolution in this country involves rhetoric, Molotov cocktails and being under 30.

To have Black Power equated with calculated acts of violence would be very unfortunate. First, if black people have learned anything over the years, it is that he who shouts revolution the loudest is one of the first to run when the action starts. Second, open calls to violence are a sure way to have one's ranks immediately infiltrated. Third—and this is as important as any reason—violent revolution in this country would fail; it would be met with the kind of repression used in Sharpeville, South Africa, in 1960, when 67 Africans were killed and 186 wounded during a demonstration against apartheid. It is clear that America is not above this. There are many white bigots who would like nothing better than to embark on a program of black genocide, even though the imposition of such repressive measures would destroy civil liberties for whites as well as for blacks. Some whites are so panicky, irrational and filled with racial hatred that they would welcome the opportunity to annihilate the black community. This was clearly shown in the senseless murder of Dr. Martin Luther King, Jr., which understandably—but nonetheless irrationally—prompted some black militants to advocate violent retaliation. Such cries for revenge intensify racial fear and animosity when the need—now more than ever—is to establish solid, stable organizations and action programs.

Many whites will take comfort in these words of caution against violence. But they should not. The truth is that the black ghettos are going to continue to blow up out of sheer frustration and rage, and no amount of rhetoric from professors writing articles in magazines (which most black people in the ghettos do not read anyway) will affect that. There comes a point beyond which people cannot be expected to endure prejudice, oppression and deprivation, and they *will* explode.

Some of us can protect our positions by calling for "law and order" during a riot, or by urging "peaceful" approaches, but we should not be confident that we are being listened to by black people legitimately fed up with intolerable conditions. If white America wants a solution to the violence in the ghettos by blacks, then let white America end the violence done to the ghettos by whites. We simply must come to understand that there can be no social order without social justice. "How long will the violence in the summers last? " another listener may ask. "How intransigent is white America? " is my answer. And the answer to that could be just more rhetoric or it could be a sincere response to legitimate demands.

Black Power must not be naive about the intentions of white decision-makers to yield anything without a struggle and a confrontation by organized power. Black people will gain only as much as they can win through their ability to organize independent bases of economic and political power—through boycotts, electoral activity, rent strikes, work stoppages, pressure-group bargaining. And it must be clear that whites will have to bargain with blacks or continue to fight them in the streets of the Detroits and the Newarks. Rather than being a call to violence, this is a clear recognition that the ghetto rebellions, in addition to producing the possibility of apartheid-type repression, have been functional in moving *some* whites to see that viable solutions must be sought.

Black Power is concerned with organizing the rage of black people and with putting new, hard questions and demands to white America. As we do this, white America's responses will be crucial to the questions of violence and viability. Black Power must (1) deal with the obviously growing alienation of black people and their distrust of the institutions of this society; (2) work to create new values and to build a new sense of community and of belonging, and (3) work to establish legitimate new institutions that make participants, not recipients, out of a people traditionally excluded from the fundamentally racist processes of this country. There is nothing glamorous about this; it involves persistence and hard, tedious, day-to-day work.

Black Power rejects the lessons of slavery and segregation that caused black people to look upon themselves with hatred and disdain. To be "integrated" it was necessary to deny one's heritage, one's own culture, to be ashamed of one's black skin, thick lips and kinky hair. In their book, "Racial Crisis in America," two Florida State University sociologists, Lewis M. Killian and Charles M. Grigg, wrote: "At the present time, integration as a solution to the race problem demands that the Negro foreswear his identity as a Negro. But for a lasting solution, the meaning of 'American' must lose its implicit racial modifier, 'white.'" The black man must change his demeaning conception of himself; he must develop a sense of pride and self-respect. Then, if integration comes, it will deal with people who are psychologically and mentally healthy, with people who have a sense of their history and of themselves as whole human beings.

In the process of creating these new values, Black Power will, its advocates hope, build a new sense of community among black people. It will try to forge a bond in the black community between those who have "made it" and those "on the bottom." It will bring an end to the internal back-biting and suspicious bickering, the squabbling over tactics and personalities so characteristic of the black community. If Black Power can produce this unity, that in itself will be revolutionary, for the black community and for the country.

Black power recognizes that new forms of decision-making must be implemented in the black community. One purpose, clearly, is to overcome the alienation and distrust.

Let me deal with this specifically by looking at the situation in terms of "internal" and "external" ghetto problems and approaches. When I speak of internal problems, I refer to such things as exploitative merchants who invade the black communities, to absentee slumlords, to inferior schools and arbitrary law enforcement, to black people unable to develop their own independent economic and political bases. There are, of course, many problems facing black people which must be dealt with outside the ghettos: jobs, open occupancy, medical care, higher education.

The solution of the internal problems does not require the presence of massive numbers of whites marching arm in arm with blacks. Local all-black groups can organize boycotts of disreputable merchants and of those employers in the black communities who fail to hire and promote black people. Already, we see this approach spreading across the country with Operation Breadbasket, initiated by Dr. King's Southern Christian Leadership Conference. The national director of the program, the Rev. Jesse Jackson, who was with Dr. King when he was murdered in Memphis, has established several such projects from Los Angeles to Raleigh, N. C.

In Chicago alone, in 15 months, approximately 2,000 jobs worth more than $15-million in annual income were obtained for black people. Negotiations are conducted on hiring and upgrading black people, marketing the products of black manufacturers and suppliers and providing contracts to black companies. The operation relies heavily on the support of black businessmen, who are willing to work with Operation Breadbasket because it is mutually beneficial. They derive a profit and in turn contribute to the economic development of the black community.

This is Black Power in operation. But there is not nearly enough of this kind of work going on. In some instances, there is a lack of technical know-how coupled with a lack of adequate funds. These two defects constantly plague constructive pressure-group activity in the black communities.

CORE (Congress of Racial Equality) has developed a number of cooperatives around the country. In Opelousas, La., it has organized over 300 black farmers, growers of sweet potatoes, cabbages and okra, in the Grand-Marie Co-op. They sell their produce and some of the income goes back into the co-op as dues. Initially, 20 per cent of the cooperative's members were white farmers, but most of the whites dropped out as a result of social and economic pressures from the white community. An offshoot of the Grand-Marie group is the Southern Consumers' Cooperative in Lafayette, La., which makes and sells fruit cakes and candy. It has been in existence for more than a year, employs approximately 150 black people and has led to the formation of several credit unions and buying clubs.

The major effort of Black Power-oriented CORE is in the direction of economic development. Antoine Perot, program director of CORE, says: "One big need in the black community is to develop capital-producing instruments which create jobs. Otherwise, we are stuck with the one-crop commodity—labor —which does not produce wealth. Mere jobs are not enough. These will simply perpetuate black dependency."

Thus, small and medium-sized businesses are being developed in the black communities of Chicago, San Francisco, Detroit, Cleveland, New York and several other urban centers. CORE hopes to call on some successful black businessmen around the country as consultants, and it is optimistic that they will respond favorably with their know-how and, in some instances, their money. The goal is to free as many black people as possible from economic dependency on the white man. It has been this dependency in many places that has hampered effective independent political organizing.

In New York, Black Power, in the way we see it, operates through a group called N.E.G.R.O. (National Economic Growth and Reconstruction Organization). Its acronym does not sit too well with some advocates of black consciousness who see in the use of the term "Negro" an indication of less than sufficient racial pride. Started in 1964, the group deals with economic self-help for the black community: a hospital in Queens, a chemical corporation, a textile company and a construction company. N.E.G.R.O., with an annual payroll of $1-million and assets of $3-million, is headed by Dr. Thomas W. Matthew, a neurosurgeon who has been accused of failing to file Federal income-tax returns for 1961, 1962 and 1963. He has asserted that he will pay all the Government says he owes, but not until "my patient is cured or one of us dies." His patient is the black community, and the emphasis of his group is on aiding blacks and reducing reliance on the white man. The organization creates a sense of identity and cohesiveness that is painfully lacking in much of the black community.

In helping oneself and one's race through hard work, N.E.G.R.O. would appear to be following the Puritan ethic of work and achievement: if you work hard, you will succeed. One gets the impression that the organization is not necessarily idealistic about this. It believes that black people will never develop in this country as long as they must depend on handouts from the white man. This is realism, whatever ethic it is identified with. And this, too, is Black Power in operation.

More frequently than not, projects will not use the term "Black Power," but that is hardly necessary. There is, for instance, the Poor People's Corporation, formed by a former S.N.C.C. (Student Nonviolent Coordinating Committee) worker, Jessie Norris, in August, 1965. It has set up 15 cooperatives in Mississippi, employing about 200 black people. The employees, all shareholders, make handbags, hats, dresses, quilts, dolls and other hand-craft items that are marketed through Liberty House in Jackson, Miss. Always sensitive to the development of the black community, the Poor People's Corporation passed a rule that only registered voters could work in the co-ops.

These enterprises are small; they do not threaten the economic structure of this society, but their members look upon them as vital for the development of the black people. Their purpose is to establish a modicum of economic self-sufficiency without focusing too much attention on the impact they will have on the American economic system.

Absolutely crucial to the development of Black Power is the black middle class. These are people with sorely needed skills. There has been a lot of discussion about where the black middle class stands in relation to Black Power. Some people adopt the view that most members of the class opt out of the race (or at least try to do so); they get good jobs, a nice home, two cars, and forget about the masses of blacks who have not "made it." This has been largely true. Many middle-class blacks simply do not feel an obligation to help the less fortunate members of their race.

There is, however, a growing awareness among black middle-class people of their role in the black revolution. On Jan. 20, a small group of them (known, appropriately enough, as the Catalysts) called an all-day conference in a South Side Chicago church to discuss ways of linking black middle-class professionals with black people in the lower class. Present were about 370 people of all sorts: teachers, social workers, lawyers, accountants, three physicians, housewives, writers. They met in workshops to discuss ways of making their skills and positions relevant to the black society, and they held no press conferences. Though programs of action developed, the truth is that they remain the exception, not the rule, in the black middle class.

Another group has been formed by black teachers in Chicago, Detroit and New York, and plans are being made to expand. In Chicago, the organization is called the Association of Afro-American Educators. These are people who have traditionally been the strongest supporters of the status quo. Education is intended to develop people who will support the existing values of the society, and "Negro" teachers have been helping this process over the years. But now some of them (more than 250 met on Feb. 12 in Chicago) are organizing and beginning to redefine, first, their role as black educators vis-à-vis the black revolution, and, second, the issues as they see them. Their motivation is outlined in the following statement:

"By tapping our vast resources of black intellectual expertise, we shall generate new ideas for *meaningful* educational programs, curricula and instructional materials which will contribute substantially toward raising the educational achievement of black children.

"Our purpose is to extricate ourselves momentarily from the dominant society in order to realign our priorities, to mobilize and to 'get ourselves together' to do what must be done by those best equipped to do it."

This is what they *say*; whether they can pull it off will depend initially on their ability to bring along their black colleagues, many of whom, admittedly, do not see the efficacy of such an attitude. Unless the link is made between the black middle-class professionals and the black masses, Black Power will probably die on the speaker's platform.

Another important phenomenon in the development of Black Power is the burgeoning of black students' groups on college campuses across the country. I have visited 17 such campuses—from Harvard to Virginia to Wisconsin to U.C.L.A.—since October. The students are discussing problems of identity, of relevant curricula at their universities, of ways of helping their people when they graduate. Clearly, one sees in these hundreds (the figure could be in the thousands) of black students a little bit of Booker T. Washington (self-help and the dignity of common labor) and a lot of W. E. B. DuBois (vigorous insistence on equality and the liberal education of the most talented black men).

These are the people who are planning to implement social, political and economic Black Power in their home towns. They will run for public office, aware that Richard Hatcher started from a political base in the black community. He would not be Mayor of Gary, Ind., today if he had not first mobilized the black voters. Some people point out that he had to have white support. This is true; in many instances such support is necessary, but internal unity is necessary first.

This brings us to a consideration of the external problems of the black community. It is clear that black people will need the help of whites at many places along the line. There simply are not sufficient economic resources—actual or potential—in the black community for a total, unilateral, boot-strap operation. Why should there be? Black people have been the target of deliberate denial for centuries, and racist America has done its job well. This is a serious problem that must be faced by Black Power advocates. On the one hand, they recognize the need to be independent of "the white power structure." And on the other, they must frequently turn to that structure for help—technical and financial. Thus, the rhetoric and the reality often clash.

Resolution probably lies in the realization by white America that it is in her interest not to have a weak, dependent, alienated black community inhabiting the inner cities and blowing them up periodically. Society needs stability, and as long as there is a sizable powerless, restless group within it which considers the society illegitimate, stability is not possible. However it is calculated, the situation calls for a black-white rapprochement which may well come only through additional confrontations and crises. More frequently than not, the self-interest of the dominant society is not clearly perceived until the brink is reached.

There are many ways whites can relate to this phenomenon. First, they must recognize that blacks are going to insist on an equitable distribution of *decision-making power.* Anything less will simply be perpetuating a welfare mentality among blacks. And if the society thinks only in terms of *giving* more jobs, better schools and more housing, the result will be the creation of more black recipients still dependent on whites.

The equitable distribution of power must result from a conviction that it is a matter of mutual self-interest, not from the feelings of guilt and altruism that were evident at the National Conference of New Politics convention in Chicago in August. An equitable distribution means that black men will have to occupy positions of political power in precincts, counties, Congressional districts and cities where their numbers and organization warrant. It means the end of absentee white ward committeemen and precinct captains in Chicago's black precincts.

But this situation is much easier described than achieved. Black Americans generally are no more likely to vote independently than other Americans. In many Northern urban areas, especially, the job of wooing the black vote away from the Democratic party is gigantic. The established machine has the resources: patronage, tradition, apathy. In some instances the change will take a catalytic event—a major racial incident, a dramatic black candidate, a serious boner by the white establishment (such as splitting the white vote). The mere call to "blackness" simply is not enough, even where the numbers are right.

In addition, many of the problems facing black people can be solved only to the extent that whites are willing to see such imperatives as an open housing market and an expanding job market. White groups must continue to bring as much pressure as possible on local and national decision-makers to adopt sound policy in these fields. These enlightened whites *will* be able to work with Black Power groups.

There are many things which flow from this orientation to Black Power. It is not necessary that blacks create parallel agencies—political or economic—in all fields and places. In some areas, it is possible to work within, say, the two-party system. Richard Hatcher did so in Gary, but he first had to organize black voters to fight the Democratic machine in the primary. The same is true of Mayor Carl Stokes in Cleveland. At some point it may be wise to work with the existing agencies, but this must be done only from a base of independent, not subordinated, power.

On the other hand, dealing with a racist organization like George Wallace's Democratic party in Alabama would require forming an independent group. The same is true with some labor unions, especially in the South, which still practice discrimination despite the condemnation of such a policy by their parent unions. Many union locals are willing to work with their black members on such matters as wages and working conditions, but refuse to join the fight for open housing laws.

The point is that black people must become much more pragmatic in their approach. Whether we try to work within or outside a particular agency should depend entirely on a hard-nosed, calculated examination of potential success in each situation—a careful analysis of cost and benefit. Thus, when we negotiate the test will be: How will black people, not some political machine downtown or some labor union boss across town, benefit from this?

Black Power must insist that the institutions in the black community be

led by and, wherever possible, staffed by blacks. This is advisable psychologically, and it is necessary as a challenge to the myth that black people are incapable of leadership. Admittedly, this violates the principle of egalitarianism ("We
hire on the basis of merit alone, not color"). What black and white America
must understand is that egalitarianism is just a principle and it implies a notion
of "colorblindness" which is deceptive. It must be clear by now that any society
which has been color-conscious all its life to the detriment of a particular group
cannot simply become color-blind and expect that group to compete on equal
terms.

Black Power clearly recognizes the need to perpetuate color consciousness,
but in a positive way—to improve a group, not to subject it. When principles like
egalitarianism have been so flagrantly violated for so long, it does not make sense
to think that the victim of that violation can be equipped to benefit from
opportunities simply upon their pronouncement. Obviously, some positive form
of special treatment must be used to overcome centuries of negative special
treatment.

This has been the argument of the Nation of Islam (the so-called Black
Muslims) for years; it has also been the position of the National Urban League
since its proposal for preferential treatment (the Domestic Marshall Plan, which
urged a "special effort to overcome serious disabilities resulting from historic
handicaps") was issued at its 1963 Denver convention. This is not racism. It is
not intended to penalize or subordinate another group; its goal is the positive
uplift of a deliberately repressed group. Thus, when some Black Power advocates
call for the appointment of black people to head community-action poverty
programs and to serve as school principals, they have in mind the deliberate
projection of blacks into positions of leadership. This is important to give other
black people a feeling of ability to achieve, if nothing else. And it is especially
important for young black children.

An example of concentrated special treatment is the plan some of us are
proposing for a new approach to education in some of the black ghettos. It goes
beyond the decentralization plans in the Bundy Report; it goes beyond the
community involvement at I.S. 201 in Harlem. It attempts to build on the idea
proposed by Harlem CORE last year for an independent Board of Education for
Harlem.

Harlem CORE and the New York Urban League saw the Bundy Report as
a "step toward creating a structure which would bring meaningful education to
the children of New York." CORE, led by Roy Innis, suggested an autonomous
Harlem school system, chartered by the State Legislature and responsible to the
state. "It will be run by an elected school board and an appointed administrator,
as most school boards are," CORE said. "The elected members will be Harlem
residents. It is important that much of the detailed planning and structure be the
work of the Harlem community." Funds would come from city, state and Federal governments and from private sources. In describing the long-range goal of
the proposal, CORE says: "Some have felt it is to create a permanently separate
educational system. Others have felt it is a necessary step toward eventual
integration. In any case, the ultimate outcome of this plan will be to make it
possible for Harlem to choose."

Some of us propose that education in the black community should be family-oriented, not simply child-oriented. In many of the vast urban black ghettos (which will not be desegregated in the foreseeable future) the school should become the focal point of the community. This we call the Family-Community-School-Comprehensive Plan. School would cease to be a 9-to-3, September-to-June, time-off-for-good-behavior institution. It would involve education and training for the entire family—all year round, day and evening. Black parents would be intimately involved as students, decision-makers, teachers. This is much more than a revised notion of adult education courses in the evening or the use of mothers as teachers' aides.

This plan would make the educational system the center of community life. We could have community health clinics and recreational programs built into the educational system. Above all, we could reorient the demeaning public welfare system, which sends caseworkers to "investigate" families. Why could we not funnel public assistance through the community educational program?

One major advantage would be the elimination of some of the bureaucratic chaos in which five to ten governmental agencies zero in on the black family on welfare, seldom if ever coordinating their programs. The welfare department, for one, while it would not need to be altered in other parts of the state, would have to work jointly with the educational system in the black community. This would obviously require administrative reorganization, which would not necessarily reduce bureaucracy but would consolidate and centralize it. In addition to being "investigators," for example, some caseworkers (with substantially reduced case loads) could become teachers of budgetary management, and family health consultants could report the economic needs of the family.

The teachers for such a system would be specially trained in a program similar to the National Teacher Corps, and recruits could include professionals as well as mothers who could teach classes in child-rearing, home economics, art, music or any number of skills they obviously possess. Unemployed fathers could learn new skills or teach the ones they know. The curriculum would be both academic and vocational, and it would contain courses in the culture and history of black people. The school would belong to the community. It would be a union of children, parents, teachers, social workers, psychologists, urban planners, doctors, community organizers. It would become a major vehicle for fashioning a sense of pride and group identity.

I see no reason why the local law-enforcement agency could not be integrated into this system. Perhaps this could take the form of training "community service officers," or junior policemen, as suggested in the report of the President's Commission on Civil Disorders. Or the local police precinct could be based in the school, working with the people on such things as crime prevention, first aid and the training of police officers. In this way, mutual trust could be developed between the black community and the police.

Coordinating these programs would present problems to be worked out on the basis of the community involved, the agencies involved and the size of the system. It seems quite obvious that in innovations of this sort there will be a tremendous amount of chaos and uncertainty and there will be mistakes. This is understandable; it is the price to be paid for social change under circumstances of widespread alienation and deprivation. The recent furor about the Malcolm X memorial program at I.S. 201 in Harlem offers an example of the kind of problem to be anticipated. Rather than worrying about what one person said from a stage at a particular meeting, the authorities should be concerned about how the Board of Education will cooperate to transfer power to the community school board. When the transfer is made, confusion regarding lines of authority and program and curriculum content can be reduced.

The longer the delay in making the transfer, however, the greater the likeihood of disruption. One can expect misunderstanding, great differences of opinion and a relatively low return on efforts at the beginning of such new programs. New standards of evaluation are being set, and the experimental concept developed at P.S. 201 should not be jeopardized by isolated incidents. It would be surprising if everything went smoothly from the outset.

Some programs *will* flounder, some will collapse out of sheer incompetence and faulty conception, but this presents an opportunity to build on mistakes. The precise details of the Comprehensive Plan would have to be worked out in conjunction with each community and agency involved. But the *idea* is seriously proposed. We must begin to think in entirely new terms of citizen involvement and decision-making.

Black Power has been accused of emphasizing decentralization, of over-looking the obvious trend toward consolidation. This is not true with the kind of Black Power described here, which is ultimately not separatist or isolationist. Some Black Power advocates are aware that this country is simultaneously experiencing centralization and decentralization. As the Federal Government becomes more involved (and it must) in the lives of people, it is imperative that we broaden the base of citizen participation. It will be the new forms, new agencies and structures developed by Black Power that will link these centralizing and decentralizing trends.

Black Power structures at the local level will activate people, instill faith (not alienation) and provide a habit of organization and a consciousness of ability. Alienation will be overcome and trust in society restored. It will be through these local agencies that the centralized forces will operate, not through insensitive, unresponsive city halls. Billions of dollars will be needed each year, and these funds must be provided through a more direct route from their sources to the people.

Black Power is a developmental process; it cannot be an end in itself. To the extent that black Americans can organize, and to the extent that white Americans can keep from panicking and begin to respond rationally to the demands of that organization—to that extent can we get on with the protracted business of creating not just law and order but a free and open society.

FOR WHITE AND BLACK, COMMUNITY CONTROL IS THE ISSUE

Nathan Glazer

It may in the end turn out a tragedy that the issue of community control of schools was first raised on such a massive scale in New York City, where it inevitably became entangled in the escalating mutual distrust and dislike of Negroes and Jews, and in the increasingly fierce if ritualized conflicts that characterize labor-management relations between civil-service unions and government in New York City. We cannot wish away the reality that in New York City a public-school population with a majority of Negro and Puerto Rican children is now taught by a teaching staff with a majority of Jews; nor can we wish away the reality that New York City's teachers have followed in the path of transit workers, sanitation workers and social-service workers in militantly fighting for the defense and expansion of their salaries and privileges.

But both these special factors will have consequences far beyond the boundaries of New York City because New York is also the capital of the mass media and the seat and learning situation of many intellectuals—and they are likely to draw, indeed already have drawn, conclusions from the terrible teachers' strike that will not apply and should not apply to "community control" and parental participation" in general, and not even in New York City.

The issue that has exploded in New York City—and increasingly we can expect it to come up all over the country—is one, we should be clear, of "community control," and not really one of "decentralization," even if that is the way most people refer to it. "Decentralization" means a pattern of organization in which decisions are made at the local level rather than centrally—but these decisions can be made by the agents of the central authority without the participation of the local community. "Community control" means a pattern of organization in which the local community has power over decisions. You can have decentralization without community control (though if you have decentralization the local community people will at least know where to go to complain or put on pressure); you cannot have community control without some substantial measure of decentralization. Nor does community control mean *total* community control. Local officials can be removed by the state. If the state will not act, and the supression of rights is too blatant, the Federal Government may intervene (Little Rock). Thus community control is never and need not be total. Nor is it nor need it be a mandate for the teaching of race prejudice or the suppression of rights—though it has been used for these and other evil ends.

Many of us are beginning to forget that the fight for community control, and for the restriction and the breaking up of the powers of great bureaucracies, particularly where they affect the ordinary day-to-day life of people, has been under way for perhaps 15 years, and that it is not a product of the black revolution alone. Indeed, for 15 or 20 years, the middle class has shown a growing discontent with the bureaucracies that control the ordinary social services that affect citizens. It did this long before it was forced to be concerned with the problems of the urban black poor, and even in countries where the issue of race did not intertwine with and complicate all other problems.

Fifteen years ago we were in the middle of the first burst of literature on the "suburbanization" of American life. At that time, suburbanites were not attacked for abandoning the central cities to their difficult problems of increasing crime, rising welfare loads, intractable educational problems, and to their prospect of racial violence—while to some extent some of these were problems even then, none were anything like the major issues they have become since. At that time, if we recall, the suburbanites were criticized for depriving *themselves* and their children of the rich urban experience—varied ethnic groups, income groups of different levels, cultural opportunities, more interesting politics and the like. And the suburbanites' argument—where they had defenders, at any rate—was that they were exchanging a situation in which they were the object of distant and indifferent bureaucratic forces to one in which they had direct access to and direct influence over government.

Thus I recall an article by Harry Gersh in Commentary describing his move from Brooklyn to Westchester—and reporting with wonder that when the garbage was not collected there was someone to *call,* and he could expect a response. Here was a middle-class citizen who nevertheless found he exchanged powerlessness in the city for some power in the suburbs. Robert Wood, in his book "Suburbia," did present a criticism of the suburbanite for leaving the arena of major political decisions and did warn that if the middle-class population moved off to local municipalities of a narrower class and ethnic range, it would be more difficult to deal with the great problems of the society, and in particular those that became evident in central cities.

Yet to many the main effect of the book was to underline how much the suburbanite gained by living in a small community which, even if it was economically part of a larger metropolis, had a narrow range of citizens and problems. Here he gained direct access and some modicum of control. If he had a position on a public issue, his fellow citizens were likely to agree with him in larger numbers than in the city, because their interests were the same. And if he had a point of view on elementary education, on zoning, on snow removal, on library services, not only would he find that he could organize some of his neighbors who agreed with him, but also that it was possible to influence local officials to take account of that point of view; or if they did not, it was possible to replace them with his friends and neighbors. It was a heady sense of power for people long deprived of much capacity to influence government—and it was a powerful attraction to get out from under the swelling and impervious bureaucracies of the central city.

The middle class thus led the way to the discovery that the urban bureaucracies, made increasingly insensitive by the replacement of political bosses by municipal unions, could be got out from under—by moving. Let us recall, too, who were the first critics of public housing. They were the planners and the middle-class reformers, not the poor who lived in public housing, or those who spoke for them as their militant leaders. The critics were Lewis Mumford, Catherine Bauer Wurster, Elizabeth Wood, Paul and Percival Goodman.

These men and women in varying degrees knew the situation in public housing and spoke from experience as well as from a general theoretical opinion, but in attacking the massive public-housing projects that began to rise in New York City and elsewhere shortly after World War II, they combined esthetic with social criticism. They attacked the public housing bureaucracies, in Washington and in New York City, which made it impossible, it appeared, to design more attractive and human-scale projects. The middle class despaired of bureaucracy in housing first—not that of course it meant that much to the middle class, which in any case lived in other settings.

And we can make the same point about the critics of urban renewal and urban expressways. The most influential single book on urban renewal was perhaps Herbert Gans's "The Urban Villagers," which told with controlled objectivity and yet with passion the story of the destruction, by urban renewal, of the West End of Boston, and in particular of its working-class, second-generation, Italian community. The West End was not Greenwich Village, but it had an Italian community, cheap and small-scale housing, a pleasant site near downtown, the urban amenities of small stores and street life celebrated by Jane Jacobs in "The Death and Life of Great American Cities." The West Ender, as Gans described him, was certainly attached to his community and his housing—but he was incapable of fighting for it, for he had no well-developed political skills.

But a sociologist and intellectual like Herb Gans was able to arouse other people—sociologists, intellectuals and others—to the enormity of the crime against the West End, and when in New York the urban-renewal authorities tried to move into the West Village—a similar community, but with many more intellectuals and writers—the community fought back, bitterly. Jane Jacobs, Eric Wensberg, and others were deeply involved in that fight, and it took several years, in the early sixties, to finally bring the project to a halt—almost.

I recall the bitterness felt by those involved in that fight at the power and the imperviousness of the urban-renewal authorities. These had full-time staffs of publicity men, planners, lawyers, administrators, Federal money—and plenty of time. The local residents had, in this case, writing and political skills, but they fought part-time against the full-timers. And it was at that time that there first developed and became prominent among younger, radical planners such ideas as the one that the community, like the large central bureaucracy, deserves to have its own full-time staff, its planners and advocates so it will not have to exhaust its energies and its money to fighting a public bureaucracy—formally its "servant." The feelings of the middle-class people who fought urban renewal in the

West Village, and who fought the plan for the Lower Manhattan Expressway—where again, they faced a full-time bureaucracy well supported by public funds —are to my mind very similar to the feelings now expressed by the poor and the black in many parts of our big cities. And we will not properly understand or respond to these latter feelings—if we are middle-class—unless we recall those earlier fights.

It was about the same time too—in 1961—that there was an explosion of anger against the Board of Education—and once again, it was not an explosion led by the poor and the slum dwellers. The Board of Education it turned out was incredibly incompetent in spending money to build new schools—schools needed by middle-class people moving to Queens and the Bronx, as well as by poor people living in older parts of the city. The Board of Education was replaced. A scandal—a minor scandal—helped, but the frustration of the middle classes of the City of New York at the imperviousness of the board and its agents to those who were technically its masters was undoubtedly the chief politically combustible material fueling the outburst and the subsequent change in the procedures for selecting the board—changes that, alas, seemed to accomplish nothing in making the board and the school system more responsive to people's demands.

I recall vividly—10 years ago—the horror stories that then circulated. Graduates from good schools who wanted to teach in the public schools could not get information on how to apply over the phone and would spend endless time getting information and forms from indifferent and ignorant clerks at headquarters; parents could not get information as to the zonal boundaries of various schools. Ideas for innovation—such as using parent aides in the schools, using the city's resources of writers and artists in the schools, even if not licensed—could not get a hearing. Parents were considered foreign persons in the school. They could not enter it without a permit. I recall I could not even take my 5-year-old daughter to her first class in a public school—because parents were not allowed in school. Quite mad explanations would be given—they might break a leg and the school would be responsible, etc.

The local community advisory boards for 25 new local school boards—a very meager and hardly successful attempt at some degree of decentralization and parent influence—were set up originally in 1961, not because of the pressure and urging of the poor and the black, who were then scarcely active in these matters, but at the demand of the middle classes. Martin Mayer's "The Schools," in 1961, had a great deal of powerful material condemning the impervious bureaucracy of the New York City schools—and he spoke out of a concern for education that had at that time much less to do with the black and poor as such than with a concern for education in general, which he felt was being thwarted by an over-centralized bureaucracy, too remote from any pressure that an aroused community and concerned parents could exert on it.

In our involvement with the tragic details of what happened in Ocean Hill-Brownsville, with the grim reports of racist teaching in some of the community-controlled schools, and with the reduction of the rights and privileges built up by teachers in these schools (many of whom have served loyally in situations which would probably not be tolerated for a week by those who critize them), we are in danger of forgetting that the demand for community control is based on far more than the experience of blacks and the poor. I have indicated that the experience of the middle classes of New York and other cities—their opposition to practices of urban renewal and highway construction in the central city, their frustration in their efforts to exercise some control over the content and character of teaching and the management of the school system in New York City, their unhappiness over city services that were not responsive to their needs—has led to their own style of community control: moving to towns where they have more power, or into projects which have their own police forces, or moving their children out of public schools and into private schools. Many of the children going to private schools in New York City, we should recall, are children of poorer middle-class and of working-class families. Those attending parochial schools and Jewish day schools far outnumber the children going to fashionable private schools. Of course, the issue here is not "community control" in any simple sense, for it could be argued that the parents of children in religious schools have less control, and this in one sense is true. But what they do have is the power to select an environment in which their children are educated, even if in some cases it is a more rigid and authoritarian one than that of the public schools.

But if we are to get some idea of the full force of black demands in this connection, we must look outside New York City, and outside the country, to discover how powerfully all kinds of ethnic groups are demanding substantial autonomy and even independence. The same issues are rising everywhere—indeed many might say the same irrationalities. But if everyone is becoming irrational in the same way, one cannot help feeling that we are in the grip of a movement against bureaucracy and centralization—particularly where ethnic and racial divisions are involved—that in some way has to be taken into account. Thus, the association of this movement in the United States with the black and the poor (not all the black and the poor, of course) may conceal to many of us its real power and seriousness.

The catalogue of growing ethnic passions around the world is by now familiar. What is perhaps less familiar is the virulence with which these passions are being expressed and the degree to which they are now divorced from any objective facts of repression or inferiority. Thus, the Flemings of Belgium have long felt themselves to be dominated culturally, economically and politically by the Walloons. In recent years, the French-speaking Walloon section of the country has been in economic decline, the Flemish part of the country has been economically rising. Politically it is now certainly dominant. But this has done nothing to reduce the sense of resentment of the Flemings. If anything, it seems to have increased it.

To the outsider, the demand that the partially French-speaking University of Louvain should no longer conduct any work in French—because it was situated in the Flemish part of the country!—seemed the height of irrationality. But it was fought for with violence, and the university is to be separated into two parts, with the French-speaking section re-established at great cost beyond the linguistic frontier. If this can happen in Belgium, where Walloon domination of Flemings is scarcely to be compared to the historic oppression of blacks by whites in this country, is it possible to expect that we will not begin to see the division of universities or colleges in this country?

Quebec is engaged in a process which it seems must lead to equally unhappy results. Montreal is a city that lives in fear of separatist French violence. The English-speaking already fear laws that will restrict their right to educate their children in English. The desire for freedom, it seems, among those who have suffered from an inferior status cannot be assuaged merely by the full right to conduct whatever cultural activities they wish, or by full political power, or even by economic concessions designed to raise them to the level of the formerly dominant groups. It moves on inexorably to the demand, at least among some extremists, for the full "purification" of the territory, so that just as French is seen to defile Flemish territory, English is seen to defile French territory.

One of the most striking examples of ethnic separatism is now to be found in the French-speaking section of the dominantly German-speaking canton of Bern in Switzerland. Switzerland has long seemed to many of us a remarkable model of the largest degree of community control and participatory democracy imaginable. The central government is almost without power, the name of the President is hardly known to the citizens, and even the cantons into which that small country is divided yield most of their powers to the smaller communities which make them up. These are dominated by the direct voting of citizens on every conceivable issue—in many cases by the face-to-face town meeting, which has control over a much wider range of governmental activities than the vestigial town meetings of New England. Yet full citizenship in the most decentralized of all states, with the greatest degree of popular participation in government, does not satisfy some of the French-speaking citizens of the canton of Bern. There have been bombings and the demand to establish a separate republic.

The people of Wales and Scotland, who have been the beneficiaries for decades of special programs to build up the economies of declining parts of Great Britain, also support at this point rapidly growing separatist movements, which have also engaged in some acts of violence. At present there is some concern over whether the investment of the Prince of Wales can be carried off without unpleasant incidents.

In all these cases—and in many more I could refer to—we find not only the demand for cultural opportunity, economic equality, political consideration in proportion to one's numbers in a unitary state but what to me is the irrational demand that the "foreigners," the "others," with whom one has been associated in an integrated state for centuries, be *removed*—a demand that, it is true, is held in many cases by only a few extremists but one that eventually becomes politically potent through the silencing, via public opinion, of the moderates who see no objection to the maintenance of a mixed society. Everywhere the liberal hope for mixed societies—mixed in ethnic and racial character—gives way before a demand, now coming from the ostensibly dominated rather than domineering groups, for the clearing out of the dominators, so that the formerly inferior group can conduct its own life, without involvement with others. And, of course, we see the same demand developing in black communities in this country. Undoubtedly this, too, is at present the demand of a minority. But the majority is confused, passionless—and for the most part, silent.

If one were to make a complete catalogue of the rising demand for participation, of the rising opposition to bureaucracies, even when these appear to be reasonably competent, selected by rational and objective standards, and considerate, this article would shortly be out of hand. But there is one other functional area in which black separatist demands can be matched around the world, and in situations where racial and ethnic division is not an issue—the demand for participation in university government. This has now been raised in almost every country in the world, except Russia (where perhaps it has been raised but we know nothing about it), Israel and Cuba. It has led to truly revolutionary changes. In France the universities have, for the first time since the age of Napoleon, changed their system of government to allow for elected bodies in which students will have substantial representation. There is no question that the ancient universities of Germany and Italy will undergo similar changes; the students have demonstrated that they can prevent them from operating and can even physically destroy them if they do not undergo these changes.

Thus, for a variety of reasons, we must separate the issues of community control and participation from the specific circumstances in which they have been raised in New York. These issues have been raised by the middle class as well as the poor, by whites as well as blacks, by groups that have not been oppressed—at least in recent times—as well as by groups that have been, in ethnically homogeneous societies as well as in ethnically heterogeneous ones. Clearly they reflect some worldwide movement of dissatisfaction with the modern state and its manner of operation. Even though this state is itself—in all the countries I have discussed—a democratic state, in which representatives directly elected by the people govern, through agents selected by the democratically elected representatives, it is considered by many as oppressive as if it were a dictatorship. Certainly the agencies of the modern state, in the view of many people, have escaped from popular control.

I think those who denounce the modern bureaucratic state exaggerate enormously the degree to which the agents of the state have escaped from popular control. I think they further engage in the worst kind of intellectual brainwashing when they fail to take seriously the differences between states in which there are popular elections and those in which there are not (or in which the popular elections simply approve the choices of the ruling party), states in which there are functioning civil rights from those in which there are not, states in which there is an independent judiciary from states in which there is not.

Nevertheless, one key issue has already been settled—in a formally and actually democratic state, disaffected groups, whether blacks, or the poor, or students, can act as if the state were a dictatorship, can gain wide sympathy for their position, and can maintain the kind of disruption that makes it impossible for many institutions important for the society to operate. Thus, universities can be brought to a standstill. High schools and now even elementary schools can be disrupted. The police of a democratic state can be cast in the role of oppressors —to the point where intelligent and educated people can justify the murder of the policemen of a democratic state. More or less the same thing can be done with other agencies of the state, whether highway construction agencies or urban renewal agencies, to the point indeed where they cannot operate.

Despite this, I think it is true that most people—in this country and in others—are more or less content with the operations of the bureaucracies of the democratic states: consider the votes in this country or in France, or in Germany, or in Japan. I think it is true that most of the people who man the bureaucracies are men of good will, interested in doing as good a job as is commensurate with their training, their abilities and their salaries. I think the process of selection for the bureaucracies is carried out in the democratic states with increasing concern for fairness and for merit, and that replacement of political selection and personal influence by objective tests (which probably in many cases measure nothing relevant to the job), is nevertheless an advance for justice and equity.

But all this does not seem to matter. While to most people the bureaucracies, whatever the frustrations they suffer from them, are seen as *theirs* (they are after all *related* to the teachers, policemen, civil servants, party officials, etc.), for many others, for increasingly dissident and violent minorities, the bureaucracies are seen as foreign, and when seen as foreign, everything becomes justified. Teachers can be spit upon, social workers can be physically attacked, policemen can be killed, the physical premises of government and educational institutions can be destroyed—and there will be an audience looking on, a good part of which will be sympathetic and encouraging.

This is the situation we face in many of our cities—as I have suggested, it is a situation we face in a good part of the rest of the world too.

What courses lie open to us? If we believe—as I do—that what we have is an over-all democratic and rational system, open to change, we will be tempted to consider the repression of those who act irrationally toward it. I think in most cases this will not work. Particularly in settings in which respect for the agents of authority is required, it is scarcely possible that this respect can be recreated and reawakened through repression. The police do not, after all, operate through force. Hannah Arendt has argued effectively that the state is not based on violence, physical force, but on power, and when physical violence is necessary to maintain authority, then it means power has been lost.

Now this has happened to the police in black neighborhoods. They are very often torn between the impossible choice of using violence, physical violence, in making arrests to uphold the law, or of simply abandoning any effort to uphold the law. Power has been lost, violence is necessary now if authority is to be maintained—but in a democratic society the exercise of violence, to the degree necessary to reestablish authority, is scarcely to be considered. Thus we have the result: lawlessness prevails, tempered by occasional police violence, and the chief victims are those who dwell in black neighborhoods and the few whites who must work there (storekeepers, the police, teachers, social workers).

The same thing is happening in public schools in black areas—the process is perhaps most advanced in New York, but is seen in many other cities too. The exercise of the teacher's authority, which once required only a severe look, a word, an admonishing touch, sending the student to the principal, now requires in more and more cases physical violence—we can call it restrain—direct forceful battling with rebellious students, sometimes by the teachers, sometimes by the police.

We can find the same thing in the welfare offices, and in other government offices, and even, shocking as it is to those of us raised in a setting in which libraries were to be approached in silence and books treated with care, in public libraries, which also now increasingly need guards if they are to operate—at the university level, as well as at the local level.

When authority is lost—and I think it has been lost in schools in black neighborhoods, by police in black neighborhoods and by a good number of the officials who deal with black neighborhoods—the only way it can be restored is by a change in the actual distribution of political power. I myself am not convinced that big bureaucracies in democratic states and even highly centralized ones, do not work—they work well enough when their authority is accepted. The centralized educational system of France seems to make all the people literate, and up until a few years ago seemed to select efficiently a higher civil service and other important groups of specialists to run the state. The highly centralized educational system of Japan seems to work even more efficiently if we consider such tests as learning to read and write and do mathematics. And I would wonder really whether the educational system of New York City, which seemed to have such wide aceptance among the people of the city in the thirties, has changed for the worse since then—I doubt that it has become more bureaucratic, or less responsive to public pressure, since then. The police have become more professional, less violent, more honest, and other government activities too are more honest and more efficient. David Riesman has argued that the universities and colleges are much better than they were in the thirties.

So I do not rest my argument for basic changes on the ground of the growing inadequacy of these institutions; I would rest it on the fact that they cannot gain acceptance of their authority among substantial minorities who have the power to resist any possible good they can do. At that point, I think we have to consider new forms of organization, and it is on this basis that I look favorably on plans like the Bundy proposals for breaking up the school system of New York City, and the participation of parent-elected groups in the governing of the smaller districts.

I do not want to go into the details of appropriate systems of decentralization and of greater community control for various government functions. I think we should recognize that we already have a substantial measure of community control in the form of elected bodies for municipalities, states, and the Federal Government. We have some partially working models for an increased measure of community control that could be expanded. The three demonstration districts in the school system of New York City are to my mind such partially working models.

Rhody McCoy seems to find it in his interest to insist that community control in New York City has been "destroyed" because the district was forced to take back the union teachers it tried to exclude. But no rational assessment can accept this judgment. Most of the teachers who have been accepted back formally will probably leave fairly soon—the power of the local board, the unit administrator and his staff, and the loyal teachers and students to make life unpleasant for them has already been demonstrated in a hundred ways. The demonstration unit still survives, with just about all the teachers it hired. It is getting more money, from foundations and from special programs for the educationally underprivileged. In other words, partial decentralization and community control in New York City is already a reality, and there will be more.

But leaving aside the special case of the demonstration school districts of New York City, we see other examples of decentralization and community control establishing themselves—even without benefit of over-all schemes for revision of local government—along the lines of the Bundy proposal. Thus, the Community Action programs set up under the poverty programs are established now in more than 1,000 communities. Within defined poverty areas, there are often elections or some other process for getting a representative board. The boards have powers over a budget, over a planning process for various local programs, over some on-going local programs. On occasion, their powers are expanded. For example, many of them now have some voice in allocating the substantial Federal funds now spent for the education of the poor under Title I of the Elementary and Secondary Education Act. As a result of the Green Amendment, these Community Action agencies can now only continue if the appropriate local government agrees to their continuance to administer anti-poverty programs. At the end of 1968, 883 of 913 reporting local governments elected to continue the existing Community Action agencies.

Thus the Community Action agencies, which were born in conflict, and have lived through intense conflict, have turned into really effective examples of decentralization and community control. In most communities, the locally elected power-holders, the mayors and councilmen—who of course also reflect community control, but at a higher level—have agreed that the bodies that represent poor areas for antipoverty programs should continue.

As Daniel P. Moynihan wrote at the conclusion of his "Maximum Feasible Misunderstanding," ". . . community action . . . survived: a new institution of sorts had been added to the system of American local government." And the Republican Administration has now accepted it. In the nature of things, when an institution survives, one finds things for it to do—or it finds things for itself to do. Those of us who believed that the conflicts over relatively small programs of no impact would become so fierce that communities would be torn apart with no gain have for the most part been proved wrong. While the conflicts were indeed fierce in many cities, in the end the local Community Action agencies have become established, have been accepted by local city government, have proved useful—at least useful enough so that the overwhelming majority of city governments are not prepared to abolish them.

With the rise of ever more extreme forms of black militancy, in addition, the leadership of the Community Action agencies, which seemed militant enough in 1964 and 1965, now turns out, within the political spectrum of poor black areas, to be generally somewhere in the middle. The agencies have provided a training ground for large numbers of local black community leaders, many of whom have become more militant, it is true, but many of whom are now on the first rungs of careers in electoral politics, and look forward to participating in the system as democratically elected representatives of citizens, rather than tearing it down.

The same process is now under way as we develop Model Cities agencies in many cities. These agencies will administer much larger funds, for a much greater range of city functions, than Community Action agencies. They must be set up with the approval of local elected bodies—which has somewhat muted the conflicts in their creation, for city governments now have less fear (than in the case of the Community Action agencies) that an alliance of radical Federal officials and radical local people will set up a government in opposition to them.

These agencies have a difficult task, but one no more difficult than the

Community Action agencies had. They must represent the people of a local area; they must develop a complex program with many different parts (the legislation requires that their programs have elements that try to improve housing, public safety, health, education, employment and a good deal more in the poor areas); they have to get local approval of programs that often arouse the suspicion of the city agencies in these various fields; they must get coordinated funding of all these programs from a variety of Federal agencies, etc.

Once again, to this observer at least, it appears that in our penchant for attacking all problems simultaneously and in achieving a high level of participation we may have placed a burden on Model Cities agencies that they may not be able to fulfill. Yet, in some cases with which I am familiar, I am impressed with the high level of many of those involved in developing Model Cities programs, and with the political skill with which these varied obstacles are being overcome. And once again, we are giving opportunity to new leaders, many black, who are gaining valuable experience and valuable political skills, and who see their future as dependent on their ability to deliver services to people, rather than on their ability to arouse them to a destructive rage.

Thus in a variety of ways, in various areas of government, a greater degree of decentralization and community control is being established. Whether we should try to formalize this process in the way the Bundy proposals do or in a more elaborate effort that breaks up city government into local sub-areas, with elected boards and separate administrators, I am not sure. But I am impressed by the fact that in the two cities overseas that are perhaps most comparable to New York in size, London and Tokyo, there is a system of borough (London) or ward (Tokyo) government. The boroughs or wards are smaller than our boroughs in New York—there are about 30 in both cities. They have an average population of about 300,000 each. They have elected councils or legislatures. They have control over elementary education, over health and welfare services, over some local housing programs, over libraries and recreational services. In Tokyo, at least, these wards generally have large, substantial headquarters, in which there are meeting rooms for citizens as well as government offices, and these headquarters are landmarks in a distinguished, contemporary architecture. The history of local government in England, Japan and the United States, has very little in common, yet despite this there may be advantages to this way of organizing the government of a very large city that we should consider.

There are undoubtedly safeguards we will want to consider and build in as we move toward community control. In other countries the main limitation to community control is simple efficiency, and that is one limitation here. It will not be possible for local community governments of small scale to take effective measures to improve metropolitan transportation or to control air pollution or to control air pollution, to run colleges (though some might—they do in London), or to manage the social security system. But in this country, we have other problems to contend with.

Since one of the main reasons for this drive is to increase the number of black jobholders and civil servants and to increase the control of blacks over branches of government that affect them, we cannot really fully guarantee the rights to seniority and to specific jobs of all civil servants, as one could in other countries. We will have to expect some kind of turnover as community control becomes stronger—and we need measures that cushion this transition for those hurt by it unless we are ready to go through more New York teachers' strikes. The municipal unions will also have to realize that the principle of merit alone will have to be supplemented with the principle of representativeness—as it already is perhaps in many cities outside New York, which have found it possible to recruit far more black school teachers, principals and administrators than New York has.

The argument is often made that the introduction of the principle of representativeness will mean that people recruited for public service will be less qualified or competent than those who are recruited on the principle of merit alone. A good deal depends on how we define "competence" or "qualification." If we define it only in terms of the tests that have been developed, this certainly is true. But the tests themselves are only one way to getting at competence and qualifications. Very often test-making begins to lead a life of its own, and tests are developed and used that are themselves rarely tested to find out if they really select better teachers or policemen or firemen. Other cities (for example, Philadelphia and Chicago) do seem to have much larger proportions of black principals and teachers—even taking into account their larger Negro populations —than New York does. Further, for many purposes we have to define race itself as a qualification. A Negro teacher or principal, all other things equal, will, we expect, have a better understanding of Negro pupils and parents, and will do a better job for that reason alone. We have to take this into account in making appointments.

One strong argument against a greater degree of community control for poor and black areas is that since the areas are poor, they will not be able to raise their own taxes on their own property tax base (as can suburban school districts and other governments), thus they will be dependent on the tax resources of the city, the state, and the Federal Government, and these will not be distributed to them in the measure required if these areas have a larger degree of independence. In other words, the argument is these areas need more money, not more local control, and more local control will mean less money.

I don't see the force of this argument. We have already accepted in this country—both in state aid formulas and in Federal aid formulas—the principle that resources should be distributed on the basis of need, not on the basis of a real contribution to tax revenue. This principle is often used to give more money to rural areas and Southern states, but in the Elementary and Secondary Education Act, and in other acts, we now see money flowing to poor areas of cities on the basis of need. There are also various cases working their way up through the court system that may lead to a greater measure of public money going to poor areas.

Community control as such does not carry a major threat to this process. What does is the possibility that we will see the rise to power in the new small governments of black militants who will teach race hatred and an illusory and false view of history and reality. This is real danger, and the fact is we cannot fully protect ourselves against it. We must hope that the good sense of black parents and citizens will on the whole prevail, but we must realize it has not been possible for the Federal Government to protect Negroes from local and state governments in the South that teach racial hatred and systematically prevent blacks from gaining access to equal education, equal justice, equal participation in government. We must try to prevent the systematic oppression of minorities—it will be black minorities, again—in Northern local government, as we try to prevent this oppression in Southern local government. But in view of how long it has taken us to make even the progress we have in the South, we cannot be very optimistic, and I think we must expect that some of the governments that will be set up in the Northern cities may well be oppressive, corrupt, inefficient, and irrational. Budgetary controls in the hands of cities and states may prevent the worst abuses, just as budgetary power in the hands of the Federal Government has helped move the South toward equal treatment.

In the end, I think the main redress of those who do not like the new governments that are established is the redress that is always available in a democracy—changing the government, whatever the degree of pressure or terror applied by it, or if that seems too hard, moving away. As long as these safeguards are available, we can move toward decentralization and local control.

COMPARING THE IMMIGRANT AND NEGRO EXPERIENCE

The National Advisory Commission on Civil Disorders

We have surveyed the historical background of racial discrimination and traced its effects on Negro employment, on the social structure of the ghetto community, and on the conditions of life that surround the urban Negro poor. Here we address a fundamental question that many white Americans are asking today: why has the Negro been unable to escape from poverty and the ghetto like the European immigrants?

THE MATURING ECONOMY

The changing nature of the American economy is one major reason. When the European immigrants were arriving in large numbers, America was becoming an urban-industrial society. To build its major cities and industries, America needed great pools of unskilled labor. The immigrants provided the labor, gained an economic foothold, and thereby enabled their children and grandchildren to move up to skilled, white collar, and professional employment.

Since World War II, especially, America's urban-industrial society has matured; unskilled labor is far less essential than before, and blue-collar jobs of all kinds are decreasing in number and importance as a source of new employment. The Negroes who migrated to the great urban centers lacked the skills essential

REPORT OF THE NATIONAL ADVISORY COMMISSION ON CIVIL DISORDERS, *"Comparing the Immigrant and Negro Experience," Chapter 9 (Washington, D.C.: U.S. Government Printing Office, 1968).*

to the new economy; and the schools of the ghetto have been unable to provide the education that can qualify them for decent jobs. The Negro migrant, unlike the immigrant, found little opportunity in the city; he had arrived too late, and the unskilled labor he had to offer was no longer needed.

THE DISABILITY OF RACE

Racial discrimination is undoubtedly the second major reason why the Negro has been unable to escape from poverty. The structure of discrimination has persistently narrowed his opportunities and restricted his prospects. Well before the high tide of immigration from overseas, Negroes were already relegated to the poorly paid, low status occupations. Had it not been for racial discrimination, the North might well have recruited Southern Negroes after the Civil War to provide the labor for building the burgeoning urban-industrial economy. Instead, Northern employers looked to Europe for their sources of unskilled labor. Upon the arrival of the immigrants, the Negroes were dislodged from the few urban occupations they had dominated. Not until World War II were Negroes generally hired for industrial jobs, and by that time the decline in the need for unskilled labor had already begun. European immigrants, too, suffered from discrimination, but never was it so pervasive as the prejudice against color in America, which has formed a bar to advancement, unlike any other.

ENTRY INTO THE POLITICAL SYSTEM

Political opportunities also played an important role in enabling the European immigrants to escape from poverty. The immigrants settled for the most part in rapidly growing cities that had powerful and expanding political machines, which gave them economic advantages in exchange for political support. The political machines were decentralized; and ward-level grievance machinery, as well as personal representation, enabled the immigrant to make his voice heard and his power felt. Since the local political organizations exercised considerable influence over public building in the cities, they provided employment in construction jobs for their immigrant voters. Ethnic groups often dominated one or more of the municipal services—police and fire protection, sanitation, and even public education.

By the time the Negroes arrived, the situation had altered dramatically. The great wave of public building had virtually come to an end; reform groups were beginning to attack the political machines; the machines were no longer so powerful or so well equipped to provide jobs and other favors.

Although the political machines retained their hold over the areas settled by Negroes, the scarcity of patronage jobs made them unwilling to share with the Negroes the political positions they had created in these neighborhoods. For example, Harlem was dominated by white politicians for many years after it had become a Negro ghetto; even today, New York's Lower East Side, which is now predominantly Puerto Rican, is strongly influenced by politicians of the older immigrant groups.

This pattern exists in many other American cities. Negroes are still under-represented in city councils and in most city agencies.

Segregation played a role here too. The immigrants and their descendants felt threatened by the arrival of the Negro and prevented a Negro-immigrant coalition that might have saved the old political machines. Reform groups, nominally more liberal on the race issue, were often dominated by businessmen and middle-class city residents who usually opposed coalition with any low-income group, white or black.

CULTURAL FACTORS

Cultural factors also made it easier for the immigrants to escape from poverty. They came to America from much poorer societies, with a low standard of living, and they came at a time when job aspirations were low. When most jobs in the American economy were unskilled, they sensed little deprivation in being forced to take the dirty and poorly paid jobs. Moreover, their families were large, and many breadwinners, some of whom never married, contributed to the total family income. As a result, family units managed to live even from the lowest paid jobs and still put some money aside for savings or investment, for example, to purchase a house or tenement, or to open a store or factory. Since the immigrants spoke little English and had their own ethnic culture, they needed stores to supply them with ethnic foods and other services. Since their family structures were patriarchal, men found satisfactions in family life that helped compensate for the bad jobs they had to take and the hard work they had to endure.

Negroes came to the city under quite different circumstances. Generally relegated to jobs that others would not take, they were paid too little to be able to put money in savings for new enterprises. Since they spoke English, they had no need for their own stores; besides, the areas they occupied were already filled with stores. In addition, Negroes lacked the extended family characteristic of certain European groups—each household usually had only one or two bread-winners. Moreover, Negro men had fewer cultural incentives to work in a dirty job for the sake of the family. As a result of slavery and of long periods of male unemployment afterwards, the Negro family structure had become matriarchal; the man played a secondary and marginal role in his family. For many Negro men, then, there were few of the cultural and psychological rewards of family life. A marginal figure in the family, particularly when unemployed, Negro men were often rejected by their wives or often abandoned their homes because they felt themselves useless to their families.

Although most Negro men worked as hard as the immigrants to support their families, their rewards were less. The jobs did not pay enough to enable them to support their families, for prices and living standards had risen since the immigrants had come, and the entrepreneurial opportunities that had allowed some immigrants to become independent, even rich, had vanished. Above all, Negroes suffered from segregation, which denied them access to the good jobs and the right unions, and which deprived them of the opportunity to buy real estate or obtain business loans or move out of the ghetto and bring up their children in middle-class neighborhoods. Immigrants were able to leave their ghettos as soon as they had the money; segregation has denied Negroes the opportunity to live elsewhere.

THE VITAL ELEMENT OF TIME

Finally, nostalgia makes it easy to exaggerate the ease of escape of the white immigrants from the ghettos. When the immigrants were immersed in poverty, they too lived in slums, and these neighborhoods exhibited fearfully high rates of alcoholism, desertion, illegitimacy, and the other pathologies associated with poverty. Just as some Negro men desert their families when they are unemployed and their wives can get jobs, so did the men of other ethnic groups, even though time and affluence has clouded white memories of the past.

Today, whites tend to exaggerate how well and how quickly they escaped from poverty, and contrast their experience with poverty-stricken Negroes. The fact is, among many of the Southern and Eastern Europeans who came to America in the last great wave of immigration, those who came already urbanized were the first to escape from poverty. The others who came to America from rural backgrounds, as Negroes did, are only now, after three generations, in the final stages of escaping from poverty. Until the last 10 years or so, most of these were employed in blue-collar jobs, and only a small proportion of their children were able or willing to attend college. In other words, only the third, and in many cases, only the fourth generation has been able to achieve the kind of middle-class income and status that allows it to send its children to college. Because of favorable economic and political conditions, these ethnic groups were able to escape from lower-class status to working class and lower middle-class status, but it has taken them three generations.

Negroes have been concentrated in the city for only two generations, and they have been there under much less favorable conditions. Moreover, their escape from poverty has been blocked in part by the resistance of the European ethnic groups; they have been unable to enter some unions and to move into some neighborhoods outside the ghetto because descendants of the European immigrants who control these unions and neighborhoods have not yet abandoned them for middle-class occupations and areas.

Even so, some Negroes have escaped poverty, and they have done so in only two generations; their success is less visible than that of the immigrants in many cases, for residential segregation has forced them to remain in the ghetto. Still, the proportion of nonwhites employed in white-collar, technical, and professional jobs has risen from 10.2 percent in 1950 to 20.8 percent in 1966, and the proportion attending college has risen an equal amount. Indeed, the development of a small but steadily increasing Negro middle class while the greater part of the Negro population is stagnating economically is creating a growing gap between Negro haves and have-nots.

This gap, as well as the awareness of its existence by those left behind, undoubtedly adds to the feelings of desperation and anger which breed civil disorders. Low-income Negroes realize that segregation and lack of job opportunities have made it possible for only a small proportion of all Negroes to

4

THE SCARS OF URBAN ALIENATION

"This is our basic conclusion," the National Advisory Commission On Civil Disorders announced, "our nation is moving toward two societies, one black, one white—separate and unequal."[1]

Polarization is not new to American life. Nor is violence. Both have been the ingredient of every human struggle to change conditions or improve life. Both are the brutal by-products of institutional repression caused or encouraged by deliberate design, innocent suspicions, or hostile attitudes.

Throughout American history the consequences of such behavior has been quite evident. British attempts, for example, to force the colonies into the Empire's niche of mercantilism, ultimately radicalized the colonies and polarized them from the mother country. The polarization intensified. Violence followed, leading eventually to rebellion and to the birth of a new nation.

Not all polarization ends so well. For two generations America was able to keep the growing division between north and south to a tolerable level of presidential electioneering and legislative maneuvering. By mid-century, however, the sectional split over slavery was beyond institutional salvation, and the nation polarized into two feuding armies.

America survived the conflict, but the wounds were deep. The scars healed slowly and unevenly. And as the nation twisted and turned into an industrial society, militancy seemed ingrained, endemic to national life. Violence came to be associated with every major chapter of life. Law and order was maintained on the frontier not by gentlemen forming civil compacts, but by vigilantes armed for action. Farmers, not by any means one of contemporary society's more radical groups, often improved their condition by physical persuasion. For pure militancy there were Shays' Rebellion in Massachusetts, the Whiskey Rebellion

[1] *Report of the National Advisory Commission on Civil Disorders* (Bantam Books, 1968), p.1.

in Western Pennsylvania, the Fries Rebellion in Eastern Pennsylvania; for sheer militant rhetoric who could match the Greenbacks, the Grange, the Farmers Alliance, the Populists and their call for "farm power."

Militancy served as the habitual factor in the struggle of other disenchanted or dispossessed elements of American society—from suffragettes to laborers. The clashes between these groups and the institutions pitted against them were some of the most brutal in the nation's history.

Perhaps the most persistent form of violence in American history has been the urban riot. Battles between immigrants and native Americans dominated many American towns from 1830 to 1860 and the period was, according to historian Richard Maxwell Brown, "the era of the greatest urban violence that America has experienced." In that one generation four cities were hit by thirty-five riots, including labor riots, election riots, anti-abolitionist riots, and anti-Negro riots, anti-Catholic riots and for some inexplicable reason, volunteer firemen riots.[2]

Race riots did not really appear until the turn of the century. Between 1915 and 1919, for example, thirty-three interracial disorders were recorded, a figure comparable to the 1960s. Unlike the contemporary race riot, however, these clashes were instigated by whites. Blacks were both the targets and the casualties. A period of relative calm was broken by the Detroit disorder of 1943, a monstrous melee that forced the Governor to send in 6000 troops. When it ended thirty-four were dead, the property damage exceeded $2 million, and fear gripped the nation.

The sixties presented a new form of urban militancy, the rebellion of disgruntled blacks. The blacks rioted, not out of malice, but out of rage. Whites were not necessarily the victims; but property was, and so was the entire system that could land white men on the moon but could not find jobs for black men on earth.

On the surface, the sixties seemed to augur an era where it appeared that most or at least many Americans had "made it." At least there was a sufficient level of affluence to stimulate a national interest in leisure time. Industries built ski slopes and beach homes. Holidaying became a national pastime. That was on the surface. Below was a cauldron of resentment at institutions, systems, bureaucrats, politicians, and a society that permitted affluence for some but poverty for so many others.

Many of those "other Americans" were white, the inhabitants of the Ozarks, Appalachia, and the cities. They were unskilled; their education was poor; they had difficulty coping with the complicated demands of their society.

Others were black. They too lived in rural shacks, but mostly in the urban hovels of the big cities. Crowded, congested, disturbed, and fiercely resentful at

---

[2] Richard Maxwell Brown, "Historical Patterns of Violence in America," in *The History of Violence in America, A Report to the National Commission on the Causes and Prevention of Violence,* Hugh Davis Graham and Ted Robert Gurr, eds., (New York: Bantam Books, 1969), p. 45.

a white, middle class America that could impose its will without sharing its security. For many years, while whites ruled, blacks could not sit on a bus, stop at a restroom, sleep in a motel—not because they were poor, or even unpleasant —but because they were black.

Blacks set out to change those conditions and to break down the institutional barriers that relegated black people to second class citizenship. They picketed, boycotted, marched, and sang. They turned an old tactic of civil disobedience into a masterful weapon for social change. There were bus boycotts in Montgomery, sit-ins in Selma, freedom rides in Mississippi. While many whites—particularly the young—held hands with their black brethren, other whites were angered, appalled by the majesty of it all. Those whites turned out dogs, used clubs, and threw black leaders into jail. But the movement would not be stopped, and across the land there was a new era of black freedom.

As the days passed, and as the restrained heroism of nonviolence faded into history, it gradually became apparent that things hadn't really changed—at least not the tangible things. Blacks could now urinate where they chose; but hovels still existed in the ghettos. Blacks could now eat where they pleased; but industries still moved to the suburbs. Blacks could now ride on buses with dignity; but slums kept getting bigger, uglier, and the rats were getting so fat that even Congress was forced to pass a rat control law.

Ultimately, the blacks blew up. The sixties was the history of that black rage. It was the history of black citizens tiring of white institutions and white myths governing their lives. It was the history of black citizens groping for a new identity, struggling for manhood, struggling for a new sense of dignity that had been brutally denied in the past. Civil disobedience was no longer valid because nonviolence had produced more rhetoric than action. In the end the blacks blew up because white America failed to listen and national institutions failed to respond to their pleas. To overcome, and to overcome in a meaningful way, blacks discovered that they needed power. Institutions are not altered by gush or, for that matter, logic. Over a period of time you can change an attitude; but an institution only gets worse. It reacts only when it is pushed to the brink by power that is equal or stronger. And the blacks came to realize that only militancy could change years of institutionalism that could plunge twenty billion dollars in a single decade to secure a victory in space but, in the process, ignore the plight of the inner city.

Black militants made it clear that things would change. They put their demands on the line: "... We want freedom; we want power to determine the destiny of our black communities," Eldridge Cleaver detailed. "We want full employment for our people ... we want housing fit for the shelter of human beings ... we want all black men to be exempt from military service ... we want decent education for black people—education that teaches us the true nature of this decadent, racist society and that teaches young black brothers and sisters their rightful place in society; for if they don't know their place in society and the world, they can't relate to anything else ... we want an end to the robbery of black people in their own community by white-racist businessmen ... we want an immediate end to police brutality and murder of black people ... we want all black men held in city, county, state and Federal jails to be released, because they haven't had fair trials; they've been tried by all-white juries, and that's like being a Jew tried in Nazi Germany ... we want black people accused of crimes to be tried by members of their peer group—a peer being one who comes from the same economic, social, religious, historical and racial community. Black people, in other words, would have to compose the jury in any trial of a black person ... we want land, we want money, we want housing, we want clothing, we want education, we want justice, we want peace." And if those demands are not met, Cleaver said, "war will come. ... Not just a race war, which in itself would destroy this country, but a guerrilla resistance movement that will amount to a second Civil War, with thousands of white John Browns fighting on the side of the blacks, plunging America into the depths of its most desperate nightmare on the way to realizing the American Dream."[3]

The black rage produced an era of new men—new militant blacks who abounded in charisma, who set styles for young blacks and taunted white adversaries, who forced confrontation one day and fed hungry ghetto children the next. The Black Panthers symbolize that breed of blacks. In the late sixties names like Stokely Carmichael, H. Rap Brown, Eldridge Cleaver, Huey Newton and Bobby Seale were as well known as some vice presidents.

How far the blacks will go in pursuing their goals and in attaining a fair share of American affluence is a question that, as Cleaver suggested, only white America can answer. Certain facts, however, have become tragically apparent. "Step by step, demonstration by demonstration, riot by riot," black historian Lerone Bennett, Jr. noted, "black people have moved to the fatal tip-point of rebellion." In social movements as in physics, actions stimulate reaction. And as blacks get more militant, whites get more antagonistic. "The other side of the coin," Bennett noted, "is creeping fascism in white America. The garrison mentality is gaining ground and the United States of America stands today in roughly the same position occupied by Germany in the 30's."[4]

Hyperbole aside, the growing polarization between black and white is the nation's most urgent social issue. More and more whites are increasingly suspicious, belligerent, and resentful of blacks. While some sympathize with black demands, few sympathize with militant tactics; and in the immediate scheme of things it is easier to show hostility than to pay higher taxes or engage in the dialogue required to ease the conditions that have stimulated the violence. So whites flee to the suburbs and draw a noose around the city, choking it off from resources that could help diminish the pressure.

Many feel that the seventies will produce a white backlash of significant dimensions; that urban whites of ethnic origin will join suburban whites in

[3] Nat Hentoff interview with Eldridge Cleaver, *Playboy Magazine,* December 1968.

[4] Lerone Bennett, Jr., "Of Time, Space and Revolution," *Ebony Magazine,* August 1969.

forging a political coalition strong enough to inhibit radical social change. The objective of that coalition may not be to contain black demands, but the result will be the same. Then there is always the danger of black extremism touching off a wave of white extremism. The physical confrontation between white construction trade workers and black laborers is typical of the new kind of polarization that is taking hold in American life.

Whites have certain objections to things they regard as "black" evils. Welfare, crime, urban plight, are not regarded by most whites as the eventual outcome of institutional racism, but as black laziness, immorality, or indifference. How deep this feeling runs and how many white Americans are carrying such antagonisms in their hearts, is not an easy question to answer. The washing away of myths, however, must precede any lessening of polarization. White and black must take a firmer grasp of their own conditions, assess each other's concerns and approach social problems with open and understanding attitudes. Otherwise polarization of sectionally divisive issues—this time the inner city versus the outer city—will lead to the nation's second internal conflagration, and one of possibly horrifying proportions.

This chapter of the anthology deals with the rage of the black and the burden of the white. It is not a pleasant story. That blacks and whites find living together hazardous and difficult is one of the nation's great tragedies. That they should continue to live so, without urgently seeking solutions, knowing the consequences of their increased antagonism, is an even greater tragedy.

In the first part of this chapter the story of the black is told. To use the contemporary idiom, the article written by black critic Julius Lester "lets it all hang out." For openers he states, "It is clear that America as it now exists must be destroyed." And he closes with "The new order is coming, child. The old order is passing away." The message in between makes it clear that America is on the brink of delirium.

Norman Mailer says the same thing in a calmer tone, and with more words. Although blacks resist white interpretations of new black concepts, Mailer shows a certain sensitivity to the black power dogma. His analysis is perceptive and tough. "The American Negro is of course not synonymous with Black Power," he writes. "But no American Negro is contemptuous of Black Power. . . ."

Violence is the ultimate expression of black rage. The next two articles examine that violence. Lee Rainwater, Senior Editor of *TRANS-action,* examines the riots of the sixties from the view of participant. "A community in which the great majority of the families must exist on significantly less than the median family income for the nation is a community of failures," he warns. Violence becomes the inevitable aggression of humans experiencing degrading conditions. They know that in America money talks and so their aggression is taken out on ghetto stores, usually owned by white retailers. The process becomes, as Rainwater points out, "a kind of primitive effort at an income redistribution which society refuses in any lawful and regularized way."

The article by the Johns Hopkins' researchers deals explicitly with the broad range of institutions at work in the ghetto that either antagonize black fury or fail to contain it. The researchers expose the attitudes of men and women who work for typical American institutions—businesses, government agencies, police departments, political machines, retail outlets and others.

Ralph Ellison the author of *Invisible Man* traces his life to Harlem in his testimony before a Senate subcommittee. "In the North, southern tradition breaks down." Ellison told the Senators, "You get to Harlem. You have expected a great deal of freedom that does not exist. Or when it does exist, you haven't been taught how to achieve it." Mr. Ellison's tone was considerably more moderate and optimistic than witnesses such as Claude Brown, who also appeared before the same committee, but even the moderate black is urging radical changes in order to accommodate the emergence of the new Negro.

The problem with being white, middle class, and moonlighting to pay off the suburban mortgages, the extra car and the new color television, is that you really have no spokesman. Blacks have produced a generation of them. When King was slain there was Abernathy. When Carmichael was deported there was Cleaver. The black spokesmen write books, debate David Susskind and fill in for Johnny Carson when he's vacationing. They are celebrities in a society that relishes celebrities.

But who speaks for the alienated, debt ridden, myth begotten white who is too proud to go on welfare or who is making just enough to survive but not enough to enjoy what he's surviving for? Some have tried, but somehow they never seem to gain excessive national political acceptance. George Wallace and Ronald Reagan come immediately to mind. There are the John Birchers and the Minutemen, but they have not yet produced a fascinating personality. At least, one hasn't seen a John Bircher on the Johnny Carson show.

The fact is that the white, middle class American—now called the forgotten, silent, or troubled American—is waiting to be spoken for. At this moment in time Spiro T. Agnew seems closest to being the spokesman for this segment of the population, described colloquially as the "hard hats."

These frustrations have not yet twisted into militancy as they have within the black. But they are welling up. Across the land there are taxpayer revolts. Black-white labor disputes have flared up. Suburban communities still continue to resist low and middle income housing projects. White groups have organized to stop bussing, fight urban renewal, kill sex education. And there is a growing white anger against student rebellions, government spending, and welfare programs.

White America's anguish is revealed in the three articles which follow. Peter Schrag, editor of *Change,* writes forcefully of a new "white power." He describes the plight of the white American, who for years has been asked to carry the burden of excessive liberalism through higher taxes. But now, Schrag notes, ". . . The liberal wisdom about welfare, ghettos, student revolt, and Vietnam has only a marginal place, if any, for the values and life of the working man.

It flies in the face of most of what he was taught to cherish and respect: hard work, order, authority, self-reliance."

Newsweek's piece on the "Troubled American" is equally revealing. With the nation's focus on the black ghettos, there is a tendency to forget that some of the poorest people in the nation are whites. Some hover a trifle above the poverty line and struggle to make ends meet. Others are in the $10,000 range but find that sending just one child to college on that income can be prohibitive. These are the "Troubled Americans." *Newsweek* seeks out their hang-ups and frustrations. This side of American life needs greater attention in the decade of the seventies.

Murray Freidman's "Is White Racism the Problem?" points to the diversity of the urban environment. The author reviews impact other ethnic groups have had, noting that "America is and always has been a nation of diverse ethnic, religious and racial groups with widely varying characteristics and qualities. . . ." Friedman reminds us of aspects of the urban environment that are easily forgotten in the current clash between blacks and whites.

1. THE BLACK MAN'S RAGE

LOOK OUT, WHITEY!
BLACK POWER'S GON' GET YOUR MAMA!

Julius Lester

It is clear that America as it now exists must be destroyed. There is no other way. It is impossible to live within this country and not become a thief or a murderer. Young blacks and young whites are beginning to say NO to thievery and murder. Black Power confronts White Power openly, and as the SNCC poet Worth Long cried: "We have found you out false-faced America. We have found you out! "

Having "found you out," we will destroy you or die in the act of destroying. That much seems inevitable. To those who fearfully wonder if America has come to the point of a race war, the answer is not certain. However, all signs would seem to say yes. Perhaps the only way that it might be avoided would be

Julius Lester, **LOOK OUT, WHITEY! BLACK POWER'S GON' GET YOUR MAMA!**, *Chapter 9. New York: The Dial Press, copyright © by Julius Lester, 1968; and London: Allison & Busby, 1970. Reprinted by permission of the publishers.*

through the ability of young white radicals to convince blacks, through their actions that they are ready to do whatever is necessary to change America.

The race war, if it comes, will come partly from the necessity for revenge. You can't do what has been done to blacks and not expect retribution. The very act of retribution is liberating, and perhaps it is no accident that the symbolism of Christianity speaks of being washed in Blood as an act of purification. Psychologically, blacks have always found an outlet for their revenge whenever planes have fallen, autos have collided, or just every day when white folks die. One old black woman in Atlanta, Georgia, calmly reads through her paper each day counting the number of white people killed the previous day in wrecks, storms, and by natural causes. When the three astronauts were killed in February, 1967, black people did not join the nation in mourning. They were white and were spending money that blacks needed. White folks trying to get to the moon, 'cause it's there. Poverty's here! Now get to that! Malcolm X spoke for all black people when a plane full of Georgians crashed in France: "Allah has blessed us. He has destroyed twenty-two of our enemies."

It is clearly written that the victim must become the executioner. The executioner preordains it when all attempts to stop the continual executions fail. To those who point to numbers and say that black people are only ten percent, it must be said as Brother Malcolm said: "It only takes a spark to light the fuse. We are that spark."

Black Power is not an isolated phenomenon. It is only another manifestation of what is transpiring in Latin America, Asia, and Africa. People are reclaiming their lives on those three continents and blacks in America are reclaiming theirs. These liberation movements are not saying give us a share; they are saying we want it all! The existence of the present system in the United States depends upon the United States taking all. This system is threatened more and more each day by the refusal of those in the Third World to be exploited. They are colonial people outside the United States; blacks are a colonial people within. Thus, we have a common enemy. As the Black Power movement becomes more politically conscious, the spiritual coalition that exists between blacks in America and the Third World will become more evident. The spiritual coalition is not new. When Italy invaded Ethiopia in 1938, blacks in Harlem held large demonstrations protesting this. During World War II, many blacks were rooting for the Japanese. Blacks cannot overlook the fact that it was the Japanese who were the guinea pigs for the atomic bomb, not the Germans. They know, too, that if the U.S. were fighting a European country, it would not use napalm, phosphorus and steel-pellet bombs, just as they know that if there had been over one hundred-thousand blacks massed before the Pentagon on October 21, 1967, they would not have been met by soldiers with unloaded guns. In fact, they know they would never have been allowed to even reach the Pentagon.

The struggle of blacks in America is inseparable from the struggle of the Third World. This is a natural coalition—a coalition of those who know that they are dispossessed. Whites in America are dispossessed also, but the difference is that they will not recognize the fact as yet. Until they do, it will not be possible to have coalitions with them, even the most radical. They must recognize the nature and character of their own oppression. At present, too many of them recognize only that they are white and identify with whites, not with the oppressed, the dispossessed. They react against being called "honky" and thereby establish the fact that they are. It is absolutely necessary for blacks to identify as blacks to win liberation. It is not necessary for whites. White radicals must learn to nonidentify as whites. White is not in the color of the skin. It is a condition of the mind: a condition that will be destroyed. It should be possible for any white radical to yell "honky" as loud as a black radical. "Honky" is a beautiful word that destroys the mystique surrounding whiteness. It is like throwing mud on a sheet. Whiteness has been used as an instrument of oppression; no white radical can identify himself by the color of his skin and expect to fight alongside blacks. Black Power liberates whites also, but they have refused to recognize this, preferring to defend their whiteness.

Black Power is not anti-white people, but is anti anything and everything that serves to oppress. If whites align themselves on the side of oppression, then Black Power must be antiwhite. That, however, is not the decision of Black Power.

For blacks, Black Power is the microscope and telescope through which they look at themselves and the world. It has enabled them to focus their energies while preparing for the day of reckoning. That day of reckoning is anticipated with eagerness by many, because it is on that day that they will truly come alive. The concept of the black man as a nation, which is only being talked about now, will become reality when violence comes. Out of the violence will come the new nation (if the violence is successful) and the new man. Frantz Fanon wrote that "For the colonised people this violence, because it constitutes their only work, invests their characters with positive and creative qualities. The practice of violence binds them together as a whole, since each individual forms a violent link in the great chain, a part of the great organism of violence which has surged upwards in reaction to the settler's violence in the beginning. The groups recognize each other and the future nation is already indivisible. The armed struggle mobilises the people; that is to say, it throws them in one way and in one direction."

It is obvious, of course, that White Power will not allow Black Power to evolve without trying to first subvert it. This is being attempted, as was mentioned in the previous chapter. This attempt will fail and White Power will have no choice but to attempt to physically crush Black Power. This is being prepared for, with intensive riot-control training for the National Guard, chemicals for the control of large crowds, and concentration camps. It is to be expected that eventually black communities across the country will be cordoned off and a South African pass-book system introduced to control the comings and goings of blacks.

At the moment, though (but, oh, how short a moment is), the tactic is one of subversion. Particular attention and energy is being given toward the subversion of SNCC. An inordinate number of SNCC men have received draft notices since January of 1967. Another tactic has been the calling of court cases to trial that have lain dormant for two or three years, cases that in many instances had been forgotten by SNCC. The most sophisticated tactic has been the legal maneuvers the government has used to keep SNCC's chairman, H. Rap Brown, confined to Manhattan Island, thus preventing him from traveling around the country and speaking. Having accomplished that, the government now seems content to take its own good time about bringing Brown's cases up for trial.

Black Power, however, will not be denied. America's time is not long and the odds are on our side.

Black Power seeks to destroy what now is, but what does it offer in replacement? Black Power is a highly moral point of view, but its morality is one that sees that a way of life flows from the economic and political realities of life. It is these that must be changed. Mrs. Ida Mae Lawrence of Rosedale, Mississippi, put it beautifully when she said, "You know, we ain't dumb, even if we are poor. We need jobs. We need houses. But even with the poverty program we ain't got nothin' but needs. . . . We is ignored by the government. The thing about property upset them, but the things about poor people don't. So there's no way out, but to begin your own beginning, whatever way you can. So far as I'm concerned, that's all I got to say about the past. We're beginning a new future."

In his 1966 Berkeley speech, Stokely Carmichael put it another way. ". . . our vision is not merely of a society in which all black men have enough to buy the good things of life. When we urge that black money go into black pockets, we mean the communal pocket. We want to see money go back into the community and used to benefit it. We want to see the cooperative concept applied in business and banking. . . . The society we seek to build among black people is not a capitalistic one. It is a society in which the spirit of community and humanistic love prevail. The word love is suspect; black expectations of what it might produce have been betrayed too often. But those were expectations of a response from the white community, which failed us. The love we seek to encourage is within the black community, the only American community where men call each other 'brother' when they meet. We can build a community of love only where we have the ability and power to do so; among blacks."

Those whites who have a similar vision and want to be a part of this new world must cast down their bucket where they are. If this kind of a world is as important and as necessary for them as it is for us, they must evolve an approach to their own communities. We must organize around blackness, because it is with the fact of our blackness that we have been clubbed. We therefore turn our blackness into a club. When this new world is as totally necessary for whites as it is for blacks, then maybe we can come together and work on some things side by side. However, we will always want to preserve our ethnicity, our community. We are a distinct cultural group, proud of our culture and our institutions, and simply want to be left alone to lead our good, black lives. In the new world, as in this one, I want to be known, not as a man who happens to be black, but as a black man. With that knowledge I can visit the graves of my slave foreparents and say, "I didn't forget about you . . . those hot days you worked in the fields, those beatings, all that shit you took and just grew stronger on. I'm still singing those songs you sang and telling those tales and passing them on to the young ones so they will know you, also. We will never forget, for your lives were lived on a spider web stretched over the mouth of hell and yet, you walked that walk and talked that talk and told it like it is. You can rest easy now. Everything's up-tight."

The old order passes away. Like the black riderless horse, boots turned the wrong way in the stirrups, following the coffin down the boulevard, it passes away. But there are no crowds to watch as it passes. There are no crowds, to mourn, to weep. No eulogies to read and no eternal flame is lit over the grave. There is no time, for there are streets to be cleaned, houses painted, and clothes washed. Everything must be scoured clean. Trash has to be thrown out. Garbage dumped and everything unfit, burned.

The new order is coming, child.

The old is passing away.

LOOKING FOR THE MEAT AND POTATOES— THOUGHTS ON BLACK POWER

Norman Mailer

"You don't even know who you are," Reginald had said. "You don't even know, the white devil has hidden it from you, that you are of a race of people of ancient civilizations, and riches in gold and kings. You don't even know your true family name, you wouldn't recognize your true language if you heard it. You have been cut off by the devil white man from all true knowledge of your own kind. You have been a victim of the evil of the devil white man ever since he murdered and raped and stole you from your native land in the seeds of your forefathers. . . ."

The Autobiography of Malcolm X

In not too many years, we will travel to the moon, and on the trip, the language will be familiar. We have not had our education for nothing—all those sanitized hours of orientation via high school, commercials, corporations and mass media have given us one expectation: no matter how beautiful, insane, dangerous, sacrilegious, explosive, holy or damned a new venture may be, count on it, fellow Americans, the language will be familiar. Are you going in for a serious operation, voting on the political future of the country, buying insurance, discussing nuclear disarmament or taking a trip to the moon? You can depend on the one great American certainty—the public vocabulary of the discussion will suggest the same relation to the resources of the English language

Norman Mailer, "Looking For The Meat and Potatoes—Thoughts On Black Power," **LOOK MAGAZINE**, *January 7, 1969. Copyright© 1969 by Norman Mailer. Reprinted by permission of the author and the author's agents, Scott Meredith Literary Agency, Inc. 580 Fifth Avenue, New York, N.Y.*

that a loaf of big-bakery bread in plastic bag and wax bears to the secret heart of wheat and butter and eggs and yeast.

Your trip to the moon will not deal needlessly with the vibrations of the heavens (now that man dares to enter eschatology) nor the metaphysical rifts in the philosophical firmament; no poets will pluck a stringed instrument to conjure with the pale shades of the white lady as you move along toward the lunar space. Rather, a voice will emerge from the loudspeaker, "This is your pilot. On our starboard bow at four o'clock directly below, you can pick out a little doojigger of land down there like a vermiform appendix, and that, as we say good-bye to the Pacific Coast, is Baja California. The spot of light at the nub, that little bitty illumination like the probe bulb in a cystoscope or comparable medical instrument is Ensenada, which the guidebooks call a jeweled resort."

Good-bye to earth, hello the moon! We will skip the technological dividend in the navigator's voice as he delivers us to that space station which will probably look like a breeding between a modern convention hall and the computer room at CBS. Plus the packaged air in the space suits when the tourists, after two days of acclimation in air-sealed moon motels, take their first reconnoiter outside in the white moon dust while their good American bowels accommodate to relative weightlessness.

All right, bright fellow, the reader now may say—what does all this have to do with Black Power? And the author, while adept at dancing in the interstices of a metaphor, is going to come back nonetheless straight and fast with this remark—our American mass-media language is not any more equipped to get into a discussion of Black Power than it is ready to serve as interpreter en route to the moon. The American language has become a conveyer belt to carry each new American generation into its ordained position in the American scene, which is to say the corporate technological world. It can deal with external descriptions of everything which enters or leaves a man, it can measure the movements of that man, it can predict until such moment as it is wrong what the man will do next, but it cannot give a spiritual preparation for our trip to the moon any more than it can talk to us about death, or the inner experiences of real sex, real danger, real dread. Or Black Power.

If the preface has not been amusing, cease at once to read, for what follows will be worse: the technological American is programmed to live with answers, which is why his trip to the moon will be needlessly God-awful; the subject of Black Power opens nothing but questions, precisely those unendurable questions which speak of premature awakenings and the hour of the wolf. But let us start with something comfortable, something we all know and may encounter with relaxation, for the matter is familiar:

> . . .*think of that black slave man filled with fear and dread, hearing the screams of his wife, his mother, his daughter being* taken—*in the barn, the kitchen, in the bushes!* . . . Think *of hearing wives, mothers, daughters, being* raped! *And you were too filled with* fear *of the rapist to do anything about it!* . . . *Turn around and look at each other, brothers and sisters, and* think *of this! You and me, polluted all these colors—and this devil has the arrogance and the gall to think we, his victims, should love* him!

> The Autobiography of Malcolm X

"Okay," you say, "I know that, I know that already. I didn't do it. My great-grandfather didn't even do it. He was a crazy Swede. He never even saw a black skin. And now for Crysake, the girls in Sweden are crazy about Floyd Patterson. I don't care, I say more power to him. All right," goes the dialogue of this splendid American now holding up a hand," all right, I know about collective responsibility. If some Scotch-Irish planter wanted to tomcat in the magnolias, then I'll agree it's easier for me than for the victim to discern subtle differences between one kind of WASP and another, I'll buy my part of the ancestral curse for that Scotch-Irish stud's particular night of pleasure, maybe I'm guilty of something myself, but there are limits, man. All right, we never gave the Negro a fair chance, and now we want to, we're willing to put up with a reasonable amount of disadvantage, in fact, discomfort, outright inequality and inefficency. I'll hire Negroes who are not as equipped in the productive scheme of things as whites; that doesn't mean we have to pay iota for iota on every endless misdemeanor of the past and suffer a vomit bag of bad manners to boot. Look, every student of revolution can tell you that the danger comes from giving the oppressed their first liberties. A poor man who wins a crazy bet always squanders it. The point, buddy, is that the present must forgive the past, there must be forgiveness for old sins, or else progress is impossible." And there is the key to the first door: progress depends upon anesthetizing the past. What if, says Black Power, we are not interested in progress, not your progress with packaged food for soul food, smog for air, hypodermics for roots, air conditioning for breeze —what if we think we have gotten strong by living without progress and your social engineering, what if we think that an insult to the blood is never to be forgotten because it keeps your life alive and reminds you to meditate before you urinate. Who are you to say that spooks don't live behind the left ear and ha'nts behind the right? Whitey, you smoke so much you can't smell, taste, or kiss—your breath is too bad. If you don't have a gun, I can poke you and run—you'll never catch me. I'm alive' cause I keep alive the curse you put in my blood. Primitive people don't forget. If they do, they turn out no better than the civilized and the sick. Who are you, Whitey, to tell me to drop my curse, and join your line of traffic going to work? I'd rather keep myself in shape and work out the curse, natural style. There's always white women, ahem! Unless we decide they're too full of your devil's disease, hypocritical pus-filled old white blood, and so we stay black with black, and repay the curse by drawing blood. That's the life-giving way to repay a curse."

"Why must you talk this way? " says the splendid American. "Can't you see that there are whites and whites, whites I do not begin to control? They wish to destroy you. They agree with your values. They are primitive whites. They think in blood for blood. In a war, they will kill you, and they will kill me."

"Well, daddy, I'm just putting you on. Didn't you ever hear of the hereafter? That's where it will all work out, there where us Blacks are the angels and honkies is the flunky. Now, let me take you by the tail, white cat, long enough to see that I want some more of these handouts, see, these homey horse balls and government aid."

The splendid American has just been left in the mire of a put-on and throwaway. How is he to know if this is spring mud or the muck of the worst Negro Hades?

> *The native's relaxation takes precisely the form of a muscular orgy in which the most acute aggressivity and the most impelling violence are canalised, transformed and conjured away. . . . At certain times on certain days, men and women come together at a given place, and there, under the solemn eye of the tribe, fling themselves into a seemingly unorganized pantomime, which is in reality extremely systematic, in which by various means—shakes of the head, bending of the spinal column, throwing of the whole body backwards—may be deciphered as in an open book the huge effort of a community to exorcise its release. If a sense of brotherhood animates the inner life of guerrilla coming together is to allow the accumulated libido, the hampered aggressivity to dissolve as in a volcanic eruption. Symbolical killings, fantastic rites, imaginary mass murders—all must be brought out. The evil humours are undammed, and flow away with a din as of molten lava. . . .*
> *Frantz Fanon—The Wretched of the Earth*

Here is the lesson learned by the struggles of present-day colonial countries to obtain their independence: a war of liberation converts the energies of criminality, assassination, religious orgy, voodoo and the dance into the determined artful phalanxes of bold guerrilla armies. A sense of brotherhood comes to replace the hitherto murderous clan relations of the natives. Once, that propensity to murder each other had proved effective in keeping the peace—for the settler. Now, these violent sentiments turn against the whites who constrain them. Just as the natives upon a time made good servants and workers for the whites, while reserving the worst of their characters for each other, now they looked to serve each other, to cleanse the furies of their exploited lives in open rude defiance against the authority.

This is the conventional explanation offered by any revolutionary spokesman for the Third World—that new world which may or may not emerge triumphant in Latin America, Asia and Africa. It is a powerful argument, an uplifting argument, it stirs the blood of anyone who has ever had a revolutionary passion, for the faith of the revolutionary (if he is revolutionary enough to have faith) is that the repressed blood of mankind is ultimately good and noble blood. Its goodness may be glimpsed in the emotions of release. If a sense of brotherhood animates the inner life of guerrilla armies, then it does not matter how violent they are to their foe. That violence safeguards the sanctity of their new family relations.

If this is the holy paradigm of the colonial revolutionary, its beauty has been confirmed in places, denied in others. While the struggles of the NFL and the North Vietnamese finally proved impressive even to the most gung ho Marine officers in Southeast Asia, the horrors of the war in Biafra go far toward proving the opposite. The suspicion remains that beneath the rhetoric of revolution, another war, quite separate from a revolutionary war, is also being waged, and the forces of revolution in the world are as divided by this concealed war as the civilized powers who would restrain them. It is as if one war goes on between the privileged and the oppressed to determine how the productive wealth of civilization will be divided; the other war, the seed contained within this first war, derives from a notion that the wealth of civilization is not wealth but a corporate productive poisoning of the wellsprings, avatars and conduits of nature; the power of civilization is therefore equal to the destruction of life itself. It is, of course, a perspective open to the wealthy as well as to the poor—not every mill owner who kills the fish in his local rivers with the wastes from his factory is opposed to protecting our wilderness preserve, not at all, some even serve on the State Conservation Committee. And our First Lady would try to keep billboards from defacing those new highways which amputate the ecology through which they pass. Of course, her husband helped to build those highways. But then the rich, unless altogether elegant, are inevitably comic. It is in the worldwide militancy of the underprivileged, undernourished and exploited that the potential horror of this future war (concealed beneath the present war) will make itself most evident. For the armies of the impoverished, unknown to themselves, are already divided. Once victorious over the wealthy West—if ever! —they could only have a new war. It would take place between those forces on their side who are programmatic, scientific, more or less Socialist, and near maniac in their desire to bring technological culture at the fastest possible rate into every backward land, and those more traditional and/or primitive forces in the revolution of the Third World who reject not only the exploitation of the Western world but reject the West as well, in toto, as a philosophy, a culture, a technique, as a way indeed of even attempting to solve the problems of man himself.

Of these colonial forces, black, brown and yellow, which look to overthrow the economic and social tyrannies of the white man, there is no force in Africa, Asia, or Latin America which we need think of as being any more essentially colonial in stance than the American Negro. Consider these remarks in *The Wretched of the Earth* about the situation of colonials:

"The colonial world is a world cut in two. The dividing line, the frontiers are shown by barracks and police stations." (Of this, it may be said that Harlem is as separate from New York as East Berlin from West Berlin.)

. . . if, in fact, my life is worth as much as the settler's, his glance no longer shrivels me up nor freezes me, and his voice no longer turns me into stone. I am no longer on tenterhooks in his presence; in fact, I don't give a damn for him. Not only does his presence no longer trouble me, but I am already preparing such efficient ambushes for him that soon there will be no way out but that of flight." (Now, whites flee the subways in New York.)

". . . there is no colonial power today which is capable of adopting the only form of contest which has a chance of succeeding, namely, the prolonged establishment of large forces of occupation." (How many divisions of paratroops would it take to occupy Chicago's South Side?)

The American Negro is of course not synonymous with Black Power. For every Black militant, there are ten Negroes who live quietly beside him in the slums, resigned for the most part to the lessons, the action and the treadmill of the slums. As many again have chosen to integrate. They live now like Negroid Whites in mixed neighborhoods, suburbs, factories, obtaining their partial peace within the white dream. But no American Negro is contemptuous of Black Power. Like the accusing finger in the dream, it is the rarest nerve in their head, the frightening pulse in their heart, equal in emotional weight to that passion which many a noble nun sought to conquer on a cold stone floor. Black Power obviously derives from a heritage of anger which makes the American Negro one man finally with the African, the Algerian and even the Vietcong—he would become schizophrenic if he tried to suppress his fury over the mutilations of the past.

The confrontation of Black Power with American life gives us then not only an opportunity to comprehend some of the forces and some of the style of that war now smoldering between the global rich and the global poor, between the culture of the past and the institutions of the future, but—since Black Power has more intimate, everyday knowledge of what it is like to live in an advanced technological society than any other guerrilla force on earth—the division of attitudes within Black Power has more to tell us about the shape of future wars and revolutions than any other militant force in the world. Technological man in his terminal diseases, dying of air he can no longer breathe, of packaged food he can just about digest, of plastic clothing his skin can hardly bear and of static before which his spirit has near expired, stands at one end of revolutionary ambition—at the other is an inchoate glimpse of a world now visited only by the primitive and the drug-ridden, a world where technology shatters before magic and electronic communication is surpassed by the psychic telegraphy of animal mood.

Most of the literature of Black Power is interested entirely, or so it would seem, in immediate political objectives of the most concrete sort. Back in 1923, Marcus Garvey, father of the Back-to-Africa movement, might have written, "When Europe was inhabited by a race of cannibals, a race of savages, naked men, heathens and pagans, Africa was peopled with a race of cultured black men, who were masters in art, science and literature, men who were cultured and refined; men who, it was said, were like the gods," but the present leaders of Black Power are concerned with political mandate and economic clout right here. Floyd McKissick of CORE: the Black Power Movement seeks to win power in a half-dozen ways. These are:

1. The growth of Black *political* power.
2. The building of Black *economic* power.
3. The improvement of the *self-image* of Black people.
4. The development of Black *leadership.*
5. The attainment of *Federal law enforcement.*
6. The mobilization of Black *consumer power.*

These demands present nothing exceptional. On their face, they are not so different from manifestos by the NAACP or planks by the Democratic party. A debater with the skill of William F. Buckley or Richard Nixon could stay afloat for hours on the life-saving claim that there is nothing in these six points antithetical to conservatives. Indeed, there is not. Not on the face. For example, here is Adam Clayton Powell, a politician most respected by Black Power militants, on some of these points. Political power: "Where we are 20% of the voters, we should command 20% of the jobs, judgeships, commissionerships, and all political appointments." Economic power: "Rather than a race primarily of consumers and stock boys, we must become a race of producers and stockbrokers." Leadership: "Black communities . . . must neither tolerate nor accept outside leadership—black or white." Federal law enforcement: "The battle against segregation in America's public school systems must become a national effort, instead of the present regional skirmish that now exists." Even consumer protest groups to stand watch on the quality of goods sold in a slum neighborhood are hardly revolutionary, more an implementation of good conservative buying practices. *Consumers Digest* is not yet at the barricades.

Indeed, which American institution of power is ready to argue with these six points? They are so rational! The power of the technological society is shared by the corporations, the military, the mass media, the trade unions and the Government. It is to the interest of each to have a society which is *rational,* even as a machine is rational. When a machine breaks down, the cause can be discovered; in fact, the cause must be capable of being discovered or we are not dealing with a machine. So the pleasure of working with machines is that malfunctions are correctable; satisfaction is guaranteed by the application of work, knowledge and reason. Hence, any race problem is anathema to power groups in the technological society, because the subject of race is irrational. At the very least, race problems seem to have the property of repelling reason. Still, the tendency of modern society to shape men for function in society like parts of a machine grows more powerful all the time. So we have the paradox of a conservative capitalistic democracy, profoundly entrenched in a racial prejudice (and hitherto profoundly attracted to racial-exploitation) now transformed into the most developed technological society in the world. The old prejudices of the men who wield power have become therefore inefficient before the needs of the social machine—so inefficient, in fact, that prejudiced as many of them still are, they consider it a measure of their responsibility to shed prejudice. (We must by now move outside the center of power before we can even find General Curtis LeMay.)

So the question may well be posed: if the demands formally presented by Black Power advocates like McKissick and Powell are thus rational, and indeed finally fit the requirements of the technological society, why then does Black Power inspire so much fear, distrust, terror, horror and even outright revulsion among the best liberal descendants of the beautiful old Eleanor Roosevelt bag and portmanteau? And the answer is that an intellectual shell game has been played up to here. We have not covered McKissick's six points, only five. The sixth (point number three) was "The improvement of the *self-image* of Black people." It is here that sheer Black hell busts loose. A technological society can deal comfortably with people who are mature, integrated, goal-oriented, flexible, responsive, group-responsive, etc., etc.—the word we cannot leave out is white or white-oriented. The technological society is not able to deal with the self-image of separate peoples and races if the development of their self-image produces personalities of an explosive individuality. We do not substitute sticks of dynamite for the teeth of a gear and assume we still have an automotive transmission.

McKissick covers his third point, of course: "Negro history, art, music and other aspects of Black culture ... make Black people aware of their contributions to the American heritage and to world civilization." Powell bastes the goose with orotundities of rhetorical gravy: "We must give our children a sense of pride in being black. The glory of our past and the dignity of our present must lead the way to the power of our future." Amen. We have been conducted around the point.

Perhaps the clue is that political Right and political Left are meaningless terms when applied conventionally to Black Power. If we are to use them at all (and it is a matter of real convenience), then we might call the more or less rational, programmatic and recognizably political arm of Black Power, presented by McKissick and Powell, as the Right Wing, since their program can conceivably be attached to the programs of the technological society, whether Democrat or Republican. The straight-out political demands of this kind of Black Power not only can be integrated (at least on paper) into the needs of the technological society, but must be, because—we would repeat—an exploited class creates disruption and therefore irrationality in a social machine; efforts to solve exploitation and disruption become mandatory for the power groups. If this last sentence sounds vaguely Marxist in cadence, the accident is near. What characterizes technological societies is that they tend to become more and more like one another. So America and the Soviet will yet have interchangeable parts, or at least be no more different than a four-door Ford from a two-door Chevrolet. It may thus be noticed that what we are calling the Right Wing of Black Power—the technological wing—is in the conventional sense interested in moving to the left. Indeed, after the Blacks attain equality —so goes the unspoken assumption—America will be able to progress toward a rational society of racial participation, etc., etc. What then is the Left Wing of Black Power? Say, let us go back to Africa, back to Garvey.

> *We must understand that we are replacing a dying culture, and we must be prepared to do this, and be absolutely conscious of what we are replacing it with. We are sons and daughters of the most ancient societies on this planet. . . . No movement shaped or contained by Western culture will ever benefit Black people. Black power must be the actual force and beauty and wisdom of Blackness . . . reordering the world.*   LeRoi Jones

Are you ready to enter the vision of the Black Left? It is profoundly anti-technological. Jump into it all at once. Here are a few remarks by Ron Karenga:

"The fact that we are Black is our ultimate reality. We were Black before we were born.

"The White boy is engaged in the worship of technology; we must not sell our souls for money and machines. We must free ourselves culturally before we proceed politically.

"Revolution to us is the creation of an alternative . . . we are not here to be taught by the world, but to teach the world."

We have left the splendid American far behind. He is a straight-punching all-out truth-sayer; he believes in speaking his mind; but if LeRoi Jones— insults absolute rejection and consummate bad-mouthing—is not too much for him, then Karenga will be his finish. Karenga obviously believes that in the root is the answer to where the last growth went wrong—so he believes in the wisdom of the blood, and blood-wisdom went out for the splendid American after reading *Lady Chatterley's Lover* in sophomore year. Life is hard enough to see straight without founding your philosophy on a metaphor.

Nonetheless the mystique of Black Power remains. Any mystique which has men ready to die for it is never without political force. The Left Wing or Black Power speaks across the void to the most powerful conservative passions—for any real conservatism is founded on regard for the animal, the oak and the field; it has instinctive detestation of science, of the creation-by-machine. Conservatism is a body of traditions which once served as the philosophical home of society. If the traditions are now withered in the hum of electronics; if the traditions have become almost hopelessly inadequate to meet the computed moves of the technological society; if conservatism has become the grumbling of the epicure at bad food, bad air, bad manners; if conservatism lost the future because it enjoyed the greed of its privileged position to that point where the exploited depths stirred in righteous rage; if the conservatives and their traditions failed because they violated the balance of society, exploited the poor too savagely and searched for justice not nearly enough; if finally the balance between property rights and the rights of men gave at last too much to the land and too little to the living blood, still conservatism and tradition had one last Herculean strength: they were of the marrow, they partook of primitive wisdom. The tradition had been founded on some half-remembered sense of primitive perception, and so was close to life and the sense of life. Tradition had appropriated the graceful movements with which primitive strangers and friends might meet in the depth of a mood, all animal in their awareness: lo! the stranger bows before the intense presence of the monarch or the chief, and the movement is later engraved upon a code of ceremony. So tradition was once a key to the primitive life still breathing within us, a key too large, idiosyncratic and unmanageable for the quick shuttles of the electronic. Standing before technology, tradition began to die, and air turned to smog. But the black man, living a life on the fringe of technological society, exploited by it, poisoned by it, half-rejected by it, gulping prison air in the fluorescent nightmare of shabby garish electric ghettos, uprooted centuries ago from his native Africa, his instincts living ergo like nerves in the limbo of an amputated limb, had thereby an experience unique to modern man—he was forced to live at one and the same time in the old primitive jungle of the slums, and the hygienic surrealistic landscape of the technological society. And as he began to arise from his exploitation, he discovered that the culture which had saved him owed more to the wit and telepathy of the jungle than the value and programs of the West. His dance had taught him more than writs and torts, his music was sweeter than Shakespeare or Bach (since music had never been a luxury to him but a need), prison had given him a culture deeper than libraries in the grove, and violence had produced an economy of personal relations as negotiable as money. The American Black had survived—of all the peoples of the Western World, he was the only one in the near seven decades of the twentieth century to have undergone the cruel weeding of real survival. So it was possible his manhood had improved while the manhood of others was being leached. He had at any rate a vision. It was that he was black, beautiful and secretly superior—he had therefore the potentiality to conceive and create a new culture (perchance a new civilization), richer, wiser, deeper, more beautiful and profound than any he had seen. (And conceivably more demanding, more torrential, more tyrannical.) But he would not know until he had power for himself. He would not know if he could provide a wiser science, subtler schooling, deeper medicine, richer victual and deeper view of creation until he had the power. So while some (the ones the Blacks called Negroes) looked to integrate into the super-suburbs of technology land (and find, was their hope, a little peace for the kids), so others dreamed of a future world which their primitive lore and sophisticated attainments might now bring. And because they were proud and loved their vision, they were warriors as well, and had a mystique which saw the cooking of food as good or bad for the soul. And taste gave the hint. That was the Left of Black Power, a movement as mysterious, dedicated, instinctive and conceivably bewitched as a gathering of Templars for the next Crusade. Soon their public fury might fall upon the fact that civilization was a trap, and therefore their wrath might be double, for they had been employed to build civilization, had received none of its gains, and yet, being allowed to enter now, now, this late, could be doomed with the rest. What a thought!

> *When the canaille rouriére took the liberty of beheading the high noblesse, it was done less, perhaps, to inherit their goods than to inherit their ancestors.*
> *Heinrich Heine*

But I am a white American, more or less, and writing for an audience of Americans, white and Negro in the main. So the splendid American would remind me that my thoughts are romantic projections, hypotheses unverifiable by any discipline, no more legitimate for discussion than melody. What, he might ask, would you do with the concrete problem before us. . . .

You mean: not jobs, not schools, not votes, not production, not consumption. . .

No, he said hoarsely, law and order.

Well, the man who sings the melody is not normally consulted for the by-laws of the Arranger's Union.

Crap and craparoola, said the splendid American, what it all comes down to is: how do you keep the peace?

I do not know. If they try to keep it by force—we will not have to wait so very long before there are Vietnams in our own cities. A race which arrives at a vision must test that vision by deeds.

Then what would you do?

If I were king?

We are a republic and will never support a king.

Ah, if I were a man who had a simple audience with Richard Milhous Nixon, I would try to say, "Remember when all else has failed, that honest hatred searches for responsibility. I would look to encourage not merely new funding for businessmen who are Black, but Black schools with their own teachers and their own texts, Black solutions to Black housing where the opportunity might be given to rebuild one's own slum room by room, personal idiosyncrasy next to mad neighbor's style, floor by floor, not block by block; I would try to recognize that an area of a city where whites fear to go at night belongs by all existential—which is to say natural —law to the Blacks, and would respect the fact, and so would encourage Black local self-government as in a separate city with a Black sanitation department run by themselves, a Black fire department, a funding for a Black concert hall, and most of all a Black police force responsible only to this city within our city and Black courts of justice for their own. There will be no peace short of the point where the Black man can measure his new superiorities and inferiorities against our own."

You are absolutely right but for one detail, said the splendid American. What will you do when they complain about the smog *our* factories push into *their* air?

Oh, I said, the Blacks are so evil their factories will push worse air back. And thus we went on arguing into the night. Yes, the times are that atrocious you can hardly catch your breath. "Confronted by outstanding merit in another, there is no way of saving one's ego except by love."

Goethe is not the worst way to say goodnight.

OPEN LETTER ON WHITE JUSTICE
AND THE RIOTS

Lee Rainwater

A great deal of the difficulty in understanding what causes riots and what might be done about them comes from a misunderstanding of exactly what their nature is. A riot seems almost always to begin with an incident in which the police make an effort at enforcing one or another law—whether the culprits involved be a tipsy driver, a traffic law violator, or the operators and patrons of a blind pig. In other words, riots grow out of efforts at social control where society's officials move in on behavior which the informal social controls of the community do not prove sufficient to contain.

As the police go about their business, a curious crowd gathers. The crowd watches what is going on and reflects on it, and some members come to deny the legitimacy of what the police are doing. Rather than responding with satisfaction to the smooth functioning of the social control forces, the crowd members respond with anger and resentment; they identify with the culprits rather than with the law. This identification often takes the form of a belief either that the culprits are innocent, or that they're being treated more roughly than is warranted or just.

The riot develops from this initial incident as the people in the crowd begin to express their anger in response to the situation—they throw rocks at the police, or make attempts to rescue the prisoners. Here they are only acting out the strong and unpleasant emotions stimulated by what they see and the meanings they assign to it. But as this process continues and people talk to each other

Lee Rainwater, "Open Letter on White Justice, and The Riots," **TRANS-ACTION,** *September, 1967. Copyright ©1967 by* **TRANS-ACTION MAGAZINE,** *New Brunswick, New Jersey. Reprinted by permission of the publisher.*

about what has happened, the matter becomes more ideological—that is, the events are interpreted in an increasingly larger context. The incident becomes an example of a society in which whites do as they please, while Negroes are held accountable for every minor infraction, even those infractions involving behavior that is not really voluntary. For example, a man may get drunk because he is depressed and discouraged about his situation, or he may spend his time on the streets and get in trouble there because he has given up looking for a job. The fury of the rioters is probably exacerbated by their weariness at trying to manage their lives in such a way that they can avoid the attentive ministrations of the social control agents (and these include truant officers, welfare investigators, and personnel officers, as well as the police).

By now the guilt or innocence of the culprits, and the manner in which the police treat them, are no longer that central. Instead, the focus is on the crowd members' general feelings that they live in a world in which they are constantly held accountable to standards of justice which are not applied to others. They feel that the merchants with whom they deal cheat them, that employers are either indifferent or exploiting toward them, that the police are disrespectful and suspicious of them. Therefore, they feel that the police (as representatives of the society at large) are perpetrating the greater evil—an evil by comparison with which the minor peccadillos of the drunken driver, traffic violator, the blind-pig patron are, in human terms, irrelevant.

Further, as incidents like this multiply, and as sophistication about Negro victimization rises in the ghetto community, it becomes increasingly possible to generalize this process without a particular incident. Following the news of the Newark, Detroit, and East Harlem riots in July, a group of Negro teenagers went on a rampage after a rock and roll concert, smashing and looting several of New York's Fifth Avenue stores. They did not need the provocation of an actual encounter with the police to touch off this vivid rejection of legal authority.

A riot is a social event which provides different opportunities to different participants. It is a short-lived "opportunity structure." Of all the aspects of the riot, this is the least well understood. There is no single "rioter," but rather many kinds of activities, each contributing a little bit to make up the total event. We know almost nothing about who takes each of the possible roles in the rioting—looter, sniper, police attacker, sympathetic bystander, ideological interpreter, and so on. It does seem that the most popular category is that of looter. This makes sense; what the rioters are saying, more than anything else, is "we haven't gotten our share." On Detroit's East and West sides the furniture and appliance stores seemed the hardest hit. "Big ticket" items are the proof of the affluent society and the looters knew exactly where to find them. In this respect the riots become a kind of primitive effort at an income redistribution which the society refuses to support in any lawful and regularized way.

The snipers, on the other hand, we can only vaguely understand. Indeed, the evidence seems to suggest that snipers are more often phantom than real; a very few snipers (perhaps none at all) are necessary to legitimate the belief of police and National Guardsmen that they are "at war" and that the danger is so great that they may fire with impunity into the rioting community. In Detroit, one such phantom sniper was apparently responsible for the National Guard machine-gunning a "white" motel near the General Motors building and inadvertently hitting an out-of-town woman staying there.

Riots are difficult to control precisely because of this voluntary division of labor among the participants. Because their many different sorts of activities require different sorts of responses, the riot becomes a highly complex event that can be brought under control only by a mass show of force (or perhaps by a show of no force at all). This, plus the fact that once the riot gets under way there is almost total denial of legitimacy to the police, means that the area must be *occupied* to be controlled—a process that calls ever further into question the legitimacy of the total society and its laws. The riots elicit from the official world exactly the kind of behavior that confirms the ghetto's estimate of white justice. The trigger-happy behavior of the National Guard and the police and the haphazard way in which arrests are or are not made deepens the conviction that being accorded justice depends more on luck than on the rule of law. The rising hysteria of the fatigued and frightened men in uniform seems to release all of their latent hostility to Negroes. In New Jersey, Los Angeles, and numerous smaller cities the civilian officials have hardly behaved better; it is to the credit of Detroit's Mayor Cavanaugh and his cabinet that no hint of such prejudice and bitterness has been apparent there.

Riots, then, provide different kinds of ghetto dwellers with different opportunities to pursue highly varied goals. The larger the riots get, the easier for individuals to become participants, and probably the more varied the goals they pursue.

In this context, it's quite clear from the data on the social characteristics of those arrested and convicted in Watts that the rioters are probably *not* exclusively "young hoodlums." For example, over half of those arrested in Watts were twenty-five years of age and over and as many as 40 percent were over thirty. Further, about two-thirds of those arrested and convicted were employed. It is certainly true that those arrested were very familiar with the law; less than 30 percent of them had no prior arrest. This, however, is not evidence that they are criminals, but only that they live in the ghetto. (Note, for example, that half of those arrested had never been convicted.) We would need more precise data to know what differences there might be between those who form some kind of active core of the rioters and those who take part more casually, by minor looting and the like. It might well be that the active core is more youthful and more solidly involved in delinquent activity than the others. But the most important fact here is that one could not make a riot of any size with the dominant proportion of the participants composed only of "young hoodlums."

There should be no mistake on this point. A very large proportion of the able-bodied members of any lower class Negro ghetto are potential participants in a riot. And, the riot has an ideological meaning for them; it is not simply a diversion which allows for criminal activity. The man who steals a six-pack of beer or breaks a store window does it not out of "criminal" motivation (it would hardly be worth his while), but because he is expressing some important feelings about his world and trying to put these feelings "on the record." If in the process he can derive some material benefit, like a television set or a new G.E. range, that is all to the good because it makes his point even clearer. Everyone in America knows that money talks. The greater the damage in terms of the financial cost of the looting and burning, the more effectively the point has been made.

But just as a riot provides a wide range of opportunities, it also involves a wide range of costs—primarily those of being killed, arrested, or burned out. It is probably true that stable working class Negroes (who are often as much prisoners of the ghetto as lower class people) are much less interested in the opportunities of riots and more concerned about the costs. They often share the feeling that legal authority is neither just nor fair, but they also have material possessions and social positions to protect. They don't want their homes burned by rioters or strafed by the National Guard. And they are concerned that their children will become involved in the riot—that they will be treated as, and may come to think of themselves as, the "young hoodlums."

Because this more stable working class in the ghetto usually supplies its "community leaders," there is real danger that any investigating committee will be misled into believing that the riots represent the feelings of only a small minority. These "respectable" spokesmen for the area must not be allowed (no matter how honest their personal views might be) to mislead an investigating group in its analysis of the nature of riot participation.

There is always deep conflict and ambivalence in the ghetto over the issue of police protection versus police harassment. The ghetto is a dangerous place for its inhabitants, and they would like to have firm and competent police surveillance. On the other hand, that very surveillance carries with it the danger of unjust and unseemly behavior by the police. Police rationality dictates that anyone in the ghetto is more suspect of crime than anyone in a white middle class neighborhood. From the police point of view, then, ghetto residents should be more willing to cooperate by answering questions and accepting arrest. The conflict built into this kind of situation can perhaps be somewhat ameliorated by more integrated police forces, and by vigorous supervision of the police to see that they are not impolite or overly aggressive. But that is no real solution to the problem.

Further, riots may well become more frequent and larger as time goes on due to the diffusion of knowledge, almost technical in nature, about how a riot is carried on. It is not too fanciful to say that anyone who watches television and reads the newspapers learns from the coverage of Watts, Hough, Newark, Harlem, and Detroit how to participate in a riot. Therefore, *without any organization at all* in the sense of a command structure, people in all parts of the nation know what to do and what roles one might take should a riot opportunity present itself. Millions of Americans today could, on request, fashion Molotov cocktails, who a year or two ago would not have known the meaning of the term. Similarly, millions of Americans now know that many rioters are not arrested and that snipers are seldom caught. There is no way of preventing the diffusion of this knowledge; we can only try to prevent the need and willingness to use it.

Finally, the particular quality of the riots reflects the Negro cultural emphasis on expressivity over instrumentality—practical, goal-directed action. A WASP riot under similar conditions would probably be a much more hardnosed and certainly much more bloody and violent event. The "carnival atmosphere" noted by observers at all major riots is probably a direct reflection of the expressive emphasis in all group activity among Negroes, whether it be church participation, the blues, a rock and roll concert, or street corner banter.

This is perhaps also part of the key to why the riots seem be be relatively unorganized, both locally and nationally. Discussion of an organized national conspiracy is probably a white projection. Whites find it very difficult to understand why Negroes aren't more efficient in their rebellion—why there is no national cadre, no command structure, no greater efficiency in doing damage. A good part of this may be because this is not the Negroes' preferred way of going about things. Rather, in the midst of an ineffable group solidarity, a kind of free enterprise prevails in which each individual works for himself, perhaps cooperating for short periods of time with others to accomplish some immediate goals, but in the main doing things his own way as an expression of his own feelings. The expressive focus may be very important in formulating an ideology, and thus ultimately have a strong effect on the frequency and nature of rioting. But, that effect is achieved not by *organization,* but rather through *communication* of a developing social doctrine.

Negro expressiveness may also account for the tremendous disjunction between the verbal communication of supposedly violent groups such as RAM and spokesmen for violence like H. Rap Brown, and the fact that organized paramilitary action seems to be virtually absent from the riots. They behave as if they were designed more for display to the white press and titillated or scandalized Negro audiences than for actual committed revolutionary action. I don't think this point about Negro expressive life style is particularly important in understanding or accounting for the riots except to the extent that it helps us understand and get behind the myths that some whites (particularly Senators Eastland and McClellan, the press, and law enforcement agencies) and some Negroes (like Carmichael in Havana) are putting forth.

When we seek the basic causes of the riots the central question is: Why are there so many Negroes for whom riots provide an opportunity for meaningful self-expression and gain? Further, why are the opportunities sought in such situations so destructive of social order? We know that in other situations which provide technical opportunity, for example, blackouts, nothing of the sort happens, although the authorities always fear that it might.

Much of the popular interpretaion of riots has turned on an understanding of the really desperate situation of the worst off in the ghettos, of those who make up the "underclass," which may include anywhere between one-third and one-half of the ghetto population. Again, however, the figures on the Watts arrestees are instructive. Two-thirds of the men arrested and convicted were employed and perhaps as many as one-third of them were earning over $300 a month. Forty percent (or over half of those who had ever been married) were living with their spouses. Thus, when a riot takes place, a significant portion even of those above the poverty line may well be drawn into participation. This should alert us to the fact that rioting is not exclusively a problem of poverty as currently defined.

One may talk about two major kinds of causative factors—one involving *class* (by which is meant simply economic deprivation and all of the cultural and social consequences that flow from it) and the other involving the inferior *caste* position of Negroes to whites. This latter factor is most directly expressed in ghetto hostility toward the police, but it is also involved in the attack the riots come to represent on the total white-dominated society. Even the Negro who is well off in class terms may feel a strong pull toward participation if he has had the experience of being interrogated and perhaps arrested in a ghetto area simply because his face is black. Where men have little to protect and where their experience of hostility and indifference from the white world is even more pervasive, as in the case of the lower class, the resistance to participation will be even less.

The fact that even a significant minority of the participants are members of seemingly stable families earning above poverty level incomes tells us something about what is involved in exclusion from ordinary American society in a city as prosperous as Detroit or Los Angeles. Whatever poverty as minimum subsistence may mean, it is quite clear that people with incomes as high as $5,000 a year are really not able to feel that they participate in the broad spectrum of average American affluence and satisfaction. A community in which the great majority of the families must exist on significantly less than the median family income for the nation is a community of failures. Inclusion in such a community, compounded as it is by belonging to a historically excluded group and the knowledge that there is a connection between racial exclusion and economic exclusion, is undersirable to those who live within its confines as well as to those outside.

Thus, the ghetto community has few informal social controls; people tend to minimize trouble by avoiding each other more than by building up informal social networks which ensure observance of common group standards. Everybody does pretty much what he wants as long as he can stay out of the clutches of the authorities. Thus, the individual has few effective sanctions available at the informal level. Even those who disapprove of rioting are powerless to do much about it by informally punishing those who participate. Any influence they might have is vitiated by the common perception of all that the authorities are just about as unjust as the law-breakers. Ghetto residents will, in desperation, call upon officialdom to punish those of their fellows who are directly making trouble for them, but they do it in much the same way that one might pay the neighborhood bully to discipline an enemy. The bully is called upon because of his power, not because of any legitimate authority.

The riots bring into high relief the ever present schism in the Negro community between those who feel they have nothing to lose, and those who want to protect what they have—while the former riot, the latter deluge the police and mayor's office with telephone calls demanding protection from the rioters, demanding that the riot be put down before their homes are burned, their community destroyed. The physical contrast in Detroit is particularly striking. Not three blocks from the 12th Street riot area are substantial homes on well--maintained tree-lined streets. Their residents, like other stable working and middle class Negro Detroiters, wanted the riots put down with all possible dispatch; the potential cost of getting even with Whitey was too great.

And then there are the Negro businessmen in the ghetto—the "soul brothers." Detroit's Grand River Boulevard, where the riot-damaged buildings string out for miles, has a great many soul brothers (and one soul mother) whose quickly inscribed signs protected them from damage while on either side the ing or burning seemed complete. But, one can't count the "soul brother" signs that are no longer there because the glass was broken; and an occasional sign is still observable when only one broken show window in a soul brother's store was required to accomplish the looting. The signs obviously provided some protection, but exactly how much they lower the risk is a moot point. If the protection is very high, it would suggest that the hostility of the more prosperous and respectable Negroes is not returned by the rioters; if protection is low the rioters might be saying, as those in Bedford-Stuyvesant are reported to have taunted Negro policemen, "Take off your black masks so we can see your white faces."

Summing up: (1) the root cause of the riots lies in a caste system deeply imbedded in our society that has created a situation in which (a) a very large proportion of Negroes are denied the opportunity to achieve an average American standard of living, and (b) even those Negroes who do, by dint of their own efforts, manage to come reasonably close to an average American standard are still subjected to special disabilities and insults because of their confinement to a ghetto community. (2) From the immediate point of view of the rioters, the most pervasive factor which prevents their achieving some sense of a decent life is that of living in poverty or near-poverty (as a rough rule from, say, having incomes less than one-half to two-thirds that of the median family income for the nation). This economic exclusion affects almost everything they do—their ability to purchase all those elements that make up the "standard package" that most American families deem their right. And the inability to earn more than this kind of poverty or near-poverty income affects the respect they are able to elicit from their own family members, members of their immediate community, and from the society at large.

It seems likely that the starting mechanisms for a riot are fairly dependent on the existence of pronounced poverty coupled with very high rates of unemployment. This, at least, would seem to be important to the extent that young men (say men under twenty-five) have a disproportionate influence on getting a riot going. This group is excluded not only from the availability of something like an average American life, but is excluded even within its own community. The older men do tend to be employed and to earn incomes reasonably close to the poverty line. It is the younger men in the ghetto who are most completely and dramatically excluded from any participation in the conventional rewards of the society.

If this diagnosis is correct—that the direct cause of participation in the riots (as opposed to the precipitating incidents) is economic marginality—it should put us on notice that no "community action" programs, whether they involve better police-community relations or rapprochement with the new black militant leaders will prevent riots. Rather, the necessary condition for any permanent solution to the riot problem will be to provide a reasonable approximation of the "average American standard of living" for every family. This means managing the society so that poverty and near-poverty are eliminated. Only then can those who now participate in and support the riots find themselves in situations where rioting has become a meaningless, useless activity. This "income strategy" has two principal elements.

The more important of these is creating work. The demand for goods and services must be manipulated in such a way that private and public employers have more jobs which they are willing to offer to relatively unskilled and "undesirable" employees because they need these employees to satisfy the demands for their products. This is the aggregate demand solution to poverty argued by James Tobin, Hyman Minsky, and others. Such a solution has the advantage that it makes maximum use of what is already our main technique for distributing goods and services to families—that is, employment. A further advantage is that an aggregate demand, full employment situation tends to upgrade wages in low wage industries and thus alleviate the problem of near-poverty and poverty among employed workers.

It might be well to design crash programs, as well as possible subsidized employment in private industry, for young workers. Such crash programs would be a dead end, however, unless they were part of an overall aggregate demand plus special-programs-for-unskilled-workers strategy.

An integral part of this strategy will probably have to be some direct planning by the government to make demand for unskilled workers roughly equal to that for more skilled workers. The most promising suggestions in this area involve the "new careers for the poor" proposals which create new kinds of jobs and avenues for advancement in public service activities. But it is very important that these programs not be developed as programs of "last resort employment," but rather as permanent programs which are productive for the entire society.

It might be well to design crash programs, as well as possible subsidized employment in private industry, for young workers. Such crash programs would be a dead end, however, unless they were part of an overall aggregate demand plus special-programs-for-unskilled-workers strategy.

It follows that the government agencies who should be responsible for solving the problems of the riots are not so much HEW, Labor, and OEO, as they are the Treasury Department, Council of Economic Advisors, and the Federal Reserve Board: OEO-type programs such as the Job Corps, which are designed only to train a small number of lower class individuals to compete more success-fully within a system that offers them little or no opportunity as long as they remain unskilled, cannot hope to solve the massive income problems of the whole disadvantaged sector. Unless the power and skills of those agencies which set basic fiscal and economic policy are brought to bear (and backed, of course, by a committed President) it is very difficult to believe that we can solve the problem of rioting—or the more general problem of poverty, and the racial caste system it supports.

The second aspect of the income strategy will involve some form of guar-anteed minimum income. We now know that the various particular plans that have been suggested—negative income tax, family allowance, upgraded welfare systems, and the like—all represent variations on a common system of income redistribution (see the work of Christopher Green recently published by The Brookings Institution). The important issue is not so much which of these plans is best as what the guaranteed minimum is to be and what the tax rate on the subsidy is to be. Given the amount of current research activity on income maintenance, the basic technical issues involved in a guaranteed income program will be resolved in the next two or three years. The real question is how we are to muster the political goodwill to put a program into effect.

A guaranteed minimum income program will be crucial for two reasons. First of all, there will always be families for whom the economy cannot provide a reasonable income on a regular and secure basis. Perhaps more important from a political point of view, a national commitment to a guaranteed minimum income will spur the government to maintain employment as fully as possible so that the maximum number of people will derive the maximum proportion of their incomes from their own earnings and not from the national dole. The political vulnerability of any group which over a period of time derives a significant proportion of its income from government transfers will always be great. Therefore, income maintenance plans can only be a form of family insurance and national political insurance, not a major way of channeling income to families.

A solution to the Negro income problem is thus the sine qua non for a permanent solution to the problem of rioting. With this achieved, tremendous pressure will be generated to move out of the ghetto. I would guess that only a small minority of current ghetto residents would prefer to stay, given a choice. This pressure will itself facilitate the development of desegregated housing; but the government must also facilitate the dispersion of ghetto residents to a more integrated life away from the central city ghettos. That dispersion would to some extent be aided by fair housing laws, but perhaps more important would be the development of government-supported programs for the expansion of middle and lower middle income housing. This would maximize the range of choice available to anyone seeking a better place to live.

It is my belief that it will prove impossible to solve the many other problems of the ghetto until the income problem is solved. Further, I believe that these other problems—education, health, political participation, and the like—would be amenable to very different and much simpler solutions if the Negro families involved had decent incomes.

The ideological developments of the past ten years in connection with the situation of the Negro American pose a challenge to the government and to white society generally. Depending on how this challenge is met, we will move more slowly or more quickly toward the basic economic solutions offered above. I see the vague and often contradictory militant civil rights ideology which has developed over the past few years as a result of two factors. First, as the nation has become more prosperous, it has become increasingly obvious that it is not necessary to have a deprived and excluded group in our midst. The dynamics of affluence themselves call into question the old caste-like racial arrangements. As some Negroes participate in that prosperity, and as they look on the tremendous affluence of white society, there is a strong push in the direction of forcing the society to accord Negroes their share. This factor was perhaps the dominant influence in the early period of the new civil rights consciousness that started in the early '60's—suddenly it seemed ridiculous to most Americans that anyone should be excluded when we have so much.

Second, and more recently, has come a new wave of black populism. The common theme running through many of the ideas of the new black militants is that Negroes have a right to their own future and their own place in the sun, not just in economic terms but as full men in society. The emphasis on blackness is a reaction to the price that white society seems to want to exact for economic payoffs, a price that seems to involve a denial of oneself as Negro and to require a tame imitation of whatever the going definition of the proper white person is. Now there is a lot of nonsense these days about what Negro culture involves and what black autonomy might mean. But, at the core of the black populist movement is a denial of the right of whites to define who the Negro is and what he may become. This is not only healthy, but much more realistic than the earlier, simple-minded integrationist myth that dominated civil rights activity for so long.

There are now, and will probably continue to be for some time, conflicts between moving toward the economic goals of the civil rights movement and the black populist goals. The political challenge for white society is to thread its way through these conflicts without denying the validity of either factor, and to select those areas in which the government can further the Negro goals (to my mind, principally the economic area) and those areas in which the main effort at constructing a new social reality will have to be made primarily by Negroes themselves.

The danger here is that the reaction to the black populist goals on the part of the government and whites generally will be so hostile that Negro leaders who emphasize such aims will be progressively alienated and provoked into activities destructive to both sets of goals. In the main, however, the mutual alienation and viciousness that has tended to dominate the civil rights-white power structure dialogue for the past two years is more a result of the government's unwillingness to make major economic commitments that it is of any inherent tendencies in the black populist movement.

In short, the government cannot give Negroes a black culture or a black consciousness, but it can manage the society in such a way as to give them a "black affluence." If the government does not do what it can do, then we can only expect the courageous and the committed in the Negro community to become more aggressive and more destructive toward the larger society which has the necessary means, but refuses to use them.

Further Reading Suggested by The Author:

Rivers of Blood, Years of Darkness by Robert Conot (Bantam Books, 1967). A carefully researched analysis of the Watts riot by a Los Angeles journalist.

Whitewash Over Watts by Robert Blauner (*Trans-action*, Vol. 3, No. 3). An analysis of the inadequacies of the McCone Commission report.

Dark Ghetto by Kenneth B. Clark (New York City: Harper & Row, 1965).

The Negro American by Talcott Parsons and Kenneth B. Clark (Boston: Houghton Mifflin Company, 1966). Collection of articles on the social, psychological, economic, and legal aspects of the contemporary situation of Negro Americans.

WHITE INSTITUTIONS AND BLACK RAGE

David Boesel, Richard Berk, W. Eugene Groves,
Bettye Eidson and Peter H. Rossi

Five summers of black rebellion have made it clear that the United States is facing a crisis of proportions not seen since the Great Depression. And one of the root causes of this crisis, it has also become clear, is the performance of white institutions, especially those institutions in the ghetto. Some of these institutions—police and retail stores, for example—have done much to antagonize Negroes; others, such as welfare departments and black political organizations, have tried to help and have failed.

Why have these white institutions helped engender black rage? One way to find out might be to study the attitudes of the men working for them—to discover what their personnel think about the racial crisis itself, about their own responsibilities, about the work they are doing. Therefore, at the request of the National Advisory Commission on Civil Disorders (the riot commission), we at Johns Hopkins University visited 15 Northern cities and questioned men and women working for six different institutional groups: major employers, retail merchants, teachers, welfare workers, political workers (all Negro), and policemen. All of the people we questioned, except the employers, work right in the ghetto, and are rank-and-file employees—the cop on the beat, the social caseworker, and so on.

EMPLOYERS' SOCIAL RESPONSIBILITY

The "employers" we questioned were the managers or personnel officers of the ten institutions in each city that employed the most people, as well as an additional 20 managers or personnel officers of the next 100 institutions. As such, they represented the most economically progressive institutions in America. And in their employment policies we could see how some of America's dominant corporate institutions impinge on the everyday lives of urban Negroes.

Businessmen are in business to make a profit. Seldom do they run their enterprises for social objectives. But since it is fashionable these days, most of the managers and personnel officers we interviewed (86 percent, in fact) accepted the proposition that they "have a social responsibility to make strong efforts to provide employment for Negroes and other minority groups." This assertion, however, is contradicted by unemployment in the Negro community today, as well as by the hiring policies of the firms themselves.

Businessmen, as a whole do not exhibit openly racist attitudes. Their position might best be described as one of "optimistic denial"—the gentlemanly white racism evident in a tacit, but often unwitting, acceptance of institutional practices that subordinate or exclude Negroes. One aspect of this optimistic denial is a nonrecognition of the seriousness of the problems that face black people. Only 21 percent of our sample thought that unemployment was a very serious problem in the nations' cities, yet 26 percent considered air pollution very serious and 31 percent considered traffic very serious. The employers' perspective is based upon their limited experience with blacks, and the experience does not give them a realistic picture of the plight of Negroes in this country. Employers don't even think that racial discrimination has much to do with the Negroes' plight; a majority (57 percent) felt that Negroes are treated at least as well as other people of the same income, and an additional 6 percent felt that Negroes are treated *better* than any other part of the population.

This optimistic denial on the part of employers ("things really aren't that bad for Negroes") is often combined with a negative image of Negroes as employees. Half of those employers interviewed (51 percent) said that Negroes are likely to have higher rates of absenteeism than whites, so that hiring many of them would probably upset production schedules. Almost a third thought that, because Negro crime rates are generally higher than white crime rates, hiring many Negroes could lead to increased theft and vandalism in their companies. About a fifth (22 percent) thought that hiring Negroes might bring "agitators and troublemakers" into their companies, and another one-fifth feared that production costs might rise because Negroes supposedly do not take orders well.

The employer's views may reflect not only traditional white prejudices, but also some occasional experience he himself has had with Negroes. Such experiences, however, may stem as much from the employer's own practices and misconceptions as from imputed cultural habits of Negroes. As Elliott Liebow observed in his study of Negro street-corner men *(Talley's Corner)*, blacks have learned to cope with life by treating menial, low-status, degrading jobs in the same way that the jobs treat them—with benign nonconcern.

Most of the employers believe that Negroes lack the preparation for anything but menial jobs. A full 83 percent said that few Negroes are qualified for professional jobs, and 69 percent thought that few are qualified for skilled positions. When it comes to unskilled jobs, of course, only 23 percent of the employers held this view. The employers seem to share a widespread assumption —one frequently used as a cover for racism—that for historical and environmental reasons Negroes have been disabled to such an extent as to make them uncompetitive in a highly competitive society. And while it is certainly true that black people have suffered from a lack of educational and other opportunities, this line of thinking—especially among whites—has a tendency to blame the past and the ghetto environment for what is perceived as Negro incompetence, thus diverting attention from *present* institutional practices. So, many employers have developed a rhetoric of concern about upgrading the so-called "hardcore unemployed" in lieu of changing their employment policies.

To a considerable extent our respondents' assessment of Negro job qualifications reflects company policy, for the criteria used in hiring skilled and professional workers tend to exclude Negroes. The criteria are (1) previous experience and (2) recommendations. It is evident that because Negroes are unlikely to have *had* previous experience in positions from which they have long been excluded, and because they are unlikely to have had much contact with people in the best position to recommend them, the criteria for "qualification" make it probable that employers will consider most Negroes unqualified.

NEGROES GET THE WORST JOBS

In short, the employers' aversion to taking risks (at least with people), reinforced by the pressure of labor unions and more general discriminatory patterns in society, means that Negroes usually get the worst jobs.

Thus, although Negroes make up 20 percent of the unskilled workers in these large corporations, they fill only a median of one percent of the professional positions and only 2 percent of the skilled positions. Moreover, the few Negroes in the higher positions are unevenly distributed among the corporations. Thirty-two percent of the companies don't report Negroes in professional positions, and 24 percent do not report any in skilled positions. If these companies are set aside, in the remaining companies the median percentage of Negroes in the two positions rises to 3 percent and 6 percent respectively. Further, in these remaining companies an even larger percentage (8 percent in both cases) of *current* positions are being filled by Negroes—which indicates, among other things, that a breakthrough has been accomplished in some companies, while in others Negro employment in the upper levels remains minimal or nonexistent.

Even among those companies that hire blacks for skilled jobs, a Negro applicant's chances of getting the job are only one-fourth as good as those of his white counterpart. For professional positions, the chances are more nearly equal: Negro applicants are about three-fourths as likely to get these jobs as are white applicants. It seems that Negroes have come closest to breaking in at the top (though across all firms only about 4 percent of the applicants for professional positions are Negro). The real stumbling-block to equal employment opportunities seems to be at the skilled level, and here it may be that union policies—and especially those of the craft unions—augment the employers' resistance to hiring Negroes for and promoting Negroes to skilled positions.

What do urban Negroes themselves think of employers' hiring practices? A survey of the same 15 cities by Angus Campbell and Howard Schuman, for the riot commission, indicates that one-third (34 percent) of the Negro men interviewed reported having been refused jobs because of racial discrimination, and 72 percent believed that some or many other black applicants are turned down for the same reason. Almost as many (68 percent) think that some or many black people miss out on promotions because of prejudice. And even when companies do hire Negroes (presumably in professional positions), this is interpreted as tokenism: 77 percent of the black respondents thought that Negroes are hired by big companies for show purposes.

The companies we studied, which have little contact with the ghetto, are very different fron the other institutions in our survey, whose contact with the ghetto is direct and immediate. The corporations are also up-to-date, well-financed, and innovative, while the white institutions inside the ghetto are outdated, underfinanced, and overloaded. In historical terms, the institutions in the ghetto represent another era of thought and organization.

GHETTO MERCHANTS

The slum merchants illustrate the tendency of ghetto institutions to hark back to earlier forms. While large corporations cooperate with one another and with the government to exert substantial control over their market, the ghetto merchant still functions in the realm of traditional laissez-faire. He is likely to be a small operator, economically marginal and with almost no ability to control his market. His main advantage over the more efficient, modern retailer is his restricted competition, for the ghetto provides a captive market. The difficulty that many blacks have in getting transportation out of the ghetto, combined with a lack of experience in comparative shopping, seems to give the local merchant a competitive aid he sorely needs to survive against the lower prices and better goods sold in other areas of the city.

The merchants in our study also illustrate the free-enterprise character of ghetto merchandising. They run very small operations—grocery stores, restaurants, clothing and liquor stores, and so on, averaging a little over three employees per business. Almost half of them (45 percent) find it difficult to "keep up with their competition" (competition mainly *within* the ghetto). Since there are almost no requirements for becoming a merchant, this group is the most heterogeneous of all those studied. They have the widest age range (from 17 through 80), the highest percentage of immigrants (15 percent), and the lowest educational levels (only 16 percent finished college).

Again in contrast to the large corporations, the ghetto merchant must live with the harsh day-to-day realities of violence and poverty. His attitudes toward Negroes, different in degree from those of the employers, are at least partly a function of his objective evaluations of his customers.

Running a business in a ghetto means facing special kinds of "overhead." Theft is an especially worrisome problem for the merchants; respondents mentioned it more frequently than any other problem. There is, of course, some basis in fact for their concern. According to the riot commission, inventory losses—ordinarily under 2 percent of sales—may be twice as great in high-crime areas (most of which are in ghettos). And for these small businesses such losses may cut substantially into a slender margin of profit.

Thus it is not surprising that, of all the occupational groups interviewed in this study, the retail merchants were among the most likely to consider Negroes violent and criminal. For example, 61 percent said that Negroes are more likely to steal than whites, and 50 percent believed that Negroes are more likely to pass bad checks. No wonder, then, that black customers may encounter unusual surveillance and suspicion when they shop.

Less understandable is the ghetto merchant's apparent ignorance of the plight of ghetto blacks. Thus, 75 percent believe that blacks get medical treatment that is equal to or better than what whites get. A majority think that Negroes are not discriminated against with regard to treatment by the police, recreation facilities and so forth. Logically enough, 51 percent of the merchants feel that Negroes are making too many demands. This percentage is the second-highest measured (the police were the least sympathetic). So the merchants (like all other groups in the survey except the black politicians) are inclined to emphasize perceived defects in the black community as a major problem in their dealings with Negroes.

The shaky economic position of the merchants, their suspicion of their Negro customers, and the high "overhead" of doing business in the ghetto (because of theft, vandalism, bad credit risks) lead many merchants to sell inferior merchandise at higher prices—and to resort to other stategems for getting money out of their customers. To elicit responses from the merchants on such delicate matters, we drew up a series of very indirect questions. The responses we obtained, though they no doubt understate the extent to which ghetto merchants provide a poor dollar value per unit of goods, are nevertheless revealing. For example, we asked the merchants to recommend various ways of "keeping up with business competition." Some 44 percent said that you should offer extra services; over a third (36 percent) said you should raise prices to cover unusually high overhead; and the same number (36 percent) said that you should buy "bargain" goods at lower prices, then sell them at regular prices. (To a small merchant, "bargain goods" ordinarily means "seconds," or slightly spoiled merchandise, because he doesn't do enough volume to gain real discounts from a wholesaler.) A smaller but still significant segment (12 percent) said that one should "bargain the selling price with each customer and take whatever breaks you can get."

The Campbell-Schuman study indicates that 56 percent of the Negroes interviewed felt that they had been overcharged in neighborhood stores (24 percent said often); 42 percent felt that they had been sold spoiled or inferior goods (13 percent said often). Given the number of ghetto stores a customer may visit every week, these data are entirely compatible with ours. Since one-third of the merchants indicated that they were not averse to buying "bargain" goods for sale in their stores, it is understandable that 42 percent of the Negroes in these areas should say that at one time or another they have been sold inferior merchandise.

It is also understandable that during the recent civil disorders many Negroes, unable to affect merchants by routine methods, struck directly at the stores, looting and burning them.

TEACHERS IN THE GHETTO

Just as ghetto merchants are in a backwater of the economy, ghetto schools are in a backwater of the educational system, experimental efforts in some cities notwithstanding.

Negroes, of course, are most likely to be served by outmoded and inadequate schools, a fact that the Coleman Report has documented in considerable detail. In metropolitan regions of the Northeast, for example, 40 percent of the Negro pupils at the secondary level attended schools in buildings over 40 years old, but only 15 percent of the whites did; the average number of pupils per room was 35 for Negroes but 28 for whites.

The teachers covered in our survey (half of whom were Negro) taught in ghetto schools at all levels. Surprisingly, 88 percent said that they were satisfied with their jobs. Their rate of leaving, however, was not consistent with this. Half of the teachers had been in their present schools for no more than four years. Breaking the figures down year by year, we find that the largest percentage (17 percent) had been there only one year. In addition, the teachers' rate of leaving increased dramatically after they had taught for five years.

While the teachers thought that education was a major problem for the cities and especially for the ghettos, they did not think that ghetto schools were a source of the difficulty. A solid majority, comparing their own schools with others in the city, thought that theirs were average, above average, or superior in seven out of eight categories. The high quality of the teaching staff, so rated by 84 percent of the respondents, was rivaled only by the high quality of the textbooks (again 84 percent). The one doubtful area, according to the teachers, was the physical plant, which seemed to them to be just barely competitive; in this respect, 44 percent considered their own schools below average or inferior.

The teachers have less confidence in their students than in themselves or their schools. On the one hand, they strongly reject the view that in ghetto schools education is sacrificed to the sheer need for order: 85 percent said it was not true that pupils in their schools were uneducable, and that teachers could do little more than maintain discipline. On the other hand, the teachers as a group could not agree that their students were as educable as they might be. There was little consensus on whether their pupils were "about average" in interest and ability: 28 percent thought that their pupils were; 41 percent thought it was partially true that they were; and 31 percent thought it was not true. But the teachers had less difficulty agreeing that their students were *not* "above average in ability and . . . generally co-operative with teachers." Agreeing on this were 59 percent of the teachers, with another 33 percent in the middle.

The real problem with education in the ghetto, as the teachers see it, is the ghetto itself. The teachers have their own version of the "Negro disability" thesis: the "cultural deprivation" theory holds that the reason for bad education in the ghetto is the student's environment rather than the schools. (See "How Teachers Learn to Help Children Fail," by Estelle Fuchs, September, 1968.) Asked to name the major problems facing their schools, the teachers most frequently mentioned community apathy; the second most-mentioned problem, a derivation of the first, was an alleged lack of preparation and motivation in the students. Fifty-nine percent of the teachers agreed to some extent that "many communities provide such a terrible environment for the pupils that education doesn't do much good in the end."

Such views are no doubt detrimental to education in the ghetto, for they imply a decided fatalism as far as teaching is concerned. If the students are deficient—improperly motivated, distracted, and so on—and if the cause of this deficiency lies in the ghetto rather than in the schools themselves, then there is little reason for a teacher to exert herself to set high standards for her students.

There is considerable question, however, whether the students in ghetto schools are as distracted as the teachers think. Events in the last few years indicate that the schools, especially the high schools and the junior high schools, are one of the strongest focuses of the current black rebellion. The student strike at Detroit's Northern High School in 1966, for example, was cohesive and well-organized. A boycott by some 2,300 students, directed against a repressive school administration, lasted over two weeks and resulted in the dismissal of the principal and the formation of a committee, including students, to investigate school conditions. The ferment in the ghetto schools across the country is also leading to the formation of permanent and independent black students' groups, such as the Modern Strivers in Washington, D.C.'s Eastern High, intent on promoting black solidarity and bringing about changes in the educational system. In light of such developments, there is reason to think that the teachers in the survey have overestimated the corrosive effects of the ghetto environment on students—and underestimated the schools' responsibility for the state of education in the ghetto.

SOCIAL WORKERS AND THE WELFARE ESTABLISHMENT

Public welfare is another area in which old ideas have been perpetuated beyond their time. The roots of the present welfare-department structure lie in the New Deal legislation of the 1930s. The public assistance provisions of the Social Security Act were designed to give aid to the helpless and the non-competitive: the aged, the blind, the "permanently and totally" disabled, and dependent children. The assumption was that the recipient, because of personal disabilities or inadequacies, could not make his way in life without outside help.

The New Deal also provided work (e.g., the W.P.A.) for the able-bodied who were assumed to be unemployed only temporarily. But as the Depression gave way to the war years and to the return of prosperity, the massive work programs for the able-bodied poor were discontinued, leaving only those programs that were premised on the notion of personal disability. To a considerable extent today's Negro poor have had to rely on the latter. Chief among these programs, of course, is Aid for Dependent Children, which has become a mainstay of welfare. And because of racial discrimination, especially in education and employment, a large part of the Negro population also experiences poverty as a permanent state.

While most of the social workers in our survey showed considerable sympathy with the Negro cause, they too felt that the root of the problem lay in weaknesses in the Negro community; and they saw their primary task as making up the supposed deficiency. A hefty majority of the respondents (78 percent) thought that a large part of their responsibility was to "teach the poor how to live"—rather than to provide the means for them to live as they like. Assuming disability, welfare has fostered dependency.

The social workers, however, are unique among the groups surveyed in that they are quite critical of their own institution. The average welfare worker is not entirely at one with the establishment for which she works. She is likely to be a college graduate who regards her job as transitional. And her lack of expertise has its advantages as well as its disadvantages, for it means that she can take a more straightforward view of the situations she is confronted with. She is not committed to bureaucracy as a way of life.

The disparity between the welfare establishment and the average welfare worker is evident in the latter's complaints about her job. The complaints she voices the most deal *not* with her clients, but with the welfare department itself and the problems of working within its present structure—the difficulty of getting things done, the red tape, the lack of adequate funds, and so on. Of the five most-mentioned difficulties of welfare work, three dealt with such intra-agency problems; the other two dealt with the living conditions of the poor.

There is a good deal of evidence to support the social worker's complaints. She complains, for example, that welfare agencies are understaffed. The survey indicates that an average caseload is 177 people, each client being visited about once a month for about 50 minutes. Even the most conscientious of caseworkers must be overwhelmed by such client-to-worker ratios.

As in the case of the schools, welfare has engendered a countervailing force among the very people it is supposed to serve. Welfare clients have become increasingly hostile to the traditional structure and philosophy of welfare departments and have formed themselves into an outspoken movement. The welfare-rights movement at this stage has aims: to obtain a more nearly adequate living base for the clients, and to overload the system with demands, thus either forcing significant changes or clearing the way for new and more appropriate institutions.

BLACK POLITICAL PARTY WORKERS

Usually when segments of major social institutions become incapable of functioning adequately, the people whom the institutions are supposed to serve have recourse to politics. In the ghetto, however, the political machinery is no better off than the other institutions. Around the turn of the century Negroes began to carve out small niches for themselves in the politics of such cities as Chicago and New York. Had Negro political organizations developed along the same lines as those of white ethnic groups, they might today provide valuable leverage for the ghetto population. But this has not happened. For one thing, the decline of the big-city machine, and its replacement in many cities by "non-political" reform governments supported by a growing middle class, began to close off a route traditionally open to minority groups. Second, black politicians have never been regarded as fullfledged political brokers by racist whites, and consequently the possibility of a Negro's becoming a powerful politician in a predominantly white city has been foreclosed (the recent election of Carl Stokes as Mayor of Cleveland and Richard D. Hatcher, Mayor of Gary, Indiana, would be exceptions). Whites have tended to put aside their differences when confronting Negro political efforts; to regard Negro demands, no matter how routine, as racial issues; and hence to severely limit the concessions made to black people.

Today the sphere of Negro politics is cramped and closely circumscribed. As Kenneth B. Clark has observed, most of the Negroes who have reached high public office have done so *not* within the context of Negro politics, but through competition in the larger society. In most cities Negro political organizations are outmoded and inadequate. Even if, as seems probable, more and more Negro mayors are elected, they will have to work within the antiquated structure of urban government, with sharply limited resources. Unless things change, the first Negro mayor of Newark, for example, will preside over a bankrupt city.

Our survey of Negro political workers in the 15 cities documents the inadequacy of Negro politics—and the inadequacy of the larger system of urban politics. The political workers, understandably, strongly sympathize with the aspirations of other black people. As ghetto politicians, they deal with the demands and frustrations of other blacks day after day. Of all the groups surveyed, they were the most closely in touch with life in the ghetto. Most of them work in the middle and lower levels of municipal politics; they talk with about 75 voters each week. These political workers are, of course, acutely aware of the precipitous rise in the demands made by the black community. Most (93 percent) agreed that in the last few years people in their districts have become more determined to get what they want. The strongest impetus of this new determination comes from the younger blacks: 92 percent of the political workers agreed that "young people have become more militant." Only a slight majority, however (56 percent), said the same of middle-aged people.

Against the pressure of rising Negro demands, urban political organizations formed in other times and on other assumptions, attentive to other interests, and constrained by severely limited resources, find themselves unable to respond satisfactorily. A majority of the political workers, in evaluating a variety of services available to people in their districts, thought that all except two— telephone service and the fire department—were either poor or fair. Worst of the lot, according to the political workers, were recreation, police protection, and building inspection.

In view of these respondents, the black community has no illusions about the ability of routine politics to meet its needs. While only 38 percent of the political workers thought that the people in their districts regarded their councilmen as friends fighting for them, 51 percent said that the people considered their councilmen "part of the city government which must be asked continually and repeatedly in order to get things done." (Since the political workers were probably talking about their fellow party members, their responses may have been more favorable than frank. A relatively high percentage of "don't know" responses supports this point).

Almost all the Negro politicians said that they received various requests from the voters for help. Asked whether they could respond to these requests "almost always, usually, or just sometimes," the largest percentage (36 percent) chose "sometimes"—which, in context, is a way of saying "seldom." Another 31 percent said they "usually" could respond to such requests, and 19 percent said "almost always." Logically enough, 60 percent of the political workers agreed that in the last few years "people have become more fed up with the system, and are becoming unwilling to work with politicians." In effect, this is an admission that they as political workers, and the system of urban politics to which they devote themselves, are failing.

When economic and social institutions fail to provide the life-chances that a substantial part of a population wants, and when political institutions fail to provide a remedy, the aspirations of the people begin to spill over into forms of activity that the dominant society regards either as unacceptable or illegitimate —crime, vandalism, noncooperation, and various forms of political protest.

Robert M. Fogelson and Robert D. Hill, in the *Supplemental Studies* for the riot commission, have reported that 50 percent to 90 percent of the Negro males in ten cities studied had arrest records. Clearly, when the majority of men in a given population are defined as criminals—at least by the police—something more than "deviant" behaviour is involved. In effect, ghetto residents—and especially the youth—and the police are in a state of subdued warfare. On the one hand, the cities are experiencing a massive and as yet inchoate social rising of the Negro population. On the other hand, the police—devoted to the racial status quo and inclined to overlook the niceties of mere law in their quest for law and order—have found a variety of means, both conventional and otherwise, for countering the aims of Negroes. In doing so, they are not only adhering to the norms of their institution, but also furthering their personal goals as well. The average policeman, recruited from a lower- or middle-class white background, frequently of "ethnic" origins, comes from a group whose social position is marginal and who feel most threatened by Negro advances.

The high arrest rate in the Negro community thus mirrors both the push of Negroes and the determined resistance of the police. As the conflict intensifies, the police are more and more losing authority in the eyes of black people; the young Negroes are especially defiant. Any type of contact between police and black people can quickly lead to a situation in which the policeman gives an order and the Negro either defies it or fails to show sufficient respect in obeying it. This in turn can lead to the Negro's arrest on a disorderly conduct charge or on a variety of other charges. (Disorderly conduct accounted for about 17 percent of the arrests in the Fogelson-Hill study.)

POLICE HARASSMENT TECHNIQUES

The police often resort to harassment as a means of keeping the Negro community off-balance. The riot commission noted that:

> *Because youths commit a large and increasing proportion of crime, police are under growing pressure from their superiors—and from the community—to deal with them forcefully. "Harassment of youths" may therefore be viewed by some police departments—and members even of the Negro community—as a proper crime prevention technique.*

The Commission added that "many departments have adopted patrol practices which, in the words of one commentator, have 'replaced harassment by individual patrolmen with harassment by entire departments.' "

Among the most common of the cops' harassment techniques are breaking up street-corner groups and stop-and-frisk tactics. Our study found that 63 percent of the ghetto police reported that they "frequently" were called upon to disperse loitering groups. About a third say they "frequently" stop and frisk people. Obviously then, the law enforcer sometimes interferes with individuals and groups who consider their activities quite legitimate and necessary. Black people in the ghetto—in the absence of adequate parks, playgrounds, jobs, and recreation facilities, and unwilling to sit in sweltering and overcrowded houses with rats and bugs—are likely to make the streets their front yards. But this territory is often made uninhabitable by the police.

Nearly a third of the white policemen in our study thought that most of the residents of their precinct (largely Negro) were not industrious. Even more striking about the attitudes of the white police working in these neighborhoods is that many of them deny the fact of Negro inequality: 20 percent say the Negro is treated better than any other part of the population, and 14 percent say he is treated equally. As for their own treatment of Negroes, the Campbell-Schuman survey reported that 43 percent of the black men, who are on the streets more than the women, thought that police use insulting language in their neighborhoods. Only 17 percent of the white males held this belief. Of the Negro men, 20 percent reported that the police insulted them personally and 28 percent said they knew someone to whom this had happened; only 9 percent and 12 percent, respectively, of the whites reported the same. Similarly, many more blacks than whites thought that the police frisked and searched people without good reason (42 percent compared to 12 percent); and that the police roughed up people unnecessarily (37 percent as compared to 10 percent). Such reports of police misconduct were most frequent among the younger Negroes, who, after all, are on the receiving end most often.

The policeman's isolation in the ghetto is evident in a number of findings. We asked the police how many people—of various types—they knew well enough in the ghetto to greet when they saw them. Eighty-nine percent of the police said they knew six or more shopowners, managers, and clerks well enough to speak with, but only 38 percent said they knew this many teenagers or youth leaders. At the same time, 39 percent said that most young adults, and 51 percent said that most adolescents, regard the police as enemies. And only 16 percent of the white policemen (37 percent of the blacks) either "often" or "sometimes" attended meetings in the neighborhood.

The police have wound up face to face with the social consequences of the problems in the ghetto created by the failure of other white institutions—though, as has been observed, they themselves have contributed to those problems in no small degree. The distant and gentlemanly white racism of employers, the discrimination of white parents who object to having their children go to school with Negroes, the disgruntlement of white taxpayers who deride the present welfare system as a sinkhole of public funds but are unwilling to see it replaced by anything more effective—the consequences of these and other forms of white racism have confronted the police with a massive control problem of the kind most evident in the riots.

In our survey, we found that the police were inclined to see the riots as the long range result of faults in the Negro community—disrespect for law, crime, broken families, etc.—rather than as responses to the stance of the white community. Indeed, nearly one-third of the white police saw the riots as the result of what they considered the basic violence and disrespect of Negroes in general, while only one-fourth attributed the riots to the failure of white institutions. More than three-fourths also regarded the riots as the immediate result of agitators and criminals—a suggestion contradicted by all the evidence accumulated by the riot commission. The police, then, share with the other groups—excepting the black politicians—a tendency to emphasize perceived defects in the black community as an explanation for the difficulties that they encounter in the ghetto.

The state of seige evident in many police departments is but an exaggerated version of a trend in the larger white society. It is the understandable, but unfortunate, response of people who are angry and confused about the widespread disruption of traditional racial patterns and who feel threatened by these changes. There is, of course, some basis for this feeling, because the Negro movement poses challenges of power and interest to many groups. To the extent that the movement is successful, the merchants, for example, will either have to reform their practices or go out of business—and for many it may be too late for reform. White suburbanites will have to cough up funds for the city, which provides most of them with employment. Police departments will have to be thoroughly restructured.

The broad social rising of Negroes is beginning to have a substantial effect upon all white institutions in the ghetto, as the situation of the merchants, the schools, and the welfare establishment illustrates. Ten years ago, these institutions (and the police, who have been affected differently) could operate pretty much unchecked by any countervailing power in the ghetto. Today, both their excesses and their inadequacies have run up against an increasingly militant black population, many of whom support violence as a means of redress. The evidence suggests that unless these institutions are transformed, the black community will make it increasingly difficult for them to function at all.

Further Reading Suggested by The Authors

Report of the National Advisory Commission on Civil Disorders (New York: Bantam Books, 1968).

Supplemental Studies for the National Advisory Commission on Civil Disorders by Robert M. Fogelson and Robert D. Hill (Washington: U.S. Government Printing Office, 1968).
Sociological studies of racial attitudes in 15 large cities, of white institutions in the ghettos of those cities, and of the characteristics of arrestees in major riots.

Dark Ghetto: Dilemmas of Social Power by Kenneth B. Clark (New York: Harper Torchbooks, 1965). One of the best studies of the ghetto and its relation to white society.

STATEMENT OF RALPH ELLISON, AUTHOR

Senator Ribicoff. Mr. Ellison, where do you live now?

Mr. Ellison. I live in New York City, Riverside Drive, at 150th Street. It isn't properly Harlem, but Harlem has a way of expanding. It goes where Negroes go, or where we go in certain numbers. So some of us think of it as Harlem, but it is really Washington Heights.

Senator Ribicoff. Where were you born?

Mr. Ellison. Oklahoma City.

Senator Ribicoff. And were you brought up in Oklahoma City?

Mr. Ellison. Yes; until I went off to college, and I went to Tuskegee, where for 3 years I worked toward a degree in music. I wanted to be a composer, but then I ran out of money, and I went to New York, and I didn't get the money to go back, so technically I am a dropout.

Senator Ribicoff. How old were you when you came to New York?

Mr. Ellison. Twenty-two.

Senator Ribicoff. And you lived in New York continuously ever since?

Mr. Ellison. Well, except for 7 months in 1937, when I lost my mother, and lived for those 7 months in Dayton, Ohio, and then I was away again for 2 years when I won the Rome Prize and lived at the American Academy in Rome —but, since then I have lived continuously in New York.

Senator Ribicoff. What was life like for you as a boy growing up in Oklahoma City?

Mr. Ellison. Well, it was the life of the average poor family. I lost my father when I was 3. My mother had two boys, and she raised us. Later on, by the time I was in high school, there was a stepfather.

We lived in what are known as three-room shotgun houses most of that time. We ate poor food, which, generally, was well prepared, sometimes not, because my brother and I we were taught to take care of ourselves when our mother went out and worked.

On the other hand, there was a relationship with the church. There was a sense of community. I was encouraged in music. My mother had some sense of the values of excellence, and she often said that she didn't care what I became as long as I tried to become one of the best. It was that kind of life.

EXTENT OF PREJUDICE IN OKLAHOMA

Senator Ribicoff. As a boy growing up in Oklahoma City, were you sensitive to, or did you encounter prejudice because of the color of your skin?

Statement of Ralph Ellison, Author. Federal Role in Urban Affairs, Hearings Before the U.S. Senate, Subcommittee on Executive Reorganization, Committee on Government Operations, August 30, 1966.

Mr. Ellison. Yes, very definitely, although racial prejudice was somewhat more muted than I experienced in the Deep South. But Oklahoma was the 46th State and had no history of slavery. It was also populated by people from all over the country, and there was a certain liberal feeling for Negroes. But you knew, nevertheless, that people despised you because of your skin, and we did have southern law.

So that I grew up in a segregated society. I never attended an unsegregated school. But although we resented segregation but we did not feel inferior because of it. We felt that it was unjust, and that we were being denied an opportunity to compete fairly with our peers. That was our basic attitude.

Senator Ribicoff. Now when you came to New York—what year again was it when you came to New York?

Mr. Ellison. In 1936.

Senator Ribicoff. 1936. Was New York a surprise to you after Oklahoma and Tuskegee?

NEGRO VIEW OF NEW YORK CITY

Mr. Ellison. It was not a complete surprise. New York was one of the great cities prominent in the Negro American myth of freedom, a myth which goes back very far into Negro and American experience. In our spirituals it was the north star and places in the North which symbolized freedom, and to that extent I expected certain things from New York. I did not, incidentally, come to New York to live especially in Harlem, although Harlem was a glamorous place, a place where wonderful music existed and where there was a great tradition of Negro American style, Negro American elegance, and so on.

But once here, what I had to do, what I had to learn was how to live in New York to discipline myself in order to discover just where I was free and was not free. In the South there were signs which told me where I could go and where I could not go. In New York there were no such signs, so I told myself, "Well, you must go out and discover its freedom for yourself, and the best way of doing it is not to dodge before someone throws a punch at you." As a consequence, I found myself going to, and being accepted in, places which might otherwise have sensed that I was intimidated and turned me away.

ELLISON'S EARLY LIFE IN NEW YORK

Senator Ribicoff. But, when you came to New York, what type of job did you get? What did you do? Were you writing then?

Mr. Ellison. At that time I still thought of myself as a musician, but I couldn't get work as a musician. I didn't have enough money to join the union. My first job was working as a counterman at the Harlem YMCA, a temporary job. But I was kept working there for a good part of a year because I was pretty good at it. I had been a waiter in Oklahoma.

The next job was very interesting. I worked briefly as a substitute receptionist and file clerk for Dr. Harry Stack Sullivan, the psychiatrist and psychoanalyst. This was a job of short duration, but one of the most interesting that I ever had.

After that, oh, I worked in factories and I sometimes had no work and slept in St. Nicholas Park below City College. I lived as I could live. Sometimes—on one occasion I slept for weeks on the daybed in a Jewish friend's livingroom. But at that point in my life, I did not view this simply as a matter of discrimination or even as hardship. It was a matter of youthful adventure and discovery and testing and a recognition that everyone was having a hard time.

CHANGES IN RACE RELATIONS IN NEW YORK CITY IN PAST 30 YEARS

Senator Ribicoff. You came to New York in 1936. Now it is 1966. In your own observations have you noticed any basic change, let us say, in the Negro community, or the relationship of the white community with the Negroes in New York between the period of 1936 and 1966—a 30 year span?

Mr. Ellison. Yes; a number of things have happened. During the WPA days, the days of relief, when everyone was undergoing the economic crisis of the Nation, there seemed to have been a closer relationship between Negroes and whites and between Harlem and the rest of the community.

In those days, for instance, the Savoy Ballroom, one of our great cultural institutions, which in the effort to build much needed public housing was destroyed, was thriving and people were coming to Harlem from all over the world. The great European and American composers were coming there to listen to jazz—Stravinsky, Poulenc. The great jazz bands were coming there. Great dancers were being created there. People from downtown were always there, because the Savoy was one of the great centers of culture in the United States, even though it was then thought of as simply a place of entertainment.

The Federal Theater was presenting excellent plays in Harlem. Some of Orson Wells' best efforts which led to his fame were produced there. What I am also trying to say is that more white people were coming into Harlem, and that there was less emphasis upon the myth of the danger to be encountered in Harlem.

It was not until the war, as I recall, that whites started staying away, and often this was done through the police department. White visitors were stopped at 110th Street and told that they shouldn't go to Harlem.

Senator Ribicoff. Do you have any idea why that was?

Mr. Ellison. I don't really understand why it was. This was before the riots of 1943. There is, of course, a traditional antagonism between the New York Police Department and Negroes.

Senator Ribicoff. This is something that was continuous?

Mr. Ellison. It was continuous enough to discourage people.

Senator Ribicoff. When you first came to New York, Harlem, was it as crowded, as teeming with people then as it is now?

Mr. Ellison. No; it wasn't as crowded. The population has since then steadily increased. But there was, Senator, I think, more optimism. When everyone in the United States is having a bad time, Negroes don't feel so bad about their own condition. On the other hand, when everyone else is enjoying prosperity, and they can't see it reflected in their own background, in their own lives, then they become highly uncomfortable about it.

DIFFERENCE IN NEGRO SITUATION IN SOUTH AND NORTH

I would like to suggest here that there is a basic difference in what has happened in the South, to the southern Negro, and what has happened to people living in such slums as Harlem.

Senator Ribicoff. I would appreciate it if you would go into this, from your own perspective—the difference of the situation of the Negro in the South and the Negro in the slums in big cities.

Mr. Ellison. Well, at Tuskegee, for instance, in Macon County, Ala., where I attended school, I knew exactly where I could go and where I could not go. The contempt which was held for me by whites was obvious in the most casual interracial contacts. I got to know Alabama and north Georgia fairly well, because I was playing trumpet in a jazz orchestra. We played in the various country clubs, and for dances for both whites and Negroes and we got to know the country people, the white people most antagonistic to my race, and there was a certain sense of security about knowing their ways. I learned that they were very interested—some of them—in provoking me to violence so that they could destroy me. And my struggle was to keep from being provoked, to keep my eye on my own goals. I was not there to hold a contest of violence with those white people. I was there to get an education and go on to the North and become a composer of symphonies.

DISCIPLINE IN LIVES OF SOUTHERN NEGROES

Now, I think that my experience, the discipline which I acquired, sums up a certain aspect of southern Negro character. We have been disciplined for over 300 years not to be provoked. We have been disciplined for over 300 years to define the nature of reality of society and the nature of the human predicament for ourselves. We have been disciplined to accept our own sense of life, regardless of what those antagonistic to us thought about us.

Now, this makes for the most complex personalities among those so disciplined, and it makes for a certain split, a certain ambivalence, within the Negro American's conception of the United States. But of one thing I am certain. We were hopeful. We made the sacrifices necessary for survival. We tried to educate our children—as we still do—and we lived as we could live and had to live, because we had great hopes in the future and great confidence in the promises of American democracy.

We Negroes have long memories. We know what went on before 1865 and after 1876. And if you think about it, there is hardly a Negro of my generation who can't touch a grandparent or two and be right back in slavery—it has been that recent. So, we have within our very lives and our memories a sense of the reality of slavery and what had been promised by emancipation. So that by 1957, when the civil rights bills began to be passed, when the law of the land began to change, we were able to transform our old discipline, our fortitude before physical provocation and casual brutilization, into an agency to help ourselves achieve the freedom which was now guaranteed by the law. To walk through hostile groups of people now became a political instrumentality, and it has worked. And even little children, little Negro children, have been disciplined to confront the new possibilities unflinchingly. And this courage is not something found overnight, but is part of a heritage of over 300 years.

In the North, southern tradition breaks down. You get to Harlem. You have expected a great deal of freedom that does not exist. Or when it does exist, you haven't been taught how to achieve it. Too often, you don't have the education or experience necessary to go into many of the jobs and places which attract you and which others take for granted, and you find yourself frustrated. Thus, when the civil rights laws began to be passed, they did not have the same impact within the northern slums because we already had certain of the rights which were symbols at least of what southern Negroes had not had.

Senator Ribicoff. In other words, basically, the civil rights laws that were passed on the Federal level were not broader than the laws that already pertained in the State of New York.

Mr. Ellison. That is true.

NEGROES' VIEWS OF CIVIL RIGHTS LAWS

Senator Ribicoff. So in a State like Senator Javits' and my own State of Connecticut, the laws we had passed on a State level went beyond the guarantees of the national laws.

What then was the impact of first, the Supreme Court decision, and later the passage of the civil rights laws on a national basis? How did the northern Negro or the Negro in Harlem regard these laws?

Mr. Ellison. Well, I will speak for one of them, myself. I regarded these laws with great relief, with a certain amount of enthusiasm, because I feel that there is bottled up in southern Negroes a great deal of strength: intellectual, physical, technical, and moral. I think that these new laws constitute one of the most important political moves affecting Negroes which has occurred since the squashing of Reconstruction, a political disaster which the new laws are attempting to correct.

I should point this out, however, that my way of thinking, there is on the political level but one American Negro experience, and it is nationwide. It is a national experience, and thus most of us, North and South, were quite overjoyed by the passage of these new laws. We were also inspired to have our beliefs in democracy reaffirmed, our sense of who we were, and what our parents and relatives were as revealed in the boycotts and marches.

The notion that Negroes suddenly became courageous with the passage of these laws amused some of us, because we knew what had always been there. We also knew that our survival had depended in part upon obeying the laws which were overturned. After all, we are a minority, and not always a nonviolent minority—and this is not through lack of physical courage. Rather, we are non-violent through wisdom.

WHAT HAPPENS TO NEGRO
WHEN HE COMES TO NORTH FROM SOUTH?

Senator Ribicoff. And yet there has been a constant exodus by Negroes from the South to the North. In the last decade a million Negroes have moved from the South to the North.

Now as we mechanize and industralize agriculture, there will be a continuation of this steady exodus. And it isn't only Negroes. The poor rural whites are moving to the cities too. What happens now to the Negro from the South when he comes to the North? What Negro folkways, what habits of the South survive in the North? Or is the Negro, when he moves from the South to the North, under some sort of trauma because of the difference between his rural life and sudden new life of a northern slum?

Mr. Ellison. Well, I have no figures on this, Senator, but I think that the shock is apt to be sustained by the second generation of southern Negroes. At least during the 1930's, 1940's and 1950's this was true. The adult who came usually found some way of bettering himself. Even though he didn't get the good job that he expected, there was a greater freedom of movement about the cities.

ATTITUDES OF NEGRO CHILDREN OF TODAY

With the children of such people, you had a different situation, because they could see what is possible within the big city. They could see the wonderful possibilities offered by the city to define one's own individuality, to amplify one's talent, to find a place for one's self.

But for many, many Negroes, this proved impossible. They came to the North with poor schooling. Very often their parents had no schooling, and thus two strikes were against them. This makes for a great deal of frustration.

Now, on the other hand, these are American children, and Americans are taught to be restless, to be mobile, to be daring. Our myths teach this, our cartoons teach us this, our athletic sports teach us this. The whole society is geared to making the individual restless, to making him test himself against the possibilities around him. He gets this from the motion pictures. He gets it from television cameras. He gets it from every avenue of life, and Negroes are as much subjected to it as anybody else.

So you see little Negro Batmen flying around Harlem just as you see little white Batmen flying around Sutton Place. It is in the blood. But while the white child who is taken with these fantasies has many opportunities for working them into real life situations, too often the Negro child is unable to do so and this leads the Negro child who identifies with the heroes and outlaws of fantasy to feel that society has designated him the outlaw, for he is treated as one. Thus his sense of being outside the law is not simply a matter of fantasy, it is a reality based on the incontrovertible fact of race. This makes for frustration and resentment. And it makes for something else, it makes for a very cynical and sometimes sharp perspective on the difference between our stated ideals and the way in which we actually live. The Negro slum child knows the difference between a dishonest policeman and an honest one because he can go around and see the numbers men paying off the police. He observes what is in the policeman's eyes when he is being ordered around.

Now that so much money has been thrown into the neighborhoods, supposedly, the papers tell us so, the slum child feels very cynically that it is being drained off somehow in graft. He doesn't know. He doesn't have the information. I don't even have it. All he knows is that this promised alleviation of his condition, isn't taking place.

Senator Ribicoff. May I say to Senator Javits and Senator Montoya I am just developing some philosophical thoughts and experiences from a sensitive and respected individual, Ralph Ellison, so if either one of you want to break in at any time with a question, please do.

Senator Javits. Senator, if I may, I would like to do that, only for this reason. I might state for the record, Mr. Chairman, that my problem has been the fact that while we have been holding these hearings, on the very things that we need to do in order to meet these conditions, hearings are going on in all executive chambers of the Senate. We are making up the poverty bill. . . . making up the civil rights bill, which is what I am called to now, and it is very difficult for a Senator, and I am so delighted that at least two of my colleagues have been able to concentrate on these hearings, though I should have as much of a vested interest in them as anybody in the Senate, as I do come from New York City and having spent my whole life there.

I would like, therefore, if you will allow me, Mr. Ellison, Senator Ribicoff has been developing your philosophy and doing extremely well, I would like to ask you just one or two rather direct and pointed questions. I think you know that I know a good deal about what you are talking, and have been there only as recently as yesterday afternoon until 4 o'clock.

The question of financing interests us very greatly. Now, I would like to answer your question. It isn't being drained off in graft, the millions that are being appropriated and that are going into these areas. It just takes so many more millions than are being appropriated to really make a measurable dent. If you relocate 10,000 families out of Harlem in a year, that is a big achievement, but it doesn't look like anything to Harlem, and the only time it begins to look like something is when you scoop a lot of young people off the street and pay them $50 a week, which is what Haryou Act and other organizations have done, and extremely important. I think they made all the difference in 1965 and some of the difference in 1966 between riots in New York and no riots. So I am not in any way apologizing. I think it is very worthwhile. But we have not yet massed the means which need to be massed, and in my judgment it is not being drained off in graft. There is inefficiency, but it is not in an intolerable sense.

Now, the thing I would like to ask you is this. As we are interested in a really massive attack, and that is what is developing in this committee, talking about very large figures in terms of $5 billion a year for New York for 10 years, and in other cities, a billion and a half a year for Detroit. The thing that troubles us is not that the money cannot be forthcoming if the credit is legitimate, and I would like to ask you this question.

What is the difference between the southern migration into New York or other places, and remember that 600,000 families have changed places in New York, 600,000 have gone to the suburbs and they have been replaced by 600,000 very heavily Puerto Rican and Negro families, what is the difference between that wave of migration and the wave of migration of my ancestors in the 1890's and the early part of the 20th century, who came into the Eastside, flooded it, had their gangsters when I was a child, and their numbers rackets and the youthful violence and many, many of the things you speak about. Certainly the dirt and the unsanitary conditions and even the inability to care for buildings that were pretty good when they got them.

Mr. Ellison. Yes.

Senator Javits. But somehow or other pulled out. Now that whole neighborhood, and I was just there yesterday, is changed into very largely Negro and Puerto Ricans and it has these terrible troubles you are talking about. Now why is that credit, why is their credit not as good as the credit of my immigrant forebears, so that one could appeal both publicly and privately, for these billions of dollars, knowing that these families would rather speedily, maybe in two decades or less, become very strong economic members of the community?

EFFECT OF FOREIGN IMMIGRATION
ON NEGROES IN LATE 19TH CENTURY

Mr. Ellison. Well, Senator, it would seem to me that the very political act which made possible the great migrations from Europe was a conscious decision to render Negroes powerless. I am speaking of the Hayes-Tilden compromise, a compromise reached after the Civil War and after reconstruction had been killed, in fact, a political act which killed reconstruction, and which got the industrialization of the United States underway.

To industrialize, you need talents, you need skills, and the Europeans brought many of these skills with them. We Negroes were kept out of it, out of the political decisions. We were removed from the competition. To that extent I think we Negroes subsidized the United States by not being there to make for racial unrest. We were not there to drive the market down for the outsiders. We were disenfranchised. So I think the Nation is obligated to recognize that Negroes subsidized the peace from 1876, when there was the threat of reopening the Civil War, until the Supreme Court decision of 1954. During those 78 years we didn't break out, as some of us are breaking out today, and this is a most important contribution to the growth of this great Nation.

As far as your question regarding credit is concerned, Negroes can't get it because businessmen customarily refuse it. One of the big problems in Watts arose because merchants there not only overcharged for inferior materials, but they sold charge accounts whenever overdue to finance companies located outside of Watts, companies which had no personal contact with the customers. I am referring to the practice known as factoring. Interest rates on such items as cars and clothing run as high as 300 percent. So you get so many things stacked against you, which accumulate, and you have nowhere to go. You don't have the instrumentalities to break out of your social and economic bind.

NEGRO ATTITUDE TOWARD HARLEM

Now beyond this, I would say that it is a misunderstanding to assume that Negroes want to break out of Harlem. They want to transform the Harlems of their country. These places are precious to them. These places are where they have dreamed, where they have lived, where they have loved, where they have worked out life as they could.

Senator Ribicoff. Will you pardon me for a second. Those bells mean there is a live quorum. If you see us leaving, that doesn't mean we are being discourteous. We will be back as soon as we answer to our names. So I will go to answer the quorum and I will be right back and Senator Javits and Senator Montoya will have questions.

Senator Javits, Go right ahead.

Mr. Ellison. I am saying that it isn't the desire to run to the suburbs or to invade "white" neighborhoods that is the main concern with my people in Harlem. They would just like to have a more human life there. A slum like Harlem just isn't a place of decay. It is also a form of historical and social memory.

ANALOGIZING NEGROES TO FOREIGN IMMIGRANTS

Senator Javits. Mr. Ellison, I gave the analogy of the Lower Eastside of New York because the Lower Eastside was in substance used as a staging area for the immigrant wave which came in the 1880's, 1890's, and before World War I, and then was left as a staging area for World War I in successive waves which populated the Bronx and Brooklyn and Queens and especially the suburbs. Now there too was a nostalgia to stay on the Lower Eastside, et cetera, but the second generation would have none of it. Now you see the same thing happening among Negroes.

Mr. Ellison. To the extent that the parents can finance it, but so few of us can. We just don't have the money to get out, and also we run into difficulty when we can, because many of the places are barred to us.

Senator Javits. Well now, do you feel—we have been talking here about the antidiscrimination in housing provision of the civil rights bill—do you feel that the dignity which is involved and the opportunity is of any importance to the Negro?

Mr. Ellison. I think it is very, very important. It is important to know that you are not being discriminated against in the abstract. The law should grant to each Negro his individuality. If he desires and has the money to go and live in a neighborhood of his choice, there is no reason why he shouldn't. Very often we won't choose to do so. But at least he is no longer, theoretically at least, set aside because of his color.

IMPORTANCE OF PERSONAL DIGNITY TO NEGROES

Senator Javits. Now do you consider this in the Negro's eye at least the equal of appropriations and antidiscrimination laws, this matter of personal dignity?

Mr. Ellison. I think it is basic to the trouble. Our laws, even some of these good laws, come across to Negroes as though we are being legislated for rather than with. It sometimes seems that we really don't exist as individuals in the minds of those who are most concerned with these laws, and there is a kind of threat in that situation. Because we feel that behind it there is a basic attitude of contempt.

Now I don't myself happen to think that. Indeed, I would think that one of the major purposes of these hearings would be to examine the details of the individual realities of Negroes.

Senator Javits. I have said many times that to my mind the most distasteful form of discrimination is the discrimination of patronization. Would you agree with that?

Mr. Ellison. I agree.

AWAKEN PUBLIC AND PRIVATE CONSCIENCE

Senator Javits. Now the last point that I would like to lay before you is this. Would it be fair to summarize your views with the feeling that what our country needs is a tremendous reawakening of conscience on this subject, which would be translated in the public realm in laws and appropriations commensurate with the need, especially the need for training? As you have pointed out, you don't come with skills because the skills have been denied Negroes for generations.

And secondly, a tremendous awakening of conscience in the private sector, that it too is a part of it and has been for decades to this denial of opportunity, and must make a special effort to enable the catchup to take place.

Mr. Ellison. Yes, Senator, I agree with that, and I would add to it that what is very necessary for all Americans, black and white alike, is to learn American history, to learn how this situation came about, to learn who benefited from the political moves and who suffered, who bore the unfairness gracefully, and who today are denied opportunity because there are those who still cannot find it within themselves to accept the necessity for change.

Somehow in our arts, in our education, we have got not only to reawaken the American conscience, but also the American consciousness, so that we will know exactly what this is all about. Then it will be seen as a national crisis, not as a Negro crisis.

Senator Javits. I agree with that. May I espouse those words with you. It is a national crisis, not a Negro crisis. I thoroughly agree with that, and I have said that myself ever since we started legislating in the civil rights field, and I would like to underline and emphasize what you say. And it, therefore, rates with the other problems created by national crises, like Vietnam, and I see no reason, with all respect, why one can't be strongly back of our policy there and strongly back of our policy here.

NEGRO CONDITIONS DURING WAR

Mr. Ellison. I certainly agree, Senator, and if I may, I would like to say something which is unpleasant about the Negro in Vietnam. Speaking historically, our condition has been bettered in this country during periods of national disaster. This was true of the Civil War when we got our freedom. It was true of the Spanish-American War when there was the beginning of the migratory movement. It was true to a large extent during the First World War. It was even more true during the depression.

We have this contradictory movement in American history: When there is a breakdown of the total structure, democracy spreads.

As much as I dislike warfare, and would like to see this thing in Vietnam ended, from a Negro point of view, from one Negro's point of view, I know that the people who are going to rule the South together under the new political situation will be black and white southerners who are fighting together in Vietnam, getting to know one another in a way that was not possible before, getting to know one another without the myths of racial inferiority or superiority. These, too, are American political realities and they have to be considered when we look at what is happening in the cities.

ELLISON VIEW OF FUTURE OF RACE RELATIONS

Senator Javits. Mr. Ellison, as one well-informed, intellectual observer, do you feel any real fear that this will blow up in some terrible purge of violence, or are you optimistic that give or take 10 percent as we say in so many things, in terms of riots or whatever else has to be endured but not condoned, we can find our way out of it now that the crisis is upon us?

Mr. Ellison. I think so, we have endured worse crises, and I think we might look very carefully at the riots to determine when we are watching episodes of the Negro rights struggle and when we are watching incidents sparked by the teenage rambunctiousness which is upon the world.

So much of what I see in the paper described as the worst thing that ever happened does not begin to touch what occurred in the Harlem riots of 1943. I covered that riot for the New York Post. If you will recall, Harlem was a shambles.

Senator Javits. I know it.

Mr. Ellison. In 1964, the riot involved only a few blocks, and I don't think it was confined simply because the police used live ammunition.

Senator Javits. Even the police methods have grown pretty considerably, especially in New York, in intelligence. They are by no means the best, and as you know, I am ardently for the Civilian Review Board.

Mr. Ellison. Yes, sir.

Senator Javits. But, nevertheless, it is a fact that police methods themselves have changed materially, isn't that true, as shown by East New York? I think they did quite an extraordinary job.

Mr. Ellison. I think so.

Senator Javits. Thank you, Mr. Chairman.

Senator Ribicoff. Thank you very much.

Senator Javits. Thank you, Mr. Ellison.

LIFE IN HARLEM

Senator Ribicoff. Mr. Ellison, yesterday we heard about some of the—let's put it mildly—seamier aspects of life in Harlem. Now, you are acquainted with Harlem. Aren't there other aspects of life in Harlem for millions of Negroes whose lot has been bettered over the past decade?

Mr. Ellison. Yes; I think so. I think that is what happened to me to an extent. There was a time when I was in Harlem every day, and also lived there. I did much research in the libraries there, in the Schomburg collection, which was very important in its way.

It isn't often mentioned these days, but Harlem is a place where there is a continuity of Negro styles. Harlem has its elegant side. Harlem is a place where you see the transformation of the southern idiom into a northern idiom. This is exciting in itself. Harlem is a place where our folklore is preserved, and transformed. It is the place where the body of Negro myth and legend thrives. It is a place where our styles, musical styles, the many styles of Negro life, find continuity and metamorphosis.

This is very important. Harlem is where a southern Negro who has a little luck, who has a little talent, can actually make himself into the man or woman of his dreams, because Harlem is a base. It is often overlooked, but most people who live in Harlem, do not work in Harlem. They spend most of their time on jobs outside of Harlem. Very many of them are intimately involved in the households of whites. Their sense of the world, therefore, is much broader than Harlem. However, there is something about Harlem which enhances whatever it is you pick up outside. It enhances it because you put the new-found values, the new-found information, the new-found styles together with what you already have, and this is inventive, this is creative. This gives the individual a sense of achieving himself. This, too, is part of Harlem.

NEGRO FEELING ABOUT HARLEM

Senator Ribicoff. Do the people who live in Harlem want to get out of Harlem? Do they look at Harlem as a prison or do they look at Harlem as a place to live in that they would like to stay in if the conditions were better? I would like to get your personal reaction. Does everybody who lives in Harlem want to get out of Harlem?

Mr. Ellison. I doubt that very seriously. I can't imagine some of these people wanting to get away from a given block or wanting to get away from a church, unless they could be assured that a branch of that church would be established in the suburbs, or wherever else they might want to go.

People want Harlem improved, not torn down. They want Harlem to remain as a base, just as people in their sections want their old blocks to remain as home base. I think it is just that simple. It is a human reaction, and the only thing that is different is that people in Harlem are usually told that they cannot get out, or if they do get out there is the threat of rioting or threats that their new neighbors will move away from them. That is the difference.

CITY AT ROOT OF NEGRO PROBLEM

Senator Ribicoff. Now I was told, and if I am incorrect, you correct me, that you once started to write an essay on the northern Negro, and realized that what you were writing about was not so much the Negro as the city. Am I correct there, before I go on?

Mr. Ellison. Yes; it is true. Back in 1948 I did write an essay about the psychological nature of the city, of Harlem, and that was included in a collection of essays of mine which was published in 1964. It was an essay entitled "Harlem is Nowhere." And I tried to describe the psychological and cultural crisis which southern Negroes encountered when they came to live in the slum of a great city.

But then when I was called to appear before this committee, I reread that essay and began to think about what I had said there and it came to me that I was really talking about the problem of the American city.

We very often get the impression that what is wrong with the American city is the Negro, when the reverse is true. What is wrong with the Negro is what we Americans have done to the American city.

Senator Ribicoff. I think that is one of the keys to this hearing. This is not just a hearing on the Negro in the American city, the Negro in American life; this is a hearing on the city and its problems and how we are organized to cope with it.

Mr. Ellison. Yes.

Senator Ribicoff. We are dealing with something bigger than just the problem of Negroes—and that is the city, and what we are trying to find out here is what is wrong with the American city, and how we can correct it. The Negro is just part of it.

Mr. Ellison. That is right.

CITY AS A PLACE TO ACHIEVE ONES CAPABILITIES

Senator Ribicoff. Do you have any thoughts of what should be done with the American city, so people can live in it and live with it and people can use it, and the city can reach what it should be in a concept of society—the best of society instead of the worst of society.

Mr. Ellison. Well, I think that one of the things that we can do about the city is to look at it, to try to see it, not merely as an instrumentality for making money, but as a place for allowing the individual to achieve his highest promise. And with that in mind, try to construct a city, or reconstruct a city, in ways which would encourage a more gracious sense of human possibility. We would teach, if at all possible, the immigrants who come, whether they are black or white or brown, that there is a certain knowledge which one must acquire in order to live in the city without adding too much discomfort to his neighbors.

I think that this is a simple matter of education. People who come from certain types of rural environment don't know how to live in cities.

ELLISON QUOTATION ON "RESPONSIBILITY"

Senator Ribicoff. I am going to read the last paragraph of your prologue. I am leaving out one word. I used a very mild word the other day and I have heard from all over the country how disturbed they were that I used this mild cuss word so I am going to leave out this one word.

Mr. Ellison. I will take responsibility for it.

Senator Ribicoff. Yes; but they won't write to you on it; they will write to me. Now in your prologue you wrote:

> *I can hear you say, "what a horribly irresponsible (blank)! " And you're right. I leap to agree with you. I am one of the most irresponsible beings that ever lived. Irresponsibility is part of my invisibility; any way you face it, it is a denial. But to whom can I be responsible, and why should I be, when you refuse to see me? And wait until I reveal how truly irresponsible I am. Responsibility rests upon recognition, and recognition is a form of agreement. Take the man whom I almost killed: Who was responsible for that near murder? —I? I don't think so, and I refuse it. I won't buy it. You can't give it to me. He bumped me; he insulted me. Shouldn't he, for his own personal safety, have recognized my hysteria, my "danger potential?" He, let us say, was lost in a dreamworld. But didn't he control that dreamworld—which, alas, is only too real!—And didn't he rule me out of it? And if he had yelled for a policeman, wouldn't I have been taken for the offending one? Yes, yes, yes! Let me agree with you, I was the irresponsible one; for I should have used my knife to protect the higher interests of society. Someday that kind of foolishness will cause us tragic trouble. All dreamers and sleepwalkers must pay the price, and even the invisible victim is responsible for the fate of all. But I shirked that responsibility; I became too snarled in the incompatible notions that buzzed within my brain. I was a coward. But what did I do to be so black and blue? Bear with me.*

Now you started writing this book in 1947. From these words you seem to have foreseen the tragic consequences of what has erupted recently in violence, in rioting all over the Nation? What did you mean that this kind of foolishness would cause us tragic trouble?

Mr. Ellison. Well, Senator, by the time I got to that, the form of the experience was underway, I was writing beyond myself.

AMERICAN ATTITUDE TOWARD VIOLENCE

I think, on the basis, however, of what was around. I saw buildings burned in the riots of 1943, and I know something about how people react. If you push them far enough, and especially if they are Americans, they will try to bring down the house, even though they will be destroyed along with it. The officer in Vietnam who ordered the napalm bombs dropped near his men was expressing a very American attitude, and we all praise him for it. The same feelings and possibilities lie within all of us, and especially those of us who come to conceive of life as a desperate situation.

AWARENESS OF NEGROES AS PEOPLE

As far as responsibility goes, I hold my own group responsible for instructing others in our view of American reality. I hold that it is necessary that we insist upon the importance of our reality. Otherwise, I must ignore the dynamics of some 90 years of history during which the American white people have been disciplined to be as vaguely aware of the humanity of Negroes as possible.

This is the reality, and I don't see how we can overcome it unless we approach it consciously. Society has been structured so that you will not know me and I will not know you. Since I am aware of this, it is my responsibility to let you know, and to accept this gulf in understanding as part of my given American situation. And when we fail to do this, then we Negroes fail our responsibility as citizens. Unfortunately, our leadership has been powerless for so long, simply because there was no legal basis upon which Negroes could be organized, that they could not give the larger American society a sense of the human complexity of this group of Americans which has grown up in this country under the condition of slavery, who survived various types of brutalization, and who is here today with much to offer the Nation, because we have lived the experience which is to be found among most colonial peoples. All of the dynamics of the future are right here among American Negroes, and we have the responsibility not to give you the cliché of sociology, but to tell you exactly what it is that we feel and how we view the world.

POTENTIAL NEGRO CONTRIBUTION TO AMERICAN LIFE

Negroes would like to be responsible for part of the life, the quality of life in the United States, not just because we are a big legal reality, not just because we are a large social reality, but because we are conscious, responsible people who have the opportunity to express that little bit of wisdom which we have gained through our denial.

Senator Ribicoff. Your words are very wise and deep, and I would hope that they would be widespread and understood. You have made a very valuable contribution.

Senator Kennedy, would you like to ask questions?

ELLISON PROJECTION OF RACE RELATIONS IN NEXT DECADE

Senator Kennedy. What is it, Mr. Ellison, do you anticipate will be the relationships of the whites and the Negroes in this country, particularly in our urban centers over the period of the next decade?

Mr. Ellison. If we have luck, Senator, proper things will be put in their proper places. A share of the responsibility for ruling, or analyzing the conditions which mar the city—and I am not just speaking of Negro slums, but of the whole city, will be assumed by Negroes. We will be able to seek out and develop those leaders who through military experience, who through experience in the arts, who through other forms of experience have acquired some vital knowledge and skills to offer to the city as a whole.

Senator Kennedy. What is the alternative to that?

Mr. Ellison. The alternative to that will be an increase among those Negroes who feel hopeless, at the very time when things seem to be changing. I think we have to recognize that the political acts which have brought Negroes the promise of more freedom by terminating 90 years or more of political practice and social custom have by the very fact of that termination created a degree of chaos. We have decreed the new but the conditions under which the new can emerge have not been created.

Senator Kennedy. Yes.

OPTIMISM OF AMERICAN NEGROES

Mr. Ellison. That is because the legislation is in many instances far ahead of the political structures which exist. People don't know quite how to use this new freedom, this new possibility of democracy. We have got to learn that. But as we learn it, I think we have to be aware that there is a crisis of optimism among Negroes.

Slavery couldn't bring this crisis about. Depressions nor wars did not bring it about. But now, in the Northern cities, there is a crisis because things don't appear to be happening fast enough.

As Senator Javits pointed out, much money has been allocated, but it takes more money to get the allocations to the people. This isn't understood by a lot of Negroes who are far away from any large sums of money. But we have to be aware that if the American Negro loses his optimistic attitude toward the American promise, the whole Nation is in trouble. Because we have been, ironically, one of the main supports of American optimism. As long as we Negroes believed in the possibility of making order out of this chaos of diversified races and religions and regions, everybody could have faith. But if the Negro loses his optimism then suddenly the supports will have been lost, for the man at the bottom will no longer believe in the burden of possibility.

Senator Kennedy. Would you agree that we are at the moment on sort of a razor's edge in the direction that we are going to ultimately be headed, as to whether we are going to fall off into this chasm of lack of hope versus the other side which gives us some opportunity for the future?

Mr. Ellison. Well, I must remain optimistic. I must remain optimistic because, fortunately, as we reach crises in the cities of the North, there is a parallel expansion of freedom for Negroes in the South. And as the next two generations, say, of college people leave the North and go South, or others remain to find places within the South—and this is very important—and as they start functioning within the governments of the South, the Negro in the northern slum is going to feel much more optimistic about his own chances. Perhaps the South is where he is going to have to look for hope, just as the Nation is going to have to look to the new South for instruction. For it might well be that the place in which the trouble started will be the place where we will begin to see the most immediate effects of the change which has been set in motion.

Relations Between Older and Younger Negroes

Senator Kennedy. Do you feel that there is a lack of identification between the young Negroes and the older generation of Negroes? Perhaps you might discuss that for a moment, and also what the relationship or the feeling among young Negroes is towards the white population.

Mr. Ellison. I don't think that there is any more lack of relationship between the young Negro and the old than there is between the young whites and the old. For one reason or the other, we have a very permissive society and the distance you get between the young and the old is generated by a complex of factors, some historical, some economic and some a mere matter of the discontinuity of memory characteristics of American society.

There is this gap in attitude between the generations because for one thing we do not transmit a knowledge of how life actually is from one generation to another. For example, at Bard College I was teaching a course in the American novel, during which I discussed the depression and the WPA. After class a very bright young woman, with whose father I once walked picket lines in New York, came up and said "Mr. Ellison, what is the WPA? "

I think Americans are going to have to realize that we have reached a plateau of our history, and that the failure not to pass on the details of the parents' past because of the cost of their success or failure, becomes dangerous. It makes for an alienation. In fact, the wealthy children of Bard College—it had one of the highest admission fees of any college—were to my mind more disadvantaged than many Negroes living in slums who have maintained a sense of the continuity of their experience. This is an educational problem, but it is also a political problem.

Senator Kennedy. If there was one thing that you could do, one thing that you would change immediately, what would that be, Mr. Ellison?

Mr. Ellison. Our way of looking at one another.

Senator Kennedy. Would you expand that?

Clichés and Stereotypes of Race Relations

Mr. Ellison. Well, by that I mean we have built up such a body of stereotypes and clichés that we can no longer see individuals. We fail to see the Negro people as Americans who share American characteristics and American history. I would like to hear less of the sociological clichés about the Negro family. They are insulting to me. They are insulting and devastating to the Negro's conception of himself, and I regard them as contemptuous of us.

I would like to hear fewer theories spun out about what I am when I am right here to be talked to, to be observed, to be visited, if one so desires. We no longer have the political system which we had before these civil rights bills were passed. That system which was supported by the myths and the cliches and the stereotypes no longer exists because the economic and political basis has steadily changed. Many white southern politicians understand this, but oddly enough, many white people in the northern cities do not, and we have to do something about that.

I think that this is more important, even more important than allocating funds.

Senator Kennedy. How can that be brought about in your judgment?

Acquaintanceship of Negro and White Youths

Mr. Ellison. Senator, I don't know. A part of it has to be done through encouraging free participation in the institutional life of this country. Somehow, young Negroes and young whites have to get to know one another. The gap is widening. We have to find some ways of restating in contemporary terms the national values, of giving them form in art, and of going back to find the political uses of folklore, of folk music, including the European, and so on. We are a diversified people, and this is a pluralistic society on every level except the political and economic—and of course our working conception of ourselves.

We must somehow make these factors manifest in the public consciouness. We must give them a hard sell. We see the gimmicky use of it. People who want to sell name brands always manage now to get a Negro into the television advertisements, even though he just runs past the scene. I look at the children's ads and frequently see little Negroes present. Perhaps this doesn't mean very much in a political way, but it does give a lot for the young Negro child who thinks, "Well, at least my existence is being recognized."

Senator Ribicoff. I am very curious, if you will pardon me a second.

Senator Kennedy. Go ahead.

Similarity of Negro and White Advertising Models

Senator Ribicoff. I watch these ads, too. Do you think that the people in charge of advertising—the Negro models they use, men and women, are those who look more like the white, the overwhelming number of whites than they do the overwhelming number of Negroes?

Mr. Ellison. Well, it is pretty hard to tell what a Negro is if we get into that, Senator. After all, there is a Congressman from Harlem who is very much a Negro, whom some would regard as anything but a Negro type. If you look at it this way, however, I think it might have some meaning: We are a new racial type blended right here on this continent in the institution of slavery, but what makes us Negroes is not race so much as our having shared a special cultural and political experience. Now our statistics, our census, our newspaper reports, always refer to whites and nonwhites. What they mean, as a friend of mine pointed out one day, is whites and part whites. It makes a lot more sense when you look at it that way.

Then coming specifically to your question, I think that the motivation of the admen, directed by fashion editors, is that they look for a certain type of Negro model who is similar to the physical type of the white models. You seldom see a fat girl modeling a dress. They like the high cheekbones and the sharp features because they photograph well. So you have really an esthetic motive working here, and I don't think it is a racial motive. And if it is, then these people really don't know what the American racial situation actually is.

Senator Ribicoff. Go ahead. I am sorry, Senator.

Senator Kennedy. That is fine. Just one final question. Would you discuss for a moment—I know you touched on it—about the Negro political leadership, whether you feel that that leadership is identified with the problems, or that the people within the ghettos identify with that, with their leadership? And, if not, what you feel can be done or whether you think this is a problem here?

Negro Political Leadership

Mr. Ellison. Well, for years most Negro politicians did not really represent Negroes. They were part of party organizations, but they had no real basis beneath them. One of the realities which always comes to mind when I see the New York Times or Time magazine foaming at the mouth over some escapade of Adam Clayton Powell, is that they think that that particular kind of rhetoric will get rid of him. But people in Harlem obviously don't want to get rid of him. He represents us. And the basis of power, to expand this a moment, is the Negro church.

Influence of Church

The Negro church is our strongest institution. The fact that Dr. Martin Luther King comes out of the church and that so much of the leadership in the South during the marches came from the church goes back to the southern Negro tradition. This institution is one of our greatest American strengths. It was a moral support of the discipline against provocation which Negroes have developed over the years.

I suspect, however, that we have reached the point now where Dr. King, or anyone like him has to become a political leader, for I think that there is a limit in this Democracy to the church's affectiveness within political situations. I suspect that some of the younger ministers recognize this, and I hope that the leaders of the two major parties, will recognize it and make use of the talent for politics which is to be found among younger Negro ministers.

Obviously, this is a good time for false leadership because almost any young man who wants to say something violent about the Government can appear on television and can be quoted in the press. He can get the basis of a following very quickly. Very often, however, it turns out that there are only a half dozen people behind him. It reminds you of the situation in a novel of Dostoevski's, wherein a would-be revolutionary came in and whispered to a group of people that he represented a worldwide organization, and they then acted, even to the point of committing murder, on the authority of a non-existent organization.

Breakdown of Political Institutions

We are living in such a time of chaos—and the chaos is within the total political structure, it isn't just in the Negro neighborhood—that we do not have political structures which can contain the energies set loose by the passage of the civil rights bills. We do not have organizations which can channelize this energy and take advantage of it, and money won't do it.

Senator Kennedy. What is the answer to that?

Mr. Ellison. Senator, I am not a politician, and I apologize for even speaking this way. I would think that you would have the skills to find out ways of doing this.

Senator Kennedy. It is not just the politicians or those in political life. It is, I suppose, a problem for all of us as citizens, white or black.

Mr. Ellison. Yes, it is.

Senator Kennedy. To find the answer to that.

Negro Participation in Government

Mr. Ellison. Senator, what I was referring to—you see, there again, is an aspect of American Negro life that we forget. We think so often that we are separate at the top, but we are only separate at the base. There is only going to be one President, whether he is black, brown, blue or green, but there will only be one. There won't be a separate one for Negroes. There will only be a certain number of Senators from a given district, so that what I am trying to say is that once the Negro gets past the Negroes' own institutions, he must become a member of the other existing institution, political and social, of this Government, of this Nation. There is nothing else, unless we are going to do what Malcolm X was suggesting—set up a separate state, which is nonsense. So somehow, we have got to find Negroes who have talent, who can function responsibly in all of the institutions of the Nation.

If we can get them into banks and into laboratories, we should be able to get them into the major political parties and be able to give them some sort of real identity with the labor unions.

Senator Kennedy. Thank you very much. Thank you, Mr. Chairman.

2. THE WHITE MAN'S BURDEN

THE FORGOTTEN AMERICAN

Peter Schrag

There is hardly a language to describe him, or even a set of social statistics. Just names: racist-bigot-redneck-ethnic-Irish-Italian-Pole-Hunkie-Yahoo. The lower middle class. A blank. The man under whose hat lies the great American desert. Who watches the tube, plays the horses, and keeps the niggers out of his union and his neighborhood. Who might vote for Wallace (but didn't). Who cheers when the cops beat up on demonstrators. Who is free, white, and twenty-one, has a job, a home, a family, and is up to his eyeballs in credit. In the guise of the working class—or the American yeoman or John Smith—he was once the hero of the civics book, the man that Andrew Jackson called "the bone and sinew of the country." Now he is "the forgotten man," perhaps the most alienated person in America.

Nothing quite fits, except perhaps omission and semi-invisibility. America is supposed to be divided between affluence and poverty, between slums and suburbs. John Kenneth Galbraith begins the forward to *The Affluent Society* with the phrase, "Since I sailed for Switzerland in the early summer of 1955 to begin work on this book . . ." But *between* slums and suburbs, between Scarsdale and Harlem, between Wellesley and Roxbury, between Shaker Heights and Hough, there are some eighty million people (depending on how you count them) who didn't sail for Switzerland in the summer of 1955, or at any other time, and who never expect to. Between slums and surburbs: South Boston and South San Francisco, Bell and Parma, Astoria and Bay Ridge, Newark, Cicero, Downey, Daly City, Charlestown, Flatbush. Union halls, American Legion posts, neighborhood bars and bowling leagues, the Ukrainian Club and the Holy Name. Main Street. To try to describe all this is like trying to describe America itself. If you look for it, you find it everywhere: the rows of frame houses overlooking the belching steel mills in Bethlehem, Pennsylvania, two-family brick houses in Canarsie (where the most common slogan, even in the middle of a political campaign, is "curb your dog"); the Fords and Chevies with a decal American flag

Peter Schrag, "The Forgotten American," **HARPER'S MAGAZINE,** *August, 1969. Copyright 1969, by Harper's Magazine, Inc. Reprinted from the August, 1969 issue of* **HARPER'S MAGAZINE** *by permission of the author.*

on the rear window (usually a cut-out from the *Reader's Digest,* and displayed in counter-protest against peaceniks and "those bastards who carry Vietcong flags in demonstrations"); the bunting on the porch rail with the inscription, "Welcome Home, Pete." The gold star in the window.

When he was Under Secretary of Housing and Urban Development, Robert C. Wood tried a definition. It is not good, but it's the best we have:

> *He is a white employed male ... earning between $5,000 and $10,000. He works regularly, steadily, dependably, wearing a blue collar or white collar. Yet the frontiers of his career expectations have been fixed since he reached the age of thirty-five, when he found that he had too many obligations, too much family, and too few skills to match opportunities with aspirations.*
>
> *This definition of the "working American" involves almost 23-million American families.*
>
> *The working American lives in the gray area fringes of a central city or in a close-in or very far-out cheaper suburban subdivision of a large metropolitan area. He is likely to own a home and a car, especially as his income begins to rise. Of those earning between $6,000 and $7,000, 70 per cent own their own homes and 94 per cent drive their own cars.*
>
> *94 per cent have no education beyond high school and 43 per cent have only completed the eighth grade.*

He does all the right things, obeys the law, goes to church and insists— usually—that his kids get a better education than he had. But the right things don't seem to be paying off. While he is making more than he ever made— perhaps more than he'd ever dreamed—he's still struggling while a lot of others— "them" (on welfare, in demonstrations, in the ghettos) are getting most of the attention. "I'm working my ass off," a guy tells you on a stoop in South Boston. "My kids don't have a place to swim, my parks are full of glass, and I'm supposed to bleed for a bunch of people on relief." In New York a man who drives a Post Office trailer truck at night (4:00 P.M. to midnight) and a cab during the day (7:00 A.M. to 2:00 P.M.), and who hustles radios for his Post Office buddies on the side, is ready, as he says, to "knock somebody's ass." "The colored guys work when they feel like it. Sometimes they show up and sometimes they don't. One guy tore up all the time cards. I'd like to see a white guy do that and get away with it."

WHAT COUNTS

Nobody knows how many people in America moonlight (half of the eighteen million families in the $5,000 to $10,000 bracket have two or more wage earners) or how many have to hustle on the side. "I don't think anybody has a single job anymore," said Nicholas Kisburg, the research director for a Teamsters Union Council in New York. "All the cops are moonlighting, and the teachers; and there's a million guys who are hustling, guys with phony social-security numbers who are hiding part of what they make so they don't get kicked out of a housing project, or guys who work as guards at sports events and get free meals that they don't want to pay taxes on. Every one of them is cheating. They are underground people—*Untermenschen.* . . . We really have no systematic data on any of this. We have no ideas of the attitudes of the white worker. (We've been too busy studying the black worker.) And yet he's the source of most of the reaction in this country."

The reaction is directed at almost every visible target: at integration and welfare, taxes and sex education, at the rich and the poor, the foundations and students, at the "smart people in the suburbs." In New York State the legislature cuts the welfare budget; in Los Angeles, the voters reelect Yorty after a whispered racial campaign against the Negro favorite. In Minneapolis a police detective named Charles Stenvig, promising "to take the handcuffs off the police," wins by a margin stunning even to his supporters: in Massachusetts the voters mail tea bags to their representatives in protest against new taxes, and in state after state legislatures are passing bills to punish student demonstrators. ("We keep talking about permissiveness in training kids," said a Los Angeles labor official, "but we forget that these are our kids.")

And yet all these things are side manifestations of a malaise that lacks a language. Whatever law and order means, for example, to a man who feels his wife is unsafe on the street after dark or in the park at any time, or whose kids get shaken down in the school yard, it also means something like normality—the demand that everybody play it by the book, that cultural and social standards be somehow restored to their civics-book simplicity, that things shouldn't be as they are but as they were supposed to be. If there is a revolution in this country —a revolt in manners, standards of dress and obscenity, and, more importantly, in our official sense of what America is—there is also a counter-revolt. Sometimes it is inarticulate, and sometimes (perhaps most of the time) people are either too confused or apathetic—or simply too polite and too decent—to declare themselves. In Astoria, Queens, a white working-class district of New York, people who make $7,000 or $8,000 a year (sometimes in two jobs) call themselves affluent, even though the Bureau of Labor Statistics regards an income of less than $9,500 in New York inadequate to a moderate standard of living. And in a similar neighborhood in Brooklyn a truck driver who earns $151 a week tells you he's doing well, living in a two-story frame house separated by a narrow driveway from similar houses, thousands of them in block after block. This year, for the first time, he will go on a cruise—he and his wife and two other couples— two weeks in the Caribbean. He went to work after World War II ($57 a week) and he has lived in the same house for twenty years, accumulating two television sets, wall-to-wall carpeting in a small living room, and a basement that he recently remodeled into a recreation room with the help of two moonlighting firemen. "We get fairly good salaries, and this is a good neighborhood, one of the few good ones left. We have no smoked Irishmen around."

Stability is what counts, stability in job and home and neighborhood, stability in the church and in friends. At night you watch television and sometimes on a weekend you go to a nice place—maybe a downtown hotel—for dinner with another couple. (Or maybe your sister, or maybe bowling, or maybe, if you're defeated, a night at the track.) The wife has the necessary appliances, often still being paid off, and the money you save goes for your daughter's orthodontist, and later for her wedding. The smoked Irishmen—the colored (no one says black; few even say Negro)—represent change and instability, kids who cause trouble in school, who get treatment that your kids never got, that you never got. ("Those fucking kids," they tell you in South Boston, "raising hell, and not one of 'em paying his own way. Their fucking mothers are all on welfare.") The black kids mean a change in the rules, a double standard in grades and discipline, and—vaguely—a challenge to all you believe right. Law and order is the stability and predictability of established ways. Law and order is equal treatment—in school, in jobs, in the courts—even if you're cheating a little yourself. The Forgotten Man is Jackson's man. He is the vestigial American democrat of 1840: "They all know that their success depends upon their own industry and economy and that they must not expect to become suddenly rich by the fruits of their toil." He is also Franklin Roosevelt's man—the man whose vote (or whose father's vote) sustained the New Deal.

There are other considerations, other styles, other problems. A postman in a Charlestown (Boston) housing project: eight children and a ninth on the way. Last year, by working overtime, his income went over $7,000. This year, because he reported it, the Housing Authority is raising his rent from $78 to $106 a month, a catastrophe for a family that pays $2.20 a day for milk, has never had a vacation, and for which an excursion is "going out for ice cream." "You try and save for something better; we hope to get out of here to someplace where the kids can play, where there's no broken glass, and then something always comes along that knocks you right back. It's like being at the bottom of the well waiting for a guy to throw you a rope." The description becomes almost Chaplinesque. Life is humble but not simple; the terrors of insolent bureaucracies and contemptuous officials produce a demonology that loses little of its horror for being partly misunderstood. You want to get a sink fixed but don't want to offend the manager; want to get an eye operation that may (or may not) have been necessitated by a military injury five years earlier, "but the Veterans Administration says I signed away my benefits"; want to complain to someone about the teen-agers who run around breaking windows and harassing women but get no response either from the management or the police. "You're afraid to complain because if they don't get you during the day they'll get you at night." Automobiles, windows, children, all become hostages to the vague terrors of everyday life; everything is vulnerable. Liabilities that began long ago cannot possibly be liquidated' "I never learned anything in that school except how to fight. I got tired of being caned by the teachers so at sixteen I quit and joined the Marines. I still don't know anything."

AT THE BOTTOM OF THE WELL

American culture? Wealth is visible, and so, now, is poverty. Both have become intimidating clichés. But the rest? A vast, complex, and disregarded world that was once—in belief, and in fact—the American middle: Greyhound and Trailways bus terminals in little cities at midnight, each of them with its neon lights and its cardboard hamburgers; acres of tar-paper beach bungalows in places like Revere and Rockaway; the hair curlers in the supermarket on Saturday, and the little girls in the communion dresses the next morning; pinball machines and the *Daily News,* the *Reader's Digest* and Ed Sullivan; houses with tiny front lawns (or even large ones) adorned with statues of the Virgin or of Sambo welcomin' de folks home; Clint Eastwood or Julie Andrews at the Palace;

the trotting tracks and the dog tracks—Aurora Downs, Connaught Park, Roose-velt, Yonkers, Rockingham, and forty others—where gray men come not for sport and beauty, but to read numbers, to study and dope. (If you win you have figured something, have in a small way controlled your world, have surmounted your impotence. If you lose, bad luck, shit. "I'll break his goddamned head.") Baseball is not the national pastime; racing is. For every man who goes to a major-league baseball game there are four who go to the track and probably four more who go to the candy store or the barbershop to make their bets. (Total track attendance in 1965: 62 million plus another 10 million who went to the dogs.)

There are places, and styles, and attitudes. If there are neighborhoods of aspiration, suburban enclaves for the mobile young executive and the aspiring worker, there are also places of limited expectation and dead-end districts where mobility is finished. But even there you can often find, however vestigial, a sense of place, the roots of old ethnic loyalties, and a passionate, if often futile, battle against intrusion and change. "Everybody around here," you are told, "pays his own way." In this world the problems are not the ABM or air pollution (have they heard of Biafra?) or the international population crisis; the problem is to get your street cleaned, your garbage collected, to get your husband home from Vietnam alive; to negotiate installment payments and to keep the schools orderly. Ask anyone in Scarsdale or Winnetka about the schools and they'll tell you about new programs, or about how many are getting into Harvard, or about the teachers; ask in Oakland or the North Side of Chicago, and they'll tell you that they have (or haven't) had trouble. Somewhere in his gut the man in those communities knows that mobility and choice in this society are limited. He cannot imagine any major change for the better; but he can imagine change for the worse. And yet for a decade he is the one who has been asked to carry the burden of social reform, to integrate his schools and his neighborhood, has been asked by comfortable people to pay the social debts due to the poor and the black. In Boston, in San Francisco, in Chicago (not to mention Newark or Oakland) he has been telling the reformers to go to hell. The Jewish school-teachers of New York and the Irish parents of Dorchester have asked the same question: "What the hell did Lindsay (or the Beacon Hill Establishment) ever do for us? "

The ambiguities and changes in American life that occupy discussions in university seminars and policy debates in Washington, and that form the back-bone of contemporary popular sociology, become increasingly the conditions of trauma and frustration in the middle. Although the New Frontier and Great Society contained some programs for those not already on the rolls of social pathology—federal aid for higher education, for example—the public priorities and the rhetoric contained little. The emphasis, properly, was on the poor, or the inner cities (*e.g.,* Negroes) and the unemployed. But in Chicago a widow with three children who earns $7,000 a year can't get them college loans because she makes too much; the money is reserved for people on relief. New schools are built in the ghetto but not in the white working-class neighborhoods where they are just as dilapidated. In Newark the head of a white vigilante group (now a city councilman) runs, among other things, on a platform opposing pro-Negro discrimination. "When pools are being built in the Central Ward—don't they think white kids have got frustration? The white can't get a job; we have to hire Negroes first." The middle class, said Congressman Roman Pucinski of Illinois, who represents a lot of it, "is in revolt. Everyone has been generous in support-ing anti-poverty. Now the middle-class American is disqualified from most of the programs."

"SOMEBODY HAS TO SAY NO..."

The frustrated middle. The liberal wisdom about welfare, ghettos, student revolt, and Vietnam has only a marginal place, if any, for the values and life of the working man. It flies in the face of most of what he was taught to cherish and respect: hard work, order, authority, self-reliance. He fought, either alone or through labor organizations, to establish the precincts he now considers his own. Union seniority, the civil-service bureaucracy, and the petty professionalism established by the merit system in the public schools become sinecures of par-ticular ethnic groups or of those who have learned to negotiate and master the system. A man who worked all his life to accumulate the points and grades and paraphernalia to become an assistant school principal (no matter how silly the requirements) is not likely to relinquish his position with equanimity. Nor is a dock worker whose only estate is his longshoreman's card. The job, the points, the credits become property:

> *Some men leave their sons money [wrote a union member to the* New York Times], *some large investments, some business connections, and some a profession. I have only one worthwhile thing to give: my trade. I hope to follow a centuries-old-tradition and sponsor my sons for an apprenticeship. For this simple father's wish, it is said that I discriminate against Negroes. Don't all of us discriminate? Which of us . . . will not choose a son over all others?*

Suddenly the rules are changing—all the rules. If you protect your job for your own you may be called a bigot. At the same time it's perfectly acceptable to shout black power and to endorse it. What does it take to be a good Ameri-can? *Give the black man a position because he is black, not because he neces-sarily works harder or does the job better.* What does it take to be a good American? Dress nicely, hold a job, be clean-cut, don't judge a man by the color of his skin or the country of his origin. What about the demands of Negroes, the long hair of the students, the dirty movies, the people who burn draft cards and American flags? Do you have to go out in the street with picket signs, do you have to burn the place down to get what you want? What does it take to be a good American? *This is a sick society, a racist society, we are fighting an immoral war.* ("I'm against the Vietnam war, too." says the truck driver in Brooklyn. "I see a good kid come home with half an arm and a leg in a brace up to here, and what's it all for? I was glad to see *my kid* flunk the Army physical. Still, somebody has to say no to these demonstrators and enforce the law.") What does it take to be a good American?

The conditions of trauma and frustration in the middle. What does it take to be a good American? Suddenly there are demands for Italian power and Polish power and Ukrainian power. In Cleveland the Poles demand a seat on the school board, and get it, and in Pittsburgh John Pankuch, the seventy-three-year-old president of the National Slovak Society demands "action, plenty of it to make up for lost time." Black power is supposed to be nothing but emulation of the ways in which other ethnic groups made it. But have they made it? In Reardon's Bar on East Eighth Street in South Boston, where the workmen come for their fish-chowder lunch and for their rye and ginger, they still identify themselves as Galway men and Kilkenny men; in the newsstand in Astoria you can buy *Il Progresso, El Tiempo,* the *Staats-Zeitung,* the *Irish World,* plus papers in Greek, Hungarian, and Polish. At the parish of Our Lady of Mount Carmel the priests hear confession in English, Italian, and Spanish and, nearby, the biggest attraction is not the stickball game, but the *bocce* court. Some of the poorest people in America are white, native, and have lived all of their lives in the same place as their fathers and grandfathers. The problems that were presumably solved in some distant past, in that prehistoric era before the textbooks were written—problems of assimilation, of upward mobility—now turn out to be very much unsolved. The melting pot and all: millions made it, millions moved to the affluent suburbs; several million—no one knows how many—did not. The median income in Irish South Boston is $5,100 a year but the community-action workers have a hard time convincing the local citizens that any white man who is not stupid or irresponsible can be poor. Pride still keeps them from applying for income supplements or Medicaid, but it does not keep them from resenting those who do. In Pittsburgh, where the members of Polish-American organizations earn an estimated $5,000 to $6,000 (and some fall below the poverty line), the Poverty Programs are nonetheless directed primarily to Negroes, and almost everywhere the thing called urban backlash associates itself in some fashion with ethnic groups whose members have themselves only a precarious hold on the security of affluence. Almost everywhere in the old cities, tribal neighborhoods and their styles are under assault by masscult. The Italian grocery gives way to the supermarket, the ma-and-pa store and the walk-up are attacked by urban renewal. And almost everywhere, that assault tends to depersonalize and to alienate. It has always been this way, but with time the brave new world that replaces old patterns becomes increasingly bureaucratized, distant, and hard to control.

Yet beyond the problems of ethnic identity, beyond the problems of Poles and Irishmen left behind, there are others more pervasive and more dangerous. For every Greek or Hungarian there are a dozen American-Americans who are past ethnic consciousness and who are as alienated, as confused, and as angry as the rest. The obvious manifestations are the same everywhere—race, taxes, welfare, students—but the threat seems invariably more cultural and psychological than economic or social. What upset the police at the Chicago convention most was not so much the politics of the demonstrators as their manners and their hair. (The barbershops in their neighborhoods don't advertise Beatle Cuts but the Flat Top and the Chicago Box.) The affront comes from middle-class people —and their children—who had been cast in the role of social exemplars (and from those cast as unfortunates worthy of public charity) who offend all the things on which working class identity is built: "hippies [said a San Francisco longshoreman] who fart around the streets and don't work"; welfare recipients who strike and march for better treatment; "all those [said a California labor official] who challenge the precepts that these people live on." If ethnic groups are beginning to organize to get theirs, so are others: police and firemen ("The cop is the new nigger"); schoolteachers; lower-middle-class housewives fighting sex education and bussing; small property owners who have no ethnic communion but a passionate interest in lower taxes, more policemen, and stiffer penalties for criminals. In San Francisco the Teamsters, who had never been known for such interests before, recently demonstrated in support of the police and law enforcement and, on another occasion, joined a group called Mothers Support Neighborhood Schools at a school-board meeting to oppose—with their presence and later apparently, with their fists—a proposal to integrate the schools through bussing. ("These people," someone said at the meeting, "do not look like mothers.")

Which is not to say that all is frustration and anger, that anybody is ready "to burn the country down." They are not even ready to elect standard model demagogues. "A lot of labor people who thought of voting for Wallace were ashamed of themselves when they realized what they were about to do," said Morris Lushewitz, an officer of New York's Central Labor Council. Because of a massive last-minute union campaign, and perhaps for other reasons, the blue-collar vote for Wallace fell far below the figures predicted by the early polls last fall. Any number of people, moreover, who are not doing well by any set of official statistics, who are earning well below the national mean ($8,000 a year), or who hold two jobs to stay above it think of themselves as affluent, and often use that word. It is almost as if not to be affluent is to be un-American. People who can't use the word tend to be angry; people who come too close to those who can't become frightened. The definition of affluence is generally pinned to what comes in, not to the quality of life as it's lived. The $8,000 son of a man who never earned more than $4,500 may, for that reason alone, believe that he's "doing all right." If life is not all right, if he can't get his curbs fixed, or his streets patrolled, if the highways are crowded and the beaches polluted, if the schools are ineffectual he is still able to call himself affluent, feels, perhaps, a social compulsion to do so. His anger, if he is angry, is not that of the wage earner resenting management—and certainly not that of the socialist ideologue asking for redistribution of wealth—but that of the consumer, the taxpayer, and the family man. (Inflation and taxes are wiping out most of the wage gains made in labor contracts signed during the past three years.) Thus he will vote for a Louise Day Hicks in Boston who promises to hold the color line in the schools or for a Charles Stenvig calling for law enforcement in Minneapolis but reject a George Wallace who seems to threaten his pocketbook. The danger is that he will identify with the politics of the Birchers and other middle-class reactionaries (who often pretend to speak for him) even though his income and style of life are far removed from theirs; that taxes, for example, will be identified with welfare rather than war, and that he will blame his limited means on the small slice of the poor rather than the fat slice of the rich.

If you sit and talk to people like Marjorie Lemlow, who heads Mothers Support Neighborhood Schools in San Francisco, or Joe Owens, a house painter who is president of a community-action organization in Boston, you quickly discover that the roots of reaction and the roots of reform are often identical, and that the response to particular situations is more often contingent on the politics of the politicians and leaders who appear to care than on the conditions of life or the ideology of the victims. Mrs. Lemlow wants to return the schools to some virtuous past; she worries about disintegration of the family and she speaks vaguely about something that she can't bring herself to call a conspiracy against Americanism. She has been accused of leading a bunch of Birchers, and she sometimes talks Birch language. But whatever the form, her sense of things comes from a small-town vision of national virtues, and her unhappiness from the assaults of urban sophistication. It just so happens that a lot of reactionaries now sing that tune, and that the liberals are indifferent.

Joe Owens—probably because of his experience as a Head Start parent, and because of his association with an effective community-action program—talks a different language. He knows, somehow, that no simple past can be restored. In his world the villains are not conspirators but bureaucrats and politicians, and he is beginning to discover that in a struggle with officials the black man in the ghetto and the working man (black or white) have the same problems. "Every time you ask for something from the politicians they treat you like a beggar, like you ought to be grateful for what you have. They try to make you feel ashamed."

WHEN HOPE BECOMES A THREAT

The imponderables are youth and tradition and change. The civics book and the institution it celebrates—however passé—still hold the world together. The revolt is in their name, not against them. And there is simple decency, the language and practice of the folksy cliché, the small town, the Boy Scout virtues, the neighborhood charity, the obligation to support the church, the rhetoric of open opportunity: "They can keep Wallace and they can keep Alabama. We didn't fight a dictator for four years so we could elect one over here." What happens when all that becomes Mickey Mouse? Is there an urban ethic to replace the values of the small town? Is there a coherent public philosophy, a consistent set of beliefs to replace family, home, and hard work? What happens when the hang-ups of upper-middle-class kids are in fashion and those of blue-collar kids are not? What happens when Doing Your Own Thing becomes not the slogan of the solitary deviant but the norm? Is it possible that as the institutions and beliefs of tradition are fashionably denigrated a blue-collar generation gap will open to the Right as well as to the Left? (There is statistical evidence, for example, that Wallace's greatest support within the unions came from people who are between twenty-one and twenty-nine, those, that is, who have the most tenuous association with the liberalism of labor). Most are politically silent, although SDS has been trying to organize blue-collar high school students, there are no Mario Savios or Mark Rudds—either of the Right or the Left—among them. At the same time the union leaders, some of them old hands from the Thirties, aren't sure that the kids are following them either. Who speaks for the son of the longshoreman or the Detroit auto worker? What happens if he doesn't get to college? What, indeed, happens when he does?

Vaguely but unmistakably the hopes that a youth-worshiping nation historically invested in its young are becoming threats. We have never been unequivocal about the symbolic patricide of Americanization and upward mobility, but if at one time mobility meant rejection of older (or European) styles it was, at least, done in the name of America. Now the labels are blurred and the objectives indistinct. Just at the moment when a tradition-bound Italian father is persuaded that he should send his sons to college—that education is the only future—the college blows up. At the moment when a parsimonious taxpayer begins to shell out for what he considers an extravagant state university system the students go on strike. Marijuana, sexual liberation, dress styles, draft resistance, even the rhetoric of change become monsters and demons in a world that appears to turn old virtues upside down. The paranoia that fastened on Communism twenty years ago (and sometimes still does) is increasingly directed to vague conspiracies undermining the schools, the family, order and discipline. "They're feeding the kids this generation-gap business," says a Chicago housewife who grinds out a campaign against sex education on a duplicating machine in her living room. "The kids are told to make their own decisions. They're all mixed up by situation ethics and open-ended questions. They're alienating children from their own parents." They? The churches, the schools, even the YMCA and the Girl Scouts, are implicated. But a major share of the villainy is now also attributed to "the social science centers," to the apostles of sensitivity training, and to what one California lady, with some embarrassment, called "nude therapy." "People with sane minds are being altered by psychological methods." The current major campaign of the John Birch Society is not directed against Communists in government or the Supreme Court, but against sex education.

(There is, of course, also sympathy with the young, especially in poorer areas where kids have no place to play. "Everybody's got to have a hobby," a South Boston adolescent told a youth worker. "Ours is throwing rocks." If people will join reactionary organizations to protect their children, they will also support others: community-action agencies which help kids get jobs; Head Start parent groups, Boys Clubs. "Getting this place cleaned up" sometimes refers to a fear of young hoods; sometimes it points to the day when there is a park or a playground or when the existing park can be used. "I want to see them grow up to have a little fun.")

CAN THE COMMON MAN COME BACK?

Beneath it all there is a more fundamental ambivalence, not only about the young, but about institutions—the schools, the churches, the Establishment—and about the future itself. In the major cities of the East (though perhaps not in the West) there is a sense that time is against you, that one is living "in one of the few decent neighborhoods left," that "if I can get $125 a week upstate (or downstate) I'll move." The institutions that were supposed to mediate social change and which, more than ever, are becoming priesthoods of information and conglomerates of social engineers, are increasingly suspect. To attack the Ford Foundation (as Wright Patman has done) is not only to fan the embers of historic populism against concentrations of wealth and power, but also to arouse those who feel that they are trapped by an alliance of upperclass Wasps and lower-class Negroes. If the foundations have done anything for the blue-collar worker he doesn't seem to be aware of it. At the same time the distrust of professional educators that characterizes the black militants is becoming increasingly prevalent among a minority of lower-middle-class whites who are beginning to discover that the schools aren't working for them either. ("Are all those new programs just a cover-up for failure?") And if the Catholic Church is under attack from its liberal members (on birth control, for example) it is also alienating the traditionalists who liked their minor saints (even if they didn't actually exist) and were perfectly content with the Latin Mass. For the alienated Catholic liberal there are other places to go; for the lower-middle-class parishioner in Chicago or Boston there are none.

Perhaps in some measure, it has always been this way. Perhaps none of this is new. And perhaps it is also true that the American lower middle has never had it so good. And yet surely there is a difference, and that is that the common man has lost his visibility and, somehow, his claim on public attention. There are old liberals and socialists—men like Michael Harrington—who believe that a new alliance can be forged for progressive social action:

> *From Marx to Mills, the Left has regarded the middle class as a stratum of hypocritical, vacillating rear-guarders. There was often sound reason for this contempt. But is it not possible that a new class is coming into being? It is not the old middle class of small property owners and entrepreneurs, nor the new middle class of managers. It is composed of scientists, technicians, teachers, and professionals in the public sector of the society. By education and work experience it is predisposed toward planning. It could be an ally of the poor and the organized workers—or their sophisticated enemy. In other words, an unprecedented social and political variable seems to be taking shape in America.*
>
> *The American worker, even when he waits on a table or holds open a door, is not servile; he does not carry himself like an inferior. The openness, frankness, and democratic manner which Tocqueville described in the last century persists to this very day. They have been a source of rudeness, contemptuous ignorance, violence— and of a creative self-confidence among great masses of people. It was in this latter spirit that the CIO was organized and the black freedom movement marched.*

There are recent indications that the white lower middle class is coming back on the roster of public priorities. Puncinski tells you that liberals in Congress are privately discussing the pressure from the middle class. There are proposals now to increase personal income-tax exemptions from $600 to $1,000 (or $1,200) for each dependent, to protect all Americans with a national insurance system covering catastrophic medical expenses, and to put a floor under all incomes. Yet these things by themselves are insufficient. Nothing is sufficient without a national sense of restoration. What Pucinski means by the middle class has, in some measure, always been represented. A physician earning $75,000 a year is also a working man but he is hardly a victim of the welfare system. Nor, by and large, are the stockholders of the Standard Oil Company or U.S. Steel. The fact that American ideals have often been corrupted in the cause of self-agrandizement does not make them any less important for the cause of social reform and justice. "As a movement with the conviction that there is more to people than greed and fear," Harrington said, "the Left must . . . also speak in the name of the historic idealism of the United States."

The issue, finally, is not *the program* but the vision, the angle of view. A huge constituency may be coming up for grabs, and there is considerable evidence that its political mobility is more sensitive than anyone can imagine, that all the sociological determinants are not as significant as the simple facts of concern and leadership. When Robert Kennedy was killed last year, thousands of working-class people who had expected to vote for him—if not hundreds of thousands—shifted their loyalties to Wallace. A man who can change from a progressive democrat into a bigot overnight deserves attention.

THE TROUBLED AMERICAN
A Special Report on the White Majority

Newsweek

All through the skittish 1960s, America has been almost obsessed with its alienated minorities—the incendiary black militant and the welfare mothers, the hedonistic hippie and the campus revolutionary. But now the pendulum of public attention is in the midst of one of those great swings that profoundly change the way the nation thinks about itself. Suddenly, the focus is on the citizen who outnumbers, outvotes and could, if he chose to, outgun the fringe rebel. After years of feeling himself a besieged minority, the man in the middle —representing America's vast white middle-class majority—is giving vent to his frustration, his disillusionment—and his anger.

"You better watch out," barks Eric Hoffer, San Francisco's bare-knuckle philosopher. "The common man is standing up and someday he's going to elect a policeman President of the United States."

How fed up is the little guy, the average white citizen who has been dubbed "the Middle American"? Is the country sliding inexorably toward an apocalyptic spasm—perhaps racial or class warfare or a turn to a grass-roots dictator who would promise to restore domestic tranquility by suppressing all dissent and unrest? To get a definitive reading on the mood of the American majority, *Newsweek* commissioned The Gallup Organization to survey the white population with special attention to the middle-income group—the blue- and white-collar families who make up three-fifths of U.S. whites.

The survey, bolstered by reports from *Newsweek* correspondents around the country, suggests that the average American is more deeply troubled about this country's future than at any time since the Great Depression. The surface concerns are easy to catalogue: a futile war abroad and a malignant racial atmosphere at home, unnerving inflation and scarifying crime rates, the implacable hostility of much of the young. But the Middle American malaise cuts much deeper—right to those fundamental questions of the sanctity of work and the

"The Troubled American," **NEWSWEEK,** *October 6, 1969. Copyright Newsweek, Inc., 1969. Reprinted by permission of the publisher.*

stability of the family, of whether a rewarding middle-class life is still possible in modern America.

America has always been the most middle-class of nations, the most generous and the most optimistic. But the pressures of the times have produced confused and contradictory impulses among the people Richard Nixon likes to call "the forgotten Americans." Himself a prototypical expression of the middle-class majority ("These are my people," he says. "We speak the same language"), the President presides over a nation nervously edging rightward in a desperate try to catch its balance after years of upheaval.

The reassertion of traditional values has festooned millions of automobile windows with American-flag decals, generated nationwide crusades to restore prayers to the schoolroom, to ban sex education, to curb pornography. The uneasy new mood has also spawned a coast-to-coast surge to law-and-order politicians—one of them a roly-poly Malaprop named Mario Procaccino, who may oust America's most outspokenly progressive major, John V. Lindsay, in New York City, once the Athens of American liberalism.

For the Negro, the turn in the tide can have the most momentous consequences. More and more American institutions are opening their doors to Negroes—mostly as a result of the social momentum generated in the Kennedy-Johnson years. Still, with the Nixon Administration setting the tone, the country seems to be retreating from active concern with its black minority—as the nation did nearly a century ago with the demise of Reconstruction. Self-reliant or self-delusive, the trend to separatism among younger blacks only intensifies the withdrawal. More ominous, even well-educated liberal whites have begun once more to speak openly of genetic differences between the races, an intellectual vogue before the turn of the century. "One has to consider the evidence that the Negro may be inherently inferior to the white and incapable of competing with him," says an MIT professor. "Look at the ones who have succeeded—they're almost all light-colored."

Such talk is only the tip of the iceberg. All around the country—especially among blue-collar workers—whites feel increasingly free to voice their prejudices and their hostility. "Everybody wants a gun," reports a community worker in a Slavic neighborhood in Milwaukee. "They think they've heard from black power, wait till they hear from white power—the little slob, GI Joe, the guy who breaks his ass and makes this country go. Boy, he's getting sick and tired of all this mess. One day he'll get fed up and when he does, look out! " A sign of the times: near-violent demonstrations by white construction workers enraged by Negro job demands in Pittsburgh last month and again last week in Chicago.

Newsweek's survey yielded provocative evidence of a deep crisis of the spirit in Middle America—but so far, at least, no real indication of outright rebellion. The average white American feels relatively optimistic about his own personal prospects, but he fears that the country itself has changed for the worse, that it will deteriorate further in years to come, that his government is not coping with its problems, that America's troubles may be so overwhelming that the nation may not be able to solve them at all. He thinks the war in Vietnam is America's most pressing concern right now, feels it was probably a mistake to send American troops to fight it, but has no clear idea how to get them home with honor. He gives President Nixon a generally favorable rating (highest in the South) and is inclined to prolong the new President's honeymoon, but he shows no deep enthusiasm for Mr. Nixon.

He bitterly opposes much of what is happening in the country. The Middle American complains that standards of morality have declined and that the exploitation of sex and nudity in the mass media erodes morals further every passing day. He is relentlessly opposed to violent tactics by blacks and campus radicals and believes that the police should have more power to curb crime and unrest. Out of perversity or ignorance, he is convinced that Negroes actually have a better chance to get ahead in America than he does and that any troubles blacks suffer are probably their own fault. Yet he does not reject black aspirations altogether. And, despite his rejection of campus revolutionaries, the average white has a favorable attitude about young people and thinks much of their criticism of the society is warranted. Perhaps most encouraging of all, the middle-class American wants the government to start moving on the nation's domestic ills. Even though he grumbles that taxes are too high, he would favor spending money on such programs as training for the unemployed and housing for the ghetto poor.

The statistics flesh out only one dimension of the story, of course. For all the essential stability the numbers indicate, the people of Middle America talk with eloquent bitterness or forlorn resignation about the state of the nation. There is a strong strain of fear in their conversation. "The honest person doesn't stand a chance because of what the Supreme Court has done" a Boston cabbie complained to a *Newsweek* correspondent. "People are scared and they've changed. Ten years ago if you were getting beaten up you could expect some help. Now people just walk by—they're afraid for their lives." In Inglewood, Calif., a dentist wonderingly recalls a confrontation with a booted band of motorcyclists' "When the light changed they didn't move off so I blew my horn. One of them yelled, 'What do you want, you old son of a bitch?' I was so scared and nervous I didn't even get their license numbers."

There is a pervasive feeling of being cheated by the affluent society. "Why, I can't even afford a color-TV set!" explodes a Los Angeles plumber. And there is the conviction that the government has its priorities wrong. "They spend $50 million to send a f——— monkey around the moon and there are people starving at home," growls a Milwaukee garage man.

But most of all there is a sense of loss and neglect. No hero to millions of Americans in life, John F. Kennedy has been elevated in death to an almost magical place in the hearts of his countrymen. "Kennedy put the spirit back in people," says a factory hand in Tyler, Texas. "He would have done some good if they would of gave him some time and hadn't killed him." And, feeling himself the spokesman of the oppressed majority, a hard-hatted San Francisco construction worker gripes: "The niggers are all organized. So are the Mexicans, even the Indians. But who the hell speaks for me?" Adds Paul Deac, head of the National Confederation of American Ethnic Groups: "We spend millions and the Negroes get everything and we get nothing."

Resentment over compensatory programs for blacks feeds the Middle American's sense of himself as the ultimate victim. The experts typically disagree over whether the middle-class white is as victimized by the society as he feels himself to be. Some contend that the white reaction is a rational response to the squeeze of taxes and inflation (despite big wage increases the average factory worker's real income has declined $1.09 per week in the past year) and the authentic danger of rising crime. Others point out that Middle Americans tend to ignore the large government subsidies they get in such benefits as tax write-offs for mortgage interest payments; still others say unrealistic expectations are bred by the myth of affluence. "Middle-class people," says University of Michigan philosopher Abraham Kaplan, "look around and say, 'We've entered paradise and it looks like the place we just left. And if this is paradise why am I so miserable?'" Then, says Kaplan, they look for scapegoats among those who are attacking middle-class values.

Indeed, the most deeply rooted source of the white American malaise is the plain fact that middle-class values are under more obdurate attack today than ever before. "The values that we held so dear are being shot to hell," says George Culberson of the government's Community Relations Service. "Everything is being attacked—what you believe in, what you learned in school, in church, from your parents. So the middle class is sort of losing heart. They had their eyes on where they were going and suddenly it's all shifting sands."

The sands are shifting beneath all the familiar totems—the work ethic, premartial chastity, the notion of postponing gratification, and filial gratitude for parental sacrifice. Middle-class folk, says philosopher Kaplan, are infuriated by college demonstrations because they "upset their image of what college is—a place where there are trees, where the kids drink cocoa, eat marshmallows, read Shakespeare and once in the spring the boys can look at the girls' underthings." Says radical writer Paul Jacobs, once a union organizer: "The notion of work that they had been brought up to deify is being undermined by the young people. The hippies, Woodstock, all those broads walking around with their boobs bouncing. Not only do young people do it, but the media seem to approve it and the upper class does these things, too." Television is the most subversive enemy of the old ways. "Through television," says Anthony Downs, a consultant to LBJ's riot commission, "we are encouraging, on the consumption side, things which are entirely inconsistent with the disciplines necessary for our production side. Look at what television advertising encourages: immediate gratification, do it now, buy it now, pay later, leisure time, hedonism."

Beyond that, TV enhances the Middle American's feeling that he is enveloped in a chaotic world he never made and cannot control. "You have violence and sex and drugs on television," says Chicago psychiatrist Dr. Jarl Dyrud, whose patients are mostly drawn from the middle class. "You have the news about the Vietnam war, the protests of the kids on campus, the protests of the blacks. It's hard to escape any more." "Every time you turn around, there's a crisis of some sort," says community organizer Saul Alinsky, a brassy anti-Establishmentarian now concentrating his efforts on white communities. "You have the black crisis, the urban crisis—it's just one goddam crisis after another. It's just too much for the average middle-class Joe to take. There's always something else to worry about. But the worst thing about it for the middle class is that they feel powerless to do anything about anything."

The more precarious a family's hold on economic security, the more menaced it feels by the pressures of black militancy and inflation. The government estimates that it costs at least $10,000 a year for a family of four to maintain a moderate standard of living—yet 26.3 million white families fall below that level. And, despite nine consecutive years of prosperity, many a breadwinner can't forget the specter of the wolf in the carport. "Blue collar and white collar alike still live too near 'layoffs,' 'reductions,' 'strikers,' 'plant relocations' to be personally secure," says former HUD Under Secretary Robert Wood, now head of the Harvard-MIT Joint Center for Urban Studies.

With little equity but his mortgaged home and his union card, the white worker is especially resistant to integration efforts that appear to threaten his small stake in the world. "I believe that an apprenticeship in my union is no more a public trust to be shared by all, than a millionaire's money is a public trust," one worker wrote to The New York Times. "Why should the government . . . have any more right to decide how I dispose of my heritage than it does how the corner grocer disposes of his? " "Second-generation people inherit from their parents a reverence for their own home," says Rep. Roman Pucinski, a Chicago Democrat who takes the pulse of his district each Saturday. "The Polish have a word, *grunt*—a base, a foundation. They know integration has to come, but their big concern is property values."

The hunt for scapegoats goes beyond the blacks to their allies: the liberal white elite. Many lower-middle-class whites feel that an unholy alliance has grown up between the liberal Establishment and Negro militants to reshape American life at their expense. School busing to achieve integration, for example, is probably the least popular social nostrum of the 1960s. And the Kerner commission's well-publicized conclusion that "white racism" is the basic cause of black riots touched off howls of indignation. "They resent their leaders' hypocrisy," says Paul Jacobs, "—especially the rich liberal politicians who send their own kids to private school."

There has always been a streak of anti-intellectualism in Middle America. It bubbles to the surface when the country feels itself betrayed—as it did in the days before Joe McCarthy's rampages. All through the late 1960s, liberals and radicals have been predicting a revival of know-nothingism. So far, it has failed to materialize to any great degree—although George Wallace did his best last year with his diatribes against "pointy heads" and such enemies of the common man. Today, a growing sense of betrayal undoubtedly is percolating in many middle-class hearts. The anti-middle-class bias of college radicals contributes to the problem. "Many of the young people see middle-class people as nothing but a bunch of big-bosomed, beer-drinking, drum-and-bugle-corps types," says Rep. Allard Lowenstein, who tries to keep up his contacts both on the campus and in his middle-class Long Island district.

S. I. Hayakawa, who became something of a middle American folk hero by suppressing demonstrations at San Francisco State College last year, thinks the educated elite is dangerously out of touch with the middle-class masses. "You and I," he tells a visitor "can live in the suburbs and demand integration in the schools downtown. We can make the moral demands and someone else has to live with them. We can say the war in Vietnam is a dirty, immoral act while our children are in college, exempt from the draft. The working people's children are in Vietnam and they're praying for victory. They want to believe America is right."

More bluntly, Eric Hoffer rages: "We are told we have to feel guilty. We've been poor all our lives and now we're being preached to by every son of a bitch who comes along. The ethnics are discovering that you can't trust those May-flower boys."

Hoffer's observation is symptomatic of the new mood of ethnic chauvin-ism taking hold in Middle America. "The rise of Negro militancy," says Con-gressman Pucinski, "has brought a revival of ethnic orientation in all the other groups." The hard truth is that the celebrated American melting pot has never worked quite so well in life as in nostalgic myth. As Nathan Glazer and Daniel P. Moynihan pointed out six years ago in "Beyond the Melting Pot," Americans tend to maintain their sense of ethnic identity far more tenaciously than was once supposed. One result of the new white nationalism is a greater willingness to express anti-black feelings-intensified by Negro job competition. "They've always been anti-Negro," says one union hand. "But they've never been pres-sured to say it publicly before."

In the current atmosphere, liberal groups are devoting new attention to the hyphenated American. The American Jewish Committee has conducted sub-stantial research on the subject, and Americans for Democratic Action is making a major thrust to try to keep ethnic voters in the Democratic coalition. "Any politician who ignores 40 million ethnics is a fool," says Leon Shull, executive director of the ADA. Paul Deac, of the Washington-based ethnic lobby, is trying to pry anti-poverty money and other considerations for his people from the Administration. "Right now, the ethnic vote is up for grabs," insists Deac. "Our people are as gun-shy of the Republicans as of the liberal Democrats. If the Republicans grab the opportunity they can forge an alliance with ethnics and remain in power for a long time."

Except for the Italians, few of the nation's later immigrant groups have had much use for the Republican Party. And no one can say for certain how successful Richard Nixon will be if he tries to entice ethnic voters into his new centrist coalition. The President's strong anti-Communist stand over the years—and his recent trip to Rumania—are likely to enhance Mr. Nixon's appeal. Just such a thrust is at the heart of a GOP battle plan devised by Kevin P. Phillips, a 28-year-old Justice Department aide, in a much-discussed book called "The Emerging Republican Majority." As Phillips envisages it, the Republicans could cement their hold by building an alliance based on the South and the traditional heartland, and whites disgruntled by Democratic "social engineering." The Pres-ident professed last week not to have read the book. And, basically, Mr. Nixon will stand or fall on his over-all ability to convince America that he can end the war, reorder priorities and bring greater stability to the U.S.

On that score, the President seems to have a number of advantages. "Nixon is tremendously reassuring to middle-class Americans," says sociologist Robert Nisbet of the University of California at Riverside. "If you started out to design a human being who would be an answer for this kind of person in this kind of time, you couldn't design a better one than Nixon. His kind of corny, square, ketchup-on-cottage-cheese image is very reassuring to these people." What's more, says Brandeis University historian John Roche, who was once LBJ's intellectual-in-residence, government—Nixon style—has reduced the level of disorder in America. "The edge is already off," says Roche, "because the election of Nixon put into office people who are not going to be responsible for demonstrations. There will be no great riots—you don't riot against your enemies but against your friends, because you know your friends don't shoot. [Attorney General John] Mitchell means business."

Even if he should end the war and further cool the ghettos and campuses, the President faces the more fundamental problem of giving the white majority a greater sense of participation and reward in the life of the society. And he must somehow accomplish this while maintaining the nation's commitments to its non-white minorities, especially the Negroes. "The ethnic groups, the Irish and the Jews don't want to penalize the Negro but they feel strongly that the rules they came up with should apply," says Roche. "To change rules now is basically unfair."

"We need more programs for Mr. Forgotten American," says a Washington liberal. The fact is, however, that very little thought has gone into the problems of the white middle class. Foundations and think tanks have primarily been concerned with the plight of the minorities. A turnabout of sorts is under way. The Harvard-MIT Joint Center for Urban Studies has made Middle America its target subject for the new year, and the Ford Foundation plans to focus some of its attention on the middle class. Concrete ideas are sparse. Mitchell Sviridoff, Ford's vice president for national affairs, speaks rather vaguely of expanding medicaid programs and of retraining the middle-aged white worker trapped in a dead-end assembly-line job.

But the underlying necessity is to find the national resources to help both the majority white and his non-white counterpart. "We've stimulated the minorities to believe that something is going to happen for them. If we slow down, as we have, their frustrations will be so seriously exacerbated that they will be pushed to more militant behavior," argues Sviridoff. "Then the majority will be pushed to more repressive behavior and we will have an absolutely impossible situation on our hands."

Some think that the problem goes far beyond the reach of even the most imaginative government. "When the hippies go to Woodstock," says Paul Jacobs, "they are building a new community of their own. The worker's community is disintegrating. He doesn't know where to find a new one. So he keeps harking back to the old days and the old values. But it is not possible to go back. And there is no new community to replace the old."

Can Middle America somehow create a new pluralist community to satisfy its new needs? On the answer to that question rests much of the destiny of the nation in the years ahead.

HOW IT FEELS TO BE CAUGHT IN THE MIDDLE

In this harvest season of 1969, that is the voice of Middle America—the white middle class, the backbone of the country, the people who have taken to thinking of themselves as "forgotten."

Newsweek's special poll of white Americans, conducted by The Gallup Organization in an unusually wide sampling of public opinion, found the white majority profoundly troubled—but not, as some have suggested, on the brink of violent rebellion. There is a heavy undertone of resentment—a dark suspicion that the rules are being changed in the middle of the game, that the dice are loaded in somebody else's favor. But at bottom, the mood adds up to a nagging sense that life is going sour-that, whatever is wrong, the whole society somehow has lost its way.

This new pessimism has serious implications for the nation, because Middle America, in a real sense, *is* America. For the *Newsweek* survey, Gallup interviewers talked to 2,165 adults comprising a cross-section of the entire white population (which, in turn, is almost 90 per cent of the total population). The sample included a middle-class group large enough for detailed analysis: 1,321 Americans with household incomes ranging from $5,000 to $15,000, representing 61 per cent of the white population.

LOOKING AHEAD: PESSIMISM

	Agree	Disagree	No Change
The U.S. has changed for the worse over the past decade	46%	36%	13%
The danger of racial violence is increasing	59%	26%	12%
The U.S. is likely to change for the worse over the next decade	58%	19%	14%
The U.S. is less able to solve its problems than it was five years ago	40%	40%	16%

Undecided omitted

By themselves, the Middle Americans are a majority of the nation—and the strength of their opinions outweighs their numbers. In the *Newsweek* Poll, the attitudes of the middle-income group showed hardly any significant variation from those of the total white group on any question.

As the Middle American sees it, his country is beset by a sea of troubles. The war in Vietnam oppresses the nation—nearly two out of three of those polled

WANTED: 'LAW AND ORDER'

	Yes	No
Local police do a good job of preventing crime	78%	16%
Police should have more power	63%	35%
Suspects who might commit another crime before they come to trial should be held without bail	68%	23%
Black militants have been treated too leniently	85%	8%
College demonstrators have been treated too leniently	84%	11%

Undecided omitted

cite it as one of America's top problems. "I don't like a war where there couldn't be a winner," complains an electrician in Mineral Wells, Texas. There is the endless, abrasive racial crisis, mentioned by 41 per cent. "We could have a civil war," warns a county employee in Stanwood, Wash. There are the nagging pocketbook issues: inflation erodes everybody's pay check, and 78 percent think Federal taxes are just plain too high. There is crime and delinquency and a gnawing feeling of powerlessness. The government, says a Chicago truck driver, "doesn't know I exist—or care." And there is a sense that solid old values are crumbling. "Seems like we have lost respect for ourselves," says a housewife in Bellefontaine Neighbors, Mo.

Save for the war, the nation's brooding is almost exclusively inward. Only 2 per cent of the sampling thought to mention nuclear war as a problem facing the country; fewer than 1 per cent listed Russia or Red China. But the internal discontents are as varied as they are pervasive. "This sex education shouldn't be in the small grades, like I heard they're going to have," said the wife of a laborer in South Bend, Ind.

For all that, most middle-class Americans expect to prosper in coming years. Nearly two-thirds of the sampling feel that five years from now they will be at least as well off as they are today—or better off. But they are afraid they will enjoy it less. Fully 46 per cent agree that the nation has changed for the worse in the past ten years. Opinion splits on whether the United States can solve its problems at all. Fifty-nine per cent believe that the danger of racial conflict is on the rise—and 58 per cent feel that the United States, on the whole, is likely to change for the worse in the years ahead.

Middle America itself is hardly monolithic; its over-all statistical unity conceals many shadings of opinions. The biggest differences match educational levels. Thus, people who went to college tend to have better jobs, earn more money and be more tolerant on racial issues and less disturbed by youth protests. Those whose education ended in grade school tend to hold blue-collar jobs—and to be financially insecure and angry over the accelerating pace of social change. The educational split was neatly shown by a question asking whether the United States is becoming too materialistic. Some 54 per cent of those who had gone to college agreed—but only 36 per cent of the grade-school group would go along.

Other significant divisions of opinion stem from age, sex and region of the country. Women, for instance, tend to be less hawkish than men on Vietnam. Westerners worry most about drugs and air pollution. And surprisingly, adults under 30 tend to disapprove of modern youth more vehemently than do people aged 30 to 55.

Despite these internal differences, however, Middle America is united in its discontent—and, increasingly, sees itself as an oppressed majority. "I think the middle class is getting the short end of the stick on everything," says a computer technician from Brooklyn. "The welfare people get out of taxes, and so do the rich," says a construction foreman in Baltimore. "The middle-class family is just forgotten."

The worst frustration is the war in Vietnam. It is, by now, a war that has come very close to home; 55 per cent of the *Newsweek* Middle American sampling said they were personally acquainted with someone who had been killed or wounded in Vietnam. Yet people are frankly and bitterly confused as to the conduct of the war, the reasons for American involvement and what should be done next.

There is general agreement on only one thing: that the war is not going well. Only 8 per cent believe that the U.S. and South Vietnam are winning. One in five said the war was being lost, and two-thirds of the sampling opted for the euphemistic "holding our own." Nearly three in five said the U.S. was justified in intervening in the war—but 70 per cent argued that, justified or not, the nation should have kept its sons at home.

At the extremes, hawks and doves were almost evenly divided. Approximately one in five said that the U.S. had "no right or reason" to fight in Vietnam; one in four said it was "our right and duty." In volunteered opinions, however, the strongest expressions were hawkish, with 21 per cent urging a more aggressive, fight-to-win policy. "I can't figure it out," complained a retired sand-and-gravel dealer in Fort Loramie, Ohio, "If you can't go into North Vietnam, what's the use of fighting? If you hit me and go into the next room and I can't follow, what the hell's the use?" "Don't bomb here, don't bomb there—it's a cuddly war," snapped a nurse who lives in East Keansburg, N.J. "They should blast them all and come home."

In contrast, the dovish opinions sounded oddly uncertain; opponents of the war cited passionless arguments on the theme that the U.S. should not have been involved in the first place, or that it was time for the war to end. "I can't remember when we started fighting there," said 22-year-old William H. Neumann Jr., manager of a restaurant in Sarasota, Fla., "but I do think we should have been out a long time ago." One of the most curious findings of the survey was the almost total absence of moral arguments against the war. Despite the clamor of the most vocal doves over the past four years, only a handful of the sampling argued that the war was simply wrong. Instead, opinions both pro and con were thoroughly pragmatic; as a New York City housewife phrased her case: "There's nothing to be gained."

On issues closer to home, the Middle American is considerably more emotional. He is in a financial vise, with inflation and rising taxes threatening what precarious security he has—and to make this threat worse, black Americans are demanding an ever-greater economic share.

Resentment of Negroes is at once the most obvious and the most complex note in the new mood of Middle America. It is not outright racism, in the sense that Negroes are hated because they are black. As recently as 1966, a *Newsweek* survey found white Americans agreeing, by more than 2 to 1, that Negroes were discriminated against and deserved better. Fully 70 per cent of whites then said that, like it or not, they would probably be living in integrated housing in five years' time—and there was a similarly grudging acceptance of black gains in jobs and education. But with this acceptance went a strong feeling among whites that Negroes were trying to win too much, too fast—and this attitude is as strong as ever.

Recent progress for Negroes—particularly in jobs, education and housing— has come partly at the expense of the middle class. What's worse, some black demands and white-liberal rhetoric have focused on the concept of reparations for years in discrimination—an idea that Middle America sees simply as a new form of reverse discrimination. "I see the Negro stepping on my rights," said a finance manager in Los Angeles. "He is asking for more than is justifiably his."

Whatever the facts of the case, a substantial minority of white America professes to believe that the black man already has the advantage. More than four out of ten in the sampling said Negroes actually have a better chance than whites to get a good job or a good education for their children, and nearly two-thirds said Negroes got preference in unemployment benefits from the government. "The Negroes think they are having a disadvantage, which is not true," said Mrs. John Tiedje, in Clarksville, N.Y. Ludicrous as the idea sounds to Negroes, many Middle Americans are convinced that police and the courts give blacks especially lenient treatment. "It looks," said an oil-refinery worker in Galena Park, Texas, "like whites don't have the rights that Negroes do."

Blacks are also perceived by many as morally different from whites: they don't seem to live by the rules of the basically Puritan white middle class. "They are given jobs by good companies and they don't work," says a New York policeman. "The backers of the Negro are making them think that we owe them jobs, and we owe them housing, food, money, for nothing." This attitude is astonishingly widespread; 73 per cent of the *Newsweek* sampling agreed that blacks "could have done something" about slum conditions, and 55 per cent thought Negroes were similarly to blame for their unemployment rate. What's more, nearly four out of five declared that half or more of the nation's welfare recipients—who tend to be thought of mainly as Negroes—could earn their own way if they tried.

With such basic attitudes, it is hardly surprising that Middle America shows little enthusiasm for what it thinks of as sacrifice to advance the black cause. In education for instance, only 2 per cent of those polled favored busing to improve racial balance in the schools. In fact, only one out of four favored further integration at all. Given their choice, nearly two-thirds would either improve Negro schools or let blacks run their own schools.

Even this attitude is not unalloyed bigotry. Unfashionable as it is to credit racial rationalizations at face value, much white middle-class opposition to integration reflects a genuine fear that the quality of education may deteriorate. And for all his resentment at black activism, the Middle American still has a

THE BLACKS: TOO MUCH, TOO SOON?

Do Negroes today have a better chance or worse chance than people like yourself—	*Better*	*Worse*	*Same*
To get well-paying jobs?	44%	21%	31%
To get a good education for their children?	41%	16%	41%
To get good housing at a reasonable cost?	35%	30%	27%
To get financial help from the government when they're out of work?	65%	4%	22%

Undecided omitted

basic sympathy for the Negro's aspirations. Significantly, nearly seven out of ten agreed that at least some of the demands presented by Negro leaders were justified. Equally to the point, the same proportion also agreed that "it will take some time" to meet the demands.

White America's prejudice is most obvious when it comes to the crime problem—which large numbers automatically associate with Negroes. "We are really afraid," said a North Carolina woman, "with the colored right in our backyard." Asked to define "law and order," an investment adviser in King of Prussia, Pa., said "Get the niggers. Nothing else."

Crime, the survey showed, is considered one of the nation's most serious problems—but oddly enough, it is generally thought to be worst in somebody else's backyard. Only 10 per cent of the sampling volunteered crime in their own listing of the nation's problems, and fewer than half considered it a serious issue in their own communities. Yet nearly two-thirds checked it off as one of the worst problems facing the cities—and suburbanites were more likely to think so than city dwellers themselves.

Despite the furor over crime in recent months, only three in ten said they had changed their habits to protect themselves; those few were mainly locking doors and windows formerly left unlatched. And despite widespread reports of an arms buildup, only 4 per cent volunteered that they kept guns to protect themselves, and fewer than 1 per cent said they had installed burglar alarms. Others mentioned tear gas and judo lessons. "We've started feeding an ugly dog," reported David Ingraham, owner of a service station in Clarksville, N.Y.

Nearly four out of five are satisfied with their local police, reporting that the officers do a good job of preventing local crime. Nonetheless, 63 per cent of the sampling said police didn't have enough power in dealing with suspected criminals, and more than two-thirds agreed that judges should have the right to deny pretrial bail to suspects considered likely to commit a crime while on the loose—a crime-fighting step of dubious constitutionality.

A significant minority worried that more police power could bring on a police state—"Hitler had law and order," observed Mrs. Marjorie Runner, a San Francisco housewife. But the majority of those polled were convinced that thugs were getting too many breaks. To most people, the possibility of added police power offers no conceivable threat to anyone but wrongdoers. "Behave yourself and there's no problem," declared a construction worker in Wichita, Kans. "I think of law and order as what I do."

BLACK SCHOOLS—OR MIXED?

What should be done about Negro demands for better education?

Improve schools where Negro children go	40%
Move toward integration	25%
Let Negroes run their own schools	24%
Integrate schools by busing children	2%
Ignore demands because they are not justified	3%

Undecided omitted

If crime is a threat to the Middle American's safety, the much-publicized youth rebellion is an equally real challenge to his self-esteem. Whether picketing on campus or parading barefoot in hippie regalia, the younger generation seems to be telling him that his way of life is corrupt, his goals worthless and his treasured institutions doomed. Logically enough, a good many middle-class citizens tend to resent the message. "It's horrible. They are going to the dogs," said Mrs. Cecil L. Davis of Wichita Falls, Texas. The overwhelming majority in the poll made it clear that they had little sympathy for the outright rebels among the younger generation; 84 per cent said campus demonstrators had been treated too leniently, and nearly three out of five said the demonstrators had little or no justification for their actions.

Nonetheless, most Middle Americans make a clear distinction between youthful rebels and the greater number of what they think of as normal youngsters. "These college rioters should be put in concentration camps," said Herbert R. Parsons Jr., a furniture store manager of Peru, Ind. "But by and large, the majority are fine young people," Some 59 per cent of those polled agreed that their impression of most young people was favorable.

And in his heart, the Middle American isn't all that sure that even the rebels are altogether wrong. Some 54 per cent of those polled, in fact, agreed that young people were not unduly critical of their country, and that criticism was actually needed. But this sentiment reflects not so much tolerance of the young as a deep-seated fear that the whole system is somehow failing, that the quality of life is declining and that the middle-class citizen's own place is no longer secure.

This painful awareness that things just aren't what they used to be is at the bottom of the nation's new discontent. "Conditions are changing for the worse," mused a farmer from Bald Knob, Ark. "Conditions are unstable, and getting worse." Solid old values seem to be deteriorating; seven-tenths of the sampling

U.S. SPENDING: NEW PRIORITIES

On which problems do you think the government should be spending more money—and on which should it be spending less money?

	More Money	Less Money
Job training for the unemployed	56%	7%
Air and water pollution	56%	3%
Fighting organized crime	55%	3%
Medical care for the old and needy	47%	5%
Fighting crime in the streets	44%	4%
Improving schools	44%	7%
Providing better housing for the poor—especially in the ghettos	39%	13%
Building highways	23%	14%
Defense expenditures	16%	26%
Space exploration	10%	56%
Foreign economic aid	6%	57%
Foreign military aid	1%	66%

agreed that people now were less religious than they were five years ago, and 86 per cent said sexual permissiveness was undermining the nation's morals. "I really worry sometimes about this country, if we don't change our ways and return to religion," said another farmer in Timmonsville, S.C.

And this erosion of values extends to the interpersonal links that foster security and stability in any society. Only 39 per cent of those polled feel most people "really care" what happens to strangers. About the same percentage said it wasn't likely that anyone would help them if they were robbed on the street in their own neighborhoods. More than half said they put only "some" trust in the news media and the Federal government to tell the truth about what was going on; some 30 per cent said they had little trust or none at all. But however skeptical, Middle Americans feel increasingly powerless to shape their own destiny. In the face of the complexity of the modern world, a bare half of the sampling thought they should have any say in their country's defense and foreign policy. "We are not well-informed enough to give solutions," said a Chicago accountant.

What the middle class does want is stability—or at least the illusion of stability. If change is inevitable, in race relations, for example, it should come without upheaval. "I think Negroes have justified reasons," said the wife of a utility serviceman in St. Paul, Minn., "but they are going about it in the wrong way with the wrong leaders."

In such a national dilemma, it would be natural for people to turn on their leaders—and there is, to be sure, no lack of grumbling in Middle America about the government. Only 24 per cent of the sampling said the government was doing a "good" or "excellent" job of dealing with the nation's problems; two-thirds said "fair" or "poor."

The grumbling is loudest, of course, over the pocketbook issues of taxes and inflation. Despite the vaunted prosperity of the nation during the 1960s, one out of every four middle-class Americans said the rising cost of living had forced a cutback on purchases; another 44 per cent said they were just managing to stay even. Nearly eight out of ten said Federal taxes were too steep, and 59 per cent thought local taxes excessive. "We had to sell our home because our taxes were too high," said G.W. Loenstein, a retired grocer in Oakland, Calif.

For the most part, however, the middle class has a weary sort of tolerance for their elected representatives. "It's not really the government's fault," said Thomas Silevitch, a Christmas-tree bulb maker in Dorchester, Mass. "The government can't solve everyone's problems." Asked to rate President Nixon's performance in office, nearly half of the sampling—49 percent—gave him favorable marks, with 31 per cent less enthusiastic and only 15 percent down-right critical. There was no great yearning for another leader; only 12 per cent thought the country would be better off with George Wallace at the helm, and a bare 10 per cent thought Hubert Humphrey would do better. But there was little enthusiasm for Mr. Nixon. In fact, people had a tendency to praise him with faint damns, explaining their ratings by saying that he had done all right so far, or seemed to be working for peace. "He is doing the best he can with the ability he has, which I don't think is too much," said a housewife in Jacksonville, Fla.

Whatever its resentments and frustrations, then, Middle America is not about to take to the barricades—or even to slump into mulish apathy. Indeed, the most encouraging finding of the *Newsweek* Poll is the extent to which people are willing to seek fresh solutions; a clear plurality of 48 per cent agreed that "we need to experiment with new ways of dealing with the nation's problems." Even the celebrated tax revolt turns out, on close scrutiny, to be a paper dragon. The chief complaint is not so much the level of taxation but rather that the government has its priorities wrong. "Nobody has the right to take a hardworking man's money and waste it, but they all do," said Mrs. Margaret Donovan, a housewife in Albany, N.Y. "Our money just isn't used right."

By a clear margin, the middle class is more concerned with solving problems than with governmental economies. Asked how the government should use any unexpected surplus in revenues, fully 48 per cent said the money should go to improve conditions in the country; only one in three favored a tax cut, and 16 per cent wanted to reduce the national debt. In specific terms, the sampling favored added spending for such programs as job training, pollution control, medicare, slum housing and crime control. But a good many thought money was being wasted in foreign aid and defense spending—and even in the afterglow of the moon landing, fully 56 per cent thought the government should spend less on space.

In the end, this willingness to tackle the nation's problems tempers Middle America's pessimism. "Change is not bad," said John King, a Mississippi cattle raiser. "But there may be a period of time when things worsen before we settle on a course again." In the long run, said the owner of a printing shop in Cleveland, "I have great confidence in our ability to find the right answers. We're great opportunists and improvisers." A touch of malaise may be fashionable, and all very well for a while, but it goes against the Middle American grain. If something has gone wrong, it will simply have to be fixed; after all, says a San Diego aircraft inspector, "We won't just sit around and let the country go down the drain." And in this troubled harvest season, the hope is that his is the real voice of the country.

THE SQUARE AMERICAN SPEAKS OUT[1]

Travels with Mister Charlie in white America. Talking to the folks. Not the Athletic Club fat cats, the poor white trash, the intellectual pointyheads, or the groovy people. Just the square American.

He wears white starched shirts, suits with baggy pants, work shirts with his name in red on the breast, white ankle-high cotton socks. Toothpicks. Lunch in a paper sack. Off-duty, bourbon and 7-up.

She wears wire-stiff bouffants, girdles, at-the-knee print dresses. She saves Green Stamps, is active in the Girl Scouts and PTA. A Bible adorns her coffee table and there's an American-flag decal on the family car. She lives for "the kids."

They live in a box-like suburban tract house or just ahead of the urban-renewal wreckers in a gritty, decayed inner-city neighborhood.

Vacation is visiting relatives, or staying home and painting the house. "Mother" doesn't play golf or have cocktail parties. A treat is dinner at the

---

[1] This segment of the report was written by Karl Fleming.

Burger King, or a movie. Family fun is a Sunday drive, a backyard hamburger barbecue, or watching TV. Television is more than ever the national narcotic for the financially immobilized. That's one reason the old spirit of neighborliness is dying.

As I rambled 5,000 miles across America, from Portland, Ore., to Springfield, Mass., from Milwaukee to Atlanta, talking to Middle Americans where I chanced upon them, they would say again and again that people just don't care about each other the way they once did.

One reason, they said, is the church. Its influence is rapidly declining and many of the once pious and faithful are now hostile and absent. Said an apostate in Minneapolis: "I used to go to church and the preacher would talk about God, Jesus and the Bible. Now he tells me why I shouldn't buy grapes."

People seemed almost pathetically eager to talk, as if nobody had ever asked before, and almost universally they were in a fretful, fearful, disquieted mood. What people seem to want above all else is order: they want everybody to just quiet down and quit threatening to destroy what they have worked so hard to build and preserve. They are hostile toward poor and rich alike—toward the poor for being on welfare, toward the rich for not paying taxes—and they are increasingly cynical about politicians.

It is a Saturday afternoon in a post-World War II neighborhood of modest GI homes on mimosa-lined streets in East Dallas, kids wheeling bikes and tricycles on the sidewalk.

Under the carport are brothers-in-law Eddie Franks and Jack Woodlee. They are pounding nails and sawing used lumber, converting the carport into a living room for Franks's three-bedroom home. Woodlee, dressed in overalls and brogans, a chubby carpenter's pencil over his ear, bites a wad out of a plug of Red Man chewing tobacco. "I got cows in the bank and money out west," he says sardonically. "Aw, hell, if the little people would stick together they could make the big boys get off their chairs and do something. But they won't."

"When taxes go up, they put them on us," says maintenance man Franks, wiping a sweaty hand on his T-shirt. "When I got married 22 years ago, I made 60 cents an hour and my wife was jerking sodas. We're not much better off now. I get mad when I see these rich kids tearing up the schools and throwing away that opportunity. I had to work. I would have liked to go to college so I could have a job where I could sit up there all day and be clean."

"Ain't no way," drawls sheet-metal worker Woodlee. "When the unions give us a raise, the supermarkets go up 2 cents on canned goods. And the politician don't help. He's only for himself."

"We shouldn't be spending all this money on foreign countries. All we get back is war," says Franks.

"The rich man ought to have to pay taxes. The country is supposed to be justice for all, not just for one or two, isn't it?" asks Woodlee. "But things ain't gonna get much better. The working man has always paid the load, fought the battles and come home with less money in his pocket."

Still, Woodlee and Franks lead relatively placid and pleasant lives within the bounds of their incomes. They enjoy their families. Most weekends, they load their pickup-truck camper and head for lake or wood to fish and hunt.

From one side of the little Wolf Lake city park in Hammond, Ind., billows of noxious smoke pour from a row of grim steel mills. From the other, plumes of nauseating fumes spew from a huge oil refinery. Blobs of green slime and yellow foam float along the shore. The narrow beach is crowded with swimmers and picnickers.

"Daddy, daddy, I went under. I was breathing and I seen bubbles," cries the dripping 5-year-old boy, rushing into the outstretched arms of truck driver Fred Huff, 41.

"Darlin', I told you to hold your breath," says Huff soothingly. He is there picnicking with his wife and four children. He rents the two-story downstairs half of a paint-peeled old wood house on nearby Carroll Street. There is a framed picture of Jesus on the dining-room wall, a single window air conditioner, under which his infant granddaughter naps on a cot when she visits.

Huff drives 2,000 miles a week through five states. He and his wife, who works as a truck-line dispatcher, earn about $10,000 a year. His eldest son, 22, lives at home, badly disabled from Vietnam mortar wounds.

"We're luckier than some. At least we got him back alive. I guess I'm more for the war than against it," Huff says uncertainly. "When some country is threatening your way of life, it has to be stopped somewhere. But I don't know. It's bad enough to lose all these boys. But for something that's pointless? No. I'm afraid it's gonna be another Korea."

Huff and his family haven't been away on vacation in ten years. But he watches the Cubs on TV, drinks a little beer and in general enjoys life. He doesn't really like Hammond. "It's just the money place to be," he says. "The steel mills and the refineries make the air so bad it smarts the old eyeballs and makes you nauseated. Everything is getting uglier and uglier. You can go 30 miles into the country and get away from it. But then it costs too much to commute. It's having an effect. People get irritated now over things they would have laughed at years ago. There's a lack of friendliness. No closeness. Half the time you don't even know who your neighbor is unless there's a fight. Something seems to have gone out of people.

"Life," he sighs, "is getting faster and furiouser. Sometimes you feel like throwing up your hands and saying to hell with it and going so far back in the hills they'll have to pipe sunshine in. We've only got a few more years to contend with it. That's why we rent, so when we're ready, all we have to do is pack and tell the kids good-by. Then mamma and I will bum around out West until we find a place. There's still a lot of beautiful country."

Of the people I talked to, the most frustrated and angry were those trapped in spirit-numbing jobs and in neighborhoods besieged by pollution, noise, traffic, decay and crime. The happiest were those whose jobs gave them some relief from tedium, and a chance to live near open fields and green trees, sunlight, creeks and country roads.

In the carpeted, brightly lit rear of Weiner's clothing store in sparkling Portland, Ore., jovial Jerry Semler is bantering with a customer.

"I'm just a shoe dog," he says. "I've been peddling shoes all my life. And in this business, if you're not happy, you're dead. I'd probably like to do something else, but I don't know what it would be.

"I love my wife. I've got three fine children. I've got a nice house in a middle-class neighborhood. Friends come over and we turn off the boob tube and talk. I get two weeks vacation a year—I go up to Lake Tahoe and booze it up a little. I'm my own man," he says happily.

Semler, 54, had a heart attack in 1956—"at 12:10, Sept. 30, sitting in a green chair"—but is as active these days as he ever was. "Whoever pulls the cards out of the rack upstairs wasn't ready to pull mine," he says.

The thing that bothers Semler the most is the war. "It just galls me every time someone is killed," he says. "Billions and billions of dollars, and I don't know how many have been killed in Vietnam. To pull their chestnuts out of the fire with the lives of our boys—unh-unh."

There is a picture of Custer's last stand on the wall. On the cluttered desk is a small American flag, the pledge inscribed on its base. Ray Brooks, shirt-sleeved editor of Sunland and Tujunga's semiweekly Record Ledger in the smoggy foothills of the Verdugo Mountains near Los Angeles, shakes his bald head sadly.

"We just seemed to be headed toward a collapse of everything," he muses. "I'm upset about the kids and the hippies and the absolute disregard for law and order and any kind of convention. It isn't the clothes. Hell, when I was a kid, I wore bell-bottom pants to school with silver bells on the side. But when I was the age of these hippies, I couldn't wait to get out and get a piece of capitalism and become part of the Establishment. But these kids grow up and don't want to be a part of it. That's what makes people mad. To these kids the future is nothing. To us, it was everything. It's sad. It's very sad."

Mrs. Emma Riel lives in a little three-bedroom home not far away from Brooks's newspaper office. To supplement her husband's $10,000 income as a sewer-equipment salesman, she sews and makes plastic-flower arrangements. Her gray hair is tied in a neat bun on the back of her head. Her pale blue eyes flash angrily. She nods toward the American flag that is mounted on the white picket fence in the front yard.

"Everybody wants the same thing: decency. But people like us don't count for anything any more," she says. "One woman can stop prayer in the schools. And a man with a prison record is patted on the head and told to go do it again. Because Mr. Warren handcuffed our police, our laws are not protecting anyone.

"And the kids—they want it all right now, the things it took us a lifetime to get. A bath, a haircut, and a good old-fashioned strap would get most of them back in line. But their mothers are too busy at cocktail parties and bridge clubs to be mothers."

Behind the long counter of the Nuttie Goodie Tea Room on Main Street in quiet Springfield, Mass., an aproned, open-faced George Layos, 36, stands frying eggs.

"I've never collected a day of welfare in my life," he says. "In my family, if you stay home and don't work, you're a bum and a criminal. These black guys think they've got it tough. When my father came to this country from Greece in

1910, he could speak five or six languages. People laughed at him and called him stupid.

"There's plenty of work around. These people just don't have backbone. They give them welfare just to keep them quiet. The police aren't tough enough. They're scared. I get nervous, too. Ten years ago if somebody came in here and gave me some baloney, I'd throw his ass out. Today, you never know if they're hopped up on dope or something. I see them take candy out of the counter and I just let them go. You never know what they're gonna do. If you and I stole a doughnut, we'd be put in jail. But they walk out with TV sets and the police are afraid to do anything about it."

The sign on the box office of Springfield's rundown Paramount Theater says, NO ONE WILL BE ALLOWED IN THE THEATER WITHOUT SHOES ON THEIR FEET. Up Main Street, in the city's biggest department store, Forbes & Wallace, dark-haired, sideburned salesman El Roth, 48, is carefully filling out a receipt. Just this morning, over eggs and toast, his daughter Barbara, 14, asked him if he thought 18-year-olds should be allowed to vote.

"Ordinarily, yes," he told her. "But the way they're acting now, I'd be afraid to let them vote."

"She just looked at me and smiled," he recalls. "But she's a good kid."

Like Layos, Roth frets about looters and lawbreakers. "People are fed up with the way 1 per cent of the population is allowed to have legal theft with police looking the other way. Looters should be shot, whether they're 6 foot 9, 2 foot 6, green or yellow. It's all just stealing," he says. "But in this store, if you see a colored person take something, you don't say anything. The store might be hit. It isn't worth a $25 sweater."

Roth has a little side business—retail clothing—and lives fairly well, although he foresees the need for a government loan to send his two children to college. But he's not happy. "The pressure of wanting material things that I don't have is always there," he says.

It is a hot, smoggy morning in San Leandro, Calif., a middle-class white enclave on the outskirts of Oakland. On the gravel apron of Dick Linton's body shop, Jacks-of-all-trades Frank Reis, 48, and David Pedroza, 44, partners in a house-repairing business, are waiting for their truck to be fixed.

They are smoking, occasionally kicking their toes into the gravel, talking to proprietor Linton, a bald, squat man of 39 in a T-shirt.

Pedroza, who wears a toothpick-thin mustache, snarls: "Look at those riots. What the f——— do you think would happen to us if we went over there and started a riot"

Says Reis with a wry grin: "They'd kill us."

"F——— right they would," says Pedroza.

"Paint your face black and you can get a new Cadillac and the county will come in and feed your family. What do they call it? Prejudice, or something? That's all they've got to holler and they've got it made. Let a f——— patrolman stop me, and I've got to pay," says Reis.

"What do you think would happen to us if we went around calling police 'pigs'? And let me be starving and steal a loaf of bread and they'd throw my ass in jail. There's nobody behind us hollering 'prejudice'," says Linton.

"There's only one way to solve this, and that's gonna be with a revolution. I'm for fighting it out between us," Pedroza says angrily.

"And I'd go for that. Just give me a machine gun," Reis agrees.

"That's why I went out and bought me some guns," says Linton.

"What do you call dragging the American flag on the ground and burning draft cards and all that s———? " asks Reis.

"Treason," says Pedroza.

"We should have a Hitler here to get rid of the troublemakers the way they did with the Jews in Germany," says Reis.

He has one of those classic Texas faces: tanned leathery cheeks, a finely cut jaw, blue eyes, strong hands with which he rolls a cigarette from a Prince Albert can. Ray Compton, 47, is a farmer who raises 100 acres of okra which he sells to 150 markets and to retail customers at the Dallas municipal market. He works long, eighteen-hour days five months a year. But the rest of the year he fishes and hunts.

Compton sits with his feet propped up on the back of his red truck, his Texas hat pushed back.

"I'm like that man on the bucking horse: I ain't going anywhere. I just want to stay where I am," he drawls. He is incensed about welfare recipients, college demonstrators, draft dodgers and such. But he doesn't think the country is collapsing.

"The old backbone of America—they're still just as good as they were 100 years ago," he says. "With them it's still the land of the free and the home of the brave. But the United States has opened its doors to so many low-classed people. I tell you what: I could get 40 or 50 of my old South Pacific buddies with grease guns and stop all these damn riots. When ol' Mayor Daley give the police in Chicago the right to shoot to kill, it stopped all of that crap, didn't it? I betcha by God if ol' Wallace runs again he'll give them a run for their money."

Earnest (Pee Wee) Hayes is 58. For 37 years he has worked the same humdrum but grueling job at the Armco steel plant in Middletown, Ohio. His father migrated north from Kentucky in the Depression. When Pee Wee started work, he earned $3.85 for an eight-hour day. Now he gets $3.96 an hour, makes $10,000-plus a year. He has money stashed in the company credit union. He gets four weeks' vacation a year, and every fifth year he gets thirteen. He has a freezer, a relatively new Buick, all but owns the $15,000 home he bought twenty years ago for $5,300. The company pays all his expenses in a gun club. And there is a generous retirement plan.

For most of his working life, Pee Wee has stood in the same little 12-by-12 area, operating a machine that shears rough edges off the long lengths of steel. "The older you get the worse it gets," he says. "The pressure and tension keep building up. More tonnage. You get behind the 8-ball. I've worked hard. I've wore out three machines.

"We do all the work. The niggers have got it made," he says. "They keep closing in and closing in, working their way into everything. Last three or four months you can't even turn on the damn TV without seeing a nigger. They're even playing cowboys.

"Us briarhoppers [transplanted Southerners] ain't gonna stand for it. And

90 per cent of Middletown is briarhoppers. And those sons of bitches will kill you, know what I mean? If a bunch of good ol' briarhopper Ku Kluxers had got ahold of Martin Luther King, he wouldn't have lived as long as he did."

In Milwaukee, they call the Menomenee valley in midtown "the Mason-Dixon line." On one side live the blacks. On the other live the working-class whites, mainly Poles. Adjacent to the white side is the oppressively Dickensian old Allen-Bradley heavy-machinery factory. Lately, Father James Groppi and some militants have been picketing, demanding more minority jobs.

Just at 3 p.m., gig grinder Ray Walczak, 44, wearily emerges from his shift and crosses the street to his rusting old '64 Buick. He is going home to pack his modest trailer, and take his son camping. But he can't resist pausing to watch the pickets.

"Look at that," he says. "Bastards don't want jobs. If you offered them jobs now, 90 per cent of them would run like hell. They ought to take machine guns and shoot the bastards. Period. The Polish race years ago didn't go out and riot and ruin people's property. It took a helluva lot of years for us to get in, and when we did, we had to take the s——— jobs. Hell, I don't know how many companies I went to back then and they'd say 'Sorry, we ain't hiring anybody right now.'

"I've been in the shops since I was 16. I worked like a goddam fool," he says bitterly. "I've been here eighteen years and if I live to be 100 I'll probably be doing the same job.

"The only raise I ever got was a union raise. I've begged and argued with the bosses, 'I'm not asking for a quarter. Just a nickel.' But never a merit raise. They say, 'Be patient, be patient.' They ought to give you a medal for patience. But they don't care. We're just peons. And if you don't like it, there's always somebody waiting for your job.

"Day after day, year after year, climbing those same steps, punching that time card. Standing in that same goddam spot grinding those same goddam holes."

Beetle-browed Balazar Smith, 53, is a plumber. He lives in the noisy glide path of planes headed for Los Angeles International Airport. But he occasionally manages to escape to the beach and to his sister's ranch in New Mexico.

Sitting in his panel truck on a quiet Inglewood street, making out a bill for $33, the charge for unstopping a residential toilet, Smith says: "When I look at my paycheck and see what they take out, I hate to work. After the Depression, I worked in a CCC camp for $30 a week. And life is almost as much of a hassle as it was then."

Smith earns about $200 a week, but he is heavily in debt, mostly because of medical bills. His wife was hospitalized for two weeks with kidney stones. Smith's insurance paid $12 a day on her room. It cost $54. "I've got to pony up about $2,300 somehow," Smith says. "But I'll pay my bills. Well, anyway, thank God my family and things have turned out all right. We've had no hippie trouble with our three children. None of that pot," he says.

Near where steelworker Jimmy Slavo, 57, lives in Hammond, Ind., there is a dingy old high school. On its grounds there is a weekend carnival and Slavo, on *this late-summer evening, is strolling about holding hands with his wife, Lula Belle, drinking a Budweiser and dipping Copenhagen snuff. Slavo has been work-ing the steel mills since 1928. He earns $3.67 an hour. His wife has been ill, and he owes $7,000 in medical bills. So he tries to work a lot of overtime. But Slavo is a steel pourer, and he works in an area where the temperature averages 115 degrees, so he can't work all the hours he'd like.*

"I sweat so much salt that when I undress, my pants stand up by them-selves," he says. "The heat knocks you on your hind end." "The heat seems to give him power," his wife says with great pride.

His gross pay averages $850 a month, but $200 automatically comes off for deductions, and the family's regular bills come to about $450—including $80 in house payments, $145 on a bank note, $40 on medical bills, $22 life insur-ance. Not much is left for operating expenses. To help feed and clothe their three children, Mrs. Slavo bakes and sews, and they keep a tiny garden in the summer. They bought a freezer four years ago, hoping they could buy bulk foodstuffs and thus save money, but for lack of cash they have only been able to fill it twice.

Slavo has never been on an airplane or in a nightclub. He and Lula Belle haven't been to a movie in ten years. For vacation, they visit relatives in Minn-esota. Mrs. Slavo said the last time she was out to dinner was on her birthday three years ago. She had fried chicken.

"Guys on relief are a lot happier," says her husband. "They got cars. They got food. I work, and what the hell have I got? I can't ask for charity. I'm too damned proud. I'll pay my bills. Anyway, to hell with the money. I've still got my wife," he says, squeezing her hand affectionately. "If sickness would stay away, we'd be happy. All I care about is my family."

Television cameras eye cars and people approaching the huge, severe-looking Massachusetts Mutual Life Insurance Co. headquarters compound in Springfield. And one has to get past a security gate to enter the building. There are 2,100 employees, 1,800 of them women. There's a company store, a bank, a credit union, umbrellas when it rains, 80-cent lunches and all kinds of recrea-tional facilities.

"It's a womb-to-tomb life," says black-haired supervisor Mark Patenaud, 26. "They lead you into the bathroom. You piddle. And then you go back and do your job. It becomes frustrating. You go home wondering, 'What the hell did I do today?' Sometimes I'd like to see some good come of what I did in a day. But you're such a small cog in such a big wheel that it all gets lost in the whole mishmash."

"Sure, I wish I was a little different," says one of his colleagues, Steve Guarrera, 33, "but, what the hell, I made this bed, I made the choice, so I have to live with it. I'm just an average slob. They wind us up in the morning and we go all day. But is that so bad? On the whole I'm happy."

"The thing is," says another employee, Roger White, 26, "you could leave here and go to work somewhere else, and how much different would it be? It might be more money, but you wouldn't necessarily be any happier."

"There's you and your family, and that's your world," says Patenaud. "If your neighbor dies tomorrow, just throw a little sand on him and that's about it. People don't want to get involved. Everybody's concern is not to be concerned."

Blue-eyed senior mechanic Bill Scudder, 33, finishes repairing a leak in the aileron-boost system of a Piedmont Airlines jet at the Atlanta Airport, wipes his hands, returns to the shop to continue his lunch—a tuna sandwich and home-made cookies.

Scudder has to feed four children on an $820-a-month salary. But he does it, even tucks away $80 a month in the company credit union. His wife bakes bread and cakes, cans beans, tomatoes and okra from a summer garden on their 240- by 240-foot lot. They chip in with neighbors to buy potatoes and meat at wholesale prices. One neighbor helped him get some used plumbing and Scudder added a bathroom to the basement of his home—for $40. For fun, his family camps. And they are deeply involved in the church and scouts.

"I guess I've been too busy to sit down and figure out what my problems are," Scudder says. "I'm happy." The big reason: he lives "in the country," 15 miles from his work. "Cities make me nervous. Country people are outgoing and friendly but city life keeps people so tense they don't want to talk to anybody," he says.

"All I want out of life is for my kids to grow up to be decent citizens. I'm happy with my family, so I'm happy with the world. All I need to do is wake up in the morning and hear the birds. That gives me joy."

IN POLITICS, IT'S THE NEW POPULISM

In Minneapolis, a policeman named Charles Stenvig becomes mayor by rolling up an astounding 62 per cent of the vote against the experienced president of the City Countil. In New York, Mayor John Lindsay and Former Mayor Robert Wagner, both liberals of national stature, bow to obscure interlopers in their parties' mayoral primaries. In Boston, grandmotherly Louise Day Hicks, whose crusade for the "forgotten man" and against school busing carried her within an inch of City Hall two years ago, leads a big field in the upcoming City Council elections. And in Newark, a onetime construction worker named Anthony Imperiale, master of karate, the bowie knife and a fleet of 72 radio cars that regularly patrol the city's white neighborhoods, confidently maps his campaign to win next year's race for mayor and "get rid of every quisling" in sight.

This is the year of the New Populism, a far-ranging, fast-spreading revolt of the little man against the Establishment at the nation's polls. Middle America, long counted upon to supply the pluralities on Election Day, is beginning to supply eye-opening victories from coast to coast. The over-all political cast of the country remains mixed, to be sure. The freshman crop of U.S. Senators elected just last year, for example, includes a significant share of conventional liberals and moderates. Only a fortnight ago, a Negro candidate topped the field in the Detroit mayoral primary, and progressive Lindsay may yet eke out a victory in New York next month. But—especially in close-to-home city politics —the frustrated middle-class majority has increasingly been turning to newfound champions drawn from its own ranks.

The seeds of popular rebellion have been long implanted beneath the surface of liberal hegemony. Even as John Kennedy and Lyndon Johnson held sway in Washington, Barry Goldwater astounded the political pros with his temporary seizure of the GOP, Ronald Reagan carried the banner of the "citizen politician" from the movie lots of the California Statehouse, and George Wallace and Lester Maddox found that fulminations against "those bureaucrats" was a sure path to popularity both in the South and, to some extent, in the rest of the nation.

But this was the year that the phenomenon finally broke the surface with a series of municipal victories impossible to dismiss as regional aberrations. And this was the year that the New Populism began to be seen more clearly for what it really is.

It is not, most politicians now agree, simply a burst of racist backlash. Though sheer bigotry has certainly played a part in fueling the little man's revolt, part of his resentment of the black man is traceable to his sense of desertion by a government that appears preoccupied with Negroes' needs and inattentive to his own. Liberals who have shouted "racism! " at white response to the black revolution are now beginning to realize that this oversimplifies the impulses involved and bolster Middle America's mounting impression that liberals neither understand nor sympathize with lower-middle class whites.

And it is not simply a swing to the political right. Though the New Populists have unquestionably turned conservative on law enforcement, they show few signs of wanting to scrap the social reforms—medicare, aid to education, and social security improvements—wrought by the liberal left. "It's a swing against anarchy," says liberal Congressman Allard Lowenstein, and indeed the disgruntlement with the progressives seems to stem far more from their permissiveness than from their programs.

Perhaps, most of all, the New Populism is a quest for recognition. "People felt that nobody was representing them and nobody was listening," says Minneapolis's Charlie Stenvig. "They felt alienated from the political system, and they'd had it up to their Adam's apples on just about everything. So they took a guy like me—four kids, an average home, a working man they could associate themselves with. They just said, 'Lookit, we're sick of you politicians'."

Stenvig was, indeed, a paragon of Middle America: the son of a telephone company employee, a Methodist of Norwegian stock, a graduate of a local high school and a local college (Augsburg), and an up-through-the-ranks detective on the police force. His opponent, by contrast, was almost pure Establishment: the son of an investment banker, a graduate of Stanford and Harvard Law, and a resident of the fashionable Kenwood suburb.

In his campaign, Stenvig pounded away at the privileged bastions of suburbia—he pledged to "bring government back to the citizens of Minneapolis and away from the influence of the golden West out there in Wayzata"—a privileged enclave on the city's fringes. To low-income whites, the suburbs are where the liberals live. "The liberal preaches from his lily-white suburb," explains United Auto Workers official Paul Schrade, while the worker usually lives on the borderline of the ghetto. The workers are on the front lines of the black-white conflict and resent the advice of rear-echelon generals."

Minneapolis's workers relish Stenvig's assault on the suburbs—"He told those rich guys to go suck a lemon," chortles one local auto mechanic—and as mayor he has kept up the attack. He has protested the financing plan for a new hospital on the ground that the suburbs would not pay enough of the tab, and he has staffed city jobs with what he calls "just average working people."

A few of these appointments have aroused the only controversy in what most people in Minneapolis agree has been an extremely hard-working, well-intentioned municipal administration. Antonio G. Felicetta, vice president of the regional joint council of the Teamsters union, created a citywide sensation recently when he delivered some pungent remarks in his new role as a member of the city Commission on Human Relations. "I'm not going to take any bull-s———," he announced to a local journalist. "If there are any grievances, I sure as hell would want to see them taken care of. But I sure as hell wouldn't want to give 'em [welfare recipients] half my goddam paycheck when I'm working and they're sitting on their asses." Felicetta was promptly denounced as a "card-carrying bigot" by a group of Minneapolis blacks, but he also received a torrent of phone calls saying "That's the way, Tony, sock it to 'em."

Middle America's radical right has always delighted in such tough words—and deeds. Newark's Tony Imperiale became an instant folk hero in these circles when he organized a band of white vigilantes in the wake of the disastrous summer riots in 1967. And last week, as he looked ahead to the day when he becomes mayor, he made plain that official investiture will not change his tune. "If any militant comes into my office, puts his ass on my desk and tells me what I have to do," he vowed, "I'll throw his ass off the wall and throw him out the door."

There is little question that Tony—38 years old, 5 feet 6 3/4 inches high and 260 pounds thick—is capable of doing just that. As he drove his volunteer ambulance—part of his vigilante patrol—past the corner of Mt. Prospect Street and Bloomfield Avenue in Newark's rugged North Ward one evening recently, he recalled an example of the sort of direct action he favors: "We came down here one night with eight guys and kicked the crap outa 22 junkies. Each time we came back to slap them around they lessened in ranks and finally took the hint." Imperiale keeps an arsenal of about 40 serviceable guns in his house, including a 14-inch-barrel scatter-gun stowed behind the couch (there have already been two attempts on his life).

Imperiale is a bit too rough-and-ready for the taste of most other politicians of the New Populism. And outside the South, most of them would disclaim any ideological kinship with Dixie's two most prominent contributions to the movement, former Alabama Gov. George Wallace and incumbent Georgia Gov. Lester Maddox. But Wallace, whose Presidential campaigns of 1964 and 1968 featured attacks on "pointy-headed intellectuals" and "briefcase-toting bureaucrats" that gave his appeal a dimension beyond sheer racism, claims paternity for much of the movement. "My vote was only the tip of the iceberg," he says. "There's others I'm responsible for: Stenvig, Mayor Yorty of Los Angeles, two mayoral candidates in New York. They were making Alabama speeches with a Minneapolis, Los Angeles and New York accent. The only thing they omitted was the drawl."

One of the things that draws the Populists together is their common wistfulness for the "old values," for traditional verities and styles of life that somehow seem to have gone awry. Lester Maddox, for example, likes to think of himself as part of "the mainstream of the thinking of the American people: the achievers, the success-makers, the builders, the individuals who like to set their own goals and accept the challenges." A number of Middle America's politicians also like to brandish the crusader's cross. "God is going to be my principal adviser," declares Charlie Stenvig, and Mary Beck, a 61-year-old Detroit council-woman who placed a strong third in last month's mayoral primary, dedicated her campaign newspaper "to the laws of God and man."

When Populists brood on the agonies of contemporary society, a certain nostalgia for a simpler life is never far from the surface. "I was born in a little town of 6,000 people," recalls Democrat Mario Procaccino, who appears to be leading Lindsay and a conservative Republican in the New York mayor's race. "We respected our parents, our teachers, and our priest or man of the cloth. We had respect for men in public office. We looked up to them . . ."

Procaccino frequently exhibits another characteristic of his new political breed: emotionalism. He wept when he announced his candidacy. Occasionally he takes his wife, Marie, and his daughter, Marierose, for an evening visit to the top of the Empire State Building. "I look out over the city and say to myself, 'What's the matter with these people? Why can't they get together?' " Many middle-class voters seem to warm to these displays of feeling, perhaps because they themselves are so upset, perhaps because they sense that their government has been run recently by soulless technocrats spouting bureaucratic jargon or political cant. "I like him because he's so emotional," beamed one housewife to her neighbor as Procaccino campaigned through Queens last week. "Any tears he sheds, you know he has heart. He doesn't fear to shed them and they bring the people closer to him."

Mayor Sam Yorty of Los Angeles is another extremely warm-blooded politician, endowed with a coloratura stumping style that ranges between acid vituperation and passionate enthusiasm. Ever since the Watts riots of 1965, he has concentrated the former on militants and the latter on guardians of law and order. This approach proved immensely popular in last spring's mayoral election, when he won an upset victory over Negro challenger Thomas Bradley. "Personally, I like the way Yorty shoots off his mouth too much," said one white-haired old man at Los Angeles's recent 188th birthday party at the Hollywood Bowl. "He'll do a better job for me than the other guy keeping down crime and taxes."

Yorty is an interesting case history in the shifting course of Middle America's mainstream. During the 1930s, he was a New Deal liberal, espousing such progressive programs as a 30-hour workweek. In the '40s, he took up the cause of zealous anti-communism, and now he is sounding the alarms of law and order. He is no political newcomer—he has been running for office ever since 1936—but today's disgruntled voters seem willing to reward the old pros pro-vided they step to the new beat.

More often, however, Middle America is turning to new political faces, even when they don't look exactly like the one in the mirror. Its latest champ-ion, S. I. Hayakawa, the feisty little professor of English who is now president of San Francisco State College, is not by nature a man of the people. "I've been, all my life, the kind of intellectual highbrow I disapprove of," he admits. But his uncompromising suppression of radical disruption at San Francisco State last fall suddenly vaulted him into political prominence: he began being mentioned as a possible opponent next year of Republican Sen. George Murphy, he started a statewide round of speech-making, and a recent Field Poll gave him a higher popularity rating than either San Francisco Mayor Joseph Alioto or California's former Democratic Assembly Speaker Jesse Unruh.

The yawning gap between the intellectual and the common man, between the governors and the governed, lies at the heart of the New Populism, and one of the first to discern it was Louise Day Hicks of Boston. A 50-year-old attorney from the predominantly Irish wards of South Boston, she pitched her 1967 mayoral campaign toward "the forgotten man," stressed the school-busing issue —and very nearly won. "I represented the alienated voter," she said last week in the midst of her new City Council campaign, "and that's who I'm representing now, except that the number has grown." Busing is no longer her main issue— some of her liberal opponents, in fact, now agree with her that the state busing law is unworkable. Now she concentrates her fire on higher taxes, declining municipal services and a government that, she contends, "is only concerned about the rich and the poor" and not about the man in the middle who pays the bills.

"The only thing saving this country," Mrs. Hicks says, "is the affluence that the middle class is feeling. But they don't realize the purchasing power is gone. When they do realize that, we're in for real trouble. There'll be a revolt— not violence, because the American people won't resort to violence, but they are going to speak up in a way to be heard."

In fact, they are already speaking up, and there is no reason to believe that November's elections will show a muting of their voices. "These people today are in revolt," warns Chicago Congressman Roman Pucinski. What's more, the middle class has become keenly aware of its political muscle and how to apply it. "The public is so much smarter than when I first started in politics," marvels Ken O'Donnell, JFK's special assistant who is running for the 1970 Democratic nomination for governor of Massachusetts. "Then it was no issue: just vote Democratic, vote Republican, and how to help your friends. What Gene McCarthy did was open the eyes of the people that they are the country. Before, it had been assumed that you couldn't bring a President down, that you couldn't fight the system. The McCarthy movement showed that you could do it after all."

The New Populism, as a matter of fact, seems to some analysts part of the same phenomenon as the New Politics. Eugene McCarthy and Robert Kennedy were trying to achieve on a national scale essentially the same goal that Charlie Stenvig and Louise Day Hicks have set on the municipal level: to bring new faces and new forces into play in the political arena, to mobilize the amateurs against the political pros, to return power to people whose voices, they believed, had been too long ignored. Of course, the McCarthy—Kennedy movement was headed in a liberal direction, while the New Populism is exhibiting a rightward bent. And the fact is that several of its new champions seem to be helping to foment, not just reflect, the public's bitterness. Still, the two movements share some common impulses, which may explain the startling number of voters who felt a kinship with both Bobby Kennedy and George Wallace during last year's campaign.

It is still much too soon to say how long the New Populism may last or what direction it may take. It has cast itself loose from the traditional political parties, neither one of which seems to hold its favor, and it has lost faith in the programs and pieties of traditional liberalism. As George Wallace puts it, "The great pointy heads who knew best how to run everybody's life have had their day." Frustrated, fearful and confused, Middle America is stirring itself to seek out new pathways, and the nation has already begun to reverberate with the commotion of its search.

INTO THE '70s—A GOP DECADE?[2]

Middle America decides who sits in the White House and it is in the dreams—and nightmares—of the middle class that the Republicans and Democrats will seek the victory formula for 1972 and 1976. Right now neither party is sure just what that formula may be.

The problem for the Republicans is simple enough, even if the answers aren't. For 1972 their hopes rest on the ability of the Nixon Administration to form a new coalition of the center—detaching at least some of those voters who would have been oriented to Roosevelt a generation ago and who supported Humphrey last year. Such a GOP coalition would have its own right wing (mostly in the South) and its own left (the Eastern Seaboard). It would not be a sharp move to the right. A militantly conservative line might attract some of George Wallace's 9.9 million supporters from the last election. But it would alienate other voters—and ignore the many populist characteristics of the Wallace vote. Mr. Nixon is much more likely to seek a new center coalition, and if he can forge such a consensus he will win.

The Nixon people know American political history. They know that outside the old Confederacy their party held general political sway for a long generation before the Great Depression and the success of Roosevelt in 1932. From the vote in 1896, when an earlier Middle America swung away from free silver and Bryan to the hoped-for stability of McKinley, right up to Roosevelt there was a long pattern of Republican rule.

But under Roosevelt a new coalition came to power in America. Save for the personalist Eisenhower years, that coalition kept power until a year ago. Even the voting in 1968 was in many ways a reaffirmation of the old Roosevelt coalition minus the South. Well-to-do and well-educated voters went Republican, despite rumbles of discontent among their young, while the poor went Democratic. Middle America split. Catholic and Jewish voters remained in the FDR pattern, voting more heavily Democratic than Protestants, while the Northern small towns and the countryside voted Republican, again in the pattern of the Roosevelt coalition. With the Negro vote going overwhelmingly to Humphrey, white Middle America edged to Mr. Nixon, but not overwhelmingly.

If the GOP is to succeed in making 1972 a triumph of the New Republicanism, it will have to break out of the tight political alignment of postwar

---

[2]This segment of the report was written By Richard M. Scammon.

America. The Republicans will have to make 1972 another 1896, with Middle America shifting as decisively to the GOP column three years hence as it did when challenged by Bryan nearly 75 years ago.

The attitudes within Middle America are a key to the probable planning of the Republicans in the '70s. These attitudes are not especially "liberal," as that word is used today. Indeed, a recent sounding of opinion in the bellwether state of California indicates that only 24 per cent of its citizens now label themselves "liberal" as against "middle-of-the-road" (27 per cent) or "conservative" (42 per cent). But neither are Middle America's attitudes hidebound, far right or reactionary.

Specifically, then, where might Republicans look to widen their slim half-million plurality of 1968 to 5 million or 10 million in 1972? One of the most immediate tests, even with the 1972 voting more than three years away, is how people react to President Nixon. The *Newsweek* Poll found the great majority positive: 79 per cent of the national total is favorably or moderately disposed to the President, only 16 per cent negative.

Statistically, Mr. Nixon registers a "highly favorable" rating among about one-third of the people of Middle America. Men rate the President a bit higher than women, older people somewhat higher than the young, Southerners higher than the rest of the country. Nowhere does the "highly favorable" rating fall below 30 per cent or rise above 37 per cent. Mr. Nixon's "unfavorable" ratings range from 5 per cent in the South to just over 18 per cent in the big cities. In every category the top of the Nixon scale considerably outweighs the bottom, with the mass remaining in the middle.

The potential political implications of these ratings are clear to me. All these groups did *not* vote Republican in the same proportions in November 1968. If blue-collar workers are not reacting in a markedly different way to President Nixon than are traditionally Republican upper-middle-income business and professional people, then the new GOP target is very obviously the manual worker.

Of course, Presidential ratings three years before the event may not have much to do with voter opinions on Election Day in 1972. Still, the groups who now approve of Mr. Nixon, but who did not support him last November, seem logical recruits for Republicans seeking to win in 1972—and beyond. In the larger sense, though, almost all of Middle America remains a Republican target. Many in Middle America are workers who have "exploded" into the middle class in the economic "great leap forward" since 1945, and many of these are trade-union members. Others are small-business men and salaried people. But, they all share in today's widened concept of the middle class. If the Nixon party can develop meaningful lines of communication to these "forgotten Americans," it may well be able to enlarge its share of Middle American strength to build itself into a virtually unassailable position in the 1970s.

Such lines of communication are not just questions of specific policies such as welfare reform, social-security increases, housing and education. Many of these are areas in which Democrats can be just as convincing as Republicans, perhaps more so. There are also important questions of style, for most of Middle America is not only middle class, it is strongly pro-middle class. Unlike upper-middle-class student rebels, the great majority does not reject middle-class values; it defends those values. The majority wants to better its situation, not overturn it.

In forming political opinion in these terms the Republicans may be the beneficiaries of Democratic mistakes. If the Democratic image in the 1970s is basically one of a party oriented away from the center, toward beard and sandal rather than toward crew cut and bowling shoe, then it seems very likely that President Nixon and the Republicans will establish a dominant position in American politics—perhaps not for a generation, as the party did after McKinley, but at least for a decade.

I doubt that the Democrats will make that mistake. Middle America controls our politics—and Middle America basically inclines neither left nor right. A swerve by the Democrats to the far left in the 1970s would end as disastrously as did 1964's right-wing adventure for the Republicans. And the Democrats have one great advantage—they remember the Goldwater experience.

Politicians are not only articulate, they are literate. They can read, and they read election statistics very clearly. While the Nixon Republicans are making every effort to win more of Middle America and to build a long-term base for their party, the Democrats will be trying just as hard to pull together the components of success as they knew them from 1932 through Lyndon Johnson—and, it might be added, almost through Hubert Humphrey's race as well. It seems likely that the real test of the Republicans' effort to move a bit more of Middle America their way will lie as much with the Democrats as with the Republicans themselves. If the Democrats can bridge their internal problems, they may well keep their share of Middle America, perhaps even move on a bit and win in 1972. But if they can't—and especially if they move away from the center—the '70s seem destined to be a Republican decade.

IS WHITE RACISM THE PROBLEM?

Murray Friedman

One of the less fortunate results of the black revolution has been the development of a by now familiar ritual in which the white liberal is accused of racism and responds by proclaiming himself and the entire society guilty as charged; the Kerner report was only the official apotheosis of this type of white response to the black challenge of the 60's. No doubt the report has performed a service in the short run by focusing the attention of great numbers of Americans

Murray Friedman, "Is White Racism the Problem?," **COMMENTARY,** *January, 1969. Reprinted from* **COMMENTARY,** *by permission; Copyright © 1969 by the American Jewish Committee.*

on the degree to which simple racism persists and operates throughout the country, but in the long run its picture of an America pervaded with an undifferentiated disease called "white racism" is unlikely to prove helpful. And even in the short run, the spread of the attitudes embodied in the report may have had a share in helping to provoke the current backlash.

It is, perhaps, understandable that blacks should take phrases like "white racism" and "white America" as adequate reflections of reality. Nevertheless, these phrases drastically obscure the true complexities of our social situation. For the truth is that there is no such entity as "white America." America is and always has been a nation of diverse ethnic, religious, and racial groups with widely varying characteristics and qualities; and conflict among these groups has been (one might say) "as American as cherry pie." According to the 1960 census, no fewer than 34 million Americans are either immigrants or the children of immigrants from Italy, Poland, Ireland, and a host of other countries. Racially, the population includes not only caucasians and 22 million blacks, but 5 million Mexican-Americans, and smaller numbers of Indians, Chinese, Japanese, and Puerto Ricans. Membership in U.S. religious bodies, finally, breaks down into 69 million Protestants (who themselves break down into 222 denominations and sects), 46 million Roman Catholics, and 5.6 million Jews.

Neither earlier restrictive immigration laws nor the forces working toward the homogenization of American life have rendered these groups obsolete. While it is true that we have carved out for ourselves a collective identity as Americans with certain common goals, values, and styles, we are still influenced in highly significant ways by our ethnic backgrounds. A number of social scientists, including Gerhard Lenski and Samuel Lubell, have even gone so far as to suggest that these factors are often more important than class. And indeed, membership in our various racial, religious, and ethnic groups largely accounts for where we live, the kinds of jobs we aspire to and hold, who our friends are, whom we marry, how we raise our children, how we vote, think, feel, and act. In a paper prepared for the National Consultation on Ethnic America last June, the sociologist Andrew Greeley reported that Germans, regardless of religion, are more likely to choose careers in science and engineering than any other group. Jews overchoose medicine and law. The Irish overchoose law, political science, history, and the diplomatic service. Polish and other Slavic groups are less likely to approve of bond issues. Poles are the most loyal to the Democratic party, while Germans and Italians are the least.

Such ethnic differences[1] are by no means mere survivals of the past, destined to disappear as immigrant memories fade. We seem, in fact, to be moving into a phase of American life in which ethnic self-confidence and self-assertion—stemming from a new recognition of group identity patterns both by the groups themselves and by the general community—are becoming more intense. The "black power" movement is only one manifestation of this. Many alienated Jews suddenly discovered their Jewishness during the Israeli War of Independence and especially the Six-Day War. Italians have recently formed organizations to counteract "Italian jokes" and the gangster image on television

---

[1] Throughout this article, references to ethnic differences include racial and religious differences.

and other media, while Mexican-Americans and Indians have been organizing themselves to achieve broadened civil rights and opportunities. At the same time large bureaucracies like the police and the schools are witnessing a growth in racial, religious, and ethnic organization for social purposes and to protect group interests.[2] To some degree, each of us is locked into the particular culture and social system of the group from which we come.

The myth, to be sure, is that we are a nation of individuals rather than of groups. "There are no minorities in the United States," Woodrow Wilson, a Presbyterian, declared in a World War I plea for unity. "There are no national minorities, racial minorities, or religious minorities. The whole concept and basis of the United States precludes them." Thirty years later, the columnist, Dorothy Thompson, warned American Jews in the pages of *Commentary* that their support of Israel was an act of disloyalty to the United States. "You cannot become true Americans if you think of yourselves in groups. America does not consist of groups. A man who thinks of himself as belonging to a particular national group in America has not become American, and the man who goes among you to trade upon your nationality is not worthy to live under the Stars and Stripes." And more recently the New York *Times* criticized Martin Luther King, Jr., and James Farmer in similar terms after the two Negro leaders had laid claim to a share of the national wealth and economic power for Negroes as a group. Terming this plea "hopelessly utopian," the *Times* declared: "The United States has never honored [such a claim] for any other group. Impoverished Negroes, like all other poor Americans, past and present, will have to achieve success on an individual basis and by individual effort."

The ideology of individualism out of which such statements come may be attractive, but it bears little relation to the American reality. Formally, of course, and to a certain extent in practice, our society lives by the individualistic principle. Universities strive for more diverse student bodies and business organizations are increasingly accepting the principle that, like government civil service, they should be open to all persons qualified for employment. But as Nathan Glazer has suggested:

> These uniform processes of selection for advancement and the pattern of freedom to start a business and make money operate not on a homogeneous mass of individuals, but on individuals as molded by a range of communities of different degrees of organization and self-consciousness with different histories and cultures.

If, however, the idea that we are a nation of individuals is largely a fiction, it has nonetheless served a useful purpose. Fashioned, in part, by older-stock groups as a means of maintaining their power and primacy, it also helped to contain the explosive possibilities of an ethnically heterogeneous society and to

---

[2] A New York City police spokesman listed the following organizations operating among members of the 28,000-member force several years ago: the Holy Name Society, an organization of Roman Catholics, with 16,500 members; the St. George Association, Protestant, 4,500 members; the Shomrim Society, Jewish, 2,270 members; the Guardian Association, Negro, 1,500 members; the St. Paul Society, Eastern Orthodox, 450 members; and the Hispanic Society, with 350 members of Spanish descent.

muffle racial divisiveness. Yet one symptom of the "demystification" of this idea has been the recognition in recent years that the older stock groups are themselves to be understood in ethnic terms. The very introduction of the term WASP into the language, as Norman Podhoretz has pointed out, signified a new realization that "white Americans of Anglo-Saxon Protestant background are an ethnic group like any other, that their characteristic qualities are by no means self-evidently superior to those of the other groups, and that neither their earlier arrival nor their majority status entitles them to exclusive possession of the national identity." As the earliest arrivals, the WASP'S were able to take possession of the choicest land, to organize and control the major businesses and industries, to run the various political institutions, and to set the tone of the national culture. These positions of dominance were in time challenged by other groups, in some cases (the Irish in city politics, the Jews in cultural life) very successfully, in others with only partial success (thus Fletcher Knebel reports that, contrary to the general impression, "the rulers of economic America—the producers, the financiers, the manufacturers, the bankers and insurers—are still overwhelmingly WASP").

But whatever the particular outcome, the pattern of ethnic "outs" pressuring the ethnic "ins" for equal rights, opportunities, and status has been followed since colonial times and has been accompanied by noisy and often violent reaction by the existing ethnic establishment. There was the growth of the Know-Nothing movement when the mid-19th century influx of Irish Catholics and other foreigners posed a challenge to Protestant control; there was the creation and resurgence of the Ku Klux Klan at every stage of the black man's movement toward equal rights; there was the organization of Parents and Taxpayers groups in the North and White Citizens Councils in the South to oppose school desegregation and Negro school gains. Bigotry and racism certainly played a part in these phenomena. Yet they are best understood not as symptoms of social illness but as expressions of the recurring battles that inevitably characterize a heterogeneous society as older and more established groups seek to ward off the demands of newer claimants to a share of position and power.

Even the recent explosions in the black ghettos have a precedent: "In an earlier period," Dennis Clark tells us, "the Irish were the riot makers of America par excellence." They, "wrote the script" for American urban violence and "black terrorists have added nothing new." So, too, with some of the educational demands of today's black militants. As late as 1906, the New York *Gaelic American* wanted Irish history taught in the New York City schools!

Racial and ethnic conflict takes its toll, but it has frequently led to beneficial results. When pressures mounted by the "outs" have caused widespread dislocation, the "ins" have often purchased community peace by making political, economic, legal, and cultural concessions. As the Irish, for example, became more fully absorbed into American life through better jobs, more security and recognition—in short, as the existing ethnic establishment made room for them—Irish violence decreased, and the Irish have, in fact, become some of the strongest proponents of the current racial status quo. The hope of achieving a similar result undoubtedly accounts in some measure for concessions which have been made to Negroes in many racially restive cities today.

Thus, when white voters in Cleveland helped elect a Negro mayor (Carl Stokes), they were not only recognizing his abilities—which are said to be considerable—but also acting in the belief that he could "cool it" more effectively than a white mayor. Nor is it a coincidence that the Los Angeles city and county school boards are now headed by Negroes.

In the past, a major barrier to the advancement of black people has been their inability to organize themselves as a group for a struggle with the various "ins." Their relative powerlessness has been as crippling as the forces of bigotry arrayed against them. As one Philadelphia militant said, "Impotence corrupts and absolute impotence corrupts absolutely." But some black power leaders have recently emerged with a better understanding than many of their integrationist colleagues of the fact that successful groups in American life must reserve a major portion of their energies for the task of racial or religious separation and communal consolidation. Divorced from posturing and provocative language, the emphasis by certain (though not all) black militants on separatism may be seen as a temporary tactic to build political and economic power in order to overcome the results of discrimination and disadvantage. "Ultimately, the gains of our struggle will be meaningful," Stokely Carmichael and Charles V. Hamilton wrote in *Black Power,* "only when consolidated by viable coalitions between blacks and whites who accept each other as co-equal partners and who identify their goals as politically and economically similar."

This is not to suggest that black power (or Jewish power or Catholic power) is the only factor in achieving group progress, or that "the American creed," of equal rights, as Gunnar Myrdal has called it, is a mere bundle of words. Indeed, the democratic tradition can act as a powerful force in advancing minority claims even when the majority does not accept its implications. Public opinion polls have reported consistently that open-housing laws are unpopular with a majority of Americans, and yet 23 states and 205 cities have enacted such legislation and the Civil Rights Act of 1968 makes it a federal responsibility. Nevertheless, the democratic ideal obviously has never guaranteed full entry into the society to ethnic out-groups. In a pluralistic society freedom is not handed out; for better or worse, it has to be fought for and won. The "outs" can attain it only by agitation and pressure, utilizing the American creed as one of their weapons.

It is important in all this to recognize that no special virtue or culpability accrues to the position of any group in this pluralistic system. At the moment the American creed sides with Negroes, Puerto Ricans, American Indians, and other minorities who have been discriminated against for so long. But we should not be surprised when Italians, Poles, Irish, or Jews respond to Negro pressures by rushing to protect vital interests which have frequently been purchased through harsh struggles of their own with the ethnic system. Here is how a skilled craftsman replies to the charge of maintaining racial discrimination in his union in a letter to the New York *Times:*

> Some men leave their sons money, some large investments, some business connections, and some a profession. I have only one worthwhile thing to give: my trade. I hope to follow a centuries-old tradition and sponsor my sons for an apprenticeship. For this simple father's wish it is said that I discriminate against Negroes. Don't all of us discriminate? Which of us when it comes to a choice will not

choose a son over all others? I believe that an apprenticeship in my union is no more a public trust, to be shared by all, than a millionaire's money is a public trust.

Surely to dismiss this letter as an expression of white racism is drastically to oversimplify the problem of discrimination. But if the impulse to protect vested interests accounts for the erecting of discriminatory barriers, no less often than simple bigotry or racism, it is also true that Americans are sometimes capable of transcending that impulse—just as they are sometimes capable of setting aside their prejudices—for the sake of greater social justice. E. Digby Baltzell has pointed out in *The Protestant Establishment* that the drive to gain equal rights and opportunities for disadvantaged minorities has frequently been led by members of older-stock groups. On the other hand, members of minority groups are not necessarily ennobled by the experience of persecution and exploitation. As Rabbi Richard Rubenstein has observed, "the extra measure of hatred the victim accumulates may make him an especially vicious victor."

Nor does the position of a given ethnic group remain static; a group can be "in" and "out" at the same time. While Jews, for example, continue to face discrimination in the "executive suite" of major industry and finance, in private clubs and elsewhere, they are in certain respects becoming an economic and cultural in-group. To the degree that they are moving from "out" to "in" (from "good guys" to "bad guys"?), they are joining the existing ethnic establishment and taking on its conservative coloration. Rabbi Rubenstein has frankly defended this change in an article, "Jews, Negroes, and the New Politics," in the *Reconstructionist:*

> *After a century of liberalism there is a very strong likelihood that the Jewish community will turn somewhat conservative in the sense that its strategy for social change involves establishment politics rather than revolutionary violence. Jews have much to conserve in America. It is no sin to conserve what one has worked with infinite difficulty to build.*

So far so good—though, regrettably, Rubenstein uses this and other arguments to urge Jews to opt out of the Negro struggle. The point, however, is that not all the groups resisting black demands today are "in" groups. Just as in a fraternity initiation the hardest knocks come from the sophomores, the most recently accepted and hence least secure group, so in ethnic struggle the greatest opposition will sometimes come from groups whose interests would seem to make them natural allies.

At the moment some of the hottest group collisions are taking place in the big-city schools. The "outs"—in this case the blacks—see the older order as maintaining and fostering basic inequities. Hence, we are now witnessing the demand for decentralization or "community control" of big-city school systems. The "ins"—in the case of New York, the Jews; in the case of Boston, the Irish—naturally see these demands as a threat. The blacks claim that the existing system of merit and experience tends to favor educators from older religio-ethnic groups; the latter fear that new and lowered criteria of advancement and promotion will destroy many of their hard-won gains. The result is increasing conflict amid charges of racism from both sides.

The underlying problem, however, is a power struggle involving the decision-making areas controlled by an older educational and ethnic establishment. At the heart of the issue is a group bargaining situation whose handling calls for enormous sensitivity and the development of procedures that will protect the interests of the conflicting groups. A similar confrontation in the 19th century which was badly handled was a major factor in the withdrawal of Catholics from the Protestant-dominated public schools and the creation of their own school system.

In the meantime, struggles among other groups persist, often also involving the schools. Frequently, these result from differences in group values and styles as well as interests. An example is the school board fight in Wayne Township, New Jersey, which attracted national attention in February 1967. The Jewish, and total, population of Wayne, a suburb of Patterson and Newark, had grown sharply since 1958, when it was a homogeneous Christian community with only 15 Jewish families. With a changing community came new pressures—burgeoning school enrollment and school costs, and anxiety over court rulings banning prayer and the reading of the Bible in public schools. There was one Jew on Wayne's nine-member school board in 1967 when two others decided to run. The vice president of the board, Newton Miller, attacked both Jewish candidates, noting, "Most Jewish people are liberals especially when it comes to spending for education." If they were elected, he warned, only two more Jewish members would be required for a Jewish majority. "Two more votes and we lose what is left of Christ in our Christmas celebrations in the schools. Think of it," Miller added.

Subsequently, the Jewish candidates were defeated amid widespread condemnation of the citizens of Wayne. The incident was cited by sociologists Rodney Stark and Stephen Steinberg as raising the "specter of political anti-Semitism in America." In their study, they concluded, "It couldn't happen here, but it did."

Miller's statements may indeed have appealed to existing anti-Semitic sentiment in Wayne. But this was not the whole story. After all, the Jewish member already on the board had been elected by the same constituency that now responded to Miller's warnings. And it must be admitted, furthermore, that by and large Jews *are* "liberals." willing to spend heavily on the education of their children just as they are desirous of eliminating religious practices from the public schools—attitudes shared, of course, by many non-Jews. Miller appealed to group interests above all: to an interest in preserving traditional religious practices in the schools and in holding down education expenditures. There was in this case genuine concern by an older religio-ethnic establishment that its way of life and values were in danger of being swept away. The votes against the Jewish members were of course illiberal votes, but that was just the point. In Wayne, charges of anti-Semitism obscured the real problem: how to reconcile differences in group values in a changing, multigroup society.

All this is not of course meant to deny the existence of racism as a force in American life, nor to underestimate the cruel and pervasive conflicts which it engenders. But it must be recognized that the crucial element in much of intergroup conflict is not how prejudiced the contending parties are, but what kinds of accommodations they are capable of making. For many years, a federal aid to education bill has been tied up in Washington, in part because of a Roman

Catholic veto. The Catholic hierarchy, whose schools have been undergoing financial crisis, and a number of Orthodox Jewish groups who also want government assistance for their schools are ranged on one side of the issue. On the other side are most Protestant and Jewish groups, along with civil-liberties and educational organizations, who are suspicious of the motives of the Catholic Church and fear that financial assistance by government to parochial schools will lead to an abandonment of the separation of church and state principle embodied in the federal and state constitutions, with the resultant destruction of the public schools. Debate now ranges in many states over providing free busing of pupils to parochial schools, supplying textbooks, auxiliary services, and equipment to non-public school students, and financing construction of buildings at church-related colleges and universities. The result has been an intensification of religious tensions.

In this controversy, however, the problem is not, as many seem to believe, mainly one of constitutional law. In spite of the First Amendment, American public education throughout our history has reflected the values and goals of a Protestant society—until, that is, Catholics and other groups began to press for, and finally obtained, a more neutral posture. The problem here is rather one of adjusting to the reality of the Catholic parochial school system—to the public service it performs and to the political power it represents. When the Constitution was adopted, Catholics numbered less than 1 per cent of the total population. Today they are the largest single religious group and they support a parochial school system which, in spite of criticism inside and outside the Church, continues to educate large numbers of Americans.[3]

It seems likely that this controversy will be resolved through a redefinition of the American public education system. Thus, secular and other aspects of parochial education that benefit the general community—subjects such as foreign languages, mathematics, physics, chemistry, and gym—will in all probability receive some form of public assistance. Indeed, this is already happening in the form of shared time or dual enrollment (parochial school children spend part of the day in public schools), aid to disadvantaged children under the Elementary and Secondary Education Act of 1965, and various other measures.

It is a tribute to our social system, proof of its workability, that the inexorable pressures of pluralistic confrontation do result in shifts in power and place. WASP control of political life in the nation's cities was displaced first by the Irish and later by other ethnic groups. The newest group moving up the political ladder is the Negro, with mayors now in Gary and Cleveland. The Negro press predicts that by 1977 there may be 21 black mayors.

There are, of course, many real differences between the Negro and other groups in this country, including the Negro's higher visibility and the traumatic impact of slavery. He is, nevertheless, involved in much the same historical process experienced by all groups, with varying success, in attempting to "make it" in American life. The idea that he faces a monolithic white world uniformly

---

[3] A study by Rev. Neil G. McCluskey in 1963 reported that 26 per cent of the children in New York, 34 per cent of those in Chicago, 39 per cent in Philadelphia, 23 per cent in Detroit, 28 per cent in Cincinnati, 30 per cent in Boston, and 42 per cent in Pittsburgh attend Roman Catholic parochial schools.

intent for racist reasons on denying him his full rights as a man is not only naive but damaging to the development of strategies which can lead to a necessary accommodation. It does no good—it does harm—to keep pointing the finger of guilt either at Americans in general or at special groups, when what is needed are methods for dealing with the real needs and fears of all groups.

As David Danzig has written: "Few people who live in socially separated ethnic communities, as most Americans do, can be persuaded that because their communities are also racially separated they are morally sick. Having come to accept their own social situation as the natural result of their ethnic affinities, mere exhortation is not likely to convince them—or, for that matter, the public at large—that they are thereby imposing upon others a condition of apartheid." Nor is exhortation likely to convince the 20 million families who earn between $5,000 and $10,000 a year that they are wrong in feeling that their own problems are being neglected in favor of the Negro. It is clear that intergroup negotiation, or bargaining, with due regard for protecting the interests of the various groups involved, is one of the major ingredients in working out racial and religious adjustments. In other words, power has to be shared—in the schools, on the job, in politics, and in every aspect of American life.

The time has come to dispense with what Peter Rose has called the "liberal rhetoric . . . of race relations." There can be no effective intergroup negotiation or bargaining unless due regard is paid to the interests of all groups. Nor will effective bargaining take place until we learn to go beyond simplistic slogans and equally simplistic appeals to the American creed.

5

THE AMERICAN RESPONSE TO THE URBAN CRISIS

The urban predicament has not gone unnoticed. Every President of this century, at least since Franklin Roosevelt, has made some stab at improving the condition of the millions of urban dwellers living in squalor and facing limited economic opportunities. John Kennedy's administration was particularly determined to elevate the cities' national status by dealing directly with big city mayors and designing programs that would rejuvenate urban life. Housing, public works, education, health, and civil rights were key aspects of the Kennedy domestic programs.

President Johnson, prior to his preoccupation with Vietnam, made a concerted effort to divert national attention to urban problems. In 1965 Johnson sent to Congress a presidential message calling the city "the center of our own society" and advocating a mass of programs to make that center a vital one.[1] With a willing Congress, the Johnson administration expanded existing national efforts in the field of housing, pollution, health, and education and initiated new efforts in the fields of poverty, hunger, higher education, safety, job training, community development, medical care, neighborhood improvement, mental health, and civil rights. During the combined Kennedy-Johnson administrations, the number of programs touching the urban environment increased from 45 to 435—literally, one for every member of the House of Representatives.

Today, somewhere in the maze of local, state and federal programs, there is a remedy for most of the problems confronting urban America: urban renewal for the slums; job retraining for the unemployed; welfare for the poor; food stamps for the hungry; social security for the old; rent supplements, federally insured mortgages, student loans, community action, day care centers, mass transit, model cities, neighborhood youth centers. Whatever the problem, someone somewhere has devised the program to handle it.

[1] Lyndon B. Johnson, Presidential Message on the Cities, March 2, 1965.

But evidence shows that the current programs have been futile, irrelevant, unimaginative, poorly administered, wasteful. Some have even been catastrophic, such as massive urban renewal that has replaced slums with higher income dwellings without compensatory housing for those the bulldozers evacuated, actually securing totally opposite results to those intended. The war on poverty was ill conceived and ill administered. Highway programs have been notorious for adding to urban congestion rather than easing it. Welfare programs have insidiously degraded generations of human beings. Busing students to produce integrated schools has been a social flop and a financial disaster. Housing programs have never met their goals. Education has been antiquated and meaningless. The vast bureaucracies spawned to administer these programs inevitably develop a dreadful life of their own, careless and neglectful of the original reason for their creation: service to the community.

The Advisory Commission on Intergovernmental Relations put it this way:

> *"The overall course of urban development generally has been disorderly, destructive, and distasteful, the deadliness of which has only begun to become apparent in the past decade. It is a product of a relative 'laissez faire' in land use—with governmental action, when occurring, being of the wrong kind, at the wrong level, and frequently for the benefit of the wrong social and economic groups. It often has tended to stultify rather than stimulate the forces of private enterprise.*
>
> *"Specifically, government at all levels has been basically passive in the migrational flow of people, in the concentration of industrial development, and in the forging of urban growth policies. Local government activity has been marked by economic competition, exclusionary zoning, and building code anarchy. State governments usually have been indifferent to urban financial and service needs and rarely willing to challenge the local government status quo. The Federal role has been wholly contradictory. On the one hand, Congress enacts areawide planning requirements, strengthens representative regional bodies, adopts programs to assist the rehabilitation of central cities. On the other hand, the Federal-State highway program, FHA's activities, the failure of a fair and uniform relocation policy, and various location decisions of the Department of Defense and other Federal agencies more often than not have collided head on with long term urban development needs.*
>
> *"The result of all this has been to accentuate wrong-way migrational patterns of people and business; to forge a white, middle- and high-income noose around the increasingly black and poor inner city; and to subject much of rural America to a continuing course of gradual erosion."*[2]

Why is this so? How is it that these ingenious programs, costing billions of tax dollars seem to have made no significant dent in the shape of urban life? How is it that a society that can master the imponderable dimensions of landing an odd-shaped module on the moon can do little to lessen the rat population in Baltimore or the garbage pile-up in Manhattan? How is it that millions of Americans live in inferior homes, have inferior diets, possess inferior educations and perform tasks considerably inferior to their own talents?

The indictment may be a trifle harsh. Undoubtedly, without these

[2]"Urban America and the Federal System," *Report to* Advisory Commission on Intergovernmental Relations, October 1969.

programs, the condition of urban life would be infinitely worse. The greatness and beauty occasionally characteristic of some urban scenes is the product of considerable work and planning. The urban condition may be disagreeable; but there are good neighborhoods, beautiful communities, and citizens who are open minded, dedicated and determined to make democracy work.

The failure is not easy to diagnose. Urbanologists offer a variety of explanations. Some, for example, have suggested that programs to cure the city reflect a white, middle-class bias with no real relevance to black ghettos, where the urban condition is the most inflammatory. "Programs," Martin Meyerson suggested, "run by middle-class professionals have evolved so that middle-class people have benefited the most." Urban renewal cleared slums but replaced them with facilities for upper-income whites. Highways paid for by all taxpayers have benefited mostly white commuters. Even current efforts at mass transit are designed to serve white collar areas rather than industrial areas. Park facilities provided through federal funds are frequently located to provide recreation for families of high income. Efforts at integration seldom affect middle-or upper-income whites who simply move to all white suburbs where blacks comprise an infinitesimal proportion of the school system. Efforts to reduce unemployment have been successful for college graduates but not for the unskilled. There are few unemployed bankers or engineers. But whites and blacks with inferior education and skills can seldom find reasonable work. All this, Meyerson suggests, has resulted because "reformers who advocate and reformers of bureaucrats who administer urban programs have engaged in unwitting hypocricy. ... The goals they have urged and the programs as they have been effectuated have reflected their class bias. They have not advanced policies and programs in their own self interest; they have merely assumed that all people view the world, or ought to view the world, as they do. ... [3]

Other urban experts suggest that the fat and flabby disease of bureaucracy is the single most depressing cause of continued urban decay. The nation has spent enough money to redo all cities and to create opportunities for all citizens; but, this line of reasoning goes, the money is squandered by inept bureaucrats whose capacity to administer imaginative programs and to understand sensitive human problems is dismally inadequate. Bureaucracy crawls when it should sprint; mumbles when it should shout. Seldom does it operate as it should. "There is mounting evidence," social critic Peter Drucker wrote bitterly, "that government is big rather than strong; that it is fat and flabby rather than powerful; that it costs a great deal but does not achieve much. There is mounting evidence that the citizen less and less believes in government and is increasingly disenchanted with it. Indeed, government is sick—and just at the time when we need a strong, healthy and vigorous government."[4]

Another reason contemporary efforts to resolve urban issues have been

[3] Martin Meyerson, "Urban Policy: Reforming Reform," *Daedalus,* Fall 1968.
[4] Peter F. Drucker, *The Age of Discontinuity,* (New York: Harper and Row, 1969), p. 212.

unsuccessful stems from the distorted concept that money—and the "bigness" that money can buy—is the answer. Through the years urban solutions have had a certain "massiveness" to them—a certain insensitivity to local conditions or human feelings. This massiveness frequently provoked rather than corrected the prevailing situation. Massive urban renewal and massive highway construction are prime examples of such practices. Jane Jacobs, a bitter critic of the reckless assault on community customs by remote and intransigent planners and administrators, put it this way:

"There is a wistful myth that if only we had enough money to spend—the figure is usually put at a hundred billion dollars—we could wipe out all our slums in ten years, reverse decay in the great, dull, gray belts that were yesterday's and day-before-yesterday's suburbs, anchor the wandering middle class and its wandering tax money, and perhaps even solve the traffic problem.

"But look what we have built with the first several billions: Low-income projects that become worse centers of delinquency, vandalism and general social hopelessness than the slums they were supposed to replace. Middle-income housing projects which are truly marvels of dullness and regimentation, seized against any buoyancy or vitality of city life. Luxury housing projects that mitigate their inanity, or try to, with a vapid vulgarity. Cultural centers that are unable to support a good bookstore. Civic centers that are avoided by everyone but bums, who have fewer choices of loitering places than others. Commercial centers that are lackluster imitations of standardized suburban chain-store shopping. Promenades that go from no place to nowhere and have no promenaders. Expressways that eviscerate great cities. This is not the rebuilding of cities. This is the sacking of cities."[5]

Other urbanologists blame poor urban conditions on the nation's historic hostility to urban life. The city, in particular, has traditionally occupied an uncertain status in American life. In 1800, when Thomas Jefferson assumed the Presidency, three of every four Americans lived on the farm. (Jefferson would have winced when the men who took the 1920 census passed the word that a clear majority of Americans had moved to the city. He had not encouraged the creation of the Census Bureau to have it preside over the dissolution of the farm!) The civil men of his era did not cherish urban life. They farmed or philosophized. To Jefferson the city in history was more conducive to inciting violence than to spawning culture. London, Paris, Madrid and other sophisticated European meccas may well have been the capitals of 18th century intellectualism, but they are also the capitals of jealous, cruel, ruthless, ambitious, and constantly conniving monarchs who spent most of their time doing in other monarchs.

Anti-urbanism persisted through the popular Jacksonian uprising where Jackson's endorsement by newly formed urban-rooted labor organizations

---

[5] Jane Jacobs, *The Death and Life of Great American Cities,* (New York: Random House—Vintage Books, 1961), p. 40.

proved highly embarrassing. After the Civil War, the urban bias intensified. The sweeping reform demanded by the "agrarian revolt" of the 1880's was directed against the vast commercial interests that were headquartered in the great cities. The bitterness toward the city reached a 19th century peak in William Jennings Bryan's famous Cross of Gold speech. The engaging figure from Nebraska put it to the city bluntly: "The great cities rest upon our bread and our fertile prairies. Burn down your cities, and leave our farms and your cities will spring up again as if by magic; but destroy our farms and the grass will grow in the streets of every city in the country."

The entrance of the twentieth century did nothing to improve urban attitudes. Immigrants who poured into the great cities at the rate of almost a half-million a year, merely exacerbated the nation's latent urban contempt. For much of America the city harbored syndicalists, radicials, socialists, anarchists, and other dangerous types. Progressives fought against trusts, monopolies, child abuse, poor wages and long hours—all evils associated with the wicked urban environment. By the 1920s anti-urbanism was downright hysterical. The hyphen-hating nativists, fire-eating prohibitionists, self-righteous fundamentalists and professional red-baiters were all, in their own fashion, expressing an anti-city thing—attitudes and behavior born and nurtured in the countryside, determined to tame the nefarious ways of city sinners.

The 1928 campaign against Al Smith was probably the nation's single most vigorous outpouring of anti-cityism." The "Happy Warrior" personified everything there was to dislike about city life: he was a product of Tammany, the dreaded political monster; he was a "wet," that is, a promoter of booze; and he was a descendant of urban immigrant Catholics—a "Tammany plug ugly"they called the poor fellow. Mr. Smith did not have a chance.

The depression and the New Deal lessened some anti-urbanism. Population shifts, rural-to-urban migration, the impact of the urban vote on electoral politics, the institutionalization of merit systems, the withering away of many of the old-line political machines, and the general economic urbanization of American life continued to diminish some of the early American antagonism to the city. But there are still urbanologists today who feel that the anti-city bias in American life is so deep and so penetrating that it subconsciously tolerates the physical inferiority, architectural mediocrity, and human degradation that by and large characterizes many American cities.

An additional reason for the nation's inability to resolve urban problems stems from a sense of narrowness. Although the nation has not hesitated to pass program after program to meet immediate urban ills, *no single responsible public body, with the power to decide and to act, has sat down to think fully about the total urban condition, its reactions to human beings, its role in the natural flow of things and its relation to each of us.* Sporadic programs have delt with sporadic issues. But they have not been fitted into a general scheme—not necessarily a master plan, but a general concept of urban living that balances neighborhood with regions and people with physical design. And for that, America's urban environment is paying a heavy price.

This chapter of the anthology deals with bureaucratic hostility, institutional failure, and creative mediocrity. It is not pleasant reading. It is always easier to *criticize* an existing program than to carry it out. And although so much appears to be ineffective, there is a great deal that is positive and constructive. There are, within the ghettos, dedicated public officials running effective social programs. There are, in certain areas, good planners sensitive to people and nature. This chapter is not a focal point of irresponsible criticism but an exploration of why a nation of such immense political, economic, and technical power should have allowed its urban condition to deteriorate to a point of embarrassment.

The first part of the chapter deals with the failure of institutions—mostly government. The Urban Coalition's assessment of the Kerner Commission report one year after the Commission warned of a divided society is indicative of institutional indifference to crises.

The second selection is a moving newspaper article on a young boy who was the most tragic kind of institutional victim—innocent. That any child should be the target of so much institutional care throughout his life and then simply die of an overdose of heroin, as if no one had ever tried to help him, is implausible. But it is true and, as one New York official put it, "There are thousands of Walter Vandermeers out there."

There follows an interview with Jane Jacobs. Jacobs has for years demanded sanity and sensitivity in American urban planning and concepts. She has tried to explain that urban life is a trifle raucous and anarchistic because of the nature of people. To destroy that freedom and openess with overzealous planning and massive programming is destructive of the environment. This interview offers a splendid development of Jane Jacobs' thoughts and ideals.

The section concludes with the article by *New York Times* editorial writer, John Hamilton, dealing with the politics of hunger. "There is," Hamilton says, "a politics of hunger in America that needs understanding, an old politics that helps explain hunger's existence and a new politics that seeks its eradication, as well as a structural politics that involves the federal system of government and permits states and localities, out of false pride or shameless bigotry, to erect barriers against federal food programs, effectively denying their benefits to millions of the poor who need and deserve them."

The next section of the chapter deals with bureaucrats, their dismal science and their inept behavior. America is a nation of commissions, a country of reports. Over the past five years there have been at least a half dozen "major" reports or commission findings on urban affairs alone. The Douglas Commission, the Kaiser Commission, the Kerner Commission, and the Eisenhower Commission are the most notable.

Two of these, the Kerner Commission and the Douglas Commission, are targets of the first two articles. Both articles show a contempt for the bureaucratic infighting that dominated both agencies. Both reveal an insight seldom realized by most Americans who read only the headlines and seldom examine what's behind them. They show bureaucracy at its worst and raise the question of how a program can possibly be carried out when there are such problems in merely preparing a report.

The final section deals with the esoteric world of planners. Lewis Mumford, one of the world's most eminent planners, speaking before a Senate subcommittee about his background, beliefs and colleagues, says, "All the colossal mistakes that have been made during the last quarter century in urban renewal, highway building, transportation, land use, and recreation, have been made by highly qualified experts and specialists—and as regards planning, I should blush to be found in their company." Mumford belittles the foolishness with which legitimate planning concepts were distorted: " . . . Every advance we projected or even succeeded in establishing eventually came to grief . . . by stupid indifference and neglect . . . by being taken up on a national scale, with all the force, the authority, and the financial resources supplied by the Federal Government. In coming to life, our good ideas were done to death, caricatured or permanently disfigured by forces—technological, bureaucratic, financial, above all perhaps financial—that we had failed sufficiently to reckon with."

The closing article is a perceptive interview by the Center for Democratic Studies with Allen Temko, noted urban affairs writer. The irony of the urban tragedy is revealed in Temko's observation that there is "no incompatibility whatever between humanism and the rational use of technology." Why then, one wonders, have not the two sat down to lunch?

CONCLUSIONS—ONE YEAR LATER

"It is time now to turn with all the purpose at our command to the major unfinished business of this nation," the Commission said a year ago. It called on the nation "to mount programs on a scale equal to the dimension of the problems; to aim these programs for high impact in the immediate future in order to close the gap between promise and performance; to undertake new initiatives and experiments that can change the system of failure and frustration that now dominates the ghetto and weakens our society." . . .

POVERTY

1. Employment and income have risen in the slum-ghetto in both absolute and relative terms. Poverty remains a pervasive fact of life there, however, and the continuing disparity between this poverty and the general affluence remains a source of alienation and discontent.

2. Further gains in employment and income in the slums and ghettos are dependent on continued prosperity. But prosperity alone will not upgrade the hard-core poor and unemployed. Specific programs are necessary to meet their special needs and problems.

3. The largest gap in these programs, as they affect employment, is lack of a public job-creation program to complement increased public-private job-training efforts.

4. Job discrimination remains a serious problem, reinforcing the concentration of minorities in low-pay, low-status occupations.

5. Increased attention has been given efforts to open business opportunities to minorities, but only limited progress has been made.

6. No progress has been made in reform of the welfare system. Judicial gains have been offset by the threat of backward steps posed by the 1967 amendments to federal welfare laws.

7. Development and public acceptance of an income-supplementation system is still not in sight.

EDUCATION

1. The major issue to emerge in the past year is that of decentralization or community control of schools. Its impact on the quality of slum-ghetto education cannot yet be evaluated.

"Conclusions," ONE YEAR LATER. Urban America, Inc., and the Urban Coalition, New York: Praeger, 1969, Chapters 4 and 10.

2. Despite a turning away of some blacks from school integration as a goal, it has been pursued with some success in small- to moderate-size cities. There is no evidence of success in big cities with substantial minority populations.

3. Federal enforcement of laws and judicial rulings against school segregation has been of limited effectiveness in the South and is only beginning in the North.

4. Direct efforts to improve ghetto schools through compensatory programs are hampered by shortages of funds and by lack of means to measure precisely their effectiveness. Federal aid each year is spread more thinly and state aid is inequitably distributed.

5. Ghetto schools continue to fail. The small amount of progress that has been made has been counterbalanced by a growing atmosphere of hostility and conflict in many cities.

ENVIRONMENT

1. Two Presidential study groups have expanded and made more precise the nation's knowledge about housing need and how to meet it. Out of their work has come Congressional commitment to a well-documented housing production goal.

2. The Housing Act of 1968 substantially expanded the programmatic tools necessary to meet this goal. But appropriations cuts pushed its attainment far into the future.

3. Passage of a federal fair housing law represented the first essential step for opening new housing choices to residents of the slums and ghettos. Its impact will be hampered by inadequate appropriations for enforcement.

4. There are as yet no sufficient means to direct federal housing and community improvement programs toward opening extra-ghetto areas to the poor and minorities. In their absence, problems of finding acceptable sites also are likely to hamper seriously realization of the 1968 act's goal for construction of subsidized housing.

5. Rehabilitation has not fulfilled its promise as a means of improving the slum-ghetto environment. The model cities program, using a redirected approach to urban renewal, continues to offer promise limited only by its level of funding. At present, however, there are no programs that seriously threaten the continued existence of the slums.

Progress in dealing with the conditions of slum-ghetto life has been nowhere near in scale with the problems. Nor has the past year seen even a serious start toward the changes in national priorities, programs, and institutions advocated by the Commission. The sense of urgency in the Commission report has not been reflected in the nation's response. . . .

"The deepening racial division is not inevitable," the Commission said a year ago. "The movement apart can be reversed. Choice is still possible. Our principal task is to define that choice and to press for a national resolution." . . .

1. Civil disorders increased in number but declined in intensity in 1968. A significant drop in the death rate was due primarily to more sophisticated re-

sponse by police and the military, resulting directly from the work of the Commission.

2. A wave of disorder struck the nation's high schools in 1968—69 and is continuing. At the same time, turbulence on college and university campuses has taken on an increasingly racial character.

3. A genuinely alarming increase in crimes of violence contributed to an atmosphere of fear inside and out of the slums and and ghettos. There was little evidence of change or reform in the criminal justice system sufficient to stem this increase.

4. Incidents involving the police continued to threaten the civil peace in the slums and ghettos. There was some evidence of a hardening of police attitudes and a weakening of traditional civil controls over their activities.

5. Structural change in local government to make it more responsive was rare. The number of black elected officials increased substantially throughout the nation and particularly in the South, but remained disproportionately low.

6. There was no evidence that any more than a small minority of the nation's Negro population was prepared to follow militant leaders toward separatism or the tactical use of violence. This minority, however, continued to have an impact beyond its numbers, particularly on the young.

7. There was striking evidence of a deepening of the movement toward black pride, black identity, and black control and improvement of ghetto neighborhoods. There were repeated suggestions that efforts toward community control and self-help had been a major contribution to the relative quiet of the summer, 1968.

8. White concern with the problems of the slums and ghettos mounted with the Commission report, the assassination of Martin Luther King, and the April disorders. It was subsumed by concern for law and order in the months following the assassination of Sen. Robert F. Kennedy, and continued to decline during the Presidential campaign. Outright resistance to slum-ghetto needs and demands intensified during the same months.

9. Black and white Americans remained far apart in their perception of slum-ghetto problems and meaning of civil disorders. The gap probably had widened by the end of the year.

10. The physical distance between the places where blacks and whites lived did not diminish during the past year and threatens to increase with population growth. The most recent trend showed a virtual stoppage in black immigration and a sharp increase in the rate of white departure; the ghettos, meanwhile, were growing in area while declining in population density. There was an increase in suburban Negro population, but there also were indications of growth in suburban ghettos.

The nation has not reversed the movement apart. Blacks and whites remain deeply divided in their perceptions and experiences of American society. The deepening of concern about conditions in the slums and ghettos on the part of some white persons and institutions has been counterbalanced—perhaps overbalanced—by a deepening of aversion and resistance on the part of others. The mood of the blacks, wherever it stands precisely in the spectrum between militancy and submission, is not moving in the direction of patience. The black neighborhoods in the cities remain slums, marked by poverty and decay; they remain ghettos, marked by racial concentration and confinement. The nation has not yet made available—to the cities or the blacks themselves—the resources to improve these neighborhoods enough to make a significant change in their residents' lives. Nor has it offered those who might want it the alternative of escape.

Neither has the nation made a choice among the alternative futures described by the Commission, which is the same as choosing what the Commission called "present policies." The present policies alternative, the Commission said, "may well involve changes in many social and economic programs—but not enough to produce fundamental alterations in the key factors of Negro concentration, racial segregation, and the lack of sufficient enrichment to arrest the decay of deprived neighborhoods."

It is worth looking again at the Commission's description of where this choice would lead:

"We believe that the present policies choice would lead to a larger number of violent incidents of the kind that have stimulated recent major disorders.

"First, it does nothing to raise the hopes, absorb the energies, or constructively challenge the talents of the rapidly growing number of young Negro men in central cities. The proportion of unemployed or underemployed among them will remain very high. These young men have contributed disproportionately to crime and violence in cities in the past, and there is danger, obviously, that they will continue to do so.

"Second, under these conditions, a rising proportion of Negroes in disadvantaged city areas might come to look upon the deprivation and segregation they suffer as proper justification for violent protest or for extending support to now isolated extremists who advocate civil disruption by guerrilla tactics.

"More incidents would not necessarily mean more or worse riots. For the near future, there is substantial likelihood that even an increased number of incidents could be controlled before becoming major disorders, if society undertakes to improve police and National Guard forces so that they can respond to potential disorders with more prompt and disciplined use of force.

"In fact, the likelihood of incidents mushrooming into major disorders would be only slightly higher in the near future under the present policies choice than under the other two possible choices. For no new policies or programs could possibly alter basic ghetto conditions immediately. And the announcement of new programs under the other choices would immediately generate new expectations. Expectations inevitably increase faster than performance. In the short run, they might even increase the level of frustration.

"In the long run, however, the present policies choice risks a seriously greater probability of major disorders, worse, possibly, than those already experienced.

"If the Negro population as a whole developed even stronger feelings of being wrongly 'penned in' and discriminated against, many of its members might come to support not only riots, but the rebellion now being preached by only a handful. Large-scale violence, followed by white retaliation, could follow. This spiral could quite conceivably lead to a kind of urban *apartheid* with semimartial law in many major cities, enforced residence of Negroes in segregated areas, and a drastic reduction in personal freedom for all Americans, particularly Negroes." The Commission's description of the immediate consequences of the present policies choice sounds strikingly like a description of the year since its report was issued: some change but not enough; more incidents but less full-scale disorder because of improved police and military response; a decline in expectations and therefore in short-run frustrations. If the Commission is equally correct about the long run, the nation in its neglect may be sowing the seeds of unprecedented future disorder and division. For a year later, we are a year closer to being two societies, black and white, increasingly separate and scarcely less unequal.

OBITUARY OF HEROIN ADDICT WHO DIED AT 12

Joseph Lelyveld

Walter Vandermeer—the youngest person ever to be reported dead of an overdose of heroin here—had been identified by many of the city's leading social service agencies as a child in desperate need of care long before his body was discovered in the common bathroom of a Harlem tenement on Dec. 14, two weeks after his twelfth birthday.

For most of these agencies he never became more than one case among thousands passing through their revolving doors. Others tried to fit him into their programs but lacked the manpower or resources to focus on him effectively. Eventually he would be shunted off to yet another institution.

It was not heartlessness or malfeasance that explain why he usually went unnoticed, just overwhelming numbers. As one school official expressed it, "There are thousands of Walter Vandermeers out there."

Along the way his case was handled by Family Court, the Society for the Prevention of Cruelty to Children, the Department of Social Services and its Bureau of Child Welfare, the Board of Education's Bureau of Attendance and Bureau for the Education of Socially Maladjusted Children, the Wiltwyck School for Boys and the Office of Probation.

Most of these agencies have refused to discuss their actions in the case on the ground that their relationship with the boy was confidential.

But interviews with neighbors, relatives and individuals in the schools and agencies through which he passed have made it possible to retrace the course of his short life and his efforts to find a foothold in a world that always seemed to him on the verge of collapse.

The agencies had exhausted their routine procedures before he died; only his file continued to move. For his last 14 months he was left to himself, with no consistent supervision or counseling of any kind, on the decaying block where he lived most of his life and died—117th Street between Eighth and Manhattan Avenues.

There he was in intimate daily contact with addicts and pushers, as if none of the overstrained agencies had heard of him or even existed. After his death, one of the block's junkies paid him this descerning tribute:

"Walter lived to be 30 in 12 years. There was nothing about the street he didn't know."

CUPCAKES AND COCA-COLA

In those months he slept at home only sporadically and attended school for a total of two and a half days.

Walter would be out late at night hawking newspapers in bars or begging for coins at the corner of Eighth Avenue. In the daytime, when most children were in school, he would station himself near a radiator in a grocery store for warmth until chased or borrow a couch to catch up on the sleep he had missed.

His diet was made up of Yankee Doodle cupcakes, Coca-Cola and, when he had the change, fish 'n' chips.

It was a life of frightening emptiness and real dangers. The only regular thing about it was a daily struggle for survival.

"Walter didn't do too bad," a junkie on the block remarked when he was dead.

"He didn't do too good," retorted a black youth, full of bitterness over what heroin has done to Harlem. "He won't see his 13th birthday."

"He didn't do too bad," the junkie repeated. "He looked after himself."

A Family Court judge, charged with the responsibility of saving such youths but lacking in most cases the means to do so, despairingly reflected:

"At least we knew about this one. There are many we haven't even counted yet. That horrible feeling just drives me crazy in the middle of the night."

The one thing the court and the various agencies to which it referred his case never knew—but might have suspected had they checked more closely into the circumstances of Walter's life—was that he was experimenting with drugs.

But even this probably would not have mattered, for no treatment centers have yet been authorized here for narcotics users under the age of 16, although youths under 16 are dying in this city of heroin overdoses at the rate of one a week.

ANGER AND FEAR

Two sides of Walter Vandermeer are remembered on his block.

One was the apprentice hustler, an angry, mistrustful youth given to violent rages in which he hurled bottles and flayed about with iron pipes.

The other was the small child who cried easily and searched continually for adult protection and warmth. Some of the older addicts, into whose orbit he gravitated in the last months of his life say he would sometimes call them "Mommy" or "Daddy" and fantasy a household into which he could move as their child.

"Walter wanted a lot of attention," said his oldest sister, Regina Price. And there were those in his family and neighborhood who tried to extend it, when they could. Given the stress of their lives, that was only now and then and never for long.

Survival on 117th Street is a hard proposition at best, and Walter's circumstances were already far from the best when he was born Dec. 1, 1957.

His mother, Mrs. Lillian Price, had come to New York from Charleston, S.C., with her husband, Cyril, in 1947, when she was 22. Her schooling had never got beyond the third grade and she was on welfare within a year. (21 years later, she is still there).

In 1949, Mrs. Price had her first children—twins—and her husband moved out.

By 1957 she was, in social-work jargon, the nominal head of a growing, desperately disorganized "multiproblem" family. Walter was her sixth child; there had been four fathers. Five more children (one of whom died in infancy) were to be born in the next seven years to Mrs. Price and a Liberian immigrant named Sunday Togbah.

FATHER DEPORTED

Walter's father, known variously as Robert or Willie Vandermeer, entered the country illegally from Surinam, having jumped ship here in 1947. Six months after Walter was born, he was found by immigration authorities while he was working as a counterman at a midtown pharmacy and deported.

But by then, it appears, Mr. Vandermeer and Mrs. Price had separated, for hardly six months after he left the country she gave birth to the first of the children she was to have with Mr. Togbah.

Only one other Vandermeer was left in the family, a brother, Anthony, three years older than Walter.

In those days, Mrs. Price and six of her children were squeezed into one room of a three-room apartment at 305 West 117th Street they somehow shared with a couple with two children of their own. (Another of Mrs. Price's children, a daughter named Beverly, was being raised by a friend.)

According to the recollection of neighbors, Walter was sniffing airplane glue by the time he was 6 and sitting in on card games on the stoops when he was 8. In school he was marked as a disruptive child who could not be contained within a classroom's four walls unless permitted to fall asleep, which he did regularly, a sign to his teachers that he was staying out nights.

AGGRESSION FLARED OUT

Public School 76 on West 121st Street gave up on him in early 1967, when he was in the third grade, soon after his ninth birthday. Walter had been out of school more days than not that year. When he was there he seemed locked in an aggressive pattern, roaming the halls and throwing punches at teachers who sought to restrain him.

Sometimes his violence could be seen as a stifled cry for attention and help. On one occasion he stormed out of an art class, only to fly into a rage because his teacher had not pursued him.

It took the threat of a court order to bring Mrs. Price to school. She said she could not handle him.

Walter was repeatedly warned to behave better, then suspended on March 2, 1967. It does not appear that the school ever attempted to arrange psychological consultations for him or his mother with the Board of Education's Bureau of Child Guidance.

After Walter's death, Assemblyman Hulan E. Jack was to charge that the school had "put the child out onto the street."

In fact, it did just the opposite by referring his case to the Society for the Prevention of Cruelty to Children, which then brought it up in Family Court on a neglect petition. However, had the Assemblyman's charge been correct, the result could hardly have been worse.

PLACED IN QUEENS SHELTER

On March 14, both Walter and his brother Tony—the two Vandermeers—were placed in the Society's Children Shelter in Queens. Later they were shifted from there to the Children's Center at Fifth Avenue and 104th Street, which is run by the Department of Social Services for children neglected by their families.

An attendance teacher, as truant officers are now called, had singled out the older boy as a youth of unusual intelligence and promise. Six months later, Tony was assigned to a home operated by a private agency in Yonkers, where he has made what is regarded as a highly successful adjustment.

But Walter got lost in the judicial maze. While one branch of Family Court found Mrs. Price unable to care for Tony, another decided in August to release Walter—the younger and more disturbed of the two boys—to her care.

Releasing Walter to Mrs. Price was tantamount to releasing him to the street (by now the family had shifted to a top-floor apartment at 2124 Eighth Avenue, near 115th Street.)

The court expected Walter to go to Public School 148, a special school for disturbed and socially maladjusted children at West End Avenue and 82nd Street. But there was no response to repeated notices sent by the school to the boy and his mother.

Meantime, members of the family recall, Tony was attempting, without success, to interest the agency that looked after him in his younger brother's plight.

Stranded, Walter at 10 was reaching for his own solutions.

One involved Mrs. Barbara Banks, who had regarded him as a godchild ever since she accompanied Mrs. Price to the hospital at the time of his birth. Around Christmas, 1967, she said, she told Walter he could move in with her and three of her children, since her eldest son was going into the Army.

"A whole lot of people told me, 'Ain't no hope for that boy,' " she said. "But I believed I could save him. He was so inquisitive, he could have been anything."

Although Walter eagerly seized the invitation, she said, she was soon forced to withdraw it, for her son was never inducted. Walter felt rejected.

Late one night he made that clear in his own way by climbing to the roof of a tenement across 117th Street and hurling a bottle through Mrs. Banks's window, raining glass on her bed.

The boy spent most of his time on the streets until April, 1968, when the Family Court assigned him to the Wiltwyck School for Boys, a treatment center for disturbed youths from the slums that had basked in the patronage of Mrs. Eleanor Roosevelt and boasted such alumni as Floyd Patterson, the boxer, and Claude Brown, the author of "Manchild in the Promised Land."

The idea was to place Walter at the school's main center at Yorktown Heights in Westchester County, but the center was full and cutting down on its staff because of a budget crisis. As a temporary alternative—to get Walter off the streets—he was put in Patterson House, at 208 East 18th Street, a "halfway house" run by the school for youths returning to their communities from the main center.

PUT ON TRANQUILIZERS

Dr. Howard A. Weiner, a psychiatrist who was then in charge of Patterson House, remembers that Walter was "extremely bright verbally" but says he was "as disturbed as any kid we had."

Like many maladjusted children from the poorest, most disorganized families, he would erupt into towering rages when he felt himself under pressure and he had to be held till he regained control. Usually that took at least an hour, so it was decided to give him 50 milligrams of the tranquilizer Thorazene four times a day.

At first, Walter showed his suspicions about his new surroundings by taking food from the table in a napkin and hiding it under his bed. Gradually, when he discovered that his stockpiles were left alone, he stopped hoarding.

After his wariness subsided, he permitted himself to draw close to his childcare counselor, John Schoonbeck, a recent graduate of the University of Michigan. Learning that they both had Dutch names, Walter eagerly proclaimed that they were "soul brothers."

'GREAT LITTLE KID'

Mr. Schoonbeck, who now is on the staff of Time magazine, says Walter was "a great little kid." Dr. Weiner credits him with giving Walter the warm, reliable affection he had rarely found in an adult.

Encouraged by his counselor, Walter finally put in an appearance at P.S. 148. In fact, in May he went to school there regularly—his first stretch of steady school attendance in more than a year and the last in his life.

Flora Boyd, a teacher at the school, says Walter had never learned to read beyond the first-grade level but thought he could catch up. "He was an intelligent little boy," she recalls. "Of course, he had a lot of problems. But he could learn."

Finally a place opened for him at Wiltwyck's pastoral upstate campus, and on June 20, Mr. Schoonbeck accompanied him to Yorktown Heights—the fifth separate institutional setting in which he had been lodged in 15 months.

Walter felt that he had been betrayed and trapped. He had never been told that his stay at Patterson House would be temporary. It was a repetition of his experience with Mrs. Banks and, predictably, he flew into a fit of anger on his first afternoon at the school.

Wiltwyck's troubles, meantime, had gone from bad to worse. In May, a third of its staff had been suspended after protesting that students were receiving inadequate clothing and food in the wake of the economy drive. They also charged that there had been instances of brutality.

In the next two months, Walter ran away at least four times. As justification, he told his family he had been beaten at the school. Wiltwyck concluded that it could not hold Walter without his mother's cooperation and that this was unavailable.

BACK IN FAMILY COURT

On Oct. 10, 1968, Wiltwyck turned Walter back to Family Court, which meant he was where he had been more than a year earlier, only more frustrated and "street-wise."

His involvement with institutions was now nearly ended.

It took warrants to bring him and his mother to court so that he could be ordered to go to school, or to Harlem Hospital for psychiatric counseling, or to one of Har-you-Act's "self-help teams." When one order was ignored, the court would simply hand down another.

Asked why the court had not placed him in a state institution—a training school or mental hospital—in order to take him off the street, a judge replied that Walter, who was too disturbed for Wiltwyck, did not seem disturbed enough.

In fact, the probation officer assigned to the case recommended last spring that he be detained in a training school. But Walter's sister Regina insisted that her mother oppose the recommendation in court. In the back of her mind were recollections of the state institutions in which she was placed after she became pregnant at the age of 12.

QUESTION OF SURVIVAL

She knew that a youth in detention had to "stay by himself" to survive, she said, for there were always homosexual fellow inmates threatening to "mess up his mind." Regina wanted Walter to receive care, but she thought the probation officer only wanted to "criticize him" and "lock him up." In her view, state institutions were no less dangerous than the streets.

The Director of Probation, John A. Wallace, agreed that a state training school probably would not have been an ideal setting for the boy, but as a practical matter, he said, it was the court's last option. The judge, however, honored the mother's objection.

Theoretically, the welfare caseworker assigned to Mrs. Price should have kept tabs on Walter. But welfare caseworkers in Harlem are responsible for 70 to 80 cases, a population of 200 or more. Mrs. Price's caseworker never entered her son's life.

On his own, Walter continued to search out adults he felt he could trust.

In November, he went down to East Sixth Street to call on John Schoonbeck, who had quit Patterson House in discouragement and was packing for a trip to Africa. Walter asked plaintively if he could come along.

FORAYS WITH GANG

On the block he had a half-dozen households where he dropped in regularly at unpredictable hours to cadge food, coins, an undemanding hour in front of a television set.

One addict said Walter tagged along after a gang that called itself Bonnie and the Seven Clydes. The gang specialized in auto thefts and shoplifting, and he accompanied it on several forays downtown.

He also teamed up, it was said, with some older youths who conducted raids into Morningside Heights and learned to snatch purses. On at least one occasion he was said to have "taken off"—that is, robbed—a drunk, although Walter never did attain 5 feet in height.

According to Regina, he bought most of his own food and clothes and sometimes had as much as $50 in his pockets. But it is doubtful that he had any regular income as a drug courier, as has been alleged, for he continued until his last days to hustle for small change, selling newspapers and delivering groceries.

In his last month, Walter's already disastrous family situation deteriorated sharply.

Last summer, Mrs. Price was living most of the time on 117th Street, although her younger children were still in the apartment on Eighth Avenue. Walter stayed on the block, too, although not with her, sometimes sleeping on a fire escape above a warehouse.

When his mother saw him, she would shout, "Go home! " Walter would shout back, "Go home yourself! "

Sometimes, neighbors say, she would call the police on her son.

TURNING TO NARCOTICS

In November, the whole family was evicted from the Eighth Avenue apartment because Mrs. Price had not paid the $73.10 monthly rent for seven months out of her $412-a-month welfare checks.

She said she was holding the money in escrow because the toilet hadn't worked for a year and a half, but never got to Rent Court to explain this to the judge, perhaps because she no longer had the money.

Tony Vandermeer became distraught when he heard the news and got permission to come down from Yonkers for a day. It was not only the eviction that alarmed him—word had also reached him that Walter had started to take drugs.

The chances are negligible that any child on 117th Street could retain much innocence about narcotics, for the block is wide open to the traffic. Everyone knows the addicts and their pushers and what stairways and landings are best avoided at what times.

Walter's brother Reggie had long been using narcotics. Sometimes he would show his "works"—the eyedropper, needle, cord and bottle cap that are the tools of the addict's vocation—to his younger brothers.

ADDICT RECALLS HIM

Interviewed briefly after Walter's death, when he was brought to the funeral home from Rikers Island, Reggie said he knew who had first given drugs to his brother and named a 17-year-old addict on 117th Street, who shall be called Theresa here.

When she was visited the next day, Theresa was sitting next to a stove with all its burners on, the only warm corner in an apartment that had been without heat all winter. She readily acknowledged that she had been on drugs for two years, had been close to Walter and had known him to be using them.

Although she denied ever having given him any herself, Theresa said she had often seen him "skin" (inject the drug beneath the surface of his skin) but had never known him to "main" (inject it directly into a vein.) Usually, she said, he skinned at the top of the stairs at 303 West 117th Street or in an apartment next door at 301 shared by two of her fellow addicts.

At 301, the two addicts—call them Mary Lou and Lizzie—also denied ever having sold or given drugs to Walter, but Mary Lou said he would often ask for them. She said that she had seen him "snort" (inhale heroin) and that she had occasionally allowed him to watch while she "mained."

Sometimes she would think of Walter as "a little man," Lizzie said. At other times she would see him as an abandoned child and haul him to the bathroom to scrub him in the tub. Treated like a child, he would behave like one, she said.

The two addicts said they found it hard to imagine his locking himself in the bathroom across the street to "shoot up" by himself.

"Walter was scared of the needle," Lizzie said, laughing indulgently as one might in recalling a baby's first steps. "He'd always say, 'Wait. Don't hurt me. Let me get myself together. Please Wait! '"

BROTHER'S ANGER ERUPTS

After the funeral, Tony Vandermeer rushed Lizzie, overturning a floral wreath and shouting, "You killed my brother! " He had heard stories on the block that Lizzie and Theresa had dragged his brother's body on the morning of Dec. 14 from 301 and across 117th Street to 310, where it was found.

Lizzie acknowledged that she had a loud argument with Walter the night before he died over $9—the change left from $25 he had given her to buy him some clothes—but insisted she had not seen him after that.

"Tony really didn't know me at all," she said. "He just had nobody else to blame."

Another addict—known here as Sugar—moved off the block as soon as the body was found. Walter had been especially close to him since the summer, it was said, and sometimes called him "Daddy."

A lanky, good-looking youth who now works at two jobs to keep up with the "Jones's" (his habit) Sugar still returns to the block late at night to make his connection.

The other night at about 12:30 A.M. he came ambling into Mary Lou's apartment on the heels of two pushers—one wearing a leather tunic, the other done out in a frilly shirt with lace cuffs like an 18th-century gentleman.

After an interlude in a bedroom, Sugar appeared rolling down his sleeve and adjusting his cuff link. Behind his dark glasses his eyelids were drooping. His only response to a question about Walter was a perfunctory expression of "shock" over his death.

"But something had to happen," Sugar drawled sleepily. "He was always hanging around."

Dr. Michael Baden, an assistant medical examiner, who examined the body at the scene, said it looked to him like "a typical overdose case." But he cautioned that his office never classified narcotics overdoses as homicides, suicides or accidents, for medical evidence on this point is invariably moot.

Curiously, chemical tests failed to reveal any trace of heroin in the eyedropper found next to Walter in the sink—a hint, by no means conclusive, that it might have been planted.

The autopsy proved that Walter had been using drugs for at least three months—possibly longer—but the absence of any track marks on his arms indicated he had probably yet to become a full-fledged addict.

He had also yet to give up on himself. About a month before he died, Walter received a new pair of shoes from Mrs. Carletha Morrison, one of the women on the block whom he would allow to mother him. He said he would save them for going back to school.

A SCHOOL DROP-IN

According to both Regina and Mrs. Morrison, he seemed to think he could not go to school until his mother took him to court. No one seemed to realize that he was still enrolled at P. S. 148, where he had appeared only three times the previous year.

When the school reminded the Bureau of Attendance of his truancy, it was told to stop sending in reports on the boy because Family Court had his case "under advisement"—a bureaucratic formula that seemed to have no specific application.

Occasionally last fall, Walter would drop into the class of his younger brother "Doe" at P. S. 76 and would be allowed by the teacher to stay. He even asked his brother to teach him reading.

"I gave him my book and any words he didn't know I told him," said "Doe," who is 11.

He was also looking forward to Christmas. Regina had promised to buy him a pair of expensive alligator shoes and a blue pullover. In addition, she said she would treat him to ice skating in Central Park and a movie downtown, probably "The Ten Commandments."

Everyone noticed a macabre touch in a legend stamped on the cheap "Snoopy" sweatshirt Walter was wearing when he died.

"I wish I could bite somebody," it said. "I need to relieve my inner tensions."

"When I heard that I broke down," Regina said. "That was him. That was the way he felt."

JANE JACOBS:
AGAINST URBAN RENEWAL, FOR URBAN LIFE

Leticia Kent

Urban critic Jane Jacobs opens her morning mail: three invitations to speak at universities; a query from "Who's Who of American Women" (which is promptly discarded); an advance copy of her new book, "The Economy of Cities," and several letters from community groups seeking advice on how to save themselves from the bulldozer. She chain-smokes as she reads, absently dropping live ashes onto the letters. "There's a housing shortage, but we're still bulldozing livable housing. We know better. I'm worried," she confides, her kindly, owlish expression less kindly.

With the publication in 1961 of her first book, "The Death and Life of Great American Cities," Jane Jacobs became one of the first liberal voices raised against the liberal programs of urban renewal and city planning. The book was an attack on then-current city planning and rebuilding. It suggested new principles and different methods from those then in use. Stressing the need of cities for economic and social diversity, Mrs. Jacobs accused orthodox planners of seeing the complexities of cities as "mere disorder." Consequently, she said, planning solutions were simplistic and destructive of cities. "There is a quality even meaner than outright ugliness or disorder," she wrote, "and this meaner

Leticia Kent, "Jane Jacobs: Against Urban Renewal, for Urban Life," **THE NEW YORK TIMES MAGAZINE**, *May 25, 1969. Copyright 1969 by The New York Times Company. Reprinted by permission.*

quality is the dishonest mask of pretended order, achieved by ignoring or suppressing the real order that is struggling to exist and to be served."

"The Death and Life of Great American Cities" was first panned by liberals, then hailed by liberals and conservatives alike. It became required reading in American colleges, and was followed by British, German, Spanish, Japanese and Czech editions. The book is now considered a classic and is being added to the "Modern Library." But, according to Mrs. Jacobs, "it has not made the slightest difference in what is actually being done. Most of the same mistakes are still being compulsively repeated."

Jane Jacobs was born in Scranton, Pa., in 1916, and now lives in Toronto. From 1952 to 1962, she was an associate editor of Architectural Forum in New York. Gradually she became increasingly skeptical of conventional city-planning beliefs as she noticed that the city rebuilding projects she was assigned to write about, once completed, seemed "neither safe, interesting, alive, nor good economics for cities." In 1965, Mrs. Jacobs served on both President Johnson's task force on natural beauty and Mayor Lindsay's task force on housing. She is a consultant to the urban-legal program of Osgood Hall, the law school of York University in Toronto, and is at work on her third book—about the governments of cities and of nations as they relate to cities.

Even though Jane Jacobs is discouraged about the stagnation of our cities, she is one of the few urban critics who likes cities, views them as primary economic organs, and does not advocate abandoning them.

Mrs. Jacobs, who describes herself as a "puzzle-solver," absently fiddled with a complex jigsaw puzzle called "Equivocation II," but she did not equivocate when her visitor asked questions. She met every question head-on, viewing each city problem posed as a puzzle capable of being solved.

Are the problems of cities insoluble?

No, of course not. The current acute problems—pollution, noise, automobile congestion, bad housing, and so on—are not nearly so difficult as the problem of bringing epidemics under control. That was a marvelous achievement of cities during the close of the last century and the earlier part of this one. Consider, too, how many problems had to be solved to electrify city industries, streets and homes, or in the job of equipping large, old cities with indoor plumbing and telephones. Mundane problems like these were solved rather magnificently in American cities, not so very long ago. I doubt that current problems are actually any harder.

Then why aren't we solving them?

We're stagnating. Our economy is not casting up *new* goods and services to meet practical problems as it did in the past. The urban crisis amounts to much more than visible physical deterioration, although that has drawn the most attention over the past 25 years. The crisis involves the *whole* economy, because a society's innovatons are created first in cities. Then they go into towns and countrysides.

But aren't our city problems mainly social?

The social problems are part and parcel of economic stagnation.

Why are the cities stagnating?

For decades now, we've been trying to solve their practical problems by "subtracting the problem," which seldom works. For instance, epidemics were not controlled by sending afflicted people out of town. Just so, city blight is not eliminated by clearance; no air pollution or noise by zoning industry away from residential areas; nor traffic congestion by building expressways to take cars off the streets. When a serious practical problem appears in a city it is countered only by adding new kinds of products and services. Combating epidemics required hundreds of them: laboratory work and the laboratories themselves, statistical and other public health services, serum manufacturing, inoculations, water testing and treatment, scientific instruments, antiseptics and so on.

Similarly, overcoming automobile congestion and its serious consequences requires hundreds of new services along with many new types of land and water vehicles to make up for our long stultification in transportation. To solve problems, instead of evading them, takes creativity and the solutions are not necessarily obvious until after the fact. To keep a society's older work from deteriorating also requires constant creativity. Older ways of organizing the work and carrying it on don't serve any longer when the scale of the work expands or becomes more complex. Witness the postal system and the public schools.

The United States was such a creative country. What happened?

When a country's economy stultifies and stagnates, it's because one small decision after another is made in favor of the status quo instead of in favor of new enterprises. Think of all the seemingly small regulations that obstruct change: transportation franchises, union rules, building codes, zoning ordinances. . . . Also, there is little capital in America now for new ideas, and a good deal is wasted on useless studies of problems. Worst of all is racial discrimination. This hampers the blacks, who now form a big proportion of the urban population, in solving problems by adding their own innovations into the economy. From new answers come true economic growth and abundance. Our problems today are not the result of "rapid progress" or of overproduction. They pile up because of lack of progresss and much undone work.

But everybody, in government and out, wants to see the cities' problems solved, don't they?

There is no point in pretending that economic development is in everyone's interest. Development of new kinds of city transportation would badly hurt the automobile, oil and highway-building establishments, including their unions. In developing economies, even the well-established goods and services are directly affected. And so are those whose goods and services are indirectly affected. And so are those whose economic and social power are tied up with those established activities. When I implied that the United States was no longer creative, I meant that the status quo was effectively resisting change.

Hasn't the status quo always resisted change?

Yes. But in this era of big business and big unions, the intransigence of the status quo is bigger, too. And big government, which derives its power from these big interests, seems to have abrogated its vital role of protecting weak and still incipient interests. Think of all the allies in government of the automobile, oil and highway-building establishments, and of the laws that enforce these interests' economic ascendancy.

Aren't large cities certain to be in serious trouble because of their size? Isn't their trouble that they're too big?

No. What we now think of as practical, moderate-sized cities are practical only because many problems were solved in the past in cities that seemed to have grown impracticably large. To limit the size of great cities, because of the acute problems that arise in them, is profoundly reactionary. And it is futile, because moderate-sized cities are not immune to stagnation and decay; in fact, they are more vulnerable than the large cities.

But isn't the bureaucracy you complained of a result of city size?

Yes, in part. When a city reaches large size, it can't be governed any more as if it were a town. It has to be governmentally divided, I think. Take New York. Back before the turn of the century, it was five cities. It was probably a mistake to consolidate them into one. Even five autonomous city governments are probably not enough for New York now. Just because a city is a huge economic unit, it does not follow that it must be a huge governmental unit. You need differing administrative approaches and lots of experimenting which you can't get very well under centralized government. I think it is also questionable that large nations are really viable governmental units any longer. They may be obsolete—like dinosaurs. The viable nations of the future may be on the scale of Sweden or Holland, rather than on the scale of the United States, China or the Soviet Union.

Would the urban crisis be solved if the money going into Vietnam were poured into cities instead?

Not necessarily. People who believe the crux of the crisis is money may be terribly disappointed when more money is available. Money without good ideas of how to use it doesn't solve anything. It can make matters worse. Suppose there was more money for expressways through cities or for urban renewal as it's currently practiced.

But given enough authority, as well as money, can't the Federal Government solve the urban crisis?

No, the Federal Government and its programs are a large part of the disease. City problems can only be solved locally, to begin with, and at an even lower level than the centralized city government. Of course, when a problem has been solved successfully, that is, innovations have been made even in one neighborhood, they can quickly be copied.

Solutions to practical problems almost all begin humbly. Humble people are usually affected by city problems long before the well-to-do are, and they notice and understand the problems first. The first hospitals were very humble enterprises. So were the first automobiles, airplanes, clothing factories, department stores and supermarkets. When humble people doing ordinary work are not also solving problems, the problems just do not get solved.

How can money be used creatively to rejuvenate cities?

By financing multitudes of small experiments—not dreamed up in remote bureaucracies, but undertaken by people who see how some new product or service can profitably and logically be added to whatever it is they are already doing or can help solve some practical problem they themsevles are facing. This is exactly how most innovations first arose. The first Ford factory was a wooden building in a coal yard, financed by the carpenter who built it. Many such experiments will fail—before Henry Ford succeeded, he failed twice—but some will succeed and grow. Private capital used to be used this way. At present, there are almost no sources—private or public—for such money. It isn't that there is not enough money—think of what only a mile or two of expressway costs—but that it is not ventured for development of new goods and services.

Why isn't private capital used innovatingly any more?

Private capital goes increasingly into well-worn grooves like the stock market, the insurance companies and the big banks, which tend to dismiss out of hand ideas for genuinely new and unproved goods and services.

What role should the Federal Government assume in relation to cities?

The single most salutary thing it could do would bè to repeal its housing, urban-renewal, model-cities and highway legislation, and hand responsibility for such matters, along with the tax money, back to localities. They could hardly do worse than under the present arrangement.

But aren't problems such as pollution, housing and transportation at least regional?

All that means is that they are widespread, that they aren't being solved in any particular locality and so there is nothing for other places to copy.

What about Secretary of Housing and Urban Development George Romney's recently announced plans for pooling the separate housing needs of the major states and cities into a single mass market and encouraging mass production techniques originated in the auto industry in Detroit?

In the first place, successful new mass-production industries are not created like that. Consider the automobile industry itself. There wasn't some decision made in Washington that the whole country was to switch from horses. Rather, thousands of small automobile companies and parts-makers arose. Most of them failed, but many succeeded. Then came the merger stage: surviving companies were consolidated. It would have been ineffective to ask the railroads, which were the big, successful companies of the time, to develop the automobile.

But wouldn't Romney's proposed national codes help expedite housing?

They would stultify development. Every building code soon comes to represent a net of vested interests in methods, materials and equipment that meet the code requirements. Buckminster Fuller found it almost impossible, for years, to construct geodesic domes because in so many places where the domes could otherwise have been tried out, the codes forbade this construction. Of course, the authors of codes had never conceived of such a thing as the geodesic dome. Luckily, Fuller found some backward places where its usefulness could be demonstrated. Frank Lloyd Wright frequently had similar troubles. In postwar New York, concrete-block walls had to be built behind curtain-wall construction for the sake of the codes. While Nervi in Italy and Candella in Mexico were building concrete-shell structures much admired in the United States, there were no American cities where similar methods were allowed.

Would it be better to have no building codes?
No, we need them to prevent catastrophes. But we need lots of different codes—not standardization. In fact, we need less standardization than we have right now, so there will be opportunity, in different places, to develop and demonstrate differing new things. In a way, we have a sample of the wrong kind of national code in our public-housing regulations. They are stultifying—socially, economically, and esthetically. So are the national F.H.A. regulations that decreed our look-alike suburbs. I don't think much new development can be achieved under any one code, no matter how farsightedly it is drawn. It would be better if a code specifies only performance requirements, and avoids being specific about means, but the whole point of the Romney proposal is to standardize means and materials.

Another mistake in the proposal is that it implies that only a few models of housing will satisfy the country's needs. One trouble now is that too few types are being built, too much fixation on the high-rise apartment on the one hand, and the single-family house—sometimes modified as a town house—on the other hand. This is one of the defects that led to so much bulldozing. If you're going to have standard housing of very few types, you've got to make standard sites too.

But wouldn't the automobile companies be efficient producers of housing?
Hardly. According to Fortune magazine, they don't produce automobiles efficiently anymore. And imagine returning the ranch houses to Detroit because the double-hung windows are loose or the furnaces may explode. I suspect the automobile companies are becoming as moribund, as incapable of making significant innovations, as the railroads became in their time. And, you know, you don't need automobile-type mass production to get efficiency and economy. The electronics industry is carried on by thousands of small companies, as well as some big ones. But these small companies have not disappeared into a few large mass-production companies as the automobile companies did. Instead, they've multiplied. This is because the electronics industry is based on a type of production more advanced than mass production. It's based on differentiation, on many different companies supplying many different kinds of equipment to satisfy many different needs.

What do you think should be done about the housing problem, instead?
All over the country, people in cities have suggested ways of adding to the housing supply by building on vacant lots, on parking lots and on sites of abandoned structures.This differentiated approach to construction is more eco-

nomical than mass production, which needs large, standard, bulldozed sites. And differentiated schemes are natural candidates for new techniques and materials that are precluded in mass production. But these grass-roots solutions to the housing shortage have been stymied because they don't fit in with the housing-project vision or they transgress zoning regulations. Then, too, large interests have a stake in city housing shortages.

But is there enough vacant and abandoned land in cities on which to build and overcome the shortage?
For all practical purposes, there is. It will be years before we exhaust these possibilities even with much greater housing production than we have now. The Metropolitan Council on Housing, after surveying parts of 22 of New York's 87 residential districts, estimated in a published report that there was enough available land in the five boroughs to build 100,000 new family units of housing. A surprising variety of sites was found—junkyards, abandoned schools, unused carbarns—most of them in Manhattan, Brooklyn and the Bronx. And the survey excluded vast numbers of small sites which I think could and should be used. A similar study of vacant land in Manhattan was released by Manhattan's borough president, Percy Sutton.

Some officials claim that neighborhoods obstruct housing programs.
Of course they do, and doubtless they will continue to as long as policies and decisions are made remotely by the bureaucracies.

Are New Towns a promising solution to the urban crisis?
Look at all the stagnant, dying little towns there are now. Why should we expect New Towns to be any more vital? Just because the buildings, roads, playgrounds and community halls are new? New Towns—in this country or anywhere else—depend on industries spun off from cities. They don't create their own economic base, the way cities do. When the cities are decaying, in time there is no growing economic base for New Towns. Most of what are called New Towns are really only suburbs of cities, in any case.
If we were to pour available capital and effort into New Towns instead of into starting to solve our many acute city problems, New Town building could actually reinforce the country's ominous stagnation.

Is massive urban renewal clearance ever justified in a city?
No. There is an economic necessity for old buildings mixed with new. Cities *need* old buildings to incubate new enterprises. Trial, error and experimentation, from which new ideas come, is precluded in the high-overhead economy of new construction. Also when an area is all new, it offers no possibilities for social diversity.

Then are new urban developments doomed to remain monotonous and dull?
Yes, under any of the planning precepts that are practiced today. A rigid and "finished" physical environment is incompatible with accommodating the future.

Edward Logue says that a lot of trouble in the cities is that they are black ghettos ringed by white suburbs and that the suburbs must be opened up to the blacks and more whites must come back to the cities.

Behind a statement like that is an assumption that blacks are not going to solve problems either for themselves or for the cities, that the cities can only be rescued by whites. I don't believe this. Moreover, there are already blacks in many suburbs—Plainfield, White Plains, Nassau County, for instance. This has solved nothing, either for the society or for the blacks. Again, it's like trying to overcome epidemics by sending the afflicted people out of town. It's an evasion.

Would birth control solve the problems of the urban poor?

The idea that poor people are poor because there are too many of them is a vicious idea, and nothing in the real world backs it up. Latin America is very underpopulated in general, and, of course, it's very poor. Japan and Western Europe are very heavily populated and well-off. I don't think you can make any correlation between numbers of people and their economic condition. Ireland was terribly depopulated by famine and emigration, but the Irish remained very poor while their population sank to about a quarter of what it had been. Does this mean that the solution for the urban poor is to reduce them to a quarter of their population? Nonsense. The economies of people are just *not* like the economies of animals. Animals live on what nature provides more or less ready made. People develop new goods and services, new resources, new means of abundance. And it takes more hands and heads to do this. You actually *need* a growing population in a developing economy.

Will education solve the problem of the urban poor, then?

Education, by itself, does not bring prosperity or opportunity. It can frustrate people in stagnant economies. According to Scientific American, India has about the highest population of unemployed and underemployed college graduates in the world. A labor leader in the United States once remarked, you just get more highly educated unemployed. Education, by itself, fails to create an advancing society. On the other hand, if there actually is opportunity, if we're not going to have a regimented and uncreative "industrial state," then education can make a very great difference.

Galbraith says the future economy of the country is going to be in the hands of the Government and the very large corporations. A lot of people on the left, such as Michael Harrington, agree with this assumption.

Galbraith assumes that this arrangement, with some adjustments such as guaranteed incomes, will permit the gross national product to continue to grow and the country to prosper, at least materially. Harrington makes a similar assumption. I disagree. Developing economies, which are the only economies that prosper, require that large numbers of young, new enterprises continually arise. The processes of development depend on this, far more than upon the research-and-development work of already large, existing corporations. Indeed, this is one reason large corporations buy up so many small companies: if they could depend on their own creativity for their growth, this would not be necessary.

Do you have any attitude toward a national guaranteed income? Is that a possible solution to urban poverty?

It is another kind of welfare payment and will accomplish what welfare does, no more, no less. The guaranteed annual income, like the poverty program, does not get at the underlying problem of undone work in the society.

Is the urban crisis less acute in Marxist countries?

The Marxist countries have one inherent advantage, which is that Marxist revolutions have occurred in backward countries. And backward countries have a lot of catching up to do. The big test of Marxist governments will be whether they are able to develop beyond merely imitating the goods and services of more advanced economies. (Nobody in a backward country has to prove that chest X-rays are workable and useful, that automobiles are better than horses, that cameras take pictures, or that tractors can be used on farms.) The Soviet Union, at present, is plagued by many of the same unsolved problems and undone work as the United States. Probably the most creative present-day economy is Japan's. Its astonishingly high growth rates are based on many innovations—including differentiated production methods. Japan is ahead of us in transportation and in waste recycling, among other things.

Theoretically, at least, isn't it easier to control urban development under Communism than capitalism?

The real problem is not control, but creativity. I don't think any existing ideology describes economic reality very well. It's more fruitful to try to learn by examining how things work, rather than leaping to conclusions about how they "should" work.

Isn't automation beginning to make much urban work unnecessary?

It reduces the labor required for some kinds of already existing work, like any labor-saving devices, but it does not take over work that is not being done at all. If we are to continue developing, we will certainly need continual automating, to release people for new kinds of work. I don't see automation as meaning there will be less total work to do—unless, of course, we continue to stagnate.

Many planners seem to think you have a poor regard for the profession of city planning. Is this true?

Yes. The planners' greatest shortcoming, I think, is lack of intellectual curiosity about how cities work. They are taught to see the intricacy of cities as mere disorder. Since most of them believe what they have been taught, they do not inquire about the processes that lie behind the intricacy. I doubt that knowledgeable city planning will come out of the present profession. It is more likely to arise as an offshoot of economics.

Do you see pollution as a planning problem or as an economic problem?

I see it as an economic opportunity. Great wealth can be extracted from waste materials that are reclaimed and recycled instead of dumped into the air and the water, to say nothing of the economic advantages of the clean water and air that will result. Waste recycling is going to afford economic opportunity, in particular to the cities that make the first effective advances in recycling their own wastes. As the work develops locally, such cities will have new growth industries. They will have many new devices and services to export to other places, as well as reclaimed raw materials.

Can you illustrate what you mean by waste recycling?

Yes. Sulfur dioxide is the second major source of air pollution in the United States because we burn huge quanities of coal and oil that contain sulfur. But sulfur dioxide can be captured in the fuel stacks at power plants and other places and converted to sulfuric acid, which, of course, is one of the most basic and heavily used chemicals in modern economies. Another kind of waste recycling is illustrated by the enormous second-hand machinery industry that has grown up in Chicago in the last 20 years.

What cities do you think are most likely to incubate new waste-recycling industries?

We can be certain they will be very large cities because the greatest and the most complex markets for the hundreds of new devices and services required are in large cities. But they will not necessarily be American cities. Japan, and possible Continental Europe, may well take the lead in this work.

Are you pessimistic about the future of American cities?

Temperamentally, I'm an optimist and tend to look on the bright side. But I can't see much happening—apart from protest, which is a hopeful sign—that justifies optimism. Historically, societies have often got into so much trouble that their decline, at some point, has become irreversible. This seems clear by hindsight, but evidently it isn't clear that a critical point is being reached at the very time it is happening. I don't know whether we've reached such a point yet or whether we are still capable of reversing direction. Of course, it is necessary to keep trying. There's nothing else to do.

You have emphasized the importance of social, economic and physical diversity in cities. Can you have democracy without diversity?

No.

THE POLITICS OF HUNGER

John A. Hamilton

There is hunger in America. Those who live well in a land fat with agricultural surpluses are beginning to grasp this paradoxical fact. It has recently been irrefutably documented by medical surveys, and, in May, President Nixon ended a policy debate within his Administration by announcing that "there can be no doubt" about its existence.

Hunger stunts the body. It dulls the mind. It causes lassitude and disease, such as rickets and goiter, and in extreme cases, according to nutritional experts, the risk of irreversible brain damage among the very young. It contributes to a nagging incidence of tuberculosis and to appallingly high infant mortality rates.

It reflects grossly distorted national priorities and a callousness of conscience. It recalls the depths of the Depression and lines from John Steinbeck's *The Grapes of Wrath,* written three decades ago but as searingly appropriate now as they were then:

"There is a crime that goes beyond denunciation. There is a sorrow here that weeping cannot symbolize. There is a failure that topples all our success.

There is also a politics of hunger in America that needs understanding, an old politics that helps explain hunger's existence and a new politics that seeks its eradication, as well as a structural politics that involves the federal system of government and permits states and localities, out of false pride or shameless bigotry, to erect barriers against federal food programs, effectively denying their benefits to millions of the poor who need and deserve them.

Mrs. Mary Addison is among those millions. She is a black, withered woman of sixty-five who has played a role in the politics of hunger—the old, the new, and the structural. She has known hunger. She sits alone most of the time in the shadows of her bare board, windowless shack that rests on cinder blocks just above the flat, sandy land at Combers Camp in Collier County, Florida.

Mrs. Addison was the first resident interviewed by members of the Select Senate Committee on Nutrition and Human Needs at its initial stop in the series of field trips that will take it crisscrossing the nation, from Florida to South Dakota, from Massachusetts to California, as it seeks to expose hunger. One day several weeks ago, members of the committee, along with a host of reporters, photographers, television cameramen and their light crews, swept through Combers Camp like a marauding army, and Mrs. Addison shared the glare of

John A. Hamilton, "The Politics of Hunger," **SATURDAY REVIEW**, June 21, 1969. Copy right 1969, Saturday Review, Inc. Reprinted by permission of the author and the publisher.

national publicity with Senator George McGovern, Democrat of South Dakota, who serves as committee chairman.

But she shared it only briefly. There was a handshake, a few words, the bright lights and whirring cameras, and then the committee was gone. Mrs. Addison's surname was listed incorrectly as "Adderson" on the tour program, and this is the way it was transmitted to the nation.

The next day, sitting alone in the shadows once more, Mrs. Addison traced a lifetime of toil in the fields that had reaped a harvest of bitter hardship for her and her husband. She had just received a letter bringing still more bad news, although it appeared that she could not read and that its message would remain a merciful mystery to her. As sunlight filtered through the screen door making the deep lines in her face clearly visible, she spoke softly and pleasantly.

"He don't get much work anymore," she said, referring to her husband, who is sixty-eight, and who had left at 5 that morning for the day-haul labor pickup point. She said that he goes anyway, hoping. "He don't see too good. Picking tomatoes, they say he misses too many of the pinks."

The story of hunger in America is a story of extreme privation, and often of crushing tragedy. Mrs. Addison told how her husband had lost the sight in one eye and had damaged the sight in the other after working in a field freshly sprayed with pesticides.

"He knowed it had been sprayed," she said, "but he was hot and sweaty on the bus riding back from the field, and he forgot hisself. He took out a handkerchief and wiped it over his face. That's when he said it happened. He said a skim come over his eye."

Mrs. Addison's left leg had been amputated a year ago following a circulatory ailment. Recalling that a welfare worker had promised her an artificial limb, she remained resolutely optimistic about her own handicap.

"I sure could use that limb," she said.

She unfolded the letter she had just received. It was a form letter from the Florida State Welfare Department rejecting her application for old age assistance. A typed sentence in the large blank space provided for individual messages said: "Your application has been pending for more than thirty days and the artificial limb you desire has not been secured and you are not eligible without the allowance for this in your budget."

During the previous day's tour, a member of the Select Senate Committee had reported seeing only dried beans and fatback in the Addison shack. A hostile and defensive local official, closely trailing the committee, reported opening the refrigerator and finding it "stuffed with meat." A subsequent examination supported the local official—to an extent. The refrigerator contained two large plastic bags of frozen neck bones and pigtails. They are sold five pounds for 89 cents.

There is hunger in America because there is poverty in America, a more wretchedly abject and pathetically hopeless poverty than even some of the nation's most zealous social reformers have realized. In describing the deprivation in *The Other America*—the poor, tucked-away, and forgotten America that languishes in remote areas and economic backwaters—Michael Harrington discounted the presence of hunger. He assumed that a generally affluent land would at least have drawn a line somewhere this side of hunger.

It was an unwarranted assumption, as the medical surveys reveal.

The Department of Agriculture estimates that it takes about $1,200 a year to feed a family of four a minimally adequate diet, and the Office of Economic Opportunity, using this figure, calculates that there are as many as fourteen to fifteen million Americans living in families unable to afford this much for food. Nutritional ignorance, considered widespread, probably accounts for inadequate diets in many families with incomes above the poverty level.

Other figures also help sketch the dimensions of a problem that hangs like a dark cloud over the land; it is there, vast and forbidding, but not susceptible to precise measurement. The federal government estimates that there are about twenty-two million Americans who live below the official poverty line of $3,335 annual income for a family of four. Federal food programs supplementing the diets of the needy reach only six million Americans.

The Select Senate Committee on Nutrition and Human Needs stirs up all these figures and estimates that there are, roughly, ten million hungry Americans. It is a guess, but it is one that respected nutritionists also make.

The old politics of hunger, which can be blamed for its extent, has been a quiet and subtle sort of thing, an exchange of favors and votes, and then a diversion of tax revenues to large farm interests by those who smoke cigars and know where power lies. Public policies have been shaped to favor farmers with lavish subsidies that promote food scarcity and that keep prices high while ignoring the plight of the poor who have not had enough food to eat, including some citrus workers found deficient in the vitamins fresh fruits supply. The old politics of hunger has been played in the dim lights of the cloakrooms and committee chambers.

The new politics of hunger, in contrast, has turned into a brassy, center-stage production. Its practitioners are on the side of the angels, of course, but they also know that political careers feed on favorable publicity. They are latter-day knights who consider hunger a dragon and draw their swords against it, in prime time if possible. It is not easy to criticize them, as President Nixon's communications director, Herbert Klein, found out.

When Mr. Klein accused the Select Senate Committee of trying to make hunger "a political cause," and when he criticized its members for "traipsing around the country with television cameras," he seemed to join the dragon. Members of the committee treated him as if he had. They drew their swords and handed him his head.

To Senator McGovern, it seemed that Klein was "aligning himself with those few of Florida's state and local officials who refuse to face up to the problem of hunger, and who react defensively to the fact that our committee has turned the public spotlight on an outrageous situation—the existence of hunger in the world's richest nation."

To Senator Jacob Javits, responding stiffly to his fellow Republican: "The assault on America's conscience by malnutrition amounting to hunger . . . is bigger than anybody's remarks about politics."

When the Senate Rules Committee, playing the old politics of hunger, lopped almost in half the Select Committee's request for investigating funds, Senator McGovern, playing the new politics of hunger, took his case to the floor. The Senate restored the funds.

The new politics with its ultimate weapon, the public spotlight, has brought other developments to a healthy bloom. The Nixon Administration's revisions of the leftover Johnson budget for the next fiscal year increased amounts devoted to food programs by only $15 million, with the increase earmarked for nutritional education programs. The skimpiness of the effort caused critics to brand it as the Administration's "thin" nutritional program.

After a tour of poverty areas in the nation's capital during which mothers testified that their children often have nothing to eat, the Select Committee invited Secretary of Agriculture Clifford M. Hardin and Secretary of Health, Education and Welfare Robert H. Finch to appear at a full-dress, televised public hearing to explain the Administration's food program. The two secretaries had long been urging President Nixon to launch an expanded anti-hunger campaign. They requested a delay. The committee granted one. The President issued his statement on hunger on the eve of their committee appearance.

The statement represents a bold, forthright commitment to end hunger, but it also reflects the Administration's intense, behind-the-scenes debate over budgetary priorities. Hardin and Finch had been on one side. Dr. Arthur F. Burns, the President's senior adviser with Cabinet rank, had been on the other. He worried about inflation and looked on any spending scheme with a cold and fishy eye.

"If there were hunger and the budget stood in the way, I'd say to hell with the budget," he insisted to one visitor making clear at the same time that he doubted hunger existed. He demanded that Hardin and Finch supply firmer facts and figures. Presidential Assistant Daniel Patrick Moynihan, the once ebullient Democrat who now serves as the increasingly testy and difficult staff director of Mr. Nixon's Urban Affairs Council, seems to have played a strangely ambivalent, middle role, wanting to end hunger but not wanting any anti-hunger program to jeopardize proposed welfare reforms which he considers more basic. He berated critics of the Administration's anti-hunger effort, while at the same time writing President Nixon a weasel-worded private memorandum denying that American youngsters suffer from malnutrition's most severe consequences as do some youngsters in other lands around the globe. It was his "suspicion," he said in the memorandum, that malnutrition caused no mental retardation here.

The President's statement of hunger exhibited its own ambivalence. It first announced that "the moment is at hand to put an end to hunger in America," and then postponed any real effort for more than a year. The present $1.5 billion overall food effort will be increased to $2.5 billion, but not until fiscal year 1971. A more modest $270 million will be added to present efforts in the latter half of fiscal year 1970. The statement also recommended a number of worthwhile reforms in the execution of existing programs.

Would any of this—even the commitment—have been announced if the Select Committee had closed up shop? In time, perhaps. In Dr. Burns's own good time.

The old politics of hunger has also had its showdowns. Its heroes, though unsung nationally, have had their victories in the past and the current budget reflects them. It allots $4.5 billion for an array of farm price-support programs and only $564 million for family food programs. Other funds go into school lunch and school breakfast programs to swell the total food program considerably, but these programs tend to benefit middle-class children more than very poor children whose schools may not even have cafeterias. Thus, as far as the poor are concerned, the nation spends eight times as much making food scarce as it does making it available.

The two federal food programs for needy families are the food stamp program and the commodity distribution program. Neither is adequately financed. They are mutually exclusive—a county that has one cannot have the other—and they are optional with the states and localities, with far too many opting out.

The food stamp program stretches the food dollars of the poor. Depending on family size and income, a needy family might be able to purchase $40 worth of stamps redeemable for $60 worth of food at the grocery store.

The commodity distribution program is linked directly to the farm price-support program. It offers eligible families up to twenty-two items free each month. All twenty-two, however, are never available at any one time, and those distributed tend to be those then in surplus.

Florida has been one of seven states refusing to certify families for the food stamp program. Collier County has been one of several hundred across the nation also refusing to shoulder the modest costs of maintaining a food distribution center and participating in the commodity distribution program. The poor in Collier County, including its 22,000 migrant farm laborers essential to its $40-million agricultural economy, are denied all family food-program benefits.

As the Select Senate Committee toured the county, the Florida cabinet voted for the state to begin participation in the food stamp program. The Office of Economic Opportunity authorized a local community action agency to ignore local official sentiment and to serve as a commodity distribution center if the Department of Agriculture agrees to make commodities available.

The nation's twisted agricultural priorities manifestly need straightening. The farmers do not have to be cut off from all subsidy help, but the poor must be given proper consideration. To expand domestic food markets by subsidizing the poor would make more sense than to restrict production by subsidizing the farmers. Existing food programs should be made complementary, rather than mutually exclusive. Their funding must be more generous, and their administration more humane.

Shaped by farm interests in the Congress, these programs are administered by the Department of Agriculture which frankly looks upon them not as programs to feed the poor but as programs to prop up farm prices. Their administration has been rigidly restrictive. The department has set the price of food stamps so high that many of the poor in the states participating in this program have been unable to afford them. The law requires the department to charge the poor a price "equivalent to their normal expenditure for food." Most American families spend 17 per cent of their income for food, and although the poor may spend a slightly larger percentage, the department has charged them as much as 30 per cent and even 50 per cent for food stamps.

Former Secretary of Agriculture Orville Freeman conceded violating the law in testimony before the Select Senate Committee shortly before his leaving office. He said, in circumlocutory fashion: "Where we now have food stamp programs in effect, to lower the requirements to what people are actually spending for food now, which is what the law provides, I mean, honestly, strictly speaking, where we are not squaring with the congressional directive, which is that people should pay in only as much as they have been spending for food. We can't do that because we don't have enough money."

The secretary's testimony indicts both the administration and the funding of the food stamp program. It is relevant to several lawsuits that have been filed by the poor in Mississippi and elsewhere charging the Department of Agriculture with pegging food-stamp prices at unlawful levels, preventing "hundreds of thousands of hungry and undernourished Mississippians from obtaining vital federal food assistance."

Not long ago, when several Mississippi counties switched from a free commodity distribution program to a food stamp program, the participation of the poor declined sharply. In Sunflower County, for example, it declined from 18,540 persons to 7,856 persons. The disparity between policies is egregiously clear in this country. The poor have been forced to go hungry while Senator James O. Eastland's Sunflower County plantation, according to the Senator himself, received $113,275 in federal subsidies last year and $157,930 the year before.

This disparity recalls what the Citizens Crusade Against Poverty said in a report it sponsored on hunger in America:

> The failure of federal efforts to feed the poor cannot be divorced from the nation's agricultural policy, the congressional committees that dictate that policy, and the Department of Agriculture that implements it; for hunger and malnutrition in a country of abundance must be seen as consequences of a political and economic system that spends billions to remove food from the market, to limit production, to retire land from production, to guarantee and sustain profits for the producer.

A roster of congressional committees that dictate agricultural policy shows Allen J. Ellender of Louisiana as chairman of the Senate Agriculture Committee, W. R. Poage of Texas as chairman of the House Agriculture Committee, and Jamie L. Whitten of Mississippi as chairman of the Agricultural Appropriations Subcommittee. All of these men are tied to the nation's agricultural interests and to Southern traditions. None has been conspicuous in his advocacy of programs for the poor.

This is probably less true of Senator Ellender, however, than of the others. He is not responsible for the food stamp plan. Its enactment several years ago resulted from the dedicated and unremitting effort of Missouri Congresswoman Leonor Sullivan. He is nonetheless a warm supporter of this plan, and its future rests largely with him.

Crusty and conservative at seventy-eight, Ellender took the Collier County tour with the Select Senate Committee. At first, he complained that the tour was hitting only the worst of the labor camps and not any of the best. He called for balance, and he worried out loud to photographers viewing the squalor through their lenses about the propaganda value their pictures would have for the Communists.

"All of the children seem happy," he told reporters at one of the early stops. "I haven't heard anybody say they are hungry," he commented at another point. But, as the tour progressed, he seemed to be genuinely moved by what he saw, and he underwent a change.

"There are some bad conditions," he finally admitted, adding that he had seen "more hunger" than he had expected to see, and that perhaps both the food stamp and commodity distribution programs could be made complementary and offered generally across the nation.

Senator Ernest F. Hollings of South Carolina did not make the Collier County tour, but he has become an even firmer convert. His testimony before the Select Committee was part confession and part resolution. As a state official, he had seen hunger and shut his conscience to the suffering. Now he wants to alleviate it. His appeal caused Secretary of Agriculture Hardin to launch a pilot food stamp plan in two South Carolina counties. The plan provides free stamps for a limited number of needy families.

Still others in Congress, weighing the power of the old politics of hunger against the potential of the new, have proved fence straddlers or worse. Politics to them is not a cloakroom backslap or television extravaganza so much as a guerrilla war, and they seem to play one role by day and another by night. They speak against hunger, and vote, in effect, for it. Their names merit mentioning: William H. Ayers of Ohio, Catherine May of Washington, Robert H. Michel of Illinois, Rogers C. B. Morton of Maryland, Albert H. Quie of Minnesota, Charles M. Teague of California, and Charles E. Goodell of New York, now a Senator.

In April, last year, they all voted against extending the 1964 Food Stamp Act. It was extended despite their opposition.

In May, they joined other colleagues in a "Coalition to Help Malnourished Americans."

In July, they voted against increasing the authorization for the food stamp plan—all of them except Mr. Goodell who did not vote. The increase was approved anyway.

State and local officials, as the touring Senators discovered, can also prove troublesome. They can refuse to participate in optional federal food programs, as they have done throughout Florida and especially in Collier County, where tuberculosis is a major problem and the infant mortality rate among nonwhites is six times the national average.

"They are not Collier County people," said one local official, referring to the county's migrant laborers and denying all responsibility for them. Florida Governor Claude Kirk angrily appeared at a public hearing to insist on a continuing role for the states even though Florida's role in the food stamp plan has been an obstructionist one.

"We do not want to quibble over words, but 'malnutrition' is not quite what we found," commented a team of doctors who made a nutritional study in Mississippi for the Southern Regional Council. "The boys and girls we saw were hungry . . . weak, in pain, sick; their lives are being shortened. . . . They are suffering from hunger and disease, and directly or indirectly they are dying from them—which is exactly what 'starvation' means."

Dr. Arnold E. Schaefer of the Public Health Service heads the first official government survey of hunger in America, and he released its initial findings in recent testimony to the Select Senate Committee. "Our studies to date clearly indicate that there is malnutrition, and in our opinion it occurs in an unexpectedly large proportion of our sample population," he said.

Another group of nutritionists consider malnutrition so prevalent as to "constitute a danger to the nation." They said that ill-nourished mothers give birth to ill-nourished children and, among poor families that produce 20 per cent of all the nation's children, the odds are three to five times as high that a child will be mentally retarded.

Hunger accompanies poverty, and to eliminate poverty would be to eliminate hunger. Poverty, however, is a complicated collection of problems, and hunger—when it is not considered a dragon—is nothing more than an empty ice box. It is amenable to immediate improvement because American agriculture produces more than enough food to go around. The nation needs a better distribution system, that's all.

Hunger can be eliminated. The Nixon Administration's delayed action and still inadequate response can be accelerated and expanded, and the nation's millions of poor—its endangered children and its abused elderly, its Mrs. "Addersons"—can emerge from their shadow worlds. Success can come, not because "hunger knows no politics" (as Senator McGovern once proclaimed in a lofty absurdity), but because it does know politics. It knows the public spotlight.

Dismissed recently by Harrington as simply too incredible in a generally prosperous land, hunger has now been exposed as disgracefully prevalent and as fully deserving of Steinbeck's Depression era terms: "a crime" and "a sorrow" and "a failure." Hunger in America knows a growing public outrage that could become a profound political force. Hopefully, it will. For if it does, it will prevail.

2. **THE ANTICS OF BUREAUCRATS**

WHITE ON BLACK:
The Riot Commission and The Rhetoric of Reform

Andrew Kopkind

"As America gets worse and worse," Murray Kempton once wrote, "its reports get better and better." No report of a commission investigating America's recent crises has found so warm a public welcome as the Kerner Commission's study of the season of civil disorders in the summer of 1967. In its official and private editions the "Riot Commission" Report has sold almost two million copies. Countless critiques and analyses have greeted it in the press, and it has turned to grist for thesis-mills in the nation's graduate schools and colleges. The careers of several Commissioners, staff officials and consultants have been considerably enhanced by their association with the Report (and only a few reputations have suffered). All in all, the Report has become a basic document in the platform of American liberals for social reform, a catalogue of problems and a program of solutions.

But by and large, those who were cheered by the Report's solemn plati-tudes or impressed by its torrent of statistics missed its essential political func-tions and its crucial social consequences. It presented—and legitimized—a specific view of the riots and a particular understanding of America that now constitutes the standard approach to the treatment of social ills. The Commission was able to do that job because of the way it was set up, staffed, manipulated and terminated; because of the promises and rewards it offered those who worked for it; because of its punishments for criticism and dissension; and because of its calculated presentation to the public through press and mass media.

Reportage and analysis of the Commission's work have largely failed, and for the same reasons: Reporters and analysts became deeply implicated in the "success" of the Report. Although there was an unusual amount of reportable conflicts during the Commission's seven months of operation, reporters never got past the vague rumors of friction between liberal and conservative forces, or the whispered hints of White House interference. The firing of 120 staff members in late 1967 was never explained; the substantial hostility of black staffers towards the Commission's own "institutional" racism was never men-tioned; the "underground" Commission document, "The Harvest of American

*Andrew D. Kopkind, "White on Black: The Riot Commission and the Rhetoric of Reform," **HARD TIMES**, September 15, 1969. Copyright © 1969. The New Weekly Project, Inc. Reprinted by permission of the author and publisher.*

Racism," was never examined; the White House veto on employment of staff and consultants active in anti-war work was never disclosed; the tacit agreement to "forget" the war in Vietnam throughout the Commission's investigations and its Report was overlooked; and the secret plan of Commissioner Charles ("Tex") Thornton to torpedo the Report just before launching is still an untold story.

In similar ways, the political analysts who pored over the long document never got past its liberal rhetoric and its profuse programmatics to see its political role. No one has yet detailed the Report's lasting effect on the set of signals it delivered to corporations, foundations and government planners to manage urban affairs on the model of foreign aid and counter-insurgency programs of the early Sixties.

For the Report does not exist outside of its political context. It can logically escape neither the conflicts which informed its operations, nor the uses to which it will be put. Strictures on thinking "unthinkable" thoughts about Vietnam (among other unthinkables) made impossible a realistic assessment of the nature of riotous America. Total concern for the way resources of the society are allocated—rather than control of the allocation process—eliminated discussion of the possibilities of serious social change. Acceptance of pluralistic myths about the operation of American institutions limited the Report to the exposition of a narrow ideology. Failure to analyze in any way the "white racism" asserted by the Commissioners in the Report's summary transformed that critical category into a cheap slogan. And overall, the Report's mindless attention to documenting conventional perceptions and drowning them in conventional wisdom made meaningless the Commissioners demands for social reconstruction.

The very acceptance—and acceptability—of the Report is a clue to its emptiness. It threatens no real, commanding interests. It demands, by implication or explication, no real shifts in the way power and wealth are apportioned among classes; it assumes that the political and social elites now in control will (and should) remain in their positions. By avoiding an approach to the riots as events of political insurrection, or as part of a world-wide response to an overbearing US empire, the Report makes sure that social therapy will be applied only to surface effects, not systemic faults.

President Johnson chose 11 members for his National Advisory Commission on Civil Disorders, a collection remarkable chiefly for its predictable moderation. There could, and would, be no surprises. The list was comprised of men (and one woman) representing various aspects of economic and political elites in the US: expansive corporatism (Charles B. Thornton, the President, Director and Chairman of Litton Industries); bureaucratic labor (I.W. Abel, president of the United Steel Workers); the pre-1965 civil rights establishment (Roy Wilkins, executive director of the NAACP); Republicans (Rep. William M. McCulloch, of Ohio, and Sen. Edward W. Brooke, of Massachusetts); Democrats (Rep. James Corman of California, and Sen. Fred Harris, of Oklahoma); old-style machine politics (Chairman Otto Kerner, governor of Illinois); new-style urban politics (Vice-Chairman John Lindsay, mayor of New York City); the police (Chief Herbert Jenkins, of Atlanta); and women-in-politics (Katherine Graham Penden, then Commerce Commissioner of the State of Kentucky).

Like all presidential commissions, the Kerner panel was designed not to study questions but state them, not conduct investigations but accept them, not formulate policy but confirm it. Although the Commission conducted hundreds of hours of official "hearings" and traveled in groups of two and three Commissioners to riot cities, the basic work was done by the staff—and by the scores of outside consultants, specialists and experts who were directed into the really critical policy-making roles. Together, the outsiders made up the elite of professional "urbanists" which has become the command-group for the management of social crises.

Staff Director David Ginsburg was chief political cadre for the Administration. His assignment was to manipulate the internal and external operations of the Commission so as to produce a forward-looking report and avoid the worst pitfalls of controversy, bickering and career damage. President Johnson himself appointed Ginsburg as the Director, shortly after he announced the names of the Commissioners. It was an unusual move, and a source of some suspicion afterwards; commissions like to hire their own hands. But the job of political organizer was too important to be left to any old bureaucrat. The White House had to keep control of the Commission, even indirectly—*preferably* indirectly. David Ginsburg filled the required role to perfection. A quiet, commanding West Virginia lawyer, he had first met Johnson in New Deal days, and became one of his pool of Jewish lawyers (c.f. Abe Fortas, Edwin Weisl) who are always available for odd jobs, big deals and general counsel (myths of ethnic attributes grow tall in Texas).

As Ginsburg was the political manager and manipulator of the Commission, his deputy, Victor Palmieri, was the adminstrator and theoretician. Palmieri was a young Southern California lawyer, very much in the hard-living, aggressive Kennedy style. By the time he was 35 he had become president of the Janss Corporation, one of the West's biggest land holding and development corporations.

If Ginsburg had a broad rhetorical view of the Commission's purposes, Palmieri had a much more specific notion of what it was supposed to do: "We thought we had a damn good chance of moving to a major racial conflagration. . . . The most important thing was what the response would be in the white police forces. The objective was to affect the posture of local authorities in the next summer."

President Johnson had called for two separate products from the Commission: an "interim" document in March, 1968, and a final Report by August 1. But Palmieri and Ginsburg came to believe that the schedule of separate reports would have to be discarded, if the Commission was to influence events in the summer of 1968.

It fell to Palmieri to assemble a crew of social scientists to document and analyze the "causes" of the riots, on which everyone had agreed before the Commission's work ever started. President Johnson's television speech on July 27—written in part and edited by Justice Abe Fortas—asserted that the riots then engulfing scores of cities were caused" by "ignorance, discrimination, slums, poverty, disease, not enough jobs."

It should not have been difficult to find social scientists who accepted the Commission's premises. Until very recently, there has been no tradition of radical analysis in the social sciences. Many of the most important figures in academic and political social science in the US came of age in the late Forties and Fifties, when the "end of ideology" was proclaimed. But while many social science stars agreed to "consult" with the Commission, none would undertake a full-time commitment. The staff finally had to settle for a National Institute of Mental Health psychologist, Robert Shellow, who was a commissioned officer in the Public Health Sercice.

There was also some question about the acceptability to the Administration of those academics who agreed to work in any capacity on the Report. Herbert Gans, for instance, was "vetoed" by the White House as a regular consultant because he had indulged in anti-war activities. Palmieri (who was personally very much against the war, too) succeeded in hiring Gans on a "contract" basis. The White House veto operation was run by Presidential Assistant Marvin Watson, the notorious hatchet man of the late Johnson years, who kept names of anti-war activists in a computerfile in the basement of the executive offices. Gans' name turned up as a member of a group of artists, writers and academics who declared that they would refuse tax payments as a protest against the war in Vietnam.

Within the Commission staff, Palmieri tried a management device designed to provide alternate circuits and prevent overloading on the "social science input." He laid out his system of "fail-safes" in an attempt to treat conclusively the data received from field researchers. According to Palmieri's plan, the investigative and research material would be worked over in three ways: sociologically, by Robert Shellow; journalistically, by Robert Conot, co-author of a book on the Watts riots of 1965; and practical-politically, by staff lawyers, such as Ginsburg, Palmieri and Stephen Kurzman.

What happened in the end, as Palmieri once said, was that the system had an "abort" in its critical center—the social scientific, "intellectual" effort. The fail-safe failed. To Palmieri's way of thinking, that failure gutted the whole Report. The journalistic accounts, the statistical tables and the political suggestions were never bound in a coherent analytical structure.

It was more than a month after the Commissioners were appointed that the "critical" social scientific staff began its work. Having failed to enlist the undivided attentions of the top men at the universities and research centers around the country, Director Robert Shellow called for their recommendations for bright young assistants to round out his department. In time, he was provided with a half-dozen full and part-time men, three undergraduate "interns" from Antioch College, and scores of consultants who would fly to Washington at $100 or $150 per diem.

Like many government agencies, bureaus and departments plowing the new fields of "social technology"—education, urban development, anti-poverty, welfare, health and civil rights—the Commission drew to it every academic entrepreneur with a scheme to sell. Some were more successful than others: Washington is full of small research firms where returned VISTAs, Peace Corpsmen or Appalachian Volunteers can earn 12 or 15 thousand dollars a year trading on their brief associations with the poor, black and oppressed. Such operations are often run by the returnees' old bosses at the various government agencies which funded the volunteer projects in the first place.

The Commission signed a contract, quite early in the game, with the TransCentury Corporation, a Washington-based research, training and job-placement company run by Warren Wiggins, a former deputy director of the Peace Corps, and staffed in large measure by returned volunteers and their friends. Several TransCenturions joined the Commission staff. The company itself won its $18,000 contract to recruit staff.

Hundreds of thousands of dollars went into research contracts. The Bureau of Applied Social Science Research at Columbia (where several Commission contractors and consultants, including Herbert Gans, now work) got $45,540 for a study of arrest records of rioters. A University of Michigan spin-off research department got $45,488 for a study of the life habits of rioters. The International Association of Chiefs of Police won a $38,000 contract for a study of police preparedness.

One of the most important Commission research contracts was given to Systemetrics, a subsidiary of the Real Estate Research Corporation, of Chicago. Systemetrics is run by Anthony G. Downs, an old friend of Palmieri's. Downs is on the "new breed" side of a family connected with Mayor Daley's Chicago. He is a major ideologist of "downtownism" and "urban land reform."

Systemetrics was assigned two jobs: to design research and management programs for the Commission, and to combine and summarize the field research reports on 24 riots in 23 cities. The way the Systemetrics researchers perceived the riots in the 24 summaries could profoundly affect the Commissioners' understanding of the processes of conflict. If the summaries portrayed ghetto blacks as pitiable victims, surrounded by rats and roaches, and put upon by evil and prejudiced predators, that would be how the Commissioners ultimately would perceive the situation.

Systemetrics did use that approach, of course, and it was the theme of the final Report. That theme grows out of the "middle position" between reactionary and revolutionary ideologies. It expresses the notion that since the conflicts of black and white America are non-ideological, no real shifts of power are needed to correct them. The problems which were seen in the American cities in the summer of 1967 did not represent contradictions within the whole political economy, but malfunctions of one or another institution—the failure to get food or money or jobs to the black people and whites in the same income group, to establish lines of communication between "control authorities" and the people they "serve." Racial prejudice, practiced by individuals alone or in groups, compounds the problems. But there is no real answer to prejudice; the "solution" to racial and urban problems must always be put in technical terms. And although it may be extremely difficult, solutions can be produced by the existing political elites.

Much of the foundation for that "middle position" was laid in an early paper written for the Commission by Howard Margolis, of the Institute for Defense Analysis, the secret war research corporation. The memorandum—never made public—reportedly laid out three possible perspectives for the Commissioners to ponder: 1) the "right wing" theory that a conspiracy lay behind the riots, and that program recommendations should emphasize the restoration of "law and order"; 2) the "left wing" theory, that the riots represented a parapolitical rebellion of the black poor in America, and that only radical social change could integrate that rebellion into a new American "system"; and 3) the "middle position," focussing on the presumably "neutral" problems of migration, urban overpopulation, and historical Negro underprivilege. Programs designed to deal with those problems implied no threat to the current organization of corporate capitalism in America.

The central contradiction of the entire Commission operation was embedded in the "middle position." As Margolis—and other staff assistants who read it in the first months of the Commission's autumn—understood, the position did not fit the realities of the black rebellions of the summer. The problem was not that it was "wrong," but that it didn't represent the forces at work in the country. Its presentation was meant to serve a single political purpose.

For that reason, its unquestioned reception created a constellation of problems for the Commission staff, for the Commissioners themselves, and for the final Report. The contradiction between theory and reality hampered the work of the field investigators, who felt themselves pulled apart between the blacks they were interviewing and the Commission they were serving. It created fatal tensions within the social science section, which was charged with integrating research materials and historical perspectives in a framework which was abstracted from real conditions. It made the official "hearings" before the full Commission quite irrelevant, for it gave values to the parameters of testimony before anyone ever was heard. And finally, it denied meaning to the Report, for it based programs on unrealistic theories.

The field investigation teams were the first to feel the tensions. Teams of six investigators were sent to each of 23 cities. In each city, "sub-teams" of two people would speak with officials, private citizens in positions of power, and ghetto residents and activists. The teams were organized on racial lines. According to a memorandum from David Ginsburg to the Commission staff, it was to be assumed that "only Negroes would be able to obtain information from residents in the ghetto areas." Whites, Ginsburg added, would be sent to interview officials and private citizens.

It was not long, however, before the black investigators began to sense that they were being used for purposes of which they were at least partly suspicious; specifically, they were worried that the reports of their interviews would be misrepresented when shown to the higher levels of the Commission staff, or that information on militants might ultimately be passed on to law enforcement agencies, despite official assurance that it would go only as far as the National Archives.

Many black staffers remained convinced that "the whole thing was a racist operation," as one of the field investigators put it. All the top policy-making jobs were held by whites, except for the post of general counsel, which had been given to a black man, Merle McCurdy. There were only a few "token" black consultants in the long list appended to the Report. Overall, the Report was always thought of as a white document written by white writers and aimed at a white audience—*about* black people. It was primarily a response to the white response to the riots. It was supposed to prescribe policy for black people, not for whites. Although it named "white racism," it did not describe white racist society.

The central contradiction of the Commission—between what was politic and what was real—was felt most strongly by the social science section, under Research Director Robert Shellow. It was expressed primarily in the drafting of the document, "The Harvest of American Racism," and "Harvest's" eventual rejection by Palmieri; and by the firing of Shellow and his entire staff in late December, 1967. Although perceptions of the reasons for the firings differ widely, the context of contradictions is hardly arguable: The Report was intended to serve particular political ends, and "Harvest" and the social scientists interfered.

Shellow had four assistants working on "Harvest": David Boesel, Louis Goldberg, Gary T. Marx and David Sears. All of them were young social scientists with liberal or radical tendencies. To them, the riots were not incoherent freakouts, but rather specific (though unplanned) responses to oppression. They could not be understood without a conception of black struggle against white domination; and the "causes" could not be found in the obviously bad living conditions, but in the distribution of power in the total system. In other words, the riots were rebellions.

By early November, the Shellow section began to feel the critical press of time. No underlings had yet been told that there would be only one Report—instead of the March interim document and the August final version—so the summary analysis of the whole summer of riots would have to be finished by the end of November to meet the interim deadline. "We were working around the clock," Boesel said. "We slept in our offices—they brought in cots—and we never left. It was crazy. We'd be found in our underwear darting across the hall in the mornings, just before people came to work. But we were really excited. We thought our case studies would be the guts of the Report. We thought our original doubts about how the Commission would operate were proving unfounded, and that we'd be able to say what we wanted."

What they wanted to say was contained in a 176-page document of forceful impressions, if somewhat limited analysis. "The Harvest of American Racism" was hardly the kind of work that a government agency would be happy to endorse. It did not couch its ideology in the conventions of "neutrality," but stated its positions boldly. It also was confused and inconsistent even in its own terms, and mixed traditional liberal assumptions which even the Commission would find perfectly acceptable with radical notions about the nature of oppression and the development of rebellion. The most extraordinary part was the last chapter: "America on the Brink: White Racism and Black Rebellion." Written in rather heated language, it went further than most top staff officials thought prudent in charging that racism infused all American institutions, and characterized the riots as a first step in a developing black revolution, in which Negroes will "feel it is legitimate and necessary to use violence against the social order. A truly revolutionary spirit has begun to take hold . . . an unwillingness to compromise or wait any longer, to risk death rather than have their people continue in a subordinate status."

Both Palmieri and Ginsburg admit that they were appalled when they read "Harvest." Ginsburg, who was thought to be the soul of genteel manners and quiet control, spoke of the document in four-letter words. Palmieri said he fairly threw it across the room when Shellow gave it to him. The real problem was not that it was poorly done (it was no worse a job than much of the finished Report) but that it defied the categories that the top officials had established for the "social science input."

Palmieri "fired" Shellow on the spot, although the actual process of separation was much more ambiguous and drawn out. But from that point on, Shellow was excluded from all important Commission activities. "Harvest" was popped down a memory hold.

At length, Palmieri gave up entirely on "social science input," a notion in which he once placed so much confidence, and gave the analysis section of the Report to Stephen Kurzman, a lawyer who was a deputy director of the Commission, to complete. Kurzman turned out a quick, lawyer-like job, incorporating those notions in the "Harvest" thesis which were acceptable from the start, but removing the more threatening ideas.

Many of the 120 investigators and social scientists "released" from the Commission staff in December, 1967, will always believe that the firings were ordered by the Johnson Administration. But there is every reason to believe that the action was undertaken by Palmieri (with Ginsburg concurring) because of the failure of Shellow's group to produce an "acceptable" analytical section.

The Commissioners themselves knew little of the firings, or of the controversy surrounding them, until the few speculative reports in the press were seen. On December 8, Ginsburg gave the Commission the news: "It was simply flabbergasting," a staff member reported. "Ginsburg said that the publication of the Report in March wouldn't really mean the end of the Commission, that there would be supplemental reports and such. And the Commissioners allowed themselves to be deluded. 'Oh, well,' Kerner said, 'if it's not really going to be the end of the Commission, then I guess it's all right.' He fell right in line, then Harris behind him, then Brooke. The rest of them sort of looked at one another. The decision was made in just 14 minutes."

From the beginning, it was clear that John Lindsay was the chief spokesman for the liberal position, and Tex Thornton was the heavy for the conservatives. Lindsay's closest allies were Senator Harris, Chief Jenkins, and Roy Wilkins. Thornton had only Mrs. Peden as a full-time cohort. The others roamed around the middle, or, like Brooke, who had the worst attendance record, roamed elsewhere.

What the "liberal" side meant first of all was a full acceptance of the "middle position" as laid out long before in the Margolis memo. Beyond that, it entailed a rhetorical emphasis on the horrors of life for ghetto blacks, and a sense—as Hubert Humphrey once expressed it—that things were bad enough to explain (but not excuse) rioting. There was no agreement, however, that the riots were a positive or beneficial political act (as "Harvest" had proposed); nor, of course, was there any idea that the failure of black Americans to achieve equality with whites was a structural failure of the American political and economic system.

The "conservative" side grudgingly accepted that same "middle position" thesis, but emphasized the bad character of the criminal element in the ghettoes rather than the conditions of life there. Secret minutes of a Commission meeting of November 10, 1967, taken by a staff member, illustrate Thornton's attitudes; in this instance, he was responding to a discussion on "what causes riots";

"In re 'bitterness and despair': We're playing right into the hands of the militants who will use it as justification for violence. Maybe bitterness and an element of despair; but only two or three percent actually start the riots. It's also the rewards, the benefit from free burglary. Put in . . . 'an increasing lack of respect for the law': That's what it is, and the Report has to bring this out loud and clear. There's little restraint to participation in disorders. . . . Improve the police departments: The military should train soldiers about to come out of the service in law enforcement work. Help solve big recruitment problem. There are up to 60,000 coming out per year. . . . No question that show of restraining force, quickly applied, actually has restraining effect. Show of military force (even with no bullets or bayonets fixed) quickly stopped militants. We should provide maybe that federal troops be made available on standby basis as a precautionary measure.

"Let's not mention about the slave background and the poor Negro. Sins of forefathers idea will fall on deaf ears. Only 10 to 15 percent of whites had slave-owning forefathers.

"No law and no courts will change the attitude of the whites. Labor unions have this very bad attitude, as does the so-called establishment. . . . Open housing helps force Negroes onto whites and releases hostile attitudes. . . . If we voice poverty, etc., as a cause of riots, 30 million poor people will use it as an excuse to riot."

On the other hand, Lindsay thought that the Report, even in its finished form, was "wishy-washy." He was particularly angry that no mention was made of the war in Vietnam as a contributing factor to the riot process. But in a meeting of the Commission to debate the point of "mentioning" the war, Lindsay was voted down. Although there is no reason to think that President Johnson directed Ginsburg to avoid mention of the war, it is clear that Ginsburg was doing Johnson's bidding: That, indeed, was his function, and the reason he was picked to head the Commission staff—by the President himself. Early fears that Lindsay entertained about Ginsburg's "daily" contact with Johnson were irrelevant. Ginsburg didn't *have* to see Johnson.

There was, however, one exception. Late in 1967, Thornton grew anxious about the final Report's "liberalism." He was particularly worried that it would suggest legislation for enormous federal expenditures; and, more than that, that it would generate "expectations" in the black community which could never be fulfilled, and which would lead to more rioting. Thornton went to George Mahon, the Texas Democrat who heads the House Appropriations Committee, and asked him to intercede with the White House on behalf of the "conservative" side of the Commission. Mahon, Thornton and the President were, of course, all Texans. Mahon and Thornton were also allied through Litton Industries' intense interest in government appropriations.

On the night before the final meeting, Lindsay and his personal staff put together what he describes as an "end game." The plan was that Lindsay would "assume" at the next day's meeting that a summary would preceed the full Report. He would then read just such a summary—written in an all-night session by his aides. In promoting the summary, Lindsay would tell how deeply he felt about the issues it raised. The implication was that he would not sign the Report if the summary were not included. The move had three objectives. First, Lindsay's "support" of the Report (with summary) would put the burden of "dissent" on the conservative side. Second, Lindsay got his own summary into the hopper before any others. Finally, the gambit would lay the emotional and intellectual basis for Lindsay's personal dissent, should his summary be defeated, or if the conservatives won their points.

But the game worked smoothly. At first, Thornton and Corman argued against Lindsay's summary, but Thornton's attempt to put together a majority against it (and, by implication, against the Report as it stood) came to nothing.

Could the Report have gone either way? Palmieri, for instance, thought there was a real danger that it could turn into an obviously illiberal document. But the structure of the Commission and the context in which it operated suggest that its tone could have hardly been other than "liberal." The finished product almost exactly reproduced the ideological sense given it by President Johnson more than half a year earlier. The choice of Commissioners, staff, consultants and contractors led in the same direction. The political constituency foremost in the directors' minds—the audience to which the Report was played —had been conditioned to expect and accept a catalogue of ills and a list of reforms.

According to the directors, the real fights in the Commission came over the introduction to the "Recommendations for National Action." That 70-page chapter was supposed to outline the scope of a national program of social reforms, in employment, education, welfare and housing, with no "price tag" attached.

The chapter was based on a thorough memorandum of program recommendations drawn up for the Commission by Anthony Downs, of Systemetrics.

The importance of the Downs strategy is not in the specifics of its programs, which in many cases are considered desirable by most right-thinking people, but in the nature of its political demands. Continuing, reinforcing—and to some degree setting the ideology of the Commission, it assumes the dominance of the same elites now in power, minus the old fogeys and plus the new technocrats. While its theory of programming may be dynamic, its theory of power is static.

BEHIND THE SCENES...
AND UNDER THE RUG

Howard E. Shuman

Last December, the Douglas Commission completed a two-year study of urban problems which has since been called "the most exhaustive of its kind ever undertaken for the federal government." By almost any standard—but certainly by that of weight and volume—the description was apt. In mimeographed form, The Commission's final report, *Building the American City,* was so mammoth that the Commission furnished reporters with shopping bags in which to lug it away. Even in published form, it would put James Michener to shame: the report runs to 502 large, double-column pages. More important, the Presidentially appointed group, formally called the National Commission on Urban Problems, delved deeply into its work and came up with revelations that could be extremely useful in fashioning America's urban destiny.

While the hearings, studies, and final report are now public, little has thus far been revealed concerning the Commission's formation or the misleading promises, defensive reactions, and hostility within the Johnson Administration that characterized its two-year charter.

GENESIS

One day in late November, 1966, Special Assistant to the President Joseph Califano called at the Old Senate Office Building to talk with Senator Paul H. Douglas. The Senator was licking his wounds at the time. Earlier in the month he had lost his race for a fourth term when a coalition of negative events and a young and glamorous opponent, Charles H. Percy (R-III.), combined to defeat him.

Califano urged Douglas to head a Presidential Commission that President Johnson had proposed in both his 1965 message on the cities and in his 1966 Syracuse speech. The Commission, Califano said, would examine urban problems, with emphasis on housing and community life as well as such mundane topics as building codes, zoning, and taxation.

Although the catastrophic 1967 riots were yet to come, this was a time when the sickness of cities was nonetheless approaching the top of the nation's domestic agenda. The Johnson Administration seemed to feel that it would be a

Howard E. Shuman, "Behind the Scenes . . . and Under the Rug," **THE WASHINGTON MONTHLY,** *July, 1969. Reprinted from* **THE WASHINGTON MONTHLY** *by permission of the author and the publisher.*

considerable coup to get a man of Paul Douglas's knowledge and stature to head a Commission on Urban Problems. The Senator had managed the landmark 1949 Housing Act in the Senate; he had been the second-ranking member of the Senate Banking Committee, which handled housing legislation; he had introduced the original Model Cities bill; and he had been involved in every major piece of housing legislation for over 18 years.

A few days later, in my role as the Senator's administrative assistant, I looked up the legislative authority for the Commission. To my surprise, I found that the 1965 Housing Act authorized a "committee" under the Secretary of Housing and Urban Development—not a "Commission" reporting directly to the President. The sum of $1.5 million had been appropriated to carry out its work.

I relayed my findings to Senator Douglas and urged him to turn down Califano's proposal unless: (1) the Senator were to head a Commission, rather than a "committee;" (2) the Commission would be independent of HUD and report directly to the President; and (3) the Commission's charter clearly included housing and urban affairs, as well as the narrower topics of codes, zoning, and taxation. The Senator agreed. He dispatched me to the White House to negotiate the points.

Both Larry Levinson, Califano's agent, and Under Secretary of HUD Robert C. Wood greeted the conditions with favor and even enthusiasm. This was not surprising. Wood himself had chaired a 1964 task force which had proposed a new Hoover Commission to look at ways to redesign the government to meet problems brought on by the "urban dynamic." And the President had said publicly, only a few months earlier, that he would appoint a "Commission" of distinguished citizens to study urban affairs. For these and other reasons, the White House accepted the Senator's conditions with alacrity.

Although we did not know it at the time, this was not the case with Secretary Robert C. Weaver and the HUD bureaucracy. In fact, HUD had gone to great and devious lengths to avoid just such a Commission as the President had originally proposed. When the President issued his 1965 housing message calling for a Commission, the HUD legal experts quietly downgraded it by writing legislation that would establish nothing more than a "committee" under the thumb of the Secretary. This had been done with the Secretary's approval.

After the White House staff agreed with our proposal, Levinson, some other White House staff assistants, and I jointly drafted a press release announcing the Commission and its broad objectives. Then we worked it over again into what was to be the final version of the release. In the meantime, Senator Douglas sought direct confirmation of the understanding from the President. In a phone conversation between the Senator and the President, Mr. Johnson offered no objection to Douglas's conditions.

The White House agreed to the Senator's request that a woman, a Negro, and some academic types—then the neglected minorities—be represented on the Commission. All parties also agreed that the formation of "The Commission on the Problems of the American City" as a valuable "new addition" to a government-wide effort to ". . . not only avert the growing deterioration of our central cities, but to bring about an urban renaissance" would be announced before the Christmas holidays so that Senator Douglas could get the Commission underway before leaving on a short vacation after a crowded and tumultuous year.

Time passed from late November, to early December, and on through the Christmas holidays. No announcement. Finally, the Senator left Washington for his much-needed vacation.

In early January, I visited Secretary Weaver to discuss the Commission's organization. With a frantic wave of his hand, he urged me to work on the arrangements at home and to stay out of sight. If I occupied a spot either at HUD or at the Executive Office Building, he said, word of the still-unannounced Commission might leak out. He was insistent and highly nervous about this. I thought at the time that the Secretary was the most insecure public figure that I had ever met. (It was only later that I learned of the reasons for his agitated state: he had recently undergone a Presidential tonguelashing over his inept showing before the Ribicoff Committee, and the White House had just killed his embryonic Comsat housing proposal because word about it leaked out prematurely.)

Late in the afternoon on January 12, Levinson called me—not, as I expected, to say that the announcement was imminent, but to say that it had been made. I scurried over and picked up a copy of the release, which the White House had unobtrusively issued at five o'clock on a Friday afternoon, along with a handful of minor appointments. As any reporter knows, this is the least favorable time and day for news to be announced.

But even worse, I found that the language in the release was a far cry from what all parties had agreed to. It assigned the Commission only a twofold charter:

"First; to work with the Department of Housing and Urban Development and conduct a penetrating review of zoning, housing, and building codes, taxation, and development standards. . . .

"Second; to recommend the solutions, particularly those ways in which the effort of the Federal Government, private industry, and local communities can be marshalled to increase the supply of low-cost decent housing."

What should we do? Should we go along with the announcement or withdraw from the whole affair? The agreement had been violated, but the release did include the important issue of how to provide an abundance of housing for low-income families. Both White House assistant Levinson and Under Secretary Wood claimed that the change was a formality; its sole intention was to keep the Commission's functions technically in harmony with the legislation. They explained that the President had, in fact, established a Commission which was to work *with* but not *under*, the Secretary of HUD, but which was to report to Mr. Johnson.

The Senator was in the Caribbean at the time and not immediately available. After consulting briefly with trusted friends, I decided against making a public objection to our revised charter. (I had been appointed executive director of the Commission.) Our independence seemed secure enough so that, given continuing White House support, I felt we could function as independently as a Commission should.

Thus, the Commission's birth was not a happy event, or even a very public one. There was no Oval Room pageantry, no dispensing of Presidential ballpoints, and only minor mention in the few newspapers which carried the announcement at all. For months afterward, old friends asked what had become of us. At times we felt like former Russian political figures, references to whom had been expunged from all public records.

HELMSMANSHIP

Larry Levinson's parting shot as I left the White House that evening in January, 1967, had been: "If you have any trouble with those HUD bureaucrats, just let us know."

Trouble was not long in coming. Secretary Weaver, who it was now clear had spent the time from early December until January 12 trying to retrieve for himself what the White House had given us, sent Douglas an insulting memo stating that the Commission ". . . will develop . . . an agreed-upon [with HUD] budget" for the Commission's operation. We knew that control of the purse strings was vital to our independence. We politely, but firmly, told him "no."

Weaver decreed that at least one HUD employee must attend all of our meetings. We declined to honor this as a "right," but we did agree—I now think wrongly—to "invite" a HUD representative to each of the formal Commission meetings. This was a mistake because every criticism of HUD during both our private sessions and our public hearings went to the Secretary from his inside agent.

The Secretary's memo even outlined what our general study areas were to be and specified that we should set up five study panels—one each on building codes, housing codes, zoning, taxation, and development standards. He did not even mention the real meat: housing programs and broader urban problems. In sum, his "directive" was generally unacceptable if we were to function as an independent body.

The memo died but the ensuing struggle over staff, funds, and operations continued. When the Secretary learned that Douglas was determined (with the Commission's concurrence) to embark on a series of hearings in the ghettos of 22 major cities of the country, the fur flew again. He claimed that we were exceeding our authority and purpose. But the real fact was that he feared such hearings would embarrass HUD. We went ahead with our plans. As it turned out, those sessions provided a common and unifying experience for the entire Commission: without them a unanimous and hard-hitting final report would have eluded us. In the end it was the very best thing we could have done.

The hearings infuriated Secretary Weaver and HUD. In New Haven, HUD's showcase for urban renewal, we sensed great local hostility to the program. Over $800 per capita had been spent—the highest rate in the country—but the community was seething and later erupted in a riot. Unknown to us until the end of our day of hearings there, the New Haven police had been stationed inside and outside the hall in case our hearings got out of hand. We prevented that by welcoming the views of unscheduled as well as scheduled witnesses. In fact, the "walk-in" witnesses talked with a fire and an eloquence which the others did not match.

Everywhere we went—Baltimore, Boston, Detroit, San Francisco, New York, Philadelphia, among other places—witnesses scathingly criticized the HUD and FHA bureaucracy and told of unbelievable delays in processing housing programs.

As Commissioners Richard O'Neill and Jeh Johnson wrote in the summary of the Commission's final report:

> The civil disorders of the hot summer of 1967 followed us and preceded us. We saw the ugly burned-out urban streets that were still smoldering in some places, and we sensed the tension and anxiety in communities that would erupt not too long after our being there.
>
> We could have stayed in Washington and gathered statistics, but statistics do not tell enough about a slum. One has to see and touch and smell a slum before one fully appreciates the real urgency of the problem.

As the disturbing facts emerged, the Secretary repeatedly denounced our activities to the White House and claimed that we had exceeded our scope (if not our grasp). In private conversations with Commission members, his lieutenants spoke of our efforts with a rage and fury which had to be heard to be believed. They were especially sensitive to our report on HUD's neglect of the housing needs of the large poor family.

What we found included:

1. While the 1949 Housing Act authorized 800,000 units of public housing to be built in six years, only two-thirds of that six-year total had been built in almost 20 years.

2. In 1967, only 30,000 public-housing units a year were being built. Of these, more than half were efficiency and one-bedroom apartments for the elderly. Much of the remainder was built in the smaller cities. In other words, virtually no housing was being built in the ghettos of the United States for the poor families—particularly poor Negro families—who needed it most.

3. The moderate-income housing program (known in the trade as the 221 (d) (3) program) authorized 45,000 units a year since its beginning in 1961. Yet it took six years to build the number of units authorized for a single year.

4. Urban renewal had destroyed 400,000 units of housing for poor people. But on the sites it had bulldozed, the program had planned to build only 20,000 public housing units, or one-twentieth the number of units destroyed.

5. When HUD claimed that the major reason for the low production of all forms of subsidized housing was the lack of sites, we established that over half the land in the urban renewal areas of the central cities had not yet been "committed" to any building whatsoever. There were sites in abundance.

In Detroit and Cleveland, for example, vast acreages were lying idle when those two cities blew up. In Detroit, hundreds of sites had been bulldozed. As a result, excessive overcrowding existed in the riot areas while the urban renewal land lay idle. Future plans provided no remedy; they called for a medical center, luxury housing, an industrial park, and athletic facilities for Wayne State University.

Unlike Governor George Romney of Michigan (now Secretary of HUD), members of our Commission did not claim that urban renewal was a cause of the Detroit riots. All our members said was that it had not helped to prevent them. But this modest and restrained claim infuriated Secretary Weaver and his urban-renewal bureaucracy when transmitted back to them by our HUD travelling informant.

6. All in all, government action had destroyed far more housing units for the poor than it had built. While about two million units of housing had been destroyed by urban renewal, highway programs, demolitions for public housing, code enforcement, and other actions, only a million units of subsidized housing had been created. Our projections—based on the present pace of construction—showed that this pattern would continue.

7. Processing time for all major programs was so slow that it strained the Commission's credulity. One-third of the completed urban-renewal projects had taken longer than nine years. Public housing routinely took three to four years to complete. The same was generally true for the moderate-income program.

8. Up until the 1967 riots, the FHA had refused to guarantee housing loans in what were called "red-lined areas" in the central cities. These areas were so named for the mythical red lines drawn on city maps by the banks, savings and loan institutions, and the FHA. The red lines embraced ghetto areas where the banks automatically refused to grant loans and the FHA automatically refused to guarantee them. Thus, the official policy of the United States was against insuring housing where it was needed most.

9. The value of government housing subsidies for the upper 20 per cent of income groups in the 1960's—through the deduction of property taxes and interest paid on mortgages by homeowners—was twice that of housing subsidies for the bottom 20 per cent of income groups, as measured by direct housing subsidies and welfare payments. While ignoring the poor, and especially the Negro poor, HUD and FHA had helped to provide vast opportunities for the white middle and upper classes. Here, they were a big success.

We thought the facts enumerated above were important in evolving public policies. HUD wanted them swept under the rug. But the cities were blowing up and lack of housing was a major cause.

HOME STRETCH

In spite of HUD's opposition, the Commission pushed ahead. By the fall of 1968, it had published five volumes of hearings, as well as individual studies on housing programs, zoning exclusions, land use, property taxes and their regressive impact, and building and housing codes. The 16 members, all private citizens, had met for more than 70 days. Attendance at meetings and hearings had been phenomenal. The final report went through four major revisions in which the Commission or its subcommittees examined it line by line. Huge portions were written by individual members as well as by key members of the staff.

During the first week of November, 1968, we sent one copy of the final draft to Secretary Weaver and one copy to the White House. Chairman Douglas then wrote Califano, requesting a time for the Commission to present its report to the President. There was no reply. Phone calls to Califano went unreturned.

When called at the White House, he was "at home." When called at home, he was "in the shower." He was at home or in the shower for almost a month.

Finally, Califano agreed to meet with Douglas on December 3rd at 12 noon at the White House. Douglas cooled his heels there for more than an hour. When Califano arrived, he asked whether the report was unanimous. It was. This news apparently came as a surprise to him, since one of Secretary Weaver's themes to the White House had been that the Commission was wracked with dissension.

Douglas again requested an opportunity for the members to present the report to the President and to be thanked by him for their diligence and devotion. Califano replied that Mr. Johnson was angry about press reports of the critical studies issued previously by the Commission. According to Califano, the President became incensed every time the Commission issued one.

The Senator told Califano that the study reports were truthful. He also argued that the final report was honest and comprehensive; it was, he said, the kind of report that the President likes. Douglas was aware of the President's populist streak and visceral reaction for the poor; indeed, it was one thing they had shared in common in the 18 years since they entered the Senate together.

In what was clearly an intended slight, Califano then insisted that the report be submitted to President-elect Nixon, rather than to President Johnson. Douglas firmly told him "no." The law prescribed that it be submitted by December 31, and he had promised his former colleagues in the House and Senate that it would be released as soon as possible. Besides, he had no intention of sending it to anyone but the President of the United States. It would break the law to withhold the report until Mr. Nixon was sworn in. Douglas flatly refused to report to a non-President, as Califano insisted.

In fact, he told Califano, he intended to release it for Sunday, December 15.

"I can't tell the President that," Califano said.

"I don't care what you tell the President," Douglas replied. "But I am telling you. We are releasing the report."

That ended the conference.

As a hedge against any attempt at suppression, we Xeroxed a dozen copies and got them into the hands of *The Washington Post, The New York Times*, and the wire services. We also bought 2,000 mimeographed copies for immediate distribution. It was these copies—each almost a foot thick—that reporters carried away in shopping bags.

The White House made two final attempts to upstage the report's December 15 release date. The President was scheduled to dedicate some lowcost housing units in Texas on Saturday, December 14—coverage of which could have competed with release of the Commission's report in the Sunday papers. The plan called for the President to take attention away from news of the report by dedicating the units. But the President upset the applecart. Speaking extemporaneously at the dedication ceremonies, Mr. Johnson said that one of his biggest disappointments had been the government's failure to provide a decent home for all American families. His unexpected but deeply felt statement—which squared with the thrust of our findings—complemented the story of the Commission's report.

In a second attempt to upstage the Commission report, some White House staff members dusted off an unknown internal HUD report on city and suburban problems and leaked it to *The New York Times* for use on Sunday December 15. If our report had not been in the hands of the wire services, the *Times,* and other newspapers several days in advance, this action by the White House might have knocked the story of our report off the front page and relegated it to the dustbins of history. This White House-HUD effort failed, and the Douglas report made the front page of almost every major paper in the country. The leaked "suburban" report, which the *Times* used on Page 1 along with the story of the Douglas report, is still buried in the HUD files. It has never been publicly released.

UNDER THE KNIFE

The crowning blow came on December 31. Under Section 301 of the Housing Act of 1965, the Secretary of HUD was required to submit our report to Congress. By this time Secretary Weaver had left the government and Robert Wood, the Commission's early supporter, was in charge of HUD. In carrying out his legal obligations, he transmitted to Congress and the President less than half of the Commission's final report.

Wood refused to send those sections which criticized public housing (or lack of it), urban renewal, and other HUD programs. All criticisms of FHA's red-lining, the paucity of housing for the poor and the Negro poor, the lengthy delays in processing time, and the excessive demolitions ended up on the cutting-room floor. So did the 50 detailed recommendations on how to speed up and improve the programs and to build more housing for the poor. Sections on population, poverty, and race went out, as did those on the need for larger urban government units, on city neighborhood organization, and on the design and improvement of the urban environment.

Among the most glaring omissions was a detailed chapter on revenue-sharing. This chapter, written by Allen Manvel of the Commission's staff, proposed that federal funds by-pass the states and go directly to the larger cities. It provided a formula for channeling rewards to states and cities which made an extra fiscal effort. This chapter and its detailed recommendations were left out because the White House opposed revenue-sharing.

When I told Secretary Wood that I felt his failure to transmit the complete version of our report was a needless and hostile act that only served to demean him, he claimed that he had left out only those sections which, in his view, had gone beyond the scope of our charter. That seemed odd, coming from the man who was the first to welcome a broad authority for the Commission.

The basic problem, of course, was that the Commission worked hard and wrote an honest, full report. In massive detail, it provided the facts about the past and suggested, in equal detail, a program for the future.

Commissions are generally established to buy time on an immediate and politically tender issue—or, as someone else has said, to treat the politics of a situation rather than the situation itself. They are expected to go into seclusion and not rock the boat. They usually report many months later—after public clamor has died down—and their work gets filed with the great unread literature of the world.

But Commissions are worthwhile only if they tell the truth, act independently, and detail past mistakes in such a way that the chances of future improvement are enhanced. This goal, even when sought by an individual Commission, is almost never shared by the federal agencies whose work comes under its scrutiny. In the case of the Douglas Commission—even during the legislative drafting period—HUD tried to turn the President's proposal for a Commission reporting to him into a committee dominated by the Secretary.

These plans backfired on the Secretary and the permanent bureaucracy when Douglas insisted on an independent role. In hindsight it is clear that the Secretary saw the Commission idea as a threat. He worked from the beginning to control and thwart the Commission's inquiry and conclusions. The White House staff, originally enthusiastic, was caught between the Commission's public criticisms of HUD and Secretary Weaver's contention that those criticisms put the Administration in a bad light. Eventually, they caved in to the Secretary's importunings.

But what if they had used the Commission ". . . to add significantly to the momentum of our existing urban programs" and to help bring about an "urban renaissance," as those agreed-upon drafts of its charter had proposed? Instead of acting defensively about HUD's miserable track record, suppose the Secretary and the White House had welcomed the Commission's activities as a lever to jolt the FHA, to light fires under the bureaucracy, and to help transform HUD from an agency hostile to the housing needs of the poor into one which seeks to meet their legitimate housing needs?

That was perhaps too large an order for either HUD or the White House staff to accept.

But the voluminous Commission work is there. As the hearings, studies, and final report are read and acted upon, the country may yet benefit from the fierce independence of a working Commission and its energetic, intellectually honest members. Such would not have been the case if it had abjectly succumbed to HUD's pressures and accepted a role as HUD's handmaiden and apologist. That would merely have helped to perpetuate what unkind persons call the Department of No Housing (for the poor) and Urban Development.

STATEMENT OF LEWIS MUMFORD,
AUTHOR OF "THE CITY IN HISTORY"

Senator Ribicoff. We welcome you today, Mr. Mumford.

I really didn't know that the New York Times was going to review your new book today.

Mr. Mumford. Nor did I.

Senator Ribicoff. But it is a good coincidence. I think I would like to read a passage of the New York Times review. It says that your new book opens with a passage from a book you wrote in 1944, "The Condition of Man." The passage is the following:

> *Ritual, art, poesy, drama, music, dance, philosophy, science, myth, religion are all as essential to man as his daily bread: man's true life consists not alone in the work activities that directly sustain him but are symbolic activities which gives significance both to the processes of work and their ultimate products and consummation.*

There is no question that you are a humanist. I think that, of all the witnesses we have had, you occupy a different niche. We are delighted that you are here. I know there is much of value that you can tell us. Why don't you proceed at your own pace?

Mr. Mumford. Mr. Chairman, honorable members of the subcommittee: though it is a privilege to appear before this subcommittee to explore subjects of such vital importance as those you have under review, Mr. Danaceau will bear witness that it is not a privilege I sought. On the contrary, I have undertaken this task with great reluctance, since the conclusions I have come to as a student of urbanism, regionalism, and technology in the course of a half century of study do not lend themselves easily to a summary statement, still less to a series of pat recommendations.

What has brought me here, despite this reluctance, is merely a sense of duty as an American citizen, one who has actively promoted regional development and "urban renewal"—Heaven help me, I invented the word! —and yet is sufficiently detached from the responsibilities of office and the restrictive discipline of specialized research to be free to bring before you certain fundamental issues that as yet have scarcely been opened up, much less defined, discussed, and debated.

Statement of Lewis Mumford, Author. Hearings Before the U.S. Senate, Subcommittee on Executive Reorganization, Committee on Government Operations, April 21, 1967.

Do not, I beg, misread my occupational qualifications. By profession, I am a writer—not an architect, an engineer, or a city planner; and though I have been a professor of city and regional planning at the University of Pennsylvania I have no wish to appear before you as an urban specialist, an expert, an authority. But please do not read any false humility into this statement. All the colossal mistakes that have been made during the last quarter century in urban renewal, highway building, transportation, land use, and recreation, have been made by highly qualified experts and specialists—and as regards planning, I should blush to be found in their company.

MUMFORD A GENERALIST

While I have prudently reminded you of my limitations, I nevertheless have one genuine qualification, unfortunately still a rare one, that of a generalist, equally at home in many different areas of life and thought. My specialty is that of bringing the scattered specialisms together, to form an overall pattern that the specialist, precisely because of his overconcentration on one small section of existence, fatally overlooks or deliberately ignores. Emerson described his ideal of the American scholar as "man thinking"; and it is only insofar as I have been a scholar in this special sense, dedicated to seeing life steadily and seeing it whole, that I venture to appear before you.

I shall not waste time listing any other qualifications I may have; for what they are worth, you will find them in any "Who's Who" or biographical dictionary. But I must lay the ground for the constructive criticism I shall eventually make by briefly summarizing the experience that has led me to my present views.

While still at college—in fact, when only 18—I came under the influence of the Scots thinker, Prof. Patrick Geddes, who shares with Ebenezer Howard, Raymond Unwin, and our own Frederick Law Olmsted, Sr., the distinction not merely of reviving the art of town planning, but of awakening fresh interest in the nature and function of cities. Though there are now scores of books and college courses available on every aspect or urbanism, half a century ago you could almost count them on the fingers of one hand.

As a disciple of Geddes, I learned to study cities and regions at first hand, living in them, working in them, not least surveying every part of them on foot: not only my native city, New York, but many others, large and small— Philadelphia, Pittsburgh, Boston, London, Edinburgh, Honolulu, Berkeley, Geneva—not to speak of smaller places like Palo Alto, Middletown, Hanover, and the Dutchess County hamlet of a dozen houses where I find the seclusion necessary for the writing of my books.

More than five-sevenths of my life has been spent in cities, mostly in great metropolises; and when in "The Culture of Cities," in 1938, I painted a picture of the prospective disintegration of megalopolis, my experience and my historic researches enabled me to anticipate by 30 years the conditions that you are now belatedly trying to cope with; for the formidable disorders I described in detail were already visible elsewhere, in London and Paris since the 18th century, and had become chronic in every congested urban center for the whole last century.

No small part of this ugly urban barbarization has been due to sheer physical congestion: a diagnosis now confirmed by scientific experiments with rats—for, when they are placed in equally congested quarters, they exhibit the same symptoms of stress, alienation, hostility, sexual perversion, parental incompetence, and rabid violence that we now find in megalopolis.

REGIONAL PLANNING ASSOCIATION OF AMERICA FORMED

My interest in cities brought me, as early as 1923, into close relations with a group of men whose human vision and practical judgment, had they been heeded in any large way, could have transformed American housing and planning. If their basic proposals had been carried further, we might have averted the grim conditions you now face.

In the early twenties this group incorporated itself into the Regional Planning Association of America, a small body, with never over 20 members, not to be confused with a quite different group, with a more conventional metropolitan approach, indeed a diametrically opposite one, the Regional Plan Association of New York. Such fresh, humanly significant ideas as came into planning and housing during the twenties and thirties was in no small measure the work of these two groups.

EXPERIMENTAL "NEW TOWNS" DEVELOPED

In urban planning, the two leaders of my own group were Clarence Stein and Henry Wright. They pioneered in the planning of a highly successful housing project for mixed-income families, Sunnyside Gardens in Long Island City. And out of that experiment, with the help of a socially responsible realtor of considerable wealth, Alexander Bing, grew an even more important experiment, the proposed new town of Radburn, N.J. Though Radburn's career as a new town was abruptly cut short by the depression, it made a contribution in design that has had a worldwide influence.

Radburn was conceived originally as an experimental model under private enterprise for a series of new towns; and some of its principles were, in fact, partly embodied in the abortive Greenbelt towns, which unfortunately never became real towns, built by the Federal Government between 1935 and 1940. During the next 25 years Clarence Stein and I kept alive, almost singlehandedly, the fundamental ideas of the new towns movement.

NEW TOWNS SHOULD BE COMPETENT COMMUNITIES

We held that further increase of population in already congested centers should be met, not by intensifying the congestion in high-rise buildings, not by adding endless acres and square miles of suburbs, with ever-longer and more time-wasting journeys to work, but by building new planned communities on a better model; many sided, balanced, self-maintaining: in a word, to use your chairman's excellent term, "competent." We conceived that these communities, fully equipped for industry, business, social life, and culture, would be linked together with the central metropolis in a new kind of urban pattern. This pattern would permanently preserve the countryside for farming and recreation, and bring together the neighborhood, the city, and the metropolis in a new constellation, which we called the regional city.

Not merely was I an intellectual associate of Stein and Wright in these activities, but I was equally a close colleague of Benton MacKaye, another member of our group; he who is best known to you, perhaps, as the shrewd Yankee whose activities as forester, conservationist, and geotect led to his projecting the Appalachian Trail. Unlike most bold dreamers, he has lived to see his dream completely realized through the voluntary cooperation of local groups, without any Government aid whatever.

REGIONAL PLANNING CONCEPT

Like myself, MacKaye had served as researcher for the New York State Housing and Regional Planning Commission, of which Stein was chairman and Henry Wright planning adviser. The hearings and reports of that commission played a decisive part in the whole movement for government action, State and Federal, to build and subsidize adequate housing for the lower income groups; and so laid the foundations for the large-scale Federal program that was begun during the depression and expanded after the Second World War.

The final report of Stein's commission, "A Regional Plan for the State of New York," was so farsighted and far reaching that, some 40 years later, it still served as the basis for a similar project by Governor Rockefeller's Office of Regional Development—though unfortunately he has not seen fit to follow it up.

In 1925 MacKaye and I edited the regional planning number of the Survey Graphic; the first time in which the ideas of regionalism and regional planning were set forth and treated as the essential key to anything fit to be called sound urban or metropolitan development. That number demonstrated the approaching strangulation of life in the great cities, dying because of that cancerous overgrowth and congestion which many highly esteemed experts, like Jane Jacobs and Charles Abrams mistakenly confuse with economic dynamism and social vitality. But we also showed the importance of the electricity grid, the radio, and the motor highway in making possible a more balanced population pattern, distributed over a much wider area than the biggest metropolis, preserving the essential resources of the countryside, in a permanent green matrix, instead of wiping out every natural advantage by affluent suburban and slummy subsuburban expansion and sprawl.

A TOWNLESS HIGHWAY SUGGESTED

One more point, and this biographic preface is done. Though MacKaye had laid down the main outlines for an effective regional approach to metropolitan problems, in his 1928 book, "The New Exploration"—a classic introduction now republished as a University of Illinois paperback—he added a new and important project in 1931—his plan for the townless highway. His article on this subject, which appeared in Harper's, was the very first one in which all the main elements of a new type of motor highway, which we now call the throughway or expressway, were put together. In the Appalachian Trail and the townless highway, this spiritual descendent of Thoreau effectually visualized the transportation backbone of a better environment and proved how much more practical he was than the "practical," specialists, who keep so closely to their familiar mole runs that they remain blind and baffled even when, by accident, they come above ground to the light.

Now, why, you must be asking yourselves, have I used up your time in rehearsing these past efforts at planning? Not, certainly, to claim priority over those who are advancing many of these same ideas now, as if for the first time; such a claim would be too picayune for words. And certainly not to boast of our successes, though when the Tennessee Valley project was first put forward by President Roosevelt—whom, when Governor, we had chosen as chief speaker for our regional planning conference at the University of Virginia in 1931—we momentarily exulted in the thought that our 10 years of preparatory thinking and experimenting had not been in vain.

FAILURE OF PLANNING EFFORTS

No; my reason for telling you these things is due to the realization that every advance we projected or even succeeded in establishing eventually came to grief; sometimes, like the regional plan for the State of New York, by stupid indifference and neglect; but even more, I regret to say, by being taken up on a national scale, with all the force, the authority, and the financial resources supplied by the Federal Government. In coming to life, our good ideas were done to death, caricatured or permanently disfigured by forces—technological, bureaucratic, financial, above all perhaps financial—that we had failed sufficiently to reckon with.

Certainly, no group worked harder than we did to establish governmental responsibility, State and Federal, for producing and subsidizing good housing for the lower income groups. But what was the result? Federal housing had hardly gotten underway before the financial bureaucratic process and the bulldozer mind had wiped out our new concepts for a better urban community, and produced those nightmares of urban anonymity and human desolation that dominate the skyline today—those high-rise housing developments in whose design only financial and mechanical calculations have played a part.

Everything that Jane Jacobs has said in condemnation of these sterile— indeed, humanly hostile—projects, is true. But, I hasten to add, they would not be any better if, on her pet formula, the designers had multiplied the number of streets and lined them with shops, and thus produced even more stifling and strangulating forms of congestion. The rapes, the robberies, the destructive delinquencies, the ever-threatening violence, for which she naively believes she has found a simple planning antidote, would still be there, since these are symptoms, not just of bad planning, or even of poverty, but of a radically deficient and depleted mode of life, a life from which both the most destitute slumdwellers and the most affluent suburbanites equally, though in different ways, now suffer. There is no planning cure for this machine-centered existence which produces only psychotic stresses, meaningless "happenings," and murderous fantasies of revenge.

CAN PRESENT EFFORTS SUCCEED?

On the basis of this wholesale reversal of our good intentions I must ask you: Is there any reason to suppose that a massive effort by the Federal Government to wipe out the existing slums—however we may define them—will succeed any better than those we have been building on a large scale all over the country since 1947?

Is there any plausible reason for expecting any better results from wholesale Government intervention, under our present auspices, no matter how much money you are prepared to spend? If you embark on such a program without asking far more fundamental questions about the reasons for our past failures, and if you fail to set up more human goals than those which our expanding economy now pursues, you will be throwing public money down the drain. And worse: in the course of doing this, you will bring about even more villainous conditions than those which you are trying to correct; for you will wipe out on a greater scale than ever what is left of neighborly life, social cooperation, and human identity in our already depressed and congested urban areas. If you want to know the human reactions to this, read Studs Terkel's recent eye-opening book, "Division Street." Let me respectfully suggest unless we challenge the current money-oriented, computer-directed American way of life, all we can soberly expect is more and more of worse and worse.

FAILURE OF THE TOWNLESS HIGHWAY PLAN

Or take another failure: what happened to MacKaye's conception of the townless highway. When he put forth this proposal, he sought to apply to the motorway efficient transportation principles, like that of an independent right-of-way, with access only at reserved intervals, that had long been incorporated in the railroad line. He did not for a moment anticipate that, in the working out of this system, the extravagant Federal subsidies would incite the highway engineers to repeat all the dismal planning errors committed originally by the railroad engineers—such as invading the center of the city and preempting its most valuable urban land for eight-lane highways and parking lots and garages.

Unfortunately, the highway engineers took over every feature of MacKaye's plan except the most important one: that it should be "townless"; that is, that it should bypass every urban center, small or big. Indeed, with all the insolence of an overcoddled public authority, they have not merely become specialists in despoiling beautiful landscapes and violating land dedicated to national and local parks, but they actively welcome further urban congestion and blight as the best possible justification for still more highway and bridge and tunnel building. When the city does not create sufficient congestion, these authorities bring it about themselves, as the Port of New York Authority proposes with its 110-story buildings for the World Trade Center.

As a result, these incontinent erections and compulsive congestions are steadily breaking down variety and continuity in urban life, wiping out centers for human contacts, obstructing the social opportunities, and undermining further the intimate face-to-face cooperations that the city exists to promote.

There is no use in your voting huge sums for housing and so-called urban renewal while a large part of the funds you have allotted to highway building are still being misused for wholesale urban destruction.

URBAN AND REGIONAL PLANNING SHOULD BE COMBINED

I have only touched, necessarily in a sketchy way, on the dismaying results that followed from carrying out, through Federal agencies and Federal funds, some of the very policies that the regional planning association and its various active members not merely advocated but participated in. But what of our other contributions—those that were only half carried out, or not carried out at all?

There I have to expose another kind of failure, equally serious. In the 1930's the ideas of regional planning seemed about to bear promising fruit not only in the founding of the TVA, with its combination of electrification, improved soil management and farming, and general regional rehabilitation, but in the founding of the National Resources Planning Board, later called the National Resources Committee, which encouraged each State to prepare regional plans, based on more sufficient knowledge, for the better development of its own resources. From the beginning, unfortunately, compartmentalized habits of thinking kept regional planning entirely separate from urban planning—which is an absurdity. But if the planning boards had not been disbanded, the very necessities of economic and social life would eventually have brought them together.

FEAR OF PLANNING LED TO BAD PLANNING

Unfortunately, your predecessors in the Congress developed an almost pathological fear of planning, and hated the very word; though no great enterprise of any kind, as A.T.&T. or General Electric or DuPont would tell you, can be carried on without long-term planning of the most detailed sort, carefully coordinated, and constantly corrected in the light of new conditions and fresh appraisals—what is now, in the jargon of the computer specialists, called feedback.

The result of this rejection of planning was not, of course, that we have done away with planning: the result is rather that our country has been the victim of the worst kind of planning possible, that in which each governmental bureau or division, each industry or business, thinks only of its own needs and aims, and tries to seize, for its own narrow purposes, the largest share of the budget, the biggest staff, the greatest amount of power—or, in business, the greatest possible financial return. At the highway conference which I attended, held by the Connecticut General Life Insurance Co. in 1957, it turned out that the Federal head of housing and the Federal head of highway building had never met, still less exchanged views, until that occasion, though neither could possibly do his work intelligently without reference to the other.

If the surveys and inventories of resources undertaken by the regional planning boards in many States had been continued over the last quarter century, you would not only have an adequate local basis for highway planning, which has been done, so far, with callous indifference to local needs and with no effort to establish a better regional pattern, but you would likewise have a good notion—as you do not in the least have now—of where the new housing, the new neighborhoods, the new towns should be built. I fear that you may be taking for granted the notion that the foul and crowded slums of the past should be replaced by more orderly, more sanitary housing, at equally congested densities, on the same sites. That assumption needs critical reconsideration. It is far from obvious.

Had the State planning agencies supplied the necessary feedback they might have kept our successive housing authorities from making the errors about the location and density of housing that already have been made—or worse ones you may now be tempted to make on an even larger scale. If active regional planning boards had been created and maintained, our country would have produced a large corps of trained minds, architects, planners, geotects, regional surveyors, who would now be able to do the job without too much direction from Washington, because they would have accumulated an immense amount of detailed first hand knowledge of the basic natural and human resources. That knowledge cannot be derived solely from statistics, is not transferable to computers, and is not achievable by any crash programs for education.

NEW URBAN PATTERN OF REGIONALISM NEEDED

May I suggest, then, that if you are not to do far more damage than good in establishing a new housing policy, you must first prepare to rebuild the effective organs for regional planning and regional government, on a State and interstate basis. This will also mean assembling, in the eight or ten major regions of the country, the Federal agencies that will or should, at various points, participate in this program. The Regional Development Council of America, a group that after 1945 continued the older Regional Plan Association, proposed such a permanent descentalization of related Federal activities in 1950, but Mr. Stein could get no one in Washington to take this proposal seriously.

Surely it is time that there was a general realization of the fact that we must deliberately contrive a new urban pattern; one which will more effectively mobilize the immense resources of our great metropolises without accepting the intolerable congestion that has driven increasing numbers of people to seek—at whatever sacrifices of time and social opportunity—at least a temporary breathing space in less congested urban areas. The new form of the city must be conceived on a regional scale not subordinated to a single dominant center, but as a network of cities of different forms and sizes, set in the midst of publicly protected open spaces permanently dedicated to agriculture and recreation. In such a regional scheme the great metropolises would be only "prima inter pares"—the first among equals.

This is the organic type of city that the technology of our time, the electric grid, the telephone, the radio, television, fast transportation, information storage and transmission, has made possible. A handful of planners, notably Christopher Tunnard, has seen the implications of this new scale in urban planning, but most of our planning authorities still remain, like a worn out scratched phonograph record, with the needle stuck in the old metropolitan groove. Many people, since the publication of Jean Gottmann's monumental survey, have tried to take comfort in the thought that the present disorder and disintegrating urban mass, which Gottmann has popularized as megalopolis, is in fact the modern form of the city, new, dynamic, and inevitable, whether we like it or not.

That is a slushy idea, worthy only of a Marshall McLuhan or a Timothy Leary. You might say of this sprawling megalopolitan nonentity, this "anticity," to use McLuhan's go-go terminology—that "the mess is the message." And the more massive the mess, the more muddled the message.

TECHNOLOGY OF THE "MEGAMACHINE"

Now, I have had to explain to myself how it came that the ideas we put forward during the last half century often proved politically and financially acceptable, but only at the price of being sterilized, dehumanized, and degraded. The full explanation dawned on me only recently in the course of an analysis I have been making, in a book soon to be published, on the basic assumptions and goals that have governed all large-scale technology, since the pyramid age in Egypt some 5,000 years ago.

From the earliest stages of civilization on, as I read the evidence, the most striking advances in mass technology have been the outcome of centralized organizations, deliberately expanding power in every form—mechanical power, political power, military power, financial power, and not least the scientific power of accurate analysis and prediction—to achieve control, the key word is control, over both the natural environment and the human community. The astounding mechanical success of these high-powered technologies is due to their method of systematically breaking down ecological complexities by eliminating the recalcitrant human factor. I have called this ancient form of mechanized organization the "megamachine." Wherever it operates, it magnifies authoritarian power and minimizes or destroys human initiative, self-direction, and self-government.

Obviously I cannot, at this hearing, present a just appraisal of the many genuine goods produced by these power systems; nor can I offer a detailed explanation of their sinister, countertendency to produce an unbalanced, deliberately wasteful, inherently destructive, and increasingly totalitarian economy, seemingly modern, but in fact based on ancient bureaucratic and military models. Even the book I have written only opens up the subject, and I have still to trace the story through the last four centuries.

POWER ECONOMY CONTRASTS WITH LIFE ECONOMY

Now, the main point to observe is that there is a deep-seated antagonism between a mechanistic, power-centered economy and the far older organic, life-centered economy; for a life economy seeks continuity, variety, orderly, and purposeful growth. Such an economy is cut to the human measure, and it respects the human scale, so that every organism, every community, every human being, shall have the variety of goods and experiences necessary for the fulfillment of his own individual life course, from birth to death.

The mark of a life economy is a respect for organic limits, it seeks not the greatest possible quantity of any particular good, but the right quantity, of the right quality, at the right place and the right time for the right purpose. Too much of any one thing is as fatal to living organisms as too little.

In contrast, a power economy is designed for the continuous and compulsory expansion of a limited number of uniform goods—those specially adapted to quantity production and remote control. Apart from enlarging the province of mechanization and automation, the chief goal of this system is to produce the greatest amount of power, prestige, or profit for the distant controllers of the megamachine. Though these modern systems produce a fantastic output of highly specialized products—motor cars, refrigerators, washing machines, rockets, nuclear bombs—they cannot, on their own terms, do justice to the far more complex and varied needs of human life, for these needs cannot be mechanized and automated, still less controlled and suppressed, without killing something essential to the life of the organism or to the self-respect of the human personality.

LIABILITIES OF OVERPRODUCTION

For the last century, we Americans have been systematically indoctrinated, with our own far from reluctant cooperation, in the virtues of mass production and have accepted, with unction, the plethora of goods offered, in which even those on public relief now participate. But we have been carefully trained to look only at the plus side of the equation, and to close our eyes to the appalling defects and failures that issue from the very success of the megamachine.

No sound public policy in housing and urban renewal can be formulated till we have reckoned with these liabilities. The overproduction of motor cars has not only wrecked our once-sufficient and well-balanced transportation system, and turned our big cities into hollow shells, exploding with violence; but it has polluted the air with lethal carbon monoxide, and even, through the use of lead in gasoline, dangerously poisoned our water and food. The chemical industry, in its undisciplined effort to sell a maximum amount of its products, has poisoned our soils and our foods with DDT, malathion, and other deadly compounds, while heedlessly befouling our water supply with detergents.

So, too, with the pharmaceutical industry, the rocket industry, the television industry, the pornography and narcotics industries. All have become immensely dynamic and profitable enterprises, automatically expanding, and by their compulsive expansion callously disregarding human health, safety, and welfare, while wiping out every trace of organic variety and human choice. As a result, the forces of life, if they break out at all, now must do so in the negative form of violence, crime, and psychotic disturbances. What we have unthinkingly accepted as brilliant technical progress has too often resulted in biological or social regression.

The point I am now making, I regret to say, challenges, not only some of the published views of your chairman, but possibly the views of the rest of this subcommittee. You accept, I take it, the current American faith in the necessity for an ever-expanding, machine-centered economy, as if this were one of the great laws of nature, or if not, then America's happiest contribution to human prosperity and freedom. I wish you were right.

TECHNOLOGY OF MEGALOPOLIS OVERLOOKS HUMAN NEEDS

But do you seriously believe that a housing industry based, as Senator Ribicoff has put it, on "the technology of megalopolis" will be any more regardful of human needs and human satisfactions, or any more eager to overcome the distortions and perversions of a power-obsessed, machine-driven, money-oriented economy? If so, you are ignoring the very factors that have mocked and ruined so many of our previous efforts at urban improvement. This expanding economy, for all its suffocating abundance of machine-made goods and gadgets, has resulted in a dismally contracted life, lived for the most part confined to a car or a television set; that is, a life so empty of vivid first-hand experiences that it might as well be lived in a space capsule, traveling from nowhere to nowhere at supersonic speeds.

Space capsules—yes, stationary space capsules—that is what most of our new buildings are, and our prefabricated foods taste increasingly like those supplied in tubes to astronauts; while in our urban planning schools I have encountered ominous designs for whole cities to be placed underground, or even underwater, so that their inhabitants may live and die without ever coming into contact with the living environment, that rich and varied environment which has been essential to the human race, for organic health, psychological stability, and cultural growth for at least 500,000 years. And in boasting of the fact that automation will soon be able to do away with all serious, humanly rewarding work, manual or mental, we are threatening to remove perhaps the most essential of all historic invention, work itself, and invention for preserving mental balance, and furthering the arts of life. These are all danger signals. Is it not time to give them heed?

RESTORATION OF NEIGHBORHOODS IS IMPORTANT

Now, your chairman, in his able speech last January, attempted to bring together what seems to me, if I may speak frankly, two altogether incompatible, in fact downright antagonistic, proposals; On one hand for restoring neighborhoods as the basic human environment; on the other for applying to housing what he called, quite properly, the technology of megalopolis, what I would call the technology of the megamachine. Senator Ribicoff wisely recognized the need to respect the small unit, the neighborhood, the small town, in order to promote those qualities we associate, at least as an ideal, with the small town—meaning, I take it, a place where everyone has an identifiable face and is a recognizable and responsible person, not just a social security number, a draft card number, or a combination of digits on a computer.

As to neighborhoods, I am entirely on his side. I have not spent part of my life in a small country community, and another part in a planned neighborhood unit, Sunnyside Gardens, Long Island, without learning to appreciate these intimate small-town virtues. And I believe the greatest defect of the U.S. Constitution was its original failure, despite the example of the New England township and the town meeting, to make this democratic local unit the basic cell of our whole system of government. For democracy, in any active sense, begins and ends in communities small enough for their members to meet face to face. Without such units, capable of independent and autonomous action, even the best contrived central governments, State or Federal, become party oriented, indifferent to criticism, resentful of correction, and in the end, all too often, highhanded and dictatorial.

MASSIVE TECHNOLOGY ELIMINATES HUMAN FACTOR

But if your purpose is to do urban planning and renewal on the basis of neighborhoods and balanced urban communities, you would, I submit, be deceiving yourselves if you imagined that a vast contribution by the Federal Government—$50 billion over 10 years has been suggested—could possibly achieve the happy results you hope for. Such a massive expenditure succeeded, we all know, in producing the atom bomb; and it has been applied with equal success, more or less, in producing rockets, space satellites, supersonic jets and similar instruments for the physical conquest of space and time, and large-scale physical destruction.

But note—this method can be applied only to those structures or machine assemblages that can be designed without the faintest regard for the human factor, and without any feedback from the human reaction. This patently leaves out the neighborhood and the city. Unless human needs and human interactions and human responses are the first consideration, the city, in any valid human sense, cannot be said to exist, for, as Sophocles long ago said, "The city is people."

Accordingly, I beg you to look a little more closely at what such a huge supply of capital, with such large prospective profits, would do. Not merely would it skyrocket already inflated land values so that a disproportionate amount would go to the property owner and real estate speculator; but even worse it would invite great megamachines to invade the building industry. With $50 billion as bait, a new kind of aerospace industry would move in, with all its typical paraphernalia of scientific research and engineering design. At that moment your plans for creating humanly satisfactory neighborhoods would go up in smoke.

"General-space housing incorporated" will solve your housing problem, swiftly and efficiently, though not painlessly, by following their own typical method, derived from the ancient pyramid builders and now applied by many other corporations: General Motors, General Electric, General Foods, all the great "General" corporations. What is this method? *Eliminate the human factor! Enforce mechanical conformity and destroy choice.* With the aid of their systems analyzers and computers, these high-powered organizations would design housing units even more prisonlike in character, if that is possible, than those we now have, and as unfit for permanent human habitation.

LARGE-SCALE URBAN RENEWAL COULD BECOME URBAN DESTRUCTION

Once started, such a scientifically ordered housing industry, commanding virtually unlimited capital at national expense, and providing, as in the Pentagon's favored industries, indecently large salaries and exorbitant profits for private investors, would be geared for further expansion. And it would achieve this expansion, not only by designing units, prefabricated for early obsolescence, but likewise by wiping out, as dangerous rivals, those parts of the remaining rural or urban environment that were built on a more human plan. In the name of urban renewal this method would complete the urban devastation and destruction that you now seek to repair. That is not a pretty prospect. But it is a realistic interpretation of what a $50 billion program, designed to use the existing power systems and feed an expanding economy, would probably do.

I have exhausted the time allotted to me, and have, I fear, more than exhausted your patience; though I have only nibbled at the edges of this difficult subject. So my final words must be brief, and I regret, mostly words of negation and caution. Go slow. Experiment with small measures and small units. Whatever you do in extending and amplifying the policies followed in the past will almost surely meet with the same embarrassments and the same dreadful failures.

Remember that you cannot overcome the metropolitan congestion of the last century, or the cataclysmic disintegration of urban life that has taken place during the last 30 years, by instituting a crash program. You are much more likely to produce more lethal congestion, more rapid disintegration, all ending in a greater social cataclysm. The time for action on a massive scale has not yet come. But the time for fresh thinking on this whole subject is long overdue.

Senator Ribicoff. Mr. Mumford, we are very grateful to you. I believe that your comments and your statement are absolutely essential to make this record complete.

I am just curious. Is there any American city that you like?

BALANCED COMMUNITIES ARE MOST EFFECTIVE

Mr. Mumford. Oh, there are many American cities that I like. There are not very many that I approve of.

Senator Ribicoff. Which ones do you approve of?

Mr. Mumford. Which ones do I approve of? The ones that have been most successful as cities have been the small towns, particularly the university towns, like Palo Alto. Now that Palo Alto has industry coming into it, and is becoming a balanced community, it might have a very good notion of what a good, effective, and thoroughly dynamic community can be, if it doesn't follow the congested model of New York and doesn't follow the equally undesirable sprawl model of Los Angeles.

OFFICE OF REGIONAL DEVELOPMENT IN NEW YORK

Senator Ribicoff. Isn't this one of our problems? I notice in an interview you gave in March to the New York Times you say: "New York, with a population of 8 million, has 2 million people too many." Let's say that we could move 2 million people out of New York. Where would we move them to?

Mr. Mumford. Why, Governor Rockefeller's Office of Regional Development has already prepared a plan for this. They have pointed out that the State of New York has 10 potential metropolises in it, each one of which could be the center of a new kind of regional development. They are, I regret to say, foolish enough to think of keeping on with the population congestion and sprawl of New York, but they see that much of the new population should go in nine other regions.

Senator Ribicoff. As a practical proposition, let's assume that we have to have a new pattern. We have to move people out of cities, create new towns. You disapprove of large injections of Federal capital. Where would you get the resources to lay out a program such as this? The resources are astronomical. Where would the financial resources come from?

PLANNING MUST COME BEFORE FINANCING

Mr. Mumford. To answer in terms of New York State would be unfair. New York State really has the financial resources for this, but there are many States that haven't. Therefore, if sufficient initiative and sufficient effort is done at the local level, at a later stage Federal help would be immensely desirable.

What I would question is whether the funds come before the planning. I think the planning must come first; and this is a long-term program, it can't be done overnight, it can't be included in the budget for 1968. The planning has to be done carefully in advance at the local level, and worked out in stages over a period of 50 years, reviewed and revised periodically in the light of fresh experience and new conditions. If you attempt a quicker program it will only freeze and permanently solidify our present errors.

Then when some sufficiently well defined idea of where the population should be, what new industries should be brought, what old industries should be brought out into the smaller regions, what new industries should be set up there—when this is understood, then is the time for calling forth State and Federal funds.

I have seen more bad thinking done as a result of having too much money at the beginning and not enough intellectual activity; so that I am suspicious of putting the funds first.

Senator Ribicoff. You described at the beginning of your testimony the frustration or the inertia that a small group of men face when they start a plan. We recognize that to get initiative going anywhere is one of the most difficult things in the world. As many have said, "To think is easy, to act is difficult." And acting in accordance with your thoughts is the most difficult thing in the world.

Where do we get the thinkers? Where do we get the planners? Where do we get the initiative? Up to the present time there hasn't been much show on any public level—Federal, State, or local—or in the private sector, There are some philosophers, some planners, such as yourself. You write books, you have ideas, you write articles, you debate. But how do we translate these ideas into realities?

Mr. Mumford. Well, a certain amount of seepage of ideas goes on, so that after a while even practical people test out the things that the thinkers provided a generation before.

NEW TOWNS MUST BE BALANCED COMMUNITIES

This is perfectly normal. You have the idea of the new town coming up spontaneously now after 50 years of thinking and propaganda, begun by Ebenezer Howard in 1898; and here in America today there are all sorts of projects for so-called new towns. They don't give promise yet as being balanced communities, because it is natural for people to do the easy things first. The difficult thing is to move industry and business out into the places that need it, and to provide them with housing.

We have many big corporations, for example, leaving New York City now. IBM, for example, recently became a neighbor of mine in Poughkeepsie, but this has been done without any planning on the part of the State to see that other coordinated industries and coordinate workers' housing is being done in this neighborhood. The result is a large part of the people who work in IBM are scattered over the countryside, when they should be put in a better kind of city. Poughkeepsie itself should be renovated very heavily, in order to make this possible.

Senator Ribicoff. Poughkeepsie is probably in as poor a position as any small community in the United States today.

Mr. Mumford. Yes, it has been a low-grade industrial community for a century.

Senator Ribicoff. This is the problem.

Anthony Downs was here yesterday. He has done a lot of thinking on the subject of new towns, both philosophically and practically. He made the statement that the whole new-town concept just won't go unless there is some planning to get jobs for people who live there.

Take the town of Columbia, which James Rouse is developing with financing by Connecticut General Life Insurance Co. I believe Connecticut General has now put up about $25 million. I have great faith in Connecticut General. But there is great difficulty in getting Columbia going, even though Columbia supposedly is a self-contained community with job opportunities and people of mixed social and economic backgrounds living together.

If you don't have the help from Government how do you get a new town going? It would be wonderful if Government didn't have to give a dime. But how do we do it?

Federal Aid for New Towns

Mr. Mumford. May I suggest that you have misunderstood me? I am not averse to Government help. I am averse to authorizing vast sums of Government money before the State and local authorities have done the necessary preparatory work. First they should know what ought to be done and where it should be done. This is a long-term program, it can't be arranged overnight, much as we would like to do it, but once the basic study has been made and the first stage of renewal has been outlined then Federal help would be immensely useful—indeed, indispensable.

We have the example of England, to help us there. The English new towns were national enterprise. They were directed from Whitehall. An enormous amount of money was sunk in them. And, fortunately, the money was first sunk in putting industry—industry and workers, housing—in the new towns. That is absolutely essential for any real program. The failure to begin with industry is why Reston is merely a middle-class suburb designed to look like a town, but it isn't a real town. It doesn't have the complexity of industrial and business enterprise that a real town needs.

VALUE OF MODEL CITIES PROGRAM

Senator Ribicoff. Would the program that Congress adopted last year, called the model cities program, would that comport with your concept of how Government goes about things? Do you or don't you like the model city concept?

Mr. Mumford. Mr. Danaceau will tell you that one of the reasons that I didn't want to come here this morning is that I have been so preoccupied with a book that I was writing that I have allowed urban affairs to drift beyond my immediate horizon, so I have never examined the model cities program. I am an ignorant man on that subject.

Senator Ribicoff. Well, then, we will pass that. I imagine the concept of the model cities is supposed to be what you are talking about—planning grants to be made to local communities to see what they could work out. It is really a "model neighborhood" program. They call it a model cities, but it envisions a model neighborhood. But let's get down to some of the problems that we have.

I would guess that what you are talking about is a "go slow" approach. You are reluctant to see any massive program undertaken by government at any level.

But consider these facts. We have 16 million poor living in the cities of America. We have another 26 million right on the edge of poverty. For all practical purposes they are in poverty. You have the great problem of the racial antagonisms. The cities are more and more becoming occupied by Negroes, and their unemployment rate is much higher. There is the great pressure for jobs, the great pressure for education, the great pressure for decent housing. Some 4 1/2 million people, in urban areas, are living in substandard housing.

A society faced with that basic social and economic stress—and we are—how slow can it go? The conditions do exist, and not much has been achieved. How do people with a sense of responsibility and who care, how do they go about correcting this, if your policy is to "go slow"? What do we do about decent housing? How do you balance esthetics and your concept of the great city or small town with the basic problems that face society today?

REBUILD CITIES WITH "ALL DELIBERATE SPEED"

Mr. Mumford. I suppose I should have said when I was suggesting the proper mood for this, we should go ahead "with all deliberate speed," to use Mr. Justice Frankfurter's famous phrase, for a simple reason. We are dealing with an immensely complex condition. It isn't something that happened yesterday. Naturally, we would like to have an answer to these related problems which would be visible within 5 or 10 years; but the sounder our constructive efforts, the less likelihood that the results will come quickly. New towns, like old Rome, are not built in a day.

I think it is well to work with a sense of urgency, but also with the realization that, just as in the case of a chronic disorder and illness, no application of a miracle drug is going to overnight abolish the disease and restore the patient completely to health. We would like to do that, but we are under very severe limitations, no matter how much money we have. We can destroy a city overnight; but a city is far too complex to be restored to health overnight.

Perhaps this is the point I should stress: That urban renewal can't be done properly by just voting money for this or that prospect. Even to vote large sums for urban research is not enough. There are plenty of people who will have research projects ready, and will take 10 years before they get to the end of them, by which time the conditions themselves will be much worse, and their program will be out of date.

We should get every local, State, and regional agency at work on these problems, and we should formulate an objective for them. We want to be able to redistribute on more rational lines the urban population of this country, which is now in great disorder. But we now allow mass technology to dictate our plans and our purposes—and this means more congestion.

POSSIBILITIES OF RELOCATING PEOPLE IN RURAL AREAS

Do you suppose that you can improve this situation without technological changes? There is an item in the paper this morning about the Negro population, something we all know. Seventy-five percent of them, perhaps more than that, used to be on the land. They have now been drawn in the last 20 years into the big cities. They are perfectly competent to work the land and to improve it greatly, and no great resources and machinery are necessary. Most people don't realize that efficient agriculture is hand agriculture. The Chinese, with a hoe, produce a higher acreage of wheat than any Western country has been able to produce with machinery. By using power machines, you can get an enormous acreage under cultivation, but the output per acre is always lower than that by hand.

Now, our whole economy assumes that everybody will stop working with his hands, and he will work a machine or he won't work at all. This is really nonsense. There is an enormous amount of cheerful manual work to be done along our roadsides that we now do by means of poisons, by means of the most ruthless kind of bulldozing. With 5 million men at work, with spades, hoes, and scythes, we could clean up our rubbish-filled landscapes, and plant trees and flowering bushes that would turn our towns and roadsides into inviting parks. This is work for men, not machines.

The enormous urban populations that we don't know what to do with in the cities could have highly useful social tasks worth economic support, if they were relocated in the rural districts from which they came, and we would probably give them a much happier life than they will ever have on relief.

Senator Ribicoff. While that may be true, how do you get them back to the farm, "once they have seen Paree"? The Negro is drawn to the city for many reasons. While the Negro came from a rural background, he now is a city person. I don't hear or see or know of any desire of the Negro to go back to the farm. They are in the city to stay. This is a condition we face.

Ninety percent of the schoolchildren in Washington are Negro. Chicago and Detroit go beyond 50 percent. Baltimore and St. Louis have an elementary school population that is more than 60 percent Negro. What do we do?

A democratic society isn't going to pick people up and send them places. This is what I am concerned with, with the immediacy of a deep social and economic problem that our society faces.

REASONS FOR MIGRATION TO CITIES

Mr. Mumford. Let's analyze, though, how this migration into the big cities came about. It came about because the large mass of Negroes in the South were living under degraded, barely human conditions. They had nothing that could be called a decent livelihood. They had only the companionship of their poor neighbors. They had a kind of local life of their own, but at the very lowest possible level, economically or educationally.

So during the war, when there were jobs in the North that offered even the Negro some opportunity, there was a wholesale migration into the North, and that has continued to increase, because conditions in the Deep South haven't become any more favorable to the Negro.

If you ask the Negro to go back to the places that he has escaped from, you would be asking for something which is humanly impossible and shouldn't be even suggested. But on the other hand, we haven't given the Negro an opportunity to make any decision, any real choices. We haven't said:

> *Do you want to live in these foul slums, where family life has become impossible, and where everybody lives in fear of each other? —or would you like, under the conditions that we can make possible, by building communities in other parts of the*

country to use a large percentage of the Negro population in the more rural areas, where these horrible features of metropolitan congestion don't exist.

We don't know what the Negro really wants. We can't possibly know until we give him an alternative. He has no alternative today.

Senator Ribicoff. But the entire farm population has been reduced by some in a decade. The whites are moving from the farm as well. It would be wonderful if we could reverse this trend. But we can't. What do we do with the condition that we are in?

MUMFORD QUESTIONS VALUE OF AFFLUENT SOCIETY

Mr. Mumford. You see, this is one of the reasons I was so reluctant to come here, because I have no simple answers to this. We are taking our orders now from our technology, that part of our technology which is immensely profitable gives us orders, and we think that we have to submit to these orders.

I can conceive that once we realize that we are being cheated, that we are not getting the sort of life, not even getting the sort of economic rewards that would really sustain life, we will think about the possibility of giving orders to our technology, of creating a more balanced technology, not completely dependent upon the overproduction, of machine goods. And once we do this, the rewards of high-energy technology will be lower, but the rewards in terms of human life will be higher.

I think that many people are fed up with the kind of civilization we have provided, and I don't think that this is a purely personal point of view. You will find the whole of the situation analyzed in this week's Life. What is the individual getting out of our affluent society? The editors of Life, who are dependent upon this technology, dependent upon the great corporations, nevertheless are asking this very pointed question, which we should be asking too.

Senator Ribicoff. I think we are. The basic purpose of these hearings is to ask some questions. One of the problems we faced at the beginning was that people weren't even asking the right questions. If we are going to try to reach the beginnings of some solutions, we had better start asking some questions.

I am going to make one comment and ask one more question and then I will turn the questions over to my colleagues.

NEGROES FACE PROBLEMS OF AN URBAN SOCIETY

Ralph Ellison, who is a sensitive writer and observer, as you are a sensitive man too, made this statement at our hearing:

Now beyond this, I would say that it is a misunderstanding to assume that Negroes want to break out of Harlem. They want to transform the Harlems of their country. These places are precious to them. These places are where they have dreamed, where they have lived, where they have loved, where they have worked out life as they could.

I think Ralph Ellison made the point that, while the Negro moved out of the rural South to see what he could find and that he found the streets weren't paved with gold in New York or Chicago, the fact remains that the Negro children today are urban children, and many problems Negroes face today are basically problems of an urban society.

Size of a Viable City

One final question, and then I will yield to my colleagues. What size unit would you suggest would be the most practical and most viable to rebuild the city? Would you do it in units of 10,000 or 20,000, or 50.000? What would, in your opinion, give a person a sense of belonging, a sense of individuality, a sense of personality? What size would you think would offer the most to the individual and the most to society?

Mr. Mumford. I don't think there is any single size. There are limits that you can establish. I think a city of over 300,000 population ceases to have many of the most valuable attributes of a city; and in England, the new towns' advocate began with an ideal of 30,000. They now have gone up to 100,000. That is a city which can have many of the attractions that a metropolis has, and yet still have some of the special local virtues that a small town has.

If you are thinking of a great metropolis like New York, and ask, "How do you make the component parts of New York more like real cities? "—I should say you should think of subcenters of an order of 25,000 or 30,000, that you can do a great deal of effective planning on that basis. I don't think there is any one ideal size; but I do think there is an upper limit. On the other hand, when you are thinking of reorganizing the new type of city on a regional scale, the metropolis of 5 million or even 8 million people may prove too small. You may want a grouping of cities amounting to as many as 10 or 15 million people, conceived as independent communities in it, but still part of a federated unified whole.

Senator Ribicoff. Senator Kennedy.

MONEY ALONE WILL NOT SOLVE CITY PROBLEMS

Senator Kennedy. I think your testimony has been most helpful, Mr. Mumford. As I understand it, it is not really in objection to the expenditure of funds but rather the idea that just the expenditure of funds is going to make the problem disappear.

The question is whether we have sat down and thought out what kind of an urban life we would like to have and what kind of life we want here in the United States for the individual. Isn't that really what we are talking about?

Mr. Mumford. Right. The money isn't enough to create the solution. That is what I am suggesting.

Senator Kennedy. And the fact is really that there isn't a city in the United States at the moment that has sat down and made a plan as to what they would do if they had the $2 billion or the $5 billion or the $10 billion that all of us talk about.

Mr. Mumford. The other point I would make, that even the biggest city cannot help itself. New York isn't powerful enough to plan for the distribution of its population. The costly metropolis can't afford to lose its taxpayers; so every prudent mayor must try to keep all the taxpayers within his bailiwick, naturally. Therefore the planning on a larger scale has to be done at a higher level, and with powerful State aid eventually. But note—in accord with the fundamental principles of the garden city, the land should be held by the community for the benefit of all its members. Otherwise, economic success will start a new cycle of congestion.

If New York or any big city should lose some of its population, there must be some method of redressing this imbalance in the tax rolls. That has to be faced.

CONCEPT OF COMMUNITY LIFE HAS BEEN LOST

Senator Kennedy. Really the whole concept of a city, of living as a community, isn't that really what we have lost more than anything else, more than the problem of the Negro coming off the farm, more than the problem of crime, is the fact that people have lost the idea of community and of the importance of themselves as individuals in our society.

Mr. Mumford. Quite right, although they regain a little of it on the individual block. There is a residue of community life, at least in poor neighborhoods. I have lived in all parts of New York, and I know there are certain areas where everybody still knows the butcher and the baker and the grocer, if they are still there, and have not turned into a supermarket.

These elementary human relationships are important and we must preserve them. This is one of the fine things that Jane Jacobs contributed to her analysis of the real life of the city. We must not break up this kind of unity. The Negroes have that to a certain degree in Harlem. They have raised their status by becoming a self-conscious kind of community, as opposed to the white community which has rejected them. So until they have something better that they can call their own, even the vilest slum is home to them, naturally.

LONG-TERM PROBLEMS MUST BE SOLVED

Senator Kennedy. I thought what you said on page 13:

> *This expanding economy, for all its suffocating abundance of machine-made goods and gadgets, has resulted in a dismally contracted life, lived for the most part confined to a car or to a television set: A life so empty of vivid first-hand experiences that it might as well be lived in a space capsule, traveling from nowhere to nowhere at supersonic speeds.*
>
> *Space capsules—yes, stationary space capsules—that is what most of our new buildings are, and our prefabricated foods taste increasingly like those supplied in tubes to astronauts . . .*

Really, unless we solve this problem, no matter what we do about some of these more obvious problems, or what appear to us to be more obvious problems, we are not going to really bring about any long-range solution.

Mr. Mumford. You see, there are really long-term problems; problems that involve radical changes in our technology are obviously long-term problems. This whole technological complex has been built up during 300 years. It isn't in a spirit of pessimism that I would say that I don't expect any profound changes to be made during the next generation. There will be palliative changes, ameliorations, not really a revolutionary change.

What I am really thinking of—as essential to effective urban renewal—is a much more profound change in our whole concept of civilization. That is something which will possibly take as long to create as our present civilization, at least 300 or 400 years. So there are no short-term solutions except the small ones. Those we must go ahead with as fast as we can.

DISSATISFICATION WITH SOCIETY IS A WORLDWIDE PROBLEM

Senator Kennedy. One last point. Do you feel that what is happening in the United States at the moment, the increase in crime, the dissatisfaction among many of our young people who are turning to narcotics or LSD, the suicide rate, the dissension which manifests itself in reference to Vietnam, but perhaps more deeply than that, dissension against the kind of life people are leading, and the kind of society that we have created at the present time, that that really is the essence of the things you are describing in your testimony.

And that unless we find the answer to that, no matter what we do about urban life or urban living or what buildings we create or how many universities we are able to build, we are not going to have the answer.

Mr. Mumford. I am in full agreement, but we must remember that this isn't just an American problem. This is a worldwide problem. It concerns our whole civilization. There isn't a single evil, a single aspect of violence or delinquency that we face in this country, that you can't find even in Sweden, supposedly a beautifully balanced, mixed economy. It is true of Russia, supposedly a Communist or a state Socialist economy.

That means to me that this is something which is deeply ingrained in our mode of thought, in our supporting technology, and the whole rigmarole of life, which is just the same essentially in Soviet Russia as it is in the United States—the underlying fact, not the superficial ones.

Senator Kennedy. I would agree. What struck me when I traveled across this country and across the world is that when you have questions from students, you have about five basic questions that are asked, whether you are in Indonesia, Japan or Kenya, Kansas or Germany, or wherever, and they all come back basically to some of the points you have raised.

Mr. Mumford. They are all the same because they arise out of the same conditions.

Senator Kennedy. Thank you very much.

Senator Ribicoff. Senator Baker.

BAKER'S SUMMARY

Senator Baker. Thank you, Mr. Chairman.

Mr. Mumford, I succumb to the temptation sometimes to try to summarize and give a superficial analysis of what I have heard for the sake of aiding my own understanding, so bear with me for a moment and I will try to touch a few of what I believe to be the salient points in your presentation, to make sure I do understand the principal thrust of this philosophy and your viewpoint.

It seems to me that your principal commentary on the current crop of proposals for new housing programs, for regional and national planning of the city and the economy, is that we really don't know enough about these factors, and about the situation involved, to allow ourselves to try to fabricate an overall comprehensive plan for a life system for the people of this Nation. And that rather than apply a poultice of $50 billion to acknowledge existing ills of the Nation, we should engage ourselves in regional and localized experimentation to add to this body of knowledge, so that we can derive answers, techniques, and evolve a new direction that will contribute something of substance to a humanized existence as distinguished from technological existence.

USE OF TECHNOLOGY TO PRODUCE A BETTER LIFE

Now, if these analyses of your thoughts are accurate, may I put this question. Do you agree, however, that the demonstrable methods of modern accelerative technology are a legitimate and a proper additional tool in determining how we best produce this new life, this more humanized life, a more orderly and more attractive life system that we all seek, and that technology itself is not antagonistic to humanity and to the human quality of existence, but rather that they go hand in hand and intelligently apply both modern technology and humanistic spirit can work side by side to produce a better life—do you agree with this?

Mr. Mumford. First of all, thank you for the summary. It is a better summary of my thought than I could give myself.

Second, let me say that I have no abstract bias against large organizations, because large organizations are sometimes the only ones that are possible.

I don't want to see a small A.T.&T., for example. I think the ideal organization for A.T.&T. is one which extends over the entire country and has a monopoly of the telephone service. I am full of admiration for the kind of planning such an organization does. It does an enormous amount of social thinking before it even locates the next telephone exchange. So it isn't a question of bias.

On the other hand, all these large organizations are governed by a money ideology. They are interested in all the problems of humanity, as long as they are sure of a guaranteed return of at least 8 percent, but hopefully much more. They will rapidly enter any field that promises more than 8 percent. If 15 is promised, they will rush in with eagerness, almost violence.

And on the other hand, if you were to say, "We appreciate your services to the community, we need your technology, we need all the skills you have assembled, but in order to balance up with other things, we guarantee only that you will get 3 1/2 or 4 percent. But you must not expect inordinate profits and you must not be tempted by them, we want you to go into phases of industry on a small scale where the profits will be small too"—this would be heresy, of course, from our present standpoint, and very unacceptable as you all know.

Senator Baker. I think it probably isn't heresy today, Mr. Mumford. As a matter of fact, I am attracted to the notion that now, today, after our population gets above the minimum starvation level, the American society is really meaning-oriented, or quality of life oriented, rather than economic or money oriented, and that is a pretty radical statement I suppose, but I believe that to be the case.

Mr. Mumford, I hope you are right.

URGENT PROBLEMS FACE CITIES

Senator Baker. I hope so, too.

Let me ask you one other question that the chairman touched on, and which I think is most pertinent to a practical consideration of the spectrum and variety of ills that our urban and rural centers suffer from.

We really have two problems. We have the problem of our current dilemma in the urban sprawl, in the impacted city areas. We have this as an immediate urgent human consideration. What do we do about this disadvantaged generation?

And then we have the second problem—and they aren't necessarily parallel, they aren't necessarily always interrelated—of what we do to plan better for the next generation.

But you can't solve one by ignoring the other. It seems to me that there has to be some application of effort to the solution of both these concepts. Would you agree with that?

LISTEN FOR LOCAL RESPONSE TO PROBLEMS

Mr. Mumford. Yes, I would agree. I would say that the most urgent thing is to help these smaller units to help themselves. They need encouragement. And the first way you encourage them is to listen to them.

I live in a small community, and people for a long time never would attend the open public meetings to discuss matters like schools and roads that relate to the real needs of the community. They let the selectmen meet and decide.

But the selectmen have made a series of very poor decisions. And to my great surprise and delight, the whole town turned out recently to speak up to the selectmen and tell them that they have got to change their policy and their plans.

Now, this is the first thing in planning—we must first listen for the local response. We have it, for example, in New York. Again, today's paper report that the board of education now, as a result of intense protest in the Negro communities of Harlem, is going to accept the people of the neighborhood as helpers and advisers in their educational program.

This is a wonderful change. It was accompanied by excessive intransigence and unreasonable demands. That is inevitable when a situation gets tense. But the upshot of it is that the board of education, which ran things highhandedly without any respect of any local community, because there wasn't in the past any local community there to talk to them, now has begun to listen. So my answer to you is this: A great many people will finally discover what I am sure all you gentlemen who have been interested in politics long ago discovered for yourselves, that the most interesting, and most arduous game in the world is the game of politics. To actually take part in managing men and managing public affairs is one of the greatest and most satisfactory arts in the world. All of us now have leisure for this occupation and the local community might play a part that it has never played before, because of that leisure.

Senator Baker. I think your point is well made, Mr. Mumford. I would like for the sake of brevity to move on to my last and concluding question.

Senator Ribicoff. I think you are doing very well. Take as much time as you want.

DUAL APPROACH TO CITY PROBLEMS

Senator Baker. Thank you, sir.

This is a two-part question—that is now and in the future, now as the palliative and the future for a better and more permanent solution—it seems to me that the question of the relationship of the city center to the Nation as a whole, both urban areas, suburban areas, medium and small towns and the like is a two-part consideration.

It seems also to me that we have got to accept the fact and probably in the light of the fact that our cities traditionally and historically have been cultural centers, have been centers of dynamic energy which lead to civilization. But at the same time, one of the greatest wastes of a national asset is the proposition that some 70 percent of our land is uninhabited.

Might not both the present and the future solutions to our quality of life dilemma be to find some better way to make the less populated areas patently attractive to new generations and to the present occupants of the more impacted areas of our urban centers, without going into some highhanded planning to move people away; but rather to make less populated areas more basically attractive to people, so they will populate them?

Would it seem to you that these dual approaches, that is upgrading the quality of the structure of urban life on the one hand, and making more attractive the quality of rural life or semirural life on the other hand, might go hand in hand? Urban and rural improvement are bound up together.

ENCOURAGE DEVELOPMENT OF NEGLECTED AREAS

Mr. Mumford. There are plenty of historical examples of that. The various communities in the South, for reasons that are sometimes excellent, attracted an enormous amount of New England industry, as you know, because there were more favorable conditions for operating in the South than there were in the North.

So Arizona and New Mexico, without any serious planning, have had their special regional resources recognized, and people have been moving into these areas in great numbers.

These things could be encouraged, of course. Admirable areas have been neglected sometimes, like the Appalachian region. The Appalachian region has wonderful qualities for living, but since the basis of industry in the Appalachian region, particularly around West Virginia and Pennsylvania, was coal mining, they created unattractive communities that nobody wanted to move into. But with a sufficient amount of resourceful planning, the whole Appalachian highlands might be a new center of a new kind of urban community.

RELATIONSHIP BETWEEN
THE HUMAN BEING AND HIS ENVIRONMENT

Senator Baker. And I sense that you and I possibly agree without saying so, that it is a basic matter of human nature that there is some interaction and relationship between the human being and his environment.

Mr. Mumford. Right.

Senator Baker. And that each takes something of the personality and character of the other, so as we change or modify and upgrade and make more attractive either an urban area or a rural area, we are likely to produce a corresponding change in the collective personality of the inhabitants of that area, which in turn will have a vast impact on the crime rate and the morality rate, on the whole range of social problems that confront the nation.

Mr. Mumford. No doubt of it. That is because the human environment is a very varied and complex one. The mechanized environment has certain virtues of its own, but it is not a complex one and it is not sufficiently varied to sustain all human activities.

GOOD BUILDINGS AND THE GOOD LIFE

An Interview with Allan Temko

Mr. Temko, what relationship exists between the architect and the city in this country?

Temko: At present there is almost none. The architect cannot do more than an individual building or group of buildings in a city. He might get an urban redevelopment project, perhaps even a large one. But none has ever been assigned a Brasilia, like Oscar Niemeyer, or a Chandigarh, like Le Corbusier. An

An interview with Allan Temko, "Good Buildings and the Good Life" 2nd Edition, CENTER MAGAZINE, *Vol. II, No. 6, November, 1969. Copyright 1969 by* CENTER MAGAZINE. *Reprinted by permission of the publisher.*

example of the lack of coördination between the architects and the city and between the architects themselves is shown in what has been happening to Rockefeller Center. Rockefeller Center was the work of a group of architects in the nineteen-thirties. It was a complex of buildings in which open space had been planned as an integral part of the composition. It was a good start but somewhat overrated because only seventeen per cent of the site had been left open—not much in view of the congestion created by the Center itself. But it was a start and it was something new in the history of private development.

Now, however, we have regressed. The Time & Life Building, though not visually an extension of Rockefeller Center, is considered a part of it, and it is only one of four huge skyscrapers that will be on the four corners adjacent to the Center. The Columbia Broadcasting System and Equitable Life Assurance occupy two of the other corners. The fourth was bought from William Zeckendorf by Uris Brothers—they put up much of the commercial hackwork in New York. The architects involved are above average. Eero Saarinen designed the CBS building. Harrison & Abramovitz did Time & Life. Skidmore, Owings & Merrill did the Equitable Building. The smallest of these skyscrapers will be the CBS building at, I believe, thirty-eight stories. But these four corporations—though two of them have high cultural pretensions—could not create one plaza between them. They were not able to put Sixth Avenue (the Avenue of the Americas) underground for a couple of blocks. They could not re-route traffic. They could not create a city-scape. All they could do was add to what Lewis Mumford calls "solidified chaos": Manhattan at its worst, skyscrapers going up without any relationship to human needs and aesthetic sensibilities.

In this "could not" is there also an element of "would not"?

Temko: They could have, but there was no political means to compel them to do it.

You mean, there was no urban authority to say, "You must do this, or that"?

Temko: Yes. There was no municipal authority or even any municipal guidance, except standard code and zoning based on speculative land values.

Is this typical of how our large American cities have grown through the years?

Temko: Yes, it helps explain the chaos. Our federally sponsored redevelopment projects are now organized, but I find most of them disappointing.

Why? Is it because the people who have ultimate control over the projects lack the experience and education to make proper decisions? That is, our borough presidents, city councils, and aldermanic bodies have the authority and responsibility for redevelopment, but no special or expert competence to exercise that authority to good effect?

Temko: A city like New York is completely out of control, both at its center and at its periphery. Even if it had a much finer municipal government, it would take a full generation to arrest the present disintegrating tendencies as far as urban life is concerned.

What is wrong?   Lewis Mumford, for example, says that our cities lack the humanist dimension and orientation, that in many instances they frustrate rather than nourish human relationships.

Temko: The modern metropolis in many respects is inhuman. There is over-congestion, an over-concentration of people. The automobile is out of control. In New York it is next to impossible to drive; this costs billions of dollars in wasted man-hours. We have no way of organizing residential and industrial patterns. Simple zoning is not the answer; it is piecemeal. I.B.M. moved its headquarters to Westchester County. They got some wonderful architecture. Saarinen, for example, did their research building. But this big corporation moved out of Manhattan and into Westchester County completely independently, without any coördination. Until such moves are coördinated and people decide what things should be in the city and what should be outside the city, we are going to be in trouble.

Are you saying that we need not only greater artistic competence in the development of our cities but also a greater measure of authority?

Temko: Yes. The very word "civic" has implications which were clear in ancient societies. The Athenian citizen, for example, took large responsibility for the physical appearance of his city.

I suppose there would be an immediate outcry if some municipal or metropolitan authority were to say to, for example, I.B.M.: "Wait, you can't move until we see whether such a move fits in with our over-all urban program." In some quarters at least, I can imagine such restraint would be labeled "authoritarianism."

Temko: The example of I.B.M. is one that may, in fact, work out very well. The point is, it may *not* work out very well, and there was no prior coördination of such a move in terms of what is good not only for I.B.M. but also for New York City and Westchester County. Freedom does imply responsibility. But even the most responsible corporation cannot now coördinate its moves with either the city or society as a whole because the means for such coördination do not exist. There is a plethora of laws, but they are working out badly.

Santa Barbara has very strict regulations on architecture, intended to make the city a Spanish-colonial stage set. In some ways it has worked out, but it has not become a visual utopia. It has, for example, the same hideous gas stations you will find in Indianapolis. Look around the San Francisco region. It is one of the most beautiful natural environments in the world and what have we done to it? We have polluted the Bay. We have ruined the hills. We have ruined the atmosphere. We have no metropolitan government. We don't even have a Bay region authority or plan. Dade County, Florida, has a metropolitan government, and Chicago has a metropolitan regional plan, but a plan with no teeth in it. Washington, D.C., has a superficially impressive plan, but none of the controls necessary for its success.

Is there some middle way between iron control on the one hand and no control at all on the other?

Temko: The Russians have an authoritarian system of planning which does not seem to be working out much differently from ours as far as overgrowth is concerned. But there is a third approach found in the Scandinavian countries and in Great Britian. The postwar British Labor government started a very bold environmental program which has been continued by the Conservatives. It includes the green belt around London, the New Towns, and very carefully designed housing. These British developments have faults, but they are so far ahead of what we have done that no real comparison is possible.

What are some of the characteristics of the ideal city from the standpoint of human relations?

Temko: We must remember that the city is made up of all kinds of individuals who wish to live in different ways. A city should provide that variety. Lake Meadows in Chicago is a significant renewal project. It was built in the nineteen-fifties by Skidmore, Owings & Merrill and was financed by the New York Life Insurance Company. It is the largest exemplification of Le Corbusier's planning ideas that I know in this country. The Lake Meadows site was one of the worst slums in the world. Certainly it was the worst I have ever seen—and I have been in China. They decided to raze it. Here was a case where they worked on a large enough scale but, architecturally and artistically, they started rather timidly. They put up five rather nondescript towers about twelve stories high in an X formation—two towers on either side and one in the center. They were stubby in outline and rather grim. They suffered from "projectitis." Ninety-nine percent of the first occupants of these five buildings were Negroes. The other one percent were young architects who moved in because of an intellectual commitment. A second group of buildings went up and this was much bolder. Here were four huge slabs, each about twenty-two stories high. They are not great, but they are excellent buildings. Two of them are about four hundred feet apart; the other two stand somewhat out and behind them, farther from the lake, and about six hundred feet apart. So you have a magnificent funnel of fresh air coming off the lake, affording great relief in the summer. These four great slab apartment houses are set in a green park: Le Corbusier's idea of skyscrapers-in-parks. In winter, of course, it is rather forbidding, with the Chicago weather. The architects originally wanted glazed, heated passageways for the winter, but they did not get them because of the cost.

What kind of tenants did they get for this second group of buildings?

Temko: I find this whole project interesting for its sociological implications. It quickly became apparent that this second group was the best housing for the money in Chicago. Whites started to move in. They included not only architects, who from the beginning saw these apartments as excellent, but also army sergeants, television repairmen, civil servants. The proportion of whites to Negroes grew to 20-80, then 30-70, and in a new series of buildings put up nearby by less gifted architects—a project called Prairie Shores—the ratio was about 50-50. The question then arose: Suppose these housing projects became totally white? I asked Fred Kramer, the Chicago financier who is actively involved in these developments, whether he had contemplated doing anything to maintain a percentage of Negroes. He said he hoped that this would take care of itself normally, that it would stabilize itself according to the proportion of Negroes and whites in the rest of the city. Recently they have added a luxurious apartment house to Lake Meadows' great group of four buildings and the rents are as high as any in Chicago, even on the North Shore. The tenants include both Negroes and whites, some with very high incomes.

Is it simply provision of green space between the buildings that makes them desirable?

Temko: The people find it attractive to live there. If you have young children, however, you probably do not want to live nineteen stories in the air. At Hyde Park, Zeckendorf's project near the University of Chicago, there is a drastically different approach to urban renewal, in which you have two big apartment houses by an excellent architect, I. M. Pei, but very close together, rather needlessly formal, and surrounded by an elliptical roadway, a "gasoline alley," so that traffic has not been removed. And in Hyde Park if you are on the inner court between the two great towers you can see the people across the way in their underwear unless they draw their blinds. One advantage of towers set very far apart, as at Lake Meadows, is the privacy afforded. Hyde Park also has little squares with town houses which are supposed to provide intimacy, like the little squares in Bloomsbury in London. But in Hyde Park they are a failure because the automobile is everywhere, taking up the center of these little court-yards and squares, which should be green. To me the present housing is inferior to what previously existed when the neighborhood was made up of free-standing one-family houses.

What about transportation? Isn't that one of the central unsolved problems of urban living?

Temko: The auto problem is out of control at present, again because of a failure of politics. I consider this primarily political, though most people do not. I think we can act only through government on all levels, federal, state and local, to get the problem of transportation under control. We are subsidizing the automobile industry. We have a fantastic national investment in automobiles. We change cars every year. We are building highways that are a feast for the bankers as well as the contractors. Meanwhile, railroads die and you cannot get money or support for alternative rapid-transit systems in our big metropolitan areas. The San Francisco Bay region has an excellent rapid-transit plan. Originally it was intended for nine counties; as finally presented it included five counties. Of those five, two counties have already withdrawn. Marin County withdrew because of a technical difficulty: a panel of engineers found that the Golden Gate Bridge could not carry trains. But San Mateo County withdrew because of irresponsible politicians, who acted against the will of many citizens, perhaps a majority.

Ideally, there should be a diversity of transportation methods in our cities, should there not? And yet there is not much that can be done if people insist on driving their cars between the suburbs where they live and the central city where they work or go to school.

Temko: Part of this is educational. The Americans get a lot of psycho-logical satisfaction, or maybe it is only an illusion of satisfaction, from their cars. The auto is a real convenience, too. The American loves to go from one place to another without changing his transportation. I don't know what the answer is, but it is a problem that must be attacked on several levels. And in many cities we do not have any good alternative to the available system of transportation.

It is said that the freeways and expressways in some cases have aggravated rather than relieved traffic congestion. At certain hours in New York or Los Angeles, for example, traffic on these roads slows down to five or six miles per hour.

Temko: Yes, and that is slower than the rate of the old horse cars. I think it was much faster to take a trolley car in Chicago thirty years ago than it is to drive your car there now. When people see the implications of some of these things they rebel.

Isn't it one of the complaints of the architects that they are not called in soon enough on the large urban renewal projects in our cities?

Temko: Yes. The Golden Gateway project in San Francisco was laid out by an architectural firm, but other things conditioned what it could do. For example, a freeway runs very close to the site where the best type of modern housing is supposed to be built. Another bad freeway borders the renewal area in southwest Washington, D. C. Why those site problems could not have been solved architecturally at an early stage, no one knows. The engineering mentality always resists this sort of intrusion by the artists and architects.

Have there been any "success stories" in the relationship of architects to urban planners in any of our cities? Have there been any instances in which competent architects have been called in at the beginning of long-range city planning, have actually planned and carried through a large-scale project?

Temko: Of course in the nineteenth century artist-designers were called in to work on a grand scale. Frederick Olmsted, the landscape architect, was one. I recently read the memoirs of T. Jefferson Coolidge, a Boston Brahmin, who spent many days on horseback with Olmsted, laying out the magnificent parks around Boston. I wonder how many of our civic leaders today would take the time, and, furthermore, would have the same keen sense of responsibility for their cities.

There has been a decline in civic responsibility then?

Temko: We do have the Blyth-Zellerbach committee in San Francisco, a group of the wealthiest and most powerful men in town. They have hired experts to see what they could do for the city. The committee has done much valuable work in redevelopment. But they suggested that the city sell some of its parks—actually sell off a few parks instead of creating new ones! Nevertheless, most businessmen are now aware of the advantages, including the financial profits, of urban renewal, and many are interested in design. The urban renewal agencies, which of course must work closely with the business community, often try hard to obtain good architecture. But most redevelopment architecture remains quite ugly.

Why is that?

Temko: For one thing, buildings look cheaper today, even when they may be quite expensive. In the old days, when a hack architect in a small town did a bank, he did it in Roman-temple style. He probably had studied at a very conservative Beaux-Arts school and would come up with something rather solid —an embellishment to the town. It was not cheap. Today most new buildings appear cheap, especially municipal buildings. Look at San Francisco's City Hall, which cost four million dollars in 1910. It is copybook architecture. But I think it is rather great as neo-classical design and an excellent building in many other ways, certainly far superior to the new buildings the city is putting up.

Why are the new buildings so ugly when they cost so much? One reason is the mechanical equipment that goes into them. Much of the money that formerly went into the structure of the building now goes into its air conditioning, electrical circuits, plumbing, and the like. A staggering amount of equipment goes into modern buildings, and it all costs money. If we could find ways to miniaturize air-conditioning systems, for example, we could put more money into the building itself.

What about the general quality of American architects? Even if you gave them more money to spend in the construction of their buildings, would they have the artistic capabilities of achieving that "more" in their architecture?

Temko: Our top architects are very good. But many of them are confused. Saarinen once pointed out that a generation ago, though there were many different architects working on the University of Chicago buildings, they were working in a discipline larger than their individual tastes. It was a neo-Gothic discipline and, I think, an erroneous one, but it existed and the individual artists harmonized their work within it. Today when four architects put up four buildings, it is going to look dreadful. There is no rapport between them.

We have talked about a number of elements that help to make a good city, such as the provision of green space and the control of the transportation problem. You also mentioned parks. Is there a general rule that the more space a city sets aside for parks the better city it will be?

Temko: The question is, what makes a good city? Today there is much talk, especially by people who have not been to Europe, that we do not need the great green spaces, that these destroy some of the urban qualities, particularly intimacy. What such people want is the nineteenth-century American city "cleaned up" a little. What they do not understand are the principles of European urbanism. When people over-value Union Square in San Francisco, for example, it is because they have not really studied the great European squares and analyzed their superiority. In those squares traffic may be banished altogether. Think of St. Peter's Square in Rome—Union Square doesn't seem much when compared to it. And even though the Place de la Concorde is cut up with traffic, it is very superior to Union Square. Then there is the Louvre, with the gardens of the Tuileries, which, in modern terms, can be seen as virtually a superblock of fifty acres in the heart of Paris, and with a river next to it. The great parks of central London probably total several hundred acres. You could throw the financial district of San Francisco into them and lose it. Golden Gateway, our huge redevelopment project on the edge of the financial district here, is only forty-odd acres.

Is it true that one of the things that make European city streets interesting and "human" is the existence of outdoor cafés as well as the parks and squares?
Temko: Yes, and these matters go deep. In this country we are all "at home" in the suburbs. The American counterpart of the Parisian who lives on the Left Bank now often lives in the suburbs, in a very fine house. We are very comfortable in the suburbs, and therefore why should we go into San Francisco or Chicago or New York? In Paris, you are likely to have something nicer outside than in your flat, especially if you don't have much money. Take the Luxembourg Gardens, a tremendous thing to have so close to the heart of a great city. And actually to see them is to know what a great city can be. In this country I don't think we have nearly enough parks. In this I would not discount Le Corbusier's skyscraper-park concept until it has been tried.

It is difficult, I suppose, for people to demand something better than what they have had if they have never been exposed to that "better," so someone has to take the lead in initiating these urban reforms.
Temko: This demands, among other things, an educational approach. An architect in Berkeley, Lois Langhorst, is trying to develop a course in the Berkeley school system, thus far for girls only, as a substitute for conventional home economics, in which they will learn something about good design rather than just how to bake a cake or sew a dress. Sir Herbert Read insists that it is all a matter of public education.

One of the best educational influences, of course, is the existence of a good piece of architecture, or a complex of buildings.
Temko: Yes. All our buildings educate us, for good or ill. The wallpaper in my parents' home, when I was a child, is with me still. The doorknob we turn, the kind of lamp we read by—these are important.

When modern architects plan a building, to what extent do they plan it with some such purpose, as Mumford, for example, says it should be planned; that is, that the building should serve personal needs, that it should be a good place in which to live or work?
Temko: One of the first things we should keep in mind about architecture is that the architect, unless he is very lucky, is not a free agent. He has a budget. He has a client. If your client is a Louis XIV and your project is Versailles, you can do what you wish as long as it pleases the prince, and the prince often wishes to do the best. Aside from a handful of older masters—Le Corbusier, Mies van der Rohe, Walter Gropius, and of course Frank Lloyd Wright—modern architects have not been "men of the Renaissance." We don't have many like them today, and those that we do have don't build enough. Furthermore, ninety per cent of the construction in this country, particularly residential construction, is done without architects.

You mentioned budget as a limiting factor. Cannot this also be stimulating —forcing the artist to rely on his imaginative faculties?

Temko: Yes. Pier Luigi Nervi, the great Italian engineer, has insisted on this. He says that in an age of general vulgarity poverty is a great force for good aesthetic design. Nervi and a whole school of modern architects, most notably Mies and his followers, believe that the best aesthetic solution is the "correct" structural solution. In this country I would say that among the new generation the foremost exponent of that view is Myron Goldsmith, an architect-engineer in the Chicago office of Skidmore, Owings & Merrill. Such "scientific" architects search for the most logical, not necessarily the cheapest, structural solution as the basis of good design. That is, they design intuitively from rational assumptions, and the results are often poetic—the poetry is in the logic. Thus they take an objective rather than subjective approach to structure. Saarinen's highly subjective TWA terminal at Idlewild (now JFK) is structurally incorrect: it is a forced use of the material; it employs industrial technology in a rather non-industrial, personal, sculptural way. Wright did this, too, although on occasion he could be a master of structural logic. But subjectivity is still a powerful force, as Le Corbusier's later work shows.

Employment of an engineer is fine, I should imagine, provided he has the qualities of an imaginative artist, and if he does have those qualities then the distinction between himself and a master architect must be a very fine one indeed.

Temko: Nervi, of course, is an artist as well as an engineer. He is one of our wisest men, a sage. He sees the architect of the future as a true master builder, unprecedented in history and comparable to the conductor of a symphony orchestra. The architect must be the coördinator of all the different elements that go into the large modern buildings of today, and yet he must also interpret them aesthetically, as Toscanini did with musical compositions.

Hasn't Nervi said that he thinks architects are not getting enough education in the structural aspects of buildings?

Temko: Yes. And he is right. In many cases the architect develops a concept for a building and then goes to the engineers and says, "Make it stand up" or "Help me to define it." Many of the big architectural firms now have their own engineering staff and this has improved design techniques considerably.

You have written an article on the experience of our architects in designing various American embassies abroad. It seems that we do have some creative architects who can produce good things if we will only get out of their way and let them work.

Temko: Again, this is related to politics. It involves freeing the architect, and especially the selection of architects, from political pressures and political considerations. The approach to the building of embassies could be a model for all government building—federal, state, and city. The Foreign Building Office in Washington saw that the problem of the embassy buildings went far beyond architectural quality; it involved the stature of our country abroad. Foreign intellectuals for years have been saying to us, "You Americans claim the United

States is the new center of cultural power and artistic influence, but look at these dreadful buildings you are putting up in our cities." So the State Department appointed a selection panel composed of very distinguished architects whose responsibility it was to select the architects who would do the consulates and embassies around the world. I think they have chosen very wisely. There are very few outstanding architectural firms that have not had a crack at an embassy.

What were some of the characteristics common to the architects on this panel? I don't mean stylistic characteristics, but approaches or philosophies, if we can use that term in this connection. Perhaps "principles" is the word I am looking for.

Temko: The panel included men like William Wurster, who is dean of architecture at the University of California, and Pietro Belluschi, dean of architecture at M.I.T. Saarinen was on it for a time. The group acted as a client on behalf of the State Department, so there were serious architects hiring other architects for the government. The panel gave the assignments and reviewed the plans. Their only common principle, as I recall, was that they wanted to show the freshness, vigor, and variety of the American approach to the problem of building. They also wanted to be sure that the building would have *local veracity,* that the one for Oslo, for instance, would be right for Oslo and not for Bangkok. Industrial technology does not belong to any country; it is international. But it can be used in many ways, and in this instance it should show the American character. Thus American character might include a willingness to find harmony with another society. I think that is praiseworthy.

It seems to me that competent, but unknown, architects today are caught in a kind of vicious circle. Until they make a great name for themselves, they are denied the kind of artistic freedom they must have to build great buildings. But they cannot make a great name for themselves until they have that freedom.

Temko: For thirty years, Mies designed largely on paper. Most of his great projects of the nineteen-twenties were never built. In fact, all of the early masters built comparatively little. We forget today how they had to fight for recognition. In the League of Nations competition in 1927, Le Corbusier prepared one of his greatest designs but it was rejected on a technicality: he had failed to use India ink in his drawings. A preposterous Beaux-Arts palace was put up instead. If the League had had the courage and decency to put up Le Corbusier's buildings, and if it had had the politics to match it, maybe we would not be in such a mess today.

Are there new young masters coming along?

Temko: Masters appear in every age. What we need is a discipline in which we will get some order and unity in our cities and countryside. I believe that in many respects our architectural schools have been greatly improved, but many young architects lack the background in the humanities that the older men had. In most instances, the modern movement has proved itself unequal to its biggest spiritual tasks. The United Nations buildings are a case in point. Le Corbusier's original concepts were weakened and devitalized by the people who did the buildings, and in fact the original concept was not one of his strongest. For one thing, the great slab of the Secretariat is wrongly oriented. It faces west and on a sunny afternoon becomes an oven. Mumford has published a great critique of the U.N. complex. He points out that the Secretariat is indistinguishable from most of the skyscrapers put up by speculative realtors in Manhattan. Why should this warren of bureaucratic offices be the image of the U.N.? Is the U.N. primarily a bureaucracy? Was the U.N. sited in the wrong place? Why was it put on a tiny plot of ground in Manhattan? Is this the calmest place for diplomatic discussions and deliberations? Le Corbusier actually had fought for a much larger site. San Francisco had offered the Presidio, with its seven hundred acres, but our State Department wanted the U.N. to be located at the heart of the most powerful American city. The site was out of the control of the architects. This is one reason why Le Corbusier withdrew—a legitimate reason. But he behaved quite foolishly at other times during the U.N. controversy.

What went wrong, besides the selection of the original site?

Temko: What would have been appropriate as a building for a world organization? The UNESCO building in Paris is also a failure, I believe, even though Nervi worked on it. I would say that the architects' responsibility in both cases—the U.N. and the UNESCO buildings—was to come up with truly great buildings. Not every architect can do that, but at certain times in history architects have consistently created buildings reflecting the greatness of their purpose. Take the Middle Ages, for instance: every one of the great Gothic cathedrals is good. Some are better than others, but all of them are good. Why? Here, the architects were working within an authentic discipline—in Gothic, not the pseudo-Gothic we see in the University of Chicago buildings or Yale University, but real Gothic. And this developed mightily as they learned new techniques. They were also expressing a spiritual, cosmological vision. As the amount of glass increased in these churches and as new structural systems were devised— for example, buttresses to make the glass walls possible—there was a concomitant theological force expressed. A cathedral was supposed to be a symbolic representation of the cosmos.

Today, the U.N. building should have been symbolic of the universal hopes of man for world peace, but our architects were unequal to this vision and aspiration. The medieval bishops of the twelfth and thirteenth centuries were equal to their vision, and the architects who worked with them were equal to it, too. Today, our politicians and diplomats don't seem to be equal to theirs.

I suppose it is true that the architecture of an age necessarily reflects the age. If our architecture is disorganized and inchoate, perhaps it is because our age is that way too. On the other hand, medieval architecture, to take your example, reflected an order and a discipline and the spiritual confidence that were in the air at the time.

Temko: I believe that as far as our environment is concerned we have anarchy. Henry Adams characterized the two periods as "medieval unity" and "modern multiplicity." Yet the modern age has certain unities, one of them being industrialism.

If we could develop a personalism as strong as our industrialism some of our urban and architectural problems might be solved.

Temko: The primacy of the person, yes. If people can be educated and have decent places in which to live, and if we can prevent war, the greatest of all the destroyers of our cities, and if we can marshal all our resources in an orderly, intelligent way, think of the potential benefits to people as individuals.

Architecture of course is only part of the problem of the cities. Conceivably we could have a great city of mediocre buildings. It might be a happy place in which to live. And you might have a beautiful city that is not a happy city. Florence has not always been a happy city.

Yet I suspect it would be difficult for anyone to be much exhilarated by mean buildings.

Temko: The architectural quality of individual buildings is perhaps less important than the over-all quality of the urban ensemble. For example, if you look at the Parisian boulevards, what you have is not building façades but street façades. You have those neutral gray walls stretching in baroque perspectives of orderly street fronts. At the end of these neutral perspectives you see a monument that may be good or bad architecturally. It might be the Opéra, which is rather a masterpiece of ostentation. Or you might see the Odéon, or the Arc de Triomphe. So the city suddenly comes into its own by the self-effacement of most of its buildings. The height of the buildings is still rigidly controlled in Paris. And up to now they have shared the same material—stone; it is a masonry city. In Paris, too, many functions will be found in one neighborhood—residential and commercial functions—which is good. The Palais-Royal, which was once a palace, is made up of a number of marvelous shops, restaurants, and a theatre on its lower level, which in places open in arcades; then, above, there are apartments. Colette lived there, Jean Cocteau lives there. It is a wonderful place to live. The Palais-Royal is an architectural entity. There is no auto traffic in its great court, which is like a park in a city. It is a super-block, but a well-designed one, and that was three hundred years ago.

I don't like to labor the traffic problem, but it seems to me that what to do with our cars remains one of the great unsolved problems in the general problem of developing beautiful and vital cities.

Temko: The car is an economic waster, a space eater, and a psyche earner. More than half the prime space in what has been downtown Los Angeles is taken up now by freeways, parking space, and garages. In San Francisco, twenty-five per cent of downtown is used for parking, and if you add the acreage covered by streets and the freeways on the periphery, perhaps half the downtown area is given over to the automobile. In other cities, certain streets are closed to traffic and it is very pleasant to be able to step off a curb and not have to dodge cars. How nice it is in London where you can walk from Piccadilly down to the great system of parks that stretch from Westminster Abbey to Buckingham Palace and beyond. There you see British businessmen stretched out on the grass taking a rather tense nap. But they use their parks. This is a mark of a great civilization.

I don't agree with Jane Jacobs' idea that we need traffic-filled streets. She loves the streets of Greenwich Village. She probably has not seen the streets in Arles or Aix-en-Provence, which are too narrow for cars and so there is no real auto traffic. Why do people love to go to Venice today? Because Venice has no cars. Why was Bermuda such a wonderful, restful resort before the cars came there? If we got rid of all cars, if someone put them all in a huge crate and dumped them into the ocean, the relief would be magnificent. Of course, we would be left with our sprawling civilization and the problems of communication. How would we do it? Well, I think we would have to rebuild our cities.

What hopes do you have that the city in America, which has so great an effect on human values, hopes, and potentialities, will rebuild itself along these personal axes, rather than along the impersonal, technological, and disorganized axes of the past? Granting that such rebuilding may take several generations, are you hopeful that we will head right?

Temko: First of all, let me say that I see no incompatibility whatever between humanism and the rational use of technology. What we find mechanical and disorganized in cities today is due to the misuse of technology. Quite simply, man has failed to use machines with sufficient boldness, sensitivity, kindness, and conviction. Yet as Mies van der Rohe said, "Wherever technology reaches its real fulfillment, it transcends itself into architecture." Everything hinges, of course, on what we mean by *real* fulfillment. This is further complicated by the limitless structural possibilities now open to mankind. "Man's structural imagination has been liberated completely," Pier Luigi Nervi has said. It is now possible to construct buildings and cities that bear resemblance to no others in history, and therefore require a new theory of planning and design.

The need for a radical urban aesthetic, uniting the art of architecture and planning with the science of building, is stragically urgent. Unfortunately, however, as the cities race chaotically towards the twenty-first century, much urban theory—to say nothing of urban practice—adheres timidly to the pre-industrial aesthetics of the nineteenth and early twentieth centuries. I have in mind the new urban sentimentality of Jane Jacobs and others, who are really arguing for a spruced-up status quo. But it is the status quo that has landed us in our present mess, and under the steady pressure of population increase the mess is rapidly growing worse. (I should qualify that: in certain fundamental respects such as public health, for example, our cities are the finest in history, but our potentialities are also the highest in history and we have not come close to attaining them.) In fact, our cities—virtually all large cities, including those subject to the authoritarian regulation of the Soviet Union—are out of control, proliferating wildly. The first step toward bringing them under control must be an analysis of those forces which are now blindly and negatively determining their fate. The next step will be to find rational means of checking those forces and, wherever possible, turning them in a more positive direction.

In this country, particularly, we must devise new controls for land use, which is now anarchic. This means the end of free enterprise in real-estate speculation, but considering the already formidable intrusion of the federal government in the land development business (through guaranteed mortgages, for example, and urban renewal legislation), we no longer have a laissez-faire economy anyway, but a mixed economy.

We must have national and regional, as well as local, planning, and it must be logically synthesized with the development of new sources of energy and new systems of transportation. Water, both as a natural resource and as a source of energy, is fundamental to the life of every individual, but nowhere in the United States is water policy truly consistent with orderly urban development. TVA was a good start, but we have retrogressed in this respect since New Deal days, and in California today we have an extravagant water-development program that I believe will cause more problems than it will solve. I would say that we must plan the environment humanely from the wilderness area in the High Sierras to the street in Los Angeles. If we do, the dividends in human happiness and creativity will be incalculable.

6

TOWARDS A NEW URBAN AMERICA

In the long sweep of history man has suffered from superstitions that drove him to burn heretics, punish dissenters, try witches, and abuse those who held views contrary to the conventional wisdom. Man has also yielded to the notion that some social issues are beyond resolution and some human conditions beyond improvement.

Ignorance and fear drive men to be intolerant of other men; indifference and rigidity prevent him from improving his environment.

The indifference and rigidity take many forms. We have seen some of them in the previous chapters: suburban Americans indifferent to the ghettos; educational leaders antagonistic to contemporary concepts; public officials oblivious to change; public agencies perverting their objectives; private institutions indulging in petty racism. "No one," Jacques Barzun once suggested, "can be sure of the future, but the past is not dumb." And the past has tried desperately to warn us of the consequences of this indifference and rigidity.

For too long the nation has refused to listen. We have plodded heedlessly —spoiling the environment, ignoring legitimate grievances, willing to pay a high price for the illusion of progress but only a cut-rate price for its reality.

The result is an urban condition that is often cruel and distorted. In too many urban places junk piles up, garbage swells, communities deteriorate, schools are inadequate, crime is rampant, and health facilities are insufficient. In too many others, skylines are marred, land is consumed ruthlessly, and industrial and municipal wastes ruin rivers and clog the air.

Such a blatant violation of the human condition defies imagination. It rests heavy on the hearts of all Americans who are proud of the greatness of our society and the strength of our system. It is incongruous and unacceptable for any society that relishes its mastery over nature to permit its urban environment to exist in a constant state of war. When it comes to imponderable programs dealing with apogees, retrogrades, rendezvous, and re-entries, the nation seems perfectly capable of setting objectives and establishing systems to meet those objectives; but when it comes to the urban environment, we seem boggled by red tape, silly superstitions, and sullen indifference.

The time has obviously come to end that. The time has come to apply the nation's social sensitivity and technical wizardry to the task of elevating urban life to a new level of excellence. "With more than half the nation's metropolitan people still living in the central cities," Dr. Abrams told a Senate committee, "and with some 320 million people destined to live in urban areas a generation hence, there is no federal urban development plan, no philosophy of urban progress, no real program for stemming urban decay—or preventing it on the city's outskirts—only a fortuitous concourse of patchwork programs accumulated over a period of more than three decades and lacking any link to long range developments, long range objectives or long range commitments."[1]

Even if the nation should make the kind of commitment required to institute significant improvements, the deeper problems that plague urban America will not disappear overnight. Institutions and attitudes are not susceptible to the same diagnosis that can cure cancer or the same skills that can place a man on the moon. Systems analysis, modular housing, mass transit, guaranteed mortgages, computerized police departments, innovative solid waste disposal systems, and other aspects of America's industrial power might well lessen the physical anguish of urban life, but such technical magic cannot move institutions or alter attitudes. Industrial ingenuity cannot force corporations to employ people regardless of the color of their skin; physical power cannot make unions desegregate; scientific discoveries cannot induce white suburbanites to welcome black neighbors, militants to stop reckless acts, or planning departments to consider human needs.

This kind of change requires not only man's best efforts to improve the physical environment, but equally diligent efforts to improve personal relations. On the part of individuals it requires a radical renewal of conscience. On the part of communities it requires a certain preliminary anguish. But under all circumstances it requires a rational relationship between blacks and whites.

In 1968, the National Advisory Commission on Civil Disorders suggested that the nation could approach its racial dilemma in three ways. First, it could continue its present policies; second, it could abandon the concept of integration and substitute instead a concept of "ghetto enrichment"; third, it could integrate and enrich at the same time. The Commission concluded that the first two policies were unacceptable, each leading in one fashion or another to a divided society with the black community, because of white power, inevitably relegated "to a permanent inferior economic status." The Commission concluded that the third alternative—a policy that included helping those who needed help and fully integrating American society—was the only sensible alternative.

[1] Charles Abrams, Testimony, "Federal Role in Urban Affairs," Hearings, *Subcommittee on Executive Reorganization, Government Operations Committee.* Government Printing Office, Washington, D.C., April 20, 1967.

That recommendation still holds considerable validity, but only if enrichment and integration are considered in their broadest context. To develop an urban environment that makes sense, both blacks and whites must view their individual environments in the total setting. They must discard fragmented views and accept what Senator Edmund Muskie has called the "fragile balance of the urban environment."

That balance requires institutions responsive to citizen requests; government programs administered by sensitive officials; businessmen interested in social improvement as well as corporate profit; public officials disdainful of demagogues; and average citizens—black or white, rich or poor, silent or loud—prepared to work together for the cause of social justice.

All this sounds exceptionally noble. Man's history has proven that nobility is not his most significant trait and that social conditions are improved more by power than by intentions. But history also shows that when man acts less than nobly, society eventually erupts. The tumult spares no one. Under these circumstances contemporary America has no alternative but to behave nobly—to provide the money, the resources, the programs, the spirit to support that nobility or there will be, as Eldridge Cleaver passingly observed, another Boston Tea Party.

Not by any means is the task of renewing the urban environment beyond the nation's moral capacity or technical potential. The concluding selections show clearly and forcefully that improvement is possible. By dealing concisely with the question of "what to do" and revealing scores of positive alternatives, the authors proclaim, even to dismal pessimists, that America can look to the future with hope.

Cataloguing urban ills is a "fancy" pastime. It occupies the opening paragraph of every book on the subject and has occupied a significant portion of this book. The real art is in finding solutions. Ideas that make sense and programs that work are considerably more difficult to come by. This chapter says succinctly: "Enough of the ills, enough of the cynicisms and the shouting. We know something is wrong. Now let's face up to it and see what can be done. Then, let's do it."

The solutions presented by various experts from various ranges of the political and economic spectrum are positive, concrete, and realistic. Some are more far reaching than others. None would destroy the American way of life (even by its most conservative definition). Some solutions require great national and personal sacrifice. But when hasn't the nation been willing to make sacrifices for what it thought was right? Other solutions require vast expenditures. But squalor is not eliminated without a price, and it has become increasingly obvious that the continued burden of mediocrity is going to be considerably more expensive than paying to stop it.

The first article, by I. F. Stone, demonstrates the latent danger of the trend as America seems to be heading towards racial conservatism during the decade of the seventies. "Without economic justice and racial reconciliation, our country has no future," Stone warns. "Nothing could be worse for America than a leadership which panders to bigotry, smugness, as the 'forgotten American' line does."

The second piece is Floyd McKissick's provocative testimony before the Senate subcommittee on Executive Reorganization. In his impassioned closing appeal, McKissick pleads, "For God's sake, end this terrible war in Vietnam . . . understand that there is no longer time for utopian dreams . . . throw out the rule-book on education . . . create jobs . . . build homes that men and women can live in . . . remember that black people are the victims of public media . . . and stop the backlashes, the hysteria. . . ."

Federal Communications Commissioner Nicholas Johnson is not an urban expert, but possesses an abrasive instinct for speaking out, never hesitating to criticize elements that inhibit dissent or discourage excellence. In his article, he makes constructive recommendations for using communications to improve urban life.

Since money is essential to constructive change, new fiscal relationships between local and federal entities are essential. Walter Heller's piece discusses "shared revenue," a concept that continues to receive increasing support.

Herbert Gans offers a practical political suggestion to lessen tensions by enhancing minority rights. Too often the groups who need help are out-voted by the groups who have the power but not the inclination to help. This frustrates the minority and drives them to seek other means of relieving their pressures. Gans suggests that we adjust to the pluralism of American life by what he calls "pluralistic rule." "A pluralistic form of democracy would not do away with majority rule," Gans writes, "but would require systems of proposing and disposing which take the needs of minorities into consideration, so that when majority rule has serious negative consequences, out-voted minorities would be able to achieve their most important demands, and not be forced to accept tokenism, or resort to despair or disruption." The Gans' proposal would have radical implications for the political process.

John Garvey's article, "What Can Europe Teach Us About Urban Growth," details some of the European schemes the author feels are worth importing.

Daniel P. Moynihan, sitting at the highest level of executive power, advises the President on urban affairs. In his speech, "Toward a National Urban Policy," he offers a comprehensive and absorbing approach to improving the urban condition.

The concluding selection, extracted from Dr. Eisenhower's Violence Commission Report, is a succinct analysis of what the future requires if we are to save the city, the suburbs and the nation from internal upheaval.

NO TIME TO PANDER TO RACIAL BIGOTRY

I. F. Stone

Before and after slavery, the Southern oligarchy stayed in power a long time by playing poor white against black. We hope that Nixon, Agnew and Attorney General Mitchell are not toying with the idea of adopting this Southern strategy by playing the white middle class against the blacks and the poor. It was racialism which wrecked the promise of Populism in the South. The GOP's strategists may see a similar hope of using racial prejudices to prevent the rebirth of that coalition which FDR organized as a successful vehicle of social reform. The first hint of this strategy appeared in Nixon's acceptance speech, when he appealed to "the great majority of Americans, the forgotten Americans, the non-shouters, the non-demonstrators." Like so many of Nixon's phrases, this was an echo of other and better voices. FDR had stirred the nation with "the forgotten man." But his was an appeal to compassion for the underprivileged. Nixon's was an appeal to the prejudices of those who had *made it* to the middle class and white collar workers now fearful of those pushing up from below.

ENCOURAGING THE KNOW NOTHINGS

We wonder whether this line is being orchestrated now by the Administration's public relations men. The press is beginning to write about this "forgotten American" in a way that tends not just to report but to legitimize racial ill-feeling, to encourage people to say things aloud they would have been ashamed to say a few years ago. An example was provided by *Newsweek's* special issue Oct. 6, "The Troubled American: A Special Report on the White Majority." There was something more than objective reporting in the slick advertising copy prose of its introduction. "America has been almost obsessed," *Newsweek* began, "with its alienated minorities—the incendiary black militant, and the welfare mothers . . . Suddenly the focus is on the citizen who outnumbers, outvotes and could, if he chose to, *outgun* the fringe rebel." The italics are ours. "How fed up," *Newsweek* continues, "is the little guy, the average white citizen . . .? Is the country sliding inexorably toward an apocalyptic spasm—perhaps racial or class warfare . . .? A community worker in a Slavic neighborhood in Milwaukee is quoted as saying, "Everybody wants a gun. They think they've heard from black power, wait till they hear from white power—the little slob, GI Joe, the

I. F. Stone, "No Time to Pander to Racial Bigotry," I. F. STONE'S WEEKLY, *October 20, 1969. Copyright 1969 by* I. F. STONE'S WEEKLY. *Reprinted by permission of the publisher.*

man who breaks his ass and makes this country go . . ." One is provoked to ask, "Go where? "

Newsweek's reporters even quote one man who said, "We should have a Hitler here to get rid of the troublemakers the way they did with the Jews in Germany"—not a remark calculated to dissuade blacks from buying guns. Carl T. Rowan spoke for the black community, and we hope for much of the white, when in his column about *Newsweek (Washington Star, Oct. 8)* he protested "innuendoes . . . that induce and feed paranoia in the average white man." To some of the misunderstandings dredged up by *Newsweek* about favoritism to blacks, Mr. Rowan replied that the ratio of blacks living below the poverty line is still more than three times that for whites.

It would be tragic if that one lunatic remark about Hitler led blacks to think this was typical of the average white man. Unfortunately *Newsweek's* presentation encouraged misunderstanding. Read carefully and thoroughly the *Newsweek* survey leaves one with quite a different impression from its opening pages. Under different instructions the same rewrite man, summing up what the reporters and the Gallup poll found, might have written quite differently. The further one reads, the more it begins to appear that the American middle class white majority is nowhere near as bad as the sensational opening portrait would lead one to believe.

STILL SYMPATHETIC TO THE BLACKS

Those phrases which sounded like a KKK speaker in a clean sheet were on page 29. But by page 45, *Newsweek's* account of its special Gallup poll leads it to admit, "For all his resentment at black activism, the Middle American still has a basic sympathy for the Negro's aspirations . . . nearly 7 out of 10 agreed that at least some of the demands presented by Negro leaders are justified." That is quite a majority. Even on law and order the poll's results differ from the stereotypes. "Only 10 percent of the sampling volunteered crime in their own listing of the nation's problems." Two-thirds didn't think police had enough power but "a significant minority worried about a police state." One housewife commented ironically, "Hitler had law and order." One furniture store manager wanted college rioters put in concentration camps but 59 percent thought well of young people and 54 percent agreed "that young people were not unduly cirtical of their country and that criticism was actually needed." Obviously the bigot and the bully are still a small, if noisy, minority. Indeed by page 48, you begin to find that the American middle class remains remarkably idealistic and liberal:

> . . . only 12 percent thought the country would be better off with George Wallace . . . there was little enthusiasm for Mr. Nixon . . . The chief complaint is not so much the level of taxation but rather that the government has its priorities wrong . . . only one in three favored a tax cut . . . the sampling favored added spending for such programs as job training, pollution control, medicare, slum housing, and crime control . . . a good many thought money was being wasted in foreign aid and defense spending—and even in the afterglow of the moon landing, fully 56 percent thought the government should spend less on space [and they were overwhelmingly fed up with the war].

Neither violence, racism nor alienation are peculiar to the United States; they are everywhere on the planetary landscape. Biafra shows what blacks can do to blacks and Ulster what whites can do to whites. The struggle in Ulster for civil rights and equal opportunity is far more bloody than ours, though the bigoted majority and the underprivileged minority look exactly alike and speak in the same brogue. The *Newsweek* survey, for all its GOP style preliminary preconceptions, shows that the white American middle class is still ready for humane and progressive leadership. History should have taught us by now that in every people there is a potential for evil as for good. Without economic justice and racial reconciliation, our country has no future. Nothing could be worse for America than a leadership which panders to bigotry and smugness, as the "forgotten American" lines does.

PRESENTATION BY FLOYD B. McKISSICK,
Former National Director, Congress of Racial Equality

INTRODUCTION

The central cities of this country are disaster areas—the debris is mounting, the walking wounded everywhere. For weeks you have been listening to the catalogue of this crisis, much as the legislators of the 18th century in the plague cities, studied the lists of the dead. It is true: . . . death is everywhere: the death of the body, the death of hope.

I am no longer certain that we can turn the tide . . . God knows we must try.

There is no time . . . there is no time to talk of the half-measures, no time to prosecute wars, no time to lash back at the angry poor, no time to moralize about an integrated utopia . . . there is no time. The seminars must end, the conferences conclude, our wisdom must now be shaped into specific weapons of change. It is in this spirit—a spirit of crisis and a spirit of fragile hope I come before you today.

I will talk about many things—of entire institutions of our society that are crumbling in the central city. I will talk about the black American—the mass of black Americans; paralyzed in poverty; unmotivated, suspicious of the white man's promise, blooded on the streets of Los Angeles and on the streets of Saigon. I will talk of racism through the entire American fabric—a racism that *cannot be changed by law alone.*

And I will talk about black power . . . black power, its consequence and its meaning.

Presentation by Floyd B. McKissick, Former National Director, Congress of Racial Equality. Hearings Before the U.S. Senate, Subcommittee on Executive Reorganization, Committee on Government Operations, 1966.

The tragedy of the recent spasm of reaction and racism in this country is best dramatized in this room . . . for it is in this room for many weeks that you gentlemen have seen in exquisite detail, the frustration, the hopelessness and the powerlessness of the American urban Negro. There is no better argument for black power—for the mobilization of the black community as a political, social and economic bloc than the words you have heard in this room. Moreover—and this is what we have always meant by Black Power—it is a rational, militant call from a whole segment of this nation's population to do what *you* have not been able to do—destroy racism in this country, create full employment in the American ghetto, revise the educational system to cope with the 20th century, and make the American ghetto a place in which it is possible to live with hope.

And once and for all—I am a man of peace, appalled by a society of violence in which I live.

I am tired of violence—not only that which has been inflicted on myself, and my children—but the deeper violence inflicted on the black child in a hopelessly antique system of education: the violence done to the Negro man and the Negro woman, torn apart by the racist employer and defeated by the humiliation of public welfare. *Do not ever forget* . . . 90 per cent of the American black community—that immobile 90 percent—which is the main subject of my discussion today—are both the children and the victims of violence.

As I proceed, gentlemen, I would ask that you keep two basic themes in mind. One: the scope of the problem facing the central city is so large and at the same time the despair and suspicion in the black community so deep that *any* solutions we discuss must be immediate and in large part be financed by the federal budget. Even more important in any such undertaking we must involve and dignify the black man as a fully enfranchised citizen—capable of administering his own recovery. Secondly, I would ask that we regard this problem in crisis terms, and for the moment set aside our understandable dreams of integration—set them aside before the "fire next time" is now. As we in CORE have studied the problems facing the mass of American black people, we found over and over again that the great moral struggle for integration has, in fact, barely touched the lives of the people. Every instinct and experience tells us that the larger battle, for real change has hardly begun. Every analysis we can find, the work of virtually every social scientist who has addressed himself to this question—leads us to the same basic conclusion—the black ghettos will not go away—they are the hard fact of our life. Any solution you may consider, which addresses itself to the cause of despair and poverty must, in fact, accept the existence of a growing ghetto and proceed immediately to the task of restoring its physical, educational and economic integrity.

Again—let me emphasize, I am not arguing *against* the past; CORE's credentials in the civil rights movement are written in blood on Mississippi and Louisiana ground—I *am* arguing *for* the future, a future in which a rich nation extends its resources and its energy and its commitment into the central cities so that those who live there may mold their hopes with their own hands, organize and act as a power for economic, political and moral force and help to rebuild this democracy as a nation of brothers.

EDUCATION

In 1954 the Supreme Court ruled that separate or segregated education is, by definition, inferior. We thought that this represented the removal of the major roadblock to full citizenship and real participation in the mainstream of American life for Black people. Now, we thought, the way was clear for every law-abiding citizen to develop to the full potential of his ability.

But the law of the land was not enforced. Twelve and a half years later only 13% of Negro children in the South attended integrated schools. Today over 50% of the children in N.Y.C. are Negro or Puerto Rican. 90% attend segregated schools. The white population in Philadelphia declined from 51% in 1961 to 43% in 1965. White enrollment in Detroit has dropped 9.2% in the last five years.

Most important, however, is the fact that the children left behind are not being taught. A recent survey of the reading levels in the segregated schools of New York shows that almost 87% of the children are reading below grade. This is compared to 50% below grade in 1954, the year of that great court decision. At this rate, by 1970 all of the children in ghetto schools in that city will be "under-achievers."

From the time a black child enters the public schools, he is fighting an uphill battle not to be pushed out of the educational system. Not the best, but the least experienced teachers are still being assigned to ghetto schools.[1] Teachers rarely teach; they keep order and impose discipline and too often hold their ghetto pupils in low esteem. "The crucial ingredient in improving education of the disadvantaged is changing the attitude of the teachers."[2] Yet, human relations courses are still nonexistent in many urban centers. Staffed by teachers and administrators from the middle class, "the American high school tends to be a white, middle-class institution loaded against the Negro, working-class pupil."[3]

The Harlems of this country are public school disaster areas. The continuing failure to educate black and poor children when education is a necessary ingredient for success in this society amounts to genocide. The fact that the "mind-killing" may be unintentional is irrelevant to the victim and of little comfort to the bereaved family.

---

[1] (New York Times, Nov, 16, 1966.) "More than 80 percent of the 1,700 college graduates trained for teaching this summer in a 7-week emergency program have been assigned to schools with heavy concentrations of disadvantaged pupils." Said one principal: "We have committed a horrible and horrendous crime in assigning these youngsters to classes that require an expert of experts."

[2] (New York Times, Dec. 1, 1966.) From a report to the President by the National Advisory Council on Education of the Disadvantaged made Nov, 30, 1966, an evaluation of the $250,000,000 spent on specific summer education projects for disadvantaged children earlier this year, went on to say: "Yet in most communities studied, the special projects for the poor 'were alarmingly deficient in facing up to this need'."

[3] (New York Times, Nov. 24, 1966.) Report submitted by Dr. Robert Vinter, associate dean of University of Michigan School of Social Workers and Dr. Rosemary Sarri, associate professor of social work, financed by the President's Committee on Juvenile Delinquency and the Department of Health, Education, and Welfare.

Integration for all children is not feasible in many large cities today. Yet parents in the black communities of our cities are no longer willing to stand by and watch their children's minds wither and die. Typical are the Negro parents at New York's widely publicized I.S.201. They demanded of the Board of Education:

1. Black authority figures (e.g., a black principal) with whom their children might be able to identify and to whose position they might aspire.

2. They insisted upon sympathetic teachers who represented black children, were supportive and encouraging and who expected black children to learn.

3. They called for a curriculum that reflected the Negro's contribution to world and American history and therefore could rebuild a self damaged by living in a world that ignored them.

4. They pledged themselves to inccreased participation in their children's lives. By being vigilant and unafraid they knew that they would compel response and respect from the school administration, the teaching staff and their own children.

In effect, they were saying to educators that if a child with native intelligence is not achieving, the fault does not lie with the child. One must assume the technique is wrong, the perception of the child is wrong. As with a doctor and a sick patient, it is more prudent to try changing the medicine and mode of treatment than to curse the patient for not getting well.[4]

Integrated quality education is still a desirable goal and there must be Federal action to insure integration wherever feasible . . . in suburban school districts, smaller cities and towns, Southern school systems, and border districts in major cities. Of all solutions proposed for the ultimate answer to the big city's educational dilemma, CORE would favor the building of centrally located, well-equipped educational complexes offering superior education to all children and the utilization of intelligent curriculums and staffs at all levels.

None of these solutions can really be considered final unless we realize this. Racism is the crux of this nation's problem. Whites must be re-educated if integration is ever to have meaning. It is time for conferences on the White Problem in America. The experts who have been called together so often to discuss the Negro must now turn their attention to white racism and violence in this society. CORE calls for a National Board of Education made up of experts, activists, parents, and administrators to develop new ideas and put them to work.

Methods of teaching black children must be improved and adopted to their needs. There must be new forms of teacher recruitment and training; the teaching profession must be made attractive to our best thinkers and leaders. There should be experimentation with ungraded classrooms in ghetto schools, team-teaching, opening schools all day, all night and all year around. Non-professionals must be used as community aides to motivate parents and children. A pupil-teacher ratio of no more than 15 to 1 is required to overcome the effects of decades of inferior education. We should consider extending education requirements downwards and upwards, guaranteeing all students at least two years

[4] Floyd B. McKissick, "Is Integration Necessary?" New Republic, Dec. 3, 1966, pp. 33-36.

of college education. We would also recommend community schools with school-parent committees which have a voice and a function.[5]

But just as important, there must be new ways to halt and reverse the spread of racism in this country. The National Board of Education must consider this problem as well. We must know why white children are more racist when they finish school then when they enter. We must know why their parents panic at the words "black power," We must know why the sickness of racism erupted in such ugly ways in Cicero, Chicago, and Philadelphia and we must know why it took its toll in the November elections. And we must devise programs to cure those ills.

We accuse school boards across the nation of being instruments of death. But the Federal Government also bears a heavy responsibility. Even experimental educational programs have too often been a rehash of tried methods that have already failed. We have not forgotten the fact that Congress passed a Civil Rights Act in education one year and cut its budget and powers the next. A similar default was congressional inaction on the Teachers Corps. We are disgusted by the Federal Government that permitted CDGM, a creative Head Start program run by the poor, to die because political forces opposed it. We are appalled at a government agency that one day cuts off funds for Chicago public schools and restores them the next. We bitterly remember the treatment of my predecessor, James Farmer, whose literacy program was dropped for political reasons. If the OEO had gone ahead with the funding of that program, tens of thousands of illiterates would today be on their way toward full participation in American life.

Here as never before there is a need for creative partnership. Parents of black and poor children must become respected partners in the coalition. Civil Rights groups have already proved that they can produce. One of the most successful Head Start programs in the country, according to Dr. Julius B. Richmond, formerly head of the National Head Start program, was run by Long Island CORE. Universities can offer new ideas. Foundations and businesses can offer funds. The public media can almost singlehandedly reverse the tide of racism, just as they reversed attitudes toward the Japanese and the Germans in a few short years. Programs featuring violence for adults and children instill the attitude that violence is a method of solving problems. Educational programs need to replace them showing that there are other ways of solving problems in a democratic society. The public needs to know what black people have contributed to the history of this nation. They need to know what black people are contributing today.

Government, if for no other reason than that of self-interest in developing productive citizens, should take the lead in creating an educational system of which we can all be proud. The right to get an education is a constitutional right. It is your responsibility to see that that right is guaranteed.

---

[5] The controversy over I.S. 201—One view and a proposal by Preston Wilcox, professor of social work, Columbia University School of Social Work.

HOUSING

Cities do not have the money to survive

The Federal Government must develop new concepts of subsidizing people, and free land to be used for human needs.

Where is this money to come from? This week Mayors around the country have been demanding cuts in the nation's space program and reallocation of funds to the cities. A few weeks delay in reaching the moon represents years of decent living for millions of Americans. Yet the housing and anti-poverty budgets are considered low-priority and "non-essential." Each year $100 million is returned as surplus by the Department of Housing and Urban Development. Why is this money returned? Why is it not used to build decent housing and create new jobs?

We must develop programs which do away with the feeling of uselessness of poor people, of black people. They have no property and no chance to own anything. Our society is based on property ownership, our personal identification comes from our jobs, yet black people have few opportunities to participate in either of these critical activities.

We must rebuild our cities to deal with the needs of the people living in them. Rehabilitation programs should be directed toward the elimination of slumlords exploiting the poor and the development of tenant ownership. They should create new jobs for ghetto residents in the rehabilitation work as well as in the management area. This will be a tremendous undertaking. It has been estimated by the Architects' Renewal Committee for Harlem that $3.8 billion is necessary for New York City for the next ten years to rehabilitate existing structures to create decent housing out of them. Another $27 billion is needed to build new units to create a sufficient supply of decent housing for the city. Another $780 million is needed just to make short-term repairs to provide decent housing while new units are being built. In addition, rent supplements will be required because rehabilitation costs will push up rents which poor people cannot pay. This will require an additional $1.1 billion per year.

This is the extent of the problem in just one city. How does the federal government deal with it? As an example, the current rent supplement program, which barely squeaked through Congress, has an appropriation of $20 million.

Nearly 80% of our citizens living in urban areas, the cities are being forced to carry the burden of our domestic problems—without any of the resources necessary to do the job.

There is only one answer: The federal government must accept its responsibility. However, history has shown that federal housing programs have never really been used for the benefit of the masses of the people.

Liberal efforts to obtain legislation to deal with slum problems have been directed toward abolishing segregated housing patterns. This approach has been destructive and has not resulted in significant increases in low-rent housing.

According to Dr. Richard Cloward and Dr. Frances Piven, in an article to be published in *The New Republic* next week, only 600,000 low-income units have been built since the start of the public housing program thirty years ago. But in less than half that time, nearly 700,000 units, mostly low-rental, have been destroyed by federal urban renewal and highway programs. In addition, federal tax incentives and mortgage programs have enabled private builders to take slum land at low costs to build middle and upper income housing. This has resulted in the dislocated being crowded into remaining ghetto areas, where the deterioration of ghetto housing has increased. People who have money already have been getting more: "To him that has, it shall be given."

New York City is a prime example. Mayor Lindsay's Housing and Urban Renewal Task Force recently reported that between 1960 and 1965 alone, the number of unsound units in the city rose from 420,000 to 525,000. During the same period, the stock of low-rental units decreased by 260,000 or almost one third. Similar statistics can be cited in Newark, Cleveland and Baltimore—cities we are particularly concerned about.

The writers contend that: "while the turmoil ranges over integration, the housing conditions of the masses of urban poor worsen. They worsen partly because the solution continues to be defined in terms of desegregation, so that the energies and attention of reformers are diverted from attempts to ameliorate housing in the ghetto itself. They worsen more because the issue of integration arouses the racism of the white majority, with the result that housing programs for the poor are defeated."

Gentlemen, the ghetto is a rotten place to live . . . and it is getting worse. We do not think that integration is the way to decent housing. We do think that federal programs, undertaken in cooperation with local communities, should now be directed to the concrete needs of the people, using all mechanisms and resources that have been so cleverly developed to raise tax revenues and sweep the poor under the rug.

The idea of a Comsat type corporation for housing, pooling the massive resources of both private industry and government, offers exciting possibilities for the creation of new housing and new jobs. We do not need new legal and administrative mechanisms so much as we need Congressional commitment and funds to be used creatively.

We propose a two-pronged approach:

The first should be massive central city rebuilding programs to be developed with ghetto residents. This should not be a continuation of token demonstration programs affecting few people, held up by the facade of token community participation. We call for rehabilitation of all existing structures in ghetto areas and the building of new public housing on under utilized sites. This must include employing and training ghetto people to do the work, and turning the ownership of the buildings over to tenant housing corporations. Let us use the financial devises of Urban Renewal in the hands of the poor so that ghetto organizations can acquire and improve slum properites and operate them as decent housing.

Let us make money available at low interest rates. Let us create and develop black contracting companies who train and hire black workers. Let us provide sufficient rent supplements so that people can pay rents increased by rehabilitation costs. Let us remove red tape and create the concept of instant money, and use it to develop our own backyards.

Let us also use federal guarantees to promote private investment in low-rent housing and to bring businesses and industries into ghetto areas. Let us bring the poor into society by providing them with an economic function, and make meeting their needs economically attractive.

The second is the construction of new cities. While many planners have looked to new towns as a solution to many urban problems, we see them as a way of dealing with the increasing migration of black farm workers to the cities. The construction of new cities offers tremendous opportunities for creation of new jobs, for the development of a whole new skilled population, and most importantly, for the creation of a new environment fit for men, black and white, to live in.

PROTECTION AND LAW ENFORCEMENT

In my opinion there were two tragic omissions on the part of the white majority in the history of this nation—two cases of reneging on the thrust of black people. One was the failure to give freed slaves forty acres and a mule, a mistake we are paying for to this very day. The other was the failure to send federal registrars into every black community of the South, the day after the Voting Rights Act of 1965 was signed.

The failure of government is clearly shown when citizens are not protected in the exercise of their fundamental rights. A government which has passed laws that it will not enforce is courting disaster. How can such a government demand respect and allegiance from the citizens it ignores?

We don't ask for any more laws. We simply demand that the constitutional rights be enforced. We are aware that political expediency determines decisions far too often. How else can we explain the practice of rewarding political retainers with judgeships when it is known that they are part of the very system that denies justice to black Americans?

A system of justice which depends upon ignorance and poverty to secure convictions is no justice. We support all reforms in this area—funds for legal assistance, bonding on personal recognizance, and so on.

The role of local law enforcement agencies in provoking rebellions in our cities has been discussed to death. We can make specific suggestions so that better qualified men would serve as policemen in our communities. It is mandatory that the nation's law enforcement agencies be men and women of high caliber, judgment and training. Mandatory human relations training provided through the assistance of Federal funds; a massive recruitment program among minority groups; the raising of wage scales comparable to the new professionalization, and access for citizens to a review board made up entirely of civilians to examine charges of police mal-practice are a minimum program.

But we are also aware of the desire of too many police forces to look upon themselves as their own lord and master. CORE reminds this nation that enforcement agencies on all levels, from the CIA to the police force of Los Angeles are responsible to the people they serve. To accept their services on any other terms is to invite totalitarianism.

EMPLOYMENT

Let's briefly review the employment situation. The statistics are familiar to all of us, but they only paint half of the picture. The other half, the solutions, will require money and determination. However, the question of financing is really not the major problem. There is a problem far deeper and greater in scope—That is the attitude of government as well as private industry as to their responsibility to the millions of poor and unemployed citizens in this country.

It is appropriate here to cite the following statistics: In August 1965, the white unemployment rate was 4.1% and the Negro unemployment rate was 7.7%. The traditional level of almost twice as many unemployed blacks as whites. Presently, white employment is down to 3.5% while at the same time, Negro unemployment has risen to the tragic figure of 8%. The gap continues to widen. Among young men of 18 to 24, the national rate of unemployment is 5 times as high for Negroes as for whites. In addition to the problem of unemployment is the hidden factor of equal pay for equal work. Negroes with Ph.D's make $4,000 less than white Ph.D's.

With statistics like these, even people educated in the public schools of our major cities can figure out that employment is a national problem and must be dealth with on a national level. And by the way, we don't agree that one national solution is to lower the unemployment rates by sending nearly 400,000 employables to a war in Southeast Asia.

The Congress of Racial Equality believes that immediate corrective measures must be instituted. The development of Negro skills is being prevented by racist practices by both government and private industry. Organized labor hasn't cleared its own house yet. The opening up of apprentice programs across the board could be a first step. For example, in New York City, according to a recent article in the New York Times, the plumbers and electricians unions continue gross discriminatory practices to the extent that only about 25 Negroes are electricians and plumbers in this great American city, the "example" of democracy.

First, we should consider creation of jobs for the poor. We do not have in mind "make work" programs, but programs which would affect the hard-core unemployed. The Scheuer Amendment to the anti-poverty act can be used as a basis if Congress will appropriate sufficient funds to make the amendment achieve the objectives for which it was designed. In such a program, jobs would have career potential and should raise the level of hope for those affected.

In such a program for example, young Negro high school graduates from the ghetto who are often found idle on the streets for lack of job opportunities, who are functionally dead as far as the American economy is concerned, can be brought back into the life of the economy by using them as teachers for elementary school children. They can teach reading and recreation activities, and be paid by the government for doing so. They can set up classes in storefronts for younger teens, churches and other private and public places. These high school graduates can thereby increase their worth to themselves and to the community, and at the same time earn money.

Secondly, thousands of ghetto dwellers can be employed in hospitals. There are tasks too numerous to mention which can be performed by unskilled persons, relieving nurses and other hospital personnel to attend to their primary tasks. Such sub-professional jobs inherently have potential for advancement. In addition, libraries are understaffed, city streets are filthy, parks need more employees. All of these and many other needs can be alleviated by giving people employment in their own communities, with the financial support and insistence of the federal government.

Employment and urban redevelopment go hand in hand. We need to construct hospitals, schools and numerous other community facilities. We need housing rehabilitation and thousands of new housing units. In this connection, the federal government should only aid those cities who demand that the labor force for these endeavors come primarily from the ghetto community. A percentage of units should be stipulated to be built by qualified Negro prime and sub-contractors, and all contractors should be required to draw some construction workers from the community. If we can force builders to observe certain requirements of structural engineering, there is no reason why we cannot certify them to observe requirements of human engineering.

Another primary concern of ours is the operation of businesses by black people in their own communities. In this too, there is much more that must be done by the federal government. It has been almost impossible for black men to obtain financing from the white banking and mortgaging community.

The recent action by the government which put the Small Business Administration under the jurisdiction of the Department of Commerce, CORE believes was a regressive act. SBA when removed from the Office of Economic Opportunity, was removed from the more progressive philosophies toward self-help programs for the poor. Since its creation, SBA has not worked effectively. It needs massive funds and drastic re-vamping to create self-help businesses in ghetto areas. In fact, to qualify for a SBA loan you really have to prove that you don't need money.

We need many more black-owned businesses in our black communities, employing local residents. Secretarial schools and small business training programs should be supported by government funds. Cooperatives and credit unions should be encouraged.

In Baltimore, for example, CORE's Target City, CORE has many success stories to its credit. Led by Walter Brooks and staff, it is an example of what CORE can do in an urban area when there is cooperation with business, local officials and government. A job training program for auto mechanics, gas station operators and small business skills was funded Monday, December 5th, as a cooperative effort by the Department of Labor, the Humble Oil Company and political leadership on local, state and federal levels.

Shortly after the first Watts riot in 1964, CORE established Operation Bootstrap, a job development agency for unemployed young men whose slogan was "Learn, Baby, Learn." Without federal grants or foundation money a self-help effort developed by CORE and the people in Watts, in cooperation with several corporations which contributed materials, facilities and training. With federal grants and foundation money, Operation Bootstrap could expand its operations and really become a unique demonstration of constructive building of a community.

In Louisiana, CORE helped to create a sweet potato cooperative which is now successfully supporting 375 Negro and white farmers.

The Congress of Racial Equality will continue to do its share; If government, private industry, and Labor do theirs, full employment and productivity can be a reality for all.

SUMMARY

In summary . . . the urban crisis must come into this room. The anguish of poor people—black people fenced into the squalid ghettoes must actually govern your deliberations. The themes repeat endlessly—the ghettoes are here, polluted by racism and cynicism—and the people are here, shattered, humiliated and vengeful. Nothing short of an immense national commitment spending the nation's resources on life as easily as we spend them on death-in-battle—nothing short of this can take us out of this dishonorable time of our history.

We in CORE will do what we can—and it will not always suit you. Today I have urged you to re-define your commitment and I have presented dozens of programs that can, if enacted and administered with integrity, reverse the river of violence and hopelnessness. And beyond all of this—I would hope that you heard me say even more—

1. For God's sake end this terrible war in Viet Nam, bring black men home to re-build their own lives, their own communities. And take the incredible costs of killing and use them to save the lives of the poor.

2. Understand that there is no longer time for the utopian dream—integration will only come when strong black men and women with pride are fully functioning in our society.

3. Throw out the rule-book of education. Create a National Board of Education dedicated to the task of stopping the maiming of black children's minds—and give them a heritage instead of a bayonet. And stop the systematic production of racists-minded white children.

4. Create jobs—real jobs, honorable work. Change the course of rivers, build highways, landscape our nation—and let us do the job. In the entire history of the immigrant American, the Northern Negro is the first to be denied the right to build his own land.

5. And build homes that men and women can live in—not just in the fringes of the city, but in the heart of the ghetto—and let those who are the veterans of the slums be the beneficiary of these homes.

6. And remember that black people are the victims of public media—the victims of stereotypes and canned violence.

7. And stop the backlashes, the hysteria . .,. because we intend to do what we must do with or without you. Twenty-two million American black people are indeed emerging into a massive political consciousness—we will be reckoned with . . . there is no form of slavery, however subtle, that we will ever countenance again.

URBAN MAN AND THE COMMUNICATIONS REVOLUTION

Nicholas Johnson

The city is man's greatest monument to the importance of communications. As a matter of logic and history, the need for contact between man and man constituted the principal impetus for the creation of cities.

But now, as critics of contemporary megalopolis are quick to point out, the city has undergone a Frankensteinian mutation. Its vast population, its crowded streets and congested living and working spaces, its cumbersome political and economic institutions, have made the city a place where communication is costly, inconvenient, and in great measure altogether impossible.

It is remarkable that professionals concerned with the future of our cities have paid communications so little heed. There can be few facts of more consequence to their projections than the exponential rate of increase in the capacity of homes and offices to send and receive information. Moreover, many familiar examples of existing technology could be put to work on the array of problems which cloud the American city's troubled entrance into the final third of the twentieth century.

As city governments consult systems engineers in attacking their problems, communications technology will be hit upon more and more as the best means of wringing more effectiveness from strained budgets. Merely to recite a characteristic list of programs and problems is to suggest the vast potential contribution which communications can make in each area.

Widespread attention has already focused on the close relationship between communications and the operations of urban police departments. The President's Commission on Law Enforcement and the Administration of Justice, in a report on science and technology prepared by the Institute for Defense Analyses, has compared police patrol systems to a living organism whose "primary input network is the public telephone system, and whose primary output network is the mobile radio police network."

As the importance of communications networks to effect crime control has become clearer to police departments, jurisdictions across the country have begun to demand, and manufacturers have begun to provide, more sophisticated devices. Radio-equipped patrol cars are commonplace. Foot patrolmen in many cities are being equipped with transmitting and receiving equipment capable of keeping contact with patrol cars or base stations. Street-corner call boxes which permit voice communication with police (and also fire) headquarters are on the market, for which the Federal Communications Commission has recently made available one narrow-band channel.

FUTURISTIC DEVICES DUE

Other devices are just over the horizon: electronic means for computer-controlled systems for locating any patrol car automatically; mobile teleprinters which transmit written orders to patrol cars and which will eventually provide mobile access to local, regional, and national computers for instantaneous data processing, storage, and retrieval; and mobile television receivers. Some day, if we so desire, we will be able to mount on the wrist of every patrolman communications equipment just as potent as that long used by Dick Tracy.

Indeed, the use of communications for crime control purposes is already one area where city governments have pioneered—and left federal communications agencies distinctly outpaced. The sliver of spectrum space allocated to the land-mobile radio service by the FCC in 1949 has been inadequate for years. In 1966 NATION'S CITIES predicted a 31 per cent increase in the need for radio frequencies for police uses by 1971. Recently the FCC has provided additional frequencies for police use. But new frequencies—and alternative systems for managing our use of current assignments—must remain among the most urgent items on the agenda of both the FCC and of local governments until this need is met.

REACHING THE PUBLIC

In such fields as housing, health care, education, welfare, legal assistance—to name just a few—we have already established massive federal and local government programs. But, as is often remarked, the people who have the problems often do not know that there are outposts of government equipped to offer a cure. And it is easy for the administrators to remain substantially ignorant of the specific needs of the people who in fact fall under their jurisdiction, or perhaps be led to believe that there is no need to be served. Those who do recognize the need spend considerable time and money trying, in various ways, to communicate with those they seek to serve.

The President's National Advisory Commission on Civil Disorders listed "effective communication between ghetto residents and local government" as the first goal in its strategy for restoring urban tranquility. The Commission's recommendation was not based on theorizing. For the Commission's investigators reported that: "Virtually every major episode of urban violence in the summer of 1967 was foreshadowed by an accumulation of unresolved grievances by ghetto residents against local authorities. . . ." The basic cause of volatile backlog of discontent was not hostile officials. It was, the Commission said, "a widening gulf in communications between local government and the residents of the erupting ghettos. . . ."

It seems to me that no governmental institution can link government to the people as well as can radio and television. And broadcasting can become even more of a two-way means of communication which allows the people to reach their government—and other people.

In New York City, for example, a leading rock and roll station has for the last three or four years run a series of remarkably successful campaigns to aid the citizenry in its efforts to locate and use government agencies responsible for housing, medical care, and racial discrimination. Several times each day, the station broadcasts one-minute spots notifying its listeners that, if they wish to rectify a matter having to do with housing, they should call a specified number. On calling, the complainant would receive information about the specific agencies that should be contacted and the nature of the process necessary to register a complaint and obtain redress.

RADIO A VITAL MEDIUM

Running this telephone service was a group of volunteer women calling itself "Call for Action." They processed 45,000 complaints about housing conditions. Over the two years, the city's housing agencies somehow were able to reduce the average time it took to process a housing complaint from more than 90 to less than 20 days. The value to the city of this imaginative—though simple—service was plainly enormous.

Some city agencies may look upon such activism by broadcasters as a threat. But certainly the dedicated governmental leader will recognize the prod of such ombudsman-style programs (a format plainly susceptible to a great variety of urban programs and problems) as an invaluable measure and guarantor of performance.

And all local agencies should recognize in television, and especially radio, a probably unparalleled means of reaching their constituencies, especially ghetto residents who are the recipients of many government services.

In many instances, the public school as we know it has been turning in a disturbingly deficient performance. Much of its inadequacies can usefully be understood as failures to communicate. As a medium, it has been cumbersome, expensive, and often altogether ineffective. And its message is too often out of step with the needs of the student seeking preparation for a role in tomorrow's economy.

SERVICE SAVINGS POSSIBLE

Here again, communications technology opens vistas that should excite educational theorist and budgetary planner alike. For example, continuing refinement of closed circuit television, teaching machines, and computer techniques promise substantial help in solving such troublesome problems as: the growing cost of assembling the burgeoning school population in adequately equipped buildings and classrooms; the difficulty of finding quality teaching personnel; and the necessity to keep good teachers abreast of fast-changing developments in their field. Broadcast or cable television systems can be used to make available these techniques of education in every individual's home—a development of increasing value in an economy where continuing technical change creates a constant need for re-education of the adult work force.

What can communications do to moderate the costs and inconveniences of that great American institution, the rush-hour traffic jam? In part, it can alleviate it: police helicopters already radio information about traffic conditions to broadcast stations which relay it to commuters, hoping thereby to permit rational individual decisions to choose one route or another. This is, of course, but a crude device.

There is no reason why the flow of traffic cannot eventually be regulated through the use of sensory devices on the scene feeding information about conditions to computers which then relay instructions to traffic lights, lane-closing and opening signals, or perhaps outright temporary roadblocks, just as feed-back flow systems control "traffic" in a steel mill or an oil refinery. At the very least we could use communications (radio and telephone) to better coordinate and distribute information about available urban transportation systems, by equipping buses with two-way radios, and by broadcasting reports about scheduling during peak-load periods.

Moreover, to some extent, communications may be able to eliminate the traffic jam altogether by obsoleting rush-hours. A housewife who can place her order by phone doesn't have to drive across town to shop. A lawyer who talks to a client by phone can do as well from across the continent as from across the hall. The small conference in the airport motel can be conducted from home with much less cost and strain with the aid of closed circuit television and long distance xerography (facsimile transmission of documents).

IMPACT ON TRANSPORTATION

In fact, any of us in the information processing business (memo writing and reading, correspondence, files, magazines and books, phone calls, newswires, computers, conferences)—and we are a growing band—will soon be able to relax and leave the driving to the non-communicative commuters. When we do so in substantial numbers we will affect the cities' "commuter problem," transportation needs and traffic patterns, and the very reason for today's central cities.

Once we recognize the impact that communications advance may have on transportation needs and patterns in the metropolis, we can see just how fundamental its role will be. If work now done in offices will not in the future require what is called "a central location," what are the implications for commercial and residential location patterns? What kinds of considerations are there in such speculations that city planners might—or must—take into account in trying to fix the shape of metropolitan areas?

Dartmouth Professor and RAND consultant John Kemeny has predicted that most of the basic functions of the central city will be wholly or partially obsoleted by 1990, when a vast computer-communications network will provide all offices and homes with video and aural contact with each other and with every conceivable kind of educational, informational, and entertainment fare. To accept a prediction like that—and it is hard to find fault with it—is not, of course, to say that cities will disappear. But it is clear that they will be radically transformed, physically as well as in many other ways. Communications advance will be the basic technological fact around which the cities of the next decades will take their shape.

COMMUNICATIONS PLANNING NEED

Otherwise said, communications will be to the last third of the twentieth century what the automobile has been to the middle third.

If we had that period to do over again, undoubtedly one of the things we could change is the failure or refusal of city planners to talk to highway engineers and vice versa—when the cities of today were on the drawing boards a decade or two or three ago. No coordinated effort was made to adapt the structure of the metropolis to the fact and implications of the automobile—or to adapt both to the human needs of the people who live and work in the city. We do not want to repeat this mistake in accommodating future technological revolutions while designing the cities of coming decades.

To take stock of the relationships between communications and urban development, we need to consider short- and long-run measures. To handle short-run problems, city governments might well consider establishing an individual or office, preferably as part of the mayor's office, specifically concerned with the totality of communications needs and activities of the city. Responsibilities of such an office might include:

Establishment of priorities in the use of mobile radio frequency space by city agencies (and possibly private users as well), as the Office of the Director of Telecommunications Management does for the Federal Government. If such offices are established by local governments, they should be accorded a formal, and to some degree autonomous, role in the decisions of the FCC on frequency allocation.

Ascertainment of the communications needs of various agencies and programs, and promotion and coordination of efforts to use the mass media to further these needs.

Consideration of whether the city should establish its own municipal radio or television broadcasting or closed-circuit media on the model of New York's highly vigorous and successful WNYC AM, FM, and TV.

Determination of how the city should use its power to franchise cable television systems. Few if any city governments have recognized the potential value to themselves of the FCC's decision not to preempt the power to license CATV systems. It not only gives the city government a handle on the future structure, content, and ownership of the communications system which will emerge within its jurisdiction over the coming decade or two. It also provides a potentially substantial source of revenue.

For its part, the FCC could, if city governments showed an interest, establish an Office of Urban Communications. Some of the matters to which this office could address itself would include:

To what extent is current research and development in communications addressed to improving communications between cities as opposed to communications within cities? To what extent does this allocation accord with the priorities of the nation?

To what extent is the current crisis in frequency allocation for landmobile radio use a matter of urban priorities? How could the present criteria for allocating frequencies, and regulating the telephone company, be revised to reflect better the needs of the mid-twentieth century metropolitan center? What procedures can be devised to better ascertain urban needs?

For the long run, we have to do two things: think and experiment. Much of both jobs must be done on a financial and institutional scale which puts them beyond the reach and responsibility (at least the direct responsibility) of individual city governments. But if the federal government, private industry, and the universities do not undertake these jobs, it will be city governments which suffer. So they may properly be burdened with responsibility for prodding others to action.

But serious analysis of the criteria and resources for designing the urban communications systems of the next decades is an urgent necessity. The alternative is to leave the field to the private—and ultimately uncoordinated—"planning" done by the managers of the communications industry.

Here is an example of the sort of intellectual tasks that demand confrontation now:

Perhaps we need to completely rethink what we are doing in the technology of mobile radio, and pursue a wholly different course to the same end. At some point, virtually every technology or system is totally abandoned in favor of a wholly new means to the same end that is cheaper and more satisfactory. Steam locomotives gave way to diesel, and both gave way to propeller airplanes, which in turn gave way to jets.

Land mobile radio frequency congestion is now so serious in the cities that we could usefully double the amount of frequency space available. But what long term solution would that provide—even if the frequencies were available? Since additional use (even with today's restraints) is growing at the rate of 20 per cent a year, we would be—within five short years—back in precisely the same bind we are today. (In fact, additional demand would undoubtedly be generated by the additional frequencies and the period would be less than five years.) Present technologies and systems simply do not appear to be adequate to the task.

CITIES WIRED FOR ACTION

What alternatives are there? We don't know. They are largely unexplored. One suggestion is that a city might be wired in such a way as to permit a mobile radio *system* to operate with perhaps hundreds or thousands more transmitters of *very low power*. Today's radio-dispatched cab must be able to transmit perhaps 30 miles—in all directions—in order to communicate with its base station. If each block were wired to receive low power transmission, and relay it by cable to its destination, the city's information system could handle much more message traffic. Such a proposal has obvious implications for public utility regulation. It may be that we will have to give more attention to common carrier mobile radio systems, and less to private as congestion becomes intolerable under our present wasteful system.

One thing is certain. We are going to have to educate ourselves in the spending of large sums of money. The military has learned that adequate planning of a relatively simple and specialized communications system cannot be done for less than tens or hundreds of millions of dollars. How much more sophisticated, costly—and significant—is the adequate design of communications systems for the daily use of millions of urban Americans. An adequate investment in such planning can pay for itself many times over. But the hundreds, and occasionally thousands, of dollars we are accustomed to spending on civilian communications planning are simply not going to do the job, and may even leave us worse off.

One of the most important areas in which we will have to invest that money is experimentaion. We will need to test individual subsystems; for example, a design for a new urban mobile communications system ought to be recipient of funds for a massive pilot program in at least one American city. We will also need to test more comprehensive systems—perhaps for a neighborhood or a single suburban or residential community, perhaps through the Model Cities program or something like it.

Finally, we do want to have some genuine model cities—like the private efforts launched in Reston, Virginia, and Columbia, Maryland, and more significant still, the Experimental City now under consideration by three federal agencies and a consortium of Minnesota interests.

We cannot—even if we would—dismantle the urban complex. But that is no reason to despair. The tools are at hand to make urban life governable and liveable—if only we will take them up. Innovations in communications technology are crashing upon us like the waves of a stormy sea upon the beach. Each brings worlds of opportunity.

The implications are there for all of us: business, universities, the arts, government. Those in the communications business and those directly responsible for our cities' welfare must make it their urgent business to take account of the communications revolution, and to put its gifts at the service of urban man.

SHOULD THE GOVERNMENT
SHARE ITS TAX TAKE?

Walter W. Heller

Washington *must* find a way to put a generous share of the huge federal fiscal dividend (the automatic increase in tax revenue associated with income growth) at the disposal of the states and cities. If it fails to do so, federalism will suffer, services will suffer, and the state-local taxpayer will suffer.

Economic growth creates a glaring fiscal gap; it bestows its revenue bounties on the federal government, whose progressive income tax is particularly responsive to growth, and imposes the major part of its burdens on state and local governments. Closing that gap must take priority over any federal tax cuts other than the removal of the 10 per cent surcharge. And even this exception may not be valid. For, as New York Governor Nelson A. Rockefeller has proposed, the revenue generated by the surcharge can easily be segregated from other federal revenue and earmarked for sharing with the states. So perhaps even the taxpayer's "divine right" to get rid of the surcharge may have to give way to the human rights of the poor, the ignorant, the ill, and the black.

For when the state-local taxpayer is beset with-and, indeed, rebelling against—a rising tide of regressive and repressive property, sales, and excise taxes, what sense would it make to weaken or dismantle the progressive and growth-responsive federal income tax? Whether our concern is for justice and efficiency in taxation, or for better balance in our federalism or, most important for a more rational system of financing our aching social needs, there is no escape from the logic of putting the power of the federal income tax at the disposal of beleaguered state and local governments.

Calling for redress of the fiscal grievances of our federalism is, of course, far from saying that state-local government has reached the end of its fiscal rope. The taxpayer's will to pay taxes may be exhausted, but his capacity is not:

Our overall tax burden—roughly 28 per cent of the GNP—falls far short of the 35-to-40 per cent levels in Germany, France, the Netherlands, and Scandinavia. Small solace, perhaps, but a strong suggestion that the U.S. taxpayer has not been squeezed dry.

Untapped and underutilized tax sources still abound in state and local

*Walter W. Heller, "Should the Government Share Its Tax Take?" * **SATURDAY RE-VIEW**, *March 22, 1969. Copyright 1969, Sautrday Review, Inc. Reprinted by permission of the author and publisher.*

finance. For example, fifteen states still have no income tax, and six still have no sales tax. If all fifty states had levied income taxes as high as those of the top ten, state income tax collections in 1966 would have been $11 billion instead of $5 billion. The same type of computation for state and local sales taxes shows a $5-billion add-on. As for that sick giant of our tax system, the property tax, the aforementioned top-ten standard adds $9.3 billion to the existing collection of $24.5 billion.

It is only fair to point out, however, that states and localities have not been exactly reticent about tapping these revenue sources. In spite of taxpayer resistance and the frequent political penalties that go with it, the fifty states have been doing a land-office business in new and used taxes. In the past ten years, the six major state taxes (sales, personal and corporate income, gasoline, cigarette, and liquor) were the subject of 309 rate increases and twenty-six new adoptions. Instead of slowing down, the pace has speeded up; in 1967-68, the states raised major taxes on eighty occasions and enacted seven new levies. Meanwhile, property tax burdens have risen faster than anyone thought possible ten years ago.

Yet, this effort has all the earmarks of a losing battle. Economic growth generates demands for new and better services while leaving a massive problem of water, air, land, and sound pollution in its wake. Population growth, especially the rapid rise of taxeaters relative to taxpayers (the number of Americans in the school-age and over-sixty-five groups is increasing more than twice as rapidly as those in-between), is straining state-local budgets. And inflation— which increases the prices of goods and services bought by state-local governments about twice as fast as the average rate of price increase in the economy— also works against state-local budgets.

In trying to meet these spending pressures, state and local governments are inhibited by fears of interstate competition, by limited jurisdiction, by reliance on taxes that respond sluggishly to economic growth, and by fears of taxpayer reprisals at the polls. But it would be a mistake to assume that the case for federal support rests wholly, or even mainly on these relentless fiscal pressures and handicaps. Far from being just a fiscal problem—a question of meeting fiscal demands from a limited taxable capacity—the issue touches on the very essence of federalism, both in a political and in a socioeconomic sense.

Indeed, it is from the realm of political philosophy—the renewed interest in making state-local government a vital, effective, and reasonably equal partner in a workable federalism—that much of the impetus for more generous levels and new forms of federal assistance has come. The financial plight of state-local government cannot alone explain the introduction of some 100 bills in Congress for various forms of revenue sharing or unconditional block grants since 1954, when my proposal for apportioning taxes was first made public and converted into a detailed plan by the Presidential task force headed by Joseph A. Pechman.

In this connection, I have been amused by how often the following sentences from my *New Dimensions of Political Economy,* published in 1966, have been quoted, especially by surprised conservatives: "The good life will not come, ready made, from some federal assembly line. It has to be custombuilt, engaging the effort and imagination and resourcefulness of the community. Whatever fiscal plan is adopted must recognize this need." In expressing similar thoughts publicly for a quarter-century, I have not been alone among liberals. Yet, the statement is now greeted as if the power and the glory of decentralization has just been revealed to us for the first time. May I add that when we are embraced by those "who stand on their states' rights so they can sit on them," we may be forgiven for wincing.

Moving from the political to the economic, one finds strong additional rationale for new and expanded federal support in the economic—or socio-economic—theory of public expenditures. It is in this theory that our vast programs of federal aid to state and local governments—projected to run at $25 billion in fiscal 1970 (triple the amount in 1960)—are firmly anchored. All too often, they are thought of simply as a piece of political pragmatism growing out of two central fiscal facts: that Washington collects more than two-thirds of the total federal, state, and local tax take; and that nearly two-thirds of government public services (leaving aside defense and social security programs) are provided by state-local government. Throw in the objective of stimulating state-local efforts through matching provisions, and, for many people, the theory of federal grants is complete.

In fact, it is only the beginning. Consider the compelling problems of poverty and race and the related problems of ignorance, disease, squalor, and hardcore unemployment. The roots of these problems are nationwide. And the efforts to overcome them by better education, training, health, welfare, and housing have nationwide effects. Yet, it is precisely these services that we entrust primarily to our circumscribed state and local units.

Clearly, then, many of the problems that the states and localities tackle are not of their own making. And their success or failure in coping with such problems will have huge spillover effects far transcending state and local lines in our mobile and interdependent society. The increasing controversy over the alleged migration of the poor from state to state in search of higher welfare benefits is only one aspect of this. So, quite apart from any fiscal need to run hat in hand to the national government, states and cities have a dignified and reasonable claim on federal funds with which to carry out national responsibilities. Only the federal government can represent the totality of benefits and strike an efficient balance between benefits and costs. Therein lies the compelling economic case for the existing system of earmarked, conditional grants-in-aid. Such grants will, indeed must, continue to be our major mechanism for transferring funds to the states and localities.

But the interests of a healthy and balanced federalism call for support of the general state-local enterprise as well as specific services. It is hard to argue that the benefits of sanitation, green space, recreation, police and fire protection, street maintenance and lighting in one community have large spillover effects on other communities. Yet, in more or less humdrum services such as these lies much of the difference between a decent environment and a squalid one, between the snug suburb and the grinding ghetto.

Given the limits and inhibitions of state-local taxation and the sharp inequalities in revenue-raising capacity—compounded by the matching requirement in most categorical grants, which pulls funds away from non-grant activities—too many of the states and the cities are forced to strike their fiscal balances at levels of services well below the needs and desires of their citizens. The absence of a system of federal transfers to serve the broad purpose of upgrading the general level of public services, especially in the poorer states, is a serious gap—both economic and political—in the fiscal structure of our federalism. Tax sharing could fill it.

FEDERAL AID TO STATE AND LOCAL GOVERNMENTS
(selected fiscal years 1949-1969) in millions of dollars

	1949	1959	1967	1968*	1969
Agriculture	86.6	322.5	448.0	599.4	644.0
Commerce and Transportation	433.6	100.6	226.3	431.7	618.6
Education	36.9	291.3	2,298.7	2,461.9	2,398.2
Health, Labor, Welfare	1,231.5	2,789.7	6,438.0	8,207.1	9,135.0
Housing, Community Development	8.6	188.4	768.3	1,185.2	1,812.5
Highway and Unemploy. Trust Funds	—	2,801.2	4,501.7	4,773.1	4,796.7
Other	5.5	319.7	1,120.2	1,239.9	1,418.0
Total	1,802.7	6,813.4	15,801.2	18,898.3	20,823.0

*Data estimated
Source: Bureau of the Budget

The core of a tax-sharing plan is the earmarking of a specified share of the federal individual income tax take for distribution to states and localities, on the basis of population, with next to no strings attached. The so-called Heller-Pechman plan has the following main elements:

The federal government would regularly route into a special trust fund 2 per cent of the federal individual income tax base (the amount reported as net taxable income by all individuals). In 1969, for example, this would come to about $7 billion, roughly 10 per cent of federal individual income tax revenues. This amount would be channeled to the states at fixed intervals, free from the uncertainties of the annual federal appropriation process.

The basic distribution would be on a straight population formula, so much per capita. Perhaps 10 per cent of the proceeds should be set aside each year as an equalization measure—to boost the share of the seventeen poorer states (which have 20 per cent of the nation's population).

To insure that the fiscal claims of the localities are met, a minimum passthrough—perhaps 50 per cent—to local units would be required. In this intrastate allocation, the financial plight of urban areas should be given special emphasis.

The widest possible discretion should be left to the state and local governments in the use of the funds, subject only to the usual accounting and auditing requirements, compliance with the Civil Rights Act, and perhaps a ban on the use of such funds for highways (for which there already is a special federal trust fund).

How well does the tax-sharing plan (also called revenue sharing, unconditional grants, and general assistance grants) measure up to the economic and sociopolitical criteria implicit in the foregoing discussion? Let me rate it briefly, and sympathetically, on six counts.

First, it would significantly relieve the immediate pressures on state-local treasuries and, more important, would make state-local revenues grow more rapidly, in response to economic growth. For example, a 2-percentage-point distribution on a straight per capita basis would provide, in 1969, $650 million each for California and New York, $420 million for Pennsylvania, $375 million for Illinois, $140 million each for Mississippi and Wisconsin, $125 million each for Louisiana and Minnesota, and about $65 million each for Arkansas and Colorado.

The striking growth potential of this source of revenue is evident in two facts: (1) had the plan been in effect in 1955, the distribution of 2 per cent of the $125-billion income-tax base in that year would have yielded a state-local tax share of about $2.5 billion; and (2) by 1972, the base should be about $450 billion, yielding a $9-billion annual share.

Second, tax sharing would serve our federalist interest in state-local vitality and independence by providing new financial elbow room, free of political penalty, for creative state and local officials. Unlike the present grants-in-aid, the tax-shared revenue would yield a dependable flow of federal funds in a form that would enlarge, not restrict, their options.

Third, tax sharing would reverse the present regressive trend in our federal-state-local tax system. It seems politically realistic to assume that the slice of federal income tax revenue put aside for the states and cities would absorb funds otherwise destined to go mainly into federal tax cuts and only partly into spending increases. Given the enormous pressures on state-local budgets, on the other hand, tax shares would go primarily into higher state-local expenditures and only in small part into a slowdown of state-local tax increases. Thus, the combination would produce a more progressive overall fiscal system.

Fourth, tax sharing—especially with the 10 per cent equalization feature—would enable the economically weaker states to upgrade the scope and quality of their services without putting crushingly heavier burdens on their citizens. Per Capita sharing itself would have a considerable equalizing effect, distributing $35 per person to all of the states, having drawn $47 per person from the ten richest and $24 per person from the ten poorest states. Setting aside an extra 10 percent for equalization would boost the allotments of the seventeen poorest states by one-third to one-half. Thus, the national interest in reducing interstate disparities in the level of services would be well served.

Fifth, the plan could readily incorporate a direct stimulus to state and local tax efforts. Indeed, the Douglas Commission (the National Commission on Urban Problems), like many other advocates of tax-sharing plans, would adjust the allotments to take account of relative state-local tax efforts. In addition, they propose a bonus for heavy reliance on individual income taxation.

A more direct stimulant to state and local efforts in the income tax field would be to enact credits against the federal income tax for state income taxes paid. For example, if the taxpayer could credit one-third or two-fifths of his state and local income tax payments directly against his federal tax liability (rather than just treat such taxes as a deduction from taxable income, as at present), it would lead to a far greater use of this fairest and most growth-oriented of all tax sources.

Ideally, income tax credits should be coupled with income tax sharing and federal aid in a balanced program of federal support. But if relentless fiscal facts require a choice, the nod must go to tax sharing because 1) credits provide no interstate income-level equalization; 2) at the outset, at least, much of the federal revenue loss becomes a taxpayer gain rather than state-local gain; and 3) since one-third of the states still lack broad-based income taxes, the credit would touch off cries of "coercion." Nevertheless, it is a splendid device that ought to have clearcut priority over further tax cuts.

Sixth, and finally, per capita revenue sharing would miss its mark if it did not relieve some of the intense fiscal pressures on local, and particularly urban, governments. The principle is easy to state. The formula to carry it out is more difficult to devise. But it can be done. The Douglas Commission has already developed an attractive formula that it describes as "deliberately 'loaded' to favor general purpose governments that are sufficiently large in population to give some prospect of viability as urban units." I would agree with the Commission that it is important not to let "no-strings" federal aid sustain and entrench thousands of small governmental units that ought to wither away—though I still prefer to see the tax-sharing funds routed through the fifty state capitals, rather than short-circuiting them by direct distribution to urban units.

Supported by the foregoing logic, espoused by both Democratic and Republican platforms and candidates in 1968, and incorporated into bills by dozens of prestigious Senators and Congressmen, one would think that tax sharing will have clear sailing as soon as our fiscal dividends permit. Not so. The way is strewn with obstacles and objections.

For example, tax sharing poses threats, or seeming threats, to special interest groups including all the way from top federal bureaucrats who see tax sharing's gain as their agencies' and programs' loss; through the powerful lobbyists for special programs such as housing, medical care, and pollution control programs, who recoil from the prospect of going back from the federal gusher to fifty state spigots; to the Senators and Congressmen who see more political mileage in tax cuts or program boosts than in getting governors and mayors out of their fiscal jam.

But, of course, opposition goes far beyond crass self-interest. It also grows out of philosophic differences and concern over the alleged shortcomings of tax sharing. There is the obvious issue of federalism versus centralism. A strong contingent in this country feels that the federal government knows best, and that state and local governments cannot be trusted. Others fear that revenue sharing or unrestricted grants will make state-local government more dependent on the federal government—a fear for which I see little or no justification.

On the issues, some would argue that it is better to relieve state-local budgets by taking over certain burdens through income-maintenance programs like the negative income tax; while others feel that too much of the revenue-sharing proceeds would go down the drain in waste and corruption. Here, one must answer in terms of a willingness to take the risks that go with an investment in the renaissance of the states and the cities. Some costs in wasted and diverted funds will undoubtedly be incurred. My assumption is that these costs will be far outweighed by the benefits of greater social stability and a more viable federalism that will flow from the higher and better levels of government services and the stimulus to state-local initiative and responsibility.

In sum, I view tax sharing as an instrument that (1) will fill a major gap in our fiscal federalism; (2) will strengthen the fabric of federalism by infusing funds *and* strength into the state-local enterprise; and (3) will increase our total governmental capacity to cope with the social crisis that confronts us. The sooner Congress gets on with the job of enacting a system of tax sharing, even if it means postponing the end of the 10 per cent surcharge, the better off we shall be.

WE WON'T END THE URBAN CRISIS
UNTIL WE END 'MAJORITY RULE'

Herbert J. Gans

In 1962, a group of us, planners and social scientists, assembled a book of essays about the city, and we called it "The Urban Condition." Had the book been published only a couple of years later, it would probably have been entitled "The Urban Problem," and today it would surely come out as "The Urban Crisis." But these catch phrases are misleading, for they divert attention from the real issues. Although American cities are in deep trouble, the real crisis is not

Herbert J. Gans, "We Won't End The Urban Crisis Until We End 'Majority Rule,'"
THE NEW YORK TIMES MAGAZINE, August 3, 1969. Copyright © 1969 by The
New York Times Company. Reprinted by permission of the author and publisher.

urban but national, and stems in large part from shortcomings in American democracy, particularly the dependence on majority rule.

The troubles of the city have been catalogued in long and by now familiar lists, but I would argue that in reality, they boil down to three: *poverty and segregation,* with all their consequences for both their victims and other urban residents; and *municipal decay,* the low quality of public services and the declining tax revenues which are rapidly leading to municipal bankruptcy. Moreover, the first two problems are actually the major cause of the third, for the inability of the poor to pay their share of keeping up the city, as well as the crime and other pathology stimulated by poverty and segregation have brought about much of the municipal decay. In addition, the fear of the ghetto poor has recently accelerated the middle-class exodus, thus depriving cities of an important source of taxes at the very moment their expenditures have been increased by the needs of the poor. Consequently, the elimination of urban poverty and segregation would go far toward relieving the other problems of the city.

Neither poverty and segregation nor municipal decay are unique to the city, however; indeed, they are often more prevalent in rural areas. More important, all three problems are caused by nationwide conditions. Poverty is to a considerable extent a by-product of the American economy, which is today growing only in the industries and services that employ the skilled, semi-professional and professional worker, and, in fact, many of the unskilled now living in urban slums were driven out of rural areas where the demand for their labor had dried up even earlier than in the cities. Municipal decay is similarly national in cause, for small communities can also no longer collect enough in taxes to provide the needed public services, and their populations, too, are becoming increasingly poor and black as the nationwide suburbanization of the middle class proceeds.

In short, the so-called urban crisis is actually an American crisis, brought on largely by our failure to deal with the twin evils of poverty and segregation. This failure has often been ascribed to a lack of national will, as if the country were an individual who could pull himself together if he only wanted to, but even the miraculous emergence of a national consensus would not be sufficient, for the sources of our failure are built into our most important economic and political institutions.

One major source of failure is the corporate economy, which has not realized, or been made to realize, that the rural and urban unskilled workers it has cast aside are part of the same economic process which has created affluence or near-affluence for most Americans. As a result, private enterprise has been able to improve productivity and profit without having to charge against its profit the third of the population which must live in poverty or near-poverty. Instead, government has been left the responsibility for this by-product of the economic process, just as it has often been given the task of removing the waste materials that are a by-product of the production process.

But government has not been able or willing to require private enterprise— and its own public agencies—to incorporate the employable poor into the economy. Not only is there as yet little recognition among the general public or most of our leaders of the extent to which urban and rural poverty result from the structure of the economy, but private enterprise is powerful enough to persuade most people that government should take care of the poor or subsidize industry to create jobs for them.

However, government—whether Federal, state or local—has not been able or willing to absorb responsibility for the poor either, and for several important political reasons.

First, most voters—and the politicians that represent them—are not inclined to give the cities the funds and powers to deal with poverty, or segregation. This disinclination is by no means as arbitrary as it may seem, for the plight of the urban poor, the anger of the rebellious, and the bankruptcy of the municipal treasury have not yet hurt or even seriously inconvenienced the vast majority of Americans.

Rural and small-town America make little use of the city anyway, except for occasional tourist forays, and the city financial institutions which play an influential part in their economies are not impaired in their functioning by the urban condition. Suburbanites may complain about the dirt, crime and traffic congestion when they commute to city jobs, but they can still get downtown without difficulty, and, besides, many of their employers are also moving out to the suburbs.

But even the city-dwellers who are neither poor nor black can pursue their daily routines unchanged, for most of them never need to enter the slum areas and ghettos. Only the urbanites who work in these areas or live near them are directly touched by the urban condition—and they are a small minority of America's voters.

Second, many Americans, regardless of where they live, are opposed to significant governmental activity on behalf of the poor and black—or, for that matter, to further governmental participation in the economy. Not only do they consider taxes an imposition on their ability to spend their earnings, but they view governmental expenditure as economic waste, whereas private enterprise expenditures are proudly counted in the Gross National Product. The average American taxpayer is generous in paying for the defense of the country and for projects that increase American power and prestige in the world, be it a war in Vietnam or a moon shot, but he is often opposed to governmental activities that help anyone other than himself. The very corporations and workers whose incomes depend on government contracts often fight against Federal support of other activities and groups—and without ever becoming aware of the contradiction.

Consequently, many taxpayers and voters refuse to see the extent to which governmental activities create jobs and provide incomes, and how much government subsidizes some sectors of American life but not others. By and large, these subsidies go to people who need them less: there are tax exemptions for home-owners, Federal highway programs and mortgage insurance for suburbanites; direct subsidies to airlines, merchant shipping, large farms, colleges and college students; and, of course, the depletion allowance for oil producers. Grants to the poor are fewer and smaller; the most significant one is public welfare, and it is called a handout, not a subsidy.

Subsidies are generally provided not on the basis of merit but power, and this is a *third* reason for the lack of action in the cities. Even though many Americans live in the city, urban areas and their political representatives have relatively little power, and the poor, of course, yet less. The poor are powerless because they are a minority of the population, are often difficult to organize, and are not even a homogeneous group with similar interests that could be organized into an effective pressure group.

The cities are relatively powerless because of the long-time gerrymandering of American state and Federal governments in favor of rural and small-town areas. As a result, rural-dominated state legislatures can use the tax receipts of the cities to subsidize their own areas, and Congressmen from these areas have been able to outvote the representatives of urban constituencies. The Supreme Court's requirement of one man-one vote is now bringing about reapportionment, but it may be too late for the cities. As more and more Americans leave for the suburbs, it appears that the cities will not be able to increase their power, for voters and politicians from rural and suburban areas who share a common interest in not helping the cities can unite against them.

In effect, then, the cities and the poor and the black are politically outnumbered. This state of affairs suggests the *fourth* and perhaps most important reason for the national failure to act: the structure of American democracy and majority rule.

America, more so than other democratic nations in the world, runs its political structure on the basis of majority rule. A majority vote in our various political institutions determines who will be nominated and elected to office, what legislation will be passed and funded, and who will be appointed to run the administering and administrative agencies. Of course, the candidates, laws and budgets which are subject to the vote of the majority are almost always determined by minorities; the only men who can run for office these days are either affluent or financed by the affluent groups who donate the campaign funds, and the legislation these men vote on is often suggested or even drafted by campaign fund donors or other small groups with specific interests in government action. Properly speaking then, American democracy allows affluent minorities to propose, and the majority to dispos ·.

There is nothing intrinsically conspiratorial about this phenomenon, for it follows from the nature of American political participation. Although every citizen is urged to be active in the affairs of his community and nation, in actual practice participation is almost entirely limited to organized interest groups or lobbies who want something from government.

As a result, legislation tends to favor the interests of the organized: of businessmen, not consumers, even though the latter are a vast majority; of landlords, not tenants; doctors, not patients. Unorganized citizens may gripe about the lack of consumer legislation or even the defense budget, but only when their interests are similar and immediately threatened so that they can organize or be organized are they able to affect governmental affairs.

This is not to say that governmental decisions often violate the wishes of a majority of Americans, for, by and large, that majority is usually happy—or at least not too unhappy—with the decisions of its governments. The almost

$100-billion spent annually for defense and space exploration are appropriated because, until recently, the majority of the voters wanted a victory in Vietnam and a man on the moon before the Russians. There is no Federal mass-transit program because the majority of Americans, even in the cities, prefer to use their cars; and Congress can pay more attention to a small number of tobacco farmers and producers than to the danger of cigarette smoking because the majority is not sufficiently concerned about this danger, and, as a recent study showed, many heavy smokers do not even believe that smoking leads to cancer or heart disease.

But while the American political structure often satisfies the majority, it also creates *outvoted minorities* who can be tyrannized and repressed by majority rule, such as the poor and the black, students, migrant workers and many others. In the past, such minorities have had to rely on the goodwill of the majority, hoping that it would act morally, but it generally offered them only charity, if that much. For example, the majority has granted the poor miserly welfare payments, and then added dehumanizing regulations for obtaining and spending the funds.

Today, many outvoted minorities have tired of waiting for an upturn in public altruism and are exerting political pressure on the majority. Thus, the poor and the black have been organizing their own pressure groups, forming coalitions with more powerful minorities (like the progressive wing of the labor movement) and getting support from liberals, other advocates of social justice and guilty whites. Indeed, such methods enabled the poor and the black to achieve the civil rights and antipoverty programs of the nineteen-sixties.

Even so, these gains, however much of an improvement they represent over the past, remain fairly small, and have not significantly improved the living conditions of large numbers in the slums and ghettos. Moreover, the activities of ghetto demonstrators and rioters have cooled some of the ardor of white liberals and trade unionists, and it is questionable whether many other groups would derive much benefit from coalition with poor or black organizations. Like all outvoted minorities, they can offer little to a coalition except the moral urgency of their cause.

Consequently, the poor and the black are caught in an almost hopeless political bind, for any programs that would produce significant gains, such as a massive antipoverty effort, an effective assault on segregation or even a workable community control scheme, are likely to be voted down by the majority, or the coalitions of minorities that make up majorities in American political life. *Moreover, since the poor and the black will probably always be out-voted by the majority, they are thus doomed to be permanently outvoted minorities.*

But if I am correct in arguing that the urban condition cannot be improved until poverty and segregation are eliminated or sharply reduced, it is likely that *under the present structure of American government there cannot be and will not be a real solution to the problem of the cities.*

The only other source of power left to outvoted minorities is *disruption,* upsetting the orderly processes of government and of daily life so as to incon-venience or threaten more powerful groups. This explains why the ghettos have rebelled, why young people sometimes resort to what adults consider to be meaningless delinquency, or students to occupations of school buildings, or workingclass people to occasionally violent forms of white backlash.

Although disruption is bitterly attacked as antisocial by defenders of the existing social order, strikes were also once considered antisocial, but are now so legitimate that they are no longer even thought of as a form of disruption. The disrupters of today do not strike, but their methods have not been so unproductive as their opponents would have us believe. The ghetto rebellions have been responsible for stimulating private enterprise to find jobs for the so-called hard-core unemployed; the sit-ins—as well as the organizational activity—of the Welfare Rights movement have won higher grants for welfare recipients in some cities and have helped to arouse the interest of the Nixon Administration in re-examining the Federal welfare program; and the uprisings by college and high school students have been effective in winning them a voice in their schools.

Needless to say, disruption also has disadvantages; the possibility that it will be accompanied by violence and that it will be followed by counter-disruption—for example, police or vigilante violence—and by political efforts of more powerful groups to wipe out the gains achieved through disruption. Thus, the backlash generated by the ghetto rebellions has been partly responsible for the cutback in antipoverty and civil-rights efforts, and the disruptions by welfare recipients and college students are now producing repressive legislation against both groups. But disruption also creates serious costs for the rest of society, particularly in terms of the polarization of opposing groups, the hardening of attitudes among other citizens, and the hysterical atmosphere which then results in more repressive legislation. Clearly, disruption is not the ideal way for out-voted minorities to achieve their demands.

Nevertheless, disruption has become an accepted political technique, and may be used more widely in the nineteen-seventies, as other groups who feel they are being shortchanged by American democracy begin to voice their demands. Consequently, perhaps the most important domestic issue before the country today is whether outvoted minorities —in the cities and elsewhere—must resort to further disruption, or whether more peaceful and productive ways of meeting their needs can be found.

If the outvoted minorities are to be properly represented in the political structure, two kinds of changes are necessary. First, they must be counted fairly, so that they are actually consulted in the decision-making process, and are not overpowered by other minorities who would be out-voted were they not affluent enough to shape the political agenda. But since even a fairer counting of the voters would still leave the outvoted minorities with little influence, ways of restricting majority rule must be found when that rule is always deaf to their demands.

Majority rule is, of course, one of the unquestioned traditions of American political life, for the first axiom of democracy has always been that the majority should decide. But democracy is not inviolably equivalent to majority rule, for government of the people, by the people and for the people need not mean that a majority is "the people." Indeed, despite its traditional usage in democracies, majority rule is little more than an easily applied quantitative formula for solving the knotty problems of how the wishes of the people are to be determined. Moreover, traditions deserve to be re-examined from time to time, particularly if society has changed since they came into being.

And American society has changed since its government was created. What might be called *majoritarian democracy* was adopted when America was a small and primarily agrarian nation, with a great degree of economic and cultural homogeneity, few conflicting interest groups, and a since-rejected tradition that the propertyless should have fewer rights than the propertied. As a result, there were few serious disputes between majorities and minorities, at least until the Civil War, and majoritarian democracy could be said to have worked. Today, however, America is a highly heterogeneous and pluralistic nation, a society of minority groups, so to speak, and every important political decision requires an intense amount of negotiation and compromise so that enough minorities can be found to create a majority coalition. And even then, America is so pluralistic that not all minorities can be accommodated and must suffer all the consequences of being outvoted.

America has been a pluralistic society for almost a century, but the short-comings of majority rule have not become a public issue before, mainly because previous generations of outvoted groups had other forms of redress. The outvoted of the past were concentrated among poor ethnic and racial minorities, as they are today, but in earlier years the economy needed their unskilled labor, so that they had less incentive to confront the majority, except to fight for the establishment of labor unions. Moreover, they had little reason even to think about majority rule, for government played a smaller role in the economy and in their lives.

Now all this has changed. When governmental policies and appropriations very nearly decide the fate of the poor, the black, draft-age college students, disadvantaged high school students, and not so affluent blue-collar workers, such groups must deal with government; and more often than not, their demands are frustrated by the workings of majority rule.

Thus, it becomes quite pertinent to ask whether majoritarian democracy is still viable, and whether the tradition of majority rule should not be re-examined. If three-fourths of the voters or of a legislative body are agreed on a course of action, it is perhaps hard to argue against majority rule, but what if that rule seriously deprives the other fourth and drives it to disruption? And what if the majority is no more than 55 per cent, and consists only of an uneasy and temporary coalition of minorities? Of if the remaining 45 per cent are unable to obtain compromises from the slender majority?

I believe that the time has come to modernize American democracy and adapt it to the needs of a pluralistic society; in short, to create a *pluralistic democracy.* A pluralistic form of democracy would not do away with majority rule, but would require systems of proposing and disposing which take the needs of minorities into consideration, so that when majority rule has serious negative consequences, outvoted minorities would be able to achieve their most important demands, and not be forced to accept tokenism, or resort to despair or disruption.

Pluralistic democracy would allow the innumerable minorities of which America is made up to live together and share the country's resources more equitably, with full recognition of their various diversities. Legislation and appropriations would be based on the principle of "live and let live," with different programs of action for different groups whenever consensus is impossible. Groups of minorities could still coalesce into a majority, but other minorities would be able to choose their own ways of using public power and funds without being punished for it by a majority.

It would take a book to describe how the American political system might be restructured to create a pluralistic democracy, but I can suggest some specific proposals toward this goal. They fall into two categories: those that incorporate outvoted minorities into the political structure by increasing the responsiveness of governments to the diversity of citizen interests—and to all citizens; and those which restrict majority rule so as to prevent the tyrannization of minorities. Many of my proposals have drawbacks, and some are outright utopian, but I suggest them more to illustrate what has to be done than to provide immediate feasible solutions.

The responsiveness of governments can be increased in several ways.

First, the one man-one vote principle must be extended to all levels of government and the political parties. County and municipal bodies need to be reapportioned to eliminate gerrymandering of the poor and the black; party leaders, high and low, should be elected by party members, and party candidates should be nominated by primaries, rather than by conventions or closed meetings of party leaders.

Second, the seniority system must be abolished in all legislatures, so that politicians can no longer obtain undue power simply because their own districts re-elect them time after time. The power of committee chairmen who may represent only a small number of voters to block legislation wanted by a larger number must also be eliminated.

Third, the administrative agencies and their bureaucracies must become more accountable, perhaps by replacing appointive officers with elective ones, or by requiring such bodies to be run by elected boards of directors.

Fourth, all election campaigns should be funded by government, to discourage the near-monopoly that wealthy individuals now have in becoming candidates, and to prevent affluent interest groups from making demands on candidates as a price for financing their campaigns. If equal amounts—and plenty of free television time—were given to all candidates, even from third, fourth and fifth parties, the diversity of the population would be better represented in the electoral process. This might lead to election by plurality rather than majority, although in a highly diverse community or state such an outcome might not be undesirable, and runoffs can always be required to produce a final majority vote.

Fifth, methods by which the citizenry communicates with its elected representatives ought to be improved. Today, legislators tend to hear only from lobbyists, people in their own social circles, and the writers of letters and newspaper editorialists—a highly biased sample of their constituencies. Indeed, the only way an ordinary citizen can communicate is by organizing or writing letters. Of course, such methods make sure that a legislator hears only from deeply interested citizens, protecting him from being overwhelmed by too much feedback, but they also discriminate against equally interested people who cannot organize or write.

One possible solution is for governments to make postage-free forms available for people who want to write letters to their representatives, to be picked up in banks, post offices, stores and taverns. Another solution is for governments to finance the establishment of regular but independently run public-opinion polls on every major issue, so that government officials can obtain adequate feedback from a random sample of their constituents, and not only on the few issues a handful of private pollsters today decide are worth polling about.

Yet another solution is for governments to encourage people to organize politically, by allowing them to claim as tax deductions the dues and contributions to lobbying organizations (other than political parties). Limits on the size of such deductions would have to be set to prevent affluent minorities from using their funds to gain extra power; and organizations of the poor, whose members cannot afford to pay dues and do not benefit from tax deductions, could be given government grants if they could prove that two-thirds of their members were poor.

Feasible methods for increasing the power of minorities at the expense of majority rule are more difficult to formulate. One approach is to enhance the power of existing institutions that represent minority interests—for example, the courts and Cabinet departments. If constitutional amendments to establish an economic and racial bill of rights could be passed, for instance, a provision giving every American citizen the right to a job or an income above the poverty-line, the power of the poor would be increased somewhat.

Cabinet departments also represent minority interests, particularly at the Federal and state levels, although more often than not they speak for affluent minorities. Nevertheless, if the Office of Economic Opportunity were raised to full Cabinet status and a Department of Minorities established in Washington, at least some new legislation and higher appropriations for the poor and the black would result. In other Cabinet departments, new bureaus should be set up to represent the interests of outvoted minorities; in Housing and Urban Development (now dominated by builders and mayors), to look after the needs of slum dwellers; in Health, Education and Welfare, to deal with the concerns of patients, students and welfare recipients, respectively. Moreover, the policy-making boards that I suggested earlier to oversee Cabinet departments and other administrative agencies should include their clients. Thus, all school boards should include some students; welfare departments, some welfare recipients; and housing agencies, some residents of public housing and F.H.A.-supported projects.

The financial power of poor minorities could be increased by extending the principles of the progressive income tax and of school-equalization payments to all governmental expenditures. Funding of government programs could be based in part on the incomes of eventual recipients, so that the lower their income, the higher the government grant. Poorer communities would thus obtain more Federal money per capita for all public services, and subsidies for mass transit programs would automatically be higher than for expressways to sub-urbia.

In addition, changes in the electoral system would be needed. One solution would be election by proportional representation. P.R. has not been popular in America, partly because it wreaks havoc with the two-party system, but it is not at all clear whether a pluralistic society is best served by a two-party system to begin with. Proportional representation by race or income would go against the American grain, but as long as racial and economic integration seems to be unachievable in the near future, this solution might be more desirable than forcing the poor or the black to resort to disruption.

Actually, proportional representation is already practiced informally in many places; in New York City, election states have always been "balanced" to include candidates from the major ethnic and religious groups. Perhaps we should even think about proportional representation by occupational groups, for job concerns are often uppermost in the voters' choices. After all, many pro-Wallace factory workers voted for Humphrey at the last minute, realizing that their job interests were more important than their fear of black militancy.

Another approach would restrict majority rule directly, by making all elections and voting procedures in legislative branches of government go through a two-step process, with majority rule applying only to the final step. This system, somewhat like the runoff used in some state and municipal elections, would require that if any legislative proposal or appropriation obtains at least 25 per cent of the total vote, it must be revised and voted on again until it is either approved by a majority or rejected by 76 per cent of the voting body. In the meantime, compromises would have to be made, either watering down the initial proposal so that a majority could accept it, or satisying other demands of the minority through the time-honored practice of log-rolling so that they would allow 76 per cent of the voting body to reject the original proposal.

For example, if at least a quarter of a Congressional committee supported a strong negative income tax, it is likely that the second vote would produce at least a weaker version of the tax that the majority could live with. Of course, such a system would work only if out-voted minority groups were able to elect representatives in the first place. (Also, it is always possible that legislators who favored a highly regressive income tax or segregationist policies would be able to obtain legislation for *their* minorities, but if an economic and racial bill of rights were added to the Constitution, such legislation would be thrown out by the courts.)

Outvoted minorities can also achieve greater political power by the altera-tion of existing political boundaries and powers so that they could even become majorities in their own bailiwicks. Current proposals for decentralization and community control are boundary-altering schemes with just this political conse-quence, and some of the disadvantages of these schemes today could be allevi-ated by my previous proposal for progressive methods of government funding to provide more money to poorer communities.

But the concept of redrawing boundaries ought to be applied more broadly, for many existing political subdivisions are anachronistic. For example, it is difficult to justify the existence of many of the states as political units today, and it might be useful to think about creating smaller and more homogeneous units in highly urbanized parts of the country, perhaps of county size, particularly in order to reduce the number of outvoted minorities. (Norman Mailer has suggested just that in proposing statehood for New York City.)

Along the same line, the old idea of replacing geographical political units by groupings along economic and other interests deserves reexamination. For instance, the welfare recipient's lot would probably be improved if he or she became part of a regional governmental body of welfare recipients which could determine how the welfare system ought to be run.

Sometimes, outvoted minorities are tyrannized because their demands are diametrically opposed to the majority's. When this happens within a school or other institution, the minority should have the right to secede, establishing its own institution without being financially punished by the majority. If some parents want a Summerhill education for their children, they should be given tax money to start their own school, just as determined black nationalists should be free to build their own community if and when public aid for new towns becomes available. In a pluralistic nation, all impulses for diversity that do not clearly harm the rest of society should be encouraged.

Finally, changes in the rules of the political system must be supplemented by changes in the economic system, for ultimately it is the major obstacle to improving the lot of many outvoted minorities—and even of the unorganized majority. Some of my earlier proposals are equally applicable here.

The one-man, one-vote principle might be extended to stockholders who elect corporate boards of directors; a Cabinet department to represent consumers and other corporate customers should be set up; feedback from stockholders and customers to the corporate "legislature" should be improved, and they, as well as workers, should sit on corporate boards. In an era when many firms are subsidized by government contracts and tax credits, it is certainly possible to argue that at least such firms should become more democratic.

Most of the proposals for a pluralistic democracy are purposely intended to enhance the power of poor and black minorities; for, as I noted earlier, this seems to me the only way of solving the problems of the cities. But such a democracy is needed by all minorities who stand in danger of being outvoted by a majority, whatever their income or color. As the current demands of more people for greater equality and more control over their lives accelerate and the role of government in society continues to mount at the same time, the need for more political pluralism will become increasingly urgent. What we so inaccurately describe as the urban crisis is in reality the beginning of a national political crisis. But it is also an opportunity for Americans to develop new ways of living together.

WHAT CAN EUROPE TEACH US ABOUT URBAN GROWTH?

John Garvey, Jr.

A wealth of urban knowledge in Western Europe is waiting to be shared.

Urban techniques from abroad can be translated, imported, and adapted right here by any American whose mind is not self-confidently closed in the mistaken belief that our country knows all there is to know about urban policy setting and problem solving.

There's a tendency by some to discount European urban experience because of a belief that the problems of the American city have no equal. Discrimination, affluence, race, status, poverty, the impact of the private car, leisure time, urban decay, regionalization, congestion—these are not confined to our country.

There are lessons to be learned in Europe. There's fresh thinking there, too, on urban problems, such as: cities as regional relay centers; abandonment of the sales tax in favor of the value added tax; the determined rebuilding of dying cities; a central city builds a new town, a non-contiguous portion of itself within its own suburban area; a country links redevelopment to expansion; supramunicipalities; a municipal home advisory service located in shopping centers; the reconciliation of the cost of public facilities to built-up areas; building "suburbs" within city limits; the concept of the dominant and the subservient community; experiments with old-fashioned, mixed land uses in newly built areas; an areawide medical data system; the separation of administrative boundaries from political boundaries; the concept of declared growth patterns; a downtown masters the automobile by narrowing, not widening, its-streets; administrative concepts keyed to the scale and pace of urbanization; and the community trust.

Relationships not yet recognizable in this country—such as the importance of urban efficiency to the national product—are met with effective measures abroad. Other new techniques can be found in such fields as: the role of industry in reaching the goals of a quality environment; the extended city-region single system concept; fringe plans for peripheral growth; the search for a new urban form; relationships of transit to predetermined density; and justifying urban growth investments by a relationship and a coordination rationale.

These are all examples of the ways by which the countries of Western Europe are shaking themselves loose from their 20th Century traditionalism. Their sights are now set on their population demands for the year 2000.

The following attempt at a summarization of new ideas and concepts does not do justice to the urban dynamics involved, to the hope and enthusiasm, to the priority importance of urbanization one finds in talking to European officials. Such a summarization reflects, but does not do justice to the most important ingredient of all: the thinking processes and the pioneering spirit of stimulated European officials.

REGIONAL POLICIES

In Western Europe, an American visitor cannot help but be impressed with a series of determined breakthroughs in developing new regional policies.

Holland is developing its eastern regions to minimize the flow of population into its present great cities and their environs. The less developed eastern regions are being promoted by accelerated public resource development and subsidies to industries.

France is redressing the imbalance created by the high concentration of the Paris metropolitan area by stimulating the growth of eight large provincial urban complexes by 1985. The concept of counter-magnets is being applied to these centers, each free from dependency upon Paris. Priorities will be given to equip each with "high level" facilities for culture, research, higher education, medical care, government, and communications. For each regional metropolis to be effective, it must have relay centers equipped to transmit their influence and that are connected to them by rapid means of communication.

England is pursuing the development of a regional plan for the entire southeast, involving major new cities, expansions of cities, and an enlargment of greenbelts. The concept is to prevent private capital from spreading endlessly to the countryside.

The Netherlands is considering another form of administration, the supra-municipal organization, for the city-region. Under this concept, policy for the city-region can be laid down while maintaining the essential function of the municipal councils. The municipal councils do not lack the strength to fulfill their individual tasks. The missing ingredient, coordinated action, would be supplied by the supra-municipal body.

Greater stress is placed upon the importance of a coordinated regional attack on the patterns and problems of urbanization by Western European countries than by the United States.

France has a National Commission for Integrated Development, a recognition that the national economy does not expand at the same rate everywhere. It is felt that planning for France must be highly interregional. Great stress is placed upon prospective environmental planning and the control of urbanization. Metropolitan areas are viewed twofold: in their urban renewal and their balanced sense.

Sweden is empowered to take the initiative in the formation of regional planning federations. It seeks to achieve desirable economic balance by regions, not by towns within a region. It has formulated the concept of the dominating and the subservient communities, between whom any perfect competition is out of the question.

The Copenhagen regional area is using as the basis of its development a private initiative "finger plan" prepared in 1947. Transit, housing, and other developments are allowed along the fingers with green space preserved between the fingers, permitting open country to push in towards the center of Copenhagen.

In France, consultative bodies advise regional prefects as to economic development and expansion plans.

NEW TOWNS

Our conception of new towns may be the types of fringe developments we have seen spring up in our suburbs, particularly since the end of World War II. These one-class neighborhoods with a thin layer of economic variation and no subsidized, low-cost housing are not new towns. New towns are communities of residence and employment, of culture and of recreation, in convenient relation to each other and to existing cities, and usually built with certain environmental objectives in mind.

England has been the pioneer country (since 1946) in new and expanding towns development. Some have the mistaken belief that much of the growth of British urban areas has been resolved by the building of new towns. This is far from a correct impression. Perhaps 5 per cent of the growth of population has gone into new and expanding towns so far.

Great Britain's new town program (24 designated since 1946) has been designed mainly to encourage the gradual dispersal of industry and population from congested cities. France's new towns program (eight urban complexes to be equipped as regional metropolises by 1985) was designed mainly to counterbalance the growth of the capital city.

Stockholm's most successful efforts have been in the development of five "sub-communities," or district centers, four within Stockholm's city limits. Dubbed locally as "sleeping towns," these independent suburbs, as they are also called are light on industry. Each features major shopping facilities, all connected by rapid transit. The fifth sub-community, Järva, is located in portions of five municipalities, one of which is Stockholm. A five-city coordinating committee has been founded for acquisition and planning. Järva may eventually become a town of its own.

In the Uusimaa Province of Finland, six national private organizations formed a Housing Foundation which has since assembled three new town sites (Tapiola, Espoo Bay, and Porkkala). Tapiola is now completed and winning international attention for its principles and achievements. The Foundation then proceeded to prepare a comprehensive developmental plan for the entire province to the year 2010, a private initiative plan. In addition to the three new towns, the plan envisions the expansion of four others.

Denmark's concept of new towns is "city sections" with decentralization as the principle objective. These sections are to be linked up with the existing metropolitan area in such a way that the region functions as an integrated whole, permitting easy access to the city center. This "city sections" plan is not similar to the satellite town principle for it is based upon a concept of a great traffic axis, along which are placed large centers with employment and supporting populations.

"Sub-centres" in Amsterdam are reserved for displacement of homes and industries, in keeping with a 15-year decentralization plan (in lobe form) to accommodate overflow. The "city fringe plan," a master plan of future growth, is the basis of city extensions and sub-center developments.

REDIRECTION OF URBANIZATION

Urban sprawl can be controlled, reshaped, thinned out, and redirected. Needless urban spread is being resisted and its trends outwitted in Western European countries. The recipe is not an easy one, for solutions involve greater use of ingredients we are not used to using: preservation of nature by permanent public green space, public ownership of land, greater involvement of the national government in planning and in development decisions.

In the various Western European countries, the national concepts of urban development are largely based upon the same fundamental principles (avoiding excessively high concentrations; developing regional centers, new towns, etc.). The differences are in the methods of implementation. The central problem appears to be a search by each country for ways to control urbanization in an acceptable form.

France uses "priority urbanization zones," which can apply to sections or entire towns to guide the direction of development projects, a method of providing for the financing of public facilities and amenities for the inhabitants. Sweden does not give its landowners an unconditional right to open their properties to dense development. Such requests for development must be found to be in the public interest.

Amsterdam gives recognition to the larger scale on which administrative authorities must think and decide. This has consequences for the administrative organization.

The concept of urban hubs in France is established as a settlement principle in underdeveloped or renovated areas. These hubs, which are to serve populations of 300,000 to 1,000,000 each with a complete range of urban components, are to be located on two major growth axes.

Copenhagen's city center is hoping to retain its existing compact and close-knit character by the carefully planned placement of "city-sections" in the outer reaches of its regional finger plan. The functions and enterprises for which central location is not absolutely essential will be removed.

The design of Stockholm's "subcommunities" has followed traditional concentration of special functions, such as residential areas, industrial areas, commercial, etc. Many people are protesting vigorously, believing such layouts to be dull and unimaginative—even if parks and footpaths connect various sections. They want to go back to the densely built-up, old-fashioned type of town with streets surrounded by shops, entertainment, small industries, etc. Such mixed uses seem more lively and have more diversity, they say.

Amsterdam's regional problem is the need to guide and control the use of space. Without this, there will be a vast area of continuous urban development in which the balance between built-up and unbuilt-up areas will be destroyed.

Denmark's regulation of built-up areas establishes three zones (inner, intermediate, and outer). Lands in the latter can be held a number of years in agricultural use. This zone has also been called a waiting zone. In Denmark, the Ministry of Culture is responsible for the preservation of nature.

REFORMING LOCAL GOVERNMENT

Amsterdam is building its own new town (Bijlmermeer), a non-contiguous section to the south of the city's limits, added to Amsterdam by Parliament for the 12-year period of development.

It was felt that the metropolitan area of Helsinki, Finland, should be viewed as a uniform area within which administration should be organized so that activities of a lower character are managed by the communities in the area. The central administration should be responsible for comprehensive duties affecting the area as a whole.

France viewed its traditional, local administrative institutions as a bottleneck to effective regional economic planning and action, and, in 1960 grouped these into 21 districts. In 1961, Sweden outlined a central government proposal whereby 900 local governments would come together in large enough clusters to sustain a diversified economy. The units have been reformed into 282 voluntary linkages and Sweden is now considering setting a target date for compulsory merger of the 282 units.

The Royal Commission on Local Government in England is expected to make its recommendations on the structure of local government this year. The Association of Municipal Corporations, in an effort to break with the traditions of the past, has proposed to the commission that local authorities be empowered to form "community trusts," a flexible, non-structured mechanism, both advisory or policy setting, for local area opinion gathering and decision making, and serving as a focus for local needs and customs.

REVITALIZATION OF DYING MUNICIPALITIES

France attempts to encourage industrial locations near medium-sized towns to maintain a certain degree of job stability in the region.

In Amsterdam, areas suffering from loss of industry, serious unemployment, etc., are rebuilt and expanded.

France is studying ways by which industrial dispersion, together with rural planning, can help small towns and rural centers.

PUBLIC FACILITIES AND SERVICES

In Stockholm, five new sub-community developments followed rapid transit lines, rather than the reverse. The object was to first create the density that can support rapid transit, and then string the communities on a radial plan along the transit line.

Stockholm locates branches of its home advisory service program in major shopping centers.

Increasing provision for malls has been made in Swedish cities. A growing consensus shares the view the automobile does not fit into the innermost portions of the city. Measures have been taken to narrow some streets and convert them to malls.

URBAN RENEWAL

France permits "Deferred Planning Zones" to facilitate the implementation of urban renewal projects. A community can take 12-year options on the land it needs for its development projects. In Sweden, such long-range acquisitions may also be designated. Cities can acquire these gradually and may even fix them up for interim occupancy.

Sweden is determined to preserve her urban cores as regional centers, realizing the need for drastic surgery if these cores are to continue to function as administrative, commercial and cultural centers.

Though urban renewal in Amsterdam costs roughly 10 times as much as urban expansion, the city is determined to give a great deal of attention to the renewal of those quarters which are out of date. Amsterdam draws a close relationship to its renewal and its expansion programs.

INDUSTRIAL DISPERSAL

The role of industry, in most Western European countries, is viewed as a helpful instrument in reaching the basic goals of the environment. Special concessions are made, encourging industrial locations that aid inadequately developed regions.

HOUSING

We have not yet established the kinds of housing institutions found in Western Europe which are able to plan long-range programs or assume responsibility for continuing development. The many small builders in the U.S. are in no position to conduct meaningful research which only contributes to rising housing costs and shortages of low-income housing. We must revolutionize our housing production.

The Scandinavian countries have outdone us, particularly in advances in the housing industry. In Sweden, two large public co-ops build 25 per cent of the housing volume. There, construction workers can count on sustained employment and the trades union itself encourages mechanization.

MUNICIPAL LAND POLICY

Urban land is an extremely valuable resource which we are too careless with. Our philosophies favor a system whereby ownership can be shortlived and speculative and with it, the best interests of the community and the best economic social values. The concept of optimum development of land is in widespread use in Western Europe where land is regulated like a public utility.

In Sweden, Stockholm has been purchasing land for over 60 years and now owns one-third of the original, central city and 85 per cent of all the rest as well as much land outside. Because of this ownership, Stockholm has been able to lead building development along rational lines. When municipal properties are developed by private enterprise, the land is leased and not sold.

Municipalities are the largest owners of land in the Netherlands for housing and related purposes, and they buy land long before they develop it. If the acquisition is in accordance with the extension plan, compensation is based on overall value after development. This has kept the price of land for city extensions low.

Land ownership in Denmark is primarily private though a few municipalities are considerable land owners. An annual land increment tax is levied on the increase of land values. This has not reduced the selling price of land. Since conditions of a seller's market exist, purchasers pay both the full price of land plus the land increment tax. This tax is now being reconsidered since it has been severely criticized.

In France, much of the land is privately owned though in urban areas, the proportion in public ownership is tending to increase. Sweden taxes the profits from property resold within 10 years of its purchase. This tax does not appear to result in a reduction of land prices.

Some local authorities in Great Britain own considerable acres of urban land. A characteristic of land tenure is the use of the leasehold system whereby the free holder grants a substantial interest in land to a leaseholder. This technique is particularly good in redevelopment since local authorities can combine the powers of landlord with those of a planning authority, enabling them to share in financial success, while at the same time attracting private investment.

FISCAL POLICIES

Indirect taxation on the value-added principle has been gaining ground in recent years. In January, Sweden adopted the value-added tax to replace the sales tax. Practically all Swedish consumption of goods and services will be taxed under the new system, compared to two-thirds of consumption under the sales tax. Principally designed to aid Swedish exports, the tax applies to the value added at each phase of production and distribution (the sales tax was levied only at the sale to the final consumer). This value-added tax, also under consideration in Britain and Norway, has been in effect in Denmark.

In the face of ever increasing land prices, Great Britain created a Land Commission to buy and sell land for development to local authorities and other public developers as well as private developers. In addition, the commission was given the responsibility to collect a betterment levy, amounting to 40 per cent of the development value, as imposed on the seller of land. The concept behind the levy is that when the value of, or interest in, a piece of land increases as a result of decisions made by the community (such as the installation of essential services, the granting of planning permissions, etc.), the community is entitled to take at least a share of that development when realized.

To a greater extent than in our country, the local governments of Western Europe depend upon shared revenues from their central governments. This is an increasingly important potential for our state governments for it removes from local governments an over-dependence upon inadequate taxing sources. For example, Amsterdam's tax base is not affected should one of its major industries move outside of its limits. Jobs are not a part of the tax base. This minimizes tendencies of local governments at fiscal zoning and permits locations of industries, jobs, and people based upon economic and social considerations and not fiscal considerations.

What are the major options in public policy available in the coming 20 to 30 years? What do we want to achieve? Where are we headed? Can we control the major trends that shape our future? The countries of Western Europe are giving these questions about their future deep thought. By remaining flexible, they are keeping their options open. They are trying to stay on top of the pace and scale of urbanization.

Ever hear of an organization known as "Group 85?" It's not a choral group, but a high level advisory body in France which has selected 1985 as the significant year in that country's urban, industrial, and agriculture future. The French Man of Tomorrow—his individual, group, and consumption needs—is being calculated closely. The findings are largely dictating guidelines for environmental planning.

How does a country make the best use of its affluence? Sweden is taking a comprehensive look at this question and the effect of its standard of living on its environment. Its visionary officials are also considering the three-dimensional city, attempting to capture the potential of the state of building technology.

In Great Britain, local authorities are required to prepare 20-year development plans, to be reviewed at least once every five years. Local communes prepare five-year flexible plans in Sweden. As far back as 1935, Amsterdam took a comprehensive look at future policies on the use of land, with population and other projections to 2000. Called the General Extension Plan, its projections have since been revised.

The planning policy of the Netherlands "is in keeping with the position the year 2000 already occupies in the minds of people in different walks of life." Though it is difficult to form a reliable picture of the changes about to occur in the present system of values and standards, such uncertainties do not relieve a person of the duty to look ahead, according to Netherlands policy.

Paris maps out guidelines to 2000 within which it sets specific goals to be reached in 10-year increments. It is accompanied by an investment plan under which work is started on infrastructure—highways, parking, rail, water, colleges —in order to lay the groundwork for guiding urban development toward the longer-term targets.

Denmark has 36 town development boards, each made up of a number of municipalities. Each must prepare a general pattern of development for 15 years. Such permits growth by stages, reconciling costs of needed public facilities.

CONCLUSION

The observations in this article are taken from a 17-day travel and study visit last fall to six Western European countries: Denmark, Finland, France, Great Britain, The Netherlands and Sweden. The visit, under the auspices of the Commission on Urban Growth, concentrated on new town inspections. This summarization is based on those observations plus information obtained from as many meetings on the side as the travel schedule would permit with national municipal association representatives, municipal and national officials, professional local government and new town corporation officers, labor, business and academic officials, etc.

At best, this summary reflects the benefits of a windshield survey. But, more importantly, what it represents is the wealth of urban experience lying near the surface, easily explorable, time permitting. Officials in every country visited were most friendly, cooperative, and eager to engage in honest give-and-take discussions on the philosophy and the practice of urbanization—mistakes as well as successes. Any discerning American urban generalist could mine the applicable gems of this vast body of urban knowledge in Western Europe.

All that need be given is a willingness to do the same and to share our experiences.

TOWARD A NATIONAL URBAN POLICY

Daniel P. Moynihan

In the spring of 1969, President Nixon met in the Cabinet room with ten mayors of American cities. They were nothing if not a variegated lot, mixing party, religion, race, region in the fine confusion of American politics. They had been chosen to be representative in this respect, and were unrepresentative only in qualities of energy and intelligence that would have set them apart in any company. What was more notable about them, however, was that in the interval between the invitation from the White House and the meeting with the President, four had announced they would not run again. The mayor of Detroit who, at the last minute, could not attend, announced *his* noncandidacy in June.

Their decisions were not a complete surprise. More and more, for the men charged with governance of our cities, politics has become the art of the impossible. It is not to be wondered that they flee. But we, in a sense, are left behind. And are in trouble.

At a time of great anxiety—a time that one of the nation's leading news magazines now routinely describes as "the most serious domestic crisis since the Civil War," a time when Richard Rovere, writing of the 1972 elections, can add parenthetically, "assuming that democracy in America survives that long"—these personal decisions may seem of small consequence; yet one suspects they are not.

Daniel P. Moynihan, **TOWARD A NATIONAL URBAN POLICY,** *Chapter 1 (New York: Basic Books, Inc., Publishers,* © *1970). Reprinted by permission of the author and the publisher.*

All agree that the tumult of the time arises, in essence, from a crisis of authority. The institutions that shaped conduct and behavior in the past are being challenged or, worse, ignored. It is in the nature of authority, as Robert A. Nisbet continues to remind us, that it is consensual, that it is not coercive. When authority systems collapse, they are replaced by power systems that *are* coercive.[1] Our vocabulary rather fails us here: the term "authority" is an unloved one, with its connotations of "authoritarianism," but there appears to be no substitute. Happily, public opinion is not so dependent on political vocabulary, certainly not on the vocabulary of political science, as some assume. For all the ambiguity of the public rhetoric of the moment, the desire of the great mass of our people is clear. They sense the advent of a power-based society and they fear it. They seek peace. They look to the restoration of legitimacy, if not in existing institutions, then in new or modified ones. They look for a lessening of violent confrontations at home, and, in great numbers, for an end to war abroad. Concern for personal safety on the part of city dwellers has become a live *political* fact, while the reappearance—what, praise God, did we do to bring this upon ourselves? —of a Stalinoid rhetoric of apocalyptic abuse on the left, and its echoes on the right, have created a public atmosphere of anxiety and portent that would seem to have touched us all. It is with every good reason that the nation gropes for some means to weather the storm of unreason that has broken upon us.

It would also seem that Americans at this moment are much preoccupied with the issue of freedom—or, rather, with new, meaningful ways in which freedom is seen to be expanded or constrained. We are, for example, beginning to evolve some sense of the meaning of group freedom. This comes after a century of preoccupation with individual rights of a kind which were seen as somehow opposed to, and even threatened by, group identities and anything so dubious in conception as *group* rights.

The Civil Rights Act of 1964 was the culmination of the political energies generated by that earlier period. The provisions which forbade employers, universities, governments, or whatever to have any knowledge of the race, religion, or national origin of individuals with which they dealt marked in some ways the high-water mark of Social Darwinism in America; its assumption that "equality" meant *only* equal opportunity did not long stand unopposed. Indeed, by 1965 the federal government had already, as best one can tell, begun to require ethnic and racial census of its own employees, and also of federal contractors and research grant recipients. To do so violated the spirit if not the letter of the Civil Rights Act, with its implicit model of the lone individual locked in equal—and remorseless—competition in the market place, but very much in harmony with the emerging sense of the 1960's that groups have identities and entitlements as well as do individuals. This view is diffusing rapidly. In Massachusetts, for example, legislation of the Civil Rights Act period, which declared any public school with more than 50 per cent black pupils to be racially "imbalanced" and in consequence illegal, is already being challenged—by precisely those who supported it in the first instance. In so far as these demands

---

[1] "The Twilight of Authority," *The Public Interest,* no. 15, Spring 1969.

have been most in evidence among black Americans, there is not the least reason to doubt that they will now diffuse to other groups, defined in various ways, and that new institutions will arise to respond to this new understanding of the nature of community.

In sum, two tendencies would appear to dominate the period. The *sense of general community is eroding,* and with it the authority of existing relationships; simultaneously, a powerful *quest for specific community is emerging* in the form of ever more intensive assertions of racial and ethnic identities. Although this is reported in the media largely in terms of black nationalism, it is just as reasonable to identify emergent attitudes in the "white working class," as part of the same phenomenon. The singular quality of these two tendencies is that they are at once complementary and opposed. While the ideas are harmonious, the practices that would seem to support one interest are typically seen as opposing the other. Thus, one need not be a moral philosopher or a social phychologist to see that much of the "crisis of the cities" arises from the interaction of these intense new demands, and the relative inability of the urban social system to respond to them.

PROGRAMS DO NOT A POLICY MAKE

Rightly or otherwise—and one is no longer sure of this—it is our tradition in such circumstances to look to government. Social responses to changed social requirements take the form, in industrial democracies, of changed government policies. This had led, in the present situation, to a reasonably inventive spate of program proposals of the kind the New Deal more or less began and which flourished most notably in the period between the presidential elections of 1960 and 1968, when the number of domestic programs of the federal government increased from 45 to 435. Understandably, however, there has been a diminution of the confidence with which such proposals were formerly regarded. To say the least, there has been a certain nonlinearity in the relationship between the number of categorical aid programs issuing forth from Washington and the degree of social satsifaction that has ensued.

Hence the issue arises as to whether the demands of the time are not to be met in terms of *policy,* as well as program. It has been said of urban planners that they have been traumatized by the realization that everything relates to everything. But this is so, and need paralyze no one; the perception of this truth can provide a powerful analytic tool.

Our problems in the area of social peace and individual or group freedom occur in urban settings. Can it be that our difficulties in coping with these problems originate, in some measure, from the inadequacies of the setting in which they arise? Crime on the streets and campus violence may mark the onset of a native nihilism: but in the first instance they represent nothing more complex than the failure of law enforcement. Black rage and white resistance. "Third World" separatism, and restricted neighborhoods all may define a collapse in the integuments of the social contract: but, again, in the first instance they represent for the most part simply the failure of urban arrangements to meet the expectations of the urban population in the areas of jobs, schools, housing, transportation, public health, administrative responsiveness, and political flexibility. If all these are related, one to the other, and if in combination they do not seem to be working well, the question arises whether the society ought not to attempt a more coherent response. In a word: ought not a national urban crisis to be met with something like a national urban policy? Ought not the vast efforts to control the situation of the present be at least informed by some sense of goals for the future?

The United States does not now have an urban policy. The idea that there might be such is new. So also is the Urban Affairs Council, established by President Nixon on January 23, 1969, as the first official act of his administration, to "advise and assist" with respect to urban affairs, specifically "in the development of a national urban policy, having regard both to immediate and to long-range concerns, and to priorities among them."

WHAT HAPPENED

The central circumstance, as stated, is that America is an urban nation, and has been for half a century.

This is not to say Americans live in *big* cities. They do not. In 1960 only 9.8 per cent of the population lived in cities of 1 million or more. Ninety-eight per cent of the units of local government have fewer than 50,000 persons. In terms of the 1960 census, only somewhat more than a quarter of congressmen represented districts in which a majority of residents lived in central city areas. The 1970 census will show that the majority of Americans in metropolitan areas in fact live in suburbs, while a great many more live in urban settlements of quite modest size. But they are not the less urban for that reason, providing conditions of living and problems of government profoundly different from that of the agricultural, small town past.

The essentials of the present "urban crisis" are simple enough to relate. Until about World War II, the growth of the city, as Otto Eckstein argues, was "a logical, economic development." At least it was such in the northeastern quadrant of the United States, where most urban troubles are supposed to exist. The political jurisdiction of the city more or less defined the area of intensive economic development, that in turn more or less defined the area of intensive settlement. Thereafter, however, economic incentives and social desires combined to produce a fractionating process that made it ever more difficult to collect enough power in any one place to provide the rudiments of effective government. As a result of or as a part of this process, the central area ceased to grow and began to decline. The core began to rot.

Two special circumstances compounded this problem. First, the extraordinary migration of the rural southern Negro to the northern city. Second, a postwar population explosion (90 million babies were born between 1946 and 1968) that placed immense pressures on municipal services, and drove many whites to the suburbs seeking relief. (Both these influences are now somewhat attenuating, but their effects will be present for at least several decades, and indeed a new baby boom may be in the offing.) As a result, the problems of economic stagnation of the central city became desperately exacerbated by those of racial tension. In the course of the 1960's tension turned into open racial strife.

City governments began to respond to the onset of economic obsolescence and social rigidity a generation or more ago, but quickly found their fiscal resources strained near to the limit. State governments became involved, and much the same process ensued. Starting in the postwar period, the federal government itself became increasingly caught up with urban problems. In recent years resources on a fairly considerable scale have flowed from Washington to the cities of the land, and will clearly continue to do so. However, in the evolution of a national urban policy, more is involved than merely the question of programs and their funding. Too many programs have produced too few results simply to accept a more or less straightforward extrapolation of past and present practices into an oversized but familiar future. *The question of method has become as salient as that of goals themselves.*

As yet, the federal government, no more than state or local government, has not found an effective *incentive* system—comparable to profit in private enterprise, p.;estige in intellectual activity, rank in military organization— whereby to shape the forces at work in urban areas in such a way that urban goals, whatever they may be, are in fact attained. This search for incentives, and the realization that present procedures such as categorical grant-in-aid programs do not seem to provide sufficiently powerful ones, must accompany and suffuse the effort to establish goals as such. We must seek, not just policy, but policy allied to a vigorous strategy for obtaining results from it.

Finally, the federal establishment must develop a much heightened sensitivity to its "hidden" urban policies. There is hardly a department or agency of the national government whose programs do not in some way have important consequences for the life of cities, and those who live in them. Frequently—one is tempted to say normally! —the political appointees and career executives concerned do *not* see themselves as involved with, much less responsible for the urban consequences of their programs and policies. They are, to their minds, simply building highways, guaranteeing mortgages, advancing agriculture, or whatever. No one has made clear to them that they are simultaneously re- distributing employment opportunities, segregating or desegregating neighbor- hoods, depopulating the countryside and filling up the slums, etc.: all these things as second and third order consequences of nominally unrelated programs. Already this institutional naivete has become cause for suspicion; in the future it simply must not be tolerated. Indeed, in the future, a primary mark of com- petence in a federal official should be the ability to see the interconnections between programs immediately at hand and the urban problems that pervade the larger society.

THE FUNDAMENTS OF URBAN POLICY

It having been long established that, with respect to general codes of behavior, eleven precepts are too many and nine too few, ten points of urban policy may be set forth, scaled roughly to correspond to a combined measure of urgency and importance.

1. The poverty and social isolation of minority groups in central cities is the single most serious problem of the American city today. It must be attacked with urgency, with a greater commitment of resources than has heretofore been the case, and with programs designed especially for this purpose.

The 1960's have seen enormous economic advances among minority groups, especially Negroes. Outside the south, 37 per cent of Negro families earn $8,000 per year or more, that being approximately the national median income. In cities in the largest metropolitan areas, 20 percent of Negro families in 1967 reported family incomes of $10,000 or over. The earnings of *young* married black couples are approaching parity with whites.

Nonetheless, certain forms of social disorganization and dependency appear to be increasing among the urban poor. Recently, Conrad Taeuber, Associate Director of the Bureau of the Census, reported that in the largest metropolitan areas—those with 1 million or more inhabitants—"the number of black families with a woman as head increased by 83 per cent since 1960; the number of black families with a man as head increased by only 15 per cent during the same period." Disorganization, isolation, and discrimination seemingly have led to violence, and this violence has in turn been increasingly politicized by those seeking a "confrontation" with "white" society.

Urban policy must have as its first goal the transformation of the urban lower class into a stable community based on dependable and adequate income flows, social equality, and social mobility. Efforts to improve the conditions of life in the present caste-created slums must never take precedence over efforts to enable the slum population to disperse thoughout the metropolitan areas involved. Urban policy accepts the reality of ethnic neighborhoods based on free choice, but asserts that the active intervention of government is called for to enable free choice to include integrated living as a normal option.

It is impossible to comprehend the situation of the black urban poor without first seeing that they have experienced not merely a major migration in the past generation, but also that they now live in a state almost of demographic seige as a result of population growth. What demographers call the "dependency ratio"—the number of children per thousand adult males—for blacks is nearly twice that for whites, and the gap widened sharply in the 1960's.

It is this factor, surely, that accounts for much of the present distress of the black urban slums. At the same time, it is fairly clear that the sharp escalation in the number of births that characterized the past twenty-five years has more or less come to an end. The number of Negro females under age five is now exactly the number aged five to nine. Thus the 1980's will see a slackening of the present severe demands on the earning power of adult Negroes, and also on the public institutions that provide services for children. But for the decade immediately ahead, those demands will continue to rise—especially for central city blacks, whose median age is a bit more than ten years below that for whites—and will claarly have a priority claim on public resources.

TABLE 1. CHILDREN PER 1000 ADULT MALES

	1960	1966
White	1,365	1,406
Negro	1,922	2,216

2. *Economic and social forces in urban areas are not self-balancing. Imbalances in industry, transportation, housing, social services, and similar elements of urban life frequently tend to become more rather than less pronounced, and this tendency is often abetted by public policies. A concept of urban balance may be tentatively set forth: a social condition in which forces tending to produce imbalance induce counterforces that simultaneously admit change while maintaining equilibrium. It must be the constant object to federal officials whose programs affect urban areas—and there are few whose do not—to seek such equilibrium.*

The evidence is considerable that many federal programs have induced sharp imbalances in the "ecology" of urban areas—the highway program, for example, is frequently charged with this, and there is wide agreement that other, specifically city-oriented programs such as urban renewal have frequently accomplished just the opposite of their nominal objectives. The reasons are increasingly evident. Cities are complex social systems. Interventions that, intentionally or not, affect one component of the system almost invariably affect second, third, and fourth components as well, and these in turn affect the first component, often in ways quite opposite to the direction of the initial intervention. Most federal urban programs have assumed fairly simple cause and effect relationships that do not exist in the complex real world. Moreover, they have typically been based on "common sense" rather than research in an area where common sense can be notoriously misleading. In the words of Jay W. Forrester, "With a high degree of confidence we can say that the intuitive solution to the problems of complex social systems will be wrong most of the time."

This doubtless is true, but it need not be a traumatizing truth. As Lee Rainwater argues, the logic of multivariate analysis, and experience with it, suggest that some components of a complex system are always vastly more important than others, so that when (if) these are accurately identified a process of analysis that begins with the assertion of chaos can in fact end by producing quite concise and purposeful social strategies.

3. *At least part of the relative ineffectiveness of the efforts of urban government to respond to urban problems derives from the fragmented and obsolescent structure of urban government itself. The federal government should constantly encourage and provide incentives for the reorganization of local government in response to the reality of metropolitan conditions. The objective of the federal government should be that local government be stronger and more effective, more visible, accessible, and meaningful to local inhabitants. To this end the federal government should discourage the creation of paragovernments designed to deal with special problems by evading or avoiding the jurisdiction of established local authorities, and should encourage effective decentralization.*

Although the "quality" of local government, especially in large cities, has been seen to improve of late, there appears to have been a decline in the vitality of local political systems, and an almost total disappearance of serious effort to reorganize metropolitan areas into new and more rational governmental jurisdictions. Federal efforts to recreate the ethnic-neighborhood-based community organization, as in the poverty program, or to induce metropolitan area planning as in various urban development programs, have had a measure of success, but nothing like that hoped for. Meanwhile the middle class norm of "participation" has diffused downward and outward, so that federal urban programs now routinely require citizen participation in the planning process and beyond; yet somehow this does not seem to have led to more competent communities. In some instances it appears rather to have escalated the level of stalemate.

It may be we have not been entirely candid with ourselves in this area. Citizen participation, as Elliott A. Krause has pointed out, is in practice a "bureaucratic ideology," a device whereby public officials induce nonpublic individuals to act in a way the officials desire. Although the putative object may be, indeed almost always is, to improve the lot of the citizen, it is not settled that the actual consequences are anything like that. The ways of the officials, of course, are often not those of the elected representatives of the people, and the "citizens" may become a rope in the tug-of-war between bureaucrat and representative. Especially in a federal system, "citizen participation" easily becomes a device whereby the far-off federal bureaucracy acquires a weapon with which to battle the elected officials of local government. Whatever the nominal intent, the normal outcome is federal support for those who would diminish the legitimacy of local government. But it is not clear that the federal purposes are typically advanced through this process. To the contrary, an all round diminishment rather than enhancement of energies seems to occur.

This would appear especially true when "citizen participation" has in effect meant putting indignant citizens on the payroll. However much these citizens may continue to "protest," the action acquires a certain hollow ring. Something like this has already happened to groups that have been openly or covertly supported by the federal government, seeking to influence public opinion on matters of public policy. This stratagem is a new practice in American democracy. It began in the field of foreign affairs, and has now spread to the domestic area. To a quite astonishing degree it will be found that those groups that nominally are pressing for social change and development in the poverty field, for example, are in fact subsidized by federal funds. This occurs in protean ways—research grants, training contracts, or whatever—and is done with the best of intentions. But, again, with what results is far from clear. Can this development, for example, account for the curious fact that there seems to be so much protest in the streets of the nation, but so little, as it were, in its legislatures? Is it the case, in other words, that the process of public subsidy is subtly debilitating?

Whatever the truth of this judgment, it is nevertheless clear that a national urban policy must look first to the vitality of the elected governments of the urban areas, and must seek to increase their capacity for independent, effective, and creative action. This suggests an effort to find some way out of the present fragmentation, and a certain restraint on the creation of federally-financed "competitive governments."

Nathan Glazer has made the useful observation that in London and Tokyo comprehensive metropolitan government is combined with a complex system of "subgovernments"—the London Boroughs—representing units of 200,000-250,000 persons. These are "real" governments, with important powers in areas such as education, welfare, and housing. In England, at all events, they are governed through an electoral system involving the national political parties in essentially their national postures. (Indeed, the boroughs make up the basic units of the parties' urban structure.) It may well be there is need for social inventions of this kind in the great American cities, especially with respect to power over matters such as welfare, education, and housing that are now subject to intense debates concerning "local control." The demand for "local control" is altogether to be welcomed. In some degree it can be seen to arise from the bureaucratic barbarities of the highway programs of the 1950's, for example. But in the largest degree it reflects the processes of democracy catching up with the content of contemporary government. As government more and more involves itself in matters that very much touch on the lives of individual citizens, those individuals seek a greater voice in the programs concerned. In the hands of ideologues or dimwits, this demand can lead to an utter paralysis of government. It has already done so in dozens of urban development situations. But approached with a measure of sensitivity—and patience—it can lead to a considerable revitalization of urban government.

4. A primary object of federal urban policy must be to restore the fiscal vitality of urban government, with the particular object of ensuring that local governments normally have enough resources on hand or available to make local initiative in public affairs a reality.

For all the rise in actual amounts, federal aid to state and local government has increased only from 12 per cent of state-local revenue in 1958 to 17 percent in 1967. Increasingly, state and local governments that try to meet their responsibilities lurch from one fiscal crisis to another. In such circumstances, the capacity for creative local government becomes least in precisely those jurisdictions where it might most be expected. As much as any other single factor, this condition may be judged to account for the malaise of city government, and especially for the reluctance of the more self-sufficient suburbs to associate themselves with the nearly bankrupt central cities. Surviving from one fiscal deadline to another, the central cities commonly adopt policies which only compound their ultimate difficulties. Yet their options are so few. As James Q. Wilson writes, "The great bulk of any city's budget is, in effect, a fixed charge the mayor is powerless to alter more than trivially." The basic equation, as it were, of American political economy is that for each one per cent increase in the Gross National Product the income of the federal government increases one and one-half per cent while the normal income of city governments rises half to three-quarters of a point at most. Hence both a clear opportunity and a no less manifest necessity exist for the federal government to adopt as a deliberate policy an increase in its aid to urban governments. This should be done in part through revenue sharing, in part through an increase in categorical assistance, hopefully in much more consolidated forms than now exist, and through credit assistance.

It may not be expected that this process will occur rapidly. The prospects for an enormous "peace and growth dividend" to follow the cessation of hostilities in Vietnam are far less bright than they were painted. But the fact is that as a nation we grow steadily richer, not poorer, and we can afford the government we need. This means, among our very first priorities, an increase in the resources available to city governments.

A clear opportunity exists for the federal government to adopt as a deliberate policy an increase in its aid to state and local governments in the aftermath of the Vietnam war. Much analysis is in order, but in approximate terms it may be argued that the present proportion of aid should be about doubled, with the immediate objective that the federal government contribution constitute one-third of state and local revenue.

5. Federal urban policy should seek to equalize the provision of public services as among different jurisdictions in metropolitan areas.

Although the standard depiction of the (black) residents of central cities as grossly deprived with respect to schools and other social services, when compared with their suburban (white) neighbors, requires endless qualification, the essential truth is that life for the well-to-do is better than life for the poor, and that these populations tend to be separated by artificial government boundaries within metropolitan areas. (The people in between may live on either side of the boundaries, and are typically overlooked altogether.) At a minimum, federal policy should seek a dollar-for-dollar equivalence in the provision of social services having most to do with economic and social opportunity. This includes, at the top of the list, public education and public safety. (Obviously there will always be some relatively small jurisdictions—"the Scarsdale school system" —that spend a great deal more than others, being richer; but there can be national or regional norms and no central city should be allowed to operate below them.)

Beyond the provision of equal resources lies the troubled and elusive question of equal results. Should equality of educational opportunity extend to equality of educational achievement (as between one group of children and another)? Should equality of police protection extend to equality of risks of criminal victimization? That is to say, should there be not only as many police, but also as few crimes in one area of the city as in another? These are hardly simple questions, but as they are increasingly posed it is increasingly evident that we shall have to try to find answers.

The area of housing is one of special and immediate urgency. In America, housing is not regarded as a public utility (and a scarce one!) as it is in many of the industrial democracies of Europe, but there can hardly be any remaining doubt that the strong and regular production of housing is nearly a public necessity. We shall not solve the problem of racial isolation without it. Housing must not only be open, *it must be available.* The process of filtration out from dense center city slums can only take place if the housing perimeter, as it were, is sufficiently porous. For too long now the production of housing has been a function, not of the need for housing as such but rather of the need to increase or decrease the money supply, or whatever. Somehow a greater regularity of effective demand must be provided the housing industry, and its level of production must be increased.

6. The federal government must assert a specific interest in the movement of people, displaced by technology or driven by poverty, from rural to urban areas, and also in the movement from densely populated central cities to suburban areas.

Much of the present urban crisis derives from the almost total absence of any provision for an orderly movement of persons off the countryside and into the city. The federal government made extraordinary, and extraordinarily successful, efforts to provide for the resettlement of Hungarian refugees in the 1950's and Cuban refugees in the 1960's. But almost nothing has been done for Americans driven from their homes by forces no less imperious.

Rural to urban migration has not stopped, and will not for some time. Increasingly, it is possible to predict where it will occur, and in what time sequence. (In 1968, for example, testing of mechanical tobacco harvesting began on the east coast and the first mechanical grape pickers were used on the west coast.) Hence, it is possible to prepare for it, both by training those who leave, and providing for them where they arrive. Doubtless the United States will remain a nation of exceptionally mobile persons, but the completely unassisted processes of the past need not continue with respect to the migration of impoverished rural populations.

There are increasing indications that the dramatic movement of Negro Americans to central city areas may be slackening, and that a counter movement to surrounding suburban areas may have begun. This process is to be encouraged in every way, especially by the maintenance of a flexible and open housing market. But it remains the case that in the next thirty years we shall add 100 million persons to our population. Knowing that, it is impossible to have no policy with respect to where they will be located. *For to let nature take its course is a policy.* To consider what might be best for all concerned and to seek to provide it is surely a more acceptable goal.

7. State government has an indispensible role in the management of urban affairs, and must be supported and encouraged by the federal government in the performance of this role.

This fact, being all but self-evident, tends to be overlooked. Indeed, the trend of recent legislative measures almost invariably prompted by executive initiatives, has been to establish a direct federal-city relationship. States have been bypassed, and doubtless some have used this as an excuse to avoid their responsibilities of providing the legal and governmental conditions under which urban problems can be effectively confronted.

It has, of course, been a tradition of social reform in America that city government is bad and that, if anything, state government is worse. This is neither true as a generalization nor useful as a principle. But it is true that, by and large, state governments (with an occasional exception such as New York— have *not* involved themselves with urban problems, and are readily enough seen by mayors as the real enemy. But this helps neither. States *must* become involved. City governments, without exception, are creatures of state governments. City boundaries, jurisdictions, and powers are given and taken away by state governments. It is surely time the federal establishment sought to lend a sense of coherence and a measure of progressivism to this fundamental process.

The role of state government in urban affairs cannot easily be overlooked (though it may be deliberately ignored on political or ideological grounds). By contrast, it is relatively easy to overlook county government, and possibly an even more serious mistake to do so. In a steadily increasing number of metropolitan areas, it is the county rather than the original core city that has become the only unit of government which makes any geographical sense. That is to say, the only unit whose boundaries contain most or all of the actual urban settlement. The powers of county government have typically lagged well behind its potential, but it may also be noted that in the few—the very few—instances of urban reorganization to take place since World War II, county government has assumed a principal, even primary role in the new arrangement.

8. *The federal government must develop and put into practice far more effective incentive systems than now exist whereby state and local governments, and private interests too, can be led to achieve the goals of federal programs.*

The typical federal grant-in-aid program provides its recipients with an immediate reward for promising to work toward some specified goal—raising the education achievement of minority children, providing medical care for the poor, cleaning up the air, reviving the downtown business district. But there is almost no reward for actually achieving such goals—and rarely any punishment for failing to do so.

There is a growing consensus that the federal government should provide market competition for public programs, or devise ways to imitate market conditions. In particular, it is increasingly agreed that federal aid should be given directly to the consumers of the programs concerned—individuals included—thus enabling them to choose among competing suppliers of the goods or services that the program is designed to provide. Probably no single development would more enliven and energize the role of government in urban affairs than a move from the *monopoly service* strategy of the grant-in-aid programs to a *market* strategy of providing the most reward to those suppliers that survive competition.

In this precise sense, it is evident that federal programs designed to assit those city-dwelling groups that are least well off, least mobile, and least able to fend for themselves must in many areas move beyond a *services* strategy to an approach that provides inducements to move from a dependent and deficient status to one of independence and sufficiency. Essentially, this is an *income* strategy, based fundamentally on the provision of incentives to increase the earnings and to expand the property base of the poorest groups.

Urban policy should in general be directed to raising the level of political activity and concentrating it in the electoral process. It is nonetheless possible and useful to be alert for areas of intense but unproductive political conflict and to devise ways to avoid such conflict through market strategies. Thus conflicts over "control" of public education systems have frequently of late taken on the aspect of disputes over control of a monopoly service, a sole source of a needed good. Clearly some of the ferocity that ensues can be avoided through free choice arrangements that, in effect, eliminate monopoly control. If we move in this direction, difficult "minimum standard" regulation problems will almost certainly arise, and must be anticipated. No arrangement meets every need, and a good deal of change is primarily to be justified on grounds that certain systems need change for their own sake. (Small school districts, controlled by locally elected boards may be just the thing for New York City, However, in Phoenix, Arizona, where they have just that, consolidation and centralization would appear to be the desire of educational reformers.) But either way, a measure of market competition can surely improve the provision of public services, much as it has proved an efficient way to obtain various public paraphernalia, from bolt-action rifles to lunar landing vehicles.

Here as elsewhere, it is essential to pursue and to identify the *hidden* urban policies of government. These are nowhere more central to the issue than in the matter of incentives. Thus, for better than half a century now, city governments with the encouragement of state and federal authorities have been seeking to direct urban investment and development in accordance with principles embodied in zoning codes, and not infrequently in accord with precise city plans. However, during this same time the tax laws have provided the utmost incentive to pursue just the opposite objectives of those incorporated in the codes and the plans. It has, for example, been estimated that returns from land speculation based on zoning code changes on average incur half the tax load of returns from investment in physical improvements. Inevitably, energy and capital have diverted *away* from pursuing the plan and *toward* subverting it. It little avails for government to deplore the evasion of its purposes in such areas. Government has in fact established two sets of purposes, and provided vastly greater inducements to pursue the implicit rather than the avowed ones. Until public authorities, and the public itself, learn to be much more alert to these situations, and far more open in discussing and managing them, we must expect the present pattern of self-defeating contradictions to continue.

9. The federal government must provide more and better information concerning urban affairs, and should sponsor extensive and sustained research into urban problems.

Much of the social progress of recent years derives from the increasing quality and quantity of government-generated statistics and government-supported research. However, there is general agreement that the time is at hand when a general consolidation is in order, bringing a measure of symmetry to the now widely dispersed (and somewhat uneven) data-collecting and research-supporting activities. Such consolidation should not be limited to urban problems, but it must surely include attention to urban questions.

The federal government should, in particular, recognize that most of the issues that appear most critical just now do so in large measure because they are so little understood. This is perhaps especially so with respect to issues of minority group education, but generally applies to all the truly difficult and elusive issues of the moment. More and better inquiry is called for. In particular, the federal government must begin to sponsor longitudinal research—i.e., research designed to follow individual and communal development over long periods of time. It should also consider providing demographic and economic projections for political subdivisions as a routine service, much as the weather and the economy are forecast. Thus, Karl Taeuber has shown how seemingly unrelated policies of local governments can increase the degree of racial and economic differentiation between political jurisdictions, especially between cities and suburbs.

Similarly, the extraordinary inquiry into the educational system begun by the U.S. Office of Education under the direction of James S. Coleman should somehow be established on an on-going basis. It is now perfectly clear that little is known about the processes whereby publicly-provided resources affect educational outcomes. The great mass of those involved in education, and of that portion of the public that interests itself in educational matters, continue undisturbed in its old beliefs. But the bases of their beliefs are already thoroughly undermined and the whole structure is likely to collapse in a panic of disillusion and despair unless something like new knowledge is developed to replace the old. Here again, longitudinal inquiries are essential. And here also, it should be insisted that however little the new understandings may have diffused beyond the academic research centers in which they originated, the American public is accustomed to the idea that understandings do change and, especially in the field of education, is quite open to experimentation and innovation.

Much of the methodology of contemporary social science originated in clinical psychology, and perhaps for that reason tends to be "deficiency-oriented." Social scientists raise social *problems,* the study of which can become a social problem in its own right if it is never balanced by the identification and analysis of social *successes.* We are not an unsuccessful country. To the contrary, few societies work as hard at their problems, solve as many, and in the process stumble on more unexpected and fulsome opportunities. The cry of the decent householder who asks why the social science profession (and the news media which increasingly follow the profession) must be ever preoccupied with juvenile delinquency and never with juvenile decency deserves to be heard. Social science like medical science has been preoccupied with pathology, with pain. A measure of inquiry into the sources of health and pleasure is overdue, and is properly a subject of federal support.

10. The federal government, by its own example, and by incentives, should seek the development of a far heightened sense of the finite resources of the natural environment, and the fundamental importance of aesthetics in successful urban growth.

The process of "uglification" may first have developed in Europe; but, as with much else, the technological breakthroughs have taken place in the United States. American cities have grown to be as ugly as they are, not as a consequence of the failure of design, but rather because of the success of a certain interaction of economic, technological, and cultural forces. It is economically efficient to exploit the natural resources of land, and air, and water by technological means that the culture does not reject, albeit that the result is an increasingly despoiled, debilitated, and now even dangerous urban environment.

It is not clear how this is to change, and so the matter which the twenty-second century, say, will almost certainly see as having been the primary urban issue of the twentieth century is ranked last in the public priorities of the moment. But there *are* signs that the culture is changing, that the frontier sense of a natural environment of unlimited resources, all but impervious to human harm, is being replaced by an acute awareness that serious, possibly irreparable harm is being done to the environment, and that somehow the process must be reversed. This *could* lead to a new, nonexploitive technology, and thence to a new structure of economic incentives.

The federal establishment is showing signs that this cultural change is affecting its actions, and so do state and city governments. But the process needs to be raised to the level of a conscious pursuit of policy. The quality of the urban environment, a measure deriving from a humane and understanding use of the natural resources together with the creative use of design in architecture and in the distribution of activities and people, must become a proclaimed concern of government. And here the federal government can lead. It must seek out its hidden policies. (The design of public housing projects, for example, surely has had the consequence of manipulating the lives of those who inhabit them. By and large the federal government set the conditions that have determined the disastrous designs of the past two decades. It is thus responsible for the results, and should force itself to realize that.) And it must be acutely aware of the force of its own example. If scientists (as we are told) in the Manhattan Project were prepared to dismiss the problem of longlived radioactive wastes as one that could be solved merely by ocean dumping, there are few grounds for amazement that business executives in Detroit for so long manufactured automobiles that emitted poison gases into the atmosphere. Both patterns of decision evolved from the primacy of economic concerns in the context of the exploitation of the natural environment in ways the culture did not forbid. There are, however, increasing signs that we are beginning to change in this respect. We may before long evolve into a society in which the understanding of and concern about environmental pollution, and the general uglification of American life, will be both culturally vibrant and politically potent.

Social peace is a primary objective of social policy. To the extent that this derives from a shared sense of the aesthetic value and historical significance of the public places of the city, the federal government has a direct interest in encouraging such qualities.

Daniel J. Elazar has observed that while Americans have been willing to become urbanized, they have adamantly resisted becoming "citified." Yet a measure of "citification" is needed. There are perhaps half a dozen cities in America whose disappearance would, apart from the inconvenience, cause any real regret. To lose one of those six would plunge much of the nation and almost all the immediate inhabitants into genuine grief. Something of value in our lives would have been lost, and we would know it. The difference between these cities that would be missed and the rest that would not, resides fundamentally in the combination of architectural beauty, social amenity, and cultural vigor that sets them apart. It has ever been such. To create such a city and to preserve it was the great ideal of the Greek civilization, and it may yet become ours as we step back ever so cautiously from the worship of the nation-state with its barbarous modernity and impotent might. We might well consider the claims for a different life asserted in the oath of the Athenian city-state:

We will ever strive for the ideals and sacred things of the city,
both alone and with many;
We will unceasingly seek to quicken the sense of public duty;
We will revere and obey the city's laws;
We will transmit this city not only not less, but greater, better and
more beautiful than it was transmitted to us.

COMMISSION STATEMENT ON VIOLENT CRIME
Homicide, Assault, Rape, Robbery: Part IV

*The National Commission on the Causes
and Prevention of Violence*

THE PREVENTION OF VIOLENT CRIME

For the past three decades, the primary concerns of our nation have been (a) the national defense, mutual security, and world peace, (b) the growth of the economy, and (c) more recently, the conquest of space. These challenges have devoured more than two-thirds of all federal expenditures, approximately one-half of federal, state and local expenditures. We have staked out vast projects to promote the general domestic welfare and to overcome some of the problems we have here analyzed—but in view of dangerous inflationary trends and an already unprecedented level of federal, state and local taxation, we have not been able to obtain funds to support such projects in a volume and manner consistent with their lofty aims. The contemporary consequence of this pattern of resource allocation is an enormous deficit of unsatisfied needs and aspirations. Nowhere is this deficit more clearly apparent than in our crime-plagued metropolitan areas, where 65 percent of our people are now living.

In the absence of the massive action that seems to be needed to overcome this deficit, our cities are being mis-shaped in other ways by actions of more affluent citizens who desire safety for themselves, their families, and their investments. The safety they are getting is not the safety without fear that comes from ameliorating the causes of violent crime; rather it is the precarious safety obtained through individual efforts at self-defense. Thus the way in which we have so far chosen to deal with the deepening problem of violent crime begins to revise the future shape of our cities. In a few more years, lacking effective public action, this is how these cities will likely look:

> Central business districts in the heart of the city, surrounded by mixed areas of accelerating deterioration, will be partially protected by large numbers of people shopping or working in commercial buildings during daytime hours, plus a substantial police presence, and will be largely deserted except for police patrols during night-time hours.
>
> High-rise apartment buildings and residential compounds protected by private guards and security devices will be fortified cells for upper-middle and high-income populations living at prime locations in the city.

The National Commission on The Causes and Prevention of Violence, **COMMISSION STATEMENT ON VIOLENT CRIME: HOMICIDE, ASSAULT, RAPE, ROBBERY** *(Washington, D.C.: U.S. Government Printing Office, November, 1969) Part IV.*

Suburban neighborhoods, geographically far removed from the central city, will be protected mainly by economic homogeneity and by distance from population groups with the higest propensities to commit crimes.

Lacking a sharp change in federal and state policies, ownership of guns will be almost universal in the suburbs, homes will be fortified by an array of devices from window grills to electronic surveillance equipment, armed citizen volunteers in cars will supplement inadequate police patrols in neighborhoods closer to the central city, and extreme left-wing and right-wing groups will have tremendous armories of weapons which could be brought into play with or without any provocation.

High-speed, patrolled expressways will be sanitized corridors connecting safe areas, and private automobiles, taxicabs, and commercial vehicles will be routinely equipped with unbreakable glass, light armor, and other security features. Inside garages or valet parking will be available at safe buildings in or near the central city. Armed guards will "ride shotgun" on all forms of public transportation.

Streets and residential neighborhoods in the central city will be unsafe in differing degrees, and the ghetto slum neighborhoods will be places of terror with widespread crime, perhaps entirely out of police control during night-time hours. Armed guards will protect all public facilities such as schools, libraries and playgrounds in these areas.

Between the unsafe, deteriorating central city on the one hand and the network of safe, prosperous areas and sanitized corridors on the other, there will be, not unnaturally, intensifying hatred and deepening division. Violence will increase further, and the defensive response of the affluent will become still more elaborate.

Individually and to a considerable extent unintentionally, we are closing ourselves into fortresses when collectively we should be building the great, open, humane city-societies of which we are capable. Public and private action must guarantee safety, security, and justice for every citizen in our metropolitan areas without sacrificing the quality of life and the other values of a free society. If the nation is not in a position to launch a full-scale war on domestic ills, especially urban ills, at this moment, because of the difficulty in freeing ourselves quickly from other obligations, we should now legally make the essential commitments and then carry them out as quickly as funds can be obtained.

What do our cities require in order to become safe from violent crime?

They surely require a modern, effective system of criminal justice of the kind we recommended in our statement on "Violence and Law Enforcement." All levels of our criminal justice process are underfunded and most are uncoordinated. Police protection and community relations are poorest in the high crime slum neighborhoods where they should be the best. Lower courts are impossibly over-burdened and badly managed, while juvenile courts have failed to live up to their original rehabilitative ideal. Correctional institutions are generally the most neglected part of the criminal justice process. *We reiterate our previous recommendations that we double our national investment in the criminal justice process, that central offices of criminal justice be created at the metropolitan level, and that complementary private citizen groups be formed.*

In addition to other long-run solutions that we suggest, other immediate steps must be taken to reduce the opportunity and incentive to commit crimes of violence. The President's Commission on Law Enforcement and Administration of Justice made many suggestions which we endorse. In particular, we emphasize the need for action such as the following (some of which are new):

Increased day and night foot-patrols of slum ghetto areas by interracial police teams, in order to discourage street crime against both blacks and whites; improved street lighting to deprive criminals of hiding places from which to ambush victims; increase in numbers and use of community neighborhood centers that provide activity so that city streets are not deserted in early evening hours.

Increased police-community relations activity in slum ghetto areas in order to secure greater understanding of ghetto residents by police, and of police by ghetto residents. Police should be encouraged to establish their residences in the cities in order to be a part of the community which they serve.

Further experimentation with carefully controlled programs that provide low cost drugs such as methadone to addicts who register, so that addicts are not compelled to resort to robbery and burglary in order to meet the needs of their addiction; increased education about the dangers of addictives and other drugs in order to reduce their use.

Identification of specific violence-prone individuals for analysis and treatment in order to reduce the likelihood of repetition; provision of special schools for education of young people with violence-prone histories, special psychiatric services and employment programs for parolees and released offenders with a history of violent criminal acts.[1]

Concealable hand-guns, a common weapon used in violent crimes, must be brought under a system of restrictive licensing as we have recommended in our earlier statement on firearms.

But safety without fear cannot be secured alone by well-trained police, efficient courts, modern correctional practices, and hand-gun licensing. True security will come only when the vast majority of our citizens voluntarily accept society's rules of conduct as binding on them. Such acceptance will prevail widely among those who enjoy by legitimate means the benefits and pleasures of life to which they believe they are entitled—who have, in short, a satisfactory stake in the system. Today the stake of our impatient urban poor is more substantial than it used to be, but unrealized expectations and needs are massive. To ensure safety in our cities, we must take effective steps toward improving the conditions of life for all the people who live there.

Safety in our cities requires nothing less than progress in reconstructing urban life.

It is not within the purpose or the competence of this Commission to detail specific programs that will contribute to this fundamentally important national goal—the goal of reconstruction of urban life. Such programs must be worked out in the normal functioning of our political processes. Many important ideas have been put forth in the reports of the National Advisory Commission on Civil Disorders, the Urban Problems Commission, the Urban Housing Committee[2] and other groups which have made the city the focal point of their studies. Indeed, as the Urban Problems Commission observed, we already have on the national agenda much of the legislation and the programs needed to do the job. Examples are the Housing Act of 1968, the Juvenile Delinquency Prevention and Control Act, the Civil Rights laws of recent years, the President's welfare reform proposal, and many other existing and proposed enactments.

[1] The Philadelphia cohort study cited above shows that out of the entire Philadelphia population of boys born in 1945 (about 10,000), less than six percent had five or more police contacts. Even though the age group from 15 to 24 includes ten such cohorts, the number of identifiable violence-prone youths in a major city such as Philadelphia is still small enough to be manageable.

[2] These reports are available for purchase from the Superintendent of Documents, U.S. Government Printing Office, Washington, D.C. 20402.

What we urge, from the standpoint of our concern, is that early and accelerated progress toward the reconstruction of urban life be made if there is to be a remission in the cancerous growth of violent crime. The programs and the proposals must be backed up by a commitment of resources commensurate with the magnitude and the importance of the goal and with the expectations which have been irreversibly raised by the small start already made.

Dr. Daniel P. Moynihan has recently outlined a ten-point national urban policy that embraces many of the recommendations of earlier Commissions and which this Commission, while not in a position to endorse in detail, believes to merit careful consideration.[3] The essentials of the ten points, together with some enlargements of our own, are as follows:

(1) The poverty and social isolation of minority groups in central cities is the single most serious problem of the American city today. In the words of the Kerner Commission, this problem must be attacked by national action that is "compassionate, massive, and sustained, backed by the resources of the most powerful and the richest nation on this earth." We must meet the 1968 Housing Act's goal of a decent home for every American within a decade; we must take more effective steps to realize the goal, first set in the Employment Act of 1946, of a useful job at a reasonable wage for all who are able to work; and we must act on current proposals that the federal government pay a basic income to those American families who cannot care for themselves.[4]

(2) Economic and social forces in urban areas are not self-balancing. There is evidence that some federal programs, such as the highway program, have produced sharp imbalances in the "ecology" of cities, and that others, such as urban renewal, have sometimes accomplished the opposite of what was intended.[5] A more sophisticated understanding and appreciation of the complexity of the urban social system is required—and this will in turn require the development of new, dependable and lasting partnerships between government, private industry, social and cultural associations and organized groups of affected citizens. Without such partnerships even the best-intentioned programs will fail or produce unforeseen disruptive effects.

(3) At least part of the relative ineffectiveness of the efforts of urban government to respond to urban problems derives from the fragmented and obsolescent structure of urban government itself. At the present time most of our metropolitan areas are mis-governed by a vast number of smaller, inde-

---

[3] Daniel P. Moynihan, "Toward a National Urban Policy," *The Public Interest,* No. 17, Fall 1969, p. 15. Dr. Moynihan has been Executive Director of the President's Urban Affairs Council and is now Counselor to the President.

[4] The President has recently made such a proposal including a work incentive formula. A somewhat different proposal has been put forward in a recent report of the President's Commission on Income Maintenance Programs.

[5] "Is the only answer to traffic congestion more and wider roads? Clearly in many localities, it is not. The dislocation of people and businesses, the distortion of land use, the erosion of the real property tax base; and the dollars and cents cost, make this an increasingly unacceptable solution." *Tomorrow's Transportation: New Systems for the Urban Future,* U.S. Dept. of Housing and Urban Development (Washington, D.C.: U.S. Government Printing Office, 1968), p. 18. See also *Urban and Rural America: Policies for Future Growth,* Advisory Commission on Intergovernmental Relations (Washington, D.C.: U.S. Government Printing Office, 1968), pp. 59-60.

pendent local governmental units—yet effective action on certain critical problems such as law enforcement, housing and zoning and revenue-raising requires governmental units coterminous with metropolitan areas. At the same time, however, many city governments suffer from being too large to be responsive to citizens, especially disadvantaged groups with special needs for public services and for increased political participation.

A dual strategy for restructuring local governments is thus required. On the one hand, steps must be taken to vest certain functions, such as the power to tax and to zone, in a higher tier of true metropolitan governments, each exercising jurisdiction over an entire metropolitan area. On the other hand, our cities must also develop a lower tier of modular neighborhood political units, operating under the direction of representatives elected by residents of the neighborhood and with the authority to determine some of the policies and to operate at the neighborhood center some of the services presently performed by city-wide agencies.[6] To provide new insights and new momentum for urban government restructuring, we suggest that the President might profitably convene an Urban Convention of delegates from all the states and major cities, as well as the national government, to advise the nation on the steps that should be taken to increase urban efficiency and accountability through structural changes in local government.

(4) A primary object of federal urban policy must be to restore the fiscal vitality of urban government, with the particular object of ensuring that local governments normally have enough resources on hand or available to make local initiative in public affairs a reality. Local governments that try to meet their responsibilities lurch from one fiscal crisis to another. Each one percent rise in the gross national product increases the income of the federal government by one and one-half percent, while the normal income of city governments increases only one-half to three-quarters percent at most. Yet federal aid to state and local governments is only 17 percent of state-local revenue, a figure which should be substantially increased as soon as possible. We also believe it is essential to insure that the cities that are most in need of federal funding will obtain their fair share from the states which receive the federal payments.

The President's revenue sharing proposal is one way to increase state and local revenues. However, it is limited both in the amounts envisioned and in the way they are proposed to be channeled. As an alternate to federal sharing of its tax revenue, consideration might be given to a plan by which a full credit against federal income taxes would be given for all state and municipal taxes up to some maximum percentage of a taxpayer's income. To prevent encroachment by state governments upon the municipal tax base, separate ceilings could be fixed for state tax credits and for municipal tax credits. Such a tax-credit plan for

---

[6] From the standpoint of reducing violence, needed services which might be provided at the neighborhood level include job counseling and training; family counseling and planning advice; medical and psychiatric care; counseling on alcohol and drugs; citizen's grievance agencies; adult education; preschool training and child care for working mothers; psychological counseling for parents during the formative child rearing years; domestic quarrel teams; suicide prevention units; youth bureaus, including counseling of youth referred for non-police action by local Juvenile Squads and Gang Control Units; and legal advice.

revenue-sharing would be simple to execute, would channel more funds directly to cities, and would eliminate competition among neighboring states and communities to lower tax rates as a means of attracting businesses and upper income residents.

(5) Federal urban policy should seek to equalize the provision of public services as among different jurisdictions in metropolitan areas. This includes, at the top of the list, public education and public safety. Not only are both of these vital parts of the public sector severely underfunded, but the available resources are not equitably distributed between, for example, the inner city and surburban areas. What constitutes an equitable distribution may not be an easy question to answer, but it is at least clear that the kinds of inner city-suburban disparities in educational expenditures and police protection reported by the Kerner Commission are *not* equitable.[7] Federal aid programs should include standards to insure that equitable allocation policies are maintained.

(6) The federal government must assert a specific interest in the movement of people, displaced by technology or driven by poverty, from rural to urban areas, and also in the movement from densely populated central cities to suburban areas. Much of the present urban crisis derives from the almost total absence of positive policies to cope with the large-scale migration of southern Negroes into northern and western cities over the past half century, when the number of Negroes living in cities rose from 2.7 million to 14.8 million. In the next 30 years our metropolitan areas will grow both absolutely and in proportion to the total population as this nation of 200 million persons becomes a nation of 300 million persons. We must do the planning and take the actions—*e.g.,* maintenance of a flexible and open housing market, creation of "new towns"—that are necessary if future urban growth is to be less productive of social and human problems than has been true of past urban growth.

(7) State government has an indispensible role in the management of urban affairs, and must be supported and encouraged by the federal government in the performance of this role. City boundaries, jurisdictions and powers are subject to the control of state governments, and the federal government must work with state governments to encourage a more progressive, responsible exercise of the state role in this process.

(8) The federal government must develop and put into practice far more effective incentive systems than now exist whereby state and local governments, and private interests too, can be led to achieve the goals of federal programs. In recent years Congress has enacted legislation under which the federal government has funded an increasing number of venturesome programs aimed at broadening the scope of individual opportunity for educational and economic achievements. Under many of these new enactments, grants-in-aid to implement the federal policies in health, education, employment and other areas of human welfare have been given not only to state and local authorities, but also to universities, private industries and a host of specially created non-profit corporations. Although these grants have been made pursuant to specified standards of performance, the results have often been disappointing, in part because there

[7]See *Report of the National Advisory Commission on Civil Disorders, op. cit.,* pp. 161-62, 241.

have been inadequate incentives for successful performance and inadequate evaluative mechanisms for determining which specific programs are most efficiently and effectively achieving the federal goals.

It is thus increasingly agreed that the federal government should sponsor and subsequently evaluate alternative—in a sense "competing"—approaches to problems whose methods of solution are imperfectly understood, as is increasingly being done in the areas of medical and legal services for the poor and educational assistance for disadvantaged children. Other methods of spurring improvement in the delivery of federally-supported services include the provision of incentives to deliver the services at the lowest possible cost (as in current efforts with regard to Medicare), and the granting of the federal assistance directly to the consumers of the programs concerned, thus enabling them to choose among competing suppliers of the goods or services that the program is designed to provide (as in the GI Bill and other federal scholarship programs).

(9) The federal government must provide more and better information concerning urban affairs, and should sponsor extensive and sustained research into urban problems. Social science research is increasingly able to supply policy-makers and the public with empirical indicators of the nature of social problems and the success or failure of efforts to solve these problems. The time is at hand when these indicators should be systematically collected and disseminated in aid of public policy at all levels.

(10) The federal government, by its own example, and by incentives, should seek the development of a far heightened sense of the finite resources of the natural environment, and the fundamental importance of aesthetics in successful urban growth. Many American cities have grown to be ugly and in-humane largely because of an unrestrained technological exploitation of the resources of land, air and water by the economically most efficient means. That there has been too little restraint is not surprising in view of the over-all American cultural context in which the natural environment was perceived as an inexhaustible frontier impervious to human harm. Today, however, the critical cultural context seems to be changing, and the "frontier spirit" is giving way to a new conservation ethic more appropriate to a crowded urban society. Government should take the lead in encouraging, and in acting consistently with, the development of this new ethic.

CONCLUSION

To summarize our basic findings:

Violent crimes are chiefly a problem of the cities of the nation, and there violent crimes are committed mainly by the young, poor, male inhabitants of the ghetto slum.

In the slums increasingly powerful social forces are generating rising levels of violent crime which, unless checked, threaten to turn our cities into defensive, fearful societies.

An improved criminal justice system is required to contain the growth of violent crime, but only progress toward urban reconstruction can reduce the strength of the crime-causing forces in the inner city and thus reverse the direction of present crime trends.

Our confidence in the correctness of these findings is strengthened by the support of the findings of the President's Commission on Law Enforcement and Administration of Justice and by subsequent events. At the end of its monumental work, in February of 1967, that Commission not only called for scores of improvements in the effectiveness and failures of the law enforcement process, it also identified the same basic causes of violent crime and said this about their cure.

"Warring on poverty, inadequate housing and unemployment, is warring on crime. A civil rights law is a law against crime. Money for schools is money against crime. Medical, psychiatric, and family-counseling services are services against crime. More broadly and most importantly every effort to improve life in America's "inner cities" is an effort against crime."

EPILOGUE

One final word. The decade of the sixties opened with a President who was determined to shatter myths. "The great enemy of truth," John Kennedy had said in those early days, "is very often not the lie—deliberate, contrived and dishonest—but the myth—persistent, persuasive and unrealistic. Too often we hold fast to the clichés of our forebearers. We subject facts to a prefabricated set of interpretations. We enjoy the comfort of opinion without the discomfort of thought."[1]

Shattering myths, splintering clichés, is never easy. It requires courage that is not found in most men. And even with courage—as Kennedy himself discovered—it does not happen readily. It took most of the sixties to discover that unrestricted technical power was not necessarily a national blessing. It took just as long to shatter the conventional conviction that racism was confined only to the south. How many myths will obscure the real issues of the future? How many myths will jeopardize public action or private support? We don't know. But we do know that whenever free men try to perform reasonable acts, the myth makers are close at hand, spreading their jargon, filling the air with deception.

Kennedy said then and it is important to say now: "As every past generation has had to disenthrall itself from an inheritance of truisms and stereotypes, so in our own time we must move on from the reassuring repetition of stale phrases to a new, difficult, but essential confrontation with reality."

If this anthology serves only to make the task of the myth maker more difficult and the efforts of the honest man more successful, then it will have served its purpose.

[1] John F. Kennedy, Commencement Address, Yale University, June 11, 1962 in *Public Papers of the Presidents* (Washington, D.C.: U.S. Government Printing Office, 1963).

542

INDEX